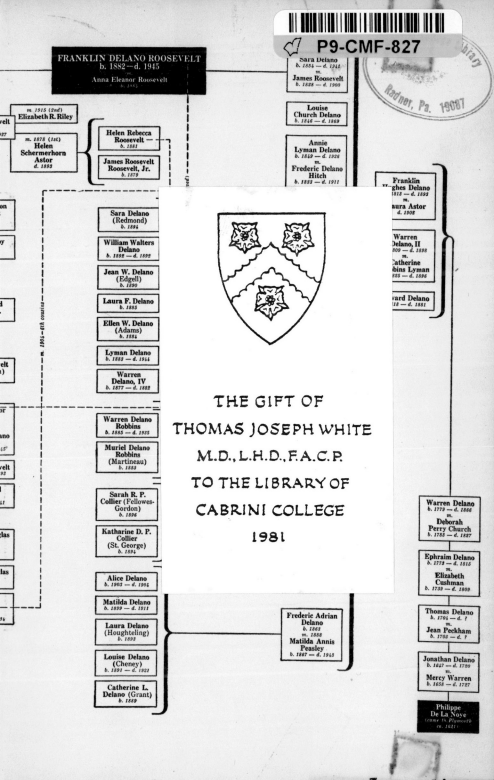

FRANKLIN DELANO ROOSEVELT
b. 1882 — d. 1945
m.
Anna Eleanor Roosevelt
b. 1885

Sara Delano
b. 1854 — d. 1941
m.
James Roosevelt
b. 1828 — d. 1900

Louise
Church Delano
b. 1846 — d. 1869

m. 1915 (2nd)
Elizabeth R. Riley
027

Helen Rebecca
Roosevelt —
b. 1881

Annie
Lyman Delano
b. 1849 — d. 1926
m.
Frederic Delano
Hitch
b. 1853 — d. 1911

m. 1878 (1st)
Helen
Schermerhorn
Astor
d. 1893

James Roosevelt
Roosevelt, Jr.
b. 1879

Franklin
Hughes Delano
1813 — d. 1893
m.
Laura Astor
d. 1902

Sara Delano
(Redmond)
b. 1894

Warren
Delano, II
1809 — d. 1898
m.
Catherine
Robbins Lyman
1825 — d. 1896

William Walters
Delano
b. 1892 — d. 1892

Jean W. Delano
(Edgell)
b. 1890

ward Delano
18 — d. 1881

Laura F. Delano
b. 1885

Ellen W. Delano
(Adams)
b. 1884

Lyman Delano
b. 1883 — d. 1944

Warren
Delano, IV
b. 1877 — d. 1882

Warren Delano
Robbins
b. 1885 — d. 1935

Muriel Delano
Robbins
(Martineau)
b. 1883

Sarah R. P.
Collier (Fellowes-
Gordon)
b. 1896

Warren Delano
b. 1779 — d. 1866
m.
Deborah
Perry Church
b. 1783 — d. 1827

Katharine D. P.
Collier
(St. George)
b. 1894

Ephraim Delano
b. 1773 — d. 1815
m.
Elizabeth
Cushman
b. 1739 — d. 1809

Alice Delano
b. 1903 — d. 1904

Matilda Delano
b. 1899 — d. 1911

Thomas Delano
b. 1704 — d. ?
m.
Jean Peckham
b. 1703 — d. ?

Laura Delano
(Houghteling)
b. 1893

Frederic Adrian
Delano
b. 1863
m. 1888
Matilda Annis
Peasley
b. 1867 — d. 1943

Jonathan Delano
b. 1647 — d. 1720
m.
Mercy Warren
b. 1658 — d. 1727

Louise Delano
(Cheney)
b. 1891 — d. 1921

Catherine L.
Delano (Grant)
b. 1889

Philippe
De La Noye
(came to Plymouth
co. 1621)

F. D. R.
His Personal Letters

1905 - 1928

F. D. R.

His Personal Letters

1905 - 1928

Foreword by

ELEANOR ROOSEVELT

Edited by

ELLIOTT ROOSEVELT

ASSISTED BY JAMES N. ROSENAU

DUELL, SLOAN AND PEARCE
New York

PRINTED IN THE
UNITED STATES OF AMERICA

Dedication

To the memory of two great Americans,
Josephus Daniels and Louis McHenry Howe

NOTE ON EDITING

The correspondence in this second volume of *F.D.R.: His Personal Letters* has been regularized in the conventional manner. Spelling errors have been corrected in almost all instances, and punctuation added or altered whenever the sense of a passage would otherwise be impaired.

Words underlined in the original letters have here been reproduced in italics.

The headings of all letters have been standardized, and, except for the occasional inclusion of the name of a hotel or boat to add interest, are restricted to place, year, month, and day of the week. Where dates (or places) cannot be definitely fixed from the original letter or from an envelope postmark, they are enclosed in brackets.

CONTENTS

ILLUSTRATIONS

KEY TO CREDITS

1 *The Franklin D. Roosevelt Library, Hyde Park, New York*
2 *Harris & Ewing Photographic News Service*
3 *Owen Winston*
4 *Acme Newspictures*
5 *Underwood & Underwood*
6 *Curtis Photo News*
7 *Originally appeared in "Sperry Scope," Vol. 10, #3, April, 1947*
Photographs not otherwise credited are from the Roosevelt family collection.

xii

INTRODUCTION

THIS SECOND volume of the personal letters of Franklin D. Roosevelt has proved to be of far different character from the first volume. In the latter were the letters of childhood and early manhood. They reflected many of the influences which played a role in the formation of F.D.R.'s character. The second volume, covering the years 1905 through 1928, presents for the first time a vivid portrait of the mature personality which the people came to know and understand during the Presidential years. One sees in these letters just what people and what events played an important part in the molding of the thoughts and acts of the President in later years.

It should be pointed out that there are far fewer personal letters available from 1905 through 1928 than in the earlier period. This is only natural when one considers that F.D.R. was forced to spend more time on official and business duties, and had less and less opportunity, as the years went by, for the writing of detailed personal letters. In addition, the great majority of these later letters were destroyed upon their receipt. It is ironical that F.D.R. should have been the only member of his family who never discarded a single item of his correspondence.

Franklin Roosevelt was not a simple personality, easy of definition and understanding. His was a highly complex and volatile mind. He was a man of great enthusiasms and tremendous energy. His curiosity was one of his dominant traits. These characteristics required a stern counterbalance of self-discipline and control. All this was intensified, as can be seen in the following pages, during the years immediately following the attack of poliomyelitis.

There is reference here to two men who entered the life of F.D.R. during this period. Josephus Daniels and Louis McHenry Howe should justly be credited with developing in Franklin D. Roosevelt a maturity and an outlook which might easily not have existed without their influence.

One woman receded in importance in the influence which she exerted. Sara Delano Roosevelt still made her personality felt in his life, but he definitely outgrew the limitations of her thinking. Another woman, Anna Eleanor Roosevelt, entered more and more into the role which she was finally to play in the evolution and growth of the man. Her patience, self-sacrifice, and wisdom, together with a firm and determined spirit, played the largest part in finally imparting to Franklin Roosevelt's character a resolute will power and staying power that made it possible for him to overcome a physical handicap and political setbacks.

It is the opinion of the editor of this volume that two people were primarily responsible for the interior survival of Franklin Roosevelt following the shattering attack of infantile paralysis. They should be credited with the amazing reactivation of his mental outlook and interest in life. Louis Howe and Anna Eleanor Roosevelt fought day and night for F.D.R.'s recovery and, during the long years of recuperation, forced his mind back into an active, aggressive interest in national and world affairs. These two, of all those who were closely associated with him, realized the innate fighting spirit of the man and the enormous scope of his intelligence. They worked on these forces and lived to see their confident beliefs confirmed beyond their fondest hopes.

In this volume of the letters historians should be able to trace, easily, the final evolution of the man that was to be.

They can see for themselves the times and the personalities responsible for that evolution. It should be remembered that this is a collection of personal letters and papers and no effort has been made to gather the material of his public life. In these letters can be seen a portrait of F.D.R. as a family man, a private personality as differentiated from a public personality.

The makeup of this volume with its chapter divisions has not been an attempt to divide F.D.R.'s life along certain lines, but rather is an arrangement based solely on the chronological grouping of the letters. No attempt has been made to edit or eliminate available material. All that could be found which truly dealt with the personal side has been included in this volume. The editing has been mainly a task of correlating these personal letters and papers to F.D.R.'s public life.

In preparing this volume, I have been aided by many people, but special mention must be made of a young man who came to work for me as my assistant in January of 1948. His name is James N. Rosenau.

I called an old friend of mine, Anthony N. B. Garvan, an instructor in American History at Bard College, during the fall of 1947. I explained that I was looking for a couple of students who would be capable of doing research work in connection with the compilation of these letters. He brought two young men down to Hyde Park for an interview, and told me that if they met my requirements, their work with me would be satisfactory credit for the winter field period which is a vital aspect of the Bard College program. Douglas B. Haviland and Mr. Rosenau then came to live at Hyde Park and work on the letters; at the conclusion of the field period, Mr. Rosenau continued on a part-time basis until his graduation in June, 1948. He wrote a brilliant thesis based on his work with the letters and graduated with top honors.

Since graduation he has remained as a full-time member of the staff, doing not only research but also performing as an excellent editorial annotator. To him go my thanks for an arduous job well done.

Two other members of my staff, Mrs. Blanche Reilly and Miss Janet B. Reinthal, deserve a very special vote of thanks from me. Their interest and devotion to the job have meant loss of home life, sleep, and recreation, but, in spite of all demands, they cheerfully went ahead to the final completion of the book.

The staff of the Franklin D. Roosevelt Memorial Library, the Archivist, Dr. Wayne C. Grover, and the staff of the Interior Department charged with the maintenance and up-keep of the site, have all contributed immensely to the preparation of this volume.

I desire particularly to thank Martin P. Claussen, former director of the Franklin D. Roosevelt Memorial Library; Herman Kahn, present director of the Library; Miss Margaret Suckley and William Nichols, members of the staff of the Library; Frederick L. Rath, Jr., historian in the National Park Service; and William A. Plog, on the staff of the National Park Service.

In particular, many others have been kind enough to answer our inquiries and provide us with material from their files and memories. My thanks go to Jonathan Daniels, Stephen Early, former Governor James M. Cox, Langdon P. Marvin, Henry Ford, II, H. Morton Merriman, Mrs. Charles S. Hamlin, Mrs. William Stanley Parker, and Owen Winston.

Finally, my mother contributed so much time from her overcrowded schedule that without her this volume would not have been possible. And in acknowledging my debt to her I include, as hardly need be pointed out, her indefatigable secretary, Miss Malvina Thompson.

ELLIOTT ROOSEVELT

Hyde Park, N. Y.

FOREWORD

BY

Eleanor Roosevelt

When the letters covering my husband's early years were published, I hoped they would be of interest to his friends. I feel sure they have been, and I think those who enjoyed the first volume will find the second even more interesting.

It is true the letters are not so frequent and there has had to be a good deal of explanatory material. The reason for this is that what happened in this second period was inevitably tied up with the history of those years, and to understand it one must have more background.

In addition, my husband wrote fewer letters—sometimes I was with him and I wrote his mother when he was too busy, but other times he wrote extremely brief notes because his time was filled to overflowing. Things could no longer be adjusted to his personal convenience. His personal convenience had to be adjusted to his obligations to the job he was doing.

These letters go to 1928, and so they cover many of the most formative years of my husband's life. In the early years, when he was the Assistant Secretary of the Navy, you very often see a young man's impatience with the way older men thought and worked. At times he was critical of his chief,

Josephus Daniels, but he learned as time went on to have a deep admiration for the qualities of character and to value the high ability of Mr. Daniels. It was his own experience that taught him it was one thing to understand and get on with naval officers, and another and perhaps even greater quality which enabled Mr. Daniels to understand and get on with Congress. What he spoke of slightingly at first, he came to admire inordinately because of all the difficulties he himself encountered.

Perhaps the experience, above all others, which shaped my husband's character along more definite lines and gave him a strength and depth that he did not have as a young man, was the long struggle with infantile paralysis. As he came gradually to realize that he was not going to get any better, he faced great bitterness, I am sure, though he never mentioned it. The only thing that stands out in my mind as evidence of how he suffered when he finally knew that he would never walk again, was the fact that I never heard him mention golf from the day he was taken ill until the end of his life. That game epitomized to him the ability to be out of doors and to enjoy the use of his body. Though he learned to bear it, I am afraid it was always a tragedy.

He soon discovered that the way to lighten all burdens is to take them cheerfully. He regained his joy in living, his hearty laughter, his ability to be happy over little things; and though I think I was too young to realize fully at the time what a remarkable fight he was making and what a victory he had won, still everyone around him sensed a little of the struggle and helped when and as they could.

I have since come to realize and to appreciate that a strength of character was built up during these years which made him able to give complete confidence to the people of the nation when they needed it, so that when he said: "The only thing we have to fear is fear itself," they knew he held that conviction. He had lived through fear and come out successfully.

I hope that to his friends, these letters will give greater understanding of how a man developed and that they will be a continuing contribution. This should be a book in their libraries which they can pick up from time to time, and obtain a little more insight and a little more inspiration to help them to enjoy life and endure its vicissitudes with greater fortitude.

F. D. R.
His Personal Letters

1905 - 1928

I

"...Having the Time of Our Lives..."

HONEYMOON TRIP

1905

IN ORDER to finish the spring term at Columbia Law School, Franklin Roosevelt and his young bride postponed their honeymoon trip for several months. Early in June, 1905, the young couple sailed for Europe and in the morning of the second day at sea commenced to inform his mother of their whereabouts and daily activities. Marriage did not sever the close tie between mother and son. As can be gathered from the letters of his early years, the strong bond between Sara and Franklin Roosevelt was destined to endure throughout their lives. Nevertheless, the tie was altered somewhat in 1905—now Anna Eleanor Roosevelt was a member of the family; now there were two persons who addressed Sara Roosevelt as "Mama," and now these same two persons were intent upon building a family of their own. To be sure, the marriage did not leave Sara Roosevelt in the background, but at the same time she was no longer the dominant figure in her son's life.

This alteration and enlargement of intimate family ties is immediately apparent in the honeymoon correspondence. The young couple took turns writing to their mother; each added notes to the letters of the other, and each occupied many paragraphs telling of the health, appearance, actions, and attitudes of the other. Jointly they pictured for Sara Roosevelt their escapades on the continent of Europe, the people they met, the things they bought. Together they revealed to her their current problems and future plans, their happiness and enthusiasm. It is this singleness of mind and action that validates the inclusion of Eleanor Roosevelt's letters in this and subsequent chapters.

∽∽

R.M.S. "OCEANIC"
JUNE 7, 1905
WEDNESDAY

Dearest Mama,

I am all unpacked and settled and F. is now getting his things in order. We haven't got any of our fruit yet as it is in the cold room, but we are looking forward to all your good things. Thank you so much dear for everything you did for us. You are always just the sweetest, dearest Mama to your children and I shall look forward to our next long evening together, when I shall want to be kissed all the time!

So far we have seen nothing of our fellow passengers, but Franklin will tell you about them the end of the trip when I won't be able to write!

Ever and ever so much love my dearest Mummy from your devoted

ELEANOR

P.S.   Forbes appeared just after you left!

"When I won't be able to write" refers to A.E.R.'s (Anna Eleanor Roosevelt, hereafter designated by her initials) fear of seasickness, an ailment that has always plagued her.

4

She was particularly fearful on this voyage because, as noted in her book *This Is My Story,* it was "terrible to be seasick with a husband . . . who seemed to think that sailing the ocean blue was a joy!" "Forbes" was William Forbes Morgan, who sixteen months earlier had married A.E.R.'s maternal aunt, Edith Livingston Hall (known by the family as "Pussie"). W. Forbes Morgan later became prominent in the liquor industry, and served as treasurer of the Democratic National Convention Committee in 1936.

∽∽

R.M.S. "OCEANIC"
JUNE 7, 1905
WEDNESDAY

Dearest Mama,

It isn't rough yet and Eleanor says she has hopes of sitting on the Captain's right for at least one meal. Eliot Cross hasn't materialized, nor has Steuart Davis, so I foresee that I shall spend most of the time talking to Mrs. Burton!

The breakfast horn is just blowing! A last chance for some people!

I think I have actually come away without leaving anything undone, except the table for Eleanor which only arrived day before yesterday. It is at the Central R.R. of New Jersey, Pier 46, and if they won't deliver it Cousin Corinne will have to send an order from the person that shipped it.

The fruit has just arrived and looks delicious and will give us much comfort. Also Aunts Annie, Jennie, Pussie, and Frances Pell sent fruit and Mrs. Hall some jellies.

The mail is about to close so I must run. We shall cable from Liverpool. "Algonac" means everything is "superfine, splendide et pas cher" as Mlle. Sandoz used to say.

Goodbye and take *very* good care of yourself and let us hear from you all the time, dearest Mama.

Ever with love

FDR

Eliot Cross and E. Steuart Davis were in the class of 1906 at Harvard. The former later became an architect, and with his brother founded the New York firm of Cross & Cross. The latter, with F.D.R.'s approval and help as Assistant Secretary of the Navy, organized and commanded the Volunteer Patrol Squadron in 1914, the organization which was the nucleus for the United States Naval Reserve that came into being a year later. "Mrs. Burton" was probably Mrs. Louise Burton, an acquaintance of the family from Millbrook, N. Y. "Cousin Corinne" was F.D.R.'s cousin and A.E.R.'s paternal aunt, Corinne Roosevelt Robinson, and the table mentioned was her wedding present to A.E.R. Her husband, Douglas Robinson, was a real estate operator in New York. "Aunt Annie" was F.D.R.'s maternal aunt, Annie Lyman Delano, who had married a distant cousin, Frederic Delano Hitch. "Aunt Jennie" was the wife of F.D.R.'s maternal uncle, Warren Delano III. Frances Pell was a childhood friend of F.D.R.; several months after this letter was written she married an Englishman, Sir Martin Archer-Shee, who for thirteen years was a Member of Parliament. Lady Archer-Shee now resides at "Pellwood," the family home in Highland Falls, N. Y. "Mrs. Hall" was A.E.R.'s grandmother, Mrs. Valentine G. Hall. "Algonac" refers to the home of the Delano family near Newburgh, N. Y.; it was often used by the family as an abbreviation for good news. "Mlle. Sandoz" was F.D.R.'s governess when he was a child, Jeanne Sandoz.

POSTED AT QUEENSTOWN
R.M.S. "OCEANIC"
JUNE 11, 1905
SUNDAY

Dearest Mama,

So far (you'll notice that this is underlined) we have had an almost perfect crossing. Thursday and Friday were almost smooth, just a slight motion and yesterday and today have

6

been just like a mill-pond—almost too smooth in fact, as the slight wind has been astern and the heat has been rather damp & oppressive.

Eleanor has been a *wonderful* sailor and hasn't *missed* a single meal or *lost* any either. She is on the Captain's right, I next, then a Mr. Lancaster, an old Liverpool merchant & quite interesting. Opposite us are a Mr. Evans, a rich Englishman, and Mr. and Mrs. Monell of Tuxedo who are building just beyond Aunt Kassie. She is pretty and very nice, but he is rather a bore, though I fancy pretty well off. The Mrs. Hunt on board is, it turns out, the one we know and she came up and introduced herself as my cousin. Also Frank Polk is on board and the Ansel Phelps (she is Coster Wilmerding's sister) who have just been married.

Our fruit is delicious but it is a case of "embrasse de riches" as we got six baskets of goodies, and are trying to do our duty to them even at the expense of chronic dyspepsia— or if it gets rough, of acute but temporary disorders.

There are also six Japs, all in the Navy, going out to take charge of the two Japanese battleships building in England. I have had several interesting talks with them though their English is not voluble, and I find myself giving out more information than I receive.

TUESDAY

We are almost in, and expect to reach Queenstown by 11 tonight and Liverpool by 1 o'clock tomorrow, and shall see the Bullochs and Maxwells and take the 5 P.M. train to London, going straight to Brown's, where we hope to be welcomed by Aunt Kassie, P.C. and Muriel.

Yesterday was a bit rolly, but not very bad as our sea-legs are really on by now, and today is glassy smooth again. Mrs. Burton and her two dear lambs have smiled at us in an affectionate way but we haven't spent *all* our spare moments with them!

7

Mrs. Hunt wants me to give you her love, we have just had a long talk. I suppose Alice is with you now—give her our best—also I am thinking of all sorts of house parties and entertainment at Hyde Park which I know you are having!

By the way we shall send a handsome wedding present to the Phelps girl from *you* and let you repay us. Isn't it good of us?

We shall write again as soon as we get to London and hope to get the first letter from you before we go to Paris Monday afternoon.

Loads of love from us both.

Ever your affectionate

F.D.R.

"Aunt Kassie" was F.D.R.'s maternal aunt, Katharine Delano, whose first husband, Charles A. Robbins, had died in 1889. In 1893 she married Hiram Price Collier, whom F.D.R. refers to as "P.C." "Muriel" was Muriel Delano Robbins, Aunt Kassie's daughter by her first marriage; she married Cyril Martineau and lives in London. "Mrs. Hunt" was, in fact, a very distant cousin of F.D.R. Frank Polk and Ansel Phelps were both in the class of 1894 at Yale. In the Wilson Administration the former was counselor for the Department of State and served two years as Under-Secretary; as will be seen from later correspondence, during the years in Washington the Polks and the Roosevelts became close friends. E. Coster Wilmerding attended Groton several years before F.D.R.; his cousin, Lucius Wilmerding, married Helene Cutting, who had been one of A.E.R.'s bridesmaids. As for the shipbuilding project of Japan, this was to support their efforts in the war with Russia which was raging at this time and which was then on the verge of a Japanese victory. In September, 1905, Russia admitted its crushing defeat and signed a treaty of peace. A treaty signed in 1902 between Great Britain and Japan that provided for benevolent neutrality in case of attack on either party by a single power explains why the Japanese were building warships in English yards. The "Bullochs" were the family of James and Irvine Bulloch, half-brothers of A.E.R.'s paternal grandmother, Martha Bulloch Roosevelt. As agents of the Confederate government, these two brothers from Georgia had gone to England at the beginning of the Civil War to organize and direct the shipping that was to run the Northern blockade of Southern ports. They were not included in the general amnesty proclaimed by President Johnson at the end of the war, and consequently settled for the rest of their lives in Liverpool. James Bulloch used to visit the United States thereafter under an assumed name. On one occasion James Roosevelt was asked to meet him at dinner and refused. He was horrified at the thought of dining with a traitor. The "Maxwells" were also members of this family, as James Bulloch's eldest daughter, Jessie, married Maxwell H. Maxwell. Both the Bullochs and the Maxwells were high-ranking officials of the Cunard Steamship Company. "Alice" was Alice Draper, a close friend of the family who later married Edward C. Carter.

〜〜

R.M.S. "OCEANIC"
JUNE 13, 1905
TUESDAY

Dearest Mama,

Franklin has already written you all about the trip so this is only a little line to tell you about him. He is looking very well and has spent most of his time *trying* to talk to the Japs. He has succeeded a few times however and they have proved interesting companions.

Captain Cameron has been very nice and the trip has been very smooth and pleasant. Franklin has been a wonderful maid and I've never been so well looked after.

The stewardess informed me the other morning that my husband must be English, he was so handsome and had the real English profile! Of course it was a great compliment but you can imagine how Franklin looked when I told him.

We have been all over the ship with the Captain and it was very interesting, but I am more sorry than ever for the Steerage passengers. Everything was very clean though and the size of the ship is overwhelming.

Your brown bag has been so comfy on cold days Mama, and we have enjoyed all the good things you sent us so much.

We hope to land in Liverpool before one tomorrow and if so we will take a five o'clock train to London.

With much, much love

Always devotedly

ELEANOR

∾

BROWN'S HOTEL, LONDON
JUNE 16, 1905
FRIDAY

Dearest Mama,

I will go back to tell you what your infants have been doing for the last three days. We got to Queenstown on Tuesday night at 11.30 p.m.—a very slow passage considering the good weather—but worse things were to come—for we ran into an hour of fog in the Irish channel, and missed the tide over the Mersey bar, not reaching the dock till 6.30 p.m. Mr. & Mrs. Maxwell met us and got us quickly through the custom house, and we then went to the Northwestern Hotel and dined. Then we went to Mrs. Bulloch's house and spent the evening with her, Mrs. Sayre, her mother, her sister and Mrs. Maxwell, talking over old days, family history, etc. They sent their love to you and asked many questions about you. We had a comfortable night in Liverpool, leaving at 8 yesterday a.m., getting here at 12. We were ushered into the royal suite, one flight up, front, price $1,000 a day—a sitting room 40 ft. by 30, a double bedroom, another ditto and a bath. Our breath was so taken away that we couldn't even protest and are now saying "Damn the expense, Wot's the odds"! Aunt Kassie met us and it was so nice to see her again. We dined with them in the evening and today they have gone to Shropshire. Muriel, alas, had just left to go with the C.L.F. Robinsons on their yacht to the Kiel Regatta and to Russia, a trip of six weeks, which sounds very delightful.

Today we have shopped wildly—saw the Reids yesterday in the palatial Dorchester House, and Eleanor's schoolmate Miss Bennett has come up to spend two days with us. Nathalie Henderson and Mrs. Thayer Robb have just been in to tea. Tomorrow p.m. we go down to Allenswood and Sunday to the polo match at Ranelagh. We go to Paris Tuesday and to Venice on Friday night. We have ordered thousands of dollars worth of clothes, and I am going to send you several cases of champagne, as I know it is needed at Hyde Park.

Ever your devoted

F.D.R.

The young couple "were ushered into the royal suite" because they had been identified with Theodore Roosevelt, then President of the United States and A.E.R.'s uncle. This identification was frequently to follow F.D.R., especially during his first years in politics. As will be seen in other letters of this chapter, F.D.R. enjoyed teasing his mother with a pretense of wild spending. Charles L. F. Robinson later became president and director of Colt's Patent Fire Arms Company. The "Reids" were acquaintances of F.D.R.'s parents and Jean Reid was a friend of A.E.R.; Whitelaw Reid, for many years successor to Horace Greeley as editor-in-chief and chief proprietor of the *New York Tribune,* was at this time United States Ambassador to England. In addition to being A.E.R.'s schoolmate, Marjorie Bennett, who later married Philip Vaughan, was also her first roommate in school. Mrs. Thayer Robb was the older sister of Nathalie Henderson; the latter married Joseph R. Swan, an investment banker. Located a short distance outside of London, "Allenswood" was the school where A.E.R. received her formal education. Her parents

having died when she was a young girl, A.E.R.'s grandmother decided that in deference to her mother's wish
she should receive part of her education abroad. When she
was fifteen A.E.R. went to England and attended Allenswood for three years.

∽

Dearest Mama,

Franklin and I were so pleased to get your two letters on
Saturday night and what exciting news! Auntie Bye had
never breathed a word to me, so you can tell Helen that so
far as I am concerned she was most discreet! November seems
very soon doesn't it? Give her my best love when you see her.
Franklin wrote you our doings up to Friday so I shall begin
on Saturday. In the A.M. we did a little shopping and then
got Nathalie Henderson and went to the Royal Academy
which was interesting as far as the Sargent's went, but seemed
to have a good deal of trash also. There is a portrait by
Collier and a picture called the "Cheat," both of which are
striking and I hear that Aunt Kassie *may* be painted by him.
After lunch we again went out and paid a number of calls
and in the evening dined at Prince's and went to see a play
called "Lady Madcap" which was most amusing. Nathalie
and a Mr. Welch went with us and he afterwards took us to
supper at the Carlton where we saw a great crowd and were
much entertained by some of the English women. It is quite
out of date over here to appear with your own face or hair.
In fact it really looks immodest! Nelly Post had sent her
electric for us to use all day and she had also given us tickets
for Ranelagh but as it rained we did not go out. Everyone
has been very kind and I think we would have lots to do even
if we stayed much longer.

Sunday A.M. we rested and went to lunch with the Reids.
I sat next to Mr. Reid! The Thayer Robbs, Nathalie, a Mrs.

Burrows, Mr. Carrolyn and Mr. Jay were the only other guests and it was very pleasant. Dorchester House is wonderful and Mrs. Reid is better than I thought she could be. Mrs. Carter gave us her carriage for the afternoon and tickets for Ranelagh so we went out and had tea there and watched the queerest conglomeration of people I've ever seen! On our way we went to see the Cholmely's and they asked many questions about you and sent you all kinds of messages. I thought Lady Cholmely charming but I am not crazy about the girls, but then I think the English artificial look prejudiced me and perhaps I shall change if we stay with them in the autumn as they asked us to do. In the evening we went back to the Reids for dinner and felt very old and very grand, the other guests being Mr. and Mrs. W. D. Sloane, Mr. and Mrs. H. Taylor, Mr. and Mrs. Higgins and Colonel Latrobe. They were all nice and we both enjoyed it.

This A.M. Franklin had to go to Baring's so I went out to Allenswood and saw Miss Samaia, but it was dreadful without Miss Souvestre. Afterwards I went and tried my habit and rough suit on at Nicoll's and I think they will be satisfactory. At 1:30 F. and I went to Mrs. Carter's for lunch, where we found Mrs. Sheffield and Mr. Jay and had a very pleasant time as both our host and hostess are too kind and dear for words. F. then went to his tailor's and Jean took me driving and left me at Lady Bridge's at five where F. joined me for tea. A Mr. Durant was there and we had a nice chat and were shown some very interesting photos of one or two Russian ships being sunk by the Japanese. The charming English women are more of a surprise to me than the uncharming ones even, for they *look* frumps even when they're not. We went later to see Mrs. and Miss Edwardes and they quite won my heart. The girl is really interesting looking and Mrs. Edwardes so nice. They spoke in the warmest way of you and she said she was writing you about some little lady who is going *perhaps* to act in America this summer. I think the loss of her son has been a dreadful blow and she talks of it frequently.

I forgot to tell you that we saw Cousin Julia Delano on Saturday and she said she was soon going home and that she was not very well.

Tonight we are packing as we leave at eleven tomorrow for Paris. Tissie has gone to St. Moritz so I doubt if I will see her at all until the autumn! Mr. Richard Mortimer is a dear to send us a wedding present and please write me what it is so I can thank him.

Hall's coat can stay hung up till the autumn, as it is to be given away and I think the autumn is a better time unless you think it will bring moths.

Everyone says F. is looking *so* well and I think he is feeling finely and so am I. Don't worry about us and take good care of your own dear self and write us *all* the news.

Best love from us both,

Your ever devoted

ELEANOR

"Auntie Bye" was A.E.R.'s paternal aunt, Anna Roosevelt, who late in her life married William Sheffield Cowles. "Helen" was F.D.R.'s half-niece, Helen Rebecca Roosevelt. She married Theodore Douglas Robinson, a sixth cousin from A.E.R.'s side of the family, who later was a member of the New York State Assembly at the same time as F.D.R. was in the State Senate. The "exciting news" refers to the birth of their son, Theodore Douglas Robinson, Jr., in November, 1905. It is not surprising that A.E.R. was only interested in the paintings by John Singer Sargent, as his portraits were for many years the leading features of exhibitions at the Royal Academy. Although American by birth, and although educated in France, it was as a British artist that Sargent won fame and the position as the most sought-after portrait painter of the day. Born in London, John Collier was another recognized portraitist of the era. Nelly Post was a schoolmate of A.E.R. Most of the people described as having attended the various luncheon and dinner parties were acquaintances of F.D.R.'s parents, and thus A.E.R. remarked that she "felt very old and grand." These were people whom the James Roosevelts had known in New York or whom they had met on their frequent trips abroad, and therefore some of them who are incidentally mentioned can no longer be identified. "Mr. Jay" was probably the noted career diplomat, Peter Augustus Jay, who was at this time visiting London from his post as Secretary of the American Legation in Constantinople; he graduated from Harvard the year F.D.R. entered, and in 1925 he was made Ambassador to Argentina, where he served for two years before retiring. "Mrs. Carter" was the wife of John R. Carter, who was at this time First Secretary of the United States Embassy in London. During previous trips to Europe F.D.R. had visited with the "Cholmely's" on their estate in Lincolnshire. Lady Cholmeley was the former Edith Sophia Rowley, and her husband, Sir Hugh Arthur Henry Cholmeley, had been a Member of Parliament before inheriting his title. Their three daughters, who were approximately F.D.R.'s age, and about whom A.E.R. felt "prejudiced," were Mary Selina, Winifred, and Aline Janetta. William Douglas Sloane was a director of the New York furniture company, W. and J. Sloane. In 1920 his widow, the former Emily T. Vanderbilt, married the noted diplomat, Henry White; the latter served as United States Ambassador to France and Italy during Theodore Roosevelt's Administration and was the only Republican member of Wilson's five-man delegation to the Paris Peace Conference in 1919. The only period that Henry White was not active in diplomatic circles was between 1893 and 1897. After the inauguration of Grover Cleveland in 1893, he was recalled from his post as First Secretary of the American Embassy in London in order to make room for a person who had made a substantial donation to the Cleveland campaign fund. The contributor: F.D.R.'s half-brother, James Roosevelt Roosevelt. "Baring's" was and is the old London bank where the Roosevelt family has always kept an account to facilitate their trips and business in Europe. Miss Samaia was the headmistress of Allenswood, succeeding Miss Souvestre after the latter's death three months before the writing of this letter. Both of these women, and especially Miss Souvestre, had played a very influential role in A.E.R.'s education and 'teen-age years. "Jean" was the daughter of Whitelaw Reid; she married the Hon. John Hubert Ward, equerry to Edward VII. It was in Lady Ward's house that the first paratrooper officers were quartered before initiating the invasion of North Africa in 1942. "Mrs. Edwardes" was the wife of Henry George Edwardes, who had become friendly with F.D.R.'s parents when they lived in Washington during the winter of 1887, he being at that time with the British legation. "Miss Edwardes" was their daughter, Sylvia Gay Edwardes, who for four years had been Maid of Honour to Queen Victoria; their son, Cecil, died earlier in 1905. Cousin Julia Delano came from Fairhaven, Mass., the first traditional home of the Delano family; F.D.R.'s great-grandfather, the original Warren Delano, settled there early in the nineteenth century. "Tissie" was A.E.R.'s maternal aunt, Elizabeth Livingston Hall; she married Stanley Mortimer, whose brother, Richard, is also mentioned in the letter. "Hall" was A.E.R.'s younger brother, G. Hall Roosevelt. After their return from Europe, Hall came to live with his sister and brother-in-law whenever he was not away at school. Although F.D.R. was nine years older than Hall, they soon became close companions and took many hunting trips together.

〰〰

37 AVENUE DE L'ALMA, PARIS
JUNE 22, 1905
THURSDAY

Dearest Mama,

Here I am writing in Aunt Doe's apartment, but I will go back and tell you first that we had a very comfortable journey leaving London at 11 a.m. and getting here at 7. The channel was perfectly smooth I am glad to say. We went straight to the France et Choiseul and Aunt Doe appeared very soon after dinner, looking quite well and happy. We drove up here for a half hour and saw Cousins Pauline and Fay.

Yesterday a.m. Aunt Doe came for us and went with us to Hugon's where Eleanor ordered a cloak and one dress, a cloth skirt and coat, very dressy. Then we went to Combe & Levy and ordered thousands of dollars worth of linen, 8 doz. tablecloths, 6 napkins, ½ pillow case and a handkerchief, all very attractive and full of holes or à jour as they say here. Then we lunched here with Aunt Doe and she took Eleanor out afterwards to buy Sarey Gamps and chests of drawers and other unmentionables. I went on a book hunt and spent all I owned in the first shop I went into and had to quit. I spent an hour with Ned Bell who is here, and have also seen Couper Lord and Duane Humphreys and Mrs. Hump. We dined with Aunt Doe and all three went to see "Manon" at the Opera Comique—very delightful and well rendered. We didn't get back till nearly 1 a.m. and were dead this morning. Today we all three went to various dressmakers, at one of which I distinguished myself by going to sleep. Eleanor got a dozen or so new dresses and two more cloaks. We haven't been to the fur place yet. I am getting Eleanor a long sable cloak and a silver fox coat for myself. We lunched with cousins Pauline and Fay and then drove out to Neuilly with Aunt Doe and saw Cousin Hortense who was very sweet and sent lots of love to you. Elsie Howland is staying with her, but mon cher Louis is now off on a trip. Loads of love. We go to Milan tomorrow night at 10.30, get there at 6 p.m. on Saturday and continue to Venice at 2 p.m. Sunday, getting there at 6.30. After that we may take a shot at the Damnation Coast or the Passion Play, according to the state of our feelings.

Ever your devoted

FDR

Don't believe *all* this letter please. I may be extravagant but—!!!

E.R.

"Aunt Doe," sometimes referred to as "Aunt Dora," was F.D.R.'s maternal aunt, Deborah Perry Delano. In 1903, several years after the death of her first husband, William Howard Forbes, she married his younger brother, Paul Forbes. The Forbes brothers were originally associated with Russell and Company, a notable firm engaged in the China trade. After thirty years of residence near Hong Kong, Aunt Doe moved to the French capital and her apartment soon became the Roosevelt family headquarters in Paris. Unmarried sisters of William and Paul Forbes were "Cousins Pauline and Fay," who had never returned to the United States after first going abroad during the Civil War. Their original crossing had been so rough that they chose to make Paris their permanent residence rather than face another. Although it was true that A.E.R. purchased the linen for her new home on the occasion mentioned, it was not in such quantities as F.D.R. describes. That A.E.R. was anxious for her mother-in-law not to be too impressed by F.D.R.'s jesting is evident from the postscript which she added. "Sarey Gamps" was another name for underclothes. As will be seen, every city that F.D.R. visited on this trip was the subject of a "book hunt." Always an energetic collector, F.D.R. especially sought old books dealing with the United States Navy, first editions, and the then-fashionable miniature books. Edward ("Ned") Bell was a classmate of F.D.R. at Harvard who later followed a varied career in the diplomatic service. J. Couper Lord and Richard Duane Humphreys were also friends of F.D.R. at both Groton and Harvard; the latter is now chairman of the board of the Mississippi Glass Company. "Cousin Hortense" Howland was a French woman who had married a brother of James Roosevelt's first wife. Mme. Howland maintained a high position in the Parisian society of the time, her salon being portrayed by Marcel Proust in his *Remembrance of Things Past* as a meeting place of the Jockey Club. Soon after the appointment of F.D.R.'s father as one of the two trustees of her estate, the other trustee absconded with all the funds. Believing he was partly responsible, from that day on James Roosevelt drew upon his own resources to provide Mme. Howland with the means to continue her style of life in Paris. "Louis" was Mme. Howland's son, while Elsie Howland was one of Louis Howland's three daughters. The "Damnation Coast" refers of course to the Dalmatian Coast.

∾

HÔTEL DE FRANCE & CHOISEULE, PARIS
JUNE 23, 1905
FRIDAY

Dearest Mama,

Franklin wrote yesterday so this is just a line to tell you that we were delighted to get your letter at Aunt Dora's last night. We dined with her and afterwards went to the Alcazar on the Champs Elysées. It was very funny and very vulgar, but as we couldn't hear very much the vulgarity didn't matter and the crowd was most amusing.

Your artistic effort looks charming and I am crazy to see it. Mme. Howland's clock is lovely, modern I think but quite charming. You would have laughed if you could have heard Mme. Howland flatter Franklin yesterday. It made him cross but I thought her most appreciative as she kept repeating "Qu'il est beau, qu'il est charmant"!

> This isn't true—Eleanor got
> buttered on both sides! FDR

Aunt Dora has been an angel and trotted from shop to shop with us every day. This A.M. we went out and Franklin got me such lovely furs. I don't think he ought to give them to me but they are wonderful and of course I am delighted with them. He has found some lovely books here too and he spent most of this afternoon rummaging round an old shop, while poor Aunt Dora and I were trying on clothes! She is dining with us to-night and seeing us off for Milan. We have

19

met 3 Bareau girls and Mme. Bareau, the latter seemed nice but the former were rather unpleasing to the eye!!!!! (FDR).

I had a sweet letter from Helen the other day. Do write us how she is. Give our love to Alice Draper and Frances if you ever see her!

Much, much love dearest from both your children.

Ever devotedly

ELEANOR

In addition to inserting the humorous note at the end of the second paragraph, F.D.R. also added the five exclamation points and his initials as a conclusion to the third paragraph. Mme. Bareau and her daughters were relatives of the Forbes family.

HÔTEL BRITANNIA, VENICE

JUNE 26, 1905

MONDAY

Dearest Mama,

Here we are, quite overcome by the wonders of Venice, and settled comfortably for ten days. Eleanor wrote you on Friday from Paris. Aunt Doe dined with us that night and saw us off at ten for Milan where we arrived at 6 the following evening after a rather long though fortunately cool journey.

We went for a little drive after dinner to get an idea of the town—which is not very impressive as the greater part is modern.

The next morning it rained and we saw the Cathedral which is fine and well proportioned, though rather ornate in style. Also we saw the Church of Santa Maria della Pietà, an interesting basilica with fascinating cloisters by Bramante which are being restored from rather rough usage as barracks by the Austrians. Unfortunately the "Last Supper" of Leo-

'nardo da Vinci is not open till the afternoon, so we had to miss it. We left Milan at 1 p.m. passing through Verona, Vicenza and Padua, and got here at seven, stepping from the station into a gondola, and got to the hotel which is on the Grand Canal and but a block from the Piazza di San Marco. I had telegraphed ahead for an excellent gondolier recommended by Cousin Julia Delano and this morning at ten we went out with him and explored the Piazza and the buildings around it. After lunch we went the whole length of the Grand Canal, examining the wonderful palaces along it and came back through the small canal, visiting three of the churches en route. Then we had tea on the Piazza and found Charlie Forbes soon after our return. We are to lunch with him on Wednesday and tomorrow go to his studio.

I think I had expected to be disappointed in Venice, but the reality is far more wonderful than the pictures I had made. We are glad that our stay will be long enough to let us assimilate the beauties of it all rather than force impressions by a hurried tour. It is deliciously cool—almost too cool for going out in the evening.

I am so glad Sarah H. has taken the house. I only hope you don't give it to her! Too bad F.P. had no news to give you.

Ever your devoted

FDR

Loads of love from us both.

The "rough usage" by the Austrians goes back to the middle of the nineteenth century and the Italian struggle for national independence. A five-day battle in March, 1848, between the Austrian garrison and the unarmed populace of Milan ended in the withdrawal of Austrian troops from the city. Although the Austrian army was forced to evacuate the whole province of Lombardy in 1859, several decades passed before the long process of restoring damaged buildings was begun. A brother of William and Paul Forbes, Charles Stuart Forbes was an artist and lived most

21

of his life abroad. "Sarah H." was Sarah Hoppin, a sister of A.E.R.'s godfather, Fred Weekes, and the daughter of F.D.R.'s cousin, Alice Delano Weekes. She married and then divorced Francis L. V. Hoppin, an architect who helped design new additions to the Roosevelt family home in Hyde Park. "F.P." was an abbreviation for Frances Pell.

〜〜

Dearest Mama,

Franklin wrote you that we had arrived and loved the place and we love it more and more every day. It isn't so much what we see, though everything is interesting, but it's the life and colour of the place which makes you feel that nothing could be quite so lovely—as long as you wished to be idle!

On Tuesday morning we went through the Doges' Palace where there are some wonderful rooms. We were shown through the prison and the spa and where the secret executions took place and the hole into which the bodies were dropped and anything more creepy I cannot imagine. It is very dark and the cells are low with nothing in some of them but a raised slab of stone for the prisoners to sleep on, and in back there is a small hole in the wall through which food was given them. Can you imagine the cruelty of those days, it must have been too awful.

I do not think that the paintings here are as fine as those in Florence, though there are some wonderful Titians and some of the churches have really fine things.

Tuesday afternoon our gondolier (who is very nice and takes a fatherly interest in all our plans and above all in Franklin's photographs) took us through some very picturesque little canals, past lovely old palaces, to see two old churches and finally to call on Mr. Forbes. His studio is charming. It's in an old palace, overlooking a lovely garden, and besides his own room he has the right to paint in the big hall, which is truly magnificent! He showed us some of his things but the only one I really cared for was the portrait of a little girl in the quaintest old fashioned red frock sitting in a big chair, looking so demure and "grande dame" and she is I believe the daughter of a small tobacco dealer! In the evening we went out again and rowed about watching the reflection of the sunset and when it grew dark we joined the other gondolas around one of the large gondolas, in which they play and sing Italian songs. It is really charming to hear them when they all sing together and they will go on forever if you will only pay them!

Yesterday, Wednesday morning, we went to a distant church, S. Giovanni and Paolo where the Doges' tombs are. We also found a funny little antiquity shop where, over the price of a fan and a bit of embroidered silk, I was told how hard it was to make anything now etc. etc. with the life history of the two little men thrown in! We lunched with Mr. Forbes and George Eustis at a little restaurant and at half past two started out for S. Lazaro, an Armenian convent near the Lido where they have some wonderful old books and a printing press. The old monk and Franklin discussed the setting up of type and improved American methods and we had a very interesting time. We then went to the Lido for tea. It is a lovely island with a splendid beach but I never saw anything like the bathing clothes the ladies wear. Their upper garment could not be called a skirt, it was hardly a frill! But Franklin says I must grow accustomed to it as France is worse! It rained in the evening so we did not go out but today is lovely again and we went to the church of St. Peter this morning as it was a festival day and there was an interesting service. On our way back we saw a little gem of a chapel, with the most wonderful wooden ceiling.

We find that the Dalmation Coast is considered hot and

unhealthy so we have given up going there and will stay here anyway till the end of next week. We cannot decide where we want to go but I think we will go through the Dolomites and the Tyrol to the Black Forest.

Thank you so much for the bills (!) and your letter of the 14th which came yesterday. We are always so glad when your letters come. A great deal of love from us both to our darling Mama,

Ever devotedly

ELEANOR

The pen and ink are both execrable.

The prisons that A.E.R. found so impressive were built toward the end of the sixteenth century for the special purpose of housing political criminals. George Eustis was an acquaintance of the family; F.D.R. and his brother, Willie Eustis, became friendly during F.D.R.'s years in the Navy Department.

HÔTEL BRITANNIA, VENICE

JULY 3, 1905

MONDAY

Dearest Mama,

Well, Frances gone and done it, ain't she, v'ot? Wasn't your son the wise one? We neither of us were surprised or shocked at the sudden change of heart—but Frances' letter of announcement to you nearly gave us hysterics—it was too delicious. Still it ought to be a splendid thing for them both. I can see large signed Titians of you chaperoning these two in August.

To go back to Thursday last—we went with C. Forbes to see Novelli act in a wonderful but hot little theatre on a back canal. He, Novelli—not Charlie—was most interesting to me in his expression and acting. I heard him say "si" once, and although this was the only word I could understand, yet it was most artistically rendered and produced such an impression on me that I shall never forget it. The next day (incidentally C. Forbes—not Novelli—dined with us before we went to the play)—the next day, as I was saying, Friday, we went to two churches or so—San Toy and Santa Claus and in one of them I drew a picture of the ceiling to be copied in the addition to the Hyde Park house. After lunch we went to a lace factory and immediately after I cabled Baring Bros. for a new letter of credit—the old one I handed "complet" to the lace man. Then we climbed a campanile on a little island and critically examined the "extensive view."

Saturday a.m. I spent at an old book store and got covered with dust and germs and secured one or two bargains. Then after lunch we went in the gondola to Murano and saw a glass factory etc. Very interesting etc.—Hot, etc.

Yesterday—the Sabbath Day—we went to rubber—*not* church—but the Museo Civile and the Academica de Belly Arty [Accademia di Belle Arti]—a few Paul Veroneses and Titians etc.—chiefly indecent infants sitting on, or falling off of, clouds—or scared apostles trying to keep the sun out of their eyes.

It has been pretty hot for the last three days—over eighty I should think—but not bad, as we take life easily. Last night we went out to the Lido and dined with George Eustis, Charlie F. and a Mr. Care who is ½ Irish and ½ Venetian and hence wholly irresistible. I am trying to recover from a slight attack of hives—feel more or less injured as I have been attacked by fleas too.

Lots of love from us both
ever yours
FDR

You will understand I know about not taking Frances' house. We want a house that we can be in at least two years without changing and also something less expensive. Thank her for offering it to us.

25

The first paragraph of this letter refers to the aforementioned marriage of Frances Pell and Martin Archer-Shee. F.D.R.'s reaction to Ermete Novelli's talent was echoed many times in Europe; with huge successes in Paris and Rome, Novelli had his own company and was one of the foremost actors of the day.

〜〜

HÔTEL BRITANNIA, VENICE
JULY 5, 1905
WEDNESDAY

Dearest Mama,

The last few days have been very hot and it does not seem to grow cooler so I think we will both be glad to get to Belluno on Friday. Franklin has felt the heat a good deal and the hives have made him feel rather miserable so I am doubly glad to get him to a bracing climate.

Last Tuesday morning we went to the Scuola St. Rocco which is a very fine building decorated by Tintoretto and some minor lights. There are also one or two of Titian's things there but I do not think they are among his best. We also saw the church and on our way back to the gondola purchased from a small metal shop two of the brass horses which they use on the gondolas and which we think will make very nice andirons. They weigh a ton but Franklin has got some old and heavy books here so I think we will put the whole lot in a case and send them straight to Paris. We also bought a few things at a fascinating antiquity shop but then the purchase of a few things is quite a business here for they seem to really enjoy the bargaining and they ask just double I think so as to be beaten down. Mr. Dominicki, the proprietor, assured me that of course he did whatever I wished though he was making nothing and yet the fans which we looked at one evening and did not take by the next morning had been reduced in price by just one half!

Tuesday afternoon we went for quite a long trip in the

gondola and had two men take us. First we stopped at Burano which is about six miles from here and most picturesque. The lace school is there and every woman seems to make lace, for you see little groups of them before every door hard at work. We got a cunning photograph of a number of little naked babies in swimming at the mouth of the canal but I don't think it can go in our book! From Burano we went on to Torcello where there is a very old church built in the basilica style about 800 and then we started back just as the sun was setting and it was too lovely. We did not get to the Vapore (the little restaurant where we take all our meals) until twenty minutes before nine. It really was a delightful excursion and as we put a sail up and sailed out the men were not overcome by the heat and Franklin was much amused by their extraordinary methods of sailing. He has decided that they start life here with white sails and then when they grow grimy with the dirt of years they paint them blue or red and feel that they have a new sail.

Wednesday morning, we again went to St. Mark's for another look at the church which is really lovely though the repairs which are going on inside rather mars the effect of the whole. Franklin says he is disappointed in it but it is the only church which he has wanted to see twice! At eleven o'clock we left for Chioggia which took us about two hours in a little steamboat. It is a queer, old little village and after lunching we walked the whole length of it and took several pictures before going for a sail on the Adriatic with three old men who looked like pirates! Like all the rest of their race they asked just double of what they eventually took with gratitude, but we had a wonderful sail and got back just in time to take the boat which landed us here at eight o'clock.

July 6th—Incidentally Franklin forgot to tell you that he met the Winslow Warren's here one day and we both called afterwards! Weren't we good? They sent you their love, Mrs. and Miss that is to say, and I believe we are to meet again at

27

Cortina! This A.M. we've been to Cook's and settled about our trip and we've visited a magnificent palace, which I fail to see how it is possible to inhabit and we have bought some red damask which they tell me is wonderful and which we think very pretty. Mr. Eustis lunched with us and Franklin is now visiting a library and taking a last look at an old book shop!

When he returns we are going to see another palace and an exhibition at the public gardens and then I hope to do a little packing before we go to dine with Mr. Forbes. He has been so very nice to us and we were so sorry he could not lunch with us to-day, but he had an old Mr. Fearing with him so we could only lunch at adjoining tables and he joined us for his smoke.

Our gondolier gentleman has presented us with a wonderful coloured picture of himself which is excellent. He also presented me the day we went to Torcello with a Tasso which he thinks is very old as he has had it thirty years. Of course it is not but it has a nice binding and I think it was very nice of him, don't you?

You must forgive me dear if my letters are long and dull for I can't write like Franklin and I'm really quite ashamed to send you such stupid epistles after his amusing ones. Anyway they carry lots of love from us both to you dearest Mama,

Ever devotedly

ELEANOR

Winslow Warren was a well-known lawyer and a friend of F.D.R.'s parents; between 1898 and 1910 he was an overseer of Harvard, a position later held by F.D.R. The early relations between A.E.R. and her mother-in-law are perhaps revealed in her apology for her "stupid epistles." Aware that her mother-in-law was at one time vigorously opposed to their marriage, an extra-special effort by A.E.R. to please Sara Roosevelt can be discerned throughout the letters written during the first few years of her marriage.

∼∼

Dearest Mama,

Just a few lines to tell you that we left our beloved Venice
yesterday, Friday morning—or rather just after lunch and
went by rail to Belluno, a three hours' journey only. You
cannot imagine what a change it was from the canals of
Venice and the Holland-like mainland behind it to the rocky
pinnacles of this part of the Alps. Belluno is a quaint old
town—but we could only take a short walk as we left this
morning in a two horse trap for the forty mile drive here.
The scenery was wonderful—less forbidding than it will be
at Cortina—and more like some of our drives in Norway
than other parts of the Alps—and the people and villages are
delightful. We lunched at Perarolo and had a two hours'
stroll after it—resuming the drive at four and getting here in
time for the best dinner we have had since leaving Paris.
This is a new hotel and apparently excellent—certainly better than any I have been to in the Swiss mountains. We stay
here tomorrow and go on to Cortina on Monday—only a
three hour drive. There we stay till about Friday, drive to
Toblach, go by rail to Meran, four hours, and thence a drive
of four days over the Stelvio and Bernina passes into the
Engadine and St. Moritz, where we expect to find Mrs.
Mortimer. We certainly struck it hot for three days in Venice
—up to 100° they said, but it was the height of luxury to
have a gondola day and night and there was always some air
on the canals. On Thursday George Eustis lunched with us
and we dined with Charlie Forbes. We bought 3 or 4 old
tapestries and a Tintoretto—the latter in his best style, and
sent a trunk with our valuables to Aunt Doe in Paris to keep
for us. Also I got an old library—about 3,000 books—and

had them shipped to London. By the way the furniture and woodwork, also mosaic floors of one of the old palaces can be got for about $60,000. If you care to have it cable me. The hives are a little better, though I got a new crop yesterday. We are both flourishing and having the time of our lives.

Loads of love

Ever

F.D.R.

P.P.S. *PRIVATE*

It is only a step (or two)—and—well—we are thinking of continuing on in October to Egypt, Ceylon, India, Burma, Siam, Cochin-China, China, Hong-Kong, Philippines, Manchuria, Japan, Honolulu, California, Yosemite, Yellowstone —and Hyde Park.

If so, we have a wonderful scheme of your coming out here the end of August and taking Muriel back in October when she goes over for the wedding. The expense of such a little trip as I have briefly sketched would be—well once more, damn the expense!

F.D.R.

The scenic comparison to Norway dates back to a trip that F.D.R. and his mother took in the summer of 1901. Although the suggested world tour was a jest and never took place, the mention of possible purchases for the Hyde Park house was made seriously by F.D.R. In this instance the purchases were not made, but the idea of adding to the family home occurs frequently in the letters of subsequent years.

∽

PALACE HÔTEL DES DOLOMITES
BORCA-S. VITO
JULY 9, 1905
SUNDAY

Dearest Mama,

Franklin posted his letter to you last night and forgot to say that we got your letters of the 18th and 26th on Friday morning before leaving Venice. It is always so splendid to hear from you and we just love your letters. I am so glad you had Helen with you for a few quiet days and I am very sorry that she is going to lead the unrestful life of Orange, though I suppose she will be quiet after the family goes to Islesboro. Is she going up there?

I am rather sorry about Frederica's engagement to Mr. Pulitzer and curious to know what stories you have heard, so do write us more fully about it.

An old gentleman named Peter Moller is staying here with a wife and daughter and son-in-law and as he introduced himself to us at Belluno, saying that Mr. Forbes had meant to do so in Venice, we are on quite friendly terms, but they are a funny family. The old gentleman I know I have read about in Dickens, his wife might be any good old farmer's lady, his daughter a spoilt woman with many clothes and his son-in-law—well, he wears gold bangles so I don't think I need say any more. Can't you see us on intimate terms?

Yesterday's drive was so lovely and this place is wonderful. I think one might grow weary of the rugged Dolomite peaks if one lived among them but to pass through they are quite magnificent. This hotel is excellent also and you will see by the envelope what a marvelous situation it has.

Incidentally the letter you enclosed to me was from Evelyn Carter and she has sent us a wedding present to Hyde Park, so do open it and tell us what it is.

Our best love to you dearest,

Devotedly

ELEANOR

Frederica Vanderbilt Webb and A.E.R. were childhood friends; three months after this letter was written she married (and later divorced) Ralph Pulitzer, who succeeded his father, Joseph Pulitzer, as a publisher of the *New York World* and the *St. Louis Post-Dispatch*. Frederica Webb's

second marriage was to Cyril H. Jones. An English girl,
Evelyn Carter used to visit Campobello Island, where she
and F.D.R. had become friends.

∾

Dearest Mama,

Here we are at Cortina and a more simple and charming
place it would be hard to imagine. The scenery is magnificent and there are any number of lovely walks and difficult
ascents to keep even energetic folks busy.

We left Borca on Monday afternoon and drove here in
about an hour and a half. There was no trouble in crossing
the frontier, we did not even open a bag, so our drive was
delightful until we reached the foot of the hill on which this
hotel is built. The road is almost perpendicular so we got
out and walked and even then the horses could hardly get
up. However when you are here you feel that the view is
worth the daily climbs! It is a queer little hotel, but the food
is good and everything is clear and fresh. The proprietress is
a funny little lady who has to be treated with great care and
who is quite capable I imagine of refusing to let you stay
if she does not like you! All the servants are maids and
they wear the peasant dress which makes them look so
picturesque.

We found the Miss Van Bibber's here and they have been
very sweet and talked a great deal of Campobello. I think
they are enjoying it immensely and I like their two friends
Mr. Frick and Miss L—— (you know her name so I won't
attempt to spell it!). We sit opposite them at table and
Franklin says he is afraid he will disgrace himself before
leaving and I must say this kind of big family effect does
make one feel on one's best behaviour!

32

Yesterday morning after breakfasting outside, we wandered down through the fields to the village and poked about till nearly lunch time. Franklin devoted two hours after that meal to accounts and then we were taken down to tea at a Mrs. January's who has the quaintest apartment in an old villa just below here. Mrs. January and her daughter spend most of the summer here and the latter takes tremendous walks alone. I feel that she would be an excellent companion for Franklin if we were staying on, as I think she is even better than Evelyn! Mrs. January says she knew me at Fontainebleau years ago, but needless to say I don't remember that meeting though I have a curious feeling that I have seen her quite lately somewhere. After tea we wandered a little way up the mountain behind the hotel to escape being present when the Moller family arrived. They asked Franklin to get them rooms but we knew the size would be a shock to them and I believe it was! Mr. and Mrs. Duer and Miss Gandy are also here and Franklin and I played bridge with the two ladies in the evening.

This morning we have again been to the village with the aforementioned Miss L—— and I have bought six of the peasants' handkerchiefs to make a kimono! They are rather brilliant colours but Miss Van Bibber has just made one so I thought I would try and see the result. We also went to the exhibition which they have of work done by the peasants in winter. Some of their inlaid wood is charming and they do filigree silver work and enamel and iron as well. We actually bought nothing, but I don't think we can hold out to the end! On our way back we met the Rainsford family and chatted a few minutes. It may be dreadful to whisper it, but, for a man who is as ill as Mr. Rainsford is, I have seldom seen a healthier looking specimen! This afternoon we are going to walk to the Belvedere where I hear one gets a lovely view. This is only about a three hour walk and we get tea up there so it sounds very easy and pleasant.

Franklin wants to add a line so I will stop. My very best love dear—

Just a line to say that we are just able to sit up and take a little nourishment. This Hotel is too angelic for me. I am even afraid to swear and have "queered" myself with several old ladies already—in fact this is an old lady's paradise Regained and I feel like Satan all right—TaTa. Lots of love.

F.D.R.

Except for the amusing last paragraph, which is more a reflection of F.D.R.'s contented mood than 'his views about old age, this letter was written by A.E.R. The "Miss Van Bibber's" were two elderly sisters who came from Baltimore and who had become acquaintances of F.D.R.'s mother at Campobello. Mr. and Mrs. Duer were relatives of Katherine A. Duer, the first wife of the celebrated Clarence H. Mackay; the latter was chairman of the board of the Postal Telegraph and Cable Corporation, a director of the Metropolitan Opera Company, and a prominent Catholic layman. Shortly after their divorce in 1914, Katherine Duer married the noted New York surgeon, Dr. Joseph A. Blake, who was in charge of a war hospital in France (vide infra). "Miss Gandy" owned a hat shop in New York, and the several days spent together in Cortina was the beginning of a lasting friendship between Kitty Gandy and the Roosevelts. The "Rainsford family" included two brothers who were F.D.R.'s schoolmates at Groton, Laurence and Kerr Rainsford. Their father, about whom A.E.R. makes "dreadful" comments, was William S. Rainsford, for twenty-three years rector of St. George's Church on Stuyvesant Square in New York City.

∾∾

MERAN, ITALY
JULY 14, 1905
FRIDAY

Thanks so much dearest Mama for your long letter which came yesterday. Franklin is going to write on Sunday so this is only a line to tell you his week in the mountains has made him look finely and this part of our trip is lovely as you can see from this.

Love

E. R.

This short note to F.D.R.'s mother was written on a postcard that pictured a typical mountain scene of the Eastern Alps: towering peaks with the town of Meran nestled in the valley.

〰〰

TRAFOI HOTEL, TRAFOI

JULY 15, 1905

SATURDAY

Dearest Mama,

Eleanor wrote you last Wednesday morning and that afternoon we took quite a climb to a "Belvedere" above Cortina and had a good view and some tea (we didn't eat the view, tho it sounds so). On Thursday morning I got up at the UnChristian hour of 7 and started at 8 with Miss Gandy to climb the Faloria, about 4,000 feet above Cortina. It took us nearly four hours up but the view was well worth the pull, and gave an idea of the wonderful colors of the Dolomites— pink, and yellow rocks, and white slopes of pure limestone— and the clouds were magnificent. We came down a landslide (it happened before we came down it, don't be worried) — almost perpendicular—and got back late for lunch. She— Miss. G.—was quite nice (smoked all my good cigarettes) and promised me a new ostrich feather hat for next winter. You know her shop in N.Y. She sent her best love to you and wants some orders. (E.R. spent the morning with the Miss Van Bibbers climbing up the landslide to meet a husband who never turned up till after they got home!)

In the forenoon we tead with the Van Bibbers who were very nice and made the hotel seem quite homelike—then we went to the village, bought some little pieces of inlaid wood

35

—the winter industry here—and left cards on Mrs. Rainsford. After supper the lady who runs the hotel and who is our bosom friend and an intimate of indeed all her guests, gave us a dance in the dining room. The hotel maids, cook etc. and some of the villagers did a "Schutplatten"—the native dance. It beats a cake walk and a court quadrille and a Robinson Virginia reel all to pieces and smacks of all three. We are going to introduce it next year. I danced with Mme. Menardi and talked to the cook and smoked with a porter and had the time of my life. The hotel is really quite like a house party—too many old ladies the only trouble—and the proprietress and waitresses are at least our equals—they consider themselves quite above many of the guests and come of old families of the Tirol with family trees a thousand years old. I felt almost ashamed to pay my bill when we left yesterday morning. We drove through two wonderful narrow valleys for four hours to Toblach, and got our last glimpse of the Dolomites when we took the train at 1. We changed at Franzenfeste, and again at Botzen and got to Meran at 5.30—the latter quite a large place and found a good hotel.

This a.m. at 7.30 we started in the landau we shall have for four days and drove up a picturesque valley with many ruined castles on the eminences, lunching at Schlanders. It was very dusty and the horse flies were so bad that I had to get out my revolver and shoot several brace. I only skinned the horse once and shot one fly off the end of the driver's nose without scratching him. Next winter I am going to take a job at the Hippodrome.

We left the main road to Landeck at about four, started up hill in a southerly direction towards the Stelvio pass and passed through a very narrow valley getting here at seven. This is 5100 feet up and right at the foot of the Ortler peaks and many glaciers. It is very shut in but the views are magnificent.

Tomorrow we actually cross the Stelvio—the highest wagon road in Europe—9200 feet—four hours up to the top (the boundary between Austria, Italy and Switzerland meeting there) and they say there is ten feet of snow on each side of the road—indeed the pass was opened only two weeks ago. Tomorrow night we spend at Bormio, on the Italian side. Monday night at Le Prese, and on Tuesday cross the Bernina down into St. Moritz.

From St. M. we shall probably go to Ulm and thence into the Black Forest the back way and spend a week at St. Blasien. The peri-mundane trip is developing.

Such a funny letter from F. P.! Almost died over it. She seems really surprised at having said "yes"! *Do* write about her!

Lots of love from us both—All well

Ever your aff.
F.D.R.

The last sentence of the first paragraph was inserted by A.E.R., and it substantiates her remark in *This Is My Story* that on this occasion she "was jealous [of Miss Gandy] beyond description and perfectly delighted when we started off again and drove out of the mountains." Mme. Menardi was the proprietor of this unique and friendly hotel in the Tirol. The First World War caused a slight alteration of F.D.R.'s comment about the Stelvio: when Austria ceded the southern Tirol to Italy under the Treaty of St. Germain, the Stelvio Pass became only the boundary between Switzerland and Italy.

∾

STELVIO PASS
JULY 16, 1905
SUNDAY

This is even more wonderful than the St. Bernard. We are on top for lunch.

F.D.R.

This brief message was written to Sara Roosevelt on a postcard portraying the Stelvio Pass as it winds through the snowcapped mountains. F.D.R. favorably compares it to the Great St. Bernard, another famous pass across the Alps that furthered the military endeavors of the ancient Romans, Charlemagne, and Napoleon.

∽

PALACE HOTEL, ST. MORITZ

JULY 19, 1905

WEDNESDAY

Dearest Mama,

Your letter of July 7th has just come and we were very sorry indeed to hear of Mrs. Grinnell's death. We have missed so often seeing the papers that this is the first we have heard of it. Could you find out whether the house in town is for rent and if it could be had for two or three years at $2,500. If it can be and the Newbold's have not already taken it, will you try to get it for us as it is just about the size we want, near you and I suppose in good order which would make it worth the extra $500.

We had a dreadful shock on arriving here yesterday for we were given two telegrams and of course at once thought something dreadful had happened. They turned out however to be the announcement of Isabella's marriage to Bob Ferguson. One was from Mrs. Selmes and the other from Mr. F. to Brother Rosy and Baring Bros. had sent it to us, so we had to send it back! I don't think anything has happened nicer than this since our own wedding but we were overcome and I can hardly believe it now! Well, now I must go back to Monday morning and our wonderful drive over the Stelvio. We started at about 8 A.M. and climbed steadily till lunch time. Franklin sent you a post card from the top where we lunched, but of course it could give you no idea of the marvellous snow peaks all around us and late as it was in the summer, there was ten feet of snow beside the road in one

38

place and the air felt as it does at Hyde Park on a brilliant February day. We had a lovely day and Franklin climbed to the highest peak and took some photographs which I hope will be good. It took us about two hours to drive down to Bormio where we spent our second night and the views all the way were enchanting. The road itself was marvellous however as it winds down along the side of an almost perpendicular mountain and we went through numerous tunnels and galleries and each time we came out the scene before us was more beautiful it seemed. Even very near the top there were beautiful wild flowers and as Franklin walked a good part of the way up he picked a number of them and the wild jasmine smells sweeter than anything I have ever had. The hotel at Bormio was comfortable and we both went to bed early after a good dinner and a little piquet. I have actually been beating Franklin lately at the game and I feel so proud that I know I must soon have a fall!

Tuesday morning we had again an early start and drove down hill all the morning through some lovely country. The villages for the most part are most picturesque and very old and their old clock towers are charming. We lunched at Tirano in a quaint old building which was once a monastery and I think part of it is still, for we caught glimpses of one or two monks gliding hurriedly through the passages. After lunch we wandered about and looked at the church which is quite fine 16th century with beautifully carved marble pillars and lovely woodwork carved and inlaid. We started to go up in the afternoon and climbed steadily until we reached Le Prese Kurhaus which is built on the lovely Poschiavo Lake. The mountains come down quite steeply all around it, and it is the most wonderful deep green colour. It looks as though the bottom could never be reached, and the trees have looked into it so long that it has taken their colour for its own. Rather to our dismay the proprietor said he had no telegram from us and had no room, but luckily he got one

for us in a villa close by so all was well! The next morning
our driver told us there had been a landslide on the road we
had come over and had we been a day later we could not have
got over! Weren't we in luck! Tuesday we started at 7.30
A.M. and climbed almost to the top of the Bernina pass
before we stopped to lunch. (You can imagine how Franklin
loves now to arise with the lark after so much practice!!) The
scenery was beautiful over this pass too but I don't think it is
as fine as the Stelvio. Unluckily Franklin's panorama got out
of order so he only got little photographs of this last day's
drive, but as it was rather cloudy and showery in the afternoon he could not have gotten very good ones with the big
Kodak anyway. Just as we were driving up the last hill to
St. Moritz, we saw a trap coming down with Auntie Tissie.
We yelled and a more surprised and bewildered person you
have never seen for she had no idea what time we would
arrive. We all hopped out and stood in the muddy road and
said polite things to each other and she asked us both to dine
here with them in the evening. She had got our rooms for us,
but her ideas of the necessities of life and ours differ, so I was
a little anxious as to what we would find awaiting us. However, we are surviving her extravagance and find ourselves
very comfortable in rooms which look over the lake and have
a nice balcony where we have breakfast and tea. After unpacking our many belongings (we now have one small
steamer trunk and hat trunk between us) we dressed and
went down to dinner. I felt very shabby in my old black
dress with wonderfully dressed ladies all about but what does
it matter. Uncle Stanley and Franklin met for the first
time and I could see that Uncle Stanley had lost his heart to
him, and he told Auntie Tissie afterwards all kinds of nice
things about him which pleased me as he is really a dear and
I wanted them to get on. We found our rooms full of flowers
which Auntie Tissie and the children had picked for us and
I also found my wedding presents here from them. Auntie

Tissie has given me a really lovely old French pendant which I think is going to be very nice under my dog collar. It is small diamonds with two emeralds and Franklin loves it and says he knows you will too, so I am crazy to show it to you! Uncle Stanley gave me a white ostrich feather fan with light tortoise shell sticks and my initials in diamonds and the children gave me a dear little chain with a little pendant parrot, very pretty and original and their own choice. Altogether I am delighted with my new presents and I do hope you will like them. Auntie Tissie says she is going to give Franklin something for the house later on but she couldn't think of anything now! I am devoutly thankful for I already begin to wonder where I am going to pack all the things we've got now!

This place is lovely. Franklin says the loveliest place we have seen yet but I can't make up my mind we've seen so much that is beautiful. This A.M. was rather rainy but we went out and saw the children at Auntie Tissie's little cottage which is next to this hotel and then we went to the bank and met Auntie Tissie who showed us the shops for cakes and soap and books. I then went to have my hair washed and so did Franklin and at quarter to one we lunched with Auntie Tissie. Afterwards Franklin found a paper and devoured it and then we all talked until Franklin had to go and get ready to play golf with Uncle Stanley when I went driving with Auntie Tissie. On my way home whom do you think I saw? Mrs. Clarence Cary! Auntie Tissie had told me she was here so I was not surprised but I am wondering a little if she will find out where we are and come to see us! Franklin and I had tea out on our balcony and mapped out our future plans a little and then went down to dinner, since when I have been writing this and he has been mending his Kodak and occasionally telling me that I have a wonderful husband, so I suppose he is being successful! We leave here on Monday for Augsburg, then to the Black Forest. I am very glad we came north for Franklin looks so well and I think he's feeling well too.

We are very sorry about Uncle Johnnie. I don't suppose he will go to Nauheim? By the way do you hear anything of Sheffield? My grandmother writes she saw in the paper he had typhoid and that is too awful and I only hope it is a mistake.

The letter you forwarded from Campobello was apparently written five years ago to Franklin by Miss Blodgett. Something very odd must have happened I think! I am so glad Frances is getting her wedding gown at Dunstan. She ought to be a lovely bride.

Your letters are so nice dear, they are just a breath of home and I wish you could see how we read and reread them when they come. I hardly dare hope that we shall get the Grinnell home but it would be nice, wouldn't it?

Much much love dearest from us both.

Ever your devoted
ELEANOR

I'm afraid parts of this letter sound quite mad and I must apologize for the tear but I can't rewrite it so please forgive me!

The wife of Irving Grinnell of New Hamburgh, N.Y., Joanna H. Grinnell was a sister of James Roosevelt's first wife. During the several months' interval between their marriage and the trip abroad, the young couple had temporarily rented a small apartment in the West Forties with the idea of establishing a more permanent residence upon their return from Europe, and thus the problem of renting and furnishing a house more or less dominates the remaining letters of this chapter. "The Newbold's" refers to the family of Thomas Newbold, Hyde Park neighbors of the Roosevelts. Isabella Selmes and A.E.R. had met and become very close friends after A.E.R. finished her education and returned from Europe. Robert Ferguson ("Mr. F."), who was eighteen years older than his bride, was also a member of the group that A.E.R. associated with prior to her marriage. Mrs. Tilden R. Selmes was Isabella's mother. "Brother Rosy" refers to F.D.R.'s half-brother, James Roosevelt Roosevelt, who was twenty-eight years his senior. Mrs. Clarence Cary was the mother of Guy and Howard Cary, schoolmates of F.D.R. at Groton; Guy Cary later became a lawyer and a member of the firm of Shearman and Sterling and Wright. "Uncle Johnnie" was F.D.R.'s paternal uncle, John Aspinwall Roosevelt. Since F.D.R.'s father used to go to the health resort at Nauheim in Germany for baths in carbonated water and other exercises calculated to relieve heart disease, the idea of a similar trip for Uncle Johnnie was suggested by the family, but he could never be induced to go. "Sheffield" was Auntie Bye's only child, William Sheffield Cowles, Jr., who later became a stock broker and a partner in the firm of Wood Walker and Company. Miss Eleanor Blodgett was F.D.R.'s godmother and perhaps Sara Roosevelt's closest friend. The tear mentioned in the postscript is exactly two and a quarter inches long in the center of one page of this twelve-page letter.

PALACE HOTEL, ST. MORITZ
JULY 22, 1905
SATURDAY

Dearest Mama,

We were so glad to get your letter of July 9th on Thursday, and *delighted* to hear about the Draper house. We had been particularly told by Kenneth Robinson that we couldn't get it—and though the price is a good deal more than we want to pay, yet we want a house for two years and you say that for $2400 Mrs. Draper will do a good job for us. It is just the right situation and size for us and our one hope is to hear very soon that you have got it for us. It would be so nice to feel that all is settled before we return. Eleanor had a very nice and amusing letter from Alice Draper and she was apparently much delighted with Hyde Park and buttered you on both sides and said things that would quite turn your head. I hope you got the cable all right—and if you succeed in getting the house and have not cabled us, could you write Lathrop at once and tell him about it and ask him to tell K. Robinson also.

We almost expired over the cable announcing Bob Ferguson's marriage to Isabella. Do write us what you have heard—was it sudden etc.?

On Wednesday—the day after we arrived here—we lunched with Tissie and Mr. M. in their little cottage and I had a game of golf with him afterwards and showed the effects of not having seen or smelt a golf stick for nearly a year. We had a quiet but ruinous dinner in the Hotel.

Thursday we drove at 11 a.m. to the Morteratsch Glacier and met Tissie and Stanley and the two children there, lunched and had a nice walk afterwards. In the evening they dined with us here.

Yesterday Stanley left to go back to America. Tissie follows in September. We had a quiet day and took tea on top of a small hill above this. Today we had another excursion—this time to the Fexthal where we met Tissie and the children and governess. After lunch we climbed quite high up and got over a dozen edelweiss. It was too lovely and I am convinced that for an all-round place this is by far the most attractive I have seen in the Alps. The valley is wonderful, with several charming lakes, and as the place itself is so high the surrounding mountains do not make it seem shut in and yet the snow effects are very fine.

Sunday July 23rd—

This morning Eleanor went to church with Tissie and I climbed a hill to recover my gold pencil which I had left there and luckily found it safe.

After lunch, Tissie, E. and I drove to Maloja, about 8 miles away and just at the point where the valley drops down into Italy. We walked up to a tiny lake at the base of two big mountains and got back just in time for dinner. Now we are packing and leave at 6 a.m. (⌒ this is a yawn) and get to

Augsburg at 7 p.m., a long day, but better than stopping at a stupid place. There we stay two days and go to Ulm for another two, then to Titisee and St. Blasien where we shall have a quiet week; then up to Feldberg to see the sunrise, to Freiburg for a day and to Strassburg and Amiens for a day each, getting to Paris about August 12th.

By the way, I don't suppose Mrs. Draper will want to start the work on the house till we get back and of course we want to choose the papers. I want the plumbing examined, even if it was put in two years ago and of course the woodwork etc. will need redoing. Eleanor says that *if* you happen to see in the paper of any sale of servants' cotton sheets, towels etc. and happen to be in town that day or could write and get us some, she would be very grateful. We are so so glad that it is really through you that we get the house—if indeed we are so lucky and it is so good of you to take all the trouble for us. Loads love from us both. We will write from Augsburg.

Ever your loving infants.

This letter was written by F.D.R. Mrs. Draper was a half-sister-in-law of Alice Draper, and it was "the Draper House" (125 East 36th Street), located only three blocks from Sara Roosevelt's home, that became the residence of F.D.R. and his bride until Sara Roosevelt purchased the plot on East 65th Street. Kenneth Robinson was a cousin of Douglas Robinson. "Lathrop" refers to Lathrop Brown, F.D.R.'s roommate for four years at Harvard and one of his most intimate friends.

〜〜

Dearest Mama,

We actually got up yesterday morning at 4:30 A.M. and left St. Moritz at 5:55 and wonderful to relate we are still alive to tell the tale! It rained all day and we hopped from one train to another four times and went through two custom houses successfully, Franklin having hid part of his cigarettes among my veils. In Brigens we had an hour to wait and the rain held up for about half an hour so we got a walk through part of the little town and it looked very quaint and attractive. About two hours before we reached here, four large and burly Germans got into our compartment while Franklin was getting some beer and as they at first paid no attention to me, I thought Franklin would find no seat on his return. However, by dint of piling coats and cameras up opposite me I succeeded in keeping it, but to my horror the train began to move and there was no Franklin and I had no ticket and no money! You can imagine my feelings but luckily we returned to the station and Franklin reappeared. Of course the Germans proceeded to make themselves comfortable and at one time I thought Franklin would burst and a duel would ensue, for one of the Germans, after pulling the blinds across *our* windows, leaned across Franklin and closed the window without so much as saying "by your leave"! However, we arrived here safely at 7:30 P.M. and the place looked very attractive even last night so we were glad we came through in a day. This is said to be the oldest hotel in Germany and it is very comfortable. We dined and went straight to bed and slept until nine o'clock this morning! We just went out and wandered up the principal street to the cathedral which is nice but nothing wonderful and then we went down to the oldest street which is fascinating. Nearly all the houses go up in a peak in front, the roofs are very steep with little staircase effects going up them, and the second story nearly always overhangs the street. Some of them have old paintings on the outside walls and even the smallest have flowers in the little square windows which gives color to all the streets. There are lots of little parks and trees everywhere and canals even through certain streets which gives them quite a rural air. We lunched at a little restaurant and then saw a very interesting old church of St. Ulrich and St. Afra. The iron screens in this church were quite beautiful, but I came away with the creeps as the small boy who kept the keys and showed us around exhibited with triumph the skeleton dressed in marvellous and gorgeous robes and laid in a glass case of St. Afra! And there were other dressed up skeletons in glass cases all around and it did seem very gruesome and horrid. After this rather doubtful pleasure we went in search of old book shops and strange to say there doesn't seem to be such a thing in Augsburg! We found only one antiquity shop where Franklin got a book of prayers in a very nice binding, the queerest old compass, broken, but in a nice old wooden case and two little boxes. Then we came back for tea and Franklin is now studying Baedeker and trying to settle our future route! He has hives again and I cannot understand it, as he seems quite well and we have been leading a very quiet life in a very cool and healthy climate since left Venice, with the exception of yesterday! I think it may be white wine which we had in St. Moritz and now that he doesn't drink it, I hope the hives will depart. I must now get ready for dinner but will finish before we leave on Thursday morning.

Wednesday evening July 26th—This morning we went to the "Rathaus" which has a wonderfully fine hall in it and various smaller rooms with fascinating woodwork and queer big stoves which reach up to the ceiling and which the little old lady caretaker endeavored to explain to me were very fine but I don't think she found me sympathetic so she finally gave it up. We then walked around for quite a while trying

47

to get some good pictures and came back to the hotel for lunch. Afterwards Franklin became so engrossed in a story of Bret Harte's (which we found in a shop where they apparently kept only Tauchnitz books published between '75 and '80!) that we did not get out till nearly four. I am reading a French book by Anatole France but he occasionally disgusts me so that I have to stop, and yet it is a mild and proper book for French, devoted so far to the problem of our future life! When we did get out we tried to see the inside of the St. Anna Kirche but only succeeded in seeing the outside as it was closed and we did not want to search for the sacristan. Then we walked to the "Stadt Gasten" which sounds very imposing but is really a very small park, quite attractive and with a restaurant where apparently all the old ladies and gentlemen and a few young ones go for coffee. It was most amusing and besides very good coffee. We got an excellent picture of a German hen party who sat near us.

We start at ten tomorrow for Ulm so I thought I had better finish to-night as we are usually hurried in the morning! From Ulm we go to Schaffhausen to see the Falls of the Rhine and drive up to St. Blasien from Albbruck on Sunday.

Poor Mama, I am afraid we've given you lots of work about the house, but I shall be so glad if we get it and it is quite near you. Much, much love from us both,

Ever your loving

ELEANOR

A cheap, paperbound collection of American and British authors (approximately five thousand different works), the "Tauchnitz books" were very familiar to English-speaking travelers on the Continent. As a part of the plan to rid Europe of its Anglo-Saxon influence, the German Army, during the Nazi occupation of France, systematically went through the French bookshops and destroyed all the books written by American and British authors—all except the Tauchnitz editions, which were published in Leipzig.

∽

Dearest Mama,

We got your nice letter of the 13th and 14th on arriving here and also several other home letters which delighted us. You don't seem to be getting many letters from us and I am wondering if they get lost for we certainly write them! Franklin will write from St. Blasien on Sunday and tell you all about this so I'll only say that our first afternoon has been very pleasant and the cathedral is very fine.

Love from us both.

ELEANOR

This brief note was written on a postcard showing the facade of the magnificent Münster in Ulm, the second largest Gothic church in Germany.

Dearest Mama,

We have just arrived in this well remembered spot and found your much appreciated letter of the 17th, but not a word yet about the house—and of course we are dying to hear if you could get it for us or not. Wasn't it sudden about Isabella and Bob Ferguson—but *so* nice. We hadn't heard a word about it or even seriously suspected it.

What an emptiness there is at Campo! I suppose you are just about starting on the Tour of the coast of Maine, but as you haven't mentioned a word about *your* plans we haven't the vaguest idea whether you are going to Portland, Maine or Portland, Oregon!

Poor Rae—the Rogers children certainly have had hard luck in the way of grey matter.

49

We are sorry about Uncle Johnnie—what a pity he can't be persuaded to go to Nauheim—it would be as much a cure for Aunt Ellen and Ellie as for him.

Last Thursday we went from Augsburg to Ulm, a short distance, in the morning. Ulm is a most enchanting old spot —not as large as Augsburg but just as interesting. Of course the Cathedral is the main "sight" and we spent half an hour in it listening to an excellent recital on the largest organ in Germany. Also the spire is the highest of any church in the world I think, but our energies lay in other directions as I discovered a wonderful old woman who knows Latin, Greek and all modern languages and supports two sons by selling old books, prints, etc. We spent much time in her garden, and I got several nice things. Also we spent part of our day in the Gewerbe Museum, an old Patrician house filled with wonderful things and we also found time to indulge in coffees and beers in the "Restaurations."

Yesterday, Saturday, we left Ulm at 10, lunched at Friedrichshafen on the Lake of Constance and got to Schaffhausen at 3. The rest of the day we spent at the falls of the Rhine nearby—first going across by bridge to the Schloss Laufen where we had some good views. Then we walked down almost *under* the Falls, so close that the spray flew over us, then got into a boat and whirled out into the boiling waters at the foot. The two rowers "worked the eddies" and we landed at the bottom of the rock which rises right in the middle of the Falls and climbed up it. Then we were whirled back to the opposite shore after a *very* rough and rather damp trip of twenty minutes. It looks anything but safe—but hundreds do it every day. The Falls exceeded my expectations, though compared to Niagara they might be called a "cunning little trickle"!

This morning we left Schaffhausen at eleven and had a nice lunch at Albbruck where the carriage was awaiting us and got here at six.

Although it is nine years since I was here, yet I remembered the Albthal quite well and the place where my bicycle chain broke and the house Mr. Dumper and I stayed in during a bad thunder storm.

But St. Blasien itself is a good deal changed. The Kurhaus is much larger and we are in it facing the Kloster Gasthof in which I was unable to get room. The Hotel Hirsh at the other end of the village is now a large first class place and there are many lodgings. The place is *jammed* with people and the band is now playing behind the Kloster—quite an innovation for me.

Thank Heavens they have a new Portier—you remember how I hated the one here before! By a show of severity I have secured a table on the verandah—the dining room has four long pigsties where the strange assortment of mortals (swine are mortal, n'est ce pas?) consume victuals.

I think we shall stay here a week, then go up the Feldberg and then to Freiburg, Strassburg, Amiens and Paris, arriving at the latter place on August 11th.

The weather is lovely and we are full of health and bursting with food (at least I am) and the only unkind word E. has ever said to me is that she would like to *see* me bust! When I *do* bust I shall go off quietly and alone as the explosion and mess would be horrible. Loads of love from us both.

Ever after

F.D.R.

"Rae" was a son of Archibald Rogers, whose family were neighbors of the Roosevelts at Hyde Park, and whose children periodically encountered difficulties in school. "Aunt Ellen" was the wife of John Aspinwall Roosevelt, the former Ellen Murray Crosby, and "Ellie" was their youngest daughter. Mr. Arthur Dumper came from Cleveland; he was F.D.R.'s tutor during the three years before he attended Groton.

Dearest Mama,

We are having such a nice lazy time here that I'm afraid my letter is bound to be unbearably dull!

Our room has a small balcony and after breakfasting out there yesterday morning we sat there and read and wrote until lunch time. Then we went down to the Tusculum waterfall and up to Gross-Herzogin-Lusien-Ruhe where we sat most of the afternoon. Several people came up there but the only people who stayed at all were an English and an American couple who sat down back of us and conversed in loud tones much to our amusement. Needless to say the Americans were common and the man had evidently been a German at no very distant date. They were impressing the English couple with their wealth and after explaining that in America there was no such thing as a season for eatables, that strawberries were much better in January than in June and that of course the price was no consideration, they proceeded to discuss the government of the country and finally the negro question while Franklin and I pretended to do accounts and in reality nearly expired with suppressed laughter! In the evening we returned to our balcony and played piquet and watched the most wonderful pinky clouds I've ever seen and listened to the band which plays every night in the Kloster garden but which sounds far nicer from here, I think. They also have a band which plays from 7 A.M. till 10 A.M. and I rather wish they had left that out of the day's programme. Franklin has been doing accounts all this morning and he is really marvellous for he always comes out exactly right!

We found a letter here from Aunt Doe and she is going to be in Paris all the time we are there which is a great relief to me as she was such a help last time. We want to go on several all day trips while we are there, to Chartres and Fontaine-bleau etc. and I hope she will go with us for she probably knows them all well.

What a wonderful trip Muriel must have had and how interesting to dine with the Emperor. I do hope we shall see her and hear all about it before we sail, but we haven't heard from any of them so we are afraid we may not see them at all. We are going to lunch so I will finish this very stupid letter later on.

Wednesday afternoon—Dearest Mama. We have just had a dreadful shock, in the shape of several letters, among them yours of July 2nd! Where they have been all this time I don't know but they were evidently sent to Hotel Faloria, Cortina and remained there a long time before they were returned to Barings. Well, we are glad to get them at last and your letter explains a number of things which we thought you spoke of very casually in the letter we got at St. Moritz. Also we have only just heard of your present to us, you dear, dear Mama. It was too sweet of you to send us such a wonderful present and I shall enjoy spending my share in London or Paris. Franklin is going to add a line at the end so I'm not thanking for him! How I would like to kiss you and *tell* you instead of writing my thanks. You don't know how pleased we both are and I can't half express the pleasurable thrills I have when I think of the fun I shall have in Paris! I do hope in the end you got Franklin's letters but both in this letter and in the one which we also received to-day of the 20th and 21st you say his letters, which are written to catch the steamer before mine, have not yet come! I don't understand it and I'm so sorry for we hoped you got letters twice a week! Now I must answer the questions in your first letter about clothes, furs etc. though as I haven't tried any of them on I can't say how they will look. Franklin's furs are lovely, a long stole and big muff of the softest, finest mink I've ever seen. Aunt Doe helped us choose them as well as everything else and of course she was a great help as she knew so much about furs compared to our ignorant selves. I am ashamed to tell you how many clothes I ordered but as you will see them all soon perhaps it is as well to prepare you! We got a white cloth evening cloak and I had my old white fur lined and arranged so that in winter it buttons into the cloak and keeps me wonderfully warm. Then I got a very grand three quarter coat and a whole dress for the afternoon in pastel blue with a short skirt to wear if I want to be a little less grand. For the evening I got a white net dress with a collar so I can have it high or low necked and black gown which Aunt Doe ordered after I left for the same kind of use. Then a pompadour silk low neck gown, a pale mauve crepe de chine high neck gown and a pale blue tea gown complete my list except for a rough tweed coat and skirt and a riding habit I ordered in London. Are you horrified at my extravagance? I am, but Franklin hasn't begun to complain as yet.

And now for your letter of the 20th which caused us great excitement! You are an angel to take so much trouble about the house and in all this hot weather too, but I am so glad you are going to see it and I do hope you will take it if it is possible! What a wonderful thing it would be if you could work the extension but we hardly dare hope for such luxury and will be quite happy if the plumbing is good and the paint and papers fresh and new. If there is a telephone please don't let it be taken out and is there a safe in the house?

Thanks so much for Cousin Alice's letter about Isabella's wedding. Helen has just written us about it too and she says they ended up by taking Ethel and Kermit to lunch at Sherry's! We think it must have been rather queer all around from the descriptions, don't you?

It rained hard all yesterday so we spent the day on our balcony, reading, writing, sewing and playing piquet. To-day has been cloudy too and it rained this morning, so I finished up the family mending and Franklin read and this afternoon we had a good walk through the woods up to the Sandboten and down by all kinds of *wrong* paths which lengthened our walk and did us lots of good! This hotel has afforded us lots of amusement for they have all kinds of strange rules and regulations! Notices such as "Türe Leise Zumachen" are everywhere and in consequence we always slam the doors. You are also requested to make no noise after 10 P.M. in your room and Franklin is not even allowed *to light* a *cigarette* after dinner on the piazza! I think we may be thrown out before Sunday, but we hope for the best!

We have been writing Aunt Doe post cards and letters quite often during the summer. Did she write you as though she did not think we wrote enough? She has been so sweet to us that I would hate her to feel we were not "aux petits soins."

I will leave the rest of the paper for Franklin, so goodbye dearest and a thousand thanks and kisses. I feel as though we would have such long arrears of kisses and cuddly times to make up when we get home! Lovingly, Eleanor.

Dearest Mama. You must have thought it very queer indeed that we did not thank you before this. With your belated letter came also one from the Barings saying £100 had been credited to my account. It is really too sweet of you and all afternoon we have been talking over what we shall get with it. Indeed we had decided not to *look,* even, at anything pretty or go near any more antiquity or book shops, but now we shall sail around Strassburg and Amiens and Paris like a "Pierp" Morgan. I shall certainly take the driving lessons unless it is frightfully hot—and you know what Paris can be the middle of August!

It is too lovely here and we spend most of the day eating and sitting on the balcony. Tomorrow we think of going up to Höchenschwand for lunch and on Saturday to Todtmos or Schluchsee for the day.   Ever your loving   FDR

Muriel's dinner with Emperor William II of Germany occurred at a time when international tension was beginning to mount; the summer of 1905 witnessed a direct conflict of French and German interests in Morocco, and the Moroccan crisis greatly solidified British and French unity against Germany. "Cousin Alice" was Mrs. John A. Weekes, the former Alice Delano. "Ethel and Kermit" were two of Theodore Roosevelt's children by his second marriage. Kermit Roosevelt afterward became active in the shipping business; he died in Alaska while serving as a major in the United States Army in 1943. Ethel Roosevelt married Dr. Richard Derby, who was a year ahead of F.D.R. at Groton and Harvard.

FELDBERG

AUGUST 7, 1905

MONDAY

We are on top of the Feldberg and the sun has just risen but the clouds prevent a view of the Alps. We get to Freiburg this afternoon.

F.D.R.

This card to F.D.R.'s mother pictures the Feldsee just as Karl Baedeker's *Handbook for Travellers* describes it, i.e., as "a gloomy little lake enclosed by precipitous pine-clad mountains." The Feldberg is the highest mountain in the Black Forest.

ZAHRINGER HOF, FREIBURG

AUGUST 7, 1905

MONDAY

Dearest Mama,

We have just got to this hotel—very well remembered by me, and I will write you before we go down to lunch as I may be too sleepy later—for we arose with the sun this

56

morning on top of the Feldberg. But I will go back to Thursday last at St. Blasien, Eleanor having written you on Wednesday. After the rain of the two previous days Thursday was clear and delightful. After lunch we took an Einspänner and drove up to Höchenschwand which you remember as a little village on top of a hill—now there is a good sized hotel and an Aussicht Thurm. The view was magnificent and clear enough for us to see all the Alps I am glad to say as it was the only sight of them we had. We walked all the way down and as usual spent a quiet evening and I paid all my bills except one from Charles & Co. that is so mixed up with your things that I will have to wait till I get back. Friday was overcast but we managed to walk up the Lehenkopf and climb the same old tower on top.

Saturday morning was lovely and we started at ten thirty in a Victoria to drive to Schluchsee as I wanted E. to see it— but before we got there it began to pour and our drive back after lunch was rather damp. That evening we had another room—a tiny one up in the Kloster as other arrivals had engaged our nice room and balcony far ahead, but it was only for the night and we didn't mind much.

Yesterday it was still raining, first cats then dogs, and we left after lunch for the Feldberg. It seemed like quite a break as we have been in St. Blasien longer than any other place except Venice and I think E. loved it just as much as I did. We reached the Feldberg Inn at 5, but alas the old Inn is now a caravansery and only the little dining room is un-changed; but there is also a huge new wing with a table d'hote of over a hundred people. In fact it is so unromantic that we had difficulty in being called at five this morning and they looked at us aghast when we demanded breakfast at 5.30. Still, we got it and walked up to Feldberg via the Bismarck Denkmal on the Seebrugg. The Tower and little boutique were just the same, but an inn has been added on the very top! The view was not wonderful, because of the mist rising after the soaking of the last few days, but still it was lovely and showed most of the Black Forest. We got back to the hotel at 7:30 and left in a few minutes for the drive down to Titisee. The moisture on all the trees and undergrowth and the bright sun made it very picturesque. We managed by much shoving to secure seats in the observation car and got here at eleven after passing through the Hollenthal—the scene of the 18 mile coast on our bicycles nine years ago.

After lunch we are going out to see the Cathedral and the old houses and tomorrow we move on to Strassburg where we should find a mail—and this will be most welcome, as we have not heard since Wednesday. We stay in Strassburg till Thursday, then go to Nancy for the night and get to Paris Friday evening. We had intended going to Amiens instead of Nancy, but found it was not on our route, and Nancy may be interesting, though we neither of us know of any particularly wonderful things to see there.

Since your delightful present to us we feel so rich that we may bring home anything from a St. Bernitte dog to a set of dining room furniture. E. thinks of having us painted by Sargent with her share of it. We are both well except for gastronomic indispositions from over-doses of solid nourishment and matitudinal headaches (on the part of your son) from over-doses of liquid refreshment. We can hardly wait to hear more about the house.

A great deal of love from us both.

Ever your devoted,   F.D.R.

ENGLISCHER HOF, STRASSBURG
AUGUST 8, 1905
TUESDAY

Dearest Mama,

We arrived here about half an hour ago and found your two letters of the 23rd and 25th with the good news in the last that you had taken the house! We are so glad and think you have done wonders for us, in the way of a good bargain. It is very nice that the work can be begun before we get home for the papering should not take very long and we will get settled so much sooner than if we waited to choose a house on our return. Altogether we feel very jubilant over it and I am looking forward so much to getting it in order with you to help us. I am afraid my unaided efforts would not be very successful! Franklin will write Mrs. Draper "a few kind words" to-morrow. We are now going out so will continue later.

Later—How very peculiarly the mails go Mama dear, and how mixed you must be when a letter from Venice reaches you at the same time as a letter from Borca written three days later! I was much relieved to know that Aunt Doe had *not* complained of our not writing and we were both glad to hear that Uncle Johnnie was better. Poor Ellie! What a strain it must be on her and on Aunt Ellen.

After Franklin wrote you yesterday we went out and walked round the "Münster" which I think lovely in spite of its many different periods of architecture and then we found a book shop, but as they didn't seem to have much or else couldn't understand us, Franklin got a catalogue to look over and we went off to the Stadt Garten for tea. This morning we returned to the book shop and Franklin got a few volumes on Maximilian in Mexico, two of which are in French, so I am going to begin my education on the subject by reading them! Franklin says I am ruining him, I read so much trash in such a short time, so he is quite pleased at the thought of a few days spent on "The Letters of Maximilian's private Secretary"! Then we went to see the old Rathaus which is very attractive and interesting I think, and walked out through the Martinsthor and passed the Schwabenthor, going up the hill to the Kanonen-platz, from which we had a magnificent view of the Münster and the city. Much to our astonishment, while we were taking a photograph up there, a man and a woman standing up spoke to us! As no one ever does such a thing we nearly fell over the parapet, but they turned out to be Americans who lived in Freiburg and I think they just had to talk to some Americans. They looked quite hungry. We only spoke for a few minutes of course but I was so sorry for the man, and I don't think he could have been home in years. After lunch we took a three o'clock train here and though we only had time for a short walk before dinner, I think we are going to like it. We went and saw the outside of the Münster but I don't like it as well as Freiburg, for though the façade and the one completed tower are wonderful, the back is very ugly and does not harmonise nearly as well as the various different styles at Freiburg. Our hotel is very nice, but as they are making alterations we can only get breakfast here, so we dined to-night at a wonderful restaurant, quite near here on a street called the Alter Wein Markt, where however there isn't a sign of any Alter Wein Markt now! Our dinner was so delicious that Franklin hasn't been able to move out of his chair since we came in!

I am so glad you went to see Helen and that she looks well. By now, you must have seen Uncle Warren and all of them and heard all about the trip. It is nice that they have enjoyed it so much and they must be glad now to get home and be quiet for a time. I suppose you will go the 10th or 15th to the coast of Maine, and though I feel sure you wish you were staying at Hyde Park, we are very glad you are going away for a time as the heat must have been very trying for you. Goodnight now dear, this doesn't go till Thursday so I shall finish at Nancy.

Nancy—August 10th. Franklin sent you a postcard yesterday so you saw that we had tea in a very pretty place! In the morning we really saw the Münster well, watched the wonderful self regulating clock (which is already half an hour

slow!) strike the quarter, whereupon a few of the figures performed, but they don't all work except at twelve o'clock and
we could not wait as we wanted to climb the tower. We only
went up 383 steps to the platform but that is very high and
the view marvellous. Franklin got several pictures from there
which ought to be good, but as he had been up to the top of
the spire once, he didn't go up this time. After that we started
to go and lunch at our restaurant but shopped several times
en route at book shops, all of which had signs outside announcing that they were "Antiquariats" but none of which
had any old books! We got lunch and returned to the hotel
for an hour's rest and then started out through the old part
of the town to see the church of St. Thomas which in itself is
quite a plain and unadorned church but in which is the tomb
of Marshal Saxe. Franklin thought it very fine and the figures
of the Marshal, descending to the tomb, which death holds
open for him while a woman representing France holds him
back are certainly wonderfully executed, but there are flags
broken and otherwise, and leopards, lions etc. around him
which I do not like quite so well, but I'm afraid I like the
plainest tombs nearly always the best. In the same church is
an old sarcophagus about a thousand years old and horror of
horrors! the mummies of the Duke of Nassau, dressed as he
was when he was killed, and his little girl aged twelve. It
seemed too dreadful to see people who had been dead only
two hundred years or so lying exposed to any curious gaze.
After this harrowing church we felt in need of refreshment
and went out to the garden of which Franklin sent you a post
card. There we had tea and got back to the city just in time
for dinner.

This A.M. we came on here and we have spent the whole
afternoon walking around. The town is attractive and there
are several fine buildings, l'Hôtel de Ville, the old ducal
palace etc., one or two very old and curious gates built in
the 14th century and one interesting church with the tomb

of Réné II, a most magnificent stone effect, coloured and gilded, quite a different style from anything we have seen before. Franklin got a nice, modern edition of the "Romaunt de la Rose" done like the old one and some curious old prints but the antiquity shops were so expensive that we decided to keep our money for Paris and he only got a small fan in one of them.

We have just come in now, 9 P.M., from a stroll in the Pepinière, the big garden here where they have a very good military band on Thursday evenings. Weren't we lucky to happen to be here to-day?

By the way if you know Katharine Timpson's address in England, will you send it to me? I have lost Cousin John's letter and I have to write and ask her for my wedding present which he left with her.

We leave for Paris at twelve o'clock to-morrow and get in at six, so we will go and see Aunt Doe after dinner and I shall be all ready on Saturday morning to start in on my shopping career with her.

Best love from us both dearest Mama,

Ever devotedly,

ELEANOR

The postcard mentioned depicts a lovely scene in the Orangerie, a beautiful park in Strassburg. Dated August 9th, 1905, the card reads: "We spent most of the morning climbing the Münster Tower and this P.M. have been to the Orangerie. We are off to Nancy tomorrow and to Paris on Friday. So glad about the house. Many many thanks." The wife of Lawrence Timpson, Katherine Timpson was A.E.R.'s distant cousin; "Cousin John" was her father, John Henry Livingston.

∾

Dearest Mama,

Just a little line, as Franklin is writing the real letter this week, to thank you for your letter about Helen and for the book, which we will both read. I was very glad to hear about Helen and it is so nice that she feels well. I wish sometimes that I could see her but one cannot have everything and I will probably see a good deal of her in October.

We got here Friday evening and went after dinner to see Aunt Doe, who had returned on our account from Berlin before Uncle Paul. She is too sweet to us and she has taken so much trouble about my clothes and she insists on having us for every meal and doing everything for us that I feel I shall never be able to thank her. A tea gown and two dresses are home and Franklin and Aunt Doe think them pretty, anyway. I had very little trouble for I never tried them on and they fit perfectly. I hope you are going to approve of everything and I think you will for you generally like what I do, but I tremble when I think of Laura's critical gaze! Ellen wrote me such an interesting letter from Lost Creek Camp, very amusing and very sweet. Franklin and I think she is growing up!

Do write us all about Frances and her Captain. Somehow I can't see her engaged. She must be funny, isn't she?

Muriel writes that the whole family may stay over here till a year from this autumn! Warren came over yesterday to stay with Aunt Doe while Aunt Kassie, Mr. Collier and Muriel are with Mr. J. H. Smith in Scotland. He is very sweet and says he hopes they will go home for a few weeks, the older members that is to say, if they decide to stay over, but I think it will be a pity if Muriel stays all that time and if Warren is left alone at home, don't you? We hope to see Muriel and

Aunt Kassie in London, but Warren and Mr. C. will be in Ireland I think.

By the way I have had another sweet wedding present from the Misses Forbes, two little diamond pins, circles like those Aunt Doe wears so much. I am delighted with them and think it so sweet of both the Misses F. to give me something.

As we haven't heard by cable I suppose we have **Mrs. Draper's** house and I am glad it is done. Franklin will return her letter and write particulars but in case he forgets I want to ask one thing, namely, please get her to whitewash the kitchen and basement if possible and are there any wash tubs?

Poor Franklin is sad at having failed in two exams, particularly as he got good marks (b) in all the others and if possible he wants to take them again this autumn, as otherwise it will mean very hard work all winter. I am not very confident about his passing but it won't hurt him to try and the work will be that much gained next winter. He found several friends here and tonight he and Warren went off on a spree with LeRoy King and George Burnett and I went to dine with Aunt Dora and played bridge with Mr. Charlie Forbes and a young Gordon Forbes who is staying with him.

I hope you enjoyed your visit to Auntie Bye; it is hard about Sheffield. Thanks for her letter which interested us both. Cousin Susie writes that Mrs. Selmes was ill and broken hearted because she felt she had nothing left now to live for, but she is very fond of Mr. Ferguson and I think she will soon find that Isabella still needs her a great deal.

Best love, dearest Mama, I do so want to kiss you and in a little over a month I will be able to. Please give my love to Miss Blodgett.

Your very devoted

ELEANOR

"Laura" and "Ellen" were daughters of Warren Delano III. The former, Laura F. Delano, was with F.D.R. at

Warm Springs when he died. The latter, Ellen W. Delano, later married Frederick B. Adams, a director of Air Reduction Corporation. "Warren" was Aunt Kassie's son by her first marriage, Warren Delano Robbins, who was appointed minister to Canada by F.D.R. in 1933. The "Misses Forbes" were the aforementioned cousins Pauline and Fay. In spite of A.E.R.'s lack of confidence, soon after returning home F.D.R. passed his makeup exams for law school and started his second year at Columbia with the proper amount of credits. LeRoy King was in the class of 1906 at Harvard. George Burnett was a brother-in-law of F.D.R.'s cousin, Lyman Delano. In addition to being her relative, "Cousin Susie" was also A.E.R.'s godmother; the former Susan Livingston Ludlow, she was married to Henry Parish, who was the second vice-president of the New York Life Insurance and Trust Company.

$\sim\sim$

IMPERIAL HOTEL, PARIS
AUGUST 14, 1905
MONDAY

Dearest Mama,

We were so glad to get your letters on our arrival here Friday night and to hear of your trip to Farmington and all about the house. Of course if Mrs. Draper can't do the third floor in white, *we* can't insist on it—but Eleanor and I think we should like to have *our* bedroom done in white—so could you tell Mrs. D. to have that room done at our expense, but not the other rooms on the third floor. Of course I mean the room which connects with the little dressing room and the bath-room. I forget whether it is front or back.

To go back—At Nancy on Friday morning we went back to the old print shop and I got some Rembrandt engravings and a cunning little original sketch by Claude Lorraine. We left Nancy at 12:30 and got to Paris at 6:30, had dinner and went around the corner to Aunt Doe's. Charley F. was there, also Gordon Forbes (of Morristown) who has just left Princeton. On Saturday we all went to the Bon Marché for socks, snout-rags, etc. and after lunch at Aunt Doe's, she and E. went to the dressmakers, and Warren (who arrived from London that morning) and I went to the bankers and various book poster and liquid refreshment shops! We met LeRoy King and George Burnett, and Jack Minturn and Stuart Preston have also turned up.

Sunday morning we unpacked all our belongings in the trunk we left here and the trunk we sent from Venice, and after lunching with Aunt Doe we all went to the Sainte Chapelle and to Notre Dame, St. Etienne and the Panthéon! In the evening Warren and I joined LeRoy and George at 7 and went on a prolonged bat. I got back at 1:30 a.m. but Warren got lost and finally returned at 4:30.

Tuesday—Uncle Paul got back last night and Cousins Fay, Charlie, and G. Forbes left for England. Yesterday morning Aunt Doe took us three for a bubble drive in the Bois and in the afternoon Warren, E. and I went to Mme. de Noel, the clairvoyant lady. We were told delightful things. E. is to inherit a fortune; Warren to marry a foreigner—not of his religion—and will live to be 105 in the shade and I am to be President of the U. S. or the Equitable, I couldn't make out which!

Last night I dined with LeRoy King, his 21st birthday dinner, and today we are off to Versailles for tea and dinner.

Forgive haste, writing and uninterestingness, but we are having a scrumptious time.

Loads of love
F.D.R.

John ("Jack") W. Minturn was a distant cousin and Groton schoolmate of F.D.R. Stuart D. Preston, who is presently associated with the Metropolitan Life Insurance Company, was a year behind F.D.R. at Harvard. Accurate as "the clairvoyant lady" may have been in her estimate of

F.D.R.'s future occupation, this prediction is merely another illustration of how F.D.R. was often associated with his eminent in-law.

〰️

Dearest Mama,

Franklin sent off his letter to you yesterday just before we left Versailles. Aunt Doe, Uncle Paul, Warren, F. and I went out by train but once there we found the crowd in the Grand Palais so great that Aunt Doe took two carriages and we drove first to the Grand Trianon which we all (except Uncle P. who preferred to sit and smoke on the railing outside) went through, and as I had never seen it I was much interested in spite of the crowd and the heat. Then we drove on to the Petit Trianon stopping a minute on the way for Warren, F. and I to go in and see the royal carriages. We did not attempt the inside of the Petit Trianon as Aunt Doe feared the heat would be too great, but we walked all about the farm and gardens and woods and then returned to our carriages and drove around the park, past the "tapis vert" and back to the Hotel des Réservoirs, which you will remember as Franklin said you spent two weeks there once. Uncle Paul took a photograph of us all sitting on the grass near the Petit Trianon and he has promised to send it to us as we took no photographs. We then went and sat down in a quiet spot and Aunt Doe read us a letter from Aunt Jennie and Uncle Warren's diary which had just come and was most interesting, so we really feel we have heard something of their trip. Finally we went back to the hotel for dinner and Warren remarked "This is the nicest part of the 24 hours"! Both Warren and F. were feeling a little weary and so food and sleep appealed to them both more than artistic beauty in palaces or gardens. Before going to the train we walked up on the terrace to see the palace but there was no moonlight which was very sad. I was fairly tired on the way home and glad to go straight to the hotel and bed but F. and Warren went off to see Jack Minturn at the Jardin de Paris and then F. came home while Warren went on to supper and got back about 2 A.M. much to Aunt Doe's anxiety. She is so afraid he will get into some scrape that I am really sorry for her for of course Warren is at an unlucky age when he thinks it big to stay out late with some fellows! Poor Aunt Doe suffers a great deal from lumbago and rheumatism and I wish she had been or would go to Aix. She does everything and never complains but I can see that it hurts her all the time. There is a chance of her crossing with Uncle P. the 30th of August, returning at once and going back to America later in the autumn, but I hope she will go to Aix instead and then come over and stay.

This morning came your dear letter of the 6th which we were delighted to get.

Later—I am so glad you gave Mr. Grinnell a message from us. I did not know him very well or I would have sent more of a message. You know now that we missed your letter telling us about Mrs. Grinnell's death and also about Uncle Johnnie so at first we did not know how ill Uncle Johnnie was and we are very glad that he seems better. We don't think a sea trip to Nova Scotia however sounds very pleasant! Poor Mrs. Edgar! I am sorry we did not say good bye but will surely bring the heather as we go to Scotland the night of the 28th and stay with Mrs. Ferguson. Bob and Isabella will be there and I had a radiantly happy letter to-day from Isabella who has just reached there.

I'm glad the house is decided on. Franklin and I have been discussing the electric light question. Of course we would rather have it than gas and you are a dear, sweet Mama, to want to put it in for us, but we are pulled in two ways for we will only have the house two years and it seems hardly wise if it is very expensive to put it in for so short a time and besides if you really want to give us something we would rather have something we can keep, such as furniture. F. says dining room furniture, chairs, etc. are quite unnecessary but I fear he will want them more when we get into the house. *In any case* he says *not* to put in electric light. You see he has come to a decision since I began this sentence.

This morning Aunt Doe and I went to the Louvre for two hours and saw the Venus, the Victory and a number of rooms but not the new ones as I wanted Franklin to go to those and he was too late to accompany us to-day. Instead he and Warren and Uncle P. went to see about bubbles and we all lunched at Aunt Doe's. Then she and I again started out and tried on clothes all the afternoon and Franklin went with Warren on Howlett's coach while the latter took a four in hand lesson. F. has arranged to take one lesson in driving a pair and a few in tandem driving as he thinks it will be more useful to him than four! They got home late and we had to rush and dress to get back to Aunt Doe for a 7:15 dinner. We found a Mr. Bob Perkins there also and he seemed very nice. We all went to the Français to see "Le Depit Amoureux" and "Andromaque," both well given and the latter quite marvellous. There is really nothing like an old classic and the French language to bring one to the highest pitch of excitement, is there? Even Warren seemed thrilled and so far he has not evinced much enthusiasm for serious things! Mr. Perkins left after the first play as he could not understand a word!

August 17th—I had to stop last night as Franklin insisted on going to bed. Poor Franklin! The hives have come again here, but he has no lumbago and seems otherwise very well, isn't it queer?

By the way I think what Laura said about Muriel was an exaggeration of her own little brain for Ellen wrote me that when Muriel came out to be brides-maid they were going to *try* and keep her for a month or so with them and now

Warren tells me Muriel may not go home at all. I hardly think however Muriel would *live* with the girls and Auntie Jennie all winter though she might like to pay them a visit. Aunt Kassie and Muriel are now staying in Scotland with J. Henry Smith and they seem to be having a very good time. Muriel goes from there to the Poor's on the 20th and joins her mother again in London on the 25th so we shall see her and I will write you more about her.

This morning we are to start at 9:30 for a long day in an automobile. We, means Aunt Doe, Uncle Paul, Warren, F. and I. We go first to Fontainebleau, lunch, see the chateau and then drive on to tea at Mme. de Mimon's and get back here about 7:30 this evening. It sounds delightful and Franklin will write you whether we get through safely or walk miles! Franklin wants to have to-day our party as Aunt Doe does so much for us all the time but so far she has insisted on doing this also. I am up early as I expect a woman to come and try some waists on this morning, but Franklin is still sleeping heavily for which I am thankful as he needs more sleep than he has had of late.

I have nearly finished Marjorie Fleming and think it so pretty. Poor little girl, what a trouble her "tempers" were and I love it where she "sinned away."

We are going some day soon to look at some furniture, as we thought we might possibly get a sofa or chairs (Louis XVI) to go with our chippendale table, as part of our present from you but we have not decided as the duty is so great that Franklin thinks we would do better at home. He got some lovely books the other day, which are being bound however so they won't reach America for some time.

I must stop as I have other letters to write this morning and I think I have told you everything, at least I seem to have covered a horrifying amount of paper!

Much, much love from both your devoted

CHILDREN

"Mrs. Edgar" was the wife of James Edgar, who was hired by James Roosevelt shortly after he purchased the Hyde Park estate in 1867, and who worked there as a farmer for more than forty years. "Bubbles" is a reference to Aunt Doe's automobile. "Howlett" was a professional horseman who enjoyed a wide reputation in and around Paris. The question of whether "we get through or walk miles" was answered by a postcard from the "Forêt de Fountainebleu" mailed several hours later: "Dearest Mama, we are here but we broke down en route. E.R." Although she died at the age of eight in 1811, Marjory Fleming's collected works, consisting of three "Journals," some verses, and a few letters, received worldwide attention when discovered and published fifty years later. In 1904 a new edition was issued and interest in her revived; the part A.E.R. refers to reads: "Yesterday I behaved exceedingly / ill and what is worse of / all is when Isabella told me / not to let my tempers get / the better of me but I did / not mind her & sinned / away which was very naughty."

∽∽

IMPERIAL HOTEL, PARIS
AUGUST 22, 1905
TUESDAY

Dearest Mama,

Our stay in Paris is nearing an end, for we leave for London on Thursday and we shall both be sorry, for our two weeks here have been very delightful, and we have been busy every moment. Last Friday I began taking driving lessons of Howlett—two lessons with a pair last week, and yesterday and today I have been driving a tandem and have my last lesson tomorrow. It is most interesting and I know it has helped me a lot already. Warren took four lessons with a four and returned to London Sunday night to go to the Dublin horse show.

Next Saturday we expect to go to the Bennetts at Dorking over Sunday and leave for Scotland Tuesday night to stay

71

with the Fergusons, see Edinburgh, etc. Then about the 6th we go to Liverpool for a night to see Mrs. Bulloch again and thence to the Foljambes for the last Sunday before we sail.

Eleanor wrote you just before we went to Fontainebleau last Thursday. We left at 9:30 and the "bubble" went very badly, one bursted tire and numerous stops, so we didn't get to F. till 2 p.m.! We had a hurried lunch and went all over the Palace which we loved. You have been there I think. At 3:30 we left and went about 50 kil. more to La Houssaye, M. de Mimon's place. Mrs. Isabelle de Mimon was waiting for us with tea and some chocolate cake which made me suffer all the way home. Their place is very attractive. The house built under Henry II, entirely surrounded by a broad moat, which however also takes in enough land for the flower garden and tennis court at the rear. Warren and I loved it and talked of copying it in A.D. 1950, and Eleanor wanted to take all the furniture back for our 14 foot mansion. We didn't leave until 7:30 but ran back quickly and had a late dinner at No. 37 at 10 o'clock.

On Friday Eleanor shopped almost all day with Aunt Doe. Warren and I drove and in the evening the dinner party we tried to get up fell through for lack of ladies and W. and I dined with LeRoy and G. Burnett. Saturday we shopped etc. and went in the evening with Aunt Doe to the Theatre Français and the Barbier de Seville, wonderfully given and so distinct that even I could understand it. On Sunday morning E. and I stayed here quietly, doing chores and writing, then lunched with Aunt Doe and spent three hours in the Louvre. I was much interested in the Musée de Marine, recently opened. We dined at 37 and Warren left at eight.

Yesterday I met E. after my drive at Risler's and we invested in a solid silver platter! It is "superfine, splendide et *trés* chère"! and we hope to get another next year like it. We want it marked with the crest, but have none here, so could you send to Aunt Doe one of our book-plates? She is going to bring it to us when she comes. In the p.m. I went with Billy Elkins along the Quai and got a few books. Mrs. E. has a bad cold, so we couldn't lunch with them yesterday, nor they drive with us tonight. Last night we went to the Opera "Lohengrin." Aunt Doe had been sent a box and we had with us M. de Jardin, a clever old Frenchman.

I got last week the report of my exams, and as I predicted failed in two and passed the others with B's! It certainly shows the uncertainty of marks, for I had expected much lower marks in some of the others and failure in one, and thought I had done as well on the two I failed as in those I passed with B. I cabled you at once for my books on Contracts and Pleading but fear you were already off for Campo, but I think you could let Harriet send them from 200 Mad. If I get them in time I am going to work the last two weeks and take the exams on Sept. 21 and 22 in the bare hope of getting thru, for otherwise I shall have to take the courses again! No more now, we are just off to Neuilly to see Cousin Hortense. We are both flourishing, but I have had hives for ten days and they won't go, so people think I have a flea that can't be killed by any method.

Ever your loving

F.D.R.

Aunt Doe's rheumatism is a good deal better and we are trying to persuade her to go to Aix.

"The Foljambes" were old friends of Sara Roosevelt; F.D.R. had visited their home at "Osberton-in-Worksop" on previous trips to England. A Member of Parliament until appointed to the peerage in 1893, Cecil George Savile Foljambe was the fourth Baron Hawkesbury, later Earl of Liverpool. William Elkins was a member of a prominent Philadelphia family and a graduate of Harvard. "Harriet" was for many years Sara Roosevelt's caretaker in New York City.

∾

Dearest Mama,

We leave to-morrow morning so I will just write a line about the last few days as London will be rather hurried I think!

Yesterday Uncle Paul, Aunt Doe, F. and I lunched in the Champs Elysées and Aunt Doe insisted on ordering so much and such very good lunch that *we* had to come home after it and rest and Uncle Paul ended by going to take a turkish bath to work off the effects! We had tea with Aunt Doe as Mme. Howland could not see us until six and then we drove out to Neuilly. It was raining but the Bois was lovely all the same and we had a nice talk with Mme. Howland, who was very sweet and showed us so many pretty things that our hearts were green with envy! Mr. Louis Howland was there so I had the pleasure of making his acquaintance! He poured a long tale of woe about his "chief" into F's ear but I don't think it matters much who his chief is for I doubt his ever being brilliant don't you? We dined and had a quiet evening with Aunt Doe. Franklin has won Uncle Paul's heart and he has promised to let him know *if* he finds anything big in Mexico and in the meantime he has presented us with a lovely little coffee pot and hot milk thing, which I fell in love with in an old silver shop. This A.M. Franklin had his last driving lesson and then Aunt Doe and I met him at a book shop. She is going to give him the "Livre d'heures," a facsimile of the Chantilly one for Christmas and we went to see about the binding and also about the sending of all the books F. has bought here. Some go with us and others do not come till January as he is leaving them to be bound. Some of the latter, very handsome French historical works he got with part of your present and also his driving lessons. After the book shop we went to a shop Aunt Doe knew of for furniture and saw lovely Louis XVI screens, one of which we got, so Mrs. Stewart has given us a screen, or rather part of one after all! F. and I then left Aunt Doe and went with the young Elkins' to lunch at Voisin's. There we saw *Mrs.* Jay Burden and *Mrs.* Harry Whitney with Mr. Bertie Goelet and Mr. Meredith Hare so you see it is not fashionable to go out with your husband! Then I took Franklin to the bank and the Louvre, magasin of course(!) and returned to find that most of the things I expected to find packed had not yet come! Aunt Doe and I then went in pursuit and were quite successful though some things are still to come to us in London. The linen looked lovely and Emma packed everything for me so I hope it will reach London safely. This evening we dined with Aunt Doe and had a quiet evening and we are now finishing up things here as we leave at 9:30 to-morrow A.M. I enclose Mrs. Draper's letter as I forgot to do so last time.

We got two letters from you yesterday A.M., the last from Fairhaven and we were glad to hear all the news. Aunt Doe is sending your shoes and miniature by Uncle Paul who sails the 30th as she seems to think it is better though we could easily take them. However, you will get them sooner as Uncle Paul leaves them at 200 when he lands. I think Aunt Doe has about decided to stay here and go to Aix which I am glad of. Good night dearest, dearest Mummy. I will finish on Friday when I have seen Muriel and Aunt Kassie.

August 25th London—Here we are back again and I really feel quite near home. We've had the most wonderful time possible but we are both anxious now to see "home and Mother" again! We had a very comfortable trip yesterday and a smooth crossing. Aunt Doe and Uncle Paul came to see us off and I think they were sorry to have us go. Aunt Doe is very gloomy about Uncle P's departure and says she will go to Aix at once and take 16 baths straight as she does not want to be there alone. I hope she will wait however and go with Aunt Kassie as Muriel told me to-day she and her mother might both go after Warren leaves. As soon as we had dined last night we went to Brown's and saw all the family except Mr. Collier and Warren who are in Dublin. We found we could not unpack till to-day, as through some mistake our rooms were only vacant this morning and last night we had to be content with a small room, which we did not much mind however as we were very tired and tumbled into bed early.

This morning Franklin went off to his tailor's and I went for Muriel. We spent the morning together trying on my riding habits etc. Muriel looks very well and seems to have had a lovely summer, but unfortunately I fear she is going to stay out here a whole year more. I think they have really settled it though Muriel still speaks of a possible flying trip with her mother across and back while Mr. Collier hunts in Ireland! F. and I lunched with Aunt Kassie and then came home and unpacked for two hours after which F. started off to do various errands and I went again for Muriel and took her to tea at Jean's. Poor Jean has been ill for a week and she is alone here just now as Mr. and Mrs. Reid are in Scotland, so she begged F. and I to dine with her which we are going to do at eight. She asked Muriel to go and stay with them at the country place they have taken and I hope Mu will go for I know she will like Jean once she knows her.

We are off to the Bennett's at 12:45 to-morrow and return on Monday and leave for Scotland Tuesday evening.

With dearest love from us both,

Ever your devoted,

ELEANOR

"Mrs. Jay Burden" was the wife of James A. Burden, who graduated from Harvard in 1893 and later became president of the Burden Iron Company. Mrs. Harry Payne Whitney, the former Gertrude Vanderbilt and wife of the noted financier, was a patron of the arts, a sculptor, and founder of the Whitney Museum of American Art. "Bertie Goelet" was Robert W. Goelet, Harvard graduate and member of a prominent New York family. Meredith Hare entered Groton in the school's first year, 1884. "Emma" was Aunt Doe's maid.

∽∽

GARLANT'S HOTEL, LONDON
AUGUST 29, 1905
TUESDAY

Dearest Mama,

Franklin will finish this but he has had a hard time packing as his clothes have not come and he has now had to go in search of them! Your letter of the 16th came last night from Campobello but as yet no books have come. It doesn't matter much however as F. got some here and if he gets the others before sailing he can work on the boat. It will be very difficult to study in Scotland anyway I feel sure.

You don't say how *you* are enjoying Campo but I am glad that Frances is happy!

We went to the Bennett's after lunch on Saturday and had a lovely drive in their auto after tea. The country round them is very pretty and we enjoyed it. After another auto drive on Monday morning we left just after lunch and on our arrival here had tea at which Moo, Warren and Miss Nicholas joined us. M., W., E., and I dined at Prince's and went to see the Spring Chicken afterwards.

This a.m. Moo and E. went out to shop and W. and I went to many places. I ordered also a tandem harness at Peat's at a horrible price! This is the effect of his tandem lessons! It has rained here steadily since we came and our Sunday was spent indoors except for a short walk to and from church.

Aunt Doe came over from Paris last night to be with Uncle P. until he sails to-morrow and they are staying at

77

Brown's. We lunched with Aunt Kassie and then came here to pack and had Uncle P., Aunt Dora, Warren, Hammie Hadden and Miss Nicholas to tea. We are now off to Scotland in great haste!

Best love from both.

Devotedly
E. R.

The part of this letter beginning " . . . after another auto . . ." and ending ". . . at a horrible price . . ." was inserted by F.D.R. "Moo" was the name by which F.D.R. had called his cousin Muriel Delano Robbins ever since childhood. Hamilton Hadden was in the class of 1908 at Harvard. Miss Nicholas was an acquaintance of the family from New York City.

∽∽

NOVAR
AUGUST 30, 1905
WEDNESDAY

Dearest Mama,

After the hurried line *we* sent off yesterday, I at once remembered something most important which I had wanted to ask of you! It is this—if Hall is not already at Groton I would like him to meet us on the dock and so I wrote and told him to let you know if he was still on the Hudson, as I felt sure you would not mind getting a permit for him when you get your own and bringing him down with you. Will it be a great bother and do you mind? I hope not, but I fear I have let you in for a good deal, however, he may be back at school.

We had a very comfortable night journey and at the station before Novar, Bob got on the train, looking much better and very happy. He only came for an hour as he is taking a cure 14 miles from here and Isabella was in bed for the day, but to-morrow they will both come here or we

78

will go there. The country is too beautiful, hills all around and a lovely firth below us. The house is run casually but comfortably and such a dear old place and Mrs. and Miss Ferguson are both very sweet. Miss Chamberlain and her Aunt came to lunch and then we had a flying visit from Mrs. Almeric Paget in an auto. Colonel Payne, her uncle, has the Ferguson's old Novar place just below this for the shooting and I hope he will ask Franklin there to shoot. She is attractive but talks about ten times faster than anyone I've ever heard! Finally Hector, Franklin, Miss F. and I went for a walk to what they call Black Rock. It is a river about 90 feet below the surface of the ground and steep black rocks go down on either side. Our whole walk was lovely and I got some heather for Mrs. Edgar! After tea I came up to lie down and started this letter while Franklin went over one of the farms with Hector and the tenant. I don't know whether he gathered any useful information or not! We had a quiet dinner and now I am adding to this while waiting for F. to come to bed.

It was so nice seeing Muriel in London and I hope we will see her again though the family all go to Leamington this Saturday. Warren goes to Ireland on the 9th for some hunting and sails from there which seems a curious arrangement as I should think they would want to see him all they can now they have apparently decided on another year over here. Muriel gave me a dear little fan in London and brought F. from Russia a very pretty cigarette box of coloured wood. She told me you had sent her such a wonderful present and she thought it so sweet and dear of you. Warren has tried to persuade her to come home but she told me she would not come without the family. However, she has decided not to marry a Lord. She says she "has seen too much of them and their ways"! A statement which made me gasp!

Thursday. This morning I went for a drive with Mrs.

Ferguson and we visited various people, first a Mrs. Munro
who sat on the edge of her chair and trembled with excitement, then an old widow, and finally the gardener at Novar
showed us the garden. Mrs. Ferguson to my surprise talked
of "peace" to them all and they all seemed to know about it
and take an interest. It is nice news isn't it? We had really
begun to think it would not be and I think Uncle Ted must
be gratified to have done so much towards it. To return
to Novar, we did not go to the house but the garden is quite
lovely, full of flowers, with the old sundial in the middle, a
pond, a few big trees and lovely paths. Mr. & Mrs. Webb
(they write books on sociology) came to lunch and Franklin
discussed the methods of learning at Harvard with the husband while I discussed the servant problem with the wife!
Incidentally, F. worked on law all the morning and this afternoon he and Hector went on a long tramp over the hills and
saw some of the queer little crofts "en route." Miss Ferguson
and I drove in a two wheeled cart called a float (isn't it a
lovely name?) to Strathpeffer 14 miles off to see Isabella. We
started in the rain and it rained most of the way there but
no one minds such trifles and I was so glad to see Isabella.
They all adore her here and she looks prettier than ever and
well too though she says she is freezing to death. It is impossible to imagine how sweet she and Bob are together for
I would not know him for the same man. He has become
demonstrative if you can believe it and they play together
like two children!

We got home here just in time for dinner and since then
Miss F. has been showing us her political cartoons which are
very amusing though I miss half the point as I don't know
the people. Both Mrs. and Miss F. sketch and paint and the
house is filled with water colours, some really lovely. This
is the country to be artistic in, the clouds and colours are
magnificent, more beautiful than anywhere we have yet
been. Mr. Hector F. gave me the sweetest little blue enamel

box this evening. It is very old battersea and I believe very rare nowadays.

To-morrow F. and I go to lunch at Strathpeffer with the Bob's and on Monday we go to Raith and from there to the Foljambe's on Wednesday.

Goodbye dearest, and much love from both.

Your devoted

CHILDREN

A sister of Neville Chamberlain, Miss Chamberlain was a friend of Mrs. W. Sheffield Cowles and a graduate of Allenswood. Mrs. Almeric Paget was the daughter of William C. Whitney, the noted financier, Secretary of the Navy in Cleveland's first administration. "Novar" was the Ferguson family home for many generations; the head of the house was traditionally known as "The Novar," and Robert Ferguson's brother Ronald had never accepted a title because he believed that the crown could not give him anything higher than "The Novar." "Hector" and "Miss (Edith) Ferguson" were Robert Ferguson's brother and sister. The "nice news" refers to the fact that several days before the writing of this letter Japanese and Russian peace plenipotentiaries had reached an agreement that brought hostilities to an end. "Uncle Ted's" role in the settlement was substantial and later proved to be a triumph for American diplomacy. Early in June, 1905, he had offered to act as mediator between the two warring nations. Shortly thereafter his good offices were accepted, and the peace conference was convened on August 9th, at Portsmouth, New Hampshire. The luncheon guests who "write books on sociology" were the noted British sociologists and economists, Beatrice and Sidney Webb, leaders of the Fabian Society (the socialist group that originated in the late nineteenth century and included George Bernard Shaw and H. G. Wells among its members). A staunch supporter of the Labor Party, Sidney Webb is supposed to have been very influential in the writing of the party's revised constitution; at least, the final version was closely in accord with his views. As a means of giving the Labor Party representation in the House of Lords, he was made Lord Passfield. Beatrice Webb collaborated with her husband on many economic works, and played a large role in the investigation of English local government that led to a revision of the English Poor Laws. They were the first couple, other than royalty, to be buried at Westminster Abbey.

∽∽

KIRCALDY

SEPTEMBER 5, 1905

TUESDAY

Dearest Mama,

Just a hurried line before the post goes to thank you for the 3 letters of the 19th, 21st and 22nd, all of which we enjoyed. F. is busy watching a bowling match or he would write.

We opened the flower show at Novar last Saturday and F. made a very good speech. I will bring you the local paper in which it was reported, though *he* says no one is to see it! We had tea that day with Miss Chamberlain and on Sunday we tead at Novar with Col. Payne and the Paget's, otherwise we were quiet walking and driving. We travelled all of Monday and were taken for a short walk by Mr. Ferguson before dinner. This place is wonderful but the country not as beautiful as the north. To-day Mr. F. took F. and me to St. Andrews and we saw the old town and they played one round on the links. The other people here are Sir A. Nicholson, wife and son (from India the latter and very important) and a dear old Lady Swinton. Tomorrow p.m. we go to the Foljambe's.

Love from both your devoted   CHILDREN

The "Mr. Ferguson" of this letter was the older brother, Sir Ronald Ferguson, who lived in the family's other home, "Raith," near Edinburgh on the Firth of Forth, and who later served for seven years as Governor-General of Australia. The "very important" person from India was probably Sir Frederick Augustus Nicholson, who enjoyed the imposing title of Knight Commander of the Indian Empire; he was a member of the Viceroy's Legislative Council, and spent many years investigating agricultural conditions in India.

∽∽

OSBERTON-IN-WORKSOP
SEPTEMBER 7, 1905
THURSDAY

Dearest Mama,

I haven't been a very good correspondent since we got to England, but I know you will realize what a rush our time here has been and how much we are succeeding in crowding into it.

The visit to Novar was delightful and quite restful as we had five days there. Eleanor has written you about the flower show. She opened it very well and wasn't a bit rattled and spoke very clearly and well—but I had an awful time of it and wasn't even introduced. I had to wander up to the front of the platform and the foolishness of my smile was only equalled by the extreme idiocy of the remarks that followed. You can imagine what a speech on gardening, and the raising of vegetables in general, by your son must have been like and I will say nothing more except that my appetite for those damned weeds has since that time departed.

At Raith we had a very good time and on Tuesday went to St. Andrews where I had a game with Ronald F. on the historic links.

Yesterday a.m. I had a long ride and E. a quiet morning and we left at 7, getting here at 8:30 p.m. after many vicissitudes, for we got out at the wrong place, got the wrong tickets and had a generally exciting time. We got to this house at 9 and Mr. Foljambe and Lady Gertrude are *just* the same, Mr. F. of course a little older and more feeble, but most delightful and Lady G. hasn't altered one scrap. The Bishop of Hull and his wife and daughter were here, also Lady G's sister. I remember the house very well and the place, and nothing is altered. This morning I began well by being late for breakfast and at twelve we all went for a walk in the gardens, the Bishop and family having departed. After lunch we went for a long drive with Mr. and Lady F. to Sherwood Forest, the scene of Robin Hood's escapades, passing thro' the Duke of Newcastle's place and two other big fellows! Tonight Mr. and Mrs. Lister-Kaye and their son and daughter dined here. I have had many long and interesting talks with Mr. Ferguson on forestry, and with Mr. Foljambe and Mr. Kaye on farming and cattle raising, and the plans for Hyde Park now include not only a new house but a new farm, cattle, trees, etc.

Friday morning—

By the way, before I forget it, will you bring down to the dock when you come to meet us a small sum of gold?! I have ordered a most wonderful tandem harness and we must pay on that as well as on the linen. I think $300 will be enough, as I shall have some myself. I hope Cousin Bammie will see that someone is there as it will expedite matters.

Today is the first fine day we have had for weeks, indeed, the first one it has not rained since August 28th! We are so accustomed to showers, Scotch mists and downpours that the sun is quite a novelty. I wonder if you saw the eclipse. We got one glimpse of it between clouds at Novar, and only half the sun was visible.

Everyone is talking about Cousin Theodore saying that he is the most prominent figure of present day history, and adopting towards our country in general a most respectful and almost loving tone. What a change has come over English opinion in the last few years! Even the French were quite enthusiastic, but the German tone seemed to hide a certain animosity and jealousy as usual.

This afternoon we are to drive over to Welbeck Abbey, the Duke of Portland's place to tea, and tomorrow we leave early for London. It will be nice to have four days to do our packing and last odd jobs, and Muriel is coming up to spend Monday and Tuesday with us. Aunt Kassie and the children are at Leamington and Warren and P.C. are hunting in Ireland.

I cannot tell you how delighted we shall both be to get home again and we speak of it every day. We ought to get in early Tuesday morning and you know how we long to see our Mummy again.

My exams are on Thursday and Friday and then we can go to Hyde Park for a few days good rest.

Au revoir for a very little while.　　Ever.　F.D.R.

Sir John Pepys Lister-Kaye was groom-in-waiting to Edward VII. "Cousin Bammie" was a childhood nickname for Mrs. W. Sheffield Cowles.

～～

This letter is the last of the honeymoon group; it is followed by a gap of twenty-one months in the family correspondence. For more than a year and a half after the return from Europe the family was united, and letters were unnecessary. If F.D.R. did write occasional notes during this period, they no longer exist. It was not until Sara Roosevelt went abroad in the summer of 1907 that the letters were resumed as a part of the daily routine. In the meantime F.D.R. had continued his studies at Columbia Law School, and in the spring of 1907 he easily passed his bar examinations (although he never bothered to complete the work for an LL.B. degree from Columbia). This interval also witnessed the advent of parental responsibilities, Anna Eleanor Roosevelt being born on May 3, 1906. Thus it was an enlarged family that F.D.R. took to Campobello for a summer of relaxation prior to starting his first job with the New York law firm of Carter, Ledyard and Milburn in September, 1907.

II

"... Foggy At Campo I Expect..."

SUMMER OF

1907

CAMPOBELLO ISLAND is at the entrance to Passamaquoddy
Bay in New Brunswick, two miles from Eastport, Maine.
James Roosevelt had purchased land on the island in 1883;
three years later a house was completed, and the Roosevelts
became permanent summer residents. Yet the possession of a
summer home in Canada did not deter Sara Roosevelt from
continuing her practice of spending occasional summers in
Europe. Her trip in 1907 was responsible for the correspondence of this chapter, a correspondence that reveals not only
the leisurely and restful life of "Campo," but that also pro-
vides an insight into the youthful enthusiasm that characterized F.D.R. on the eve of his entry into the professional
world.

Once again F.D.R. and A.E.R. took turns writing to the
former's mother, and once again the correspondence would
be conspicuously incomplete without the inclusion of
A.E.R.'s letters. Indeed, as mentioned in the second letter

of the chapter, the correspondence was considered by both
mother and children as constituting a "diary." Each day
several paragraphs describing the daily activities were added,
and about every fifth day the letter was mailed and another
one begun. Although frequent changes of authorship occur
in the letters, it is usually clearly apparent from the contents
which parts were written by F.D.R. and which entries were
made by A.E.R., and only where the changes are obscure has
the authorship been annotated. This diary form of correspondence for prolonged trips was a family habit of long
standing, dating back to the early nineteenth century and
the separation of the Delano family due to the exigencies of
the China trade, and it was a habit that F.D.R. practiced
on his official trips abroad in later years.

∞

AYER JUNCTION, MAINE
JULY 9, 1907
TUESDAY

Dearest Mama,

We are almost there now and this R.R. is without doubt
conducive to a far rougher trip than the steamers ever
thought of having. The Baby has behaved very well, except
that she insisted on waking up at 4 a.m. and talking to
Eleanor and Nurse for hours!

We have very cool weather—foggy at Campo I expect—
and the only contretemps has been the loss of dear "Duffy"
who missed connections during the night. I am telegraphing
all over the place however and expect him to turn up on
tonight's train, as he is labeled. Also *two* trunks have gone
astray somewhere though I think the most important ones
have come.

By the way I entirely forgot to get a berth for Kay for
Thursday night but will do so by wire from Eastport. Tell
him to ask for it in the name of David Kay.

I want to write a line to the steamer so must stop. Bon voyage dear Mummy—we shall miss you a very great deal. Eleanor and Anna join me in ever so much love and kisses.

Ever your devoted son

F.D.R.

Ayer Junction, the meeting place for the Maine Central and Canadian Pacific Railways, is about fifteen miles from Eastport. Purchased in Scotland on the honeymoon trip, "Duffy" was the first of many Scotch terriers owned by F.D.R. David Kay was Sara Roosevelt's butler.

∽∽

CAMPOBELLO
JULY 11, 1907
THURSDAY

Dearest Mamma,

Just a line to catch the Saturday's steamer in a great hurry. We arrived safe and sound on Tuesday and spent the rest of the day unpacking and getting the house in order. Everything was ready for us and Edgar met us at the train, but as it was a flat calm and the engine a little out of order after the trip up the Half Moon could not come over to meet us, so we took the boat to the Pool and drove up. Mr. Hubbard came over in the evening and they are all well, Parky Haven staying there. Yesterday morning Duffy and the two missing trunks arrived and in the afternoon we went to Eastport for much-needed shopping, taking Nurse and Baby with us on the Half Moon.

By the way I never gave you the list of my clothes before I left so here it is—

1 Dinner Coat, Waistcoat and Trousers.

1 Winter suit—Dark grey.

2 Pair Brown Linen or Khaki very thin Riding Trousers with belt straps and no extensions and 1 pair gaiters to match.

88

2 Evening Waistcoats, single breasted.
   All this from Tautz.

---

1 Pair black lace boots like the last.
1 Pair black Riding boots, a little bigger on the instep
   and ½ inch more at the top.
   This from Peal.

We are thinking of you on the water now passing Sandy
Hook—8:30 a.m. We are just off in the Half Moon as there
is a fine breeze and we take luncheon and get back at 2:30 to
walk the baby to Herring Cove.

Sarah comes today. Loads of love from us all and we shall
begin the diary tomorrow.

Ever your devoted

F.D.R.

Edgar McGowan was a native of Campobello hired by
the Roosevelts as a general handyman during their vacations on the island; he was a fatal victim of the flu epidemic
that occurred during the First World War. His widow, Anna
McGowan, was for many years winter caretaker of the Hyde
Park home and she is presently filling a similar job at
Campobello. The *Half Moon,* an eighteen-ton, sixty-foot
schooner, was the second family yacht to bear the name.
The first *Half Moon,* on which as a child F.D.R. frequently
sailed with his father and which was thus the original
stimulus for his lifelong interest in ships, had been lost in
1898 due to negligence of the crew. The second *Half Moon*
was purchased by James Roosevelt shortly before his death,
and as a reaction to the latter event F.D.R.'s mother was for
several years desirous of selling it. Its eventual disposition,
however, did not take place until F.D.R. sold it in 1917, a
time when private yachts were needed by the Navy to assist
in the fight against German U-boats. The "Pool" refers to
a small harbor at Campobello near the Roosevelt home;
from here a boat ran regularly back and forth to Eastport.

A summer resident of the island from Boston, Gorham Hubbard took a keen interest in the vacation activities at Campobello and was in charge of the golf club. The summer of 1907 was not a real vacation for him, however, as his wife, the former Sarah Henshaw, had died during the previous winter. An occasional visitor to Campobello, Parkman ("Parky") B. Haven was a close friend of Gorham Hubbard's from Boston. "Sarah" refers to the aforementioned Sarah Weekes Hoppin.

~~

Dearest Mama,

Franklin sent off a line this morning so I am beginning my letter this evening. Everything is quite settled now, the baby's crib arranged very nicely, the house grandly painted and your ceiling looking very nice.

F. and I. went off at ten this morning and sailed up Great South Bay, had lunch and returned about three. We found a telegram from Kay saying you had sailed comfortably and we have been thinking of you constantly and wondering who you have found on board. We took nurse and baby to Herring Cove and just before starting we had a visit from Mrs. Sturgis, Susan and young Master Clymer who is very big for seventeen months but doesn't look as healthy as Anna. The Lord's are not here yet and I haven't seen the Hubbard baby yet. Mrs. Hoppin arrived to-day but we have not been to call yet.

Friday morning—F. and the baby are playing on the floor and in a few minutes she is going to sleep in the dining room as it is raining. F. is going to meet Kay but as it is wet I am going to call on the Cochran's, Sturgis' and Hoppin! (I forgot the last lady had to be singular!)

July 13th. Kay arrived safely with Toutou yesterday and we asked him all kinds of questions about you. We are so sorry

90

the passenger list is so uninteresting and do hope someone nice turned up. Toutou misses you very much and looks for you everywhere. The baby knew his bark and called him before he got into the house! F. and I fished yesterday afternoon and caught twelve flounders, three of which we sent Sarah H. but Edgar couldn't even find a maid to leave them with so I don't suppose she knows who sent them! Mrs. Cochran has arranged for Lank to take the servants to church and we pay as we used to do on the old boat, 25 cts. the round trip.

We are reading the "Indiscreet Letters" in the evening and find them most interesting, but aren't the details gruesome? I hope your copy reached you.

A telegram from Grandma last night announced the arrival of Pussie's baby—a boy and both doing well is all I know as yet but I am glad it has at last come.

We are going for a walk so goodbye for the present.

July 14th I have just remembered that you wanted what addresses I had in Paris for children's things and I hope this will reach you in time. Leveau and Bracia, 14 Rue Clérq, 3rd floor is good for dresses. Mme. L. Marie, 121 Boul. Sébastopol—2d floor has hats for children but it is so far away and you can get them so easily elsewhere that I hardly think it is worth while your bothering to go there.

F. and I had a good sail yesterday afternoon but it was quite rough so the baby did not go. She was at the pier to meet us on our return and we are going to photograph her costume, for you can't imagine a much funnier sight, particularly when F. carries her up the hill on his back with two short legs sticking straight out on either side of his head!

This morning we are taking care of the baby and after Katherine gets home from church we are going to take Anna over to meet the little Hubbard baby. They still have a trained nurse for her so she rarely leaves the piazza except to go in the launch.

Sunday evening. The Hubbard baby is lovely, dark, but lovely red cheeks and so happy and not at all afraid. Anna thought she was to be patted like Duff, only harder, and we were obliged to restrain her fond embraces! Your three letters came from Sandy Hook and also the Marconi. We were so glad to get them and to know that you were comfortably settled and well looked after. I am writing a line to-night to Aunt Annie as you wanted us to do.

I had a letter from Helen also to-day and the hospital has disappointed her and she has no nurse and wanted to know about Nelly. I have written her that she is with you, so you will probably hear from her and I hope she will take Nelly.

We had a lovely sail this afternoon and Anna seemed to enjoy it as much as anyone and behaved beautifully though we were out till nearly six. Franklin wants to finish so goodbye dearest, love to Aunt Doe and please give all kinds of nice messages to the Miss Forbes' and anyone else you see who would like them.

In reading over the foregoing manuscript I realize that Eleanor has told you about everything and must have a strong wrist to escape the horrors of writer's cramp. The only thing she hasn't told you is that she is well and doesn't seem unhappy. I am ditto as to health and can vouch for the state of my feelings. The servants seem contented with their surroundings—the Nurse enthusiastically so—and Delia's charms seem already to have captivated Edgar, Mr. Babcock, the crew and last but by no means least that naughty naughty Scotch serving gentleman of yours.

By the way, William is again the efficient engineer steward and general third wheel of the Half Moon, and in place of Charley, we have another Blue-Nose from Shag Harbor who rejoices in the Sir Walter Scott name of Desmond Nickerson and we don't know whether to call him Desmond, Nick or Mr. Nickerson.

I have gulped down three novels since our arrival, besides

a good deal of more nutritious food in the shape of Biographies suited to the salt air. Our attempts to see [name deleted] have failed (here the Doxology should be sung), tho' we caught Mr. [name deleted] coming away from her house at 10 yesterday morning. It looked badly—especially as she was still in bed (here should be sung Hymn 142—Oh come all ye faithful) (In case we don't see [name deleted] all summer Hymn 684 should be sung—Peace, perfect Peace).

My box of wines has just arrived at Eastport so tomorrow I go to meet them and my epistles may be incoherent—more so than this one—after this. The Baby is too sweet and makes us shriek with laughter when she puts her whole hand into my cup of tea. If I don't stop I will go broke paying the postage.

Loads of love from us all.

Ever your affec. son

F.D.R.

"Mrs. Sturgis" was the wife of Dr. Russell Sturgis of Boston, a near-neighbor of the Roosevelts at Campobello. Dr. Sturgis was a descendant of the Sturgis family of Boston that had been associated with Warren Delano II in the China trade. "Susan," his daughter, was the wife of George Clymer and mother of "young Master Clymer." Another daughter, Anne (referred to in the correspondence as "Nancy"), married Sidney Archer Lord. Mr. and Mrs. Travis Cochran from Philadelphia were regular summer residents at Campobello. They owned a sloop yacht, the *Mavis,* in which they sometimes raced their neighbors in the *Half Moon.* The last sentence of the third paragraph refers to a smudge on the letter caused by an effort to reduce the Hoppin name from the plural to the singular; this was the first summer of their separation. "Toutou" was a Spitz owned by F.D.R.'s mother and given a childhood nickname of Helen Roosevelt Robinson. Edward Lank was a native of Campobello, one of the best sailors on the island, who had done much to educate F.D.R. to the sea. He rented a boat, and as there was no Catholic church on the island at this time, it was the practice for Lank to carry a church party to Eastport each Sunday. Edited by Bertram L. Simpson (pseudonym: B. L. Putnam Weale), the full title of the book described as containing "gruesome details" helps to explain A.E.R.'s impression and description: *Indiscreet Letters From Peking; being the notes of an eye-witness, which set forth in some details, from day to day, the real story of the siege and sack of a distressed capital in 1900—the year of great tribulation* . . . that is to say, the Boxer Rebellion. "Pussie's baby," W. Forbes Morgan, Jr., became a technical sergeant in the Second World War, and died at sea on his way home from the Philippines in 1945. His wife, the former Marie Newson, was secretary of the Democratic National Convention Committee in 1936. "Katherine" refers to Gorham Hubbard's daughter, who married the second Thomas Jefferson Newbold in 1914; she was at this time acting as mother to her baby sister and to her younger brother, Gorham Hubbard, Jr. Mrs. Theodore Douglas Robinson's reason for being in the hospital was the birth of her eldest daughter, who was named Helen after her mother; "Nelly" had been A.E.R.'s nurse and was at this time Sara Roosevelt's maid. "Delia" was the cook, while Mr. Babcock was the local butcher. Mrs. W. Stanley Porter, for many years a resident of Campobello, recalls the latter as being ". . . quite a character. He lived in Wilson's Beach, where he had a store, but he also had a butcher's cart with a canvas cover, and he came around three days a week. On Tuesday you would order what he would bring on Thursday, etc. He had meats and vegetables, but did not sell fish. As the horse seldom went at more than a walk, in order to get to the lower end of the island at a reasonable time, including stops along the way, he had to leave home at five A.M. to drive the eight or nine miles or so. He had about twelve children, many of them named for the summer people, but I think Mrs. Roosevelt, Sr. prevented his naming one for her husband."

94

Dearest Mama—

Since writing you on Sunday the fog has been thick outside but we have managed to have clear weather inside during the daytime. Yesterday we went up to St. Andrews with
Gorham, Katherine, G. Jr. and Mr. Haven in the launch,
lunched at the hotel, bought a Wedgwood clock and got back
here at 4:30. It made a very nice trip and though slightly
rough in Passamaquoddy Bay for a few minutes E. did not
show the least paleness of cheek or tendency to edge towards
the rail! Now we are off to Eastport to get several things.
Last night when we got back we found Nurse in tears and it
developed that she had just received a letter from her beloved son Orin. He, with another boy in his office, hired a
horse and runabout in N.Y. last Thursday and while driving Orin dropped a rein, the horse swerving across the car
tracks. A car struck them, killing the horse, demolishing the
trap and throwing them all over the place. The other boy's
leg was broken but Orin escaped with bruises. However the
worst was yet to come. The livery stable man insisted on
$500 damages and threatened to lock up Orin if his share
was not paid by today! His letter was a long drawn out
agony. It ended by my having to advance Mrs. W. $150
which I am going to telegraph him from Eastport now—also
a telegram sending him to Appleton Clark for advice, and a
letter to the same effect!

Wednesday—July 17th. Yesterday after endeavoring to
straighten out the Watson boy, we landed at the Pool, and
saw Mr. Clark about the vegetable baskets and called on Miss
Rigby for a few minutes—Mr. R. being out. Also we saw
Miss Brooks and stopped to see Nancy and her two infants
who have just arrived. Sidney Lord won't be here for several
weeks. Last night Susan and Geo. Clymer, Nancy, and Miss

French came to tea and we actually had quite a pleasant evening, with more conversation than I have heard from Sturgises for a long time!

This morning I worked on the tennis court from 9:30 to 1, and we ought to have a fairly good court when we get through with the gravel sand and clay. In the afternoon we had another good sail taking the baby and [name deleted] and this ought to last the latter for some time; it will us.

I forgot to say that yesterday afternoon we took the baby and went all the way to Pembroke and back, a total of about twenty-three miles in two hours and a half! Now the fog has closed in again for the night.

Thursday—I have just returned from Eastport whither I rowed with the Captain. It is dead calm and this afternoon E. and I are going to catch flounders from the float. E. will finish this sheet and send it to catch the Saturday steamer.

F. doesn't say I see that [name deleted] has been very kind and invited us to drive down to the pool at 4:30 to weigh the baby which we are going to do. Anna is just beginning to be a little tanned but the sailing is fine for her and she never wakes till seven in the morning! F. looks very well. He is going deep sea fishing to-morrow A.M. with Mr. Hubbard and Mr. Haven and I think he is getting full of health. We are waiting anxiously for our first cable and letter.

Much love from us both.

Anna has just given F. a hug and said Gaga.

Devotedly

ELEANOR

Appleton Clark, a lawyer, was married to John Aspinwall Roosevelt's eldest daughter, Grace Walton Roosevelt. From the very beginning of their summer residence at Campobello the Roosevelts had continued to enjoy the produce of their Hyde Park farm, and so "vegetable baskets" were shipped back and forth under the supervision of "Mr.

Clark," the customs inspector. During these early years there was only one church on the island, St. Ann's, and the rector was Hazen Rigby ("Mr. R."). He took the parish of this Anglican church in 1906 while still in his twenties, and lived there for more than eight years with his sister, Helena, who kept house for him. He was a small man—hence the later reference to a visit to "Little Rigby." Miss May Brooks came from Baltimore and was the eldest of a number of sisters; she owned a house near the Roosevelts and used to bring her family there for the summer.

∽

Dearest Mama,

It is a beautiful day, the water looks like glass this side and for little Gorham's sake I hope it is the same outside. They (Mr. Hubbard, Mr. Haven, Franklin and Gorham) left at 8 A.M. and hope to return for luncheon laden with fish! We are going to tea with Mr. Hubbard to-night. It is the first time and I think it will seem very strange without Mrs. Hubbard. [name deleted] took us to the pool yesterday and we weighed Anna in Mr. Byron's scales but of course we can't tell anything till we weigh her again but I am sure she is gaining and she looks splendidly.

Hall writes that they have had a fancy dress ball, been out camping and altogether leading what sounds like a most strenuous life so I am wondering what disease he will have when he comes up next Wednesday!

Saturday A.M. F. got home about 2:30 yesterday, very hot for the thermometer was 81 on the piazza and they didn't have wonderful fishing, but we have 3 cod which is all we can well use and they all said the morning was delightful. After tea we started to go canoeing but were met at the pier by a boat from the "Comanche" which had come in a little earlier with Gus Hemenway, Mr. Goodhue and Mr. Brooks on board. They came up to the house and as we were going out for supper we arranged to take them for a picnic on the Half Moon to-day.

Sunday morning—I have just put Anna in her carriage to go to sleep but she is talking loudly to herself and making every effort to free her legs and arms. The picnic yesterday was great fun. Mr. Haven, Katherine and little Gorham came besides the three boys and we went up to Casco Island. Mr. Hubbard had to put his launch up and couldn't come. I really didn't think he wanted to so I was not very urgent. We started with very little breeze but had a good one for returning and got here at 4:30. Miss Norris and the three boys came to supper after which we indulged in a childish game of "hearts"! We went to bed feeling that we could rival Bar Harbor for gaiety and to-day we are settling down to quiet again as the "Comanche" left this morning for Nova Scotia!

Your cable came yesterday afternoon and we are so glad you got in Friday night and had a good trip. I am sending it on to Aunt Annie as I did the Marconi for I think she likes to have us do it. She wrote us a very nice letter and told me she dreamed the other night that our Helen had twin daughters! Isn't that funny? I am sure you are enjoying this Sunday at Osberton and wish we could look in and see you there.

Toutou is absolutely wrapped up in Kay and never leaves him. He even came on our picnic yesterday and had a splendid time!

I have quite forgotten to tell you about Franklin's dream two nights ago and I know you will be amused for it was so characteristic that I had to laugh when I got over being scared! He sleeps or rather slept until this night episode occurred on the side near the windows and suddenly leaped up, turned over a chair and started to open the shutters! I grabbed his pyjama tails and asked what he wanted and received this surprising answer: "I must get it, it is very rare, the only one and a most precious book." After some persuasion he returned to bed, very angry with me and the next morning he knew nothing about it! Now I sleep on the window side as the middle of the room seems a better place to hunt for rare and precious volumes!

I called on Mrs. Gough the other day and told her you wanted to know how she was etc. etc. and she sent you all kinds of messages and hoped you would keep well.

Monday morning. Yesterday afternoon we went for a sail but it looked as though a bad storm were coming up so we came home early. We took supper with [name deleted] much against F's will but I could not think of an excuse and she heaped coals of fire on our heads by giving us a very delicious meal! Much love dear from Anna and me. Franklin is going to end up so he will send his own.

Monday Morning—Another boat has just come in and it may be some more friends to add to our gaiety, but we don't know yet. Poor William on the boat has been rather seedy, and thinks he feels worse than he really is and talked of going home to his family, but I have persuaded him to change places on deck with Desmond and let the latter do the cooking, as he thinks the cramped position over the stove may be the cause of it. It is another lovely day with a N.W. wind and I only hope it will be fine when the Parishes come next Friday from Bar Harbor.

The grocer man is here so this must go. Loads of love from us both. We should get a letter from you next Sunday or Monday.

Ever your devoted

F.D.R.

George Byron was the proprietor of the general store in Welshpool, one of Campobello's two small villages. An excellent speaker and always active in local politics, he was given a county position fifteen years later and moved away from the island. Augustus ("Gus") Hemenway, Jr., was the son of one of Boston's prominent merchants and Harvard's great patrons; like "Parky" Haven a member of the Somerset Club, he was a year behind F.D.R. in college. "Miss Norris" was either Alice or Edith Norris, nieces of Mrs. Travis Cochran, who used to spend their summers with the Cochran family. A.E.R. recalls that F.D.R.'s inclination to have dreams like the one described only existed while he was young, and that in later years none ever occurred. Mr. and Mrs. William Gough were natives of Campobello and nearby neighbors of the Roosevelts. Their three children are still residents of the island. Their youngest son, Russell, was a contemporary of F.D.R. and the two boys were close companions during F.D.R.'s early years on the island.

∞

CAMPOBELLO
JULY 22, 1907
MONDAY

Dearest Mama,

We have had a sad blow today—as William became panicky about his health, and took the Aurora to St. John to go home to his doctor and family. So now we are at sea more or less as to a man. W. is going to try to get a sailor from Shag Harbor. The Captain and I would infinitely prefer one from there to any local talent we could get, but if William is not successful in this we shall get probably either a son of Captain Dixon's from Grand Manan or else Harvey Johnston, J. Johnston's son.

We have been very very gay since last Wednesday. Last night we dined with Sarah, and tonight Gorham, Mr. Haven and Katherine dine with us. All today I have spent at the tennis court putting on sand and rolling and this afternoon had a set with Geo. Clymer. E. has looked on and talked to the various *interesting* neighbors!

Tuesday July 23rd. The dinner party last night was great

fun and Gorham, Mr. H., E. and I played bridge afterwards until 11:15—G. and I winning, much to the chagrin of Mr. Haven.

This morning Gorham, G. Jr., Mr. H. and I started at 10:30 on our second fishing expedition, to the other side of the island. We had much better luck than the first day, though the fish ran a good deal smaller. We got 99 in all, Mr. Haven and I tying for "high-line" with 26 fish apiece. We got back at five and went to tea at the [name deleted], a very quiet evening. Eleanor was overcome by the general untidyness and "sloppy weather" effect of the [name deleted] mansion, and by the bad manners and "revolting appearance" of [name deleted] (the quotations are hers!).

Wednesday July 24th. Mr. Johnston came this morning and we decided to try the salt water engine tomorrow or next day. The engine is of course all right, but if you remember the pipe seemed pretty rotten last year. Now it is all gone—crumbled to pieces from the top of the tank to the ground and we fear it is the same under ground down to the beach. If we can get water to pump up as far as the house I will have a new pipe put in up to the tank but if the water won't come up to the house it shows the whole pipe to be rotten. It seems useless expense to dig up the whole line of pipe and put in new—especially as salt water rots pipe etc. in a very few years. I am trying to work out a scheme for moving the engine up here to be used to fill the present tanks and the salt water tank from the cistern, thereby obviating the hand pumping every day. It certainly seems as if the salt water is never used to any extent for baths and doesn't work well in closets as it ruins all pipes near it. Of course I wouldn't do anything while you are away, but it's worth thinking over.

We went over to Eastport at 10:30 and I met Hall at the train. He came straight from Oyster Bay, and looks rather better than he usually does after staying with the strenuous Presidential family. While I was at the train Eleanor stayed on board and the Half Moon was warped to the dock and supplied with water. We drifted back just in time for lunch, and in the afternoon played tennis and had the Clymers to afternoon tea.

Thursday a.m. It is a vile day, chilly and beginning to rain, but we need it as it is the first for nearly two weeks, and if it pours now it may be fine by the time the Parishes come tomorrow night. Henry Parish can only stay till Tuesday as he must be back in N.Y. on Aug. 1st. Eleanor will finish this and send it for the Saturday's boat.

There really is no more news dear, except that we are all well and the Hall, Cally affair is in full swing again! The baby had toothache last night and cried for two hours but she seems all right to-day. No more teeth through but 4 very swollen back ones look as though they must soon come through. We have finished "The Indiscreet Letters" and are now beginning "A Staff Officer's Diary" by Ian Hamilton. It is two fat volumes but easy reading and most interesting to us (F. and me). Hall prefers lighter literature but is forced to listen!

Love from us all.

Ever devotedly

ELEANOR

James M. Johnston was the local plumber and Harvey was the second of his four sons, later becoming one of the prominent men on the island. "Cally" refers to another daughter of Russell Sturgis, Carolyn; in spite of the "full swing" definition of her summer romance with A.E.R.'s brother, she later married Theodore T. Scudder, who was in the class of 1911 at Harvard. The interest of F.D.R. and A.E.R. in Lieutenant General Sir Ian Hamilton's *A Staff Officer's Scrap-Book During the Russo-Japanese War* patterns their previously indicated concern. As the military representative of India with the Japanese Field Army in Manchuria during the war, Hamilton wrote a detailed account of the conflict in which the Japanese Army is continuously praised.

Dearest Mama,

I must go back to Thursday as I haven't written since then. We fished in the afternoon and came home at 4:30 to play bridge with Mr. Hubbard and Mr. Haven but our plan was frustrated as all the Island chose to come to tea! Dr. and Mrs. Lord, Miss French who is with them, George Clymer, Marius Prince and a Mr. Meyer staying with the Sturgis' and finally Mrs. Hoppin! After they left we had just time to dress for supper after which we were all obliged to betake ourselves to the Club House and dance to the music of a Victor talking machine! We (F. and I) came home at ten leaving Hall talking to Cally in the moonlight!

Friday, Hall and F. played tennis all the morning and from one o'clock to seven it poured in torrents so Mr. Haven and Mr. Hubbard came over and had their game of bridge after all. It stopped raining but was quite foggy when we started over to Eastport to meet Cousin Susie and Henry and we took an hour over, so as the train was on time F. just got to the station as it came in! Then we started to come back and a lantern was hung over the compass so F. could see it better and no one thought of its making it untrue but it did and we got lost in the fog and made circles round Treat Island and Pope's Folly before we finally reached home at ten thirty! It was really most amusing but Cousin Susie was quite tired when she got here.

F., Hall, and Cousin Henry started off at ten-thirty this morning to sail up Passamaquody Bay and back by way of Letete but Cousin Susie was too tired to get up so early so I had to stay at home too. It has cleared and the wind is fine but we have had one or two showers. We took a little walk before luncheon and now Cousin Susie has gone to rest so I hope by tomorrow she will feel well again.

The Lord's have had an anxious time with their little baby. He had erysipelas and now that that is better his digestion is very bad. He lost 1¼ lbs the week before he came up and has lost a ½ lb every week since so he weighs less than 13 lbs and is nine months old. He lies on the bed all day with his legs and arms pinned to the mattress with tapes to prevent his scratching and as he has done this for six months he is really a pitiful baby with apparently no desire to move or even cry. It does seem as though they ought to be able to do something, doesn't it?

Aunt Annie sent us two photos of Morris Brownell and his boy the other day with a letter saying it was cool on the river and she and Uncle Fred were well.

I forgot to say that I took Anna to call on Mrs. Cochran yesterday morning but the strange house and strange people were too much and she buried her face in my lap and wept. Even after the tears ceased she would only show the back of her head so our call was not a great success. She is very well and I do hope the film I sent the Obrig Camera Co. will have some good ones of her to send you. Nurse took two on the beach which are excellent but she didn't give them to me so I didn't like to ask for them!

Cousin Susie tells me Mrs. Blodgett's baby isn't coming till November and she doesn't show it at all! She also heard from them a sad piece of news. Our old nurse Madeleine died in Florence of typhoid. Wasn't it sad for her and also hard for Mrs. Dickey with that little baby over there?

A new man is coming on Monday for the boat and F. says he must be good as he's been on an English cutter. The salt water came to the house so F. is putting a new pipe up to the tank and we will soon have it. The babs has two pails brought by Edgar every other night and she bathes in them mixed with the hot water and you should see her lick her lips when she splashes it into her face.

Sunday Morning—Our sail yesterday was splendid—up the St. Croix past St. Andrews into the Magaguadavic a little way, then through Letete passage and back by way of Head Harbor. Cousin Henry loved it and I was glad he saw so much as he has to return on Tuesday night. It is a lovely day today with a strong N.W. wind and we shall sail this afternoon. There isn't much real news and Eleanor has told you all. The new man should be here tomorrow and the Captain seems pleased. Hall's affair with Cally doesn't seem to be quite so serious. We think there were other attractions at Oyster Bay which he still remembers.

The servants are off to church. Loads of love.

Ever your affect.
F.D.R.

In spite of the signature, F.D.R. wrote only the last paragraph of this letter. Marius D. Prince was a friend of the Sturgises. His family owned a house at Campobello; he later married Anne W. Snoden and moved his residence from St. Louis to California. In *This Is My Story* A.E.R. notes that due to the amusing incident of the lantern attracting the compass and to the bad weather that followed ". . . never again were we able to induce Mrs. Parish to attempt a trip to Campobello." Morris R. Brownell was a distant cousin of F.D.R.; a member of the class of 1902 at Harvard, he later established a law practice in New Bedford, where the original Warren Delano had been a whaling captain. The former Hannah L. Whitney, "Mrs. Blodgett" was the wife of Miss Eleanor Blodgett's brother, William Tilden Blodgett, who divided his life between a large farm at Beacon, N. Y., and his father's business; the first William T. Blodgett was one of the founders of the Metropolitan Museum of Art in New York. Mrs. Charles D. Dickey, formerly Louise Whitney, was a friend of F.D.R.'s mother; for

thirty years her husband was the senior partner of Brown
Brothers, the New York banking house.

∽∽

Dearest Mama,

Nothing from you yet, though we should get a letter by
tomorrow surely. Yesterday we *all* went to church, managing
with exceeding labor and shortness of breath to perambulate
the long and dreary way that leads to Little Rigby. After
lunch we drifted about the neighborhood for two hours and
came home for tea, the Infant going with us. Sweet [name
deleted] supped with us, as we couldn't play bridge on the
Sabbath and thought it an opportunity to do the necessary
with the least inconvenience to ourselves.

Tuesday—Yesterday morning was fine though very calm.
We left in the Half Moon at 10:30, taking besides the
Parishes, Katherine, Cally, and Fanny as a species of harem
for Hall. We had to use the engine and went far up into
South Bay between the Islands and landed for lunch. Cousin
Susie broiled four youthful chickens for us and we did some
canoeing before returning at three, getting home at five. The
P.'s thought the scenery lovely and seem really enthusiastic
about the place.

The evening gave us a chance for another very exciting
bridge game.

This morning was foggy outside but as Mr. P. leaves tonight it was his only chance to see the other side of the
Island and we walked over to Herring Cove and of course
got no view at all.

Later. After lunch we went out at 3:30—giving Cousin
Susie plenty of time for her post-prandial snooze—and
landed Cousin Henry at Eastport at 6 to take the night train.
He has been so nice and I am very sorry to have him go.

Thursday morning—Aug. 1. Yesterday we played tennis all morning, Mrs. P. managing to survive three sets and in the afternoon we hired Miss Elizabeth Gough to take us down to the Pool, where we weighed the Baby, who showed a gain of ½ pound for the two weeks. Thence we continued along the North Road almost to the end.

Last night Mr. Hubbard, Mr. Haven, Katherine and Cally came to supper, making eight in all, and we had bridge and euchre afterwards. Mr. Haven goes today, after a month here, and he is certainly a very nice little man—a typical Somerset Club bachelor, but an excellent person for Gorham. Laura McAllister and her two children arrive tomorrow and later the Farnhams and Clarks are coming.

Your dear letters were so welcome on Tuesday. I am so glad Nelly is so successful and that the Baltic was so comfortable. What a lot you read! Our reading hasn't progressed very far this last week. We are so anxious to hear all about Osberton and whether you saw Mrs. Bulloch and how long you stay in London and whether you see Muriel and Cyril or not!

By the way, the new man came from Barrington on Tuesday and seems all right so far and the Captain seems satisfied, so all is well.

Many thanks for my special letter. Of course Nelly would be a splendid person and I should be very angry if you didn't write me about such things, but Nurse feels now that she would like to stay and as you know Helen is very anxious to have Nelly if she will go to her. I never felt better but I have changed a good deal now and there isn't a sign as yet of my old trouble though I've been taking medicine again.

The enclosed kodaks we think very cunning and I'm sure you will like them. Please keep them for we have no duplicates and I want to put them in a book. Anna gained a little over a ½ lb and it was only 12 days so we think she is doing finely as her big teeth have bothered a good deal. She can say "bye bye" now and she tries hard to say Captain but only succeeds in saying "Cap." How nice about the laundress. Do have her come on the 12th as there are a number of fine things I'm not going to have washed here at all. Mrs. Mitchel does linen all right but fine clothes are not well ironed!

I must stop as F. is going over with Mr. Hubbard to East-port and will post this. Much, much love from us both.

Devotedly
ELEANOR

F.D.R. wrote all but the last three paragraphs of this letter. "Fanny" was Frances Sturgis, a fourth daughter of Russell Sturgis; she later married F. Haven Clark, a member of the class of 1913 at Harvard. The membership of Boston's Somerset Club was—and is—exclusive; a Somerset Club bachelor would, of course, be one of the most eligible young men in Boston. Laura and Annie Henshaw were sisters of Mrs. Gorham Hubbard; the former became Mrs. Hall Mc-Allister and the latter married Frank A. Farnham, both families being mentioned in this letter as soon to arrive at Campobello. The other expected visitors were Dr. J. Payson Clark and his sister Mary, both of whom spent frequent summers either at the local hotel or as guests of the Hub-bards. A.E.R.'s mention of having "changed a good deal" refers to the expected birth of her second child, an event that took place on December 23, 1907.

∽

CAMPOBELLO
AUGUST 3, 1907
FRIDAY

Dearest Mama,

Yesterday afternoon Cousin Susie, F., Hall and George Clymer had three very good sets of tennis and returned to tea much exhausted. I went for a lovely walk and explored some of the little paths of the Glensevern road and ended by paying Mrs. Lord a visit to ask after the baby. They still seem much worried but think the food they have now is a little better. We dined with the Cochran's and played bridge afterwards. Poor F. had to play all the evening with Miss Tappen who was too foolish for words so he felt quite indignant by the time we came home! We are still shrouded in fog and it is thicker than ever today so Cousin Susie has written and read most of the morning and F. and Hall are now fishing. Tomah and his wife are here this year and F. got him yesterday to repitch his canoe which has to be done every year.

By the way Franklin wants to know if you won't ask Aunt Jennie to let us know who she wants you to have for Ellen's wedding as he doesn't think you will have time to hear from her and then write the people yourself. We will keep our servants at Hyde Park as long as you want so you won't have to bother about anyone till you get home unless you want to.

Saturday—Yesterday afternoon Hall and F. canoed Cousin Susie and myself down to the pool and up to Friar's head. It was drizzling but Cousin Susie wanted some Wedgewood and as we can't go to St. Andrews now we contented ourselves with the Pool in the rain! After supper Mr. Hubbard came over for "bridge," and we played till eleven o'clock. Mrs. Wells and Lulie arrived a few days ago but I haven't seen them yet.

It is as foggy as ever to-day and I doubt if it ever clears! Franklin has just heard that Tom Beal and possibly Livy Davis will arrive next Tuesday and Hall expects V. Webb. They plan to go off on Wednesday, and take the trip up the Magagnadavic that F. took three years ago with Marius Prince, returning Saturday morning. I hope it will be nice so they can enjoy it.

Sunday—Yesterday morning Hall and F. played tennis between showers and in the afternoon we had the buckboard from the Owen and Mrs. Hoppin, Cally, Fannie and ourselves drove to Head Harbor. The fog lifted sufficiently to see the Island itself and we had a glimpse of one or two others and a very pleasant tea getting home about 7:30. We found your letter from Osberton and were so interested in all you saw there. Perhaps those photos may get off some day! How nice that you went to see Aunt Ella. It was just like you to be so kind and I know how much Aunt Ella must have enjoyed your visit for home people mean so much to her. I am glad Muriel is in London and so anxious to get your next letter about her and her relations-in-law.

We had a quiet evening last night and Hall supped with the Sturgis'.

Sunday Morning—I have never seen anything like this weather in my life. A whole week of it and we are getting pretty discouraged especially as Cousin Susie of course has the impression that it is not foggy or rainy at other places on the Maine Coast. Today it is raining and foggy as usual and our only hope is that it will be fine for our trip to Magagnadavic on Wednesday. We are going in two canoes.—T. P. Beal, L. Davis, V. Webb, Cooper Bryce, Hall and myself. We expect to camp in Mill Lake beyond Lake Utopia and return to the Half Moon via the L'Etang River (this time by daylight) on Saturday. Hall has gone to Church, not for the love of Church, but for the walk with his harem. Eleanor and Cousin Susie are reading aloud in the parlor and I am going to get in some naval work.

How you must have enjoyed Osberton and the dear old couple. I am overcome at Muriel's sudden enthusiasm at seeing you again. We had hardly expected it, judging by her remarks before departure!

Ever so much love dear Mummy from us both and from Hall. Anna is very well but she has had to be disciplined these last few days as she thought whenever she saw anyone they must take her out of her pen and that was an unfortunate idea as the only way to recover from it was to let her cry which she did all one rainy afternoon! Now she is quite good again and I know you feel sorry for her! Our love to Aunt Doe if you are with her.

Devotedly
ELEANOR

F.D.R. inserted the second and third paragraphs from the end of this letter. "Miss Tappen," whose bridge playing "was too foolish for words," was a friend of the Cochran family. Tomah Joseph was the last Indian chief of the Passamaquoddy tribe of central Maine; he used to visit Campobello each summer to build and repair canoes for the islanders. The Franklin D. Roosevelt Library possesses one of his products that belonged to F.D.R.; a birchbark canoe made from the bark of one tree. As can be seen from this and other letters of the chapter, Ellen Delano's marriage to Frederick B. Adams in the autumn of 1907 was a big family event that called for much preparation. Mrs. Kate Gannett Wells and her daughter, Louisa ("Lulie"), were regular summer residents. They lived in a cottage near the Roosevelts which was built by Mr. Wells, a former president of the Campobello Company, in 1883. The latter's son, Gannett, was also very active in the summer colony, and helped start the golf course. Thomas P. Beal, in F.D.R.'s class at Harvard, was one of the latter's ushers; for over twenty-five years he has been president of the Second National Bank of Boston. F.D.R.'s close friend and Harvard classmate, Livingston ("Livy") Davis, later entered the brokerage business and became a director of a score of large companies, including several railroads. In August, 1917, he was appointed special assistant to F.D.R. in the Navy Department, a position he resigned two years later to join the American Relief Administration under Herbert Hoover. A Groton friend of A.E.R.'s brother, Vanderbilt Webb later became a prominent New York lawyer and a director of Rockefeller Center, Inc. "The Owen" refers to the original hotel at Campobello. As inferred in the next to the last letter of the chapter, it was later remodeled, but eventually it was destroyed by fire. "Aunt Ella" was the wife of Irvine

S. Bulloch, the former Ella Sayre from New York. A member of the class of 1913 at Yale, Peter Cooper Bryce was another friend of Hall Roosevelt; his mother, the former Edith Cooper, was the daughter of New York's Mayor Edward Cooper, while his father, Brigadier General Lloyd Stephens Bryce, served in Congress (from 1887 to 1889) as well as in the Army. The "dear old couple" at Osberton refers to the aforementioned Foljambe family.

∽∽

Dearest Mama,

Yours from London—two delightful letters arrived today. How nice it must have been to see Muriel and Cyril and Esmond and also the Philip Martineau's; their plans sound very nice and make us more convinced than ever that Muriel will become so wedded to Cyril's life and friends, as well as to Cyril himself, that she will hesitate more and more about making visits to this country. What an amusing young person your travelling companion must have been—and how unlike any other nationality for one of her class to be making a caravan tour of the country for pleasure! You do not say how Mrs. Neale is or whether she told you anything about Lord Berkeley.

Yesterday was one of the vilest days here I have ever known. Fog and rain from the East till three o'clock when the wind ceased, and the rain came back on us with redoubled fury in a hurricane from the Northwest. We stayed in the house all day and occupied ourselves most usefully and agreeably. George Clymer came over and we worked over stamps.—I having sent to Hyde Park for my albums— for a couple of hours. In the evening a conversation on the subject of Hall's education and general knowledge resulted in a sort of questions and answers class in geography and general history led by me—and Eleanor and I were rather

112

overcome at finding (We think F.D.R. would be poor in grammar!) Cousin Susie about the foot of the class in geography and modern history, tho' (to be Irish) a little more up to date in ancient affairs!

Today of course, as Cousin Susie left, has been fine and gives promise of better weather. This morning we walked her over to Herring Cove—the first chance to get any view since she has been here. On our return E. and I went to see Laura McAllister and her two children, a girl of eleven, and boy of six, both nice looking. We left in the Half Moon at four and sailed to Wilson's Beach before leaving Cousin Susie at Eastport to take the night train back to Orange.

Wednesday Aug. 7th. We were too confident on Monday about the weather and yesterday morning the fog was thick again, everyone is growing quite cross as a result! We steamed over to meet Livy Davis, Tom Beal, V. Webb and Cooper Bryce, and Franklin laid in stores for the trip though I didn't think they would get off. In the afternoon they all played tennis while I made gun cases and tea bags and had a call from Mrs. Lord who seems much depressed about her baby. After supper we played tennis and went early to bed as they were to breakfast at 6:30. It rained hard in the evening and 5:30 this morning found us enveloped in fog but they started and are to return this afternoon if it isn't clear up there but the fog has lifted here and though the clouds are still black I hope they will have good weather.

We heard yesterday that the Winston's are coming to us on the 23rd for a few days which is very nice as Franklin was very anxious to have Owen Winston here.

I see Franklin has omitted to chronicle the exciting fact that Anna can walk from one person to another. She began on Sunday going from him to Cousin Susie and does better all the time but she loves it so that she really runs instead of walking which is the cause of many tumbles and subsequent tears! I am to take charge of her and put her to bed to-night as Nurse is going to Eastport to say goodbye to her son. He came up on Sunday for a few days rest as his back was hurt in that accident and also to say goodbye, as he has been offered a position in Chicago for a year at much better pay than he can get in New York and he is leaving almost at once.

I am glad Nelly decided to go to Helen for I am sure it will take a load off Helen's mind to know she has such a good nurse coming to her.

I must go now and leave a note for Sarah Hoppin as she invited me to drive with her this afternoon. She sent some cakes yesterday afternoon for the boys to take them and she has been altogether most attentive and sweet and I wish she wouldn't be for I feel like such a pig!

Later. I have had my supper and no boys have returned so I expect it was pleasant up the river. We had a nice afternoon but the fog is closing in again to-night. Toutou seems to have been left out of our letters and I know you will be glad to hear he is well. He is devoted to Kay but occasionally deigns to walk with us and he rarely barks! The baby and I had a lovely afternoon on the piazza and I wish you could have flown over to join us.

Ever so much love from us all.

Devotedly
ELEANOR

In addition to inserting the note about F.D.R.'s grammatical ability, A.E.R. made the August 7th entry in this letter. "Esmond" was Cyril Martineau's son by a former marriage, while "the Philip Martineau's" were his cousins. Mrs. Neale and Lord Berkeley were English friends of Sara Roosevelt from previous trips abroad; the former was the wife of Sir Henry Neale, for seven years Assistant Secretary of the Admiralty (the British equivalent of the job F.D.R. later held in the Navy Department). Owen Winston was in F.D.R.'s class at Harvard and an usher at his wedding; he later became vice-president of Brooks Brothers in New York.

Dearest Mama,

Just a line this time as Franklin if he goes to Bar Harbor will mail you his letter from there. Yesterday was lovely and half my family, Hall and Van that is to say, went to church and Toutou insisted on going also and after they had settled themselves in the front pew he rushed in and sat down, panting, in front of Hall! Wasn't it funny? Hall was quite annoyed and removed him sternly and the poor mite came home alone! The others played tennis and in the afternoon Hallowell Gardiner and Roger Pierce came in, on their little boat and we had quite a tea party in the midst of which Mrs. Hoppin came with her little pony to take F. to the woods to identify the hermit thrush! Wasn't it cunning? F. wouldn't go however, so she had to drive off alone.

This morning I sent Hall, Van and Cooper off with their lunch on a general Prince-Sturgis picnic and all the others took Billie Gough and went down to the duck ponds to shoot. F. brought Tom Beal home a little while ago and then started back to meet the others and I gave Tom his tea and sent him off in lonely state to Eastport as the fog has come in and I didn't care to get soaked! Tom sent his love to you and was very sorry you were not here.

I enclose some kodaks, but they were done in Eastport and are pretty poor.

Aug. 14th Wednesday—Yesterday morning was so foggy that we all got up and saw Van & Cooper off to their train and then Franklin decided there was no use in starting for Bar Harbor. We went over to meet Miss Spring and after lunch it looked better and Franklin, Hall and Livy started. It got better and better all the afternoon and we had a lovely sunset and in the evening I got a telegram from F. at Cutler. To-day is glorious with a splendid breeze so they should

115

reach Bar Harbor quite early. Your two letters of the 31st and Aug. 2nd came last night and I can't tell you how sorry I am that you and Aunt Doe have been so bothered by Franklin's bills. I never saw the Gateau bill but I cannot understand about Loidrault. F. will have your letters as soon as he returns and I hope he will feel as ashamed as I do and as sorry that your trip should be marred by such occurrences.

Before I forget it, Aunt Annie wrote me yesterday that she knew of a good laundress through her waitress and would write her if I thought you wanted her. I am writing her that you have already written to one that Nelly recommended but should that one not come to you I thought you might like to know of this one.

So many thanks for ordering my lingerie dear, remember I won't be a "graceful person" when you come back so don't be tempted by the pretty things! I am so well, far better than last time, but I'm sure it is to be twins for I look so enormous already! If you do see a plain white silk evening petticoat would you bring it to me for the one I got at Jones last winter is already nearly worn out and I wore my French one over a year! I am so anxious to see your pretty clothes and am looking forward to a delightful time at Hyde Park seeing all the things unpacked. The invoice came from Marshall & Snellgrove last night but the things have not yet come. What fun it is to be getting things for the houses already!

The code you sent I shall keep but I hope we won't need it. Frances' letter was too funny and I keep it for F. as he will enjoy it. I am so glad Marie is coming back with you for I know you are relieved. Kay asked F. the other day and said he hoped she would return as she was too valuable a servant to lose. Don't you think that was quite nice and discerning of him? We quite forgot to tell you the end of the Watson boy tale. His mother had to pay $250 and felt awfully about it but we lent $150 and she returned it out of her wages. His back was quite badly hurt but he got an offer of a very good place in Chicago for one year at $25 a week at first and then $30 and his trip paid. It was double what he got in New York so he came up here and said goodbye to his mother and had three days rest and is now gone. I am sorry for Nurse but it is a good chance for him and the doctor said if he was careful his back would be strong again in a year.

It is very nice having Miss Spring and she would satisfy even you for there is nothing good enough to say about Anna! She thinks she looks *very* well and is in every way perfect!

Mrs. Lord, Joe, Miss Spring and I are driving to-day to Racoon Beach with "Bessie" and taking our lunch.

I think of you now in the Dolomites and hope your drives will be lovely. I am so anxious to hear about Venice and whether the heat was too bad for you to enjoy it. Our next letter will go straight to Paris as you directed and soon F. and I will be meeting you at the steamer and how glad we shall be to see you coming in. It makes me feel quite excited to think of it for I feel already as though you had been away for the longest time!

This letter which was to be so short has grown and grown so I shall keep it and finish up to-morrow morning! Give Aunt Doe my best love and I do hope she is well and also my love to Aunt Tilly and the girls if this should get to you in time.

Thursday Aug. 15. We had a lovely picnic yesterday and the view from the other side was lovely. To-day is beautiful again and I feel sure Franklin is enjoying his trip as he couldn't have more ideal weather.

Ever so much love

ELEANOR

Robert Hallowell Gardiner was a classmate of F.D.R. and a member of the sizable Gardiner family of Gardiner,

Maine; his brother, William Tudor Gardiner, was governor of Maine from 1929 to 1933. A member of F.D.R.'s class at Harvard, Roger Pierce later became a noted corporation executive; in 1947 he was made chairman of the board of the New England Trust Company. Miss Blanche Spring had been A.E.R.'s trained nurse when Anna was born, and in subsequent years she returned to the Roosevelts whenever serious illness or a new child entered the household. The "code" refers to the family habit of using abbreviations in cablegrams, and this particular reference was probably concerned with A.E.R.'s pending confinement. "Marie" was a servant member of Sara Roosevelt's household. "Joe" refers to Nancy Lord's son, Joseph Lord, who in later years was not affected by the ill health frequently mentioned in this chapter. "Bessie" was a horse that the family rented from the village. The former Matilda Annis Peasley, "Aunt Tilly" was the wife of F.D.R.'s maternal uncle, Frederic Adrian Delano, a successful railroad administrator who served as vice-governor of the Federal Reserve Board during World War I; in 1934, F.D.R. appointed him chairman of the National Resources Planning Board. "The Girls" is a reference to Frederic Delano's daughters: Catherine, Louise, Laura, and Matilda.

∽∽

CAMPOBELLO
AUGUST 16, 1907
FRIDAY

Dearest Mama,

We had such a quiet day yesterday that I really couldn't think what we had done when I first sat down! In the morning we walked along the beach to the "Friar" as Miss Spring wanted to see him from nearby and on our way back I received a telegram from Franklin saying they reached Bar Harbor and would start for home this morning. The weather is too lovely but there is very little wind so I don't expect them till to-morrow.

We played with Anna and put her to bed so our afternoon

was well occupied and to-day we are lunching with Mrs. Hoppin and taking Anna down this afternoon to be weighed.

The invoice has come from Goode also and I suppose the things themselves will soon be here.

Saturday Aug. 17th—Contrary to my expectations the "Half Moon" sailed in last evening about six and instead of just Franklin, Hall, Livy, walking up the path I saw these three and two more, Van Webb and Maurice Smith! I was a little surprised as I hadn't had any word but the telegraph strike prevented my getting F's telegram and we managed all right as it was. Sarah H. came to supper and we had a quiet evening as the three younger boys were asked to go on a hay ride to Herring Cove the moment supper was over!

Franklin got the notices of the arrival of your packages this morning and he will finish this later, just now they are playing tennis.

Anna weighed 25 lbs yesterday, a gain of a whole pound in two weeks, wasn't that splendid? She received from Aunt Annie yesterday a floating doll as "compagnon de bain" but unfortunately its head was cracked in the mail. However, she loved it just the same and enjoys it more than most other toys! Wasn't it sweet of Aunt Annie to think of her?

Sunday morning—Our trip to Bar Harbor was a complete success. The very rough run to Cutler on Tuesday afternoon was followed by a splendid all day sail on Wednesday with a strong Northwest wind that kicked up a very troubled sea in conjunction with the old fog swell of the day before. Hall and Livy thought discretion the better part of valor and remained rolled in blankets on deck, while I steered for about ten hours. I dined with the Davis family—Mrs. Davis being a good deal better. On Thursday morning I went to the swimming pool, saw thousands of people I knew, had my hair cut, then lunched at Dr. Hasket Derby's, played tennis at the Cutting's with Lisa and Bayard and Suydam and went again to dine at the Davis'. Hall spent most of his time at the Smith's and he and Maurice Smith and Van Webb joined us on board at 10 p.m.

On Friday we got under weigh at 5 a.m. with the engine, but an increasing S.W. wind sprang up pretty soon and we made a wonderful run up the coast, getting to West Quoddy at 5 p.m.—just 12 hours for the 75 miles—and reached the mooring a little after six.

Yesterday we played tennis most of the morning and as the rain began during lunch we had a quiet little bridge party until we took Van Webb to the train at 5:30.

Today to our great surprise is almost fine, the little fog that remains disappearing under the rays of the sun. We are to play tennis this morning and L. D. goes back to his work tonight, and we think M. Smith goes tomorrow—so we shall have three days of quiet before the Winstons come to us on Friday.

Hall is to go to the Webb's at Shelburne on Sept. 8 and thence to Ne-ha-sa-ne—in the Adirondacks for a week before he returns to school so I think our trip to the woods will be unnecessary—for which I am somewhat thankful as I am much more inclined to stay here.

A great deal of love from us both.

Ever your affec son
F.D.R.

A friend of A.E.R.'s brother, Maurice Fremont Smith later became a doctor. Two of Dr. Hasket Derby's sons were college acquaintances of F.D.R., while the Doctor himself was a famous eye specialist and surgeon. He never maintained a general practice, but instead held the position of consultant to numerous Boston hospitals; a recognized litterateur and amateur landscape gardner, Dr. Derby was also a co-originator and president of the American Ophthalmological Society. The "Cuttings'" were the family of the celebrated financier and philanthropist, Robert Fulton Cutting, who was known around the turn of the century as "the first citizen of New York." R. Bayard Cutting, who died in France during World War I while working for the Red Cross, was Fulton Cutting's only child by his first marriage. Elizabeth ("Lisa") and C. Suydam Cutting were children by his second marriage; the former is now Mrs. Neville J. Booker, while the latter became a noted field-collector (especially in Central Asia) for the American and the Chicago Museums of Natural History.

∽∽

CAMPOBELLO
AUGUST 20, 1907
TUESDAY

Dearest Mama,

Livingston Davis left us on Sunday afternoon after a visit of nearly two weeks. It has been awfully nice having him and I think it did him a world of good as he was rather run down when he came, after the strain of his sister's death and his mother's long illness. We took Hall and his harem and Maurice Smith on Sunday afternoon for a nice sail before leaving Livy at the train, and dined with Sara that evening. Incidentally when at Bar Harbor I saw [name deleted], looking very cheerful, and in a moment of forgetfulness asked him to come back with us in the Half Moon to Campobello! He *roared* with laughter and said he thought it would be *such* a good joke if he *could* come, and asked me particularly to give his best love to [name deleted]! I shall do so some day soon and watch the result with interest.

Yesterday, Monday, we left in the morning at 10.30 taking Miss Spring, Hall, M. Smith, Katherine, Gorham Jr. and Cally and sailed out to the Wolves where we landed for a short time on the East Wolf. We had to use the engine most of the way back as the wind died out. The engine I am glad to say has been going splendidly ever since we went on our camping trip two weeks ago—never have I seen it go better —but it is due entirely to the cleverness and care of the Captain, who stops any little disorder before it gets very bad. Of course the engine is now eight or nine years old and a good many parts have become worn. I think that in another year from now it will be necessary to take up the question of very extensive refitting of the engine or the possible installation of a new and better type.

Today I have played tennis all morning, Eleanor and Miss Spring remaining quietly at home. After lunch Sarah came for Miss Spring and they drove down to Wilson's Beach to return the pony on which Sara has been riding for two weeks. E. and I started in the Half Moon a little later and met them down there and brought them home. We have now after supper finished an exciting game of euchre.

Wednesday Aug. 21st. I had the Half Moon hauled up today to be cleaned, and played tennis again this a.m., also helping G. Hubbard repair his hot air engine at the Club House. It has been out of order for a week and nobody seems to be able to find out the trouble, consequently the poor Hubbards have only six inches of water left in the tank! Eleanor and Miss S. have walked to Herring Cove and after lunch I canoed them both down to the Pool to see the Half Moon being scrubbed.

Thursday, Aug. 22nd. Franklin is out playing tennis so I will finish this. We had Mr. Hubbard, Mrs. Farnham and Katherine to supper last evening and as Maurice, Hall and Katherine went over to a candy bee at the Sturgis' right afterwards we "older generation" as Hall calls us (!) had a pleasant, talkative evening. Franklin and I have been working over the plans for lighting, bells and telephones which Mr. Platt sent us two days ago. All the arrangements seem very good except in one or two bedrooms where I think he has made a mistake as one would want lights over dressing tables it seems to me and not in the four corners of the room. We enclose three kodaks but they are poor, owing chiefly I think to bad developing in Eastport. Anna walks now very nicely and with more confidence and Duffy's life is becoming daily more trying! Toutou she cannot get even now though she calls him all the time! Your letters came this morning from Tai and Cortina and I am so glad you had good weather and are enjoying it with Aunt Doe. Your letter from Venice has not come yet so there is a gap in our news but we hope for it daily. No news yet from Helen and she writes that she hates waiting and misses Douglas terribly. Miss Spring and I went to pick balsam this morning and this afternoon we all go sailing including Anna, but I start early and walk to the Pool as they are having the Animal Fair and F. is going to pick me up after I have attended.

How wonderful Mme. Menardi remembered us. We never took the drive to Misurina, but I wish we had, it must be so lovely.

By the way William got better after he got home and is now on another boat. The man he sent is very nice and a good sailor.

The Winstons come to us on Sunday and Lathrop may come later. Hall was to have gone to see G'ma on the 4th and then for a week to the Webb's but G'ma does not seem really anxious to have him and writes she would rather go to New York to see him so he will stay on and go from here to Shelburne.

Ever so much love dear from us all.

Devotedly,
ELEANOR

The "Wolves" are three islands to the east of Campobello. Charles A. Platt was the architect hired by Sara Roosevelt to design the homes she was building for herself and her son on 65th Street. He established an admirable reputation in his field, being particularly noted for the Freer Art Gallery in Washington, the expansion of the University of Illinois, and the rebuilding of Phillips Andover Academy; between 1928 and his death in 1933, he was president of the American Academy in Rome.

∽

Dearest Mama,

I went to the fair yesterday and everyone told me how much you would be missed but judging from the crowd I think they must have done quite well. Franklin picked me up at the Pool but the wind was so slight that we barely got to Eastport and home by 5:30. This morning was lovely and the first thing I saw from the window on the Pell beach was a canoe and two Indians! We all bustled round and by 10:30 we were ready to start, Mrs. Hoppin taking the food in her canoe and Franklin and Hall paddling Miss Spring and me. The wind came up quite strong and going across the Duck Ponds and around Liberty Point we had quite a little sea but it was a glorious day and we reached Mill Cove by lunch time. We started again at two and paddled till we met the "Half Moon" at Mill Cove at four but this time Miss Spring went with Mrs. Hoppin so the boys had a light canoe and took keen joy in making the Indians work to keep up with them. We sailed home and got there about 6:30 and I think everyone enjoyed the day, it was so lovely and the Island beautiful. To-morrow if it stays fine we start at 9:30 and take Mrs. Hoppin and Cally with us to St. Andrews coming home I hope through Letete as I have never been through and want to see it.

Your letter from Venice and postcard from Misurina came yesterday afternoon and made us very sad that we did not drive to the latter place and very envious of those evenings in a gondola. I wonder if you are in St. Moritz still. I hope so for I feel that will do you and Aunt Doe both good. I had quite a long letter from Aunt Kassie yesterday afternoon at Fairhaven and I shall try to answer it in a few days but spending whole days on the water is not good for one's correspondence.

Sat. Aug. 24th. The morning was lovely and we started for St. Andrews and sailed up in two hours. After landing we had lunch on board but an east wind came up and it looked like rain so we came straight home. The day was delightful and the wind made our sail home more interesting and exciting! After tea and seeing Anna splash in her tub Miss Spring, Mrs. Hoppin and I walked nearly to Herring Cove and left Franklin doing stamps with George Clymer. Susan and he came to supper at 7:30 and have just left after spending a short but pleasant evening with us. Franklin is going to add to this so much love dear and goodbye for the present.

Sunday morning—25th. I can only add a line, as I am just off in the Half Moon to meet the Winstons. The wind has come out strong from the East and it is pouring so the poor Winstons will not have a pleasant arrival. I much fear that we are in for the three days' August storm. Our visitors certainly seem to have pretty hard luck! I have added quite a lot to my stamp collection and would love it if you could bring me the *new* French stamps and the 2 franc stamp too. Also the *higher* values of the German stamps!

Much love from us both.

Ever
F.D.R.

∞

CAMPOBELLO
AUGUST 28, 1907
WEDNESDAY

Dearest Mama,

The letter is a little late in beginning this week owing to various excitements, but we will go back to Sunday and try to remember everything! Mr. and Mrs. Winston came in rain and fog and we spent an absolutely inactive afternoon and evening. On Monday morning Nurse, who had been getting more and more upset in spite of all we could say, as she had never heard from her son since he wrote her he was to leave for Chicago over two weeks ago went to Eastport in the hope of getting news and got it with a vengeance. Her son had withdrawn all her savings from the bank and then no one had seen him again. She nearly had hysterics and I let her go that night to town to look for him and we are now waiting to hear what she finds and if she can return. Of course her son is a scamp or some accident has happened so either way the poor woman is in for trouble I fear. I never knew before how easy it was to take care of Anna. Of course Miss Spring helps enormously in the day and the babs has her crib in our room and is too good and sweet. Tuesday morning Franklin, Mr. Winston and Hall left for Point Lepreau and expect to return to-night. Mrs. Winston and I walked up to Friar's Head in the morning and drove up the north road in the afternoon. Mrs. Hoppin came to supper and was most charming and Mrs. Lord is lunching with us to-day. Mrs. Winston is very nice and does not seem to mind constant interruptions from Anna! Miss Spring is reading the "Woodcarver of Lympus" to her now as I write and Anna is sleeping on the sunny side of the piazza.

I have a letter from Auntie Bye this morning and she is having a lovely visit at Henderson but says Auntie Corinne does not have a moment unoccupied! I know F. will want to finish, so much love dear and he will tell you any other news.

Thursday—We returned at 8:30 last night from Pope Logan and had a satisfactory two days. We went on a hunt for cormorants, and got a nest and four young birds, to be presented to the Nat. Hist. Museum, and fished for trout yesterday morning, getting 2 very small ones! I have a certificate from Mr. McWalters showing $10,000 work done on the houses—so I shall pay him the whole $5,000 you left me and write to ask if he wants the rest now or can wait until you get back. He doesn't say a word about how the houses are progressing, so I shall ask for news. If he wants the other $5,000 at once, I will advance it for you.

I have written the Farmers Loan & Trust to send a draft for $700 to be deposited to your account at Baring's. Of course I can't trace my remittance of April to Loidrault until I get back to N.Y., and I hope that if it hasn't been cashed I can get the money back from the Express Co. I am too sorry about both the bills. I realize it was far too long to have left them, but Gateau knew I shouldn't make the final settlement for some time to come, and I simply haven't had the money till now. Hereafter I shall pay cash!

The Winstons are off this afternoon and I must close this in a hurry.

Ever your devoted

F.D.R.

"Henderson" is the Robinson family home in Mohawk, N. Y.; at the beginning of the eighteenth century it was deeded to the first member of the family to come to America by Queen Anne of England. James McWalters was the contractor for the building of the two adjoining homes into which F.D.R.'s family and his mother moved several months after the writing of this letter. F.D.R.'s apology for the unpaid book bills must have been to some extent stimulated by his mother's rather stern admonition in a letter from Paris dated July 31, 1907: ". . . To my sorrow I find poor Aunt Doe has been troubled by the knowledge that my dear boy's bills are not paid, though 2 years old. She did not say much and hesitated to tell me. I have today been to the bankers and the bills are paid. I will say nothing, as it will do no good, only it *is* a surprise as I am not accustomed to this way of doing business my dear Franklin and if you love me you will be more careful in the future."

Dearest Mama,

The Winstons left us yesterday afternoon, much to our regret, as they are a most delightful couple to have with one. In the afternoon before taking them to the train Owen and I lunched on Treat Island. He is most enthusiastic about it here, and we have seriously considered the joint purchase of Treat Island. We hear rumors that the last sale was for less than $2,000. The sale of Campobello itself seems really imminent, the old Company having apparently come to terms with the new syndicate whoever they may be, and we hear that efforts are being made to acquire the vacant privately owned lots on which the golf course is situated. In view of all this, and of the doubt as to exactly what is going to happen to this immediate locality, the purchase of Treat Island with its wonderful sites and American soil doesn't sound like a very bad proposition, does it?

This morning I played tennis and Eleanor and Miss Spring had a quiet morning at home, and this afternoon it was too calm to sail so Anna was given a short walk. I have "done stamps" with George Clymer for several hours and added about fifty to my collection.

Saturday—Aug. 31st. I spent the entire morning at Eastport getting the September 1st money. I have paid the taxes and Kay's wages, and am keeping an account for you of everything.

Who do you suppose turned up here after luncheon? Cousin Frank Lyman, come down to Eastport for the day! We had a nice talk and he is at N. Perry with the lovely "Florence" and little Joseph, the latter very well and flourishing. We are going to try to go up there some afternoon this week.

Sunday—We have had a telegram from Nurse asking us

to forward some money for her return and that she had "found loss"—whatever that means—so she will be back I hope by Tuesday, for which I shall be thankful, as the care of the baby means a good deal of work and worry for Eleanor.

Your cable was most welcome yesterday saying you would be at 12a Curzon St. on the 11th. We leave here the 10th and go straight through to Hyde Park.

Loads of love from us both in which Hall joins.

Ever your affec.
F.D.R.

The idea of purchasing nearby Treat Island was a serious one and not a jest similar to those of the previous chapter; it never materialized, however, and the fears regarding the transformation of Campobello turned out to be unwarranted. Recalling the summer of 1907, Owen Winston writes: "I remember that visit very well. Franklin and I and Hall Roosevelt went off trying to find cormorants' nests. We were fairly successful and got ourselves properly messed up. Regarding the proposed purchase of Treat Island, it was one of those dreams that both he and I really were serious about at the time, but like many youthful dreams, it didn't materialize. Campobello difficulties seemed to be resolved, and I was working hard, and it was doubtful if I could get up there very much, so the idea was dropped." "Cousin" Frank Lyman was related to F.D.R. through the latter's maternal grandmother, the former Catherine Robbins Lyman.

∽∽

CAMPOBELLO
SEPTEMBER 1, 1907
SUNDAY

Dearest Mama,

Franklin forgot to say that we received and enjoyed both your letters, the last written at St. Moritz on Aug. 20th. It is so nice being able to really *see* you in all the places and I'm so glad Aunt Doe enjoyed it with you, though very sorry that she looked so ill at St. Moritz. I do hope you will land Thursday evening and Franklin and I both expect to meet you unless something unforeseen occurs. Oh how glad we shall be dear, to have you home again, it seems so long since you left! I haven't yet heard of any special to Barrytown but I've written Aunt Jennie and if she tells me of any of the arrangements I will let you know.

You will surely have had a cable about Helen but I don't suppose many particulars. Cousin Susie writes me that the little girl was born at 4 A.M. on the 29th and weighed 8 lbs some ounces. The doctor from New York came the night before and she had a fairly easy time. I feel sure she will keep her trained nurse for six weeks so you won't be hurried about Nelly. I have not heard from either housemaid Nelly or laundress yet but suppose I will soon.

I am so glad Helen and her baby are so well and Anna won't be much older than this little girl cousin. My lady Anna is the mischief itself and I will be glad when Nurse returns to manage her, as Nurse Spring and I not being used to her have had some quite hard struggles with little tempers and wildest animal spirits which will break out at inopportune moments!

Ever your devoted

ELEANOR

Don't you think these kodaks are cunning?

The remark that "Franklin and I both expect to meet you" is noteworthy, as it became a family tradition for Sara Roosevelt always to be welcomed back from Europe by her children; in 1921 this habit caused some embarrassment and uncomfortable moments, for she left Europe shortly after her son had been stricken by infantile paralysis, and arrived in New York to be greeted unexpectedly by others.

Dearest Mama,

After sending off our letters yesterday, Franklin and Hall played tennis and in the evening Hall supped with the Sturgis' and F., Miss Spring and I went to Mrs. Lord's. She was very nice but I think her summer has been an awful one as she is constantly anxious about the baby who does not seem to improve. She showed me a new knitting stitch which is very pretty but should be done in absolute seclusion I think, so I doubt if I will ever use it!

This morning Hall and F. played tennis and this afternoon we all sailed and Anna was very good. A telegram from Nurse tells us she will be here in the morning and that "all is well" for which I am thankful though I fail to see how *all* can be well! I fear you will find your granddaughter a sad mischief, no one has any peace now if she is round and *out* of her pen and her greatest joy is wheeling her baby carriage up and down the grass road to the gate so you can see that she is strong! Her big teeth seem to bother her a good deal but they are not through yet and I am sorry as I hoped they would be through before we left here. I can hardly believe that we go a week from to-morrow. Franklin has written Elespie, Plog, Bullimore and Edgar, and Kay goes down on the 6th to have a day in New York to deposit his money (?) and then he will help Elespie. I do hope some of Uncle Fred's family will come to Hyde Park for I would like to have them. Caroline Wilmerding and Lathrop come to us over the first Sunday that we are home and I think F. wants the deRhams the next but I shan't ask them till we get home. I wanted G'ma to come down for a night but she wrote me she couldn't leave Tivoli where there seem to be many complications. I will write Aunt Annie a line later on and see if I can find out anything about Aunt Tilly's plans.

We think of you now in Paris and I do hope Aunt Doe has allowed you to have a few meetings outside 37 Ave. de l'Alma! Dear Aunt Doe, what a trial it must be not to have you and all Uncle Fred's family constantly under her roof!

I feel sure Toutou will bark himself into a fit with joy on your return but he is quite well now in spite of his wonderful behaviour and Kay has taken care of him.

Wednesday—Yesterday and to-day have been rainy and foggy. In the morning yesterday, George Clymer went over to Eastport with F. and Hall and they brought Nurse back. She looks as though the week in town had aged her but seems resigned and cheerful and like a sensible woman will try to forget about her son's behaviour I hope. He is married and he took all the money to furnish his flat and he has become a Roman Catholic like his wife and he meant to write his mother as far as I can gather after frightening her into a state of forgiveness. It is too bad but her savings are gone and she has to work and of course she will make it up sometime with her son but he is evidently a fool as well as several other less pretty things. I think the longer she can keep clear of him the better. Anna is very happy to have her back but I am glad to say I think she missed me a little last night! Franklin spent the afternoon in stamps which are just now a tremendous interest and Miss Spring and I went to call on Mrs. Hoppin and took a short walk.

This morning we have been reading "Paul Jones" by Buell and sewing and Franklin has done a little writing and a little more stamps and talked long with Mr. Johnston. Just before lunch F. and I went to call on Mrs. Wells and I know he will want to tell you about the sale of Island which seems probable so I will stop.

Thursday Sept. 5th—Dearest Mummy.   I must add a little before Franklin finishes as your two letters have just come from St. Moritz—the last to me on Aug. 27th. I will wear anything of yours that will go on dear but I doubt if anything will fit me. I seem to carry this baby very differently from Anna, it is very low down and I think I look worse now than I did near the end last time! In taking my waist measure to have the dress for Ellen's wedding begun I found I was 34 inches already. It is a very active infant or infants(!) and I have never felt so well but it will stick out in front and I have great difficulty in keeping my clothes from rising up to my chin! Miss Spring says if it is twins she will run away!

I haven't heard from a laundress yet and if none writes me before the 12th I shall cable you to know if I can engage one when I am in town on the 17th to see Hall off to school. I don't want to go down again before meeting you and I don't want to discourage a new woman by having too big a wash awaiting her arrival!

I had a letter from Aunt Jennie this morning and she says a special will leave New York on the 28th at 9:30; returning it will reach there 6:30 so she doesn't think of anyone who cannot come that way. She says Ellen is only going to have Laura as bridesmaid and Mr. Adams will have six ushers and his brother for best man. Several of Ellen's friends will not be able to be there which is a disappointment. A Mr. Battershal of Albany who is a great friend of Mr. Adams' is to perform the ceremony. Perhaps if Helen and Teddy can leave the baby they will come to Hyde Park if Uncle Fred's family are all going to Algonac or Steen Valetje; anyway I will find out from Aunt Annie after we get home what her arrangements are.

Thursday—Kay is leaving this afternoon and will take this to post in Boston. We shall be left to the tender mercies of the brilliant Delia from now on. Kay has been *so* satisfactory and nice all summer and we shall really miss him.

Lulie and Mrs. Wells have been here this morning and examined our cistern as they are thinking of putting in one. Mr. Johnston has a scheme for enlarging our own cistern and if the hotel remains closed this will be the best solution of the water question, as the hotel engine and pipes won't last much longer. You can look over the plan when you arrive and pass on it. Just now the hotel question is as follows: A perfect agreement has been reached on all points except one—the fertilizer factory at Eastport. If the evil smell can be stopped the Island will pass into the hands of the new company—chiefly New York men, represented here by Mr. Merriman, whom you may have seen last summer. The smell is to be passed upon in Eastport this evening by a meeting of the board of trade. The idea of the new Co. is to remodel the present hotels and to build possibly a few cottages—also to keep a lot of sheep and do some intelligent wood cutting. All this I get from Lulie, and in spite of the source I think the information is substantially correct.

It is still vile weather—fog and rain—the third day—but we don't much mind as the weather for the past month was really very good. Hall leaves us on Sunday for Shelburne to stay with Van Webb.

We have enjoyed your letters on the driving trip and from St. Moritz so much—it brings back our own trip of two years ago so vividly.

George Clymer and I have bought an old stamp collection and are very busy over it. My interest in my collection has really revived! And I find it a pretty good one to use as a foundation.

While in England do you think you could get me an unused £1 stamp and also an unused 10 shillings?

I hope Messrs. Barings & Co. have got the $700.00 I sent. I have a receipt from the Farmers' Loan & Trust for it.

Loads of love from us both.

F.D.R.

William A. Plog (pronounced "Plow") came to work for James Roosevelt as grounds superintendent of the Hyde Park estate on November 3, 1897, and he still holds this position in 1948. As but one small incident in Mr. Plog's long and remarkable record of faithful service, it is noteworthy that after F.D.R.'s death he refused a family pension and entered the National Park Service to continue his work. Plog's account book of this period shows that Arthur Bullimore was hired as a coachman by Sara Roosevelt on March 17, 1906, the first anniversary of F.D.R.'s marriage; his book has no record of "Elespie," but A.E.R. recalls that, next to F.D.R.'s retired nurse, she was the oldest servant in the Hyde Park home in 1907. As previously noted, James Edgar was the farmer on the estate at this time. A sister of Lucius Wilmerding, Caroline Wilmerding later married John B. Trevor, who was two years ahead of F.D.R. at Harvard. Henry C. de Rham was a classmate of F.D.R., and in later years their friendship encompassed politics when the former became chairman of the Putnam County (N. Y.) Democratic Committee. His first wife, the former Frances A. Dana, was a granddaughter of Henry Wadsworth Longfellow and of Richard H. Dana, author of *Two Years Before the Mast*. Augustus C. Buell's two-volume work on *Paul Jones, Founder of the American Navy*, comprised only a small part of F.D.R.'s large collection on the life and times of John Paul Jones; indeed, his fascination for this naval figure later led F.D.R. to attempt to write a "little volume" on Jones. In this recently discovered and unfinished document (numbering five handwritten pages), which was begun during the quiet days spent recuperating from infantile paralysis, F.D.R. suggests that much of the material on Jones is "romance" and unhistorical, that unfortunately "John Paul Jones surpasses all in the pure fabrication of untruthful 'facts'," and that therefore his work is written "with the hope of correcting many still existing misconceptions" alleged to surround the career and life of Jones. Contrary to popular opinion and many historical interpretations, F.D.R. contended that Jones "was not the greatest naval commander of all time, he was not essentially a great American patriot, he was not either the 'founder' or the 'father' of the American Navy." It would seem that F.D.R.'s fascination for Jones resided in the simple fact that "it was he above all others who lifted the somewhat drab record of the revolutionary navy of the United States into world history." As for the "hotel question," Mr. H. Morton Merriman recollects that "in 1906 two businessmen from New York came to Campobello to look over the property of the Campobello Island Club. They were very much interested but insisted something must be done to eliminate the odor of the fertilizer plant from the Seacoast Canning Company of Eastport, which with the wind from that direction was very objectionable on Campobello. The Seacoast Company agreed to make certain changes which would eliminate the odor and a contract was signed to purchase the holdings of the Campobello Island Company consisting of some 5000 acres and two hotels. Then came the panic of 1907 and some members of the Syndicate could not make good their subscriptions. The plan for the rehabilitation of the hotels had to be deferred, but the Owen Hotel, another property, was leased and operated for several years, rather unsuccessfully, and the Syndicate lost interest in the property which passed into other hands."

∽∾

CAMPOBELLO
SEPTEMBER 6, 1907
FRIDAY

Dearest Mama,

This will be our last epistle to you, unless I succeed in catching you at Queenstown by a line on the outgoing White Star boat. Just think—when you get back in less than three weeks I shall be a full-fledged office boy seeking my first afternoon off to go to a wedding.

The invitations have just come and seem to be correct in every way! The special train leaves N. Y. at 9:35 a.m. and the wedding is set for 12:30. Eleanor has a letter from Aunt Jennie in which she says she hopes and trusts that she will do all that is right on the day of the ceremony. What she thinks she may or might do I don't know—but the remark sounds either like a bad man from the West or an intended suicide. If she faints I shall pray that it be not into my arms!

We are wondering very much whether the Toms will come back with you. What a horrid time they must have had. If they do return on the Baltic give them our love and don't go too near Julia as you know her aim is sometimes poor. Has Mr. Newbold got a new pair of trousers? Or Mary a new black and white check? Or Mrs. N. any new unmentionable combinations to take the place of the suit on the scarecrow?

Today is the fourth day of fog—but the back of the storm is broken and it is going to clear up. Yesterday we did very little out of doors, but were busy and contented in the house. Today we have. We drove the baby down to the Pool and found she had gained ½ pound more—25½ in all and a new tooth is through today, making the second large one, whatever they are called.

We, or rather I, am paying every bill I can, so you won't find much to do in that line when you get back.

Saturday 7th.

Last night we supped with dear [name deleted] and had a most exciting evening, for which we were secretly prepared. At about nine a horrible crash was heard on the long piazza, much exciting the household. Then five minutes later another awful crash from the kitchen, followed by piercing screams from the maids. We rushed out to find them almost in hysterics and—not a sign of anything or anyone, except a large croquet ball on the floor and a lot of cakes gone from the kitchen table. [name deleted] took it quite well but had Gough's boy to sleep in the house. Perhaps the younger society of the cottages might know something about it—but remember please that this hint is to go no further!

This morning I went to Eastport, E. and Miss S. going also for the sail, and sent sundry express packages and got money to go home with. After lunch we three went for another sail and the wind left us off Wilson's Beach. We found the "Mavis" stuck for good, and towed her home with all the Cochrans on board. The engine has really been splendid this summer, tho' I must tap on wood for the next three days. We have burned less gasoline than usual I think—only two barrels from Wadsworth. Jimmy, the new man is excellent and I hope the Captain can get him again next summer. His (Captain's) expense accounts have been low I think and he will leave here about three days after we do, as I want him first to take up the mooring entirely. It must be fairly bad in condition as it has been down three years, I think, and when put down again it can come a little more to the south—more in the position of the mooring of the old Half Moon.

We haven't been able to get to Perry to see Cousin Frank Lyman as the weather has been so bad this week. We hear that they have at last had rain on the Hudson but I fear things will be pretty dry and burned.

I have had one letter from Jim and two from Plog—both several weeks ago—all well then. Kay went back on Thursday—goes up today and will get the silver from the bank on Monday.

F. seems to have told all there is to tell so I will only add love from us all. Devotedly.

ELEANOR

P. S.   We have a number of amusing kodaks but I don't send them for fear they should miss you.

E. R.

"The Tom's" was an abbreviation for the family of Thomas Newbold. They had some illness abroad which explains their "horrid time." F.D.R.'s warning about Thomas Newbold's second daughter, Julia, refers to her inclination to be seasick; she later married William Redmond Cross, who was a prominent New York banker and vice-president of the American Geographical Society.

〜〜

138

After writing all but the last paragraph of this letter, F.D.R. did not take pen to write a member of his family for almost a year. The task of writing daily letters to his mother was turned over to A.E.R.; henceforth Sara Roosevelt received only an occasional letter from her son. This does not mean that F.D.R. became less and less attentive, but rather that he was able to spare less and less time from his work to manifest his devotion when separated from his mother. F.D.R.'s work during the winter of 1907-08 was precisely as he predicted in this last letter from Campobello: "a full-fledged office boy." He was assigned the usual routine jobs of a young lawyer, ranging from actual case work to legal research to running errands. Yet this brief, uneventful period of F.D.R.'s eventful career was perhaps far more significant than it appears to be on the surface, perhaps far more formative than simply the experience of acquiring practical law techniques and contacts: for this early inter-lude as a fledgling lawyer was his first real introduction to some of the various classes of society not encompassed by his heritage and education. A listing in the Social Register and four years at Harvard had not provided F.D.R. with direct knowledge of how most men lived and thought; his life prior to September, 1907, had been a thoroughly shel-tered one. The actualities of law, which not infrequently required him to meet, interview, and advise all kinds of people with all kinds of problems, brought F.D.R. at least partly out from under the shelter. The three years spent with Carter, Ledyard and Milburn constituted F.D.R.'s first immediate and real contact with the world that existed beyond Hyde Park, Campobello, Cambridge, and 65th Street. In view of the social and political philosophy he evolved in later years, this first contact cannot be regarded lightly, refined and negligible as it may have been.

III

"...A Succession of Wonderful Valleys and Hills..."

CAMPING TRIPS

1908

WITH HIS ENTRY into the professional world, F.D.R. relinquished the right to prolonged vacations; the practicing lawyer also differed from the student of law in that he could not spend the summer months as he pleased. In June of 1908, however, F.D.R. was allowed a week away from the office to join his uncle, Warren Delano, on a trip to Kentucky and Tennessee. Although ostensibly the trip was a business one (intended to straighten out family interests in some coal mines), it can be seen from the letters that F.D.R. was far more enamored of the people and the countryside he encountered on this first journey south of Washington, D. C.

∽∽

The next letter is chronologically the first existing letter written by F.D.R. as a husband to his wife, whom he almost always addressed as "Babs." A.E.R. cannot recall any particular reason for this nickname, but presumably it stemmed from the affectionate use of the word "Baby."

HOTEL JOHNSON
PENNINGTON GAP, VA.
JUNE 12, 1908
FRIDAY

My own dear Babs—

The letterhead will explain to you where we are just as well as I could without the aid of a map. Suffice it to say that we are spending the night here, having arrived at 9:30 P.M. We are in the point of Virginia which runs down to where Kentucky and Tennessee join. Tomorrow we leave at 7 A.M., take the train down the valley about 20 miles to a place called Hagan, get out horses there and ride over the mountains over Boone's Trail to Harlan in Kentucky, our headquarters. Next Thursday night we come out to the R.R. at Pinesville, far to the S.W. of this, take train on Friday to Knoxville, Tenn. and get to Washington some time on Sunday. I thought that if I can't get to Seabright on Sunday evening I will spend the day at the White House, provided any of the family are there, and take the night train to N. Y.

I hope you understand from my scribble on the train last night that you can telegraph me c/o Mr. W. W. Duffield, Harlan, Ky. up to Wednesday A.M.

As to letters, you can write up to Wednesday noon to c/o Post Office, Knoxville, Tenn. and telegrams up to Friday c/o Western Union Office, Knoxville, Tenn.

The trip today has been so wonderful to me that I can't begin to tell you about it now. We woke up near Hagerstown, Maryland, and ever since have been coming through Virginia, the valley of Virginia or rather a succession of wonderful valleys and hills. In some places we were over 2,000 feet up, and the train ran thró gorges that for sheer beauty beat anything that we saw in the Black Forest.

Loads of love, my own dearest. I do hope you are taking very good care of yourself and that the lambs are well. I am so anxious to hear how Anna likes Seabright.

It is now 11 o'clock and I have had a bath and am almost asleep.

Ever your own devoted,

F.

At the time this letter was written, six-month-old James was recovering from pneumonia, and in order to be near the doctor and F.D.R.'s law office, A.E.R. broke with family tradition and did not move the household to Campobello for the summer. Instead, the summer was divided between Hyde Park and a house rented on the boardwalk at Seabright, N. J., which is mentioned here as F.D.R.'s objective upon his return from Tennessee.

HOTEL JOHNSON
PENNINGTON GAP, VA.
JUNE 15, 1908
MONDAY

Dearest Babbie—

This letterhead is erroneous as to our location, as we have come many miles into the mountains, staying at Mr. Henry Smith's house about three miles from Harlan.

We got up on Saturday morning at Pennington at 6 A.M., took the train about 18 miles down the valley to Hagan and found the horses waiting at the station. We had been joined by a Mr. Whiteley of Baltimore, the manager of some iron mines just south of Hagan, and we rode down the railway as far as the mines and came to the path running into Kentucky over the Cumberland Mountain which Daniel Boone came over on his first westward journey. If you can imagine a succession of ridges, each fifteen hundred or so feet above the valleys, running up at a very precipitous angle and covered with marvelous trees and an undergrowth of rhododendrons and holly, you can get a general idea of the country. The path was just about the steepest kind that I would care to take a horse up, following generally a water course filled with boulders and ledges of rock. We formed a cavalcade of five, Mr. Whiteley, Mr. Wolf, the superintendent of the Boone's Path Iron Co., Uncle Warren, Mr. Sewell, W.D.'s local attorney, and your hubby. My horse is small but wiry and sure footed. Uncle Warren rode a mule, as the horse intended for him had a sore back.

We got to the top of the Cumberland Mountain about 10 o'clock and had one of the most magnificent views I have ever seen, looking to the South over the angle of Virginia almost to the mountains of North Carolina and Tennessee, and to the Northward over the Harlan County, Kentucky, section that Uncle Warren and Davis are interested in. We continued along the ridge for a mile or so, got lost, came over the top and started down into the valley over what they thought was a trail. I thought otherwise—for half an hour we slipped, slid and fell down the slope, the horses slipping, sliding and almost falling on top of us, and ended up in a heap in the stream at the bottom. Uncle Warren said it was about the roughest ride he has ever had here. We rode N.E. along the creek about five or six miles, when Mr. Whiteley and Wolf left us to recross the ridge to their mine.

We had some chocolate and spring water for lunch at 2 o'clock and then started up over Black Mountain on a so-called wagon road—positively the worst road I have ever seen or imagined and one which was not really easy to traverse on horseback. We dropped down into this valley along Catron's Creek, and came to the house at about 6:30, having done 22 or 23 miles in all, most of it on the roughest trail and worst road in a county famous throughout the land for bad trails and worse roads.

This house belongs to Mr. Henry Smith, about the most prosperous farmer of the county and his bottomlands along the valley are splendid.

I must close this long epistle hurriedly, as the mail is going. Will add this p.m.

Ever,

Your devoted F.

✖

My own dearest—

I had to close abruptly my last missive as the mail decided to start out to the railroad a little ahead of time. I will take this up where I left off.

On Sunday we breakfasted very late at Mr. Smith's, 7 o'clock, and sat around for an hour, discussing legal and political affairs, and soon after rode into Harlan, about 3½ miles, which means about 7 miles anywhere else, because of the horrible condition of the roads here.

On arrival at Harlan we were met by Mr. Duffield, the manager of Kentenia, and by most of the famous men of the town—sat around "chewing the rag," lunched at the Imperial Hotel, which is conducted by the County Judge, Judge Lewis. He and his wife do all the work and he waits on table. He is 29 only and they have been married 15 years and have two children.

We climbed to the top of the small hill close to the town and rode back to Smith's after a severe thunderstorm. Last night I sat up till eleven discussing law with Mr. Sewell, and was up at 6 this morning. We rode into Harlan again in time for lunch and are now ensconced here, saddle bags and all, at Judge Lewis' Hotel.

This afternoon we are just back from a ride of five or six miles up Martin's Fork, the most beautiful country we have seen yet. The sides of the valley going up 2,000 feet, heavily wooded with great poplars, chestnuts and a dozen or two other deciduous trees and every mile or so a fertile "bottom" with fine crops and a stream of splendid water.

I will add to this in the morning.

Tuesday—Can't add, just off for an all day ride up Clover Fork. Loads of love as always and kiss the chicks. My one regret is that you aren't with me and when living is a little less rough you should come here.

Ever your devoted F.

∞

F.D.R. returned from his short Southern trip to spend the summer commuting between his office and Seabright. Several months later he took another brief leave from his work, this time to go hunting with his brother-in-law. The letters again portray the youthful spirit and ubiquitous curiosity that especially marked F.D.R. during this more-or-less quiet period of his life. Unlike those written after 1913, these early letters do not indicate a keen sense of responsibility and concern for the events and trends of the world at large. Doubtless F.D.R. was interested in the national and international conditions of the time, but the pressing responsibility he felt for the state of things in later years does not become apparent in his correspondence until after he had taken on public duties in the New York State Senate and in the Navy Department. Yet, even at the time that he was leaving for Newfoundland in 1908, events and trends throughout the world were taking on a definite shape, a form in which F.D.R. was soon to be deeply entangled. In Europe the pot was beginning to simmer as Austria-Hungary announced her intention to annex Herzegovina and Bosnia, thereby causing great unrest in the Balkans. Although the Dual Monarchy overcame British, French, and Russian protests against her aggressive tactics and won a decisive victory on the diplomatic level, Serbian resentment had been stimulated to a point of intense hatred and the following months witnessed the reorganization and enlargement of Serbia's army. In the United States, 1908 was marked by the exit of A.E.R.'s "Uncle Ted" from the White House and the election of William Howard Taft.

∞

Dearest Babbie—

So far everything is proceeding with entire success. We had a comfortable trip on the night before last, caught the 8 A.M. out of Boston and played piquet most of yesterday. We just made connections at St. John, N.B. at 11 last night and found a section awaiting us in the sleeper. We left the latter at 7 this morning and are waiting here until 9:20 to take the local train to North Sydney, where we should arrive tonight at about 7.

Luckily the weather is cool, though the dust is bad as there has been no rain for some time. This part of the country is not very thrilling to travel through as you can imagine.

Here comes the train. Will drop you a line tomorrow from Deer Lake before we go into the woods.

Keep very well dearest and give my very best love to the chicks. I really miss you more than I can say and it is going to seem a very long time.

Hall sends a great deal of love. He is fine and a nice comfortable sort of travelling companion.

Love to Mama.

Ever your devoted

F.

∞

NORTH SYDNEY, CAPE BRETON
AUGUST 30, 1908
SUNDAY

On board S.S. "Bruce" en route to N.F.

Dearest Babbie:

I wrote you a line at Truro, N.S. this morning and since then we have had an interesting and comfortable journey to North Sydney on Cape Breton Island.

To our surprise we had a parlor car all the way. The

scenery was not particularly interesting in Nova Scotia—too much like that between Washington Junction and Eastport, but at about three o'clock we suddenly came out on one of the strange natural waterways that one reads of in the geographies, the Gut of Canseau—a "straight" thirty or forty miles long and from half a mile to a mile wide and very much reminding me of the Hudson. The whole train was slowly backed on a ferryboat and we sailed gaily across to the other side,—Cape Breton Island. I made friends with the Captain and went up on the bridge—an affair suspended far up between a smoke-stack on either side—and I got some good snapshops of the queer craft and the entrainment.

Almost the whole trip across C.B. Island was skirting the shores of one or the other of the wonderful Bras d'Or Lakes, which are salt and yet completely landlocked except for the narrow openings into the sea. Do you remember last summer at Campo when I spoke about wanting so much to see them?

The train took us straight to the wharf and we have a comfy cabin on board. We have been out to get a light supper in the town and now are waiting for the Montreal train to arrive before steaming out into the Gulf of St. Lawrence. As there is no boat back from Port-aux-Basques till Monday I will finish this tomorrow night when we arrive at Mr. Geo. Nichols' place at Deer Lake. We can get our license all right tomorrow morning, I hear.

Sunday night—Deer Lake, N. F. Dearest—We had a comfortable and smooth night on the boat and got to Port-aux-Basques at 7 A.M. The coast and harbor were just like the first glimpse we had of Norway 7 years ago. We found the license official awaiting us at the Custom House and the train left at 8. For two hours or so we skirted the wild coast and for the rest of the day have been coming up the Bay of Islands, the lower Humber River and Deer Lake, getting to Deer Lake Station at 5 after a pretty rough day, but the wild scenery was well worth it.

Mr. Nichols met us and rowed us across Deer Lake, about ¾ mile and another ½ mile up the Humber River to this settlement which consists of four houses! Everything is ready for us and this house where we sleep tonight is Mr. N's mother's, she a nice old lady and very anxious about our poor appetites!

We are off tomorrow about 7 in boats and go up the Humber just as Uncle Warren did and not to Grand Lake as we had first planned.

It seems an age since we have been gone and I miss you and the chicks very, very much. Loads and loads of love.

Your devoted F.

∞

WESTERN UNION TELEGRAPH COMPANY
NORTH SYDNEY
SEPTEMBER 12, 1908

To Mrs. F. D. Roosevelt, Seabright
Fine trip one head each taking Plant Line boat Halifax to Boston tonight wire me Touraine.

Franklin

∞

F.D.R. returned to New York from the Hotel Touraine in Boston and started his second winter with Carter, Ledyard and Milburn. Except for the occasions when his mother vacated 65th Street for her Hyde Park home, there was no necessity for writing letters during the winter of 1908-09. One such occasion accounts for the following letter.

49 E. 65TH ST., NEW YORK
DECEMBER 5, 1908
SATURDAY

Dearest Mama
This to explain vagaries of milk cans.
Supposing for the sake of argument that we receive a can of that fluid which is the source of human kindness on a

bright afternoon of a Monday about an hour after the sun
has passed the meridian. Now that can sits here, getting clean
but empty till the same hour of a Tuesday, then makes an
expedition without expedition to the platform of my client
the American Express Company—sits there till night because the 3:40 Schnellzug won't carry an empty and under
the light of the moon is carried to the place where all good
people go—Poughkeepsie—is transferred there to a Dienst-
zug of some kind and gets to H.P. about 8:30 on Wednesday—sits with Mr. Cummings till Thursday morning when
the dear Jim comes into his own again.

We can't see any way to hasten matters, can you? If they
arrive later than this it is fault of Ex. Co. and I'll raise thunder. We feel terribly about the locks and hope the last two
arrived in better condition.

Just off to dine with Uncle Warren. Eleanor is lying down.
Kids well.

Lots of love

F.D.R.

Like the vegetables at Campobello, the milk for F.D.R.'s
family in New York was shipped to him from the Hyde Park
farm, and this amusing letter explains the delays involved
in returning the empty cans and the failure to properly lock
them. The various stages mentioned in the "expedition"
refer to an express train (Schnellzug), a local train (Dienst-
zug), a former Hyde Park station master (Mr. Cummings),
and the farmer on the estate ("Jim" Edgar).

This explanation of the "vagaries of milk cans" is also
the last existing family letter written by F.D.R. before he
entered the field that was to be his main occupation for the
rest of his life. However, the new role of a politician did not
alter the general nature of F.D.R.'s personal letters. As will
be seen, nowhere in his later correspondence is there even
a faint intimation that F.D.R. the politician was wielding
the pen. Whether lettered with *The White House, The*

Governor's Mansion, or *The Office of the Assistant Secretary of the Navy,* F.D.R.'s letters are always those of a family man, be it husband, son, or father. It is true that after 1910 he is far more concerned with the national stage and the world scene, but always secondarily to his interest in the same routine family matters that account for the unity of all families. His personal letters clearly reveal that politics for F.D.R. was a business, not a way of life, and in this sense the transition from the letters of 1908 to those of 1911 is not as significant as the official record would seem to indicate. There actually was no transition. Law work continued as usual, except that F.D.R.'s proficiency as a lawyer steadily improved and he began to win the respect of his firm as a specialist in Admiralty law. His New York home continued as the focal point of his activities, although he visited Hyde Park and Dutchess County more frequently than in the past. In 1909 another son, Franklin D. Roosevelt, Jr., entered the Roosevelt household, only to die of influenza eight months later; but the family again numbered five ten months after this tragedy, when Elliott Roosevelt (named after A.E.R.'s father) was born on September 23, 1910.

IV

"...*I Dropped a Bomb in the Senate*..."

STATE SENATOR

1911-1912

THE DEMOCRATIC NOMINATION for state senator from New
York's 26th Senatorial District (comprising Dutchess, Putnam, and Columbia counties) was considered political
suicide in 1910. Republicans had held the post for thirty-
two years, the last Democratic senator having been F.D.R.'s
Hyde Park neighbor, Thomas Jefferson Newbold, who himself had been preceded by twenty-eight years of Republican
occupation. Even the apparent fact that 1910 was to be a
Democratic year could not induce Lewis Stuyvesant Chanler
to relinquish his Assembly seat and accept the Democratic
nomination for senator from the 26th. It was an honor that
only an inexperienced politician, someone who had nothing
to lose and everything to gain, would have been willing to
accept. The Democratic leaders of the district, particularly
Mayor John K. Sague of Poughkeepsie, found such a person
in F.D.R.—a candidate, moreover, who would pay for his
own campaign, and who was blessed with a surname that at
this time completely dominated America's political scene.

A half-century later it is easy to generalize about the reasons which led F.D.R. to accept the nomination; it is much more difficult to note the specific motivations that guided him. From the viewpoint of history, the decision was an important one, but regarded through F.D.R.'s eyes in 1910 it was the natural thing to do. There was no real decision to make, no crucial moment to be resolved; F.D.R. desired to enter politics and public service, and the offer of Mayor Sague and his associates was a good way to begin. His inclination to engage in politics was created and heightened partly by the exciting example of his "Uncle Ted," partly by the convincing arguments of his Poughkeepsie friends, but in the main it was fostered by factors within himself. This tendency, shown in previous letters, actively to seek and enjoy new experiences did not exclude politics; the spirit of adventure and the thrill of answering a challenge were instinctive features of his character, and they were not insignificant contributions to his acceptance of the nomination—indeed, they were the difference between making a decision and taking a natural step.

Idealism, too, was an innate feature that, to some extent at least, influenced his actions. Party machines and "boss rule" were the key to New York State politics in 1910, with Tammany Hall in the center of the rigid network, and these undenied violations of democratic principles inspired F.D.R. to the point of idealism. His two-year record in the State Senate was just as idealistic as it was successful, and it was only his success (and the success of his progressive associates) that reduced idealistic notions about good government and equal representation to a precedent for practical action.

These were the personal factors which lay behind F.D.R.'s candidacy for public office in 1910. They were of such a nature that to attribute great deliberation and prolonged uncertainty to his acceptance of the nomination would be erroneous. Except for the usual considerations involved in the voluntary change of one's place of business, F.D.R.'s entry into politics was as natural and unrestrained as his subsequent ascent of the political ladder.

At first the members of Dutchess County's Democratic Committee had hoped to enter F.D.R. in the race for assemblyman from the Second District, as this position largely comprised the city population of Poughkeepsie, which had elected a Democrat in 1909. For this very reason, however, Chanler refused to give up his seat and enter the senatorial race, where the farm vote—invariably Republican—was the deciding factor. Hence the original plans had to be reversed, and F.D.R. was offered the Senate nomination. Although a mere formality, the latter event officially took place on October 6, 1910; it was reported the next day by Poughkeepsie's Republican paper, the *Daily Eagle,* as follows:

... The Senatorial convention was held first. The convention was scheduled for one o'clock but it was 2:15 before it was finally called to order by Frank B. Lown, a member of the senatorial committee. John E. Mack nominated the permanent chairman of the convention, William Church Osborne, of Putnam County, and he was chosen unanimously. Mr. Osborne expressed his thanks for the honor conferred upon him and then asked for the further pleasure of the convention. John Hannigan nominated Homer W. Guernsey for secretary and his election was unanimous.

There being no contests, the roll call was dispensed with and the convention at once proceeded to the nomination of a candidate for senator. District Attorney John E. Mack placed in nomination Franklin D. Roosevelt; Mr. Mack said that if the Democratic party was to carry on the affairs of the nation, it must weigh its candidates. There was a pause of considerable length before John J. Meara seconded the nomination. There being no further nominations the secretary was directed to cast one ballot for Mr. Roosevelt. Mr. Mallory of Columbia County then moved that the chair appoint a committee of three to escort the nominee before the convention. Mr. Mallory, Mr. Perkins of Dutchess and Mr. Townsend of Putnam were appointed.

In accepting the nomination, Mr. Roosevelt said among other things:

"I thank you heartily for the honor you have done me and the confidence you have reposed in me by nominating me for the State Senate. But even more do I thank you for giving me an opportunity to advance the cause of good government under the banner of the Democratic party this year.

"As you know, I accept this nomination with absolute independence. I am pledged to no man; I am influenced by no special interests, and so I shall remain.

"In the coming campaign I need not tell you that I do not intend to sit still. We are going to have a very strenuous month.

"Gentlemen, I count on your active support. We have real issues and an excellent platform to lay before the people, and with the aid of the independent thinking voters of these counties we have little to fear from the result on November eighth."

Mr. Mack moved that the senatorial committee be continued and that it have the power to fill vacancies, which was adopted.

After the adjournment of the convention, Mr. Osborne asked all the delegates to step forward and shake hands with Mr. Roosevelt.

Editorial comment on F.D.R.'s entry into politics was brief; he was an unknown quantity and the local editors therefore used his candidacy largely as a vehicle for the expression of their heavily weighted opinions. The hostile *Eagle* bitterly viewed the nomination in financial terms:

Well, the Democrats have made their nominations and put their ticket in the field—all except the city ticket. They have made a new and valuable discovery, Franklin D. Roosevelt, younger son of the late James Roosevelt of Hyde Park.

This is one of the exceptional branches of the Roosevelt family that is Democratic in politics. Young Mr. Roosevelt is a graduate of Harvard and this is his first jump into politics. Presumably his contribution to the campaign funds goes well above four figures—hence the value of his discovery, which we doubt not was made by that astute politician, Mr. Perkins. Senator Schlosser, we imagine, will not be greatly disturbed by Mr. Roosevelt's candidacy.

Somewhat at a loss for words but in favor of his nomination, Poughkeepsie's leading Democratic paper, the *Evening Enterprise,* editorialized:

> . . . Mr. Roosevelt, the nominee of the party for the office of state senator, is more of a stranger than either of the other nominees, but he is spoken of as a young man of high ideals and lofty impulses and he has the character and the ability to take a place in the legislature of the state and fill it to the entire satisfaction of the people who comprise the senatorial district.

F.D.R. immediately set about fulfilling his promise not "to sit still" during the pre-election period. He had exactly a month to conduct his campaign, not a long time in view of the very limited transportation facilities. A horse and buggy would not have enabled him to tour the three counties effectively, so he hired an automobile and joined forces with Richard E. Connell, who was the traditional Democratic nominee for Congress from the 21st District. Mr. Connell was famous in the area for his fiery speeches, which usually concluded with a peroration on the American flag. However, his pyrotechnic oratory had never won him the election, and it is still recalled in Poughkeepsie that each defeat so spurred his ambition to be elected that eventually he commenced befriending children in order that some day they might vote for him.

155

Both Mr. Connell and a bright-red Maxwell touring car added unusual color to F.D.R.'s first political campaign; indeed, it was a whirlwind campaign the like of which the 26th District had never before seen. Disregarding weather, the candidates drove all over the district, stopping to talk with anyone who would listen. The *Evening Enterprise* reported the campaign at quite some length, but the unfriendly *Eagle* only mentioned F.D.R. twice during the month between October and November 8th. One was a brief notation at the end of an article headlined "Democrats Hold a Mass Meeting" (dated November 4th): ". . . at the conclusion of the mayor's speech, Captain Zabriskie announced that Richard E. Connell and Franklin D. Roosevelt had been stalled somewhere in Putnam County and were not present. He paid his compliments to them and then . . ." The other was a violent editorial denouncing F.D.R. on the ground that he was not really a resident of Hyde Park, which thereafter became known as the "non-resident issue" of the campaign. Typical of the yellow journalism that marked the election year of 1910, the accusation was an unfair one, and it began a mild battle of words among Poughkeepsie's four newspapers (three dailies and a weekly).

The farmer vote was the main objective of F.D.R. and Connell, the city electorate being left to the persuasive tactics of the party organization. It is recalled that on one occasion F.D.R. devoted an entire speech to his plans for supporting legislation that would supply the farmer with uniform apple barrels. Emphasizing the need for "good government" and the evils of machine politics, in addition to agricultural matters, F.D.R. made an average of ten speeches each day. The notes for one of these speeches were found among his personal correspondence and they are worth quoting. Hastily penciled by F.D.R. on the stationery of Poughkeepsie's leading hotel, they illustrate the nature of his campaign, as well as his technique of outlining a speech.

En route to Campobello in 1907—"Dearest Mama,
We are almost there now. . . . The Baby [Anna]
has behaved very well. . . ."

During the summer of 1908 the need for F.D.R. to be near his law office and for baby James to be near his doctor led the young Roosevelts to forsake Campobello and rent a house on the shore at Seabright, New Jersey, where this picture of 26-year-old F.D.R. was taken.

Young Eleanor Roosevelt with James, her second child and eldest son.

Family picnic at Campobello—Cousin Laura Delano, Mrs. James R. Roosevelt, James R. Roosevelt, F.D.R., E.R., Sara Delano Roosevelt, Uncle Warren Delano, Cousin Frederick B. Adams and his wife Ellen Delano Adams.

At Campobello in 1907—Mr. and Mrs. Livingston Davis, Mr. and Mrs. Archer Martin, Franklin and Eleanor Roosevelt—"After supper we played tennis and went early to bed."

During the last summer of freedom before settling
down to law practice—Cooper Bryce, F.D.R.,
Hall Roosevelt, and Vanderbilt Webb aboard the
Half Moon.

"Duffy," bought in Scotland on their honeymoon,
was the first of many Scotch Terriers the Roosevelts owned.

On the lawn at Campobello in 1912—F.D.R. and the new baby, Elliott Roosevelt, who was named for his maternal grandfather.

Anna on her pony, with her father, mother, and grandmother.

Sara Delano Roosevelt with Anna and James in 1908.

F.D.R. and Anna, with Eleanor Roosevelt, Miss Spring, and Mrs. Owen Winston in the background.

"We had a lovely sail this afternoon and Anna
seemed to enjoy it."

THE ASSISTANT SECRETARY OF THE NAVY.
WASHINGTON.

Monday
Mar. 17
1913

Dearest Mama —

I am baptized, confirmed, sworn in, vaccinated — and somewhat at sea! For over an hour I have been signing papers which had to be accepted on faith — but I hope luck will keep me out of jail — All well, but I will have to very like a new turbine to master this job — but it will be done even if it takes all summer —

Your affec son
Franklin D Roosevelt

F.D.R., sworn in as Assistant Secretary of the Navy on his eighth wedding anniversary, signed his report of the first day's activities with a flourish which did not escape his mother's attention.

During his third summer as Assistant Secretary—
"We spent an hour going over the range and
watching rifle and machine gun drill."

MEMORANDUM.

OFFICE OF THE ASSISTANT SECRETARY.

Secnav

1. I beg to report

(a) That I have just signed a requisition (with 4 copies attached) calling for purchase of 8 carpet tacks

Astnav.

Assistant Secretary

Why this wanton extravagance? I am sure that two would suffice —

From the Astnav to the Secnav, a memorandum covering a requisition for eight carpet tacks. The Secnav's notation—"Why this wanton extravagance?"

F.D.R. and Josephus Daniels standing on the
balcony of the old War and Navy Building gazing
over at the White House. In later years Josephus
Daniels used to tell the story that he was teasing
Franklin Roosevelt at the time that the picture
was taken and that he had just said, "I suppose
you think you will be the next Roosevelt after
T.R. to occupy that house?"

A meeting in Washington in 1917 of the Wage Scale Committee—Walter Lippmann, F.D.R., and William Blackmer.

In 1944 Admiral Byrd scribbled a note to President
Roosevelt on an old picture which included in the
foreground Assistant Secretary of the Navy
Franklin D. Roosevelt and in the background
Navy Lieutenant Richard E. Byrd.

Humboldt the great traveller once said: "You can tell the character of the people in a house by looking at the outside." This is even more true of a community—and I think I can truthfully say that of all the villages of Dutchess County, and I have been in pretty nearly every one, there are very few that appear as favorably as Pleasant Valley. This Library Building, the splendid trees, and the generally neat and prosperous appearance of the community as a whole all point out that the people inside are made of the right stuff.

You look here as if you stand for progress.

And it is just this standing for something that I want to say a word about.

Doughnut

There is just the same difference between the man who stands for something positive and he who stands for something merely negative.

Carlisle calls them constructive man and the stationary man.

And he goes on to prove that the stationary man is more than that—he is a destructive man, and then he goes on and utters his cry:

"Rise, you people of England, rise up and *make* something."

This country has progressed since its beginnings more than any other probably in the history of the world. And it is due to one thing more than any other, it is a country where more men than in other countries have made things.

Not confined to material side of life—

Take the example set by our Social Service. . . .

157

Pinned to the first page of the notes is a newspaper clipping which F.D.R. undoubtedly incorporated into his speech; it reads: ". . . the following splendid lines by Abraham Lincoln: 'I am not bound to win, but I am bound to be true. I am not bound to succeed, but I am bound to live up to what light I have. I must stand with anybody that stands right, and PART with him when he goes wrong.' " The town of Pleasant Valley is near Poughkeepsie; on election day it reacted to F.D.R.'s praise by according him a twenty-vote margin (175 to 155) over his opponent, John F. Schlosser of Fishkill. The word "doughnut" was inserted to remind F.D.R. to elaborate on one of his favorite comparisons: the fact that government cannot function properly if it contains a hole similar to the one that characterizes a doughnut, that unlike a doughnut government is an entirety in which the slightest defection infects all of the parts.

∽

F.D.R. was elected to the State Senate on November 8, 1910, receiving 15,708 votes to Schlosser's 14,568; the same general results were repeated everywhere in the nation. In New York State the Democrats gained control of both houses of the Legislature; the same was true for the House of Representatives in Washington, Richard E. Connell at long last becoming one of its members. In New Jersey the trend was expressed in the election of Woodrow Wilson to the governorship. Thus was the stage set for a rapid series of events that lifted F.D.R. permanently into the public eye and that brought him permanently into the field of politics.

If any doubt remained after the election about F.D.R.'s serious and energetic attitude toward his new occupation, it was soon dispelled. He moved his whole family to Albany and took up legislating as a full-time task, a move not usually undertaken at the state level of politics and only possible for those who possess financial independence. On January 1,

1911, having rented the 65th Street home, the Roosevelts took up residence in a house on State Street near the Capitol. This date not only marked the first day of F.D.R.'s public service, but also the first day in which A.E.R. had complete charge of her own home. F.D.R.'s mother did not move to Albany with her children, thereby ending five years of A.E.R.'s dependence upon her in running the household affairs of the family. Nor was it long before those household problems became acute, as the following months witnessed the transformation of her house into the central meeting place for eighteen men who astounded the country by their successful opposition to the dictates of Tammany Hall.

It is interesting that, years later, F.D.R. was the leading figure in the destruction of the vehicle whereby he first experienced nationwide acclaim. To all intents and purposes it was the New Deal that put an end to the intense interest with which people followed state politics prior to 1933. This interest continued after F.D.R. entered the White House, but everywhere it was subordinated to an interest in the activities of the federal government. Such a subordination was a fundamental requisite of the New Deal program, as the latter's success largely depended on a shift of interest from the state capitals to Washington. State-federal cooperation was encouraged by F.D.R., but the system he headed was nevertheless geared to the predominance of the federal government in all spheres, including public opinion. This was not so for the first three decades of the twentieth century, and it was particularly untrue for the era immediately prior to World War I. Washington was generally considered a faroff place, and the legislation it produced was viewed as having no real effect either upon the everyday life of a person or upon a community. The state capital was the place where the individual's interests were furthered or hampered. Newspapers devoted many more column inches to the news emanating from their state capitals than to the affairs of

Congress; editorials, too, were largely of a local nature prior to 1933. And the central attraction of this nationwide interest in state government was Albany, especially in 1911. New York State, by virtue of its size and wealth, had always been a leader in the politics of the country; therefore, within three months after he had entered the Senate chambers at Albany, F.D.R.'s fight against the election of William F. Sheehan for United States Senator brought him national acclaim.

The story of F.D.R.'s dramatic entry into politics has often been recounted, and it is necessary to review here only the essentials of the rebellion against Tammany. The first important business before the Legislature in January of 1911 was the election of a replacement for Senator Chauncey Depew, whose term expired on March fourth. Prior to the adoption of the Seventeenth Amendment to the Constitution in 1913, United States Senators did not enter office by popular elections, but rather by the elective consent of the state legislatures. Democratic control of the new legislature of 1911 meant that Republican Depew could hardly hope for reelection; but it also meant that the Democrats would have to agree upon a candidate before a decision could be reached. One hundred and one constituted a majority of both houses, and the minimum amount of votes necessary for election. At the separate Democratic and Republican caucuses prior to the official election, a majority for one candidate bound all those present to vote thereafter according to the majority decision of their party. These were the technical aspects of what F.D.R. later called the "Sheehan business," and since Democratic representation in the Legislature numbered one hundred and fourteen, the apparent simplicity with which they might elect a Senator could only be disturbed by the question of who attended the party caucus. In 1911 such a disturbance occurred in the caucus of New York's Democratic legislators, while the Republicans renominated Depew.

"Blue-Eyed Billy" Sheehan was the choice of Tammany Hall and of its powerful leader, Charles F. Murphy. The more progressive elements of the party favored Edward M. Shepard, an independent Democrat whom Murphy could not find acceptable. Although there was no personal resentment involved, the progressive elements regarded Sheehan as a perfect example of the type of man produced by machine politics, and even if Shepard could not be elected, they were determined to prevent the nomination and subsequent election of Sheehan. F.D.R. was not the leader of the pro-Shepard faction (although earlier he had announced his preference for Shepard); rather, he led the anti-Sheehan movement. This distinction became an important one on the day of the Democratic caucus: as Murphy had lined up a strong following for Sheehan, those who were willing to vote for Shepard but abide by the majority decision attended the caucus, while those not willing to risk a Sheehan majority and the sacrifice of their independent vote did not attend. F.D.R. persuaded eighteen Democratic assemblymen to join him at his house on State Street while the caucus was taking place. Hence, while Sheehan received sixty-two votes and a majority of the caucus, only ninety-one representatives took part in the meeting, ten less than the number necessary for nomination. The next day the first ballot for Senator was taken in the Legislature, Sheehan receiving ninety-one votes, Depew all of the Republican's eighty votes, while the remainder were cast mostly by F.D.R.'s "band of insurgents" and were split among several other candidates.

This successful resistance to Tammany immediately became front-page news throughout the country, although editors speculated that it could not endure for very long. Unfriendly writers insisted that the "insurgents" were only seeking publicity, but later events proved the accusation to be distinctly false, as their final compromise on a candidate bore out their original intention only to block Sheehan, not to be a dictatorial minority. Under a two-inch headline proclaiming "THE LEGISLATURE IS DEADLOCKED," the *Evening Enterprise* on January 17, 1911, carried a subhead announcing "Senator Roosevelt One of the Big Men in Albany Today." On the same day the *New York World* reported:

> The most active of the "insurgent" Democrats in the new state legislature here, who are opposing the caucus selection for United States Senator, is State Senator Franklin D. Roosevelt of Dutchess County. He is regarded the commander of the opposition.
>
> A distant relative of Col. Roosevevlt, he is 32 years of age, of spare figure and lean intellectual face, suggesting in appearance a student of divinity rather than a practical politician. Gold bowed spectacles loop his long thin nose, and a frock coat drapes his figure. He is wealthy, possessing, according to his friends, a fortune of considerable size, and is able and of pleasing personality.

Even the antagonistic *Eagle* editorialized that "Senator Franklin D. Roosevelt is starting well."

For more than ten weeks F.D.R. and his associates resisted severe pressure from Tammany to relinquish their hold over the Legislature, the pressure tactics varying from giving F.D.R. a chairmanship in the Senate (of the Forest, Fish and Game Committee) to brutally cutting off the incomes of some of the insurgents who depended upon party patronage. The resistance never weakened, however, and toward the end of March Tammany submitted to the selection of a compromise candidate. Although he was chosen by Murphy, the insurgents agreed to support State Supreme Court Justice James A. O'Gorman, who was then nominated by a caucus that numbered exactly one hundred and one votes (some of the insurgents not having heard of the new caucus in time to be present). Hence, on the sixty-fourth ballot, the "Sheehan business" came to an end with the election of O'Gorman by 112 votes to 80 for Depew.

This three-month battle in New York over the election of a Senator eventually had a threefold effect upon the political life of the nation: it paved the way for the adoption of the Seventeenth Amendment; it was a solidifying event for the progressive Democrats in the country, thereby playing an important role in the Democratic convention of 1912 and the Presidential nomination of Woodrow Wilson; and it resulted in the dismissal of any remaining doubts F.D.R. may have had about his fondness for politics, much less his ability as a politician.

Unfortunately, this momentous period of F.D.R.'s career was not recorded in his personal correspondence, as his immediate family was united and as A.E.R. wrote the necessary letters to Sara Roosevelt. His own letters do not resume until A.E.R. took the children to Campobello for the summer of 1911, leaving F.D.R. behind to pursue his responsibilities as a legislator in Albany.

∾

HYDE PARK, N.Y.
JULY 1, 1911
SATURDAY

Dearest—

Your telegram came about an hour ago, and I was thankful to get it as I was getting very worried. I had expected one from Portland, but am glad you all got there all right. I am just this minute dressed,—just three days since I came down and I feel a good deal like a rag and have lost nearly ten pounds. Throat still a bit swollen and right ear hurts occasionally, but Dr. thinks there is no more danger there. I now hope to get away on Tuesday, reaching Campo Wednesday. I can't tell you how I miss you and Mama does not in the least make up. I do hope you have found things in a semblance of order, and that the chicks are all right. I am sure they are delighted at being there again. The Campo is all I need now and I will surely be up.

Loads of love and kisses.

Ever your devoted
F.

In addition to his required presence in Albany during the summer months, F.D.R. also had to spend some time in Dutchess County attending to the needs and complaints of his constituents; thus his letters constantly refer to travel plans for moving back and forth between Albany, Hyde Park, and Campobello. At the latter place he now owned his own home, by virtue of a gift from his mother. After the death in 1910 of a Campobello neighbor, Mrs. Kuhn from Boston, it was found in her will that the first purchase right of her house and property should be offered to Sara Roosevelt. As F.D.R.'s family was expanding beyond the capacity of the original house, his mother purchased the property and gave it to him as a present.

∽

HYDE PARK, N.Y.
JULY 14, 1911
FRIDAY

Dearest Lamb—

Here I am, back from Albany at 1:30 and was delighted to get your telegram from Boston and to hear that Maude and the children go to you on Monday. It will be so nice for you and I hope they will stay till after I get up.

Yesterday I got to the Senate just in time for the debate on the race track gambling bill and I am glad to say we finally defeated it, 22 to 20, not getting thro' until 8 P.M. I had a simple dinner at the Fort Orange Club and was in bed at 11 feeling none the worse for the day. This morning I did a lot of correspondence and attended the ten minute session, catching the 12 m. train to Poughkeepsie where Mama met me. I feel really much stronger and more like myself. They expect to adjourn next week and talk about Wednesday or Thursday, but I personally look for Friday or Saturday and I very much fear they will make the assinine mistake of not passing the Direct Primary Bill. It will be a hectic week—all night sessions, etc., but I will take all the care of myself possible.

Loads of love to the chicks.

Ever your devoted

F.

I will go to the Dr. tomorrow morning, and also the barber.

"Maude" refers to A.E.R.'s maternal aunt, Maude Livingston Hall, who had recently divorced Lawrence Waterbury and was spending the summer at Campobello with her children, Nancy and Lawrence, Jr. Her second husband was David Gray, a noted writer and diplomat who served as United States Minister to Ireland between 1940 and 1947. Sponsored by R. T. Wilson, Jr., president of the Saratoga Association, and introduced into the Senate by Senator Robert H. Gittins, the "race track gambling bill" was a Tammany reaction to the Agnew-Hart law of 1908 and 1910 which held race-track directors personally liable for all gambling that took place at a track, and thus forced the closure of all the race-tracks in New York. The Gittins bill was designed to relieve the directors of this liability. The pleasure F.D.R. derived from defeating the bill was momentarily interrupted, a week later, when the bill was reconsidered and passed by the necessary twenty-six votes, this change being due to a shift of one vote and the presence of five senators who were absent when the first ballot was taken. The next day, however, the bill was voted upon in the Assembly, where the final tally lacked thirteen votes of the necessary seventy-six. There was much talk during the following weeks about bringing the Gittins bill up again, but the necessary support could never be mustered and it was finally abandoned for the year. Albany's Fort Orange Club catered particularly to the "country-gentleman" members of the Legislature; F.D.R. was a member of the club and used to spend his off-hours there when the family was away.

F.D.R.'s predictions of "an assinine mistake" and "a hectic week" were not ill-founded: the Direct Primary Bill did not become law until the Legislature reconvened in September, and almost every day of the week following this letter the *New York Times* reported legislative sessions as having taken place in the "wee sma' hours of the morning." Greatly stimulated by the prolonged Senate battle over the nomination of Sheehan and by the fast-growing opposition to machine politics in general, the question of direct primaries for the nomination of candidates for public office dominated the Legislature during the summer of 1911. Indeed, although somewhat less concerned with particular personalities, the legislative battle over direct primaries was just as fierce as the "Sheehan business." It pitted Democratic Governor John A. Dix against Tammany Hall and Charles F. Murphy, Republican against Republican, and the final resolution was such a compromise that no faction could claim victory. Considered frequently by previous Legislatures, the matter came to a head in 1911 as a result of the "Sheehan business" and because of the inclusion of a direct primary plank in the 1910 election platform of both parties. In 1910 the Republican-controlled Legislature had killed the direct nominations bill sponsored by Charles E. Hughes (Dix's predecessor); the next year Tammany attempted to do the same to Dix's request for a law which would insure all "party voters the right to nominate all candidates for elective offices." Campaign pledges, however, received little consideration when the Ferris-Blauvelt bill came before the Legislature during the week that this letter was written. Aware of the threat to machine politics, Tammany Hall was opposed to any direct primary law, but was willing to compromise on the lower elective offices where their control would not be endangered. The Republicans, recognizing their minority position, made a pretense at liberalism in order to embarrass the Democrats. F.D.R. and his progressive members of the Legislature were the third faction, their position being based on a sincere desire to establish a real direct primary law. Thus the original Direct Primary Bill, which F.D.R. feared would not be passed, was revised several days later by Tammany leaders with new provisions reducing direct primaries to an absurdity. The new bill not only called forth a strong denunciatory message from Governor Dix (mentioned in the next letter), but it also put F.D.R. in the reversed position of temporarily trying to prevent passage of the revised Ferris-Blauvelt bill. Three days later, on July 21, 1911, Dix succumbed to Tammany pressure, withdrew his opposition, and urged immediate passage of the revised bill. That evening the bill was voted upon in the Senate and failed of passage by six votes; the Legislature then recessed and the matter was postponed until September. The new legislative session witnessed a continuation of the argument until the progressive elements realized that neither side was interested in the passage of an effective direct primary law, and compromised for an amended version of the revised Ferris-Blauvelt bill. It was passed by the Senate on October 4th, by the Assembly on October 6th, and it was approved and signed on October 19th by Governor Dix.

∽

ALBANY, N.Y.
JULY 18, 1911
TUESDAY

Dearest Babby—

Here I am back again in Albany for what I hope is the final week. I raised a riot this a.m. in the Senate when the Governor's message in favor of direct primaries was read by moving to instruct the Judiciary Committee to report a bill conforming with the message. It upset the plans of the organization and precipitated a 3-hour angry debate, and although beaten the motion has served to wake people up about Direct Nominations and may help to give us a good law, though we have only three days more.

I am feeling stronger and had my sinuses washed out yesterday for the last time. Dr. Dobson wants to poke the tonsils once more before I go away, so I will have to go to Poughkeepsie once for a very short time. Also I have to spend one day in New York to order my western things. So if we don't adjourn till Saturday I couldn't leave till Monday, getting to Campo Tuesday a.m. What do you hear from L. P. Marvin? and Hooker?

I can't imagine what has happened to Hall's and my sleeping bags. Have you looked on the Half Moon?

A call of the house is ordered.

Ever your devoted

F.

Langdon P. Marvin and Henry S. Hooker were associated with F.D.R. at Carter, Ledyard & Milburn; in 1911 the three of them formed a law firm of their own, Marvin, Hooker & Roosevelt, with F.D.R. being a more-or-less inactive partner because of his legislative duties. The partnership continued throughout F.D.R.'s years in the Navy Department, terminating in 1920 when the firm of Emmet, Marvin & Roosevelt was organized. In 1924 infantile paralysis forced F.D.R. to end his business association with Langdon Marvin; Mr. Marvin recalls the causes of this break as follows: "After the infantile, when he was able to come downtown, he could not come to our office which was then at 52 Wall Street with a high front stoop, but he did go to the Fidelity & Deposit Company's office at 120 Broadway. After a while, when he had been appointed as a receiver by some court, he wrote me that he had better withdraw his name from our firm as he was going to have some letterheads made with 120 Broadway as his address; so reluctantly we parted as partners." F.D.R. and Langdon Marvin nevertheless remained close friends, and the latter formed the new firm of Emmet, Marvin & Martin. Henry Hooker also continued in close friendship with F.D.R.; in 1948 he represented President Truman at the unveiling of the statue of F.D.R. in Grosvenor Square, London.

∽∽

Dearest Mama—

I have just received your dear letter of last night, and this may catch you in N. Y. before you get away. I got here all right last night and we sat until 11:30 p.m.

Today I dropped a bomb in the Senate by a motion in favor of immediate action on Direct Primaries. It provoked a heated 3-hour discussion and I was called some choice names, but it has had a good effect and may hasten matters. But on the other hand it may prolong the session thro' our attempt to give the State an honest bill.

It is now 6 p.m. and we shall probably sit here until midnight. I am going to send out for a glass of milk soon.

Give my love to Aunt Doe and goodbye. I'm locked in and will send this out by page.

Loads of love. You can count on my getting to Campo at the earliest possible moment.

Ever

F.D.R.

∽∽

The Legislature began its long summer recess on July 22, 1911, and F.D.R. hurriedly left Albany to get "to Campobello at the earliest possible moment." As the Legislature did not reconvene until September 7th, he was able to enjoy a long stay on the island. A highlight of this vacation was a brief sailing trip on the *Half Moon* with Livingston Davis; following the Maine coastline southward, they stopped at Cutler and Bar Harbor, from where F.D.R. mailed the next two letters to his wife.

Dearest E

It is Thursday a.m. and we are still stuck in Cutler Harbor
—fog very thick, but a chance of clearing today when we go
on Westward if possible. John Pratt has just left by rail for
Bar Harbor.

It is the last chance to send ashore—possibly! All well and
having a good time.

Loads of love.

F.

A member of the Pratt family of Standard Oil prominence, John Teele Pratt started as a lawyer and later became a noted financier; like F.D.R., he began (in 1900) to
practice law with Carter, Ledyard & Milburn, but left there
a year before F.D.R. entered the firm. His wife, the former
Ruth Sears Baker, was elected to the 71st and 72nd Con-
gresses, the first Congresswoman from New York State.

BAR HARBOR, ME.
[AUGUST 11, 1911]
FRIDAY

Dearest Babbie —

My hand is so stiff from handling ropes, etc., that the pen
won't work quite right. We got away from Cutler yesterday
at lunch time, and in spite of a head tide got into Jonesport
before dark, had a walk on shore and a comfortable night.
This morning we started at 4:30, ran 100 feet and ran on a
mud bank where we stuck for over two hours—no damage
to the boat. We have had a fine run today getting here at two
thirty, but it was pretty wet as we caught two heavy downpours. I wrote you from Cutler that John Pratt had left us.
We have come ashore, Capt. Field going to his sister-in-law.

170

Liv. and I have visited the Lawrences and saw Sally, then to the Pratts who were not in, and we are now here, hoping J.T.P. will telephone us to come to dinner!

In all this time we have done little but sit in Cutler harbor, but yesterday and today were good from a cruising point of view.

We are thinking of starting back tomorrow afternoon, but I suppose I ought to go to N. E. Harbor to see Cousin Susie, so Liv. and I may drive over there and spend the afternoon, in which event we will start back at the crack of dawn on Sunday. You can count on our being home via Half Moon or rail Monday night at the latest.

We have had several amusing incidents. Capt. Field *talks more* than a politician and I ought to know! We like him, but sometimes have to climb to the masthead to escape the chatter!

I am longing to see you again and the chicks. Give my love and kisses to them, also Maude and hers.

Ever your devoted

F.

My health is *wonderful* and you won't know me! We had the tablecloth on for *one* meal!

"The Lawrences" refers to the family of William Lawrence, one of Groton's first trustees and at this time Bishop of Massachusetts. His daughter, Sarah ("Sally"), married Charles L. Slattery, who succeeded his father-in-law in the Massachusetts episcopate.

∽

ALBANY, N.Y.
[SEPTEMBER 12, 1911]
TUESDAY

Dearest Babbie—

I got here at 4 p.m. yesterday after a comfortable journey and plunged at once into the Charter business and my divorce bill. By great good luck the divorce resolution passed the Senate *unanimously* last night and the Assembly *unanimously* today!

The Charter amendments are in, and not satisfactory yet, though 40 improvements have been made. I am holding out on the veto power and the Civil Service and have enough support to defeat the Charter.

The Mayor sent Mr. Creelman up to see me and the latest rumour is that they will give in!

Meanwhile, we are to hold only perfunctory sessions until Wednesday next, but I have so much to do on the Charter and the Reapportionment that I will stay here probably till Thursday and then go to Hudson and Poughkeepsie. Then on Saturday I must attend the Putnam County convention. I have thought of going back to Campo, but fear it is unwise in every way. I do so wish you could be here and I miss you terribly. Loads of love and kisses to the chicks and *do* take very good care of yourself.

Ever your devoted

F.

F.D.R.'s divorce resolution called on New York's Congressional representatives to initiate action toward the enactment of a uniform federal divorce law. His attitude toward the subject was reported on September 8, 1911, by the *New York Times:* "Senator Roosevelt does not believe that a Federal divorce law should be as rigid as the statute enacted in this state, where absolute divorce can be obtained on only one ground. But, on the other hand, he believes that 'the divorce laws of Nevada and some other Western states are too lax.' "

Although devoted to two entirely different matters, the Cullen-Foley New York City Charter bill and the Congressional Reapportionment bill were intricately tied together during the September session of the Legislature, and this link was largely provided by F.D.R. His vigorous opposition to both bills enabled Tammany leaders to bargain one for the other with him. He was opposed to the Tammany-sponsored Charter bill because of the power it would give to the city's political machine; in particular he objected to the insuperable veto power accorded to the mayor (at this time Democrat William J. Gaynor) over public franchises and to the lack of state supervision over the municipal Civil Service Board (which was at this time presided over by Mayor Gaynor's emissary to F.D.R., James Creelman, who was also a well-known New York newspaper editor). Whereas Republican opposition to the Charter was based on the contention that the 1909 municipal elections would be annulled, F.D.R. was only opposed to certain chapters of the bill and merely sought amendments to them. Among other Congressional alterations, the Reapportionment bill proposed a change of the 26th District lines from Dutchess, Putnam, Columbia, and Greene counties to Orange, Putnam, and Dutchess, and F.D.R. disapproved on the ground that such a change would unquestionably make the 26th a Republican district. Hence, when Tammany realized that it lacked the necessary number of votes to put the Charter bill to a test, F.D.R. was approached on the possibility of shifting his vote on the Charter in exchange for an adjustment of the 26th District lines.

On September 30, 1911, the *New York Times* reported legislative circles in Albany as being "stunned" by an overnight shift of F.D.R.'s feelings on the Charter bill and the simultaneous report of the Reapportionment Committee that "the new Congressional district of Senator Roosevelt will be composed of the Counties of Dutchess, Putnam, and Greene, a district providing a fair fighting chance for a popular Democrat." The next day, however, the insurgent Democrats were bombarded by telegrams from an aroused constituency which protested their support of the Charter, and consequently the following evening witnessed another complete reversal of the situation. F.D.R. once again announced his opposition to the Cullen-Foley bill, and the Reapportionment Committee amended its report to the extent that the 26th District again included Orange, Putnam, and Dutchess Counties. Thus, on October 1st, the Reapportionment bill was passed by both houses of the Legislature and the Cullen-Foley bill was killed for the year. Throughout the confused maneuverings on both bills F.D.R. claimed that his vote on the Charter was not dependent upon the arrangement of Congressional districts, that given certain amendments he would vote for the Charter. In spite of the several reversals that occurred, these claims appeared to be substantiated by this and the next letter to his wife.

∽∽

HYDE PARK, N.Y.
[SEPTEMBER 14, 1911]
THURSDAY

Dearest Babs—

I got here finally at 11 last night after a day of conferences in Albany, with another in Poughkeepsie in the evening. I think I wrote you that Dutchess has been put in with Orange and Putnam in the new Congressional district and it seems pretty rough on poor old Connell. Everybody is up in arms about it here and I am doing my best to get it changed, but I don't personally think there is any chance, as Speaker Frisbie wants Schoharie put in with Greene County and this will spoil our District and make it unquestionably Republican.

Today, I have been in Poughkeepsie all a.m. and had a ride after lunch, thence back to see Perkins and now I have just finished talking to Mama. She began about the New York house. I told her we had made all arrangements to have all the servants board out. She was quite upset and although I said it didn't matter I *think* she has written you to have the servants stay! I don't know quite what to say about it; it would certainly be nice to have them there in November and December, but on the other hand we have practically decided not to. Do just as you think best dearest and you know I'll

174

back you up! I haven't had a line from you and suppose you wrote to Albany.

Friday 2 p.m. I'm just back from another morning in Poughkeepsie and go to W. C. Osborn's at Garrison for the night, thence to Carmel for the Putnam Convention tomorrow and home here in the afternoon.

I haven't heard yet from Portland but expect to tomorrow, when I will wire you.

Loads of love to the chicks. By the way, as you have seen by the papers we have no real business day at Albany until Wednesday, but they hope to end Thursday and I will hasten to Campo. But of course there is the possibility of no action until Friday or Saturday and in that case I would have to wait and meet you in Boston on Monday.

I miss you dreadfully and our lovely summer has spoiled me for being away.

Ever your devoted
F.

Although the passage of the Reapportionment bill Republicanized the old 21st Congressional District (and renamed it the 26th), it was never "rough on poor old Connell," as Richard Connell died during his first term in office and never had the opportunity to seek reelection. F.D.R. and Daniel Frisbie, who came from Schoharie County and was at this time Speaker of the Assembly, often found themselves partners in the various fights over progressive legislation, but on the Reapportionment issue they were opponents. Any change in F.D.R.'s district required a subsequent alteration of Frisbie's 27th District, and since Democratic Greene County could easily have been placed in either the 26th or 27th Districts, F.D.R. and Speaker Frisbie were forced to contest one another over the placement of this county. Edward E. Perkins was chairman of the Dutchess County Democratic Committee and one of F.D.R.'s early political mentors. A prominent lawyer and always active in the political and welfare circles of New York State, William

Church Osborn was at this time legal adviser to Governor Dix; included among his numerous outside activities of later years were the presidencies of the Metropolitan Museum of Art (for six years) and the Children's Aid Society. During World War II his son, Major General Frederick Osborn, was Director of the Information and Education Service of the Army, and in 1947 was appointed deputy representative of the United States on the United Nations Atomic Energy Commission.

∽

Dearest Babs—

Mama says "Tell E. I forgot to write her I will send the milk down the week she is in N.Y."!

I got back here last night at seven. On Friday, Jeff and Julia who were spending Sunday at the Osborn's took me down with them in their new F.I.A.T., arriving just in time for dinner. We had a quiet evening, running up to the H. F. Osborn's for a few minutes, where I saw the Sangers. Yesterday at nine Mr. Osborn and I motored over to Carmel, a trip of nearly two hours. We saw numbers of political friends but left again at noon, as we suspected some kind of a deal in the Convention and didn't want to get mixed up in it in any way. We suspect that Jack Yale is arranging to have no nomination made against him, giving the Democrats some of the County offices instead.

We got back at 2:30 and went to the Garrison Horse Show. I saw many of our friends there and Mr. O. introduced me to the local people. Eleanor Mortimer was there but I thought it wise not to mention H. Hooker! I got back just in time for dinner.

Monday. I didn't finish this yesterday as I rode all morning and had Frank Cleary and others come in the p.m. and Aunt Ellen and Ellie came to dinner. Now I am just back from another long ride and am going to H. P. and Poughkeepsie this afternoon.

At last I have a letter from you! The others must have gone to Albany and New York. I know you will rather enjoy this quiet week. I still hope to get off Friday and reach Campo Saturday a.m.

Loads of love to you dearest, and kiss the chicks. It is *horrid* here without you.

Ever your devoted

F.

The F.I.A.T. Automobile Company of Turin, Italy, opened its first U. S. factory at Poughkeepsie in 1911, and Jefferson and Julia Newbold's "new F.I.A.T." (35 horsepower) was one of the first of its kind to be operated in this country; F.D.R. later purchased a secondhand one for himself from W. Forbes Morgan. A cousin of William Church Osborn, Henry Fairfield Osborn was an internationally known paleontologist, his achievements ranging from numerous books to innumerable medals to the presidency of countless scientific societies. One of these organizations, the New York Zoological Society, was later headed by his son, Fairfield Osborn, a naturalist also prominent in scientific circles. "The Sangers" refers to Henry F. Osborn's daughter, Virginia, and her husband Ralph Sanger, a Harvard graduate and New York stockbroker. A Republican from Putnam County, John R. Yale was a member of the Assembly for more than a decade, and his long service thus enabled him to arrange "to have no nomination made against him" at the Putnam County Convention. As he was reelected to the Assembly without opposition several months later, F.D.R.'s "suspicions" proved to be well-founded. Later the wife of Maxime H. Furlaud, Eleanor Mortimer was a niece of A.E.R.'s Aunt Tissie (Mrs. Stanley Mortimer). Frank Cleary lived all his life in Hyde Park, spending fourteen years as superintendent of the nearby Wales estate and later as a foreman with the New York Central Railroad.

∽∽

Except for some difficulties involved in the announcement of his support of woman suffrage, the half-year interval between this letter and the next was a relatively quiet one for F.D.R. and his family. The Legislature's adjournment on October 6th ended the longest legislative session in the history of the state, and F.D.R.'s role in the establishment of this record was not a small one. F.D.R. spent the following month actively engaged in the campaign for positions in the new Assembly. Although his term in the Senate did not expire for another year, he toured the state urging the election of progressive assemblymen. His efforts were in vain, however, as Tammany fulfilled its boast of preventing insurgent Democrats who had voted against Sheehan from returning to the Assembly by throwing its weight behind Republican candidates. On the other hand, in New York City, Tammany control showed signs of weakening, and the final result of Tammany's weaknesses and revengeful tactics was a large (50) Republican majority in the 1912 Assembly.

Yet this otherwise quiet winter of 1911-12 did contain a significant experience for F.D.R.: his first meeting with Woodrow Wilson. They spent several hours together late in 1911. It was only natural that the New Jersey Governor and the New York State Senator should meet; both had gained varying measures of national recognition for their support of progressive legislation during the preceding year, and the advance of the progressive movement had reached a point where organization of its leaders was both possible and necessary. Unfortunately, F.D.R.'s personal correspondence does not include a record of his first meeting with Wilson, but his subsequent efforts toward the creation of a New York delegation for Wilson at the 1912 convention indicate that he was highly impressed by the occasion. Thus, at the same time that F.D.R. wrote the next letter he was busily assisting in the formation of an organization (called the New York State Wilson Conference) that would publicize the Wilson movement and attempt to win him delegates to the national convention.

Dearest Mama—

We were so glad to get your telegram today, and the plants are too lovely and make the house very bright and cheerful.

The Emmets and Forbes' are nice guests, the latter has gone down this afternoon and we are just back from tea at the Henry Sages'.

I went yesterday to the sprayer people and saw the outfit. They will for $200 send the engine, tank etc. all complete on a framework which is ready to bolt on one of our wagons. In addition they will add free another spraying pole adapted for throwing a high stream into shade trees. It will be shipped as soon as the boats start running, about a week they think.

I enclose my cheque for $1414.73, being $1377.98 for taxes on house 49 East 65, and $36.75 for water tax.

When at Hyde Park tomorrow I will go over the locations for planting the 8,000 trees, and also see how they are getting on with the clearing for new pasture.

Much love from us both.

Ever your affectionate

F.D.R.

This letter was written on F.D.R.'s seventh wedding anniversary, which explains his mother's telegram and the new plants she sent as a present. "The Emmets" refers to the family of Grenville T. Emmet, who later became F.D.R.'s law partner in the firm of Emmet, Marvin & Roosevelt. The other weekend guests, the "Forbes'," were probably relatives of F.D.R.'s Aunt Doe (Mrs. Paul R. Forbes). Henry M. Sage, a friend of the family, entered the State Senate with F.D.R. in 1910; he was a Republican from the 28th District, and was reelected to the Senate four times.

～～

Several weeks after writing this letter about the spraying and planting of trees at Hyde Park, F.D.R. took advantage of a legislative recess and went on a prolonged trip to Jamaica and Panama. His companions were his brother-in-law, who was about to graduate from Harvard but made the trip with the permission of the college authorities, and J. Mayhew Wainwright, then a member of the State Senate from Westchester and later a member of Congress for nine years. A.E.R., not wishing to be away from her children for a long time and being fearful of sea travel, did not make the trip, but met F.D.R. at New Orleans and journeyed with him to New Mexico for a visit with Isabella and Robert Ferguson. It was not F.D.R.'s first visit to the Caribbean, his mother having taken him on a cruise to Puerto Rico and Cuba in 1904 in an effort to dissuade him of his engagement to A.E.R.

The eight-year interval between these two trips had brought an immense change to the Caribbean: the Panama Canal. F.D.R.'s first cruise occurred during the months when formal negotiations for the start of the Canal project were in progress under the dynamic leadership of "Uncle Ted," and by the end of 1904 active operations had commenced on the Isthmus. Although the following three years were devoted to preliminary work such as ridding the Canal Zone of yellow fever and malaria, by the time F.D.R. arrived at Colon (this city at the Atlantic terminus of the Canal was originally called Aspinwall after its founder William H. Aspinwall, who was F.D.R.'s great-uncle) in 1912 the actual excavation and construction work was nearing completion.

∾

ON BOARD S.S. "CARILLO"
BETWEEN CUBA AND JAMAICA
APRIL 17, 1912
WEDNESDAY

Dearest Mama—

I have written about sixteen pages to Eleanor and she will doubtless read it to you. All can be said in a nutshell:

180

weather perfect, sea like the much overworked mill pond, boat roomy and cool, food and all appointments excellent. If one came down fifty times, nothing could have been smoother or more delightful in every way than this trip. As you know we came through the Eastern end of the Bahama group and therefore far to the west of the "Prinzessin's" course to St. Thomas and far to the east of the return course from Havana homewards. But today we have been for many hours in sight of the Eastern End of Cuba and you will remember the wonderful mountains on the southeast coast.

Tomorrow we reach Kingston early and I am planning to engage a motor to take us to Spanish Town, Rio Cobre, Bog Walk and New Castle, the encampment up in the hills. In this way I think we can see it all in one day for tomorrow evening we leave for Colon.

It seems so natural to be down in these seas again and I only wish you were with us, and I almost expect to see you every time I go on deck.

The special cooling apparatus is going today and it would be uncomfortably hot without it.

The passengers are not an inspiring lot, but there [are] several young engineers and others bound for the West Coast of So. America. Also a young clergyman named Scott, an assistant at St. George's and the *right kind* of a cleric.

We all go about in our shirts, no coats except at meals, but trousers of course. The few women are also still entirely covered, but we anticipate what greater heat will bring forth.

Loads of love. I will write you from Panama, and you should get it May 1st.

Ever your affectionate son

F.D.R.

Hall is I think having a very good time. Mayhew Wainwright is one of the most delightful travelling companions I have known and he is always in good spirits and ready to do things.

∽∽

181

During the course of the trip F.D.R. collected an album of postcards, passenger lists, maps, and other trivia which appealed to him. He arranged them in chronological order and annotated each item with a brief note concerning its history and purpose. The next letter was found lying loose at the back of the album. As it was never completed, there is no way of knowing whether F.D.R. intended it to be the first pages of a diary or a letter to his family, but it fits nicely into the account of his trip.

ANCON, CANAL ZONE
APRIL 18, 1912
THURSDAY

A Further Account of an Unsentimental Journey of Two Politicians and an Undergraduate—

It must be undisputed that Swedish exercises are harmful to the lady. The evening before reaching Kingston I attempted [to] make some of these gyrations in a cabin about six feet square and unwittingly stopped the blades of an electric fan with my thumb. Pond's Extract and iodine may save the nail.

We were on deck at daylight in time to see the great mountains East of Kingston Harbor poking pink heads through the low morning mists. They are lower and further back from the sea near Kingston, allowing a wider shelf on the coast, and it is this alluvial low-land which has been the most subject to devastating earthquakes. At the mouth of the harbor on the end of a long bar which protects Kingston from the sea once stood the infamous Port Royal—rich, degraded rendezvous of buccaneers and royally commissioned pirates like Sir Henry Morgan—a city which sank to its merited fate beneath the waters in 1693. Not far away on the bar lay two wrecks, one of the "Prinzessin Victoria Luise" which carried me here in 1904, the other that of a Hamburg boat which struck just after the great earthquake of 1907, the lighthouse having been demolished.

We came to dock at eight, and found another "Victoria

Luise," formerly the "Deutschland," with a huge tourist menagerie on board. An hour sufficed to buy some white clothes, and "Jippi-Jappa" hats and to engage an automobile from a Long Island Yankee. Five of us including G.H.R., Mayhew Wainwright, W. Arthur Murphy, a young Baltimorean going down to the nitrate mines in Chile, his companion and myself, were soon whirled away over a very dusty road to Spanish Town, the old capital, about 12 miles to the West. We saw the old church with its interesting monuments, especially the statue of Lady Elgin and the slab in the floor to the memory of a "Colbeck of Colbeck who came with the forces who conquered the Island and having performed various services both civil and military—with great applause he departed this life on the ——— day of ——— 1692." Showing the importance of correct punctuation. We also rediscovered the signatures of "Mrs. James Roosevelt and F. D. Roosevelt Feb. 25, 1904" in the old church register.

By good luck we discovered a woman who showed us over the "King's House" or former residence of the royal governors. It must have been abandoned about two generations ago when the Capitol was moved to Kingston, yet the building is unchanged and the big state room, the long banquet hall and the stables and slave quarters and kitchens in the rear show how magnificently the old governors ruled. By great good fortune the earthquake of 1907 did little harm to Spanish Town, and the statue of Rodney and fine old buildings around the Square remain as they were when I was here before.

We continued on by the excellent road which skirts the Rio Cobre through its rocky tropical course to Bog Walk. I had forgotten how magnificent the cliffs and defiles are, covered with great creepers and clinging crooked trunks of trees. At Rio Cobre we decided to go on and see the Natural Bridge, a very curious formation where the stream has broken through a cliff. The plantations in this part of the

Island were interesting, and a drink of cocoanut water, procured by a naked colored boy from the top of the tallest tree, did much to make us forget the dust. Back here on the Island the temperature is much lower than in Kingston. It can afford to be.

∽∽

ANCON, CANAL ZONE
APRIL 22, 1912
MONDAY

Dearest Mama—

I find a six-day boat leaves tomorrow, so I will send off a few lines to tell of the progress of the trip. Eleanor will have left for New Orleans before this reaches you.

I sent an awkward scrawl on our arrival in Colon Saturday; please forgive the script, but I had stuck my right thumb into an electric fan just before reaching Kingston. It is now healed and I do not expect to lose the nail.

The day in Kingston last Thursday was, as usual there, *very* hot and dusty, but we took a motor on arrival at eight, ran out to Spanish Town, saw the fascinating old church, with the old register containing our names under date of Feb. 25th, 1904! We also went over the old Governor's House which you and I did not do. It was well worth it, showing the pomp and circumstance in which the old Royal Governors lived. Thence we motored on to Rio Cobre and Bog Walk and I must confess that I had quite forgotten how very wonderful that drive is. You and I turned back at Bog Walk Station, but having a motor enabled us to go on six or seven miles thro' the plantation country to the Natural Bridge, a very wonderful formation of rocks. As before we sent a colored boy up a tree for fresh cocoanuts to quench our thirst.

We got back to the Myrtle Bank Hotel (new of course, as the old one went down in the earthquake and cost several lives) just in time [to] make several purchases of hats, clothes, etc., and to greet a crowd of Americans off the "Victoria

Luise" (old "Deutschland") including the Wm. Loebs, R. A. C. Smiths, etc. By the way the wrecks of the poor old "Prinzessin V. L." and of another Hamburg boat still lie on the ocean side of the long reef guarding the harbor. We sailed at four and hence had no time to get up to New Castle where the troops are garrisoned.

The trip to Colon was hotter and uneventful, except for a travelling American circus on board bound for the Zone and the West Coast of South America.

Colon came in sight at noon Saturday, two hours ahead of time and we had time to drive around the town of Colon proper (under Panama control) and the adjoining Cristobal (under our control and the true northern terminal of the Canal). The American quarters were a revelation, spotless and comfortable, yet with an air of absolute efficiency. Here are located the Commissary headquarters, cold storage plant for the whole Zone etc. The ice cream factory alone is the largest in the world!

The observation parlor car on the rear of the train gave us splendid glimpses of the Canal as we came across, reaching Panama at 6:50 just at dark, but still light enough to see the waters of the Pacific. This hotel is just above the town and our rooms overlook the Bay of Panama. We are most comfortable and of course under management of the I.C.C. (Isthmian Canal Commission).

On our way over we met a Mr. Wait, who is on the harbor work at Colon and had run across for a spree here. We promptly dined together, and later he took us all over the city, so that by 2 a.m. we had been introduced to all the tricks of the trade. It is a most interesting place, every tongue and nationality, but clean and fairly orderly—a very different Panama than under the French. Like Colon, although surrounded by the Zone, it is under Panama control and is only subject to us in the matter of sanitation, orderliness, etc.

Yesterday morning we drove out to Balboa, the Pacific

terminus of the Canal and site of the future docks and harbor. Tremendous operations now in progress, thence through the wonderful hospital grounds on the hill back of the hotel.

At four we took the train back to Culebra, the location of the Great Cut and home of the Administration. Commissioner Rousseau was waiting to meet us and we called on Goethals and had a nice long talk. We all dined with Mr. & Mrs. Rousseau, had a delightful evening and took the train back at nine. Mrs. Rousseau was the daughter of Herbert Squires, our first minister here and a very intimate friend of Wainwright's. In fact the latter is the executor of Mr. Squires and Trustee for his children, so we were all received with open arms.

This morning we left at 6:30 by train back to Culebra (½ hour). Rousseau met us with an observation engine and took us for two hours through the length of the great Cut, nearly nine miles. We ran over tracks and switches among the blasts and drills and steam shovels and dump trains, the whole trip personally conducted by Commissioner Rousseau, who, I take it, is probably more the right-hand man of Goethals than anybody else. At ten we attended a lecture on the Canal given in the Model Room for tourists on the sight-seeing train, and afterwards we three lunched with the Rousseaus, meeting Mr. Carlos Arosemera, (the Secretary of Public Works of the Republic of Panama and nephew of the President) as well as his brother and two sisters.

Most of the afternoon we spent inspecting the great locks of Pedro Miguel (called here Peter McGill) and Miraflores, the latter a double flight of locks. These locks raise the vessels 85 feet to the level of the cut.

I can't begin to describe it and have become so enthusiastic that if I didn't stop I would write all night. The two things that impress the most are the Culebra cut, because of the colossal hole made in the ground, and the locks because of the engineering problems and size. Imagine an intricate concrete structure nearly a mile long and three or four hundred feet wide, with double gates of steel weighing 700 tons apiece!

Goethals said in his quiet way last night: "We like to have Americans come down, because they all say it makes them better Americans."

Tonight, after visiting a tailor, we are having a quiet evening and going to bed early, for it is pretty tiring to go all day in the heat, tho' the early mornings and evenings are delightfully cool. Tomorrow we leave at 6:30 again for Gatun, the great dam at the Atlantic end forty miles from here which will impound a lake of 160 square miles! We return at two and drive out to see the ruins of Old Panama six miles from here. It was sacked and destroyed by Sir Henry Morgan the Buccaneer in 1671! Wednesday we inspect the Pacific end harbor works in the Commission launch and sail Thursday afternoon from Colon.

Your very welcome cable dated Friday was delivered this (Monday) evening and I promptly answered. I was beginning to get anxious.

The Titanic tragedy is too horrible. We know practically no details, only scraps here and there. I am counting on your saving all the papers for every day I am away up to April 30th when we reach N. Orleans.

I am so glad Eleanor was able to move the chicks down today. It will give her time to get well settled. Give them all a great many kisses and hugs from Father. I will send a line by Thursday's direct boat to N.Y. but you will hardly get it before another line from N. Orleans.

I only wish you could see this wonder of the world, greater than the Tower of Babel or the Pyramids.

Your affectionate son
Franklin D. Roosevelt

By the way we sail on the "Abangarez"—*not* the "Parismina."

F.D.R. had first met William Loeb at the White House, where the latter spent nearly eight years as a secretary to Theodore Roosevelt; at the time of their meeting in Jamaica, he was Collector of the Port of New York. Robert A. C. Smith later became chairman of the board of the White Rock Mineral Spring Company. In 1912 Congress showed its appreciation of Harry H. Rousseau's work on the Canal by promoting him to the rank of rear admiral, and he later became vice-chairman of the U. S. Shipping Board. To historians of the Panama Canal the name of George Washington Goethals is practically synonymous with that of the Canal itself; he was not only chief engineer of the Canal for seven years and the first civil governor of the Panama Canal Zone, but he is also credited with having given to the personnel of the project the esprit de corps that accounted for the swift construction of the Canal.

∽

ON BOARD S.S. "ABANGAREZ"
APRIL 29, 1912
MONDAY

Dearest Mama;

We are approaching the Mississippi, and should pass into the mouth at 3 this afternoon reaching New Orleans shortly after midnight. I hope we shall get through the customs in time for me to meet Eleanor's train at 7:50 tomorrow morning. We have a wireless saying the flood situation around New Orleans is very bad, and I only hope E's train will get through all right.

I wrote you last Monday night, I think. The next day we spent the morning going over the Gatun dam and triple flight of locks, confirming our feeling of the tremendous size and importance of the work. The dam is simply a healthy and growing young mountain which has been moved into the valley. It is so big that it is part of the natural landscape and in a year or so when vegetation has completely covered

188

it and the Gatun Lake is filled people will wonder what all the talk of the dam was about. In the afternoon we drove out to Old Panama, all that is left of the magnificent city sacked and destroyed by Sir Henry Morgan the buccaneer in 1671. Its ruins are more extensive and remarkable than we had any idea of. Many people go to the Isthmus and are too lazy or indifferent to go out but there is quite enough left to give an excellent idea of what a centre of Spanish power and riches existed here when the Pilgrims and Puritans had only a precarious foothold in New England. It was in fact an old city when destroyed nearly two and a half centuries ago.

On Wednesday Mr. Rousseau took us in the Commission launch to see the completed sea level section of the Canal on the Pacific side, with the work being done on the new docks, terminals and workshops at Balboa, and the break-water out to the Islands which are being fortified in the strongest possible way.

That afternoon we did a little more shopping. Hall and Mr. Wainwright spent a quiet evening and I took the train at five out to Corozal to dine with Bill Clark '03 of Pittsburgh, who preceded me as President of the "Crimson." We had a nice swim in the salt water of the completed section and dined in the regular Commission "mess." Food as good and all as well appointed as in the Tivoli Hotel and supplied to all "gold" employees (i.e. white men) at 30 cents a meal. Clark is in charge of the construction of one of the lock gates and we spent the evening at the Y.M.C.A. with a couple of hundred young Americans who are all making good and have to a man the same kind of spirit which is putting the Canal through ahead of time.

Thursday we paid a farewell visit to the American consul, Mr. Snyder, who had called on us, and took the train back to Colon at eleven, sailing at three. The voyage has been uneventful but interesting because of our fellow passengers: one army major, many Canal employees with wives and children, going home for the annual vacation, several Yanks from the West Coast of So. America and the Lord knows where.

I will wire you after meeting Eleanor tomorrow. Give the chicks my love, and sister a big kiss for her birthday. I am so sorry we are to be away for it. Much love.

Your affec. son
F.D.R.

∽∽

The year that followed F.D.R.'s return from Panama and his visit with the Fergusons in New Mexico was a momentous one for the Roosevelt family. Throughout the world a new world was making. In the Balkans tension was mounting beyond the sphere of diplomacy. A series of secret treaties, providing for mutual protection against outside interference, were concluded between Serbia, Bulgaria, Greece, and Montenegro during the summer of 1912, and thereafter the war spirit developed swiftly in the Balkan peninsula. This new spirit soon came into direct conflict with the expanding Turkish Empire, and in October a general war broke out between the four Balkan states and Turkey. The Balkan Wars committed the European powers to a renewal of their war preparations and to a strengthening of their alliances. While France ordered its entire fleet to the Mediterranean, the German Reichstag passed a defense bill that called for a great increase in naval and military expenditures. To be sure, 1912 also witnessed diplomatic efforts by all the powers to avert the oncoming crisis, but the era of imperialism had already run its course and diplomacy could only briefly postpone the inevitable.

In the United States the national political scene reduced the impending war in Europe to a matter of secondary importance. The growth of great enterprises in the two preceding decades had given rise to innumerable economic and social problems that fifteen years of Republican leadership had failed to solve. The election year of 1912 was the culmination of all the unrest and discontent that had naturally accompanied the advent of giant corporations around the turn of the century. In spite of the widespread existence of "boss rule," public opinion throughout the country clamored for a change. In June, 1912, the Republicans met in Chicago, disregarded the demand for change, and renominated William Howard Taft. Theodore Roosevelt, upset by the trends that followed his departure from the White House in 1908, broke from the Republican Party when it failed to nominate him, and called for the creation of a new party which would cure the fallacies of the existing system by greater government participation in the economic and social life of the nation. The Progressive Party, known as the "Bull Moose," convened on August 5th and nominated T.R. by acclamation.

However, the appeal for change was mainly directed at the Democratic Party, especially at its progressive element which had caught and pleased the public eye. The Democrats met in Baltimore at the end of June and the convention soon turned into a bitter struggle between the supporters of Woodrow Wilson and Champ Clark, who was at this time Speaker of the House. It took 46 ballots, frequent riots on the convention floor, and the oratory of William Jennings Bryan for the turbulent convention to reach a decision: Woodrow Wilson and his "New Freedom."

F.D.R. had gone to Baltimore several weeks before the convention opened, as an advance guard for the Wilson movement. He took A.E.R. with him and they rented a house with several other couples. However, as noted in *This Is My Story,* A.E.R. soon "decided my husband would hardly miss my company, as I rarely laid eyes on him, and the children should go to Campobello, so I went home and took them up there and waited to hear the result." Almost oblivious of his wife's departure, F.D.R. was all over the city attempting to line up support for Wilson. At the convention he organized a rally for his candidate just at the crucial time when Clark had gained a majority of the votes and seemed headed quickly toward the necessary two-thirds mark. Along with Bryan's oratory, this rally, which reached riotous proportions, has often been considered a turning point of the convention; but regardless of the validity of this interpretation, there can be no doubt that F.D.R.'s activities at the Baltimore convention had two important consequences for him. It meant his graduation from the party's state organization and his entrance into politics on a national scale; henceforth, he was recognized everywhere as one of the party's key men in New York. Secondly, it was at this convention that he first met (and impressed) Josephus Daniels, who subsequently became Wilson's Secretary of the Navy and F.D.R.'s "Chief."

On the other hand, at the time that he sent the following telegram, the progressive movement's convention victory meant far more to F.D.R. than any advantageous connections he may have made in Baltimore.

NEW YORK
JULY 2, 1912

Mrs. F. D. Roosevelt
Campobello, Eastport, Me.

Wilson nominated this afternoon all my plans vague splendid triumph.

Franklin

∞

F.D.R.'s "vague" plans soon became those of regaining his seat in the State Senate, a task which first required his renomination by the party. Circumstances had changed somewhat since his 1910 campaign. He was no longer an unknown quantity, but a well-known and controversial figure possessed of numerous enemies within the party machine. His startling two-year record in the Senate had stirred up antagonisms among Dutchess County's Old Guard, which was also under pressure from Tammany to prevent the reelection of any insurgents instrumental in Sheehan's defeat. Thus, admirable as it was, F.D.R. could not stand on his record alone; both his nomination and election necessitated stumping the district and combating the defamation of his progressive record.

Dearest Babbie—

I am just back from a long day in which I have covered 150 miles in the machine. I have seen all the "henchmen" in Claverack, Hillsdale, Copake, Ancram, Pine Plains, Bangall, Stanfordville, Clinton and Salt Point! I ran straight up to Columbia County, then turned East, came down the Harlem Valley and thence home. The day was perfect, the machine went well, and I can truthfully say that it was really very pleasant—a change from the day before, which I spent in Poughkeepsie. It appears that Tammany and the "Interests" are really making an effort to prevent my renomination. This is being done by several agents who are trying to stir up the old Sheehan business and are taking advantage of the starting of the Empire State Democracy to howl about "Discord" etc. Of course the trouble is that Perkins has no spine, but he knows now that if he listens to orders from 14th St. he will have a perfectly delightful little fight on his hands that will not stop easily or quickly. Columbia's machine is against me because of patronage troubles. Putnam is for me, so Dutchess must decide. The Enterprise, Eagle and two Fishkill papers have come out for me editorially, and none have dared to oppose me openly.

I dined at the Newbold's last night and will again tonight. Tomorrow I lunch with Aunt Ellen and Ellie. Last night I attended Mr. Landon's reception to the Fire Department of Hyde Park and Staatsburg and we both made speeches about clean elections this fall.

It is still heavenly weather and delightfully cool. Monday morning I go to N. Y. and the big State-wide meeting of the

Empire State Democracy is to be at the Hotel Astor in the evening.

It is too bad you have had such rain. Perhaps the change of the moon tomorrow will bring sunshine. The crops however have been wonderful on the place,—good hay, rye, wheat, and the oats are just going in, over 300 bushels from North Farm lot and fine straw. The corn also on the avenue is the best in the County. Indeed East of here it has been so dry that nearly all the crops are failures. Why doesn't Edgar build those steps? I told him all about them before I left and he promised to start on them at once.

Sunday p.m. I slipped up on Church as I have been writing madly all morning. Had a nice lunch at Aunt Ellen's and took Rev. Newton home.

Give the chicks a great deal of love and kisses.

Ever your devoted

F.

The Empire State Democracy had been organized, ten days prior to this letter, by F.D.R. and seventy members of the Democratic Party's progressive element. Its purpose was to carry on Wilson's campaign in New York and to oppose Tammany domination of the State ticket. As mentioned in the letter, the organization convened again on July 29th, and the *New York Times* reported that the evening was spent "savagely assailing" Charles F. Murphy: "Murphy was called 'an ignorant, stupid, arrogant leader,' under whom the Democratic Party of the city had steadily lost votes, and the prediction was made that if he was allowed to control the party in the State there would be an even worse state of affairs."

F.D.R.'s editorial support from the local newspapers was actually the same editorial published by the *Fishkill Herald* and reprinted in the other three papers mentioned. The *Daily Eagle* made necessary changes and carried it as follows: "It seems hardly possible that the local Democratic bosses can be in earnest in their efforts to turn down Senator

Franklin D. Roosevelt. The *Eagle is,* of course, not in sympathy with many of Senator Roosevelt's ideas, but it is only fair to say that his record has been an extraordinarily good one for a young man in his first term. He took the lead of the anti-Tammany men in the State Senate almost from the start and he fought the Tammany men to a standstill. To be sure, the fight on the senatorship did not come out quite as many people expected. It resulted in the defeat of William F. Sheehan only to elect another Tammany man, Senator O'Gorman, but Senator Roosevelt's record did not stop there. He was the champion of practically all of the good legislation passed, so far as we know, and an opponent of most of the bad legislation. Certainly he was nobody's man and was not even bossed by Ed Perkins. If the local Democrats are going to try to turn him down, he will certainly be justified in making the strongest kind of a fight in the primaries for a renomination and even in putting up an independent ticket, should the bosses be able to defeat him in the primary."

Francis G. Landon had been a Republican member of the Assembly for many years until he was defeated by Robert W. Chanler in 1903, the year that F.D.R. cast his first vote. F.D.R.'s speech at Landon's reception for the Staatsburg Fire Department was reported by the *Eagle* very briefly, but the parade of fire-fighting equipment which preceded the speeches was accorded a lengthy description.

The Reverend Edward Pearsons Newton was the rector of St. James's Church in Hyde Park from 1912 until he died in 1926. To commemorate the church's centenary anniversary in 1911, he compiled a detailed account of its history, which was then privately published under the title of *Historical Notes of Saint James Parish.* This work contains a long entry about F.D.R.'s father, who was senior warden of the church for seven years, and who is recalled with great affection: "He spent as much of his time each year as his manifold duties would permit, at his country place, in Hyde Park, which he dearly loved, and took an active interest in the local affairs of the town, having been for years especially devoted to the welfare of the public school. As vestryman and warden he served Saint James parish with constant zeal. Actively useful as a businessman, a philanthropic and public spirited citizen, he was the very ideal of a gentleman of the old school, witnessing by his kindliness and charm of manner to the nobility and honor of his inner Christian character."

∾∾

After writing this letter F.D.R. spent the next few weeks on his campaign for the nomination, and on August 24th he wired A.E.R. the results of his efforts.

POUGHKEEPSIE, N. Y.

AUGUST 24, 1912

Mrs. F. D. Roosevelt
Campobello

Received designation by unanimous vote. Will wire Sunday if I can leave.

Franklin

The *New York Times* of August 25, 1912, was somewhat more explicit about the nomination:

> Poughkeepsie, N. Y., August 24. State Senator Franklin D. Roosevelt, who headed the revolt against Sheehan, which resulted in the election of Judge O'Gorman as Senator from the State of New York, received the primary designation for renomination at the Democratic Senatorial Committee meeting in this city today.
>
> Senator Roosevelt in his speech of acceptance said that he realized that Democrats disagreed over some steps he had taken, but in everything he tried to represent the majority of his constituents. Senator Roosevelt is one of the active leaders fighting Charles F. Murphy of Tammany Hall.
>
> Before the Senatorial Committee met it was understood that Columbia County and two Dutchess committeemen were against him, but at the committee meeting everything was harmonious, and the vote for Mr. Roosevelt was unanimous.

∾∾

F.D.R.'s opponents in his second political campaign were Republican Jacob G. Southard, and George A. Vossler of the Bull Moose Party, but it turned out that typhoid fever was his most dangerous competitor. F.D.R. came down with the disease toward the end of September, just as he was about to begin his campaign in earnest, and he was bedridden until after the election. Due to party organization and loyalty, the inability to conduct a campaign probably would not have seriously harmed F.D.R.'s chances for election under ordinary circumstances, but 1912 was a Presidential year and the farm vote was bound to be much heavier than in 1910. Besides, Tammany was particularly anxious to prevent the reelection of the leading figure in Sheehan's defeat. F.D.R. coped with the emergency by hiring a campaign manager to keep his name at least before the electorate of the 26th District. During his first winter in Albany F.D.R. had become friendly with the upstate political correspondent of the *New York Herald,* Louis McHenry Howe, and as the latter was fully acquainted with the politics of New York State and heartily approved of F.D.R.'s progressive efforts, he was the ideal man to conduct the campaign. Howe was given a leave of absence by his editor and took on the job; the election returns later proved that he was the margin of victory.

In order to sell a man who could not make public appearances, Howe was forced to use political methods never before experienced by the residents of the Hudson Valley. Full-page advertisements urging F.D.R.'s election soon appeared in the local newspapers, and posters, pamphlets, and letters also carried F.D.R.'s pledge to continue the fight for progressive legislation throughout the district. Such was Louis McHenry Howe's first job for F.D.R.

On election day F.D.R. received 15,590 votes to 13,889 for Southard and 2,628 for Vossler. The election also put the Democratic Party back into control of the State Legislature; perhaps even more important to F.D.R.'s future career, the Presidential contest was won by Wilson.

F.D.R. never finished his second term in the State Senate.

Early in March, 1913, he journeyed to Washington to attend
Wilson's inauguration. During his visit he renewed his acquaintance with Josephus Daniels, who then offered him
the job of Assistant Secretary of the Navy. In his book, *The
Wilson Era*, Josephus Daniels recalls that F.D.R. accepted
the offer without hesitating for a second. The United States
Navy, which formerly had been one of F.D.R.'s favorite
hobbies, thus became his major occupation.

V

". . . I Am Baptized, Confirmed, Sworn in, Vaccinated—
and Somewhat at Sea! . . ."

ASSISTANT SECRETARY OF THE NAVY

1913

WHILE F.D.R. returned to Albany to close his affairs in the Legislature, Wilson approved his appointment and the Senate quickly confirmed it. Several weeks later, on his eighth wedding anniversary, F.D.R. took the oath of his new office and hastened to inform his mother of the occasion.

WASHINGTON
MARCH 17, 1913
MONDAY

Dearest Mama

I am baptized, confirmed, sworn in, vaccinated—and somewhat at sea! For over an hour I have been signing papers which had to be accepted on faith—but I hope luck will keep me out of jail.

All well, but I will have to work like a new turbine to master this job—but it will be done even if it takes all summer.

Your affec. son
FRANKLIN D. ROOSEVELT

As this letter is one of the very few in his personal correspondence that bears F.D.R.'s full name, it would seem that in signing the papers left by his predecessor the full signature had become an unconscious habit. Sara Roosevelt answered this letter on March 18, 1913, and also had some comments to make about his signature: "My dearest Franklin—You can't imagine the happiness you gave me by writing to me yesterday. I just *knew* it was a *very* big job, and everything so new that it will take time to fit *into* it. Try not to write your signature too small, as it gets a cramped look and is not distinct. So many public men have such awful signatures, and so unreadable. . . ."

∽∽

WASHINGTON

MARCH 19, 1913

WEDNESDAY

Dearest Babbie

Mr. Daniels is away and will be tomorrow also, so I am Acting Secretary and up to my ears. I must have signed three or four hundred papers today and am *beginning* to catch on.

Monday evening I dined with Ned Bell and yesterday lunched with Charley McCawley and his wife and Uncle Will and Major Leonard! Last night I dined with Nick and Alice and Miss Elkins was there. We went on to "The Daughter of Heaven," Pierre Loti's play and went back for eggs afterwards. Today I lunched with Uncle Will and tonight give a dinner for Helen and Lathrop! Going some!

It is now six and I go to visit Senator Gore. Loads of love. No letter from you today, but I may find one at the hotel.

Your devoted

F.

At the time this letter was written Colonel Charles L. McCawley was second in command of the Marine Quartermaster Corps. He had entered the Marines in 1897 when his father, Major General Charles G. McCawley, was Commander of the Corps; and almost his entire service thereafter had been spent in Washington, where he cut a prominent figure in the city's society. In May, 1913, Josephus Daniels, pursuing his policy of not allowing any officers to stay in Washington for a long assignment, ordered McCawley transferred to San Francisco. This order shocked Washington society and Daniels was subsequently bombarded with pleas that it be revoked. Although Senators, no less, called on him and reminded him that appropriations for the Navy required their approval, Daniels resisted the pressure and stood by his order. However, shortly before McCawley was to board the train for California, the Chief of the Quartermaster Department, General Frank L. Denny, resigned, and McCawley automatically took his place, a job which required his presence in Washington and which he held until he retired in 1929.

"Uncle Will" refers to William Sheffield Cowles, the husband of A.E.R.'s aunt, Anna Roosevelt; formerly a rear admiral and naval attache to the American Embassy in London, he had retired from the Navy in 1908 and divided his time between his home in Farmington, Connecticut, and his Washington house at 1733 N Street. The latter acquired the title of the "Little White House" when Theodore Roosevelt lived there while waiting for Mrs. McKinley to move out of the White House in 1901, and it was this house that F.D.R. rented for his family in the autumn of 1913.

A lawyer, Major Henry Leonard entered the Marines in 1898 to fight in the Spanish-American War, and remained in the Corps to serve in China during the Boxer Rebellion; while storming Tientsin in July, 1900, he was wounded in the arm and later had to have it amputated. He nevertheless returned to active duty during both World Wars, and won recognition as a leading authority on military law. A colorful figure in Washington law circles, as counsel for the defense he became intricately involved in the court martial of Major General Smedley D. Butler in 1931, when the latter was tried for having asserted in a Philadelphia speech that Mussolini had killed a child in a "hit and run" auto-mobile accident. The case proved very embarrassing for the Services and the State Department, especially for the American Ambassador to Italy, John W. Garrett, who was Leonard's brother-in-law. While Butler was freed with a public reprimand, informed sources in Washington contended that the Navy had allowed Leonard to write the lenient reprimand in exchange for a retraction by Butler of his statement.

F.D.R.'s dinner with Nicholas and Alice Longworth might almost be considered part of his official introduction to his new job. Theodore Roosevelt's celebrated daughter was a leading figure in Washington society from the time of her father's residence in the White House through her husband's thirteen terms in the House of Representatives. In *This Is My Story* A.E.R. recalls her cousin's home as "the center of gaiety and of interesting gatherings. Everyone who came to Washington coveted an introduction to her and an invitation to her house."

Lathrop Brown had married Helen Hooper in 1911, and moved to Washington two years later when he was elected to Congress from New York's First District; in 1917 he became an assistant to the Secretary of the Interior, but resigned his position the next year to enlist in the Tank Corps as a private.

Blinded in childhood by a prank of his playmates, Thomas Pryor Gore, a Democrat from Oklahoma, served in the Senate from 1907 to 1921, and again from 1931 to 1937; as he was also a member of the Executive Committee of the National Democratic Committee at the time of this letter, F.D.R. had to visit him regarding the politics of naval appointments.

∾

WASHINGTON
MAY 14, 1913
WEDNESDAY

Dearest Mama,

Your "doggy" letter I found last night at the house and am so sorry the people are not enthusiastic about the new

"Duffy." Also I'm very sorry your letter came two days after I had written to order a Scottie from a lady in Clinton, N. Y. and of course I can't now withdraw the order. So at any moment you may get a letter from her or a telegram saying the dog is shipped! He is nearly three months old and I particularly want him to get accustomed to the children, so that we can take him to Campobello with us—and I know he won't really be any trouble at Hyde Park.

I am busy every second but hope to leave Friday and get to Hyde Park Saturday morning, though this may not be possible.

A great deal of love

F.D.R.

∽

Around the time that F.D.R. was solving the problems involved in the purchase of a new "Duffy," a tragic event occurred which forced him also to write a "doggy" letter. This tragedy was the death of Sara Roosevelt's closest companion, "Toutou." The Thomas Newbolds were having tea with her on the south veranda and Toutou entertained the gathering by playing with the Newbolds' Irish terrier on the lawn. Suddenly, as Sara Roosevelt watched, the Newbolds' dog grabbed Toutou, gave him one violent shake, and killed him. Like the Newbold dog, F.D.R. and A.E.R. had often found Toutou a little too "yappy," but realizing his mother's sorrow at losing her companion, F.D.R. wrote her a condolent letter to insure her of his sympathy. This letter, which he failed to date, is placed next in the correspondence.

49 E. 65 ST., NEW YORK

Dearest Mama—

I am really and honestly distressed at the tragedy, for it really is a tragedy, poor little mite, what a horrible and unlooked for fate.

203

You know I really, really was devoted to the doggy. He was so brave and faithful and so absolutely dependable in what he was meant to do, give the alarm. If I was ever harsh to him it was for the sake of discipline and not because I wasn't really fond of him.

The poor Toms must feel awfully; it is really almost as bad for them as for you; I don't suppose there was any possible way of preventing it—one can't watch a dog every minute and it was just the hardest piece of luck that that one corrective shake was too much for his wee but ferocious little body.

Eleanor too feels really sad about it.

I hear the Welshes are coming.

Ever in haste
F.D.R.

Joseph W. Welsh spent his entire law career associated with Carter, Ledyard & Milburn, from 1901 until his death in 1932; as a member of the firm, he handled many cases for the New York Stock Exchange.

While A.E.R. took the children to Campobello, F.D.R. spent the summer of 1913 in Washington, journeying to the Canadian island and to Hyde Park whenever his work would permit it. This procedure was followed every year but one during his seven years in the Navy Department, and since he rarely had to write letters between October and June, the separation from his family in the summer months accounts for the existence of more than a fragmentary correspondence during his Navy years. Even the summer correspondences contain numerous intervals when no letters are available, but as the letters fully portray the kind of life F.D.R. led in Washington, it has not been thought necessary to explain his activities during these brief periods.

Dearest Mummy

It's nine o'clock and I'm really feeling better tho' Tummy isn't according to Hoyle yet. The amusing thing I referred to was that the Doctor almost fainted when I told him I had taken 6 grains of Calomel. Apparently 2 grains is a large dose! However he remarked that as long as I was alive I had better take some more Pluto water and I'm also taking Bismarck or Bismouth or Bismuth powders—and I am really feeling better, tho' it has been 91° all day.

I came home at 4 for milk, went to the moving picture exhibition at 5 and came back here for a banquet of milk toast, rice and hot milk. Soon, after writing Eleanor, I'm going to bed.

I loved having you, and you saved my life, but I'm *too* sorry we couldn't have done some nice things together. I will drop you a line tomorrow.

Your affec.

F.D.R.

Love to Nellie. I will write her some day!

As Sara Roosevelt was always worried about her son's health, F.D.R. felt obliged to write this and the next letter assuring her of the good progress of his temporary stomach ailment. "Nellie" refers to Miss Eleanor Blodgett.

∽

Dearest Mama

I'm quite cured and not in the least salivated (which by the way means that your teeth drop out and you foam at the mouth), and now after a *very* busy day I'm off at 4 p.m. to play golf. Tomorrow also I am to golf so you will see what very good care I'm taking of myself. So far I have maintained my diet of milk toast, rice and hot milk, but digestion is restored. Tonight I am dining with Capt. Rogers to meet the British Commission of Naval officers and tomorrow I am giving them a luncheon at the Army and Navy Club!

In awful haste as my trolley car goes in 4 minutes.

Affec

F.D.R.

During his seven years in the Navy Department, F.D.R. played golf almost every time he could spare several hours away from the office. The frequent allusions to his favorite sport are noteworthy in that "golf" was the one word F.D.R. consciously dropped from his vocabulary after he was stricken by infantile paralysis. "Capt. Rogers" is probably a misspelt reference to Thomas S. Rodgers, at this time Director of Naval Intelligence; in 1916 he was promoted to rear admiral and put in command of a battleship division of the Atlantic Fleet.

∾∾

WASHINGTON

JULY 29, 1913

TUESDAY

Dearest Mama

I haven't written you anything about Warren because nothing was decided. He was *not* ordered to Mexico, but his Ambassador was asked if he, Warren, could conveniently go. In the meantime I stopped it, though I don't want it thought that I can get him any place he wants. It was a compliment to have thought of him for Mexico, and under the rules of the Service there are few places he can go to. South America is the most probable and I am trying to get him Secy of Legation at Montevideo, Uruguay. He can't go to the Argentine as he is not far enough advanced—nor to Chile. Montevideo is a good climate—healthy—and one night by steamer from

Buenos Ayres. Of course it is possible he may *have* to go to Mexico City as the most available person, but it would only mean dividing the family until conditions there get better or else explode. Personally if I were in the Dip. Service I would beg for Mexico, as it is the only place just now where there is real action.

I enclose letter from Plog for you to read and destroy. Tonight I go out to Doughreghen Manor and stay with Lathrop and Helen.

This is a *very* hot day, but I keep exceedingly well and am careful of my grub.

Love to Aunt Ellen, Ellie and Roosevelt.

Affec.

F.D.R.

At the time this letter was written, F.D.R.'s cousin, Warren Delano Robbins, held the post of Third Secretary of the U.S. Embassy in Paris. Anxious for a change of scenery and a chance for promotion in the hierarchical diplomatic service, he had written F.D.R. for advice on the possibilities of a transfer. He was subsequently offered the third secretariat in Mexico, and again wrote F.D.R., asking the latter's assistance in stopping the appointment because he did not consider it a promotion. The matter was settled the following year when he was transferred from Paris to the post of Second Secretary of the American Legation in Guatemala.

F.D.R.'s personal preference for Mexico is indicative of his desire to lead an active life at the expense of a secure one, a desire which later led to efforts to resign his civilian post and enlist in the Navy. Indeed, the situation in Mexico in the summer of 1913 was far from being inactive for the 50,000 Americans residing there. United States relations with Mexico had been relatively good during the three-decade dictatorship of Porfirio Diaz (1887-1911), but within Mexico itself this period witnessed the reduction of the masses to a state of peonage. The strong-arm rule of Diaz brought order to the country, order which permitted foreign exploitation of Mexico's natural resources but which also brought poverty and insecurity to the average Mexican. The United States outstripped all its foreign competitors for Mexico's rich oilfields, and by 1913 American interests in Mexico totaled one billion dollars, more than the investments of all other foreign countries combined. At the same time as foreign interests in Mexico were expanding, however, the Mexican people found an able leader who championed their cause. In May, 1911, Francisco Madero drove Diaz into exile and six months later was officially elected to the Mexican presidency.

The following months were marked by counter-revolutionary disturbances in Mexico, culminating in February, 1913, with the deposition of Madero by General Victoriano Huerta. Several days later the former was murdered under circumstances which indicated that the latter had ordered his death. President Taft, with only a few weeks left of his term, continued his foreign policy of non-intervention and turned the question of American action over to his successor for settlement. Breaking with a tradition that went back to the days of Thomas Jefferson, Wilson refused to accord official recognition to Huerta's government. In the form of unwillingness to be a party to Huerta's bloody subjection of the Mexican masses, Wilson's idealism thus clashed with the time-honored precedent of recognizing established governments, regardless of how they came into power. Resisting the pressure of British and American investors, who were losing thousands of dollars each day of non-recognition, Wilson proclaimed that he was far more concerned about Mexico's "submerged eighty-five per cent" than adherence to diplomatic traditions. In the place of official recognition, Wilson established a new policy which he called "watchful waiting." Thus, in the summer of 1913, "conditions" in Mexico were very unsettled—likely to "explode," in F.D.R.'s estimation.

"Roosevelt" refers to Roosevelt Clark, who was the son of Aunt Ellen's eldest daughter, Mrs. Appleton Clark.

~~

Dearest Babs

We—Prof. Coolidge, E. Bell, Jack White and myself—
left the Navy on the "Sylph" at 12:30 on Saturday and
steamed down the Potomac, getting into St. Mary's Bay near
the mouth of the River at 8:30. It was a heavenly day and we
got thoroughly cooled and rested. Incidentally I did some
quiet work on the Navy Estimates. Mr. Coolidge was delightful and I have never had such interesting conversation on
that kind of a trip. We covered every country on the globe!
Sunday morning we went overboard for a dip before breakfast and then went ashore to see the monument and site of
the first settlement of Lord Baltimore on a promontory.
Nothing is left of the old State House, but its location and
Maltese Cross shape are marked by stones.

Then we went across the Bay and visited Portobello
Manor, and old Hebb place, now owned by some people
named Hyatt from N.Y. The house is small but has some delightful old woodwork and mantles. After lunch we got
under weigh again and ran up the Potomac 25 miles and
went ashore to try to find Stratford, the old Lee place where
R.E.L. was born. Luckily, for no one was sure of the location,
we found it 1½ miles back from the River. It is a wonderful
old brick house shaped thus

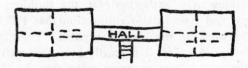

It has huge chimneys and the woodwork tho' brown
painted could be made lovely.

Wed.

I thought I had finished this yesterday.

After "Stratford" we returned on board, had a quiet night at anchor, and got back at nine Monday morning.

Today I'm back from Lathrop's and feeling very well. Just off to golf!

Your devoted

F

Professor Archibald Cary Coolidge had been F.D.R.'s first adviser at Harvard, where he taught history for twenty-eight years; a month after this weekend on the Potomac, Coolidge left for Germany to spend a year as an exchange professor at the University of Berlin. At the time of this letter Edward Bell was attached to the State Department's Division of Latin American Affairs. John Campbell White was Henry White's (*vide supra*) son by his first marriage to Margaret Rutherfurd. In 1913 he was associated with the *Baltimore Sun,* but, like his father, he later became a noted diplomat, serving as U.S. Ambassador to Haiti and Peru before retiring in 1945.

F.D.R.'s vessel for this brief vacation on the Potomac, the *Sylph,* was one of two yachts provided by the Navy for the personal use of the President. However, Wilson preferred the larger of the two, the *Mayflower,* and rarely used the *Sylph.* Thus the latter was often used by the Secretary of the Navy and the Assistant Secretary for inspection trips along the New England coast and the Potomac.

During the first two years of the Wilson Administration, appropriations were authorized for the building of five battleships, and it is in this connection that F.D.R. "did some quiet work on the Navy Estimates." The expansion of the Navy under Taft had hardly been perceptible, and by 1913 there was alarm in many circles that the Navy was inadequately equipped to protect the country's expanding interests. While Josephus Daniels handled the task of acquiring Congressional approval for the expansion program,

F.D.R. was charged with the supervision of subsidiary construction, i.e., navy yards, training camps, and the numerous other preparatory aspects involved in the final launching of a naval armada.

∞

Dearest Babs—

We are nearing Washington on our return from a very delightful trip. The party includes Senator Brandegee of Connecticut, 1st Assistant Sec'y of State Osborne, Assistant Sec'y of War Breckinridge, Assistant Attorney General Graham, U. S. Treasurer Burke, Commissioner of Corporations Davies, Mr. John Sidney Webb, Louis Howe and mineself. In spite of the downpour Friday night it was not rough in Chesapeake Bay and we reached Hampton Roads at 8:30 Saturday a.m. Admirals Badger, Winslow, Beatty, and Boush came on board, and also Major ——— from Fort Monroe to call on Breckinridge. At ten I began the farewell visits to the flagships, going on board the Wyoming, Arkansas, Connecticut and Rhode Island, the latter the flagship of the 2nd Division of 4 ships which leaves for Mexico next Wednesday. On returning to the Dolphin at 12:30 we started out ahead of the fleet and anchored just inside the Capes. Soon the nine battleships bound for the Mediterranean came along, the three colliers and the supply ship having gone out earlier. The big gray fellows were magnificent as they went past, with all hands at the rail, and I only wish a hundred thousand people could have seen them. The Connecticut had trouble—only one engine working—but it was evidently not serious as she kept on going.

We returned at once to Old Point, went ashore and inspected the coast defence guns and mortars and attended the war game at the Artillery School. Then back to the

Dolphin for a very good dinner. Last night we lay quietly at anchor, getting under weigh early this morning and stopping at Tangier Sound to go over the wrecked old San Marcos which has been so successfully used as a target. Since then we have been running up the Potomac under heavenly skies and with wonderful color effects on the banks. We are dining on board and expect to dock at eight.

Let me know what time to expect you, it will be so nice to have you back again.

Love to the chicks and Mama. By the way I want Vincent Astor to lunch with us at Hyde Park next Sunday if possible.

Ever your devoted

The occasion for this letter was the departure of an impressive fleet of nine battleships on a seven-week cruise of the Mediterranean, the first fleet to visit Europe under the Wilson Administration. Most of the ships were products of the naval expansion program inaugurated in 1912, and for the times they were the finest examples of naval construction and equipment in the world. The *New York Times* of October 26, 1913, editorialized that "the object of such a cruise is practice for the crews, real experience in seamanship . . . this relief from the monotonous routine of naval life in times of peace helps to improve the men by enlarging their outlook." The *Times* also suggested "that no harm can come of this notable exhibition of our naval development," a statement which was perhaps more closely in accord with the purposes envisioned by government circles.

The vessel that carried F.D.R.'s official party, the *Dolphin,* was a yacht provided for the use of the Secretary of the Navy. Built by J. Roach & Co., a private concern, and completed in 1885 as a dispatch boat, the 1500-ton *Dolphin* did not meet the specifications demanded by President Cleveland, and was subsequently rejected as a fighting ship by the government. A close personal friend of Secretary of the

Navy William E. Chandler, Roach had won the contracts for all the ships built during the Arthur Administration, but he and his company were ruined by the failure of the *Dolphin* to meet the tests required by Cleveland. During the trials it was found that the *Dolphin*'s speed was low (15.5 knots), its shaft broke, its most important gun was inaccurate, and it had great difficulty withstanding a heavy sea. Although it saw light service in the Spanish-American War, the *Dolphin* thus became a yacht for the use of government officials.

Frank B. Brandegee served in the Senate from 1909 to 1921, and his presence on the *Dolphin* was probably due to his position as chairman of the Senate Committee on Interoceanic Canals. The varied career of John E. Osborne began with an apprenticeship to a druggist, and thereafter it included an M.D. from the University of Vermont, a period as surgeon for the Union Pacific Railroad, the governorship of Wyoming for four years, and election to the Fifty-fifth Congress. He was appointed First Assistant Secretary of State in 1913, resigning from that position three years later. Henry Breckinridge was commissioned a major in the infantry in 1917, and participated in the Battle of St. Mihiel and the Meuse-Argonne offensive. In 1932, a prominent New York lawyer, he attended the turbulent Democratic convention in Chicago and seconded the Presidential nomination of Harry F. Byrd, who then withdrew on the fourth ballot in favor of F.D.R. Samuel J. Graham continued in the capacity here mentioned until 1919, when he became a judge of the United States Court of Claims, a position he held until his retirement eleven years later. John Burke had been the governor of North Dakota for four years prior to his entrance into Wilson's Cabinet in 1913. Joseph E. Davies later became United States Ambassador to Russia in F.D.R.'s Administration, a job which provided the material for his controversial book, *Mission to Moscow*. A member of the class of 1882 at Harvard, John Sidney Webb was a lawyer in Washington at the time of this letter. As for the presence of Louis Howe among the official party, F.D.R.

had brought his campaign manager to Washington as his special assistant soon after entering the Navy Department.

Admiral Charles J. Badger was at this time Commander-in-Chief of the Atlantic Fleet, while Rear Admiral Cameron Winslow commanded the Fleet's First Division, Rear Admiral Frank E. Beatty the Washington Navy Yard, and Rear Admiral Clifford J. Boush the Fleet's Third Division. F.D.R. evidently forgot the name of Breckinridge's visitor from Fort Monroe, as the original letter contains a blank space following the gentleman's rank.

Son of John Jacob Astor and a nephew of James Roosevelt Roosevelt's first wife, Vincent Astor was a Dutchess County neighbor of F.D.R.; it was on his yacht, the *Nourmahal,* that F.D.R. vacationed after his election in 1932.

This is the last existing personal letter written by F.D.R. in 1913. Although perhaps not revealed by the sparse correspondence, his first nine and a half months in the Navy Department turned out just as he predicted at the outset: working "like a turbine to master this job." By the time he journeyed to Hyde Park for the Christmas holidays, F.D.R. had not only mastered his new job, but had also won the approval of his civilian superiors and the respect of the Navy's high-ranking officers. Indeed, the highly successful Mediterranean cruise of nine first-line warships was in part testimony to F.D.R.'s quick mastery of official naval matters.

VI

"... These Are History-Making Days..."

ASSISTANT SECRETARY OF THE NAVY

1914

AT THE TIME F.D.R. was writing the next two letters concerning his personal finances, the crisis in Europe was swelling to catastrophic proportions. As soon as the First Balkan War had been concluded with the signing of a peace treaty in London on May 30, 1913, the victorious Balkan countries proceeded to argue over the spoils. The Treaty of London, which was supervised and arranged by the European powers, limited Turkey's European possessions to Constantinople and a small area in eastern Thrace, the remaining territory of European Turkey being ceded to the Balkan allies. During the summer of 1913 the Balkan nations fought one another over the disposition of their new territorial acquisitions. Bulgaria, desirous of dominating the Balkans, suddenly attacked Serbia and Greece, who were then joined by Rumania in the battle against the Bulgarian forces. Due to European pressure, the Second Bulgarian War was quickly ended; a new treaty was arranged at Bucharest on August

10th, one which humiliated Bulgaria and raised Serbia to the number-one position in the Balkans.

The continuously shifting scene resulting from the Balkan Wars had far-reaching repercussions in Europe. Austria-Hungary became fearful of Serbia's rapidly growing power, and only strong German and Italian opposition prevented the Dual Monarchy from attacking Serbia in the autumn of 1913. Russia, too, was interested in Balkan affairs, especially in preventing Austria-Hungary's southward expansion; thus the period between the Treaty of Bucharest and July, 1914, was marked by the efforts of both powers to construct Balkan alliances in such a way as to block the advance of the other. The Russian Ambassador at Paris, Izvolski, convinced the French government of the necessity for "Balkanizing" the Franco-Russian alliance, and thereafter the French press was subsidized by Russian funds in order to make the French people conscious of Balkan affairs. At the same time a diplomatic correspondence between Britain and France was transforming the friendly *entente cordiale* into a Franco-British alliance against Germany, while the latter nation was busily carrying out its military and naval expansion program.

Thus, in brief, an outline of the tightening process of Europe's alliances as 1914 opened and F.D.R. informed his mother that Christmas vacation had ended for his children and that they were both "back at school."

WASHINGTON
[JANUARY 6, 1914]
TUESDAY

Dearest Ma

Ongfang I have found the Dec. 1 accounts of the place and enclose them.

I had a nice visit from Uncle Warren yesterday. He came to lunch and again to tea, and the children adored him. Elliott has several times today asked for Uncullel Waa.

The rain has stopped at last and Anna and James are both back at school. Lots of love.

Your affect.   FDR

"Ongfang" was F.D.R.'s slang for the French *enfin*.

∼∽

WASHINGTON
[JANUARY 7, 1914]
WEDNESDAY

Dearest Mama—

Yes actually another letter within twenty-four hours. Here is Anna's cheque from Southern Pacific stock—to be deposited in the Poughkeepsie Savings Bank.

We are just back from a delightful dinner at Justice Holmes' and we stopped in at the Mrs. Marshall Field dance for a few minutes afterwards.

Your affec
F.D.R.

Oliver Wendell Holmes made it a practice to lunch on occasional Sundays with some of the younger men in the government, and during the Wilson Administration he and F.D.R. became good friends. Formerly Mrs. Delia Spencer Caton, Mrs. Marshall Field was the second wife of the founder of Chicago's famous department store; she was a prominent dowager in Washington society at the time of this letter, her dances being among the highlights of the social season.

∼∽

Except for an inspection trip to the West Coast, F.D.R. spent the spring of 1914 engaged in the usual Washington routine. This is not to say that it was an inactive period; the business of naval expansion continued at a rapid pace, and each step forward uncovered new problems of policy and construction. In addition, not only did the mounting crisis in Europe require continual adjustments within the Navy

Department, but the situation in Mexico, which had swiftly become explosive, likewise necessitated numerous revisions of naval policy.

Formally demanding Huerta's resignation on November 13, 1913, Wilson added an aggressive character to his policy of "watchful waiting." This shift was further implemented three months later when the United States lifted the arms embargo imposed under Taft, thereby allowing for the shipment of war materials to Huerta's two leading opponents, Carranza and Villa. While Wilson was besieged by American and European oil interests to intervene in Mexico and restore order, Huerta stubbornly continued his antagonistic policy, using the hostility of the "Colossus of the North" to strengthen his position within Mexico.

On April 9, 1914, the explosion that F.D.R. had predicted nine months earlier in a letter to his mother occurred at Tampico, and at the center of this explosion was the *Dolphin*. Its colors plainly displayed, the *Dolphin* had entered the port to load supplies, and while engaged in this task the crew was arrested by a Mexican force. Although the Americans were released shortly thereafter, Huerta refused to proffer a satisfactory formal apology to the commanding officer, Admiral Mayo, who had demanded a public raising of the American flag followed by a 21-gun salute. Huerta's evasive tactics in not saluting the flag aroused the war spirit in the United States, and on April 20, 1914, Wilson asked Congress for authority to use armed force in Mexico. However, between the consent of the House on the 21st and the Senate authorization on the 22nd, the situation blew wide open: a German merchantman, weighted down with a cargo of arms which were to be used by Huerta against the United States, began to unload at Vera Cruz. The next day, with Wilson's approval and with considerable loss of life, American forces assaulted and captured Vera Cruz. While the crisis fanned the war spirit to a high pitch in the United

States, it left Wilson with two distasteful alternatives, either a costly war in violation of his announced policy or a humiliating withdrawal from Mexico. Fortunately, before Wilson had time to make a decision, the difficult situation was resolved by an offer from Argentina, Brazil, and Chile to act as mediators.

As the representatives of the mediators, of Mexico, and of the United States were convening in Niagara Falls late in May, 1914, and as the crisis in Europe approached the breaking-point, F.D.R. returned from a weekend in New York and informed his wife that "I have my hands full."

WASHINGTON
[SPRING, 1914]
TUESDAY

Dearest Babs—

Arrived safely and came to house and Albert telephoned Miss Mercer who later came and cleaned up. Then a long day at the office and dinner alone at 7:30, after which I dressed and went to the reception for the visiting So. and Central Americans at the Pan American building and came home at 10:30.

Tonight I dine with Uncle Fred at the club to meet the Chilean part of the Conference.

Now I am just back from lunch with the Spring-Rices— a very nice Prof. Young there from Calcutta—studying our educational system. I gave him letters to Uncle Ted, Nicholas Murray Butler and Prof. H. F. Osborn.

I do hope Rosy is better, do let me know.

If I don't hear from you I will leave Saturday at 12:30 for Wilmington via Penn. R.R.

It is delightful and cool. Mr. D. leaves tonight for a day so I have my hands full!

Lots of love and kiss the chicks.

Your devoted

F.

Although this letter cannot be dated to the day, from the references to James Roosevelt Roosevelt's operation and to the visiting delegates from the Niagara Conference it appears to have been written either late in May or early in June, 1914.

Albert was F.D.R.'s chauffeur and general handyman in Washington, while Miss Lucy Mercer was A.E.R.'s part-time secretary; in 1920 she became the second wife of Winthrop Rutherfurd, who was a descendant of the first governors of New York and Massachusetts, Peter Stuyvesant and John Winthrop, and a leading figure in society for more than a half-century. It was necessary for the wives of all officials to have secretaries; Miss Lucy Mercer was well acquainted with the social obligations of an Assistant Secretary's wife, and arranged her calling list and handled her invitations, besides any correspondence of an official nature.

After a varied career in the foreign service, Sir Cecil Arthur Spring-Rice in 1912 became Britain's Ambassador to the United States, a post he held until shortly before his death in 1918. He was known to his associates as "Springy." When a young man he had come to the United States as Third Secretary of the Embassy, and became a close friend of T.R.'s family; this friendship continued through the years and was the basis of a close association with F.D.R., who was also attracted by Springy's great knowledge of American history. F.D.R.'s letter of introduction to Nicholas Murray Butler, Columbia University's eminent president, was written more as Assistant Secretary of the Navy than as a close personal friend.

∽

WASHINGTON
JUNE 26, 1914
FRIDAY

Dearest Mama—

I almost paid the enclosed by mistake and shudder at the thought of almost losing $3.02! I tried this morning to get off and surprise you at Hyde Park tomorrow, but it is impossible as the sale of the ships to Greece has given me a lot of extra work and now the Venezuelan Minister has taken it into his head to die and Billy Phillips and I have got to embalm him and send him to La Guayra on a battleship after funerals etc.

I have a line from Helen saying her Father is really better and that she had a very satisfactory talk with you and that you were *splendid*.

By the way, why don't you come down here between July 13 and 17 or between July 20 and 24 if it isn't too hot? Lots of love.

Your affec.

F.D.R.

"The sale of the ships to Greece" was a not altogether insignificant factor in the course of subsequent events in the Balkans. Several months prior to this letter the Greek government had sent representatives to call on Daniels with an offer to purchase two U.S. battleships, the *Idaho* and the *Mississippi*. Built under conditions similar to those that produced the *Dolphin*, these warships were considered by American naval authorities as "Navy orphans," i.e., they were much smaller than the standard dreadnoughts and much less suitable to naval warfare. Aware that Daniels and Congress might thus be willing to part with the two ships, and desirous of further protecting herself against possible attack by any of her neighbors, Greece began negotiations for their purchase. With the consent of Wilson, Daniels agreed to the proposal, thereby causing F.D.R. "extra work" in the preparation of an appropriate bill for submission to Congress. The sale was authorized in the Naval Appropriation Act of June 30, 1914, and eight days later an official ceremony marked the delivery of a check for $12,535,275.96 to Daniels in full payment for the ships. Contending that the sale should have been made on the open market, Turkey raised a vigorous protest; and in view of the intense hostility which characterized Greco-Turkish relations at the time, it does not seem unreasonable to conclude that the addition of the warships to the Greek Navy played a large role in the prevention of war between the two countries.

Señor Ezequiel Rojas, Venezuelan Minister to the United States for four years, died at the age of eighty-three in Atlantic City the day before F.D.R. wrote this letter; after lying in state his body was taken on the *Sylph* to Hampton Roads, thence to the Venezuelan capital on the battleship *Kansas*. Rojas had been identified with Venezuelan politics all his life, his long career including the presidency of the Venezuelan National Congress, as well as several imprisonments and a number of years in exile. From 1893 to 1898 he was Minister of Foreign Affairs, a period which witnessed the famous dispute between England, Venezuela, and the United States over the definition of the boundary dividing British Guiana and Venezuela.

William Phillips and his wife, the former Caroline Astor Drayton, were old friends of the Roosevelts; they were especially close during F.D.R.'s years in the Navy Department, forming with F.D.R. and A.E.R. part of the small coterie that met informally every few weeks in order to escape Washington protocol. At this time Third Assistant Secretary of State, "Billy" Phillips was beginning a long and varied career in the diplomatic service; under F.D.R. he served as Ambassador to Italy, and as political officer on General Dwight D. Eisenhower's staff in London during World War II.

At the same time that F.D.R. was writing this letter, the heir to the Austrian and Hungarian thrones, Archduke Franz Ferdinand, was setting out for a visit to Sarajevo, the capital of Bosnia.

∽

WASHINGTON
JULY 14, [1914]
TUESDAY

Dearest Babs—

I sent you a line in Mama's letter from Hyde Park, left at 6, stopped at Aunt Ellen's to say goodbye, got to N. Y. at 8:30 and had nearly an hour with Rosy. He seemed much better than when I saw him last and was quite cheerful, sitting in a reclining wheelchair on a balcony on the 15th floor. I got here yesterday morning after a very hot night on the train, had a bath and delicious breakfast and came to the Dept. to find not only a vast accumulation, but also an interesting situation in Haiti and Santo Domingo, with a hurry call for marines from the State Department. I saw the President about it, also Mr. Bryan and Bill Phillips, and by 5 p.m. had 700 marines and two ships in motion towards Guantanamo. I dined with Caroline, Billy and A. Peters at the Shoreham and went to bed early.

It is not really hot today, only very muggy, and I am in excellent condition.

My trip down was a great success, and I got in 22 holes of golf on Friday afternoon at the Essex County Country Club with Livy. The launching went off well, and I escaped most of the banquet afterwards (including the speeches) by running for the Federal Express to Poughkeepsie. The Daniels' went to Newport and are now on the Dolphin returning to Washington, so I am alone these three days.

Lots of love to Maude and David. Kiss the chicks and heaps for yourself.

Your devoted

F.

The "interesting situation" in Haiti and Santo Domingo involved far more than the dispatch of an emergency force of marines to Guantanamo, the United States naval base on the southwest end of Cuba which is within easy striking distance of both republics. Although the immediate issue was the unrest and revolutionary spirit that prevailed on the Caribbean island and thereby threatened American lives and property, the overall situation seriously jeopardized the Monroe Doctrine and American supremacy in the vicinity of the Panama Canal.

The difficult problem of U.S. relations with the island republics of the Caribbean first became acute in 1904 when successive revolutions caused the bankruptcy of Santo Domingo. With a debt at this time of thirty-two million dollars and a revenue of less than one-third of the interest on the debt, Santo Domingo's European creditors were threatening to collect by force unless the United States would guarantee efficient management of its finances. Announcing that under such circumstances the U.S. was bound by the Monroe Doctrine to intervene, Theodore Roosevelt negotiated a treaty with Santo Domingo whereby the United States was the receiver for the bankrupt republic and the authority which appointed an official to collect the revenues. This policy existed for two years under "executive agreement" until the Senate finally ratified the treaty in 1907. Even though American management of Santo Domingo's finances helped to restore its solvency and satisfied its creditors in Europe, the establishment of a financial guardianship caused much strife within the Dominican Republic, and the next decade witnessed the development of revolutionary parties opposed to U.S. domination.

In 1914 revolutions again swept the island, and in July the unstable conditions led the United States to insist that a new treaty be arranged that would strengthen its control. The president of Santo Domingo refused to sign the agreement, thereby intensifying the disorder. This was the Dominican situation when F.D.R. ordered the marines to Guantanamo, and it grew progressively worse in the following months; in 1916 the U.S. finally established a military government over Santo Domingo that lasted for eight years.

The crisis in Haiti at this time was identical to the situation in Santo Domingo in 1904. The country's financial condition bordered on complete collapse, and on June 14, 1914, France and Germany demanded control of Haitian finances, thus leaving America once again faced with the alternative of allowing European footholds in the Caribbean or of intervening in Haitian affairs and accepting responsibility for the reimbursement of Haiti's European creditors. The Haitian government, however, refused to submit to an American financial protectorate, riots followed; thus the situation in Haiti was also "interesting" at the time F.D.R. wrote this letter. In 1915 the revolution broke forth violently in Haiti, and the U.S. temporarily settled the financial question by ordering the marines from Guantanamo to Port au Prince. After ten months of American military control of Haiti a treaty almost identical to the American-Domingo Convention of 1907 was proclaimed. Order was subsequently restored to the Caribbean, and American supremacy over the Panama Canal remained unimpaired. The Monroe Doctrine, on the other hand, had undergone a slight alteration: the century-long verbal guarantee that the United States would assist its hemispheric neighbors in the case of European intervention no longer excluded American intervention in the affairs of its neighbors. This "big brother" policy lasted until 1933 when it was replaced by the "good neighbor" policy.

In later years one of F.D.R.'s favorite anecdotes was the occasion of his interview with William Jennings Bryan mentioned in this letter. It seems that the Secretary of State came rushing into his office and demanded, "I must have a battleship at Guantanamo by tomorrow morning." F.D.R. replied that this was impossible because the nearest dreadnought was at least four days' travel time away from the Caribbean. Bryan again insisted, "But I must, I must have it. American lives are endangered at Haiti." F.D.R. repeated the impossibility of granting such a request, but added that "we have a gunboat in the vicinity that could be in Guantanamo Bay within twenty-four hours." Whereupon Bryan exclaimed, "Oh, that's all right; when I say 'battleship,' I mean anything that goes and has some guns on it."

Andrew J. Peters was at this time serving his fourth term in Congress, but he resigned a month later to become Assistant Secretary of the Treasury. He was Boston's mayor in 1919 when its policemen went on strike, an event which attracted the interest of the entire country and became a major issue of the 1920 campaign; while the governor of

Massachusetts, Calvin Coolidge, neatly sidestepped the strike "against the public safety," Peters distinguished himself by assuming command and calling out the State Guard. His wife, the former Martha Phillips, a sister of William Phillips, is described by A.E.R. in *This Is My Story* as one of the two women (Alice Longworth being the other) in the capital who were not "slaves of the Washington social system."

As F.D.R. had been inspecting New England naval stations during the previous week, he was able to be present at the launching of the battleship *Nevada* in Quincy, Massachusetts. Considered at the time to be the best fighting ship ever built for the Navy, the *Nevada* was christened by ten-year-old Eleanor Anne Siebert, niece of Governor Tasker L. Oddie of Nevada and great-great-great-granddaughter of Benjamin Stoddert, the first Secretary of the Navy. So that the new battleship could bear its name, its predecessor, the monitor *Nevada*, was renamed the *Tonopah*. Included among the speakers whom F.D.R. "escaped" were Nevada's Senator Key Pittman, Massachusetts' Governor David I. Walsh, Boston's Mayor James M. Curley, and Josephus Daniels.

〜〜

WASHINGTON
[JULY 16, 1914]
THURSDAY

Dearest Babs.

Just a hurried [note] to tell you all is well. Huerta is out and I am at the Department working on a thousand things. J.D. is not back till tomorrow morning.

Your devoted   F.

In spite of the failure of the Niagara Falls conference to settle the Mexican situation, Wilson continued to press for Huerta's resignation. The latter proved unable to maintain his resistance, and went into voluntary exile several hours before F.D.R. scribbled this brief note to his wife.

Although Carranza's refusal to accept the settlement proposed at Niagara Falls canceled the good work of the conference, the meetings nevertheless succeeded in averting a war and in assuring other countries that the United States did not have aggressive designs on its weak neighbors. On the other hand, the disappearance of Huerta from the scene did not alleviate the plight of troubled Mexico. Carranza, Huerta's successor, did not carry out the reforms he had previously advocated, and was soon challenged by Villa and his supporters. In 1915, therefore, Mexico entered into an even bloodier phase of its prolonged revolution, a phase which included the massacre of eighteen American citizens and the subsequent invasion of Mexico by an American force under General John J. Pershing.

∿

WASHINGTON
JULY 18, [1914]
SATURDAY

Dearest Mama—

Mr. Daniels only got back yesterday and I have been having such a strenuous time that I haven't had a minute even to write a line. When I got here Monday morning I found a critical situation in Haiti and San Domingo and after several conferences with the President and the Secretary of State I sent a regiment of Marines to Guantanamo. Then old Uncle Huerta climbed down and the whole situation has required my being at my desk not only all day but also in the evenings. It has been very hot and very moist. I fear you have not had weather for crop harvesting.

I haven't been able to decide about going to Campo, whether next Sunday the 26th or the following week. I wired Uncle Warren last night asking him to accompany me on a destroyer to the opening of the Cape Cod Canal from Fairhaven on the 29th. I wish you could be there, but by then you will be in the wilds of Maine or New Hampshire.

I hope to get a game of golf tomorrow p.m. but must

227

return to Dept. in the evening. A great deal of love to Aunt
Kassie and the two children. I suppose cunning little Kassie
can toddle about and begin to lisp a few words. Sallie from
all accounts must be a bouncing baby.

Your affec. son
F.D.R.

After five years of difficult labor and much scandal, the
Cape Cod Canal was formally opened on July 29, 1914,
with an impressive ceremony described by F.D.R. in a
later letter to A.E.R. Over eight miles long, the Canal connected Cape Cod Bay with Buzzards Bay and shortened
the water route between New York and Boston by nearly
seventy-five miles. Built by the Boston, Cape Cod, and
New York Canal Company, the Canal also offered an al-
ternate route to some of the most dangerous shoals along
the coast, and consequently at the opening ceremonies it
was often referred to as "the greatest life-saving institution
on the Atlantic."

"Little Kassie" and "Sallie" were Aunt Kassie's daughters
by her second marriage, Katharine and Sara Collier, who
were at this time twenty and eighteen years old. By in-
ferring that they were very small children, F.D.R. was
teasing his mother, who had written him of the arrival of
Aunt Kassie and "her two babies." In 1917 Katharine D.P.
Collier married George B. St. George; in 1946 she was
elected to Congress on the Republican ticket from New
York's Twenty-ninth District; and in 1948 she was a keynote
speaker at the Republican National Convention in Philadelphia. Sara R.P. Collier later became Mrs. Charles Fellowes-Gordon; F.D.R. was her godfather.

∽∽

WASHINGTON
JULY 19, 1914
SUNDAY

Dearest Babs—

Here endeth one week of real old-fashioned activity! Up
to yesterday afternoon I seemed to live at the office. You have

probably read in the "Times" some of the results—first came the Haitian troubles, with the outfitting of a new expeditionary force and many conferences with the President and the Secretary of State, then the resignation of Huerta, bringing to an end the time-worn cry of "Huerta must go," but plunging us into all sorts of new difficulties—entre nous without resulting to date in any *definite* policy of construction.

We drift on from day to day as usual—where it has been a success so far, the time has come for a concrete program.

Every evening I have been at the Dept. and have succeeded in cleaning up the last of the annual contracts that have been bothering us for three months.

Politically there is little change. I *might* declare myself a candidate for U. S. Senator in the Democratic and Progressive Primaries. The Governorship is, thank God, out of the question.

As to next year *if* I am still Assistant Secretary—a new bill is before Congress providing for three National Commissioners to the Panama Pacific Exposition, two from the Executive Departments and one from civil life, the latter to get $5,000 and devote his whole time to it. It is planned that Bill Phillips and I are to be the two from the Government, and we should have to spend less time than originally thought, going out February 1 for a month, and once in the summer and once at the close.

Yesterday p.m. I golfed and went to the Dept. in the evening, today I have played 45 holes and am nearly dead! I am just in after dining with Paymaster and Mrs. Heap and John McIlhenny. Luckily yesterday and today were delightfully cool and dry. I have dined at home almost every evening.

I will wire you tomorrow or Tuesday whether I can go up next Sunday or the following.

The Cape Cod Canal opening is Wednesday, the 29th and

I will either take it in on the way back from Campo or on the way up.

A great deal of love to the chicks. I miss you all so much! I really would like to be in the Senate just so as to get a summer really with my family once in every three or four years!

Take very good care of yourself! Your devoted

F

F.D.R.'s idea of entering the senatorial primaries was mainly stimulated by William G. McAdoo, who was anxious to construct a Democratic organization in New York that could successfully oppose Tammany Hall. Although at the time of this letter there was still some doubt in F.D.R.'s mind as to the advisability of declaring himself a candidate, exactly one month later his candidacy was announced.

As Congress approved the bill providing for three national commissioners to the Panama-Pacific International Exposition, and as F.D.R. was "still Assistant Secretary" in 1915, the proposed trip to San Francisco became a reality the following February. The Exposition was primarily a cultural one in celebration of the new era of world trade which commenced with the opening of the Panama Canal. Although the World War delayed the expansion of trade and upset the plans for an international naval parade to mark the opening of the Canal, the Exposition was a huge artistic and financial success. Running from February to December, it entertained nearly nineteen million visitors and made a net profit in excess of one million dollars; thirty-nine foreign nations and thirty-seven states and three territories of the United States were represented at the Exposition. Representing the President, Vice-President Thomas R. Marshall officiated at the formal dedication, and it was for this occasion that a Vice-President's flag was originated. Although almost all the high government officials had a special flag, no emblem had ever been designed for the Vice-President. Josephus Daniels and F.D.R. therefore conceived a white flag with an American eagle which was to be displayed on naval vessels whenever they entertained the Vice-President, and which has since become the official insignia of that office.

Samuel L. Heap was then pay director in charge of the Navy Allotment Office in Washington. John A. McIlhenny, an old friend of Theodore Roosevelt and one of his Rough Riders, was at this time president of the Civil Service Commission; during his years in Washington he was one of F.D.R.'s favorite golf partners.

∽

WASHINGTON
[JULY 22, 1914]
WEDNESDAY

Dear Babs—

I'm *too* sad about the bunny's demise, and only hope the funeral and making of the tombstone will console the chicks. I wonder if it was the lop-sided one?

It may be impossible to get off this Sunday as J. D. may go [to] Raleigh and won't know till tomorrow. In that case I will come up right after the launching or baptism or whatever it is of the Cape Cod Canal, arriving Thursday 11:30 a.m. Liv. Davis and Alice and Morris Brownell and Laura go with me, and we start from Fairhaven at 10:30 a.m.

I have been as usual going every second, at the office till 7:30 last night, so today I left at 4 and played one round of golf with L. Heap, dined here alone and now go back to bed!

I'm so sorry I missed Hemenway et al.

Lots of love. Kiss the chicks.

Your devoted

F

F.D.R.'s sadness over "the bunny's demise" was a response to a description contained in A.E.R.'s letter of July 19, 1914: ". . . We had a tragedy yesterday, one of the bunnies died. Nobody seems able to explain it, unless it was the cold and damp. So now Edgar is putting them in the pump house at night when it isn't warm and pleasant. The chicks were very sad but they buried it with great ceremony and are going to put a mound of stones above him today, and this seems to be a great consolation! . . ."

∽∽

Because of the imminence of war in Europe, F.D.R.'s vacation in Maine after the opening of the Cape Cod Canal was cut short by a telegram requesting his immediate return to Washington. The last days of July had witnessed a complete deterioration of diplomatic efforts to prevent Archduke Ferdinand's assassination from mushrooming into a general war. Following the Sarajevo incident, Austria-Hungary sent an ultimatum to Serbia which was purposely designed to be so harsh that Serbia could not accept it. Claiming that acceptance would be a violation of her sovereignty, Serbia on July 25th rejected the parts which dealt with this issue, and suggested referring the whole matter to the Hague Court. Austria-Hungary, however, anxious to defeat Serbia in a local war, announced that the reply to the ultimatum was unsatisfactory and declared war on Serbia three days later. On July 29th, Russia, fearful of losing her influence in the Balkans, declared mobilization against the Dual Monarchy; this in turn brought forth an ultimatum from Berlin which stated that unless Russia halted her mobilization in twelve hours Germany would mobilize; and when Russia did not reply, Germany declared war—several hours before F.D.R. wrote the next letter to his wife. By August 24th the entangling alliances had fully unwound and Europe was engaged in a general war.

∽∽

[AUGUST 1, 1914]
SATURDAY

Dearest Babs—

I am on the train returning to Washington after dedicating the Maine anchor at Reading, Pa. The latest news is that

232

Germany has declared war against Russia. A complete smash up is inevitable, and there are a great many problems for us to consider. Mr. D. totally fails to grasp the situation and I am to see the President Monday a.m. to go over our own situation.

The Canal opening was a great success but was not over till 7 p.m. so I couldn't get to Washington till 1:30 p.m. Thursday. I worked at office both evenings and go there all day tomorrow. These are history-making days. It will be the greatest war in the world's history. All well.

Love

FDR

The dedication of an anchor from the battleship *Maine* caused as much turmoil in the city of Reading as the excitement created in the entire country by the destruction of this famous vessel in 1898. Fourteen years had passed since the blowing-up of the *Maine* before the ship was finally raised from Havana harbor and towed out to be sunk at sea. During the process of recovering the wreck, numerous relics of the *Maine* were returned to the United States and distributed to various municipalities as historical mementos. Occasionally controversies arose over the distribution of the relics, although none of the arguments were as severe as the Reading episode; in fact, the controversies were often quite amusing, as in the case of a small town in Ohio, which, after making strenuous efforts to secure the captain's bathtub as a souvenir, became so sensitive to the many jests made at its expense that it requested permission to return that object (a neighboring town was not so sensitive, however, and the bathtub still occupies an honored position in Ohio).

In Reading the controversy arose out of a local political situation and subsequently became so bitter that Daniels found it necessary to send F.D.R. to the dedication ceremonies to represent the government and resolve the matter. It began early in 1914 when Congressman John H. Rothermel, then seeking his fifth Democratic nomination from the Reading district, announced that he had obtained the *Maine* anchor for Reading. The enthusiasm which greeted his announcement, however, was of short duration; contending that any number of cities had received *Maine* anchors and that they thus could be had for the asking, the supporters of his opponent for the nomination, Arthur G. Dewalt, accused Rothermel of seeking votes on the basis of an achievement which was not as distinctive as he claimed. The issue was hotly contested at a local level until an emissary of Dewalt's returned from a visit to the Washington Navy Yard and announced that the anchor sent to Reading was indeed a fraud, that it had never been a part of the Maine. Angered at the attack upon the integrity of the Navy Department, Daniels entered the argument and stated that no doubt existed as to the origin of the anchor, that it was on the *Maine* when the ship exploded. But in spite of Daniels' statement and F.D.R.'s presentation address, Dewalt won the nomination.

The *Reading Eagle* of August 1, 1914, carried F.D.R.'s entire address to the citizens of Reading. A few excerpts reveal that F.D.R. not only explained the history of the anchor, but also profited by the occasion to express some of his views on government:

. . . The Maine was not at anchor at the time of the explosion, but was moored to a buoy. Consequently, all six of the Maine's anchors were on board at the time, and the four largest anchors were carried down with the wreck of the bow.

She carried six anchors, designated as follows: Two bowers, weighing about 10,000 pounds each, which were the anchors ordinarily used, and were carried one on each side of the bow. Next to these came the two sheet anchors of approximately the same size and intended to be used in addition to the bowers when necessary to ride out a gale. There were also two smaller anchors, one called the stream anchor of about 3,500 pounds, and one, the stern anchor, of 2,800 pounds. . . .

In the process of raising the wreck, it was found that certain parts were so deeply buried in the mud as to make recovery impossible, and among these articles were most of the anchors.

The anchor now in Reading, however, was recovered and was sent to the Navy Yard at Key West, Florida. From Key West the anchor, together with a gun and two pumps which had also been recovered, were shipped to the Navy Yard, Norfolk, Virginia, on the naval collier Caesar, where they arrived on April 30, 1913.

The Caesar being unable to proceed up the Potomac, these relics were loaded to a barge and towed by the naval tug Hercules to the Navy Yard, Washington, where they were stowed until the anchor was asked for by Mr. Stratton, the mayor of Reading, and at the solicitation of Mr. Rothermel the Department granted the request and ordered the anchor shipped to that city.

This Anchor Was on the Maine.

It has come to my ears that certain persons, who must have had either a strongly perverted sense of humor or a malicious design to circulate a falsehood, have suggested that the national government has deliberately attempted to perpetrate a fraud on the city of Reading by sending it an anchor which was not one of the anchors of the Maine. I have briefly outlined the history of the anchor that is being dedicated today in the city of Reading. There is, of course, absolutely no question that this anchor was on the Maine at the time she was blown up in Havana Harbor; that it was raised from the wreck 14 years afterwards, taken to Key West, Florida, then to Norfolk, Va.; from Norfolk to Washington and thence to its present resting place. Its history is complete and absolutely authenticated, but I cannot refrain from suggesting my disappointment that there can exist in any community people so small as to allow personal or political jealousies to influence them so far that they publicly doubt the honesty of the national government.

It so happens that a few years ago I had the honor of being a member of the upper house of the New York Legislature. As such I had an opportunity of becoming pretty well acquainted with the workings of a state govern-

235

ment. I can assure you that I saw enough of that state government to convince me that there was a vast amount of room for improvement, both in its honesty and in its efficiency. Naturally, also, I have read and heard much about the state's government of the commonwealth of Pennsylvania, and it is not going too far to say that the sentiment which I have expressed about the government of my own state could be applied with at least equal force to the government of this state. But I can also say this: since I came to Washington in March, 1913, I have been every day struck by the fact that the standards of Albany and of Harrisburg are by no means the standards of Washington, for in the national capital I have found on the part of the members of the administration a sincere and successful desire to manage and maintain the government of the nation for the sole benefit of the people who go to make up that nation.

There have been two kinds of successful politics devised in our system of government up to the present time. The first is the kind which seeks to build up party strength by obtaining for that party power based on the personal domination of a few men and the perpetuation in places of authority of these few men and their own appointed successors. That has been in the past, we must admit it to our shame, a successful kind of politics, but the day of its success has just about come to an end. The administration in Washington believes in a very different kind of successful politics. It goes back to the fundamental theory that the success of a government depends upon the freely expressed consent of the governed. It is seeking so to handle the affairs of the nation that no man, no group and no class shall have privilege to the exclusion of any other man or group or class to the end that there may be equal opportunity for all. The administration believes that the national government should be conducted for the benefit of the 99 per cent. and not, as has sometimes been the case in the past, for the benefit of the 1 per cent. . . .

∽∽

My own Dearest—

At last I have time to write you a real letter. I posted a line on the train last night, and on arrival went straight to the Department, where as I expected, I found everything asleep and apparently utterly oblivious to the fact that the most terrible drama in history was about to be enacted.

To go back many days, I got to Boston all right on Wednesday morning and a telegram from Livy said he and Alice could not go to the opening of the Cape Cod Canal because of the business crisis. I found Captain Coffman on the special train and we arrived New Bedford 10:30 where the Brownells, Howes, Bertie Hamlin, Anna H. and Robert McAdoo were waiting. We all boarded the McDougal, now commanded by nice Leigh Palmer and the flotilla started for Buzzards Bay headed by Rose Standish with the Belmonts and guests on board, the McDougal second, and after us about ten large yachts. Off the harbor a division of six destroyers fell in line as escort, and two submarines were off the entrance to the Canal. We steamed slowly through, taking about an hour and a half, and the spectacle was intensely impressive. A great many thousand people lined the banks all the way, with countless automobiles and much noise of welcome. The flotilla turned in Massachusetts Bay and the return trip was exciting enough as the current running with us was altogether too strong for safe navigation by a destroyer at slow speed. Palmer handled his ship beautifully and at the village of Buzzards Bay we went ashore in the launch for the ceremonies. The people on the Rose Standish were not so fortunate as the current was too strong to make a landing and they had to go out into the Bay, turn around and come back against the tide. They arrived an hour late and the exercises began, Seth Low presiding, and speeches by August Belmont, W. Barclay Parsons, Gov. Walsh, Charles Hamlin and myself. As a result we got through at six, had to go seven miles in the launch to meet the McDougal in the Bay, dropped the Brownells and Hamlins at New Bedford, but it was too late for me to catch the boat to N. Y. so I tried for the Fall River boat by keeping on to Newport. I missed it there by ½ hour and also the last train to Providence, so with the Howes I chartered a sea-going auto for Fall River! There (it being now quarter past midnight) the last trolley had left for Providence, so I dropped the Howes (to go to her Mother) and sped on in my auto at top speed feeling very much like P. Revere. We made a record run, reaching the Providence station just as the midnight train from Boston pulled in at 1:20 a.m.! I breakfasted during my hour in N. Y. on Thursday morning and took the 8:08 on here.

To my astonishment on reaching the Dept. nobody seemed the least bit excited about the European crisis—Mr. Daniels feeling chiefly very sad that his faith in human nature and civilization and similar idealistic nonsense was receiving such a rude shock. So I started in alone to get things ready and prepare plans for what *ought* to be done by the Navy end of things. Friday I worked all day on these lines, and actually succeeded in getting one ship north from Mexico.

These dear good people like W.J.B. and J.D. have as much conception of what a general European war means as Elliott has of higher mathematics. They really believe that because we are neutral we can go about our business as usual. To my horror, *just for example,* J. D. told the newspaper men he thought favorably of sending our fleet to Europe to bring back marooned Americans!

Aside from the fact that tourists (female etc.) couldn't sleep in hammocks and that battleships haven't got passenger accommodations, he totally fails to grasp the fact that this war between the other powers is going inevitably to give rise to a hundred different complications in which we shall have a direct interest. Questions of refugees, of neutrality, of commerce are even now appearing and we should unquestionably gather our fleet together and get it into the highest state of efficiency. We still have 12 battleships at Vera Cruz—their "materiel" has suffered somewhat, their "personnel" a great deal! The rest of the fleet is scattered to the four winds—they should be assembled and prepared. Some fine day the State Department will want the *moral* backing of a "fleet in being" and it *won't be there.*

All this sounds like borrowing trouble I know but it is *my* duty to keep the Navy in a position where no chances, even the most remote, are taken. Today we are taking chances and I nearly boil over when I see the cheery "mañana" way of doing business.

Two hours ago a telegram from Badger came in asking for information about the war and instructions as to neutrality. Nobody had thought it necessary to keep him in touch! And yet he has a German, a French and an English cruiser off Vera Cruz!

Naturally I am worried about Coz. Susie and Henry and Aunt Jennie and Laura and Sara. Also of course Rosy and Betty are on the Kronprinzessin Cecilie due in Plymouth tonight or tomorrow morning. I have thought of telegraphing Bell in London to look out for them, but it can't really do any good. If they land safely they will be all right and England is not yet openly involved.

There seems no hope now of averting the crash. Germany has invaded France according to this afternoon's report. The best that can be expected is either a sharp, complete and quick victory by one side, a most unlikely occurrence, or a speedy realization of impending bankruptcy by all, and cessation by mutual consent, but this too is I think unlikely as history shows that money in spite of what the bankers say

239

is not an essential to the conduct of a war by a determined nation.

Rather than long drawn-out struggle I hope England will join in and with France and Russia force peace *at Berlin!*

The Reading unveiling of the Maine anchor was a great success—fine parade, lots of bands—ending with an impassioned oration by hubby to 5,000 people in the park!

I have deposited $332 in Met. Bank. A great deal of love to the chicks and Mama and A. Annie and a great big hug for yourself.

Your devoted   F

News reports of the Cape Cod Canal ceremonies indicate that the *Rose Standish* was an excursion steamer and that the *McDougal* was the only destroyer of the flotilla able to pass through the Canal. Captain DeWitt Coffman was at this time commandant of the Boston Navy Yard and an essential dignitary at the opening ceremonies. As a vice admiral, he commanded the Atlantic Fleet during the first summer of American participation in World War I.

Charles Sumner Hamlin, then Assistant Secretary of the Treasury, was several months subsequent appointed a governor of the Federal Reserve Board, which position he held until 1936. F.D.R. had first become acquainted with him at Harvard, where he directed a government course that F.D.R. took during the first term of his third year. Hamlin's young guests aboard the *McDougal* were his wife, "Bertie," his daughter, Anna, and the third son of his superior. Fifteen years old at the time of this letter, Robert H. McAdoo enlisted in the Navy in 1917; after the war he became an investment banker. His mother was William Gibbs McAdoo's first wife, the former Sarah Fleming; his eminent father, whose second marriage was to Eleanor Randolph Wilson, the President's daughter, was a key figure in the Democratic Party for more than two decades, serving as Wilson's first Secretary of the Treasury and later in the Senate.

As F.D.R.'s letters contain very few comments about the people he knew only casually, it is interesting that both references to Leigh C. Palmer in the correspondence include complimentary adjectives. Formerly a naval aide to President Taft, in 1916 Palmer was promoted to the rank of rear admiral and made Chief of the Bureau of Navigation, a position described by Daniels in *The Wilson Era* as the "closest to the Secretary."

Seth Low, one-time president of Columbia University and mayor of New York, presided at the dedication exercises in his then capacity as head of the Chamber of Commerce of New York State. A prominent banker, August Belmont was the president of the Boston, Cape Cod, and New York Canal Company; as a candidate for the Democratic Presidential nomination in 1912, he was the object of Bryan's famous resolution asking for the convention to proclaim itself "opposed to the nomination of any candidate who is the representative of or under obligation to J. Pierpont Morgan, Thomas F. Ryan, August Belmont, or any other member of the privilege-hunting and favor-seeking class." William Barclay Parsons was chief engineer of the Cape Cod Canal; in 1916 he became chairman of the Chicago Transit Commission, having previously been chief engineer of New York's Rapid Transit Commission for ten years. Governor of Massachusetts for two years, David I. Walsh later represented his state in the Senate for more than a quarter of a century.

F.D.R.'s criticism of William Jennings Bryan ("W.J.B.") was due mainly to his youthful enthusiasm, and was only partly valid. Bryan had a better "conception of what a general European war means" than F.D.R. could perceive at this time, but because of his complete pacifism Bryan preferred not to recognize the connection between European wars and the welfare of the United States, a preference which later forced him to resign from Wilson's Cabinet. Bryan was a statesman of the first order and a champion of peace; and his efforts to secure worldwide approval of peace treaties providing for a "cooling time" prior to any declaration of war were overlooked by F.D.R. in the excitement of the moment. Although the letter would seem to indicate otherwise, Josephus Daniels' pacifistic views were far more reasonable than those of Bryan, as F.D.R. later came to realize. At the same time, of course, F.D.R.'s criticism is indicative of his well-known facility for being able to grasp swiftly the real implications of a crisis, and to act accordingly without hesitation.

Edward Bell had been transferred from his Washington post earlier in the year to London, where he served as Second Secretary of the American Embassy during the first four years of the war. Then vacationing in England with her mother and sister, Sara Delano was the youngest daughter of Warren Delano III; she later married Roland L. Redmond, senior partner of Carter, Ledyard & Milburn, and president of the Metropolitan Museum of Art. F.D.R.'s fears about the proximity of his other relatives to the war proved to be unwarranted, especially his concern for the safety of his half-brother, who arrived in Bar Harbor, Maine, instead of Plymouth, England. Unbeknown to F.D.R. at the time, the *Kronprinzessin Cecilie,* when approximately one thousand miles from Plymouth, had been ordered to return to America by its company's offices in Bremen. Realizing that the liner, which was weighted down with over thirteen million dollars in gold and silver, would make a prize capture for British or French warships, the German officials preferred to have it returned to the neutral waters of the United States rather than risk continuation of its passage to a German port. James Roosevelt Roosevelt's reason for being on the *Kronprinzessin Cecilie* was twofold: to recuperate abroad from his operation, and to enjoy a belated honeymoon with his second wife, the former Elizabeth R. Riley, whom he had married shortly before entering the hospital. After their unexpected return to the Atlantic coast, the newlyweds vacationed at Campobello.

Dearest E.

Alive and very well and keen about everything. *I* am *running* the real work, although Josephus is here! He is bewildered by it all, very sweet but very sad!

Not very hot so far.

Your devoted

F

The somewhat derogatory remarks about Josephus Daniels in the letters of this chapter are far more illustrative of the growth of F.D.R.'s personality than of Daniels' competence as a Secretary of the Navy. Because of the entirely different backgrounds and personalities which J.D. and F.D.R. brought to the Navy Department in 1913, it was almost inevitable that at first the younger man should find fault with his superior. Daniels' lack of concern for longstanding traditions of naval etiquette, his preference for prolonged deliberation at the expense of quick decisions, his shrewd, country-editor type of mind, and his mature understanding of Washington politics were characteristics that clashed with F.D.R.'s youthful and impetuous enthusiasm.

Daniels was never disturbed by his own very limited knowledge of navigation and of naval techniques, but always felt that his task was an administrative one in which a command of naval science was not a prerequisite. However, he considered naval etiquette to be an administrative question, a question of morale, and thus antagonized almost all the high-ranking officers by attempting to replace outworn naval traditions with a more democratic system. He housed officers and enlisted men in the same barracks, reformed the promotion system, allowed enlisted men to enter the Academy at Annapolis, changed the uniforms to provide greater comfort, and altered many other traditional

243

restrictions which were no longer applicable to a modern navy. At first F.D.R.'s fondness for the traditions of the Navy caused him to agree with the protesting officers, who also resented Daniels for his limited understanding of technical naval matters and for his insistence upon keeping final authority in civilian hands. As a result the admirals played up to F.D.R. and brought him all their complaints, thereby further encouraging his early criticism of Daniels; indeed, in order to obtain official approval of their requisitions and other papers, some of the officers even went so far as to hold the documents until J.D. left Washington, and then presented them to F.D.R. for his signature as Acting Secretary. On the other hand, the enthusiasm which made F.D.R. the favorite of the ranking officers did not produce the same results with Congressional committees. As Daniels achieved successes on Capitol Hill where F.D.R. continuously failed, the latter soon learned that there was a vast difference between getting something done in the Department and obtaining action by Congress.

The particular cause for F.D.R.'s criticism in the letters of this chapter was Daniels' pacifistic views regarding the crisis in Europe and his contemplative method of handling crucial situations. While F.D.R. wanted to take swift action, Daniels preferred a more cautious approach. In addition, F.D.R. had realized, before J.D. did, that war was not only bound to occur in Europe, but also that it was eventually destined to involve the United States. Although they agreed on the necessity for expanding the Navy, their differing opinions of the world situation often made F.D.R. quite contemptuous of "Mr. D." in the early years of their association.

However, as will be seen in subsequent correspondence, F.D.R. gradually changed his estimate of Josephus Daniels, coming to have a profound respect and a great affection for him. As he became less impetuous and more mature, F.D.R. began to realize that the editor from North Carolina was much more capable and shrewd than he had originally thought. His youthful remarks about Daniels should there-

fore be regarded as a temporary attitude, and it would
not be incorrect to credit the "Sec Nav" with having been
a major influence in F.D.R.'s life. An influence which
F.D.R. himself acknowledged when he resigned from the
Navy Department (see Chapter XI). As to how Daniels
himself regarded their early relationship, one finds in his
book, *The Wilson Era,* the following comment: "[F.D.R.]
was young then and made some mistakes. Upon reflection,
although I was older, I made mistakes too."

∽∽

WASHINGTON
[AUGUST 7, 1914]
FRIDAY

Dearest Babs—

Gee! But these are the strenuous days! I'm going home to
bed after three nights at the various Departments up till
nearly 3 a.m.

Now at last some order is coming out of chaos. I have been
serving on two boards appointed by the President and representing our Department as Mr. D. didn't seem anxious to do
it himself. The other Heads of Department, Garrison,
McAdoo and Sweet (Redfield being away) have served, but
Lansing has represented the State Department.

The first of these boards has had to do with neutrality,
and the Navy is now watching things along the coast—you
will read of the "Warrington" holding the Kronprinzessin
fast in Bar Harbor. Most of the reports of foreign cruisers
off the coast have really been of *my* destroyers!

The other board has been the Relief Board. We have got
the Tennessee off and the North Carolina goes tonight. *I*
suggested Breckinridge after declining myself to take charge.

It is too terrible about Mrs. Wilson. We knew on Wednesday afternoon that there was little hope and the end
came last night. The President has been truly wonderful,
but I dread a breakdown. The funeral is Monday at the

White House. I don't yet know whether Assistant Secretaries will be expected to go or not. The interment will be private, probably in Georgia.

It is hot again, but one does not think of heat these days. I feel hurt because the Emperor William has left the U. S. out —he has declared war against everybody else.

The Belgians are putting up a glorious and unexpected resistance. Still this *lack* of news is driving us all wild and we are not forgetting that the little that comes through is from the Franco-English side.

The Germans may be doing more than we suspect. Everybody here feels that this country as a whole sympathizes with the allies against Germany.

Loads of love to the chicks.

Your devoted F.

A vice-chancellor of New Jersey for nine years prior to Wilson's election, Secretary of War Lindley M. Garrison had entered the Cabinet because of his abilities as a jurist and because of his residence in Wilson's home state. Less progressive than his associates, he resigned in 1916 after a disagreement with Wilson over military policies. Edwin F. Sweet, previously a lawyer and member of Congress, served as Assistant Secretary of Commerce throughout the entire eight years of the Wilson Administration; his superior, William C. Redfield, retired from the Commerce post in Wilson's Cabinet in November, 1919. The latter was a champion of tariff reform, and spent the rest of his life writing about his experiences with the federal government, in addition to holding the presidency of the National Institute of the Social Sciences. Robert Lansing was at this time a counsellor for the State Department; in 1915 he succeeded Bryan as Secretary of State. He was a member of Wilson's five-man peace delegation to Paris in 1919, later recording his impressions of the peace conference in several highly illuminating books.

Guided by Wilson's strong neutrality proclamation issued on August 4th, which committed the United States to complete neutrality and made it a crime for anyone to be partial beyond the "free expression of opinion," the Navy undertook the task of "watching things along the coast," i.e., protecting the neutrality of American ports, preventing the shipment of munitions to any belligerent, and guarding against any other acts of an unfriendly nature. Thus the revenue cutter *Androscoggin* and destroyer *Warrington* were ordered to Bar Harbor as a precaution against any attempts by Germany's enemies to seize the precious cargo of the *Kronprinzessin Cecilie;* the ship's gold was subsequently placed in the vaults of the Subtreasury and the Guaranty Trust Company. Reports of "foreign cruisers off the coast" occupied many newspaper columns during the first weeks following the outbreak of war in Europe, but these same reports invariably quoted "an amateur wireless operator" as their source; later reports, however, admitted that in actuality the ships were U.S. destroyers, a fact which did not surprise F.D.R.

The neutrality board was organized to handle the task of transforming the principles of Wilson's proclamation into practical realities. The task proved to be extremely difficult: neutrality "in fact as well as in name" only applies to disinterested parties, and it soon became evident that the United States could not maintain a disinterested attitude toward the course of world events.

The purpose of the relief board was that of assisting Americans stranded in Europe by the war. To this end the armored cruisers mentioned were loaded with $2,500,000 in gold allocated by Congress to subsidize the credit of Americans abroad. The *Tennessee* also carried over $5,000,-000 in gold shipped by American banking houses for the relief of their patrons abroad. F.D.R.'s suggestion of Henry Breckinridge for the chairmanship was accepted, and the latter spent the next few months in Europe supervising the distribution of the funds and expediting the swift return of American citizens to the United States.

Ellen Louise Axson Wilson first met Woodrow Wilson

through her brother, Stockton Axson, a professor at Princeton, and thereafter she played an important part in her husband's career. A constructive critic in all matters, she was particularly helpful in writing speeches and planning political strategy. During her nineteen months' residency in the White House, Ellen Wilson was active in settlement-house work, arousing the Administration to alleviate Washington slum conditions. She died shortly after the marriage of her daughters, Eleanor and Jessie, to William G. McAdoo and Francis B. Sayre (now U.S. representative in the Trustee Council of the United Nations); a third daughter, Margaret, never married. Although Wilson did not have a breakdown to the extent feared by F.D.R., the *New York Times* on August 12, 1914, reported that at the burial services in Rome, Georgia, "the President's form was visibly broken by emotion and tears streamed down his cheeks."

F.D.R. was correct in thinking that "the Germans may be doing more than we suspect." Although temporarily set back by the stubborn resistance of the Belgian Army, within several weeks after the writing of this letter the German advance into France had reached the gates of Paris, only to be halted by the First Battle of the Marne during the week of September 6th. Thereafter the war in the West ceased as a conflict of movement, and over a line extending from the Alps to the Channel it settled into a trench warfare that lasted nearly four years. In the East, the Russian armies seeking to overrun East Prussia were badly defeated in the Battle of Tannenberg during the last week of August. Thus by the end of 1914 it was everywhere evident that the "war to end wars" was not going to be a swift one.

∽

WASHINGTON
AUGUST 10, 1914
MONDAY

Dearest Babs—

The heat has come again, and today is the third scorcher, but one doesn't have much time to think about it. There is little real news from Europe. The fact that though the city of Liege has been abandoned the forts still hold out is still the chief item. The Belgian defense has been as magnificent as unexpected. I hear on good authority that the French War College figured on only three days of delay to the German advance by the Belgian forces. Thank God England has gone in in earnest. Now she has landed 20,000 with 80,000 more to go on this first movement. This move and the Belgian resistance make it possible to threaten the German right. Their left has fallen back at Mulhausen before the French advance. But of course these are all purely preliminary moves and the main attack on both sides remains undisclosed.

I've been disappointed that England has been unable to force a naval action—of course it is the obvious course for Germany to hold her main fleet back and try to wear out the blockading enemy with torpedo and submarine attacks in foggy and night conditions.

My work has continued absorbing. Yesterday, however, after work at the office in the morning I got in a round of golf.

Caroline is here for a week with Billy Phillips, also Mrs. Hamlin here for a day looking for a house. Uncle Fred arrived this morning, was sworn in as a member and vice governor (Hamlin being governor) of the Federal Reserve Board. He lunched with me and returned to Chicago at 3. He gets back Thursday and comes to 1733 N.

I'm so glad to think of Miss Spring getting to you Wednesday and only wish Ely could get there before the 18th. *Please* on *receipt* of this wire me whether Miss S. thinks I had better come at once or can stay till the 17th. I still hope to come the 15th, and can of course come any day but I may be able to accomplish more by staying two days longer.

We have straightened out most of the preliminary fundamentals of neutrality both as to radio communication and as to ships and cargoes, and from now on probably concrete and individual cases only will arise.

Also there is little more to do about relief of Americans in Europe till we get further reports.

Tell Sister and James that I have loved their letters but that there is hardly time enough to eat!

Mrs. Wilson's funeral was today, only family and Cabinet and House and Senate Committees.

Loads of love. I long to be with you dearest these days and you are constantly in my thoughts.

Your devoted

F

The detailed plans for the arrival of F.D.R., Miss Spring, and Dr. Albert Ely (the Roosevelts' family physician from New York) at Campobello concern the birth of F.D.R.'s fourth child, Franklin D. Roosevelt, Jr. Although Miss Spring and F.D.R. were present for the occasion, Dr. Ely never came. The baby was born on August 17, 1914, and the attending doctor was an old friend from nearby Lubec, Dr. Bennett, who was also the first doctor to examine F.D.R. when he was stricken with infantile paralysis.

∽∽

Shortly before he left for Campobello, F.D.R. announced that he would enter the New York senatorial primaries. On August 14, 1914, the *Poughkeepsie Eagle* briefly carried his announcement as follows·

Franklin D. Roosevelt, of New York, Assistant Secretary of the Navy, today announced his candidacy for the Democratic nomination for the United States Senate. In his statement Mr. Roosevelt said that he believed the coming campaign in New York will determine whether the State "is to be found on the side of reactionary politics and politicians, or on the side of intelligent progress and honest administration of government."

Mr. Roosevelt has been in close touch with the President and other administration officials, and has been consulted on many New York political matters. It is not believed, however, that the President will announce himself in favor of his primary campaign.

As F.D.R.'s opponent in the primaries was the President's Ambassador to Germany, James W. Gerard, Wilson did not openly support F.D.R.'s candidacy, thereby substantiating the belief expressed by the *Eagle*.

Hence, in addition to handling the problems created by the war, F.D.R. spent the next six weeks campaigning for the senatorial nomination, a job made somewhat easier by Gerard's decision not to return from Germany to conduct his own campaign. The major issues of the primary contest centered around the question of Tammany support and the other controversies arising out of the marked difference between Wilson and the Old Guard Democrats. Assisted by Tammany pressure, opposition to F.D.R. arose from all quarters, and included some of his early supporters in Poughkeepsie. His opponents obscured their objections to his progressive record by making an issue out of F.D.R.'s age, which at this time was thirty-two. But even the Republican *Eagle* rebelled against the contention that F.D.R. was too young to serve in the United States Senate, and on August 24th expressed these views editorially:

. . . If it be true that the old guard Democrats of Poughkeepsie and Dutchess County, in conference assembled, have turned down the candidacy of Hon. Franklin D. Roosevelt for the United States Senate, it seems to the *Eagle* that the action was both unkind and discourteous—contrary to all the best principles of political etiquette. Mr. Roosevelt may be conceded to be young, but he is not too young to be eligible under the constitution to a seat in the United States Senate. In fact he has a considerable margin to his credit above the required thirty years. Besides that he has served with distinction in the Senate of the State of New York and is now the Assistant Secretary of the Navy, a position of great responsibility in which all authorities agree he is making good.

These things being true, if Secretary Roosevelt desires to enter the lists, in accordance with the provisions of the direct primary, and contest for the Democrat nomination for United States Senator we see no reason why he should not do so, and having done so all the rules of political etiquette require that the Democrats of his own district should stand by him. If some of them dislike him, or disapprove his record or his action in certain matters such as the election of the last United States Senator, they might at least sink their differences for the time being. We shall probably be accused of saying this about Secretary Roosevelt on the theory that he will be an easy man for Mr. Calder or Mr. Wadsworth to beat if nominated. To that we may add that we believe that the Republican nominee will surely be elected, but we do not believe Mr. Roosevelt can be any more easily beaten than William Church Osborne or William Randolph Hearst, both of whom are mentioned as probable candidates.

Astounded by the *Eagle's* editorials, the *Evening Enterprise* reprinted it that night with the following remarks:

Inasmuch as the politics of the Poughkeepsie *Eagle* are Republican, naturally the views of its editors and those of the *Enterprise* are often at variance, and therefore with especial pleasure does the *Enterprise* today find itself in harmonious accord with the admirable sentiments expressed by the *Eagle* this morning. In common with other people, the *Eagle* deplores the tendency among some members of the Democratic party to deny to Franklin D. Roosevelt the right to even run in the primaries of his party for the nomination for the United States Senate. The theory of the primary is equal opportunity to all candidates. Having brought upon themselves the rebuke of a disinterested newspaper, these Democrats should now see that the only sensible course is to accord to Mr. Roosevelt the same treatment which they will desire for all Democratic primary candidates. . . .

∞

WASHINGTON
[SEPTEMBER, 1914]
TUESDAY

Dearest Babs,

Just got here after a busy day in New York. I saw many people, attended my meeting, dined at the Racquet Club with Harry, Lang, Arthur Woods and Phil Carroll, then Harry, Lang and I went to the "Girl from Utah," a *fairly* good show only.

Now I am very sleepy, but must do much work today, dance and dine with the Phillips' and then on to the house warming and then another dose of the midnight train.

All goes well at the house.

Love to all the chicks and much for yourself.

Your devoted   F

The exact date of this letter cannot be definitely ascertained, but from the mention of political activities and the "Girl from Utah" it was probably written in September, 1914. The *New York Times* was even more critical of the Broadway musical than F.D.R., reviewing the opening on August 25, 1914, in no uncertain terms:

. . . the audiences that seek out a theatre in New York where a modern musical company is playing do not look for much more than two hours of fooling with an orchestral accompaniment, but even the least exacting might find the fooling in the "Girl from Utah" a trifle tedious and the music endowed with little more than a capacity to set the foot a-tapping were it not for the fact that, after all, it is just a nondescript jumble arranged for the purpose of setting off the talents of Donald Bryan, Julia Sanderson, and Joseph Cawthorn.

In addition to his law partners, F.D.R.'s other dinner companions included New York City's police commissioner and an old friend from Baltimore. F.D.R. had first met Arthur Woods at Groton, where the latter was a master from 1893 to 1909. In 1914 he received his appointment in the New York Police Department, where he made a notable reputation, resigning to enter the Army as a lieutenant colonel in 1918; in later years he was a trustee for numerous organizations, including the Rockefeller Foundation. A member of a prominent Baltimore family, Philip Carroll was two years ahead of F.D.R. at Harvard.

∽∽

My own dearest—

Safely back in Washington last night at 11 o'clock. I find the work enormous as Mr. D. is away and the campaign work needs lots of personal straightening out.

The trip down was a wonderful success. We stopped at York Harbor and saw Isabella and the children.

I will write again this evening but will let this go off quickly now. No word from Campo till Mama's wire this morning.

I so hope all goes well with my darling and the little babs. Kiss him for me and the three grown up chicks too.

I have given up Champlain and go to Buffalo instead. Plans not yet complete.

Your devoted

F

∽

WASHINGTON
[SEPTEMBER 10, 1914]
THURSDAY

Dearest Babs,

I have been at the grindstone fairly steadily since the hour I arrived at the office Tuesday night till 12 and last night till one. This afternoon I leave at 4 for New York, have a conference with the Mayor tonight, and leave in the morning for Buffalo, having given up Plattsburgh. I speak in Buffalo Friday night and spend Saturday and Sunday in West part of State then work East and end up in New York City the end of the next week.

Loads of love and kiss the little Babs.

Your devoted

F

New York's mayor at this time was John Purroy Mitchel, a lawyer and former Collector of the Port of New York; at the end of his term in 1917 he was commissioned a major in the aviation corps, and was killed in action six months later at the age of thirty-nine. As can be seen from these few letters written in September, F.D.R. conducted his senatorial campaign in the same vigorous manner as the previous ones, except that this time his travels had to include the entire state rather than just its 26th District.

∽∾

[SEPTEMBER 28, 1914]
MONDAY

Dearest Babbie,

A very restful day and so far a successful trip, but I hate much to be gone so long and wish you could be with me.

I was late getting to Buffalo so missed the train for Batavia, but got them to stop an express. A large luncheon of the Chamber of Commerce proved easy to talk to and afterwards I went to Bert Scatcherd's house until my train back to Buffalo at 5. He is the brother of Mrs. George Milburn.

The Saturn Club dinner was rather difficult as it has been their big annual spree and this year's drought changed its character. I was rather unsuccessful in trying to cheer them up and deliver a serious speech at one and the same time.

I spent the night with the Evan Hollisters and we reminisced over that famous day at Niagara when we saw the ice bridge break. They sent many messages to you. Yesterday I left Buffalo at 9:30, got to Binghamton at 2, and was entertained by the Fancher Hopkins' and addressed a crowded church-full in the evening.

Kiss the chicks. Thursday seems still very far off. I will wire on Wednesday.

Your devoted

John George Milburn, Jr., met his wife, the former Madeleine Scatcherd, while studying law at the Buffalo Law School. He started practicing law in his father's Buffalo firm, Rogers, Locke & Milburn, and came to New York with his father around the turn of the century when the latter joined the firm of Carter & Ledyard; in 1914 he was made a partner in Carter, Ledyard & Milburn, and retired in 1927. He was a brother of Devereux Milburn, the polo internationalist. A member of the class of 1897 at Harvard and one-time holder of the intercollegiate half-mile record, Evan Hollister was a well-known Buffalo lawyer, later serving as vice-president of the New York Bar Association; the "famous day at Niagara" occurred during F.D.R.'s first months in the State Senate. Fancher M. Hopkins was the president and treasurer of the Binghamton Cadillac Corporation; in addition, he handled the duties of Binghamton's postmaster for more than fifteen years.

∽∾

Although "successful," F.D.R.'s upstate speaking tour proved to be in vain: the day after writing this letter Gerard defeated him in the primaries, F.D.R. receiving less than half the total votes. He concluded a congratulatory cable to Gerard in Berlin with an offer to assist the Ambassador in his campaign; however, the offer contained one reservation: "Will make active campaign for you if you declare unalterable opposition to Murphy's leadership and all he stands for." In *The Wilson Era* Josephus Daniels observed that the defeat "hurt Roosevelt," while the local newspapers quoted F.D.R. as having "cheerily" remarked "never mind; we paved the way."

∽∾

WASHINGTON
[OCTOBER, 1914]
WEDNESDAY

Dearest Babs,

The enclosed is the truth and even if it gets me into trouble I am perfectly ready to stand by it. The country needs the truth about the Army and Navy instead of a lot of the soft mush about everlasting peace which so many statesmen are handing out to a gullible public.

All is well here. The Secretary left yesterday morning. I spent most of last evening with Mr. Milburn who came down to the meeting of the Bar Association. The servants have safely arrived.

Tomorrow I hope to play golf in the morning with John McIlhenny.

I do hope the little Babs progresses and that Nurse does too!

Lots of love and kisses.

F

As the enclosure mentioned was not preserved, the exact date of this letter cannot be fixed, but from the references to the arrival of the servants and to the improved health of "the little Babs" an approximate estimate would be October, 1914. Because of the new addition to the family A.E.R. had delayed her departure from Campobello until late in September, and then spent a recuperative month at Hyde Park, sending the servants to Washington just before moving there herself. This approximate date is further substantiated by a prepared statement F.D.R. issued to the press on Wednesday, October 21st, in which he outlined the numerous deficiencies of the Navy in order "to call attention to certain facts which have perhaps been misunderstood by some." In all likelihood this statement was "the enclosed" in this letter to A.E.R.

〰〰

WASHINGTON
[OCTOBER, 1914]
FRIDAY

Dearest Babs,

I shall not go to the Rhode Island meeting on Sunday but will go to Hyde Park, thank God, getting there Saturday night late if possible, otherwise Sunday morning. Did you see my article in the papers—they all gave it much and prominent space—also editorial comment today.

I dined last night with General Wood, Captain McCoy, Gerald Morgan and Basil Miles, most interesting. They seem to feel the allies will hold out.

Your devoted

F

The date of this letter is also uncertain, but the mention of "my article" suggests the possibility that it was written two days after the preceding letter. Editorial comment on the prepared statement referred to in the preceding footnote generally agreed that F.D.R. had explained the deficiencies of the Navy in "lucid" terms.

In 1914 Major General Leonard Wood ended four years of service as the Chief of Staff of the United States Army, and took on the responsibility for the organization and training of several divisions and numerous smaller units during the war; in 1921 he voluntarily resigned from the Army to accept an appointment as Governor General of the Philippine Islands. Major General Frank R. McCoy was a captain on the general staff of the Army in 1914, having previously served as an aide-de-camp to Wood in Cuba and the Philippines; also an aide-de-camp to T.R. during the latter's last two years in the White House, McCoy later became the A.E.F.'s Director General of Transportation. Gerald Morgan, a war correspondent during World War I, married F.D.R.'s childhood neighbor, friend, and playmate, Mary Newbold. F.D.R.'s fourth dinner partner, Basil Miles, was at this time working for the U.S. Chamber of Commerce, having formerly been a secretary of the embassies in Moscow and Berlin; he was attached to the State Department in charge of Russian affairs between 1917 and 1919, a period which was marked by the Russian Revolution and the inception of the U.S.S.R.

〜〜

Dearest Babs,

We had a packed and enthusiastic meeting here last night. Mr. Noone, candidate for Governor, and Congressman Stevens were the other speakers, and I want you to meet Stevens when you get to Washington. I am very much impressed by him.

The visit to Groton was well worth while. I breakfasted in Boston and got out to school at 10:30. Had a nice talk with Mrs. Peabody and the Rector, saw all the Masters, and Sheffield and Quentin, lunched with the school, took a train at 3:30 through cow paths to Nashua and then another to Concord.

Today I leave soon for Peterborough, stopping at several smaller places enroute, and tonight I hope to get down via auto or buggy to the line of the Fitchburg and board the 2 a.m. sleeper for Troy.

I will wire from Dunkirk (on Lake Erie) tomorrow night what time I get to Poughkeepsie Thursday morning.

A great deal of love and kiss the chicks.

Your devoted

F

The German naval toast has been "Zum Tag". The enclosed is strong.

F.D.R. spent a good many days of October, 1914, campaigning for the Congressional candidates on the Democratic ticket, which explains his presence at the Concord rally. Albert W. Noone, a wealthy woolen manufacturer, had won the Democratic nomination for governor after a prolonged battle with New Hampshire's party machine, while Congressman Raymond B. Stevens was at this time a candidate for United States Senator from New Hampshire. A Harvard graduate, the latter became a vice-chairman of the U.S. Shipping Board in 1917, and under F.D.R. was made a member of the Federal Trade Commission in 1933. Noone and Stevens, along with James W. Gerard, were defeated in the November elections, which almost halved the Democratic majority in Congress.

The first volume of F.D.R.'s letters, *Early Years,* should be consulted for a full account of the role that Groton's founder, the Reverend Endicott Peabody, played in his life. Even before his sons were old enough to attend the school, F.D.R. visited Groton whenever he was in the vicinity. William Sheffield Cowles, Jr., *(q.v.)* and Quentin Roosevelt were at this time in the fifth form at Groton, the latter standing second in his class. Quentin was Theodore Roosevelt's youngest child. He interrupted his education during his sophomore year at Harvard to enlist in the Canadian Aviation Corps; after the American entrance into the war he transferred to the U.S. Army, and lost his life in aerial combat in July, 1918.

The enclosed article about the German naval toast "to the day" has not been preserved, although in all probability it dealt with the war at sea, which at this time had already witnessed the sinking of five British warships by German submarines or mines.

∽∽

WASHINGTON
[DECEMBER 17, 1914]
THURSDAY

Dearest Mama—

Elliott is normal this morning so I see no reason why I should not come on Saturday night midnight, reaching the house at 7:45 a.m. Sunday, breakfasting and going up at 8:45. Also don't you think we could take Anna and James too? They would love it so and by coming back at 4 they could be in bed early enough.

The hearings before the Naval Committee are over— really great fun and not so much of a strain, as the members who tried to quizz me and put me in a hole did not know much about their subject and I was able not only to parry but to come back at them with thrusts that went home. Also I was able to get in my own views without particular embarrassment to the Secretary.

If I don't hear from you I shall carry out the Saturday night plan and expect a lovely day at Hyde Park with you and A. & J.

Always your affec
FDR

The strong statements concerning the plight of American military preparedness that emanated from all quarters, especially from the executive offices of the Navy Department, during the first months following the outbreak of war in Europe finally initiated long hearings on the subject. F.D.R.'s first significant encounter with a Congressional committee, which he found to be "really great fun," was reported on December 17, 1914, by the *New York Times* as follows:

The necessity for a large naval reserve and a definite and scientific estimate of the relative strength of the United States Navy were included in statements made today by Franklin D. Roosevelt, Assistant Secretary of the Navy, before the House Naval Committee.

As Mr. Roosevelt was beginning his statement Representative Hobson, who yesterday urged that Theodore Roosevelt, a relative, by the way, of the Assistant Secretary, be called to give his views on national defense and who had wired the ex-President to learn if he would consent to appear, showed to his fellow-committeemen a telegram he had received from Col. Roosevelt, as follows:

"Thanks for your telegram. I do not see what I can add, other than what I have again and again written, and do not believe I would serve any useful purpose by appearing. It does not seem to me that it would be well to take any public action in the matter. I would come if I could do any good, but I do not believe it would do any good."

Assistant Secretary Roosevelt was asked whether the United States stood second or third among the nations in naval strength. This question and others were asked by Representative Kelley of Michigan, representing Mr. Gardner of Massachusetts, who, although present, was not permitted to interrogate witnesses himself. Mr. Gardner had insisted that there should come from some authoritative source an estimate of the strength of our navy according to the Kretschmer formula. Assistant Secretary Roosevelt explained what the Kretschmer formula was.

"There are four factors," said he. "A certain ship is taken account of in tonnage, armor, gun power, steaming capacity and other elements, and she is rated as having 100 per cent of efficiency. Every other ship in the navy is given a percentage based on that standard.

"The General Board has been working out the efficiency and strength of our navy by the Kretschmer formula, modified in some particulars. We took the *Delaware* as the standard. She was estimated first as to her offensive power, gun fire, torpedoes, and all that. Then she was rated as to defensive efficiency—her armor, interior, construction and protection against submarines, also her size and buoyancy as affecting her cruising radius. The third estimate was as to her tactical ability, including her speed and efficiency in manoeuvers. The fourth estimate covered her strategical points, such as her endurance, her capacity for supplies, ammunition and fuel and her radius of action.

"In rating ships different values are given. In the battleship type offensive efficiency counts sixty points, defensive twenty-five, tactical efficiency ten, and strategical five points. In the battlecruiser type the offensive efficiency counts fifty, defensive twenty, tactical twenty, and strategical ten. In armored cruisers, offensive efficiency counts forty-five points, defensive twenty-five, tactical twenty, and strategical ten. In scouts offensive efficiency counts twenty-five points, defensive ten, tactical fifty, and strategical fifteen.

"On that formula the General Board has figured out a comparison between our navy and those of four countries which, for the sake of neutral propriety, I will not name. Their computations apply to armored ships only."

The Assistant Secretary gave the following list as showing

the relative standing in which, parenthetically, the nations included are indicated: First (England), 7768.05; second (Germany), 3818.70; third (United States), 3562.70; fourth (France), 2208.74.

Mr. Roosevelt said that he had no hesitancy in saying that the third navy was that of the United States, and that judged by other standards as well, it was his opinion that we stood third at this time. The comparison, he pointed out, did not include submarines, destroyers, scouts, or auxiliaries of any kind.

"Suppose you include all types?" was suggested.

"Well, then," replied the Assistant Secretary, "the comparison would be less favorable to the United States."

Mr. Roosevelt took up first the subject of the enlisted personnel of the navy, and said that in case of war the present force of 51,000 men would have to be very much increased, probably by 50,000 men. The available force from the present Naval Militia he put at 7,000. Several members expressed surprise at this low estimate. Mr. Roosevelt said it was safe to rely on no more than half of the enrolled strength.

Asked why the Naval Militia was not more attractive to young men, Mr. Roosevelt said he thought it was due to not having enough good vessels.

"I am firmly convinced," he added, "that there should be a large and well-drilled national naval reserve independent of the State Militia. We can get such a reserve, first, by keeping track of every man who goes out of the navy. Every ex-enlisted man willing to enter a national reserve and others who successfully undergo an examination as to fitness should be enrolled. Duty in the reserve should be made attractive."

Chairman Padgett said that a bill was under consideration to accomplish just what Mr. Roosevelt had proposed.

Mr. Roosevelt said those who desired to create a naval reserve were not agreed that service should be compulsory, but there should be a reserve of 25,000 ex-enlisted men, the number available now.

"Lacking such a reserve," he said, "we should have to train a large number of men in the emergency of war. It would take nine months to make an ordinary seaman of the average raw man. It would be rare to make a good gun pointer from raw material in a year."

Asked what sort of ships the Naval Reserve should have, Mr. Roosevelt said that a ship of light draught and with plenty of berths made the ideal reserve ship. He said the navy had no such ships available.

Discussing the conditions of the vessels in reserve, Mr. Roosevelt said the theory was that they could be sent to sea in twenty-four hours, but it was the average opinion of captains that they could not be made ready for battle in less than three months.

"A battleship in reserve could go to sea tomorrow," said Mr. Roosevelt, "but it would take three months to shake her down. Two-thirds of her crew would be new to the ship and would have to fit themselves to her. This would be true even if they had come from other ships."

"It is a necessity as a matter of economy that all our ships should not be in commission all the time," continued the Assistant Secretary. "No navy does that except that of one country."

Every member of the committee seemed intent to know what power it was that kept its entire navy always in commission. It was something unheard of.

"What country is that?" demanded several members in unison.

"Haiti," replied Mr. Roosevelt. "She has two gunboats and they are in commission all the year around."

"Do we lack officers or men that we cannot keep all our ships in commission?" was asked.

"We do not lack officers," was the reply, "and I have said that one additional full class of men from the Naval Academy would be a great help to us—say 125 more officers. Our enlisted men are of a high order of ability. They come up to a high standard of efficiency, and so we do not need so many officers."

Mr. Roosevelt gave a history of the methods followed in supplying the navy with coal. When he entered the department, he said, no advertisements for bids were published— there was a list of approved coals, so that there was no competition. All that had been changed. The bids last April were all at the uniform price of $2.90 a ton, and Secretary

Daniels had charged that there was a telegraphic combination among the bidders. In the June bids there was actual competition.

To questions as to unpreparedness of the navy, Mr. Roosevelt said we were less prepared than nations now at war, for they had the stimulus of war.

"From confidential reports," he added, "I am certain other nations have very greatly increased their submarine strength, a fact which Congress should consider in framing the Naval bill."

Questioned about the shortage of men in the navy, Mr. Roosevelt said:

"We are from 30,000 to 50,000 men short of the needs of the navy as laid down in the confidential war plans of the War College."

It was on this grave note that 1914, a year of many "history making days," ended for F.D.R.

VII

"... The Bullet May Bounce Back on Me..."

ASSISTANT SECRETARY OF THE NAVY

1915

F.D.R. SPENT the first few months of 1915 mainly engaged in fulfilling his duties as commissioner to the Panama-Pacific International Exposition. A.E.R. joined him on the journey to San Francisco, and in *This Is My Story* she recalls some of the amusing incidents that occurred during their trip, concluding with "we found ourselves immersed in the usual round of official engagements." The return trip was made via New Mexico and a visit with the Fergusons; A.E.R. notes in her book that the "visit had to be short and we hurried back to our children and our duties in Washington," where F.D.R.'s correspondence was resumed when A.E.R. departed for occasional visits to Hyde Park and a summer at Campobello.

∽

WASHINGTON
TUESDAY

Dearest Babs,

Hard at work and keen to see you and the little Babs to-morrow afternoon. I arrive about 4:30 and must leave again at 5:40 for Staten Island.

Last night I dined with Uncle Fred and Ralph Sanger at the Club. Today Sir C. Spring-Rice lunched with me. He is much better and his family arrive tomorrow. Von Bernstorff was at the next table, trying to hear what we were talking about! Springy and Von B. would kill each other if they had a chance!

I just *know* I shall do some awful unneutral thing before I get through!

Loads of love

F

The exact date of this letter is uncertain, but the reference to the arrival of Springy's family indicates that it was written early in 1915. The British Ambassador had returned to the United States from a brief trip to London for war conferences on August 22, 1914, while his wife remained in England to enlist as a Red Cross nurse; however, later letters of this chapter refer to Lady Spring-Rice as being a resident of Washington, and thus this letter is placed at this point in the correspondence.

Ralph Sanger (*vide supra*) was commissioned a captain in the infantry in 1917 and was killed in a flying accident a year later in France.

Count Johann Heinrich von Bernstorff came to Washington as the German Ambassador in 1909, and remained in this capacity until the severance of U.S.-German relations in 1917. A strong advocate of keeping the United States neutral, his position became a precarious one when the militarists gained complete control of Germany's wartime efforts in the autumn of 1916; after the war he excited much controversy in Germany by stating that war with the United States could have been avoided if Germany had pursued the proper policy. In *This Is My Story* A.E.R. notes that although von Bernstorff was conscious "of the general antagonism growing around him . . . he had a few warm friends and went his way serenely enough in Washington society," which explains his presence "at the next table."

The problem of doing "some awful unneutral thing" was further complicated on May 7, 1915, when the Cunard liner *Lusitania* was torpedoed and sunk off the southern coast of Ireland with the loss of 124 American lives. Although the German government answered Wilson's first note of protest with an expression of regret that Americans had perished, Germany refused to be held responsible for the loss on the grounds that the *Lusitania* was carried on the navy's reserve list and therefore was a British warship. Hence, beginning with the sinking of the *Lusitania*, the war at sea gradually brought an end to the strict neutrality of the United States; the "free expression of opinion" did not protect American lives on the high seas, and public opinion in the country was aroused to the point of not being satisfied with merely the right to express itself.

∽

WASHINGTON
THURSDAY

Dearest,

The Sec'y is back, but I have only seen him for a moment and he seems cheerful and still glad to see me! We have had no real talk however and won't till this afternoon.

I am lunching with the Spring-Rices today. Last night I dined at home alone and went to bed early. Tonight Uncle Fred and I dine alone at home.

It is warm and lovely here. Lots of correspondence to catch up on.

Love and kisses to you all.

Your devoted

F

This letter also lacks a specific date, but the intimation of friction between F.D.R. and Josephus Daniels suggests that it was written at about the same time as the next letter.

∽

Dearest Babs,

I arrived safely yesterday a.m., very sleepy after dinner, play and supper the night before and sitting up talking to George Marvin in the stateroom until 2 a.m.!

Quantities of things to do at the office and dinner at the Daniels', who were cordial (!) but no reference was made to the New York episodes.

I still hope to get the midnight Friday, but you needn't tell political friends at Hyde Park that I get there till Sunday!

All well, love to Mama and kiss the chicks.

Lyman comes this evening for 3 hours and dines with me.

Your devoted F

The year in which this letter was written is estimated from the date and day of the week; the only possible alternative to this correlation is 1920, but 1915 appears to be the more likely choice from the reference to F.D.R.'s strained relations with his superior. Although the exact nature of the "New York episodes" has been lost to history, it seems very probable that they were the result of some incident surrounding the reception given by New York City to the Atlantic Fleet in the middle of May, 1915. On this occasion the entire Fleet was anchored in the Hudson, the naval parade was reviewed by Wilson, many speeches were delivered, and in general the city went all-out in its welcome to the Fleet, which subsequently engaged in war games off the coast. The particular incident during this week in New York which caused the friction was possibly a disagreement over naval policies, as witness the speeches F.D.R. and J.D. delivered at the Navy League banquet. Where Daniels continuously praised the "forward-looking Sixty-third Congress," F.D.R. spoke of Congress in much less polite terms; the *Army and Navy Journal* of May 22,

1915, reported part of F.D.R.'s speech as follows: "Most of
our citizens don't know what national defense means. Our
extraordinary good fortune in our early wars has blinded
us to facts. Let us learn to trust to the judgment of the real
experts, the naval officers. Let us insist that Congress shall
carry out their recommendations." Commenting on the
Navy ceremonies in New York, the *Philadelphia Evening
Telegram* at least partially perceived the friction between
F.D.R. and J.D. when it editorialized on May 17, 1915, that
F.D.R. "seems not to be so self-satisfied as his Chief" in
regard to the accomplishments and expansion of the Navy.
That the friction emanated from the Fleet's reception in
New York is perhaps further substantiated by another remark Daniels made in his speech: after warning against the
optimists who do not see the necessity for continued naval
expansion, Daniels then berated the "depressing pessimists,
who are resolved not to see anything but the hole in the
doughnut,"—which, it will be recalled, was one of F.D.R.'s
favorite analogies, having been included in his notes for the
speech before the citizens of Pleasant Valley in 1910.

F.D.R.'s acquaintance with George D. Marvin began at
Groton, where the latter was a master from 1899 to 1902.
After serving with the United States Consulate in China and
the Embassy in Paris, he became an editorial writer for the
New York Press in 1911; in 1914 he was made Washington
editor of *World's Work,* in which capacity he occasionally
solicited F.D.R. for articles on naval preparedness. Like his
father, Frederic A. Delano, Lyman Delano, a first cousin
of F.D.R., was a prominent railroad official, and became
board chairman of the Atlantic Coast Line.

〰

WASHINGTON
[JUNE 10, 1915]
THURSDAY

Dearest Babs,

These are the hectic days all right! What d' y' think of
W. Jay B.? It's all too long to write about, but I can only say
I'm disgusted clear through. J.D. will *not* resign!

Last night I spoke at the R.R.Y.M.C.A. Banquet and tonight I address the Spanish War Veterans.

Tomorrow night praise God I shall take the midnight and arrive Poughkeepsie at 10:30 Saturday a.m. Please meet me; I must dash straight to vestry meeting.

All well and cool still. Love to the chicks.

Your devoted

F

William Jennings Bryan's unexpected resignation as Secretary of State on June 8, 1915, caused great commotion in Washington, as can be gathered from F.D.R.'s opening sentence. Contrary to an oft-expressed notion that he resigned in order to enter the 1916 contest for the Democratic Presidential nomination, Bryan tendered his resignation primarily because his pacifistic views toward the war in Europe had come to conflict with the foreign policy pursued by Wilson. The particular incident which occasioned his departure was Wilson's second note to Germany regarding the sinking of the *Lusitania*. Wilson demanded that Germany end its "ruthless" submarine campaign, and if this was not done, the United States would henceforth hold Germany strictly responsible. Bryan's conscience would not allow him to sign this note which he considered to be tantamount to a declaration of war, and he therefore resigned from the Cabinet (his wife later stated that he had signed the first note because it was only an announcement of the United States position on the submarine war). The controversial note was subsequently approved by the Cabinet and dispatched to Berlin; two weeks later, on June 23rd, Lansing succeeded Bryan. Many circles in Washington expected that Daniels, known to be more in sympathy with Bryan's views than any of the other Cabinet members, would also refuse to approve the note and tender his resignation. However, as he said in *The Wilson Era*, Daniels "did not believe the note would lead to war"; hence F.D.R. writes that "J.D. will *not* resign."

The banquet given by the Terminal Y.M.C.A. was in

celebration of its seventh anniversary. On June 11, 1915, the *Washington Herald* reported that F.D.R. urged more adequate preparedness for possible war in his address to the United Spanish War Veterans of the Admiral George Dewey Naval Camp, No. 7, but quoted only one brief excerpt from the speech: "It is better for us as a nation to feel that we are perfectly safe than it is for us to live in fear by reason of the fact that all the downstairs windows are unlocked and that the burglar and enemy may at any time enter."

∽∽

WASHINGTON
JULY 15, 1915
THURSDAY

Dearest Mama—

Hand is a bit out of practice, same as feet, but today the latter have carried me from my room to the porch, albeit somewhat groggily.

Sunday we leave at 9 a.m. getting to N.Y. at 1:57, and it will be very delightful to see you again and to "ride" in that comfortable old Cadillac to the E. 23 St. landing. You must come on board with us and see us installed and we shall not get under weigh until 3 o'clock.

I do so love the kimono and it is a real beauty. I have received visitors in it two days and at last I have something respectable and not bulky to take on visits to the country houses of my rich friends!

Later—The Dolphin will not arrive 23 St. until four o'clock so we will all go to the house from the train and spend 2 hours there.

The Spring-Rices, Willerts, Mrs. Lane, W. Phillips etc. have all been here this afternoon.

All goes well and it will be so nice to see you in N.Y. Sunday.

Always your affec.
F.D.R.

The "Willerts" became close friends of the Roosevelts during the war years in Washington, where Sir Arthur Willert served from 1910 to 1920 as the chief correspondent of the London *Times* in the United States. In 1921 he joined the British Foreign Office and subsequently became head of its News Department, also serving as a member of the United Kingdom delegations to four international post-war conferences and to meetings of the League of Nations.

The former Ann Wintermute, "Mrs. Lane" was the wife of Wilson's distinguished Secretary of the Interior, Franklin K. Lane. Described by Daniels in *The Wilson Era* as having "a genius for friendship" and everywhere known as a "forceful and progressive" man, Lane started as a lawyer in San Francisco and rose to political prominence mainly as a result of his work on the Hetch-Hetchy power and water project (which brought water into San Francisco from the Sierras). His work impressed T.R. and in 1906 he was appointed to the Interstate Commerce Commission, where he made a notable record in fighting important cases through to Supreme Court decisions. He became chairman of the I.C.C. in 1913, but resigned shortly thereafter to accept the appointment in Wilson's Cabinet. In the Interior Department he established many new precedents, and was especially instrumental in the mobilization of U.S. resources for war in 1917. Along with the Millers (*vide infra*) and Phillips' the Lanes joined the Roosevelts in the small coterie that met informally every few weeks during the Wilson Administration.   .

This letter was written shortly before F.D.R. departed for a recuperative vacation at Campobello. Late in the evening of July 1, 1915, he had been stricken with acute appendicitis and rushed to the Washington Naval Hospital, where his appendix was removed. While it took A.E.R. several days to make the trip from Campobello, Sara Roosevelt arrived at his bedside the next day, bringing with her a new kimono which F.D.R. found worthy of wear when visiting his "rich friends."

Although F.D.R. was teasing his mother by grading his

friends according to their wealth, this remark is indicative
of a growing discord between F.D.R. and his mother over
the values of their common heritage. It was inevitable that
F.D.R. should come to reject the *noblesse oblige* concepts
that characterized his mother's generation, and it was only
the strong ties of affection that reduced this clash to a simple
family disagreement understood and accepted by both parties. The basic area of disagreement concerned the end to
which their affluent Hudson Valley heritage was to be put:
for Sara Roosevelt her heritage constituted an ultimate in
life whereby she could set "a great example" for others,
while F.D.R. envisioned the same heritage as merely a mode,
the physical way one lived, and considered that apart from
this mode there existed a whole set of standards which
guided daily actions and long-range ideas. These variances,
which it should be emphasized again were calmly accepted
as an aspect of Roosevelt family life, are clearly revealed in
a letter written by F.D.R.'s mother on October 14, 1917.
Hence, although the particular issue which guided Sara
Roosevelt's pen is unknown, and although chronologically
out of order, it seems appropriate to include this letter at
this point in the correspondence.

NEW YORK

OCTOBER 14, 1917

SUNDAY

Dearest Franklin and Dearest Eleanor,

I feel *too* badly that I let you go without your pearl
collar, *too* stupid of me! Do wear the velvet one Aunt Doe
gave you! I think of you almost in New York and I am sorry
to feel that Franklin *is* tired and that my views are not his,
but perhaps dear Franklin you may on second thoughts or
third thoughts see that I am not so far wrong. The foolish
old saying "noblesse oblige" is good and "honneur oblige"
possibly expresses it better for most of us. One can be
democratic as one likes, but if we love our own, and if we
love our neighbor, we owe a great example, and my constant
feeling is that through neglect or laziness I am not doing my

part toward those around me. After I got home, I sat in the library for nearly an hour reading, and as I put down my book and left the delightful room and the two fine portraits, I thought: after all, would it not be better just to spend all one has at once in this time of suffering and need, and not think of the future; for with the *trend* to "shirt sleeves," and the ideas of what men should do in always being all things to all men and striving to give up the old fashioned traditions of family life, simple home pleasures and refinements, and the traditions some of us love best, of what use is it to *keep up* things, to hold on to dignity and all I stood up for this evening. Do not say that I *misunderstood*, I understand perfectly, but I cannot believe that my precious Franklin really feels as he expressed himself. Well, I hope that while I live I may keep my "old fashioned" theories and that *at least* in my own family I may continue to feel that *home* is the best and happiest place and that my son and daughter and their children will live in peace and keep from the tarnish which seems to affect so many. Mrs. Newbold's theory that children are "always just like their parents" is pretty true, as *example* is what really counts.

When I *talk* I find I usually arouse opposition, which seems odd, but is perhaps my own fault, and tends to lower my opinion of myself, which is doubtless salutary. I doubt if you will have time dear Franklin to read this, and if you do, it may not please you. My love to our fine little James, and to you two dear ones.

Devotedly

MAMA

∽

WASHINGTON·
[SUMMER, 1915]
WEDNESDAY

Dearest Babs,

Martha is much troubled because two large pieces of stuff have come and they are not similar in design to the stuff she already had and she thinks you want the curtains to be all the same kind. If she is right and you want the stuff returned wire me on receipt of this and I will bring it on with me when I come. I *may* leave tomorrow Friday on the midnight as this will give me all day in New York and an opportunity to go to Brooks to replace stolen clothes. However, I will telegraph you if I can get off.

I am just back from Annapolis. It has poured all day so the water drill, dress parade etc. had to be called off, and I spent most of the time going over the very unfortunate and disagreeable cases of "gouging" i.e., cheating at exams, and made my report to the Sec'y on my return an hour ago.

Last night I dined with Helen Morton, only the Willy Eustis's there.

I enclose under separate cover a bunch of mail! All well. Love to Cozs. Susie and Henry.

I miss you so much.

Your devoted

F.

As "the disagreeable cases of 'gouging'" at Annapolis spanned the entire summer of 1915, this letter cannot be given a more specific date. The trial of seven midshipmen for stealing examination papers and cribbing on exams began on July 13th, and the cases continued for the two following months, with accusations of guilt being freely tossed in every direction, from Daniels on down. Stating that the defense was attempting to use political pressure to prevent the punishment of the guilty midshipmen, Rear Admiral William F. Fullam, the superintendent of the Naval Academy, recommended their dismissal. Resenting this indictment, the defense charged Fullam and the other officers of the board with "prejudice, unfairness, and lack of capacity," and claimed that Fullam in his turn had brought politics to bear to prevent a fair hearing of the cases; that he had conducted a newspaper campaign to prejudice the general public, as well as Josephus Daniels.

Exactly what F.D.R.'s "report to the Secretary" contained is not revealed by his naval papers in the Franklin D. Roosevelt Library.

Helen Morton was the daughter of Levi P. Morton, one-time governor of New York and Vice-President of the United States in the Harrison Administration. The Mortons were Dutchess County friends of the Roosevelts, living at nearby Rhinebeck. Another daughter, Edith, married William C. Eustis, who graduated from Harvard in 1887 and lived in Washington; during the war years F.D.R. frequently spent evenings with the Eustis family.

∽∽

ON TRAIN TO NEW YORK
[AUGUST 14, 1915]
SATURDAY

Dearest Babs,

It is hotter 'n hinges but all goes well. We got in on time in Boston, Walter Bradley met me, and we all went to South Station for breakfast, which Mama took with Miss McLean, while I sat with W. B. at another table and talked submarines! Miss McL. left us at New London and now I am talking to Ma.

I hope to see Mr. Koen for a few minutes and then take the 3:35 up to Steen Valetje.

I just hate to be going back—it was such a wonderful three weeks in spite of not being able to do everything. But I know you will have everything go well and it is really a comfort to know definitely that "certain person" will not torment much longer! Kiss the chicks and tell Elliott not to forget about his promise to learn to tell time.

Your devoted
F.

A member of the class of 1905, Walter H. Bradley was a close friend of F.D.R. at Harvard; at this writing he was a manufacturer in Boston. Terence A. Koen was a partner with Francis L. V. Hoppin in the New York architectural firm of Hoppin and Koen. F.D.R.'s desire to confer with this gentleman came in connection with the proposed plans to enlarge the Hyde Park home. In the autumn of 1915 these plans were carried out: the south and north wings were added and outside alterations were made on the front. These were the last major structural changes to be made on the house.

Located a few miles north of Hyde Park at Barrytown, Steen Valetje was an ancestral home of the Delano family. The estate had come to F.D.R.'s great-uncle, Franklin Hughes Delano, as a gift from the latter's father-in-law, William B. Astor, and passed in turn to Warren Delano III. A.E.R. recalls that during F.D.R.'s recuperative three weeks at Campobello (which had ended just prior to this letter), he had a nurse whom he did not like, hence the reference to "that certain person."

∽

WASHINGTON
AUGUST 16, [1915]
MONDAY

Dearest Babbie—

I am here again at the house and everything is as if I had never left it. Millie and Francis greeted me this morning, also Prior, who had been advanced to Clark's place. I found Mr. Daniels at the office at 9:30 and soon after Howe & McCarthy both arrived from the Federal.

Things in the Department seem to be fairly quiet, though there is of course an immense amount of work to be caught up with and the estimates must be taken up in a day or so. Mr. D. leaves on Friday for two weeks.

Today I lunched with Mr. Lansing and Andrew Peters and Frank Polk. I think there is a possibility that the latter may be offered the position of Counselor of the State Department. It would be awfully nice if he gets it.

There is little in the way of news. I saw Colville Barclay, who is in charge. Springy returns the end of the week—Adolph Miller is back, though I have not seen him. Tonight

I am dining quietly at home and it is pretty hot, and the heat and dampness combined have given me lumbago or rheumatism between the shoulders. Otherwise I am very fit.

Kiss all the chicks. I am too sorry not to be able to be there for the Babs first anniversary. Many kisses too for you dearest and do take very, very good care of yourself.

Your ever devoted

"Millie and Francis" were servants who took care of F.D.R. and the 1733 N Street house during the summers when A.E.R. was at Campobello, just as they had taken care of W. Sheffield Cowles in earlier years during the absences of A.E.R.'s Auntie Bye. Prior and Clark were messengers in the Navy Department; in 1933 F.D.R. transferred Samuel Prior to a clerkship in the White House.

A graduate of Georgetown University Law School, Charles H. McCarthy had been the private secretary to the Assistant Secretary of the Navy since T.R.'s Administration. He left this post during the war years to join the Emergency Fleet Corporation, but returned to F.D.R. in 1920 to become manager of his Vice-Presidential headquarters.

As previously noted, Frank Polk received his appointment in the State Department shortly after F.D.R. wrote this letter. Sir Colville Barclay's varied career in the foreign service found him at this time a counsellor to the British Embassy in Washington, a post he held until 1918 when he became Minister Plenipotentiary to the United States. Adolph C. Miller and his wife, the former Mary Sprague, were the fourth couple in the group with which F.D.R. and A.E.R. were particularly intimate during the early years in Washington. An old friend of the Lanes from California, Adolph Miller was Flood Professor of Economics at the University of California from 1902 until 1913, when he became Lane's assistant in the Interior Department; in 1914 he was made a member of the Federal Reserve Board, a position he held for twenty-two years.

[AUGUST 18, 1915]
Dearest Babs—

Yesterday afternoon I moved out to the McIlhenny's for three nights as it is vastly cooler at Chevy Chase. I return to 1733 on Friday as J. D. leaves that day and I want to be in close touch in case anything blows up. Yours has just come telling of A & J's upsets and I am glad they seem to be slight.

If everything is quiet I shall run down late Saturday afternoon to the Eustis's at Leesburg and come back Monday morning.

Today is much cooler and I am well though back is still rheumatic.

Too bad your fog still continues. Loads of love and kiss the chicks.

Your devoted F.

Springy spent an hour with me this afternoon and seems very worried over the financial situation, though the cotton troubles seem to be clearing.

Chevy Chase is located on the outskirts of the District of Columbia, in Maryland; F.D.R. frequently played golf at the Chevy Chase Club.

The worries of Sir Cecil Spring-Rice over the "financial situation" concerned the drain on Allied financial resources caused by the war. Later in the month an Anglo-French Commission was established to arrange for a billion dollar credit in the United States that would help finance the war effort of the Allies. Although not an economist, Springy was directly involved in the negotiations because of the diplomatic aspects of the loan, particularly the problem created by Russia's demand for a share in the fund and the opposition of numerous American bankers to the extension of aid to Russia. The difficulties between the Anglo-French Commission and the American bankers for a long time appeared to be irreconcilable and required Springy's close attention. American terms were finally accepted, and in October, 1915, a 5% five-year loan for $500,000,000 was signed (the proceeds to be divided equally between the British and the French). Repaid on maturity in 1920, this loan marked the first time in the history of the British Empire that it borrowed extensively from a foreign nation.

The "clearing" of Springy's "cotton troubles" was in effect the end of a significant phase of United States neutrality during the first three years of the war. The first months of the war in Europe had created a serious controversy between the United States and Great Britain over the British blockade of Germany. Determined to starve its enemy into submission, the British established an illegal blockade at the outset of the war and continuously added to the list of contraband goods which had previously been free from seizure and which were destined for delivery to civilian populations rather than armed forces. Ignoring the rules of blockade, which required interception of contraband to take place near enemy ports, the British also stopped neutral vessels on the high seas and brought them to British ports for examination, often detaining them for a prolonged period; in addition, the British seized merchantmen bound for neutral countries on the ground that the cargoes were destined for Germany. These practices greatly injured American commerce abroad and brought forth lively protests against Britain's action by both official and unofficial circles in the United States, where it was also suspected that Britain was not half so much interested in starving Germany's civilian population and thereby reducing German military power as it was in preventing American goods from being placed on legitimate European markets. Bryan's protests to England failed to end these practices for two reasons: the American Ambassador at London, Walter Hines Page, convinced that an Allied victory was absolutely essential to the welfare of the United States, did not pursue strict neutrality and refused to press the protests upon the British Foreign Minister, Sir Edward Grey; secondly, the Germans claimed that their submarine attacks were launched because of the illegal blockade, and it was not long before public opinion became more concerned about American lives than American goods.

At the time of Springy's "cotton troubles" cotton had not yet been declared contraband, the British authorities claiming that by not so declaring they were favoring American cotton exporters, as otherwise cotton could be seized without payment. The "troubles" arose from the detainment of numerous shipments of American cotton in British ports, an embarrassing position for the English representative in Washington, who was personally liked by everyone he met. Cotton was placed on the contraband list three days after this letter was written, and eventual U.S. acceptance of this act marked the beginning of a new phase of American neutrality; namely, a policy of benevolent neutrality in regard to the British blockade.

∽

WASHINGTON
[AUGUST 19, 1915]
THURSDAY

Dearest Babs—

Just a dozen lines in haste to tell you all is well with me and lumbago is nearly gone but a slight cold in the head seems to be replacing it!

I am still at the McI's and go to Camp Winthrop tomorrow for the afternoon in the "Sylph." Then Saturday p.m. I go to Leesburg.

It is still cool today after a drop in temperature yesterday of 40°!

Loads of love.   Your devoted   F

∽

WASHINGTON
[AUGUST 21, 1915]
SATURDAY

Dearest Babs—

It has been a joy to get your letters and to know that all goes well and that the little Babs enjoyed his birthday. I feel terribly that I could not have been there and I miss you all so much. Yesterday we had a most successful trip on the "Sylph" to Indian Head or rather Camp Winthrop, the rifle range just below there. General Barnett, Capt. McKean, Capt. Harlee and John McIlhenny went with me and we spent an hour going over the range and watching the rifle and machine gun drill. Then we drove over the reservation and had supper with Capt. & Mrs. Price and returned in the cool of the evening. We passed the Dolphin, J. D. and family on board, on the way up and exchanged felicitations by signal. He is to be gone till September 4 unless things break loose in the meantime. I have seen Lansing today and am worried about the Arabic and I think the President will really act as soon as we can get the facts. But it seems very hard to wait until Germany tells us her version and I personally doubt if I should be quite so polite.

This p.m. I leave at 5 p.m. to go to the Eustis's at Leesburg and will be in touch with Washington by telephone.

Your devoted

F

Major General George Barnett was Commandant of the Marine Corps from 1914 to 1920. At this time assigned to duty in Washington with the Navy Department, Joseph S. McKean was later promoted to rear admiral and made Assistant Chief of Operations. On the occasion of F.D.R.'s trip to Indian Head, Marine Captain William C. Harlee was the Navy Department's assistant director of gunnery exercises and engineering performances, a job he held for six years; the author of numerous military manuals, he retired in 1935 and was promoted to brigadier general seven years later. Charles F. B. Price was at this time commandant of the Marine Corps rifle range at Winthrop, Md.; during World War II he served as commanding general of the Samoan Defense Force.

Just as it was generally accepted that the German government had agreed to no further repetitions of the *Lusitania* disaster, the White Star liner *Arabic* was sunk by a German submarine off the southern coast of Ireland. Forty-four people, including two Americans, lost their lives, and the event astounded both the United States public and the government; public opinion, led by the press all over the country, was aroused to call for severance of relations with Germany. After the American Ambassador presented the United States protests, which claimed that the *Arabic* was unarmed, that it carried no war munitions, and that it had not attempted to ram the German submarine, it became evident that the German government was in a mood for explanations and not defiance. As noted in the next letter, on August 24th the Germans asked for a delay in order to assemble the facts of the case. On September 1, 1915, Ambassador von Bernstorff gave Lansing a note in which it was pointed out that Germany had agreed, prior to the *Arabic* disaster and as a result of the *Lusitania* protests, to renounce sinkings of unarmed liners without warning. In effect, therefore, Germany admitted the sinking was wrong, claiming that it must have been accomplished by an error on the part of the submarine commander and not as a result of government orders. This note greatly pacified the aroused American public.

Several weeks later, after conferring with the submarine commander who had sunk the *Arabic,* Germany presented another reply which stated that Commander Schneider had surfaced and was about to sink a British ship, the *Dunsley,* when he saw the *Arabic* approaching with the apparent intention of ramming his submarine. He was forced to submerge and fire a torpedo out of self-protection; therefore, the Germans argued, indemnity for American lives lost was not payable. However, on October 5, 1915, Germany retreated from this position and von Bernstorff notified Lansing that Germany would indemnify the United States for the two American lives lost.

Dearest Babs—

I did not write yesterday as every second of the day was more than occupied. I lunched with Henry Breckinridge to meet Senhor Cardoso, the Brazilian Minister to Mexico, who has handled our affairs there in excellent manner since O'Shaughnessy left. Last night I attended the official dinner by the Lansings to the same gentleman and it was a delight to see a Secretary of State who is a gentleman and knows how to treat Ambassadors and Ministers from other civilized nations.

The Sunday at Leesburg was delightful, no one else at the Eustis's and we did nothing except for a motor drive to the Henry Fairfax's for tea. They live in the old President Monroe house and keep it up excellently. I am a little at sea in regard to next Sunday and even about when I can get away. But this p.m. the request of Germany for a wait until they can get facts makes the situation less strained.

It is warmer today but still not bad. I lunched with Lansing and am dining with the Willerts, with whom I shall talk about Campobello.

Kiss the chicks. Loads of love and a longing to get back to you all.

Your devoted

F

As a result of the seizure of Vera Cruz in April, 1914, Huerta severed diplomatic relations between Mexico and the United States; and on April 22nd of that year the charge d'affaires of the American Embassy, Nelson O'Shaughnessy, was given his passports. Between O'Shaughnessy's departure and the resumption of formal relations in December, 1915, the archives of the Embassy in Mexico were in the charge of the Brazilian Minister to Mexico, Senor Cardoso.

F.D.R.'s remarks about Lansing are less praise of the new Secretary of State than they are the results of his embittered feelings toward Bryan, who was at this time urging strict neutrality in a speaking tour of the country as a "private citizen." These comments are another example of the impatient attitude F.D.R. had toward anyone who did not hold views similar to his own during this period of his life.

∞

Dearest Babs—

I had a nice dinner at the Willerts last night, George Marvin and Walter Howe there too. The W's fear they cannot get off at all.

Tonight I go with Springy and Lady S.R. to dine on the Raleigh Roof. It is still not hot and I am in great good luck.

I love the description of Elliott's spanking!

My plans are vague and I may not get up till the 6th but will know in a few days. I want to take in a visit to Plattsburg if possible.

Loads of love and kiss the chicks. Tell James I will not forget his tool box.

Your devoted
F.

A member of the class of 1901 at Yale, Walter B. Howe lived in Washington and was a social acquaintance of F.D.R. The "description of Elliott's spanking" is contained in A.E.R.'s letter of August 22, 1915, as follows: "Elliott bit James hard the other day and I explained that no matter whose fault it was boys didn't bite. His feelings were much hurt and he made such a long upper lip he looked like a rabbit, but at the end of the spanking (with my slipper) he said 'It didn't hurt very much mother!'"

∞

Dearest Mama—

I have been so abominably rushed since getting back here from Leesburg on Monday morning that I have had no time to send you a line and I had hoped to be able definitely to tell you about plans. But things are too uncertain, though I *hope* to be able to leave here Saturday noon and go to Tuxedo in time for dinner.

I should like to go to Hyde Park the next day, Sunday, right after lunch, see the house, and take the Federal back to Washington. I cannot decide definitely until Friday as I must judge by the situation in Haiti as well as by the Arabic matter, though the latter looks less alarming since Bernstorff's more conciliatory attitude. If I cannot go, I shall leave here the following Saturday the 4th, take in Hyde Park that p.m., leave for Plattsburg that night and thence to Campobello, getting there Tuesday by train or destroyer.

I had a delightful Sunday at the Eustis's and went all over the President Monroe house now owned by the Henry Fairfax's.

Monday I lunched with Henry Breckinridge to meet Senhor Cardoso, the Brazilian minister to Mexico, who has so well handled our interests there since O'Shaughnessy left. That evening I dined with the Lansings to meet the same dusky gentleman and his duskier wife and daughter. Last night I dined with the Arthur Willerts, he the London Times correspondent. Tonight I dine with Springy and Lady S.R., she having just come down for a few days.

I am well and the heat has not been severe at any time.

Love to Aunt K and the little girls. If I go to Tuxedo my godkind must promise not to kick me in the stomach.

Always your affec

F.D.R.

The "situation in Haiti" at this time was approaching the climax of direct American intervention and military control of the island republic. On July 26, 1915, two hundred political prisoners were massacred at Port au Prince by order of a follower of the Haitian president, Vilbrun Guillaume Sam, who was at this time seeking refuge in the French legation. A party of the mourners at the funeral of the victims entered the legation, dragged the president out, and handed him over to the mob. Two hours after his death U.S. Marines landed at Port au Prince and subsequently restored order; on September 23rd, the commanding U.S. officer, Rear Admiral William B. Caperton (later a full admiral and commander-in-chief of the Pacific Fleet), declared martial law.

∽

WASHINGTON
AUGUST 28, 1915
SATURDAY

My own Dearest

I have been so worried about the baby's strange upset and as there was no letter from you this morning I wired to get the latest news. Just now on coming back from the Department I find your welcome telegram and letter and am greatly relieved. I suppose it must have been stomach and the poor lamb must have had a most uncomfortable time.

Last night I dined quietly at home. In the afternoon I had a long talk with the President about various routine matters, but especially about the Council of National Defense which I am trying to get started. It seems that I can accomplish little just now as the President does not want to "rattle the sword" while Germany seems anxious to meet us more than half way, but he was interested and will I think really take it up soon.

I decided to stay "on the job" over Sunday as Haiti is not a calm spot and there might be important dispatches from Admiral Caperton.

Tonight I dine with the Lanes who are just back.

Sunday—We were all alone last night and both the Lanes in fine form. They sent you much love. I have been cleaning house all morning and afternoon and my desk looks like a desert! I think I have got rid of 100 lbs. of papers etc., it would rejoice your heart! Now I am going down to the Club to dine, and at 8:30 Arthur Woods comes from N. Y. and will stay with [me] at 1733 for a couple of days.

As to plans, I hope to leave Friday midnight, spend Saturday at Hyde Park, get to Plattsburg Sunday morning, leave there Sunday night for Boston and get to you Tuesday morning. I have written Liv. of change of plans and I have not heard whether he will come up with me or come later and go after moose on the 15th.

Kiss the chicks and I do hope you didn't get too tired over the babs upset and that you are taking very good care of yourself. It rained hard all yesterday, is clear today and so far no heat. I am in luck!

Your devoted

F.

F.D.R. was a year ahead of his time with the idea of a Council of National Defense, as Congress did not authorize this organization until August, 1916, and Wilson did not announce his appointments to the Council's advisory commission until the following October. When finally established, the Council not only proved to be an effective "rattling of the sword," but also a significant step toward preparedness for war. Accorded large powers, including the placement of "orders for war material directly with any source of supply," the Council was organized in such a way as to "render possible in time of need the immediate concentration and utilization of the resources of the nation." While the Council itself was comprised of six members of the Cabinet (with the Secretary of War as chairman), its non-partisan advisory commission was made up of leaders in industry, labor, and science, and thus the nation's resources were harnessed for a united war effort.

〰

Dearest Mama

I did not dare leave Washington this Sunday, as the situation in Haiti is ticklish and also I am expecting Arthur Woods this afternoon to stay with me. I so wish I could have got up to Tuxedo but the distance is so great I could not have kept in touch by telephone. Now I hope to leave on the Friday midnight for N.Y., see Hoppin and Koen Sat. a.m., take the 11:15 up to Hyde Park and leave that night about 9 for Plattsburg where I will spend Sunday and go on to Campobello via Boston. Do join me in N.Y. or else meet me by motor at Fishkill?

Last night I dined at the Lanes, no one else there. On Friday I had a long talk with the President, chiefly on Haiti and the new Council of National Defense which I hope to put through *in time*.

It has poured here all yesterday and last night but is clear now and still very cool.

Tomorrow night I am giving a dinner for the Spring-Rices, Lanes and Andrew Peters at the Dower House down the river. I do hope it will be a nice evening.

Today I have been cleaning house at 1733 N. and the sitting room looks spotless and very empty as I shovelled several tons of old papers into the waste paper basket.

Love to Aunt Kassie and the girls. By staying in Washington I have [at] least escaped their brutal treatment! Slap my godchild on the bare wrist—yes I said wrist—and tell her that though I grieve I love her still.

Always your affec

F.D.R.

Dearest Babs—

I have given up Plattsburg, as they practically close there on Saturday and I will therefore go to Hyde Park Saturday night, spend the night at Aunt Ellen's, go up to the house early Sunday a.m., leave at 11:20, and catch the 3 o'clock from New York to Boston, so I will be with you on Monday morning. For this I am very thankful as it gives me one more day with you.

By the way I think I forgot to mention that I deposited the $300 in the Nat. Met. Bank a week ago.

I have been really busy every second during the past few days, with quantities of troubles from unexpected sources, chiefly labor. Today I sprang an announcement of the National Naval Reserve, and trust J. D. will like it! It is of the utmost importance and I have failed for a year to get him to take any action, though he has never objected to it. Now I have gone ahead and pulled the trigger myself. I suppose the bullet may bounce back on me, but it is not revolutionary nor alarmist and is just common sense. Last night I dined at the Lanes, Adolph Miller and Andrew Peters also there. Tonight I am at home and tomorrow at A. Miller's to meet Mr. Peters and the Lanes!

Yesterday came a letter from the Secretary telling me to send Fullam to Puget Sound, and Eberle to the Academy— awful row in the service which believe Fullam is being punished for the midshipmen's troubles. Mrs. F. called me on the telephone and raised the roof. I am *very* sorry, but orders is orders! Thank James and Anna for their letters—it is good to hear from them "au naturel" without having their letters dictated by an "institutrice"!

The party at the Dower House was a great success. Arthur Woods left the next day and he *may* come up on the 12th to go after moose with us. The Drs. at the Naval Hospital said it would do me good.

Loads of love to you all and I can hardly wait for Monday to arrive.

Your devoted
F.

Ever since his entrance into the Navy Department the establishment of a naval reserve had been one of F.D.R.'s pet projects; it was an important aspect of his frequently reiterated demand for increased preparedness through greater naval strength. However, the "trigger" he pulled was not so dangerous as his letter would seem to indicate, for his announcement did not officially establish the National Naval Reserve, but merely outlined "the plans of the Navy Department" for its organization. This announcement was carried by the *New York Times* on September 3, 1915, as follows:

1. RETIRED OFFICERS AND FORMER ENLISTED MEN OF THE NAVY.—The organization of retired officers already exists, and a step toward securing a reserve of former enlisted men was taken last Spring by Congress. While the results of this examination have not been large during the two months it has been in effect—115 men have enrolled up to Sept. 1, 1915—it is believed that an increasing number of men whose enlistments expire will take advantage of the opportunity offered, and it is already having the effect of increasing the number of re-enlistments.

2. OTHER BRANCHES OF THE FEDERAL AND STATE GOVERNMENTS.—This means the co-ordination of the Coast Guard, i.e., the Reserve Cutter and Life Saving Services, the Lighthouse Service, the Coast Survey, the State nautical training schools, harbor police, etc., in such manner as to fit readily into the naval service at short notice. Little legislation is necessary to accomplish this, and the organization of the work is already under way.

3. VOLUNTEER CIVILIANS.—It is believed that the reserve of personnel should total 50,000 officers and men. What is particularly desired is not merely numbers, but individuals

who will be capable of doing the highly specialized service which exists in modern navies. For instance, in wartime the navy would need the services of possibly 1,000 additional radio operators; it would require local pilots for inside waters, helmsmen, gunners, gasoline motor experts, signal men, etc., besides, of course, first-class seamen. The department has had many letters asking whether an opportunity could be given to individuals to take courses of training in these specialties, and if the general plan is approved, it is hoped that next summer courses of instruction can be started, using reserve or other available ships, and giving to those who desire it three or four weeks of training so that they could become of some definite use if called upon.

Any amateur operator, any yachtsman or motorboat enthusiast, in fact, any citizen with intelligence and application could learn how to fit into some place where he might be needed. Possibly some form of certificate could be given at the close of instruction, showing exactly what services the individual is capable of performing, the holder to be under no further obligation than to keep the Navy Department, at stated periods, informed of his address.

4. MERCHANT VESSELS, YACHTS, AND POWER BOATS.—It is obvious that the navy would need a great number of auxiliary ships as patrol boats. Steps have already been taken to organize the merchant shipping, but much remains to be done. Modern naval operations have shown the great need of a large number of small and fast yachts and motor boats of a type as seaworthy as possible. The department has already endeavored to cooperate with the power squadrons, and it will be possible, in connection with the training of volunteer civilians, to list all suitable vessels and to train their crews in the duties that could be expected. This training would be given in conjunction with the use of naval vessels in the summer time, and would be in charge of regular officers.

As will be seen in Chapter VIII, this plan became a reality nine months later.

The transfer of Fullam from Annapolis marked the end of the prolonged trial of the cheating cases at the Academy. Earlier, on August 16th, two of the seven midshipmen were dismissed from the service, and as five men were acquitted, Fullam subsequently requested his own transfer (evidently unbeknown to "Mrs. F.") on the grounds that the failure to uphold his recommendations would make it impossible for him to maintain discipline. After Fullam received his new assignment to command the Pacific Reserve Fleet, almost a nominal command, it was charged that his transfer was the result of resentment on the part of politicians who were interested in the midshipmen whose dismissal Fullam had recommended; Daniels' reply to this charge was a simple one: "rot." Fullam's successor, Rear Admiral Edward W. Eberle (at this time a captain and Commandant of the Washington Navy Yard), is described by Daniels in *The Wilson Era* as "one of the finest Naval officers that ever commanded a fleet."

∽∽

WASHINGTON
[SEPTEMBER 2, 1915]
THURSDAY

Dearest Mama—

I am too sorry I shall miss you but there seemed no way for me to leave here even for a night. Mr. Daniels will be here for a few hours tomorrow and goes on to Raleigh for Sat. and Sunday, returning Monday. So I can leave on Saturday afternoon; I have given up the Plattsburg trip as the camp practically ends Saturday, and I shall try to take in the 2nd encampment on my way back from Campobello. I shall get to N.Y. at 5:55 and take the 6:36 up river getting to Poughkeepsie at 8:59. I shall spend the night at Aunt Ellen's and am writing her. On Sunday morning I will go up to the house at 9 and take the 11:10 back to N.Y., thence the 3 p.m. to Boston and thence the 10 p.m. to Campo.

Therefore will you write or telegraph Butler—if he is back —to meet me Poughkeepsie Sat. night at 8:59? If I don't hear from you I will know it is all right.

I am having a hectic lot of work and will get off by the

skin of my teeth if nothing blows up in the meantime. Last night I dined with the Lanes, and tomorrow with Adolph Miller.

It is still most delightfully cool and so much so that one has to wear a waistcoat—think of this for Washington at the time of year.

So many thanks for the book. I shall read it on the train.

The baby seems to have had quite an upset with a high temperature, but is recovered and waiting for good weather to go out again.

By the way *what* have H. & K. told you about the Library? Do please not let any contract till I have a chance to see the offer and to go into details of construction, as I have several "thoughts" and there is much to be decided about shelves etc.

A great deal of love.

Your affec. son

F.D.R.

The contemplated visit to Plattsburg, N.Y., was in connection with F.D.R.'s work on the creation of a National Naval Reserve. Under the direction of Major General Leonard Wood, on August 10, 1915, the Army had established a summer military camp at Plattsburg organized along the same lines that F.D.R. proposed for the training of civilians in a naval reserve. Indeed, in an article entitled *The Naval Plattsburg* that F.D.R. published in *Outlook* on June 28, 1916, he admitted that in planning a naval training cruise for civilians during the summer of 1916 the Navy Department "has taken a leaf out of the note-book of the army. . . ."

William A. Plog's account book *(vide supra)* shows that Westley Butler came to work for Sara Roosevelt as a coachman in September, 1909. Visitors to the F.D.R. National Historic Site know "the Library" as the large living room that comprises the ground floor of the south wing.

∾∾

Dearest Babs—

After telling you that I had nothing in particular "on" for this week I got back three hours late yesterday morning or rather noon to find delegations of workmen, College Presidents, ornery politicians and weeping females waiting for me. Result was I went home exhausted at 7:30 to find Robert Neeser at the house, I having forgotten entirely that he was coming to spend the night! Hence I talked about every Naval engagement from Salamis to Falkland Isles with him up to 1 a.m.! Tonight he dines with me at Club and leaves on midnight, so I hope to get an hour or two of sleep tonight.

Tomorrow the Inventors come in force, but I am dodging the trip to Mt. Vernon. Most of these worthies are like Henry Ford, who until he saw a chance for publicity free of charge, thought a submarine was something to eat!

Loads of love and I hope James' tummy is better.

Your devoted and harassed

FDR

Robert W. Neeser was a naval historian who frequently came to F.D.R. for information to be included in his many articles and books on the Navy; in 1917 he was made assistant to the American naval attache in Paris. As can be gathered from this letter, F.D.R. was never particularly disturbed by any sleep he lost in exchange for a scholarly discussion of naval history.

The criticism of Henry Ford was partially stimulated by the latter's condemnation of preparedness and his charge that the Navy League was supported by munition manufacturers. Several weeks prior to this letter Ford's avid pacifism had led him to announce that he was setting aside one million dollars to combat preparedness in the

United States and other neutral countries, an announcement which doubtless irked F.D.R. Hoping to bring about a conference of the belligerents that would get the soldiers "out of the trenches by Christmas," Ford in December, 1915, chartered the steamer *Oscar II* and with a party of pacifists sailed for Europe. However, the celebrated peace delegation could nowhere obtain official recognition, dissension over the principles of peace arose within the party, and Ford returned to the U.S. with his mission a complete failure.

∽∾

This little birthday gift is the first earnest of Hubby's efforts as an author—and he hopes you will use at least a little part for something really and truly your own, and not all for household linen or baby's didies.

Exactly what were the literary "efforts" referred to in this brief note to A.E.R. on her thirty-first birthday cannot be determined. At this time F.D.R. was writing numerous articles on naval preparedness and other related subjects, and which of these provided the "first earnest" is open to speculation. Among the possibilities are a series of articles for the Newspaper Enterprise Association, *The Cost of the United States Navy* in the September issue of *The Economic World,* and *The Future of the Submarine* in the October 15, 1915, issue of the *North American Review.*

∽∾

Dearest Mama—

I haven't heard a word about the library estimates and wonder why they have been so long—of course before making any award it will be absolutely necessary to make one or two small changes in the details shown on the last plans.

I spoke to Frank Hoppin about these, but do not for a moment think they are in and it is vital that I should make sure.

I am a little in doubt as to whether you want me to write the Lamonts about the elevator, or to wait till they write me. They did this last year and I paid something like $60 or $70 for a new wire rope. I imagine they will do so again if they do anything more to the elevator.

Eleanor says to tell you that there is a case of chicken pox in James' class so he is home for a few days; also that the children's umbrellas have been discovered, though they seem to me somewhat inadequate in size and if anyone wants to give Anna and James a Xmas stocking present, umbrellas would be most useful!

Please tell Aunt Annie I much appreciate the splendid way she is keeping me in touch with the Newburgh political situation. It is really a great help and I will write her in a few days to give her the news from this end, though there is nothing definite yet about the Postmastership.

All is well here, and though it is a vile day, we went to church this morning. Last night the dinner at the Japanese Embassy was most interesting. It was the official dinner to the Administration in honor of the Coronation of the Emperor and we got there as I happen to be Acting Sec'y just now. Mr. Daniels has had awfully hard luck in losing his printing establishment by fire twice in two years and he is a good deal at Raleigh these days.

Much love. I hope to get off for New Brunswick Saturday.

Your affec son   FDR

Thomas W. Lamont, who with his family rented the 65th Street house during F.D.R.'s years in the Navy Department, was a member of J. P. Morgan & Co. for more than thirty years, becoming chairman of the board in 1943. "Aunt Annie" (Mrs. Frederic Delano Hitch) lived most of her life at Algonac and was a great benefactress of the town of Newburgh; she frequently wrote F.D.R. on the status of Hudson River politics. Although Yoshihito became the 124th Emperor of Japan on his father's death in 1912, because of a period of national mourning he did not officially ascend the throne until the formal coronation on November 10, 1915. His regime, proclaimed "Taisho" (Righteousness), was marked by his own ill health; in 1921 his son, Hirohito, was named Prince Regent, and rose to the throne five years later when his father died. The entire plant and building of *The News and Observer* was destroyed by the second fire on November 6th, but, operating temporarily from the plant of *The Raleigh Times,* Daniels had his paper on the stands "as usual" the following morning.

~~~

MEMORANDUM

OFFICE OF THE ASSISTANT SECRETARY

Secnav—

1. I beg to report

(a) That I have just signed a requisition (with 4 copies attached) calling for purchase of 8 carpet tacks.

Astnav.

Why this wanton extravagance? I am sure that two would suffice.

J.D.

This penciled memorandum to Josephus Daniels, and the latter's curt reply, was found among F.D.R.'s personal correspondence and is an appropriate conclusion to this chapter. In spite of his mockery of government red tape, F.D.R. overlooked one of the most important entries on all official forms: the date. Nevertheless, it is significant that by the close of 1915 the friction between F.D.R. and J.D. was gradually being replaced by an intimacy that can be detected in this note.

~~~

VIII

"...I Hope to God I Don't Grow Reactionary with Advancing Years..."

ASSISTANT SECRETARY OF THE NAVY

1916

THE YEAR 1916 was a Presidential election year in the United States, and the ensuing political battle was fought largely in the arena erected by the war in Europe. The internal program originally sponsored by the "New Freedom" was not nearly so important as the question of continued American neutrality. The political issues were clouded by those of neutrality and preparedness, and vice versa. Yet, amidst the vast confusion caused by the entanglement of American politics with a general European war, one fact stood out as clear as the fact of the election itself: the contradiction between America's efforts both to avoid entering the war and to protect her interests and honor was rapidly looming larger and larger. The country's approach to the point where this contradiction had to be resolved was perhaps best illustrated in successive statements by Woodrow Wilson. In August, 1914, he had urged strict neutrality "in thought as well as in act"; five months later he had advised against preparedness; but in January, 1916, during the course of a speaking tour of the Middle West, Wilson repeatedly recommended that military preparedness be undertaken throughout the country "without losing a day." Although he continued his efforts to bring about a cessation of the conflict abroad, as the person upon whom the burden of the contradiction between "honor" and neutrality largely resided, Wilson soon came to realize the hopelessness of strict abstinence from the affairs of Europe.

∞

For F.D.R., the swift movement of events toward climax was temporarily subordinated to the problem of curing a throat infection which had gotten the better of him during the early weeks of 1916. In February he spent two weeks on the boardwalk at Atlantic City, from where he wrote the next letter to his wife.

HOTEL CHELSEA
ATLANTIC CITY, N. J.
[FEBRUARY 21, 1916]
MONDAY

Dearest Babs—

This "health resort" is purgatory, the place of departed spirits. It is a heavenly day and my throat is, if anything, a little redder, but what I fail to understand is how anybody can stay here more than 24 hours without wanting to murder somebody. Except for throat I feel better as to strength.

I shall return Friday if I can stick it out that long.

Yours has just come and I do hope FDR Jr.'s cold is not bad. Kiss all the chicks and tell them home is best, and take very good care of yourself.

Your affectionate but mad clear through

F.

In *This Is My Story* A.E.R. recalls F.D.R.'s abbreviated trip to "purgatory": "He was supposed to take a two-week vacation, but the inactivity was more than he could bear, and in a week he was back at work again." Shortly after F.D.R.'s return, on March 13, 1916, John Aspinwall Roosevelt was born and the Roosevelt family now numbered seven.

∽

Eight days later the world situation was further complicated by a German torpedo which sank the French passenger steamer *Sussex* without warning; two Americans were included in the casualty list of eighty. Wilson then sent Germany an ultimatum which demanded that the imperial government either change and greatly modify its "present methods of submarine warfare against passenger and freight-carrying vessels," or the U.S. would sever diplomatic relations. This note brought forth a promise from Germany that merchantmen would not be sunk "without warning and without saving human lives." The *"Sussex* pledge" brought momentary peace to U.S.-German relations, and it also proved an important political tool for the Democratic Party, which convened in St. Louis on June 15th to renominate Wilson and Marshall. The party boasted that in the *Sussex* pledge Wilson had won a recognition of American rights. "He kept us out of war" became the Democratic campaign slogan.

Hoping that the Republicans would nominate T.R., the Progressive Party convened in the same city (Chicago) and on the same day (June 10th) as the G.O.P. But the Progressives were destined to be disappointed, for their absence from Republican circles left the party under the control of the conservatives, men who were not disposed to forgive T.R. for leading the revolt which made possible Wilson's election in 1912. Hence, while the Progressive convention again nominated T.R., Charles Evans Hughes, former governor of New York and at the time associate justice of the Supreme Court, was chosen the Republican standard-bearer. T.R., aware of his minority position and convinced that a third candidate would again indirectly help Wilson, declined the Progressive nomination (thereby killing the movement) and gave his support to Hughes's candidacy.

Amid political maneuverings and diplomatic dealings Congress went ahead with legislation designed to increase military and economic preparedness. Several conflicting plans calling for the expansion of the Army were brought forth, and Congress spent the spring of 1916 wrangling over the passage of the Army bill. Secretary of War Garrison supported a plan to enlarge the Regular Army greatly, and when Wilson refused to support him, he resigned and was succeeded by Newton D. Baker, the efficient mayor of Cleveland. On June 3rd, Congress finally reached a legislative decision and passed the National Defense Act. In addition to authorizing the enlargement of the Regular Army to a quarter-million men in five years, the Defense Act also called for the "federalization" of the National Guard, for the establishment of civilian training camps, and for the construction of a $20,000,000 munitions plant.

After subsidizing Army preparedness, Congress turned its attention to increasing American naval strength. The preparation of an appropriate Naval bill thus became the main occupation of the Navy Department during. the summer of 1916. This task was not an easy one; once the differences within the Department were straightened out, it was necessary to contend with various obstacles to Congressional approval. As can be gathered from the remaining letters of this chapter, F.D.R. did not entirely agree with all the provisions proposed by either Josephus Daniels or Congress, but at the same time he was pleased to see the actuality of steps toward preparedness.

Such, then, was the world and national scene as F.D.R. returned to Washington after a short visit with his family at Campobello, and commenced his correspondence for the summer of 1916.

Dearest Babs,

All is well, except for an accumulation of about 3½ feet of mail! The Sec'y is still busy with the Naval Bill and I am trying though I fear in vain to eliminate a number of fool features in it and to get into it a few more really constructive items. The Mexican situation is going through one of its periodically peaceful revivals, but the pendulum will swing back to intervention in a week or a month or a year. I don't care much which as it is sure to come and at least Army and Navy are gaining by every hour's delay.

I am dining quietly at home and going to bed early. I lunched with Lathrop, whose contest comes up in Committee next week. He looks badly, but Helen is all right again as are the children.

The infantile paralysis in N. Y. and vicinity is appalling. *Please* kill all the flies I left. I think it really important. Tomorrow I golf with J.A. McI. and dine with Warren out in the country at the Howards.

I miss you all so much. It was *such* a short visit. Loads of love and kiss the chicks.

Your devoted

F

Lathrop Brown's "contest" was a seesaw affair that lasted for nearly two years. It began when he ran for reelection to Congress from New York's First District in 1914. According to the first unofficial returns on election day, he received one more vote than his Republican opponent, Frederick B. Hicks; the next unofficial count gave Hicks a majority of fifteen votes; and thereafter the case traveled from court to court over a period of thirteen months, with each side claiming that the votes had been tabulated improperly. Brown won the fight in the State Supreme Court and

Appellate Division, but lost in the Court of Appeals. This latter court decided in December, 1915, that Hicks was the winner by ten votes, and for the remainder of Hicks's term Brown unsuccessfully attempted to carry the contest to the floor of Congress, an attempt referred to by F.D.R. in this letter.

The infantile epidemic of 1916 was a very severe one, particularly during the summer in upstate New York, and F.D.R.'s fears for the health of his children were those of parents all along the eastern seaboard.

When asked about the meaning of "all the flies I left," A.E.R. recalled that "there was a window at Campo looking out on the water that trapped flies. They settled there by the thousands and we used to spend large amounts of time swatting them. He is probably referring to the fact that he spent quite a lot of time swatting flies, and to kill the rest." George Howard and his family were social acquaintances whom F.D.R. had met in Washington.

∾

WASHINGTON
[JULY 10, 1916]
MONDAY

Dearest Babs,

There isn't any news of interest down here and a summer which I had expected to be full of excitement and action is turning out rather tame. The heat however is with us at last. Saturday afternoon I golfed, then dined at the George Howards', taking out Warren and Leland Harrison. Yesterday I golfed both morning and afternoon spending the whole day at Chevy Chase. We (about 10 of us) had planned to dine out at Lock Tavern but a driving rain prevented and it continues to shower today.

I am too sorry about the Half Moon's accident, it must have been quite a hard crash and I do hope you weren't worried.

I saw M. de Laboulaye today. They are well and at Chevy

Chase about two blocks to the *left* of the circle as you go out. I thought he looked better. I shall dine there soon.

The Navy bill is put off in the Senate for a few days and J.D. leaves tomorrow to spend three days in North Carolina so I shall be alone.

Kiss the chicks and take very good care of yourself, dearest. I long so to be with you and this bachelor life isn't what it's cracked up to be even though I dine Tuesday with A. Legare, Wednesday with F. Polk, and Thursday with H. Fletcher!

Your devoted

F

Leland Harrison, several years behind F.D.R. at Harvard, was a career diplomat at this time assigned to Washington on special duty; formerly attached to the U.S. Embassies in Tokyo, Peking, and London, he was counselor to the Embassy in Paris during the peace conferences in 1919.

A.E.R.'s letter of July 8, 1916, describes the *Half Moon* accident as follows: "There was a strong breeze this a.m. and I went to Eastport at 10:30 taking Blanche, A. & J. and Elliott. We went over fast with the wind but alas! we did not get back so successfully. We really had quite an accident and carried away the bowsprit, owing to the fact that the Captain didn't realize the strength of the tide. He anchored too near the St. Croix and she dragged, then he only had her under the mainsail and jib and when he tried to get off we went straight into the wharf before he could get her to turn. I am sorry for the Captain, he is so upset and I hope I have done what Mama would have me do in telling him to get what must be done, done at the pool, doing all he can himself. James was the only child who seemed scared and he asked me if we were going to sink!"

Lefebvre de Laboulaye was the Second Secretary of the French Embassy in Washington. He and his wife, Marie, became close friends of the Roosevelts during the early years in the capital; in *This Is My Story* A.E.R. writes of

Mme. de Laboulaye as "one of the finest characters it has ever been my good fortune to know." Lt. Commander Alex B. Legare, who graduated in the class of 1883 at Annapolis, was at this time attached to the Office of Naval Intelligence. Henry Fletcher was in the diplomatic service.

∾

HYDE PARK, N. Y.
[JULY 16, 1916]
SUNDAY

Dearest Babs—

I have been very remiss about writing and telegraphed you today that all is well. The heat in Washington was so fierce all of last week that it just about got my goat. It was in the upper 90's for five days and the nights were the kind that meant baths at 2 a.m. During the day the office itself got so baked that the fans did little good and when I got off in the afternoons I spent the hours until midnight driving the car around the country. It was a real comfort to have the car and Warren, Lathrop (who was there two days), Fletcher, Harrison and others were also appreciative of it. Friday evening I sweltered at the 14th of July dinner at the Jusserands'. They all sent you much love and wished you could have been there. The Springy's, Laboulayes, de Penas, Duc and Duchesse of Richelieu, Barclay, Martin, Brambilla, etc., and the Haveniths.

It was otherwise a dull week enlivened only by the loss of the Hector, everyone on board saved I am thankful to say.

Yesterday I got here at 10:30, rode in the a.m. and the trip to the Ashokan Dam was interesting but I was so exhausted I almost went to sleep all the way back.

Today it is warm, only about 86 so I shall know what to expect tomorrow! I spend the night at Tuxedo, go to Philadelphia in the a.m., attend a Civilian Cruise luncheon, spend afternoon at Navy Yard and go back to Washington at 6 p.m.

I will know this week when I can get off. If I have to attend the Saratoga Conference August 4th, I will go to Campo the 25th, getting there 26th. That would be fine. I just hate to think of not seeing you for another two weeks. Kiss the chicks. I will write them this week.

Your devoted

F

From the time they arrived at the French Embassy in February, 1903, Jean Adrian Jusserand and his wife, the former Eliza Richards of Paris, were colorful figures in Washington. The Ambassador was also justly famous as a literary critic and historian, his *Literary History of the English People* being a standard work. Dr. Carlos M. de Pena and Emmanuel Havenith were at this time the Uruguayan and Belgian ministers to the United States. Unlike the other guests at M. Jusserand's Bastille Day dinner, the Duc and Duchesse de Richelieu held no official position in Washington. "Barclay" was the aforementioned Colville Barclay, while "Martin" was probably Commander Antonin Martin, at this time naval attache to the French Embassy. A counselor in the Italian Embassy, Giuseppe Brambilla was the husband of Julia Meyer, daughter of Daniels' predecessor in the Navy Department, George von L. Meyer.

The *Hector,* a large naval collier, was carrying sixty marines to Santo Domingo when it was caught in a hurricane sixty miles off Charleston; blown aground off Cape Romain, it was destroyed by the heavy sea after six hours of heroic rescue work which succeeded in saving all on board with injury to only four men.

COMMITTEE ON APPROPRIATIONS

House of Representatives

WASHINGTON

[JULY 19, 1916]

WEDNESDAY

Dearest Babs,

I am up here at the Capitol spending most of the day trying to get appropriations past Congressman Fitzgerald and Uncle Joe Cannon and will probably be at it again tomorrow. It is not cheerful work with the temperature at 94°!

I had quite a hectic three days. Sunday Mama and I left Hyde Park at 4:30, motored to Tuxedo where we spent the night. Aunts Kassie, Annie and Dora and the two girls made it so lively that Aunt Annie didn't go to sleep after dinner. I smashed my front tooth as a little incident of the evening! Monday at eight, Mama, Sallie and I motored to New York stopping at Dr. Dailey's, who was out of town, made an appointment for the next day and then I went to Philadelphia, lunched with Mr. Alex van Rensselaer and others interested in the Navy Cruise, went to the Navy Yard with Admiral Grant and Capt. Russell, made complete inspection, reviewed the 200 civilian rookies, had supper with them in the Marine Barracks and returned to New York getting to 47 at 10 p.m.

Yesterday I got to Dailey's at 8:45, and in less than two hours he had put on a new tooth, filled a cavity and dismissed me until November! It is a beautiful tooth, more artistic than the last and only shows what a dentist can do when he too is anxious to get away to the country!

I caught the 11:08 to Washington getting to Department in time to sign mail, clean up my desk and have Gardner Bradley to dine with me at the Club.

I shall probably stick here pretty close this week, including Saturday and Sunday, as the Sec'y goes away for three days and I want to get off the 27th arriving Campo the 28th if possible.

I am too sorry little Babs has been upset but as nothing further has come from you since your Sunday letter, I suppose he is getting his tummy straightened out again. Also I am glad the calomel seems to have worked at last on James. It is very delightful for the chicks to have friends with a pony!

Caroline is here with William, though I have not seen her yet. Tonight I dine with the Laboulayes.

Loads of love and kiss the chicks. I wish I could see Franklin and Henry playing together.

Your devoted
F.

Representatives John Joseph Fitzgerald (D.) and Joseph G. Cannon (R.) were members of the Committee on Appropriations; the former was chairman at this time; the latter, always known as "Uncle Joe," had been speaker—and dictator—of the House for a decade prior to Wilson's election.

As F.D.R. announced that "Philadelphia will get a dry dock over a thousand feet in length and as wide or wider than the Panama Canal," the Philadelphia newspapers made much of his inspection of the two hundred naval volunteers in training at the city's Navy Yard; his supper with the "civilian rookies," for example, was reported as "possibly the most democratic proceeding ever enacted in any military post of the Government—at a bare board table and on a wooden bench sat the second highest officer of the United States Navy eating from heavy chinaware such as is used by privates in the service." Alexander van Rensselaer was chairman of the Philadelphia Committee of the Association of Naval Volunteers, while Rear Admiral Albert W. Grant was at this time in command of the Atlantic Fleet's

,submarine force; Captain Robert Lee Russell was the commandant of the Philadelphia Navy Yard.

Two years ahead of F.D.R. at Harvard, Joseph Gardner Bradley was a well-known coal operator. He later held the presidencies of the National Coal Association and the American Mining Congress. Young Franklin's playmate was Henry Parish Roosevelt, A.E.R.'s nephew and the eldest son of Hall Roosevelt.

∽∽

COMMITTEE ON APPROPRIATIONS
House of Representatives

WASHINGTON
[JULY 19, 1916]
WEDNESDAY

Dearest Mama,

I am sitting up here waiting for the House Committee to give us a hearing on additional clerical and drafting force for the Department and it looks as if I'll be here all day.

Yesterday was a complete success and you ought to see my new mouth! The night before I got back from Philadelphia at ten-thirty, had a comfy night at 47 and was on the dot of nine at Dailey's office. He removed remains of old tip, put on a new one, a beauty and much more artistic than its predecessor, filled a tooth and let me go at 10:45! I commandeered a taxi, got my bag, caught the 11:08 to Washington, got to Department in time to sign mail, clean up three days work, and then Gardner Bradley dined with me at the Club! I am not to go back to Dailey till after Election Day! Therefore I won't come on this Sunday, especially as J.D. is to be away, though I do wish I could be with you at Hyde Park. But it is best, and I will be able to go up to Campo direct Thursday the 27th.

It is hot and sticky, only 90° in this room but equal to
100 on the River.

Much love.

Affec.

FDR

∾

WASHINGTON

[JULY 23, 1916]

SUNDAY

Dearest Babs,

It is still near the boiling point here, no relief even at
night. Yesterday I golfed in the afternoon and dined with
Col. O'Brien and the other British attachés—a nice evening,
though thoroughly British! Today I go out for 9 holes at
noon, more than that would be suicide and then after
lunch R. Huidekoper, C. McCawley, J. McIlhenny, Jack
Wilkins, Fred Chapin and I go down to the Patuxent Club
for a turtle soup dinner! It may be cooler there and at all
events we get a nice run in the motor.

I still hope to get off without fail Wednesday midnight,
arriving Eastport Friday morning by *train*.

Everything here is quiet, even politically and people agree
that Hughes has hurt his chances greatly by not starting his
campaign *at once* when he was a new story.

I am to attend the State Committee meeting in New York
at noon August 4th. That means, I fear, that I must leave
Campo the morning of the 3rd or even the night before.

I am so glad Wee Babs is better, and that the big ones
really like the pool.

A great deal of love. I long for Friday.

Your devoted

F

Reginald S. Huidekoper, class of 1898 at Harvard, was
at this time a lawyer in Washington with the firm of

312

Wilson, Huidekoper and Lesh; between 1909 and 1914 he served as Assistant District Attorney for the capital. Treasurer of the Wilkins Securities Corporation, John F. Wilkins was a Washington businessman and a golfing acquaintance of F.D.R.; Frederick E. Chapin, a lawyer, was another.

∾

Dearest Babs,

Here I am, alone as Mama stayed down, Aunt Doe's sailing being postponed to tomorrow noon. I had to come up as I had appointments with Townsend, Herrick, etc. in Poughkeepsie, so after arriving there at 2:30 I spent three hours with them and am now having a comfy evening expecting burglars to walk in on me in the big room. My peregrinations of the last few days have been highly varied.

On Thursday I spent the morning at the Boston Navy Yard, took train to Gloucester after lunch, conferred with various people about Naval Reserve, took train to Prides Crossing where I was met by Jeff, dined with him and Catherine, and then train into Boston and the midnight to New York.

Friday, breakfasted with Mama, spent the morning at Nat. Dem. Headquarters where I had talks with Vance McCormick, Robert Woolley, Hugh Wallace, Norman Mack, etc., and gave out the interview about the prospects in Maine which you may have seen in the Times.

Then I went downtown, lunched with Lang, saw several political callers, went to Racquet Club, Harvard Club, two picture shops (to look at Naval prints and bought nothing—honest!), then home and to dine with Mama and Aunt Doe at Uncle Warren's house. After dinner the latter gave the usual line of talk "agin the government" and I delivered eulogy per contra. Think it did Aunt Doe good at least.

This morning Mama and I spent two hours at Caldwell's looking over fixtures and Mama brings some up in the car tomorrow afternoon to try.

It is hot and prospects are hotter.

Sunday a.m. Prospects materialized. It is *awfully* hot! I was up till three a.m. waiting for the burglars! Clements, Robert and Duffy also looking for them most of the night. I wish they had come!

Your letter is here. I am too sorry about Bab's digestion but do try not to wean him. It would be an awful trip to come here, also the infantile paralysis is gaining, 6 more cases in Poughkeepsie, and the heat is really severe after Campo.

Loads of love, kiss the chicks.

Devotedly

F

John E. Townsend and Thaddeus J. Herrick were political friends of F.D.R. from Poughkeepsie; Townsend had been sheriff of Dutchess County from 1909 to 1912, and was at this time Poughkeepsie's postmaster; while Thaddeus Herrick operated a lumber yard in Rhinebeck and served as county clerk prior to holding the chairmanship of the Dutchess County Democratic Committee.

Vance McCormick, a former mayor of Harrisburg, Pa., became a close associate of Woodrow Wilson and played a conspicuous role in the latter's first Presidential nomination. He twice declined Cabinet posts. Between 1916 and 1919 he was chairman of the Democratic National Committee, and has often been regarded as the main difference between victory and defeat in the close election of 1916. Robert W. Woolley, one-time sports editor for the *New York World,* was the Democratic Committee's Chairman of Publications during the 1912 campaign; in 1915 Wilson appointed him to the directorship of the Mint. A key figure in the Democratic Party since Cleveland's Administration, Hugh C. Wallace was a delegate to the 1916 convention from Tacoma, Wash.; his wife, the former Mildred Fuller, was the daughter of Melville W. Fuller, late Chief Justice of the Supreme Court. Founder, editor, and publisher of the *Buffalo Times*, Norman Mack was another important person in Wilson's political scheme, having served as national chairman of the Democratic Party from 1908 to 1912.

The *Times* interview "about the prospects in Maine" was printed the same day that F.D.R. wrote this letter; excerpts from it follow:

Returning from a week's trip in Eastern Maine, Franklin D. Roosevelt, Assistant Secretary of the Navy, reported to Vance C. McCormick, chairman of the Democratic National Committee, that he had discovered nothing for the Democrats to be alarmed about in that State this year. He said he found a distinct trend to President Wilson among the people there generally and especially among Republicans.

"While I was in Maine," said Assistant Secretary Roosevelt, "the Hughes speech of acceptance was published and I made particular efforts to find out how the Republicans and Progressives felt about it. I was greatly surprised at the number who felt that the speech was wholly inconclusive, who had hoped for a definite statement along constructive lines but felt that they had received nothing but clever words which could be construed into almost any line of policy at the desire of the construer.

"A large number of the men whom I talked with— factory hands, mechanics, and storekeepers—were regular Republicans who had never voted for a Democrat. These men did not wish to announce publicly that they would vote for Wilson, but told me that this was their present intention. . . ."

Warren Delano III, an ardent Republican, often engaged in long arguments with F.D.R. over the policies of the Wilson Administration; as will be seen in a later letter of this chapter, Wilson's reelection recalled this particular after-dinner controversy to F.D.R., and stimulated him to send an interesting wire to his uncle.

During the months of July and August, residents of the

large estates between Hyde Park and Rhinebeck were tormented by a series of burglaries that continued for several weeks without the slightest clue as to the identity of the perpetrator. Each succeeding robbery redoubled the efforts of what the *Poughkeepsie Eagle* termed "the millionaire colony" to apprehend the thief. Hence, during his visit to Hyde Park, F.D.R. joined his neighbors in "waiting for the burglars" during the early hours of the morning. Mr. Plog's account book has a record only of one of F.D.R.'s companions during the vigil: Robert (last name not listed), a groom in the stable who quit his job a month later. However, Mr. Plog recalls that during the burglar scare F.D.R. hired a night watchman, and it is not unlikely that this gentleman was "Clements." His third companion was the aforementioned Scotch terrier, Duffy.

∽∽

A collection of F.D.R.'s personal letters would be very incomplete if it did not contain at least one routine sample of his correspondence with Louis McHenry Howe. The following letter, although only a carbon copy and lacking a signature, was one of the many found among F.D.R.'s naval papers; chosen at random, it is similar in spirit to all the items of the F.D.R.-Howe correspondence. It is inserted at this point through the cooperation of the Franklin D. Roosevelt Library.

WASHINGTON
[AUGUST 8, 1916]
TUESDAY

Dear Louis:

I did not change my mind about the Saratoga trip, as the State Committee meeting was held in New York August 2nd, two days earlier than originally planned, and I had to miss it, sending my proxy to John Sague. However, the unofficial Convention takes place Friday and I leave here Thursday night, getting to Saratoga about 1 p.m. Friday. Much apparent opposition to Seabury by Tammany. I can't make out whether it is the real goods or not. If you want to come to Saratoga do so, but I don't think it essential and I don't want to "butt in" on your drying out process. I shall spend Friday night at Schenectady with Hall, and I suppose the Convention will last over Saturday and I hope to get back to Hyde Park Saturday evening.

I will take up the question of the three civilian assistant shop superintendents and agree entirely with Wright. Also I will take up Adams' matter.

Did you see my interview in last Saturday's paper about the outlook in Maine?

Everything quiet here; heat still awful. Naval bill won't go through for another two weeks. While I was away Secretary baptized my Naval Civilian Training Cruise as the "John Paul Jones Cruise." What do you know about that! It is an awful mistake to leave the Department for more than five minutes and a half at a time!

As ever yours,
[F.D.R.]

Louis McH. Howe
Westport Point, Mass.

Although never in perfect health, Louis Howe tended to exaggerate his maladies, and not infrequently he requested leave from the office to pursue his "drying out process." F.D.R. always granted these requests, as he sympathized with his friend's hypochondria and maintained a policy of not "butting in."

Major J. E. M. Wright was at this time in charge of the collection of salvage material in the machinery division of the Norfolk Navy Yard. It had been proposed that Wright be promoted to a shop superintendent, but the latter felt that his age and poor physical condition prevented him from handling the job efficiently. He therefore requested a promotion without a change of duties, and since he had served the Navy for a number of years, F.D.R. agreed "entirely" with his suggestion. The exact nature of the "Adams' matter" cannot be determined, but it is known to have concerned L. S. Adams, the industrial manager of the Portsmouth Navy Yard.

The "John Paul Jones Cruise" (so-named because its participants were the nucleus of a new navy, as were the men who served with John Paul Jones) began on August 15, 1916, and was the climax of F.D.R.'s efforts to establish an adequate naval reserve. The number of enrollments in the reserve far exceeded F.D.R.'s expectations; indeed, the Navy Department was able to assign nine battleships to the cruise, each carrying a full quota of recruits. Extensive war games and target practice were held throughout the month that followed, and at the conclusion of the cruise it was everywhere considered to have been a great success. Henceforth the U.S.N.R. was an integral part of American military power.

∽

WASHINGTON
[AUGUST 8, 1916]
TUESDAY

Dearest Babs,

I got here again yesterday morning, had a busy day, dined at home and perspired all night. Today is still hot, but I am to dine at the Club and have a little poker party! No news, except the shooting of one of the burglars which Mama will tell you all about. Yours of Sunday is *very* welcome telling of the Babs improvement. I do hope it is permanent and I really think it would be an awful mistake to move to Hyde Park at this time of year, especially as the infantile paralysis is gaining headway rather than abating.

Wednesday. I am off to play golf with McIlhenny this afternoon and dine at Chevy Chase with him and Fred Chapin and Jack Wilkins. Tomorrow night I leave for Saratoga and will spend Friday night with Hall and Margaret, going to Hyde Park Saturday evening.

318

Our poor old Naval Bill is still a bill and not a law, but it looks as if the House would adopt the Senate increases when it comes up next Tuesday. They have agreed on a fool personnel provision which won't work as in practice it will create retirements, block promotions and do just the things it aims to prevent. They worked it out without consulting any of my board which had become expert in the figures.

Last night's little party was delightful, though I lost the large sum of $8.00.

William Phillips has gone for a month. Mrs. Polk is here with Frank and they go next week to Bar Harbor. The Lansings are back—and everybody is beginning to warm up for the campaign. I had an intimation that the New York organization would like to use me to beat Seabury out of the nomination for Governor, but I declined to flirt and the six votes of Dutchess will be for Seabury if it comes to a head.

I brought my stamp albums down here and am putting in many which have drifted in to me during the past ten years.

Kiss the chicks and give my love to Mama. I answered the enclosed in the affirmative, no one need speak of it!

I long to get back.

                                        Your devoted

                                                        F

Margaret Richardson of Boston had become the bride of A.E.R.'s brother in June, 1912, and at this time the young couple were living in Schenectady, where Hall Roosevelt was working as an engineer with General Electric.

The dissension between the House and the Senate over the "poor old Naval Bill" concerned the number of capital ships to be constructed during the first year of the building program. While the Senate provided for the construction of four battleships and four battle cruisers in 1917, the House originally authorized only five battle cruisers for the first year, but—as F.D.R. suspected—altered its position a week later and let the Senate figures prevail. As for retirements

and block promotions, Congress accepted the plans submitted by the Navy Department board, which called for
the promotion of naval officers by selection rather than by
seniority. However, the plan was amended to apply also
to officers of lower rank than that of commander, an
amendment which tended to create the block promotions
noted by F.D.R.; *i.e.,* notwithstanding the proviso for a
board of nine admirals to pass on each promotion (with
approval by six necessary for advancement), there was a
greater tendency to promote low-ranking officers en masse.
Although the Congressional committee raised the general
retirement age from 62 to 64 years, it encouraged retirements by arranging for the retirement of captains who had
not been promoted at the age of 57; commanders not promoted were to be retired at 45, and lieutenant commanders
at 40.

In New York the "warm up for the campaign" centered
around the Democratic State Convention at Saratoga. The
purpose of this meeting was to endorse candidates for the
statewide primaries to be held the following month; and as
endorsement by the Saratoga convention meant that victory
in the primaries was a virtual certainty, interest in the convention was great, with much preliminary bickering behind
the scenes.

Samuel Seabury was at this time Associate Judge of the
Court of Appeals of New York State; during F.D.R.'s governorship they were closely associated in the famous trial
of Mayor James J. Walker of New York City, Seabury personally presenting F.D.R. with the charges against Walker.

∽∽

WASHINGTON
[AUGUST 14, 1916]
MONDAY

Dearest Babs,

It never rains but it pours. On arrival today I found
Golden in hospital, car smashed badly. I am so mad clear
through that I will write when I know more about it.

And now to more pleasant things. I got to Saratoga Friday 2 p.m., found the Convention had merely met and adjourned to 8 p.m., went to the races, then supper, then convention, where I helped to put Seabury across, did my best to nominate Wm. Church Osborn for Senator but it was McCombs who "had the goods." Then spent the night at the house of McCombs, Baruch and Forbes Morgan, the latter not there.

Saturday, conferences all morning with every political potentate you ever heard of in the State from C. F. Murphy up, then to the races again with R. T. Wilson whose horse promptly won the gold cup. I caught a 5 p.m. to Poughkeepsie, got there at 10:30, all much surprised to see me and cook away!

Sunday morning I went to Poughkeepsie at noon, had a political lunch at the Nelson House, then at three up to Aunt Ellen's, then to the Dows and with Tracy to the scene of the burglar killing and to Steen Valetje for tea, then home, several candidates to see me after dinner and the Federal at 1 a.m. to Washington where I was met by Wicker, the Wales ex-man, with the news of the smash. Golden's leg broken and he may be injured internally—they won't know for another day.

It is cool fortunately and I shall dine at home and be fit by morning.

Plans are upset by Sec'y. I shall surely get to Campo the 27th though, even though I may have to return here the 1st, but I will get that holiday in *somehow*.

Loads of love. So glad Babs improves.

Your devoted

F

Golden was F.D.R.'s unfortunate chauffeur; upon his return from the hospital F.D.R. dismissed him.

The Saratoga convention "merely met and adjourned" on the first afternoon because of a sore throat which plagued the presiding officer and keynote speaker, Congressman John F. Fitzgerald *(vide supra)*. He recovered in time for the evening meeting, however, and delivered a one-hour speech which the *Poughkeepsie Eagle* reported as having been received "with vigorous applause." While Seabury's support for the governorship nomination was almost unanimous, the convention did not agree so easily upon a candidate for U.S. Senator. William Church Osborn led in the early stages of the voting, but most of the delegates switched to William F. McCombs when reminded that Osborn had approved of Mayor Mitchel's action in the New York controversy over public charities, an approval which the leaders feared would inject an unfavorable religious issue into the campaign. Although the endorsement of Seabury and McCombs was equivalent to nomination, "the leaders conformed in every respect on the surface to the spirit of the primary law," according to the *Poughkeepsie Courier* of August 13, 1916.

F.D.R.'s caustic remark about the rank and influence of Charles F. Murphy among the other politicians present at the conferences is a reflection of the aversion for this boss that began with the "Sheehan business" and subsequently marked all his efforts in New York politics. The *Courier* also reported that Murphy's role in the arranging of a Democratic slate was not an insignificant one: "Tammany maintained its policy of 'hands off' till the last moment. Charles F. Murphy said he did not care to lead and was willing to follow. The conference at which the slate was written, however, was held in Mr. Murphy's room, and it was noticed that he kept an extremely watchful eye on events."

A New York lawyer and former student of Woodrow Wilson at Princeton, William F. McCombs was a key figure in Democratic politics throughout the Wilson Administration, having managed the Presidential campaign in 1912 and having served as chairman of the Democratic National Committee for the next four years. F.D.R.'s acquaintance with Bernard M. Baruch was at this time still a casual one, based mainly on their mutual admiration for Wilson.

Two months after the Saratoga convention Wilson appointed Baruch to the Advisory Commission of the Council of National Defense. F.D.R.'s relations with Richard T. Wilson had commenced when the latter sponsored the Gittins bill which F.D.R. opposed during his first summer in the State Senate. A New York banker, Wilson still held the presidency of the Saratoga Association at the time his horse, Campfire, won the Saratoga Special ("gold cup") by two lengths over the entries of Harry Payne Whitney and August Belmont.

The series of burglaries that had alarmed Dutchess County came to an end on August 7th when a man named Fred Cramer was killed in a running fight on a wooded road of Vincent Astor's estate north of Rhinebeck. Although Cramer died in the Vassar Hospital before he could sign a confession, there were no further crimes, and Sheriff Conklin subsequently announced that evidently Cramer was a "one-man thief" and had been responsible for all the robberies.

Tracy Dows and his family were neighbors and lifelong friends of the Roosevelts. His son, Olin Dows, later became an artist; among his accomplishments are the murals which now adorn the post offices in Hyde Park and Rhinebeck.

∾∾

WASHINGTON
[AUGUST 15, 1916]
TUESDAY

Dearest Babs,

I *think* our nice Golden has been a weak, miserable wretch, though I haven't got all my proofs together. You will remember I have nearly always paid my garage bills in *cash* which I have given him to take to the Dupont people. Apparently these cash envelopes have gone into his pocket and he has requested the garage each month to send me the bill for the *past* month only and *not* the arrears! So I am out about $250.00 on that! Next I think I have been badly stung on gasoline and tires. Next I *think* he was joy-riding last

323

Sunday night and that others were in the car and were hurt too. I am now looking up other patients in other hospitals. If so, of course, I get no insurance and the car is pretty badly smashed as it turned completely over down a bank and landed back on its wheels! Damage looks like at least $500.00.

The Doctor at the hospital can't tell yet whether there are internal injuries or not. His stomach is badly bruised and much pain. One bone in leg near ankle is surely broken and X-ray will be done tonight.

I am sorry to say the Mme. de Laboulaye's little boy is very ill, acute appendicitis which they did not recognize till too late. They operated last night, peritonitis had set in and it is now touch and go. Luckily it is cool and they still hope for the best.

Naval bill comes up today and is going through all right, at least it will if our count of noses is correct. So we are very very busy. Last night I had a good long sleep in spite of so many troubles. Tonight I dine quietly with the Polks and shall not move out of Washington till I leave I hope next Monday night to join a ship at New London and go to sea to attend the Civilian Cruise and the war game, ending up in Portsmouth August 26th and Campo the 27th.

Aunt Jennie is going to Ellen's as you probably know. Some undertaking. I hear Fred is to enlarge his boat.

Loads of love and take very good care of yourself.

Your devoted

F

F.D.R.'s "count of noses" was indeed "correct," as the House approved the Senate amendment for sixteen capital ships within three years by a vote of 283 to 51. This vote wound up the prolonged consideration of the Naval bill, and on August 29, 1916, it was signed by Wilson. In its final form the bill provided for 156 ships of all classes to be built within three years, for appropriations totaling more than $600,000,000, and for an increase of naval enlisted strength to 67,800 men. At the time it was the largest appropriation ever devoted to naval expansion by any country.

The various details involved in the building program largely occupied F.D.R.'s time during the months that followed. For F.D.R. preparedness was now a reality, a welcome addition to his daily routine.

A.E.R. explains the remark about Mrs. Warren Delano III's trip to her daughter's home at Campobello by noting that "Aunt Jennie was very stout and moved with great difficulty." Frederick B. Adams, who must needs enlarge his boat, was her son-in-law.

$\sim\sim$

WASHINGTON
[AUGUST 18, 1916]
FRIDAY

Dearest Babs,

I love the pictures of my namesake, but he sure does look tough enough to be a future pugilist. I am so glad the wee Babs gains, even though slowly and 17-1 is no bad weight.

The Sec'y was accused in Congress of intention to use Dolphin to campaign in Maine—hence he is scared blue and Dolphin won't be allowed within 1000 miles of Maine till after September 11. I think *then* the Sec'y will use her for a week or so and I might get her about the 20th. I am really upset at the thought of bringing you all down by rail. There is much I.P. in Boston, Springfield, Worcester, etc., and even in Rockland and other *Maine* points. Also the various villages are keeping motorists with children out and it would be difficult to get to Hyde Park by motor, even if mine were in shape. It will take at least a month of repairs.

The Laboulaye child is better, not out of the woods yet but the peritonitis seems to be subsiding.

Yesterday I went out late and played golf and then dined at the Sec'y of State's to meet my old friend Dr. Lauro Miller, Sec'y Foreign Affairs of Brazil, a stag dinner and very nice.

325

Today I have lunched with Uncle Fred and George Rublee. It is not very hot and we have had a comfortable week.

Kiss the chicks and give Mama my love.

Your devoted

F.

During this national election year interest was centered upon the state of Maine, which holds its elections two months prior to the rest of the country. For several weeks preceding the September 11th contest the state attracted leaders from both parties, but to F.D.R. this influx of political speakers was very inconvenient, as he had planned to avoid the infantile epidemic by bringing his family from Campobello on the *Dolphin.* (Although delayed a full month by the political situation, F.D.R. was eventually able to carry out this plan, the arrangements for which more or less dominate the remaining letters of this chapter.)

Josephus Daniels' views regarding the use of the *Dolphin* were not so unreasonable as F.D.R. intimates, as witnessed by the following note to F.D.R. aboard the U.S.S. *Yankton,* dated August 21, 1916, and marked "personal" in J.D.'s own hand: "My dear Roosevelt: Refering to our conversation the other day about the DOLPHIN, it is unnecessary for me to tell you that I would love to do what you wished but I fear that it would not be the part of wisdom to do it. Mr. Padgett came in to see me this morning and said he would like to have the DOLPHIN for a few days. I told him certainly, he was the Chairman of the Naval Committee, but I pointed out the possibility of criticism, asked him to think it over and he has just now informed me that he feels it would not be wise at this time, there are so many crazy people. As you know I have sent my boys to Raleigh for the same reason. I could not get away to go with them on the DOLPHIN, combining official duty with a pleasure trip, so rather than risk adverse criticism I gave it up entirely. Don't you think it would be a mistake at this time to send the DOLPHIN into Maine upon anything except an official trip? Cordially yours, Josephus Daniels."

A prominent lawyer, George Rublee was Groton's first graduate (the only member of the class of 1886); in 1915 Wilson appointed him to the Federal Trade Commission, and he remained in Washington thereafter with the law firm of Covington, Rublee, Burling, & Shorb.

∾

ON TRAIN TO NEW LONDON, CONN.
[AUGUST 22, 1916]
TUESDAY

Dearest Babs,

We get to New London at 11:30, there board the Yankton and go off shore to the Rhode Island. I left Washington yesterday after lunch and met Livy, Henry de R. and Frances at Sherry's at 7:30, dined and we all went to the "Follies." Frances goes on to Boston and will try to arrange with Alice to meet her at Gardiner on the day train Saturday, reaching Eastport that evening.

Wasn't it too sad about the Laboulayes? On Saturday morning Mme. Jusserand told me over the telephone that he was getting on well, more comfortable and very little temperature. On Sunday afternoon they telephoned me that he died and the funeral would be at St. Paul's at 9 a.m. Monday. No flower shop was open, so I could send none, but I went to the pathetic little funeral—only the French and British Embassy people there. I feel too sorry for them.

It is simply out of the question to make the move to Hyde Park the 10th as the I. P. is no better and we can't get our car. But I hope to get the Dolphin about the 20th or perhaps a few days earlier. *No one* is thinking of moving children by rail.

I had a quiet Saturday and Sunday, golf late each afternoon. It was pretty hot and yesterday and today are broilers.

I shall be glad to get to sea. I have had a bad three weeks.
I long to get to you all.   Your devoted

                                                        F

This letter looks as if it had been written by Cousin Susie!

∽

Dearest Babs,

Back again safely at 1:40 this afternoon and was met at
station by my own car! It looks all right again but is still
without windshield and searchlight. I ran it home and it goes
all right as far as I can tell. Golden is still in hospital and will
be for four or five days more. I shall see him tomorrow and
it will be cheerful.

The dinner last night was very good. Larz Anderson,
Charlie Winslow (used to know you at Tivoli when he was
playing with Maude and Pussie), Frank Crowninshield, Alec
Legare and young Elliott. I caught the midnight by the skin
of my teeth, something like the rush of the previous night
at Eastport!

Yesterday I went down to Myopia with Liv. at 12:30 and
we lunched and then played 18 holes, saw Alice and I returned in time to dress for the dinner.

Millie and Francis are well and tonight I dine at home
with Howe and go to bed early. It is a heavenly day and not
hot.

I hear of lots of I.P. all over up-state, almost every village
of Dutchess and it doesn't seem to be decreasing yet as it is
in N.Y.

Loads of love. I just hated to go away and it will be nice
the next time to be with you *all alone.*

Kiss the chicks.   Your devoted

                                                        F.

Larz Anderson was in the class of 1888 at Harvard, and later joined the diplomatic corps, serving in London, Rome, Brussels, and Tokyo, before resigning in 1913 with the advent of a Democratic administration; during the football season Yale undergraduates are forever trying to steal the gold mountings on the posts of the Larz Anderson Bridge at Harvard. His wife, the former Isabel Perkins, wrote numerous books for children and was a ranking official of the Red Cross during World War I. A pioneer American collector of modern French art, Frank Crowninshield was the editor of *Vanity Fair* for more than two decades. "Young Elliott" was probably John Elliott, at this time four years out of Harvard and later an investment counselor. His father, John Elliott, Sr., was a step-brother of Mrs. Theodore Roosevelt.

This is the last reference in F.D.R.'s correspondence to Mrs. W. Forbes Morgan (A.E.R.'s Aunt Pussie); four years later, in February, 1920, she and her two daughters were killed in a fire that destroyed their New York home on Ninth Street.

The emphasis upon "all alone" in the last paragraph resulted from a houseful of guests on F.D.R.'s previous visit.

∽∽

WASHINGTON
[SEPTEMBER 14, 1916]
THURSDAY

Dearest Babs,

The more I hear of conditions in New York *State* the more certain I become that we should give up Hyde Park until December 10 or 15, but we still need not decide definitely until the 20th and in the meantime I will know on Monday about the Dolphin. I feel terribly about it, as I need not tell you, but there are so *many* cases and really seems to be more a country than a city disease.

Yesterday I went out late and golfed and as a result I have not caught up with work and we have had this armor plate hearing for two days. J.D. leaves this afternoon and I shall

329

be alone tomorrow and Saturday, leaving that afternoon to spend a dreary Sunday I fear, at Winterthur all alone with Senator du Pont! If it is really too tiresome I shall come back Sunday afternoon. Tonight I dine with the McIlhennys and tomorrow at home. Howe goes to Newfoundland tomorrow and I shall try to clean up his back work for him! He is so wonderful on the big things that he lets the routine slide. I need a thoroughgoing hack without brilliancy like the faithful McCarthy to keep things running! It is warm and sticky. Kiss the chicks. I am glad Babs seems to begin to gain.

Your devoted   F

The circumstances surrounding the "armor plate hearing" received nationwide attention for more than three years. The commotion began early in the Wilson Administration when Daniels asked for bids on the armor plate for the new dreadnought *Arizona*. Only three companies in the United States made armor plate, Carnegie, Midvale, and Bethlehem, and they all submitted identical bids of $454 per ton. Although the representatives of these companies contended that they had not communicated with each other prior to making the bids, Daniels rejected the bids on the ground that not only was the price unfair, but also that it had not been arrived at by competitive bidding. Nevertheless, this did not remove the Navy Department from the mercy of the armor plate monopoly, and Daniels therefore requested Congress to allocate sufficient funds for the construction of a government plant to make armor plate and shells. This request, and the subsequent fight in Congress, reverberated throughout the country. Directed by Charles M. Schwab of Bethlehem, the armor plate group conducted a vast advertising campaign against the proposal. Large and attractive advertisements appeared in newspapers all over the country, including the *Raleigh News and Observer*, Daniels' paper; some of the papers (mainly those located in the same districts as the armor plate factories) supported the advertisements with editorials denouncing the government and claiming that the individual taxpayer was bound to be injured by the operation of a government-owned plant. Congress withstood the campaign, however, and appropriated $11,000,-000 for a new plant by a 58 to 23 vote in the Senate and by a proportionally similar margin in the House. The Navy Department then turned its attention to the selection of a plant site, and was subsequently bombarded by bids from more than one hundred cities throughout the eastern seaboard. Daniels appointed a special committee to hold hearings on the subject and select an appropriate locality, and it is to these hearings that F.D.R. refers in this letter. Two months later, after careful consideration and much discussion, Charleston, West Virginia, was chosen as the site for the new plant, the construction of which was never fully completed because of the return to monopoly practices under Harding.

Senator Henry A. du Pont graduated from the United States Military Academy at the head of his class in 1861; he won the Congressional Medal of Honor for gallantry at Cedar Creek in the Civil War, and was later promoted to a colonelcy. In 1906 he was elected U.S. Senator from Delaware and served in this capacity for twelve years.

〜〜

WASHINGTON
[SEPTEMBER 14, 1916]
THURSDAY

Dearest Mama—

I have been so swamped since I got here that I couldn't write you, but I have, I need not say, thought of you much during these very disgustingly trying days, and the more I think of the situation as a whole the more I begin to feel that we too must be unselfish and not go to Hyde Park till December but come straight here. But we shall not decide till the 20th and I shall telephone you on Monday about lunch time.

Everything has piled up here and I shall be alone for the next few days as J.D. departs.

331

It is warm and sticky and I shall be glad of a few more days at Campo. I shall know about the Dolphin also on Monday. Warren is here and his family arrive Monday by Federal. I would go to H.P. myself for Sunday but I can't be so far away from Dept. and I may go to Sen. du Pont's at Wilmington just for Saturday night. I wish I could do something to help but I suppose the process now is chiefly one of waiting.

Your affec. son   F.D.R.

∾

WINTERTHUR, DEL.
[SEPTEMBER 17, 1916]
SUNDAY

Dearest Babs,

You will recognize my Sunday location by the heading. Yesterday I found that I could get through the urgent department work in time to leave at 1 and I got out here to the house (by ancient horse-power) by four and found the Colonel waiting. We walked together over the place for two hours, then a dinner in state vis-à-vis served by two men, then an evening in his library discussing history and genealogy! This morning I slept till nine, breakfasted in my room, read the papers, browsed among the old du Pont French books till lunch time. Then Mrs. William du Pont, a charming widow, came in her auto and took the Colonel and me to lunch with the Coxes, he the Harlan and Hollingsworth shipbuilding head. The Russian Naval attaché and his wife (formerly Mme. Vassilief) were there. After our return the Colonel and I took another long walk and I begin to feel much the same age. Tomorrow I return by the 8 a.m. train.

In Washington there is little news. Irene and the children return tomorrow. Mama seems to feel safe about our returning to H. P. about the 10th! I will talk to her over telephone tomorrow or next day and wire you the 20th.

Your devoted
F.

The former Mme. Vassilief, wife of Commander I.V. Mishtowt, was an old acquaintance of F.D.R.'s mother. "Irene" was the wife of Warren Delano Robbins, the former Irene de Bruyn of Buenos Aires, whom he had met in 1910 while serving with the diplomatic corps in Argentina; their three children were named Warren, Edward, and Helen.

∽∽

Dearest Babbie,

Your letter about the wee Babs worried me a lot this morning but I am relieved by your telegram this evening. I wired you about Dolphin. The Secretary said he saw no reason now why I should not have her. Therefore, as he leaves for a two weeks' trip to the Middle West next Friday, I said nothing further to him but shall order the Dolphin to Eastport myself. Today I talked to Mama by telephone. She said nothing new but there are no new cases on the place and I agree with you that H. P. is really no more risk than a long autumn in Washington. But if wee Babs is all right I think we should put off leaving Campo till as late as possible. I will have Dolphin there the 2nd but if we could wait to go till 3rd, it would not get us to H. P. till 6th and by that time the Butler child might be out of quarantine and everything fumigated. When we get to New York we can lie off 81st St. West and if Solley is then regularly in town we can decide then whether to have him come aboard or take Babs to him. The former is of course preferable.

If we don't leave Campo till 3rd I think I must not come up this Saturday as Sec'y will be away and it would mean my absence for 2 weeks as I want to go on the Dolphin with you. That would get us to H. P. about Friday and I would have two days there.

333

No special news here, except meetings of Edison Boards etc. I am fearfully busy and this is the second night I am at home working.

I will tell Millie about the curtains. It is quite cold but wonderful clear weather. I may go down to Patuxent tomorrow evening to get the early morning rail bird shooting and get back by 9:30 a.m.

Why don't you let old Bennet look over the Babs again and see if his heart sounds right? If there is "dope" a quiet search would show it, but I don't believe it.

Loads of love. I just hate to have you worry so. Send the servants down by boat the 4th, not earlier as we may be delayed by weather.

Your devoted
F

I will wire Mama the 21st.

Westley Butler's daughter, Mildred, was three years old when stricken by infantile paralysis at the height of the 1916 epidemic; as the case was not a serious one, she fully recovered and now lives in Rhinebeck, N.Y. Dr. Fred P. Solley was the Roosevelt family's general practitioner.

Early in 1915 Thomas A. Edison was asked by newspaper reporters whether he could add to the terrors of war. Edison replied in the affirmative, but added that he wouldn't turn his energies in this direction "except at the call of my country." Convinced that modern warfare depended upon the continuous improvement of war techniques, Daniels was anxious to take advantage of Edison's qualification, and finally persuaded him to accept the chairmanship of the Navy Consulting Board. Composed of members of eleven leading scientific societies, the Edison boards were responsible for the coordination of military and civilian research. At an estimated cost of $5,000,000 for laboratory equipment, buildings, and research, the Consulting Board developed numerous inventions for use by the Navy. Edison's inventive genius personally accounted for an apparatus to detect submarines and a device whereby merchantmen could swiftly change their course to avoid torpedoes. There was thus good reason for Daniels to remark in *The Wilson Era* that "the story of what Edison and his associates did is a great chapter in Naval history."

~~

WASHINGTON
[SEPTEMBER 24, 1916]
SUNDAY

Dearest Babs,

I have been spending the whole day at Chevy Chase, eighteen holes in the morning with McIlhenny, Chapin and McCawley, lunch and 18 holes more, then dinner with the Millers, she just back and with lots of news of the Phillips', etc., and sent you very much love. It has been a glorious day and I am exhausted!

Yesterday the Sec'y left and turned over enough to prevent me from leaving here for a month. However, I shall get off Wednesday evening and take the day train Thursday, getting to Eastport 8:30 that night. It is an awful trip but saves me a day here. Benson is also away, and I shall have to turn over the Department to Leigh Palmer, very new on the job, but promising well—far better than Blue.

I fear you have had it pretty cold. Be careful of the sparks on the roof or too much heating of any one chimney. I am so glad the Babs is better. I have told Millie about the curtains and all is well at the house.

Lang I wrote to of course when I got your letter. I used to know her in Boston. They will indeed be an estimable couple and it will do Lang good to be married! Reggie Huidekoper also is engaged, to a du Pont of Wilmington.

By the way I had paid Trecartin and sent him a cheque, so I have written him to send either mine or yours back—if he sends mine I will give you a cheque for the amount. I

335

enclose deposit slip for $600 and will put in another $100 when I get it!

Loads of love, kiss the chicks.

Your devoted F

Rear Admiral William S. Benson was at this time Chief of Naval Operations, a job he held until his retirement in 1919; he was Wilson's naval adviser at the Paris Peace Conference, and afterward became chairman of the U.S. Shipping Board. Leigh Palmer *(vide supra)* had succeeded Rear Admiral Victor Blue as chief of the Bureau of Navigation on August 16, 1916, and was thus "very new on the job." The latter was given the command of the battleship *Texas,* but returned to his former position in December, 1918, when Palmer was made chief of staff of the American Battleship Squadron in the North Sea. In *The Wilson Era* Daniels credits Blue with having "drawn up comprehensive plans creating the naval reserve"; nevertheless, F.D.R. was critical of his administrative techniques, as witnessed by the remark in this letter. His son, Stuart Blue, was one of the first naval officer casualties of World War II, and the Navy named a destroyer *Blue* for the father and son who, as noted in Daniels' book, "illustrated the best traditions of the service."

Langdon P. Marvin and Mary Eliot Vaughan were married the following December; in 1919 F.D.R. became the godfather of Langdon P. Marvin, Jr. Reginald Huidekoper's prospective bride was Bessie C. du Pont, and their marriage took place in 1917. Earlier in the year F.D.R. had enlarged the house at Campobello, and the check to Trecartin was in payment for his services as contractor.

〜〜

CAMPOBELLO
[SEPTEMBER 30, 1916]
SATURDAY

Dearest Mama—

It is blowing hard from the S.E. and thick and dirty weather, so we can only hope it will come out strong from the

336

N.W. by Tuesday. The Dolphin should get here tomorrow. Once we get off it will take us only about 42 hours to N.Y. So if we leave Tuesday a.m. we get to N.Y. Thursday early and if we see Solley we could get up to H.P. that evening. However, I feel there is little chance of your seeing us before Friday at the earliest.

By that time I hope all will be fumigated, but anyway whether it is or not I think the children ought not to go in any of our own autos or carriages or sit behind Butler. Therefore could not Rosy or his man come down to the River to bring up Eleanor, Caton, F.D.R. Jr. and J.A.R. The rest of us can walk!

I enclose a picture of Mrs. Howard in bed. I meant to send it to her before when it came out in the Courier. It ought to be framed for Elsa and Tommy.

The baby seems a little better but not comfortable yet. Otherwise the chicks are all fine.

Much love from us all Your affec son F.D.R.

"Caton" was an English nurse A.E.R. employed for the children at this time. Thomas H. Howard was the superintendent of the Vanderbilt estate just north of Hyde Park. He and his wife, the former Rose Post, were old friends and neighbors of the Roosevelts, as were their children Elizabeth (now the wife of Congressman Robert Winthrop Kean) and Thomas, Jr. The incident of the "picture of Mrs. Howard in bed" occurred earlier in the month when a burglar entered her room while she was asleep. Awakened by the noise of the prowler, Mrs. Howard kept still and did not make a sound until the intruder had departed. This feat was fully reported by the local papers, and although not preserved, the picture F.D.R. enclosed in this letter was probably a cartoon which he had found and jestingly considered to be a good portrayal of the newspaper accounts.

After sealing this letter, F.D.R. thought of another method of getting his family safely up the steep hill that separates the Hudson River from his home, and added it to the back of the envelope: "Or you could send the Ford down and I could run the children up in it."

All of F.D.R.'s precautions and plans were carried out three days later, and the trip from Campobello to Hyde Park via the *Dolphin* proved to be an uneventful one. While the children remained in Hyde Park until the infantile epidemic had run its course and travel was safe again, A.E.R. and F.D.R. returned to Washington, where the war in Europe was momentarily overshadowed by the pending election.

∽∽

The campaign was a turbulent one, and as election day approached it became obvious that no accurate prediction could be made about the outcome. A.E.R. was visiting the children at Hyde Park during election week, and to her F.D.R. excitedly wrote the letters which follow, as the returns were coming in and as he was experiencing "the most extraordinary day of my life."

WASHINGTON
NOVEMBER 8, 1916
WEDNESDAY

Dearest Babs,

The most extraordinary day of my life. After last night, Wilson may be elected after all. It looks hopeful at noon. The reaction from yesterday is great. All well here, also the Lanes with whom I dine. I do have hopes for their sakes.

Your devoted

F.

∽∽

WASHINGTON
NOVEMBER 9, 1916
THURSDAY

Dearest Babs,

Another day of the most wild uncertainty. Returns, after conflicting, have been coming in every hour from Cal.,

338

N.M., N.D., Minn., and N.H. Without any of these Wilson seems to have 251 votes safe, 266 necessary to choice. This p.m. it appears we have N. Dakota 5 votes safe and in California (13) we are well ahead, though there are still 200 districts to hear from. Minn. (12) looks less favorable, also N. Mexico (3), but N. Hamp. (4) is getting better and we may carry it.

I dined at the Lanes', Adolph also, and they feel the strain much. Tonight I dine at home. It is warm today, real Indian summer. I have any amount of work to do and J.D. is too damned slow for words—his failure to decide the few big things holds me up all down the line.

Kiss the chicks and much love to yourself. It will be too nice to have you here next week. Curtains are up and new female, name Jenny, here. I leave Saturday noon for Chicago.

Your devoted

F.

I enclose a more complete copy of the Paine letter to Washington. Also do you want me to pay Brooks bill?

If Wilson is elected I shall wire as follows:

"W. Delano

Barrytown

The Republican party has proved to its own satisfaction I hope that the American people cannot always be bought.

FDR"

I hope to God I don't grow reactionary with advancing years.

These two letters portray the spirit and "wild uncertainty" of the circumstances surrounding Wilson's second election. Early in the morning of November 9th, before the returns came in from the West, both the *New York Times* and the *World* announced Hughes's election in banner headlines, calling it a "sweeping victory." Indeed, Hughes had gone to bed the night before confident that his next four years would be spent in the White House, and the story is told how his son replied to a late caller that the "President cannot be disturbed." As can be gathered from this letter, the next day the picture began to change, culminating in a 3773 vote majority for Wilson in California. Except for Ohio and New Hampshire, Hughes won every state north of the Mason-Dixon line and east of the Mississippi, but the thirteen electoral votes of the Golden State was the margin of victory, the final electoral tally favoring Wilson by 277 to 254.

∽∽

Excepting the Presidency, election day was won by the Republicans. The Democratic majority in the House was completely wiped out (each party electing 214 Representatives), and reduced from 16 to 12 in the Senate. Four years later this trend would prove of immense importance to the nation and especially to F.D.R. For the time being, nevertheless, the Presidential vote held the greatest significance. It meant that Wilson's leadership was desired for the pending crisis; the American people did not care to "swap horses while crossing the stream." The election was a personal triumph for the President, a vote of confidence in his efforts "to keep us out of war."

The political excitement quickly subsided, and concern for the affairs of Europe was intensified in Washington. On December 18, 1916, Wilson—regarding his reelection as an endorsement of his peace efforts—sent a note to all the belligerents requesting that they "state their views as to the terms on which the war might be concluded . . . in order that we may learn how near the haven of peace may be." His attempts at mediation, however, were not sincerely welcomed in the capitals of Europe; and thus, as A.E.R. noted in *This Is My Story,* "there was a sense of impending disaster hanging over all of us" as 1916 drew to a close.

∽∽

IX

"... I Am Inexpressibly Busy ..."

ASSISTANT SECRETARY OF THE NAVY

1917-1918

UNBEKNOWN to most of the world, a German crown council on January 9, 1917, decided that on the first day of the next month unrestricted submarine warfare would be resumed. This decision was the climax of a long struggle within Germany between the military and diplomatic factions. For nearly three years the latter group, led by Chancellor Theobald von Bethmann-Hollweg, succeeded in their efforts to have Germany pursue a policy of preventing war with the United States at any cost. Toward the end of 1916, however, sentiment in Germany began to shift to the frequently proposed argument of Generals Hindenburg and Ludendorff that a German victory could only be achieved through a resumption of unrestricted submarine warfare. The war had gone badly for the Central Powers in 1916. Their hopes for a swift and triumphant end of hostilities by a tremendous blow at Verdun went unrealized when the Allied lines held. At sea the Battle of Jutland in May, 1916, convinced the

Germans of British naval superiority. The Allied blockade, too, was taking its toll, and the advent of food riots was clear indication of an alarming internal situation. Hence, despite military successes in the East, the Germans came to realize that time was running out, and Hindenburg's contention that Germany's weakening economic and military position made an unrestricted submarine campaign essential thus became more and more plausible.

Early in December, 1916, the German high command made its last concession to Bethmann-Hollweg, consenting to postpone the submarine campaign long enough for him to attempt peace negotiations with the Allies. These proposals, which revealed Germany's precarious position through the absence of any specific terms of peace, were transmitted to the Allied governments shortly before Wilson's offer to act as mediator. Claiming that the effort to open negotiations was a war maneuver and not a genuine offer of peace, the Allies rejected the "empty and insincere" proposals on December 30th. His diplomatic efforts having failed, Bethmann-Hollweg at last agreed to Hindenburg's plan and German foreign policy came under the full sway of its military faction and its submarine commanders.

❦

For F.D.R. the early weeks of 1917 were devoted to preparations for an inspection trip to Haiti, where after a year and a half of American intervention order and solvency were slowly being restored. F.D.R. had an intense interest in the development of the island republics of the Caribbean. The road-building and public-works projects of Haiti so captured his enthusiasm that a newspaper story quoted him as having stated that "I wrote the Constitution of Haiti." (Although this was a false report, it later became an issue in his Vice-Presidential campaign and had to be vigorously denied.) It was thus with a sense of anticipation that F.D.R. wrote the next letter to his mother.

[JANUARY 21, 1917]

SUNDAY

Dearest Mama,

I am off at 3—John McIlhenny, Livingston Davis, General Barnett and Captain Keyser. Arrive Key West Tuesday a.m. and go across to Havana by destroyer, call on President Menocal Wednesday a.m., arriving Santiago by rail Thursday a.m. and Port au Prince, Haiti, Friday. The 5-day ride in Haiti starts the 29th and then another ride across Santo Domingo brings us to S.D. City the 8th and Guantanamo by boat the 10th, and home by boat arriving I hope the 15th.

I hate to leave E. and the chicks, but they are all right except for F Jr.'s tonsils. I hope you will be here when I return. You must be having a lovely trip. Love to Rosy and Betty, and a great deal for yourself.

Your affec son

FDR

The Dutchess Co. dinner was very successful and all at 47 was well.

Marine Captain Ralph S. Keyser was at this time an aide to General Barnett.

Sara Roosevelt's "trip" consisted of a visit to James Roosevelt Roosevelt and his wife, who were vacationing at Hot Springs, Arizona. Sensing her son's excitement, she answered this letter on January 27, 1917, with a few carefully chosen words of motherly advice regarding F.D.R.'s health: "Dearest Son, I have been longing for a letter from you and today brings me your welcome letter of Sunday noon the 21st just before you left, so you did write me before going so far away. You seem to have a nice party and I hope it is a very interesting trip, and hours of riding in the open air must be fine every day. I hope you took dark glasses and a pith hat for I know how you feel the tropical sun. Do you remember Nassau? You must have reached Haiti yesterday, and on Monday when we are at the Roosevelt Dam you will start on a 5 days' ride. I had three letters from Eleanor today. . . ."

The annual dinner of the Dutchess County Society was held at the Hotel Astor in New York City. The *New York Times* of January 21, 1917, reported that "practically every speaker on the long program took a fling at the advocates of 'peace at any price,'" which no doubt influenced F.D.R.'s estimate that the "dinner was very successful." After quoting in full the key speeches, the *Times* noted that "Assistant Secretary of the Navy Franklin D. Roosevelt proposed a toast to Admiral Dewey . . . [and] said he was leaving this morning for Haiti."

F.D.R. was unable to carry out his detailed plans for the inspection of Haiti. Midway through the trip he received an urgent message from Josephus Daniels requesting his immediate return to Washington—American neutrality was in its final stages and the U.S. Navy had been alerted for war. On January 31, 1917, Germany had announced to the world that the following day all vessels, neutral or belligerent, traveling within certain zones surrounding Great Britain, France, Italy, and the eastern Mediterranean would "without further notice, be prevented by all weapons." All limitations on submarine warfare were removed, except that each week one American passenger ship would be allowed to pass through a narrow safety lane in each direction between the U.S. and England. Claiming that the renewal of the unrestricted submarine campaign was a violation of the *Sussex* pledge, Wilson three days later announced to Congress that the United States was severing diplomatic relations with Germany. Earlier in the day, von Bernstorff had been handed his passports.

Wilson's action was expected by the German high command, but they believed that the war could be won through recourse to submarine warfare before American military power could effectively influence the outcome. Carrying this belief further, Zimmerman, the German secretary for foreign affairs, sought to embarrass the U.S. by instructing the German minister in Mexico to arrange an alliance between the two countries whereby Germany would provide financial support and Mexico would "reconquer the lost territory of New Mexico, Texas, and Arizona." However, at the time that he announced the severance of relations, Wilson was unaware of the extent to which Germany intended to pursue its new policy. He did not believe German submarines would actually carry out unrestricted warfare, and therefore preferred to postpone further action until "overt acts" had been committed.

But events moved swiftly. The German order was tantamount to an embargo on American shipping. Shipowners did not dare risk the loss of their merchantmen, and not one American ship left New York for the war zone during the first week after the severance of relations. Pointing this fact out to Congress, Wilson on February 26th requested authority to arm merchant vessels. On the same day eight American lives were lost when the British steamship *Laconia* was sunk without warning; three days later the Zimmerman notes to Mexico were published in the United States. On March 1st the House passed the Armed Ship bill, but Senate authorization was not forthcoming as a small group employed the filibuster to prevent passage of the measure before Congress expired on March 4th. The next week, with Congress not in session, Wilson ordered armed neutrality by executive authority. On March 15th the Czarist regime in Russia was overthrown and replaced by a coalition of popular forces known as the Kerensky government. The immediate consequence of this revolution was to remove another barrier preventing American entry into the war, for now Americans would not have "to fight side by side with the autocratic and intolerable government" of Czarist Russia. The next day the final barrier was removed when three American ships were sunk by German torpedoes; this was the "overt act," the end of neutrality and the beginning of war.

On April 2, 1917, Woodrow Wilson called Congress into special session and asked for a declaration of war against Germany. A.E.R. writes in *This Is My Story:* "Everyone wanted to hear this historic address and it was with the greatest difficulty that Franklin got me a seat. I went and listened breathlessly." This impression is easily understood, for Wilson was eloquent:

. . . With a profound sense of the solemn and even tragical character of the step I am taking and of the grave responsibilities which it involves, but in unhesitating obedience to what I deem my constitutional duty, I advise that the Congress declare the recent course of the Imperial German Government to be in fact nothing less than war against the government and people of the United States; that it formally accept the status of belligerent which has thus been thrust upon it; and that it take immediate steps not only to put the country in a more thorough state of defense but also to exert all its power and employ all its resources to bring the Government of the German Empire to terms and end the war. . . .

Congress adopted the declaration of war during the next two days, and on April 6, 1917, Wilson proclaimed that "a state of war exists between the United States and the Imperial German Government."

In *This Is My Story* A.E.R. observed that "from then on the men in the Government worked from morning until night and late into the night." As can be gathered from the letters that follow, by the time A.E.R. took the family to Campobello in July the pressure of equipping the Navy for war was beginning to tell on F.D.R. "I am unreasonable and touchy now," he admitted; and in a way this mood characterized the entire country as it went to war against a first-class foreign power for the first time in over a century, as it engaged in a battle to make the world "safe for democracy."

Dearest Babs,

I had a vile day after you left, stayed at home, coughed, dozed, tried to read and work and failed even to play Miss Millikin! But today I am practically all right and have been here at office as usual, except for lunch with the Blanpre's and am going to dine with Warren and Irene alone. I really can't stand that house all alone without you, and you were a goosy girl to think or even pretend to think that I don't want you here *all* the summer, because you know I do! But honestly *you* ought to have six weeks straight at Campo, just as *I* ought to, only you can and I can't! I *know* what a whole summer here does to people's nerves and at the end of this summer I will be like a bear with a sore head until I get a change or some cold weather—in fact as you know I am unreasonable and touchy now—but I shall try to improve.

It has been hot and wet all day and now at 6 p.m. the usual thunderstorm.

I do hope all will go well with you in Boston and that the Touraine man will meet you and fix up the tickets and checks. I am too sorry about it and will kick myself forever.

Kiss the chicks for me all round and many many for you.

Your devoted

F

I opened this from Bob as it was addressed to me!

"Miss Millikin" was a game of solitaire that F.D.R. occasionally played. The naval attache of the French Embassy in Washington, Commander de Blanpré, with his wife were close friends of the Roosevelts during these later years of the Wilson Administration. "Bob" refers to Robert Ferguson.

〰️

347

Dearest Babs,

It seems years since you left and I miss you horribly and hate the thought of the empty house. Last night I thought I heard a burglar and sat at the head of the stairs with the gun for half an hour, but it turned out to be the cat.

My cold is about gone. Today I lunched with Robert Neeser and go to Adolph's to meet the Sec'y of the Interior and Mrs. Lane at dinner!

We exercised this a.m. at 7:30 and though very hot it has since got cooler. The usual thunderstorm came up last night and another is now brewing.

Write me all about the Half Moon and the house and place. The chief thing I worry about is fire, and you must see that the extinguishers are filled, that the fireplaces in the rooms are pointed up and that no large fire is left when you go to bed.

I wonder how the chicks like Campo this year?

Evidently you told Mama I had a cold. I have had a telegram and letter!

Love and kisses to you all.

Your devoted

F

F.D.R. "exercised" under the auspices of the Navy Athletic Commission headed by Walter Camp, Yale's renowned football strategist. In *The Wilson Era* Josephus Daniels notes that, after organizing a physical fitness program for the Navy, Camp "was not content with prescribing strenuous exercises for the young men. He rented a house in Washington and made it a place for athletic exercise for members of the Cabinet and others with responsible duties. A score accepted his invitation, and every morning at seven o'clock they repaired to his place for setting-up exercises, then a rub-down and breakfast with Camp before entering upon their duties." F.D.R. was a regular member of this "score."

This is the last reference to the *Half Moon* as a family property; later in the year F.D.R. sold it to the government when private yachts were needed to assist in the campaign against German submarines.

∞

All I can say is that your latest newspaper campaign is a corker and I am proud to be the husband of the Originator, Discoverer and Inventor of the New Household Economy for Millionaires! Please have a photo taken showing the family, the ten cooperating servants, the scraps saved from the table and the hand book. I will have it published in the Sunday Times.

Honestly you have leaped into public fame, all Washington is talking of the Roosevelt plan and I begin to get telegrams of congratulation and requests for further details from Pittsburgh, New Orleans, San Francisco and other neighboring cities.

Uncle Fred says "It's fine, but Gee how mad Eleanor will be!"

All quiet and cold all gone. Dined with Adolph last night, also Mrs. Lane, Houston and Harding.

It rained today slightly but we did our exercises. I lunched on desk and dine quietly at home. I will write Sister tomorrow and have written Mama!

Your devoted

F

This jesting letter to A.E.R. refers to a nationwide news release which was published by the *New York Times* on July 17, 1917, as follows:

Washington, July 16. The food-saving program adopted at the home of Franklin D. Roosevelt, Assistant Secretary of the Navy, has been selected by the conservation section of the Food Administration as a model for other large households. Mrs. Roosevelt on her pledge card said that there were seven in the family, and that ten servants were employed. Each servant has signed a pledge card, and there are daily conferences.

Mrs. Roosevelt does the buying, the cooks see that there is no food wasted, the laundress is sparing in her use of soap, each servant has a watchful eye for evidence of short-comings on the part of the others; and all are encouraged to make helpful suggestions in the use of "left overs."

No bacon is used in the Roosevelt home; corn bread is served once a day. The consumption of laundry soap has been cut in half. Meat is served but once daily, and all "left overs" are utilized. Menu rules allow two courses for lunch-eon and three for dinner. Everybody eats fish at least once a week.

"Making the ten servants help me do my saving has not only been possible but highly profitable," said Mrs. Roose-velt today. "Since I have started following the home-card instructions prices have risen, but my bills are no larger."

A.E.R. substantiated Frederic A. Delano's remark by writ-ing to F.D.R. on July 20th that "I do think it was horrid of that woman to use my name in that way and I feel dread-fully about it because so much is not true and yet some of it I did say. I never will be caught again that's sure and I'd like to crawl away for shame."

A Harvard graduate and college president, David F. Houston held the Agriculture post in Wilson's Cabinet from 1913 until 1920, when he succeeded Carter Glass as Secretary of the Treasury, a position more compatible with Houston's wide knowledge of finance and economics. He later served as chairman of the Federal Reserve and Farm Loan Boards, and became president of the Bell Telephone Securities Company. Another of F.D.R.'s dinner com-

panions was banker William G. Harding, an associate of
Adolph Miller on the Federal Reserve Board, to which he
had been elected a governor in 1916; two years later he
became managing director of the War Finance Corporation.
"Sister" refers to F.D.R.'s daughter.

∞

Dearest Babs,

It is still cool here and all goes on quietly. Today I lunched
on my desk and am to dine at the Club.

Yours from Boston and Campo has just come and I am
overjoyed that all goes well at the place and that the journey
was not very bad. By the way, I meant to tell you that if by
any perfectly wild chance a German submarine should come
into the bay and start to shell Eastport or the Pool, I want
you to grab the children and beat it into the woods. Don't
stay to see what is going on. I am not joking about this, for
while it is 500 to 1 against the possibility, still there is just
that one chance that the Bosch will do the fool and unexpected thing.

All well. Kiss the chicks.

Your devoted

F.

∞

WASHINGTON
[JULY 23, 1917]
MONDAY

Dearest Babs,

Just back from Richmond and the Sylph—we had a bully
trip and I was particularly [glad] to see the fleet and have a
chance to talks things over firsthand with the officers. I will
write you later about it all.

Auntie Bye arrives this p.m. and I will go to meet her.

Devotedly

FDR

∞

Dearest Babs,

Since I got back on Monday morning I have been so rushed and so gay that I haven't sat down to think quietly for one second. Auntie Bye arrived at 4 p.m. and I spent an hour with her, returning to Department and then home here to dine with her. There was much to discuss and we had a delightful evening.

Yesterday I came home and lunched with her in the midst of plumbers, paperers, etc., and did the same thing today. Last night she dined with Senator Lodge and tonight goes to Alice and leaves early tomorrow morning.

Last night I dined at the Montgomery Country Club with the Billy Elkins' and tonight I go to the Barnetts' at the Marine Barracks!

———

The trip on the Sylph was a joy and a real rest, though I got in a most satisfactory visit to the fleet. Such a funny party, but it worked out *wonderfully!* The Charlie Munns, the Cary Graysons, Lucy Mercer and Nigel Law, and they all got on splendidly. We swam about four times and Sunday afternoon went up the James to Richmond. We stopped at Lower and Upper Brandon, Westover and Shirley and went all over them, getting drenched to the skin by several severe thunder storms. Those old houses are really wonderful but *not* comfy!

I found much food for thought in the fleet—things not right and due to old lady officers and lack of decision in Department. We inspected the fleet in a destroyer and lunched with Admiral Tommy Rodgers on the Arkansas.

Today I have been before the House Committee all day trying to get 147 millions!

It has been pretty hot and today a tremendous rain—3

inches and a leak in the sewing room extending to F Jr.'s
room and the dining room ceilings!

I am very well and do my exercises with regularity!

Your devoted

F

The presence of the "plumbers, paperers, etc.," was occasioned by the fact that Mrs. Cowles was doing over her
house for new tenants. The "Little White House" on N
Street was not large enough to house a family of seven comfortably and the Roosevelts were to move to 2131 R Street in
the autumn of 1917, after their return from Campobello.

Massachusetts Senator Henry Cabot Lodge was an associate of T.R., and consequently F.D.R.'s family had always
known him; after twenty-five years' service in the Senate he
became Republican Majority Leader in 1918, as well as
chairman of the Foreign Relations Committee, positions
in which he later gained added prominence as Wilson's
main adversary in the Congressional fight over the League
of Nations. Charles A. Munn was in the class of 1910 at
Harvard and an acquaintance of F.D.R. His wife, formerly
Mary Astor Paul, worked with A.E.R. in the Red Cross
during the war. Cary T. Grayson had served as a surgeon
at the White House during both T.R. and Taft's adminis-
trations, and held the rank of lieutenant commander when
he became Wilson's physician in 1913. Impressed by Grayson's abilities, Wilson three years later recommended his
appointment as Medical Director of the Navy, with a jump
in rank to rear admiral. This was considered an unprece-
dented promotion at the time, and Grayson's nomination
created a fight in the Senate that included a filibuster and
vicious accusations of favoritism directed at Wilson. The
Senate acquiesced, however, and Grayson soon proved that
he merited the advancement. He and F.D.R. became good
friends during these war years in Washington, and when
F.D.R. returned to the capital as President he made Dr.
Grayson head of the Red Cross. Nigel Law was the Third
Secretary of the British Embassy in Washington.

The "147 millions" were to be used by the Navy to purchase war materials, including ammunition, ordnance stores, clothing, yard and dock improvements, and the other miscellaneous equipment and supplies commensurate with the needs of wartime.

∽

Dearest Babs,

Yesterday I wrote you all about our trip but posted the letter in our corner box which was marked "Paint" and it occurs to me too late that perhaps the postman will hesitate to open it.

Last night I dined at the Barnetts', a large garden party of about 40 in honor of the Daniels! But as it poured we had the party without the garden and I had a very dull time sitting between Mrs. Townsend and Mrs. McCawley and chatting afterwards with Mrs. James!

It is a real scorcher today, the hottest yet.

I dine with Mrs. Lippincott and am just back from lunch with Winston Churchill. He saw the President yesterday and apparently had a pretty satisfactory talk.

Kiss the chicks. I do miss you so *very* much, but I am getting busier and busier and fear my hoped-for dash to Campo next week for two days will not materialize. Nor can I get to H.P. for Sunday, as I found my absence last Sunday has put me too far back.

Your devoted

F

Mrs. Richard H. Townsend and Mrs. Julian James were leading dowagers in Washington society at the time; the former's daughter, Mathilde, later became the second wife of Sumner Welles. Mrs. McCawley, the former Sarah H. Frelinghuysen, was the wife of Charles L. McCawley *(vide supra);* while Mrs. Lippincott was a younger Washingtonian friend of the Roosevelts.

After nearly two years of political obscurity and service in France as a major with the Grenadier Guards, Winston Churchill was appointed England's Minister of Munitions early in July, 1917. This post occasionally required his presence in the United States to secure American aid. During the first years of the war Churchill had been First Lord of the Admiralty, and was largely responsible for the preparedness of the British fleet in August, 1914. Although he had been demoted in 1915 because of internal politics and the ill-fated Dardanelles expedition, Churchill's naval record was admired in the United States, especially by the far-sighted men in the Navy Department. As can be seen in the next letter, F.D.R. in particular admired Churchill's imaginative and vigorous method of coping with war and naval problems. Some of F.D.R.'s contemporaries in the Department noted a similarity between their approaches to the conduct of the war; a comparison between Churchill's fight for the Dardanelles campaign and F.D.R.'s efforts to win approval of a mine barrage in the North Sea was not infrequently made.

It is likely that the question of bottling up Germany's submarine fleet in the North Sea was discussed in the course of Churchill's "satisfactory talk" with Wilson and during his luncheon with F.D.R. This topic was a primary consideration of American and British government circles in the summer of 1917, for the renewal of unrestricted submarine warfare was taking a heavy toll of Allied shipping. During the first three months of the submarine campaign more than two million tons had been lost by the Allies, and it became everywhere recognized that unless this situation was remedied the war would be prolonged for several years. In the Navy Department frequent cables from Admiral William S. Sims, Commander of American Naval Forces in European Waters, asking for anti-submarine craft reinforcements, were a constant reminder that new methods had to be quickly devised. Sims took an even more serious view of the Allies' precarious position than his superiors, as witnessed by a paragraph from his book written in 1921: [1]

"In the spring of 1917 the situation which we were facing was that the German submarines were destroying Allied shipping at the rate of nearly 800,000 tons a month. The one thing which was certain was that if this destruction should continue for four or five months, the Allies would be obliged to surrender unconditionally."

With the failure of existing methods to combat the U-boat menace successfully, the laying of a mine barrage across the North Sea from the Orkney Islands to the coast of Norway was proposed in order "to shut the hornets up in their nest." The summer and autumn months of 1917 were marked by American efforts to overcome British opposition to this proposal, which was considered completely impracticable by the Admiralty. There were likewise many opponents of the "infeasible" plan in the United States. Against both obstacles F.D.R. labored for many months. He had become an outspoken supporter of the North Sea operation following contact with the inventor of a mine capable of forming the 240-mile barrage; and it irked him that valuable time was being lost while the responsible officials argued. Not until November, 1917, was the barrage approved, and several months elapsed thereafter before the mines were laid.

∾

WOODLEY LANE

WASHINGTON

[AUGUST 17, 1917]

FRIDAY

Dearest Babs,

Just a line before I go in to dine at the Ohls', damn nuisance as it's lovely out here this evening.

All well and a *very* busy day.

The more I think over the talk with the President the more I am encouraged to think that he has *begun* to catch

[1] *Victory at Sea* by William S. Sims, New York, 1921.

on, but then it will take lots more of the Churchill type of attack. I lunched with Willert and there is nothing more to do till Northcliffe comes down next Wednesday.

Kiss the chicks and loads of love. Your devoted F

In the interval between this and the preceding letter there was a recurrence of F.D.R.'s throat infection, and A.E.R. journeyed to Washington to be with him while he spent a week in the hospital. After his recovery and her departure, he wrote this note from the Phillips residence at Woodley Lane in the outskirts of Washington.

Joseph Kingsley Ohl had been the Washington correspondent of the *New York Herald* from 1896 to 1906, and at this writing was on the paper's editorial staff. Shortly thereafter he became the *Herald*'s editor-in-chief. As for the "talk with the President," although undoubtedly it was in connection with the North Sea barrage, even A.E.R. was somewhat confused by the reference, for she replied on August 21st: "Your letter of Friday came last night and I was glad of a word at last but can't help wondering if you wrote before, for you allude to your talk with the President but don't tell me when or anything."

That founder of the British popular press, Alfred Harmsworth, Lord Northcliffe, controlled seven English newspapers at the outbreak of the war in 1914, including the London *Times* and *Daily Mail*. The much-abused "Northcliffe press" became a valuable morale factor in England during the conflict, and Northcliffe himself wrote the famous story from Verdun in 1916 which startled and pleased the Allied world by claiming that the city was "unlikely to be taken." After turning down a number of cabinet posts, in June of 1917 Northcliffe was persuaded to accept the chairmanship of the British War Mission to the United States, a job he held until the following November. In recognition of his services in Washington he was created a viscount.

Dearest Babs,

I had a very occupied Sunday, starting off for golf at 9 with McIlhenny, Legare, and McCawley, quick lunch at Chevy Chase, then in to town and off in car at 2:30 to the Horsey's place near Harper's Ferry. Lucy Mercer went and the Graysons and we got there at 5:30, walked over the farm—a very rich one and run by the two sisters—had supper with them and several neighbors, left at nine and got home at midnight! The day was magnificent, but the road more dusty and even more crowded than when we went to Gettysburg.

By the way, they handed in a record amount of sweaters and other wooleys on Saturday and all wanted to know how the Daniels-Thompson row would affect the work. I told them to sit tight, keep on knitting and not rock the boat!

I hope to see Northcliffe on Wednesday and will then wire you what day I arrive!

Loads of love and kisses.

Your devoted

F

I enclose the cheques for taxes, please *endorse* them over to the collectors.

The "Daniels-Thompson row" created a nationwide commotion and was the climax of Daniels' prolonged fight against the Navy League, which frequently challenged his authority. The "row" began on August 14, 1917, when the League issued a gratuitous statement to the effect that the investigation of the recent explosion at the Mare Island Navy Yard had been "blocked" by the demand of "labor influences." Aroused by the "false and slanderous" accusation, Daniels wrote the president of the Navy League, Colonel Robert M. Thompson, and asked him and the other officers of the League to resign their positions in view of the "treasonable action by the League toward the government and a gross slander of patriotic workers in the Navy Yard." In his reply Thompson offered to resign if Daniels would quit his post in Wilson's Cabinet. Two days later Daniels issued orders barring officers and agents of the Navy League from any naval ship, station, or reservation, and he further declared that until the League had "purged itself" of its officers the Navy would receive no contributions from that organization, "not even a postage stamp." With this move the dispute threatened catastrophe to the efforts of some 400,000 women who comprised the membership of the Comforts Committee of the Navy League, and who were mainly engaged in knitting "sweaters and other wooleys" for the Navy.

A.E.R. was an active member of the Comforts Committee and on August 21, 1917, wrote F.D.R. her views on the controversy: "What a mess about the Navy League but I think Mr. D. has made a mistake to refuse all garments from them. People will be discouraged and the volume of work will take forever to pick up if it does at all." Sara Roosevelt, too, had some comments on the subject (in a separate letter written the same day from Campobello): "What you wrote about the row between Mr. D. and Col. T. is reassuring. I confess Eleanor and I are both troubled and I do think constant changes and reorganizations of Leagues hurts them and takes away interest. We have even in Hyde Park 130 members, all knitting hard, and I am also vice-chairman of the Woman's Section of the Navy League in New York and am writing letters, begging for Christmas bags and donations. I suppose Sec. D. is very angry, but he ought not to interfere with the work. Perhaps Col. Thompson will resign! A young man wrote one of the Porters that it was a scandal the way the men go for the sweaters, mufflers, etc., which are given, when they can perfectly afford to buy them. He is in Captain Gibbons' boat, or training camp? He wrote some men just wear the sweaters under their own under-flannels. There certainly are a great number of people who long to get all they can for nothing, even when they are comfortably off."

Nevertheless, public opinion generally upheld Daniels' action, as did a later report on the Mare Island explosion which proved the League's charges to be distinctly false. In the meantime, a director of the Comforts Committee, Mrs. Edward T. Stotesbury of Philadelphia, resigned from the League and became the head of a Red Cross auxiliary which undertook the job of collecting the knitted garments. Maintaining his refusal to deal with the Comforts Committee amidst accusations that he was denying enlisted men their sweaters, Daniels recognized Mrs. Stotesbury's rival organization; thereafter (as he noted in *The Wilson Era*) "there was no lack of gifts to Naval personnel." Eventually Thompson withdrew his charges and Daniels relaxed his orders against the League; in the long run the episode tended to have a beneficial effect upon the somewhat autocratic League.

∽

WASHINGTON
SEPTEMBER 9, 1917
SUNDAY

Dearest Babs,

A very busy day, consisting of steady golf, 36 holes, from 9 a.m. to 6 p.m. with an hour out for sandwich and rest. The usual crowd of my contemporaries, McIlhenny, Legare, McCawley, Hollis, and we dined quietly at a very dry Metropolitan Club and now home at nine. Yesterday the usual work and dinner at home.

Monday. Nothing exciting today. I lunched with Mr. and Mrs. Homer at the Shoreham and am just back from dinner with eight of the British Embassy "boys" out at Woodley in the old Grover Cleveland house near the Cathedral. It is frightfully cold. I only hope it will get warmer for your trip tomorrow.

Yours has come telling of the safe arrival of the tickets and I hope all will go well on the trip and that Huckins will meet you all right.

Tuesday. Still very cold but the papers say warmer. I dine with Hohler tonight—Springy is back, and I think Senator Lodge is to be the fourth.

No news, except that apparently Daniels has chucked the Comforts Committee entirely and is trying to organize a rival set under the Red Cross and to be directed by Mrs. Stotesbury. The end is not yet as the League (or at least the Comforts Com.) is I think going to fight back.

You are entirely disconnected and Lucy Mercer and Mrs. Munn are closing up the loose ends.

Give a great deal of love to Hall, Margaret and the babies and kiss Anna for me. I hope she is loving her first grown up visiting party.

Your devoted

F

The reference to "the usual crowd of my contemporaries" is a facetious one, as F.D.R. was by ten years the youngest member of the group. One of the Metropolitan Club dining companions was Henry French Hollis, the first Massachusetts Democrat since 1852 to be elected to the Senate; he served from 1913 to 1919. Mr. and Mrs. Arthur P. Homer were friends of the Roosevelts from Boston. Huckins replaced the unfortunate Golden as F.D.R.'s chauffeur. Sir Thomas Beaumont Hohler was at this time counselor of the British Embassy in Washington.

WASHINGTON

OCTOBER 10, 1917

WEDNESDAY

Dearest Babs,

Sallie got here safely and we had a nice dinner à quatre. All is well and the servants have not left in a body. That is all I know about it except that Maude and Sallie expect to continue to jolly them along!

I am really too sad that you will not be here for tomorrow.

I did so want to be with you the 11th. We shall drink your health and we all miss you so much.

James is well and apparently very happy and keen about the School.

I am inexpressibly busy, something new turning up every minute, so that I am really forced to put off the less important stuff and am behind in the work and trying to catch up.

Give my love to Elliott.

Very many happy returns of the day from

Your devoted

F

Questioned about the first paragraph of this letter, A.E.R. explained that "probably I was worried because they were having so many guests and the servants were trying to get the house ready. I thought they were going to leave in a body and remonstrated."

ON TRAIN [TO NEW YORK]

SATURDAY

Dearest Babs,

We are on time so far and I still hope to catch the 6:55 up river. I entirely forgot your necklace in the rush of departure and you will find it in my cupboard under my soft shirts.

I hope the canteen went well this morning and that you will all enjoy the football game this afternoon.

The Willard Straights are on the train and I am just going to pay them a visit in their drawing room.

This car has a flat wheel, as an expert in penmanship could tell without this information.

If my train is very late on Tuesday morning, i.e., after 9:30, I will go straight to the office and telephone you from there and come home for lunch.

Your devoted

F

The exact date of this letter cannot be ascertained. It is placed at this point in the correspondence because of the reference to A.E.R.'s canteen work and the mention of a football game, *i.e.,* the latter event places it in the autumn months and the former in either 1917 or 1918. In *This Is My Story* A.E.R. fully outlined her work in the Red Cross canteen during these war years, and as can be gathered from her remarks, it was an invaluable experience:

"I think I learned then that practically no one in the world is entirely bad or entirely good, and that motives are often more important than actions. I had spent most of my life in an atmosphere where everyone was sure of what was right and what was wrong. . . . Out of these contacts with human beings during the war I became a more tolerant person, far less sure of my own beliefs and methods of action, but I think more determined to try for certain ultimate objectives."

Willard Straight was married to Dorothy Payne Whitney; he was a Morgan partner and she the daughter of William C. Whitney, Cleveland's Secretary of the Navy. They were among the founders and permanent supporters of *The New Republic;* their son, Michael Straight, is the present editor of that liberal weekly.

∞

WASHINGTON
[OCTOBER 29, 1917]
MONDAY

Dearest Babs,

Back again safely and found Livy still here, though the Houstons had gone yesterday. The Davis' have taken the McComb house on N. H. Avenue just below N. and are delighted with it. Livy will return to Boston Thursday and not come back till the 6th or 7th.

I have seen Pollen and later Lord Northcliffe, and have given the Sec'y a very stinging memorandum and sent a copy to the President. Some day they will be interesting reading!

All is well and peaceful in the house. I forget whether you spend the night in New York tomorrow so will send this to Hyde Park.

Your devoted

F

Arthur Pollen was a British naval expert connected with Northcliffe's War Mission. Carbon copies of the "stinging memorandum" to Josephus Daniels and the letter to President Wilson were found among F.D.R.'s naval papers at the Franklin D. Roosevelt Library. Although not personal letters, in view of the remark that "some day they will make interesting reading," they are included herewith in the correspondence.

OCTOBER 29, 1917

CONFIDENTIAL

MEMORANDUM FOR THE SECRETARY:

SUBJECT: Proposed measures to close English Channel and North Sea against submarines by mine barrage.

1. This is, of course, nothing more nor less than a resurrection of my proposition, which, with all earnestness possible, I called to the attention of the President, the Secretary of the Navy, the Chief of Operations, the General Board, Admiral Sims (and through him the British Admiralty), Admiral de Chair (and through him also the British Admiralty) and Admiral Chocheprat (and through him the French Ministry of Marine) during the months of May and June past.

2. While I have never claimed that the proposed plan was an infallible one, and while, quite properly, I have never attempted to lay down the exact location or the exact type of mines, etc., to be used in the barrage, I did state, and still

state, that every consideration of common sense requires that the attempt be made, first in the English Channel and then in the North Sea.

3. But above all, starting when the Balfour and Viviani Missions were here in May, I reiterated the need for haste. I know how unseemly it is to seem to say "I told you so," but it is a literal fact that, while the British Admiralty may be blamed in part, our own Navy Department is at least largely responsible for failing to consider this proposition seriously during all of these months—May, June, July, August, September and October—which have gone over the dam beyond recall.

4. Now, this is the milk in the cocoanut: The powers that be seem at last willing to take up this proposition seriously. Unless we are willing to throw up our hands and say it is too late, we must admit that the same need for immediate haste exists today as existed last May. We have done altogether too much amiable "consideration" of this matter. If it is to be carried out at all it must be carried out with a different spirit from any of the operations up to now. It will require prompt decision all along the line and an immediate carrying out of the procurement of the material—mines and ships.

5. To accomplish the above it should be placed in the hands of one man on our part and one man on the part of the British. These two men should receive orders from their governments, not as to details, but simply orders to carry out the plan. *And most important of all, these men should have all the authority requisite to do this.* This is a bigger matter than sending destroyers abroad or a division of battleships, or building a bunch of new destroyers—it is vital to the winning of the war. Its success cannot be guaranteed. No military or naval operation can be guaranteed. But if it works it will be the biggest single factor in winning the war. I have seen something during the past four and a

half years of how our present Navy Department organization works and it so happens that I am also fairly familiar with the way the British Admiralty works. If the suggested plan is carried out solely under the present organizations its chance of success will, in my judgment, be seriously diminished. You need somebody with imagination and authority to make the try.

6. I know you will not mind my sending a copy of this to the President, as I have discussed it with him several times.

[FRANKLIN D. ROOSEVELT]
Assistant Secretary of the Navy

❦

OCTOBER 29, 1917

Dear Mr. President:

I am very sorry to bother you, but in view of our several talks during the summer I am sending a copy of a memorandum which I have just given to the Secretary. As you probably know, Admiral Mayo reported on his return that the British Admiralty would like "serious consideration" of the Straits of Dover and Scotland to Norway barriers, and a week or so later we telegraphed Admiral Sims to ask whether the British Admiralty really approved attempting the plan. We received an affirmative reply a few days ago and now our General Board has also approved.

This much has been accomplished in six months, but it is my duty to tell you that if the plan is put into execution with the same speed and method employed in the past other priceless months will be wasted and the success of the plan will be jeopardized. I can only repeat what I have told the Secretary: Some one person in whom you have confidence should be given the order and the necessary authority to execute the plan without delay, and he, working with an Englishman clothed with the same orders and authority, will succeed if success is possible.

I dislike exaggeration, but it is really true that the elimination of all submarines from the waters between the United States and Europe must of necessity be a vital factor in winning the war.

Faithfully yours,

[FRANKLIN D. ROOSEVELT]

The President,
The White House.

The British approval of the North Sea barrage constituted a willingness to allow the United States to carry out the project without further objections or interference. This concession, plus an offer to use British mines and put down part of the barrage, were the fruits of Admiral Henry T. Mayo's trip to England in September. There followed a favorable report by the British Admiralty, by the General Board of the U.S. Navy, and finally by Josephus Daniels, and on the day after F.D.R. wrote these memoranda the barrage was approved by Wilson and his Cabinet. The direction of the mining operation was subsequently given to Rear Admiral Joseph Strauss, and within two months the tremendous operation commenced. Completed in October of 1918, the barrage cost $80,000,000 and required 22 million pounds of TNT and 50 million feet of wire cable. Some 70,000 mines were laid, of which the U.S. Navy supplied more than three-quarters. The project was finished too late in the war to be fully effective, but even during its short duration it accounted for eight and one-half per cent of all the submarines sunk. Furthermore, the mutiny of the German Navy, an event which precipitated the armistice, was partly due to the fear instilled in the personnel of the fleet by the mines guarding the entrance to the North Sea. "One of the wonders of the war," Sims later remarked. Only time vitiated F.D.R.'s prediction that "it will be the biggest single factor in winning the war."

Dearest Babs,

Mrs. Martin has found a K.M. and wired you yesterday, I hope in time to prevent you from going to New York.

The Secretary has decided not to go away today, but he may tomorrow *or* Monday! So in view of this charming uncertainty and of the really important labor work I am on in connection with Shipping Board I will stay till Monday noon.

All well. Livy left last night. We both called on Aunt Kassie and Sallie before dinner.

Tonight I dine alone at home.

Kiss the chicks.

Your devoted   F

Here is Nov. 1 cheque—no it isn't—I will deposit it in Bank today—for $300.

The precious addition to the household discovered by A.E.R.'s cook, Mrs. Martin, was a kitchen maid ("K.M.").

〜〜

Dearest Babs,

I am enclosing another batch of mail and bills. Also receipt from bank showing deposit of $300 and $135 extra.

It is a heavenly day and I only wish I could get out for some golf, but I must stick to the office and try to clean up for the week. I will play tomorrow morning and work in the afternoon.

No particular news. I dined alone at home last night and dine at the Club tonight, alone also unless I pick up someone.

Your devoted   F

〜〜

Three days after F.D.R. wrote this letter Kerensky's government in Russia was overthrown by the Bolshevik Party under the leadership of Lenin. On November 7, 1917, the All-Russian Congress of Soviets passed a resolution approving the coup d'etat, thereby establishing the U.S.S.R. The immediate consequence of this upheaval, for the rest of the world, was a military one. In order to embark upon their experiment of a "dictatorship of the proletariat," the Bolsheviks deemed it necessary to withdraw from the war, which was at this time marked by sizable German advances through the Russian lines. Accordingly, within two weeks after the revolution the Commissar for Foreign Affairs, Trotsky, sent a note to the various interested governments announcing that it was the Soviet intention to sue for "a democratic peace." While the Allies ignored the proposal, the Central Powers, anxious to shift their troops from East to West, responded quickly to the invitation, and armistice negotiations were begun at Brest-Litovsk on December 3rd. A truce was signed twelve days later, whereupon the first peace conference of the war was convened. Several months of wrangling over the peace terms ensued, but on March 3, 1918, Russia acquiesced to German terms and the Treaty of Brest-Litovsk was signed.

These developments, plus a victorious campaign in Italy during the fall of 1917, led to high optimism in the war councils of the Central Powers during the opening months of 1918. Confident that the added strength transferred from the eastern to the western front would end the war before sufficient American manpower could be landed in France, Germany repudiated Wilson's famous Fourteen Points announced on January 8, 1918, and began planning for the "final offensive."

And F.D.R. wrote his mother on the occasion of her succumbing to the grippe.

Dearest Mama,

We got back from the Lanes' a few minutes ago and found Aunt Annie's telegram that you are a little better and temperature nearly normal. Naturally we are much upset, knowing nothing about it all except your letter telling of a little cold and a dose of castor oil! I am too too sorry and so wish you had had Durrant telephone as I would have come right on. Now I have just talked to Aunt Jennie on the telephone and feel relieved though it does seem that you have one of those same old vile colds on the chest. I do hope you will give in to it absolutely and not *move* out of the house till it is absolutely gone.

All is well here. The chicks cured all at the same time so we feel more cheerful. Though a holiday I have been at the office, taking James with me for an hour this morning and working with my private secretary for two hours this afternoon. Eleanor has been at the canteen from 12 to 6:30. It has snowed again, only two inches but enough to make holiday golf game impossible. Tomorrow night we have a dinner of 18, trying to have the people we ought to have but don't want to have! I do hope all will go well and that Ely is giving you real attention with a firm hand! I *hope* to get on March 2 but can't tell yet.

Much love from us all.

Your affectionate son

F.D.R.

Durrant was Sara Roosevelt's waitress for a number of years. There is a disparity between F.D.R.'s tally of "the people we ought to have" and A.E.R.'s old "Dinner Record" of these early years in Washington, which lists twenty-four persons for dinner at eight p.m. on February 23, 1918.

〜〜

370

During the interval between this and the next letter the German Army unleashed its attack upon the Allied lines in France. On March 21, 1918, a force of more than five hundred thousand men suddenly drove against the fifty-mile sector between La Fère and Arras. This was the area where the British and French forces met, where the lack of a unified command was expected to reveal the greatest vulnerability; and it was Hindenburg's plan to isolate the British and drive them into the sea. Outmanned three or four to one, the British retreated and lost contact with the French on the second day, and the German plan appeared headed toward success; but on March 26th contact with the French was restored and the breakthrough prevented. On the same day, having learned the difficult way, the Allies decided that a unified command was imperative, and General Ferdinand Foch was subsequently made Commander-in-Chief of the Allied Armies. The Battle of the Somme raged until the latter part of April, resulting in a British retreat of thirty-five miles and a casualty list of over three hundred thousand men. This crisis of the war is reflected in the following letter, in which F.D.R. remarks "I am somewhat blue."

WASHINGTON
[MARCH 28, 1918]
THURSDAY

Dearest Mama,

I have been trying to write you for many days about many things, first of all to give you loads of thanks. I have loved my very extra nice shirts and ties and they will make me very comfy and cool this summer. And you have saved my life, or, rather, the various Doctors' lives, by making it possible for me to pay them promptly! I really think it has been wise to have this wholesale butchery of Anna and James. They are getting over the operations excellently and I feel sure they will both benefit.

I enclose a tax blank for the Half Moon. You should send it with cheque for $45.75 to Roscoe Irwin, Collector of In-

371

ternal Revenue, Albany, N. Y. as that is where you pay your Income Tax and it is better to keep it all in one District.

Now in regard to 49 East 65. Mrs. Grenville Emmet's cousin is willing to rent it for $5,000 a year for two or possibly 3 years. Possibly she might even go up to $5500 if we do a good deal of repainting, etc. It seems to me best therefore, if you could go to Mrs. Lamont and tell her this quite frankly and say that of course we want the Lamonts to have first chance. I think we should agree if the Lamonts want it for only one year to do an amount of painting and repairs equal only to the amount of rent they pay in excess of the present $4500, and we should *try* to get them to take it for two years at $5500 and we should put $1000 into repairs, etc. This would give $5000 a year *net* for each of the two years.

Let me know as soon as you can, for if the Lamonts don't want it, I must get hold of Pauline.

Sunday. I enclose an insurance card on my life but your pocket! Due April 5th! That policy must be nearly paid up isn't it? I think it was a 20-year one?

Also the tax return on the Half Moon which I mention above, you must swear to it.

We have been to hear Archbishop Lang this morning. I have been in conference all afternoon with Leonard Wood. I am somewhat blue.

Not much likelihood of my going over, though they ought to send me. You will have plenty of notice!

Lots of love. All well.

Your affec. son
FDR

The Most Reverend Cosmo Gordon Lang, then Archbishop of York, had come to the United States earlier in the month in response to an invitation from the war commission of the Protestant Episcopal Church asking him to preach in large eastern cities and universities. Speaking several times a day, he urged a united effort to crush "the menace of a power which claimed world dominion and which acknowledged no law but that of its own armed force."

The idea of an inspection of naval activities in European waters by a civilian official of the Department had occurred to F.D.R. as early as 1914. His first efforts to win approval of the proposal failed when the English and French authorities rejected the proposition, and F.D.R. let the matter drop for the time being. In 1918, however, urged on by a desire to see active service, F.D.R. brought the idea forward again. "One of us ought to go and see the war in progress with his own eyes, else he is a chess player moving his pieces in the dark," J.D. quotes F.D.R. in *The Wilson Era*. Yet it required not a little persuasion by F.D.R. to win approval of the trip, as can be gathered from the concluding remarks to this letter.

He had further reason for "blue" spirits in the failure of his attempts to resign from the Department and go abroad as a naval officer. He was of course told that the most valuable service he could give to the country was the one he was performing—small consolation to any young man whose friends are under fire. And when he finally did win the promise of a lieutenant commander's commission in Admiral Plunkett's naval railway battery of 14-inch guns, the war was virtually over and he was bedridden with pneumonia. Nevertheless, he partially realized his desire to enter the war zone. By the late spring of 1918 the strain on the Navy Department had eased sufficiently to enable either J.D. or himself to leave Washington long enough to make a thorough inspection of U.S. naval forces in European waters. Wilson preferred to have Daniels remain in the capital, thus F.D.R. was designated for the trip, which comprises the correspondence of Chapter X.

∿

X

"... Tell Them of the Wonderful Things Our Country Is Doing Here..."

EUROPEAN INSPECTION TRIP

Summer, 1918

IN SANCTIONING F.D.R.'s trip Daniels listed four specific tasks for the Assistant Secretary to perform during his visit to England and the other Allied countries. First, F.D.R. was to inspect the American naval forces with particular attention to administrative and business organization, such as expenditures, leases of buildings and land, and other contracts. Second, he was to consult with the other government branches in order to coordinate naval activities with their enterprises. Third, he was to gather information pertaining to general conditions abroad and their applicability to naval affairs. Last, he was to investigate any other matters which he considered advisable. As will be seen, these duties required a variety of activities during the trip, including interviews with the heads of governments and other Allied war leaders, inspections of naval stations, and journeys to the combat zone.

Livingston Davis went along as F.D.R.'s civilian aide and

Captain Edward McCauley, Jr., was chosen as his chief of staff; Commander Victor S. Jackson and Lieutenant Commander Elliot C. Brown comprised the rest of his naval staff. Mr. Renah F. Camalier as his private secretary and Marine Sergeant W. W. Stratton as his orderly completed the group. Davis, Brown, and Camalier sailed on the British Admiralty transport *Olympic* on July 12, 1918, while F.D.R., McCauley, and Stratton departed three days earlier aboard the U.S.S. *Dyer*.

During the course of the trip F.D.R. kept a personal diary of his activities. This record, plus detailed letters to his family and notes that he dictated but did not mail for security reasons, were all merged into a single account of the trip by A.E.R. after the war. F.D.R.'s wordage was retained, but repetitions and other incidental data were omitted in the process of compiling the material. As F.D.R. did not complete his personal diary and as some later letters were lost, the final account only covers the first half of the trip. Except for deletions by the censor, this letter-diary is otherwise given here in full.

Tuesday, July 9. We went on board the U.S.S. DYER, Brooklyn, N.Y., at 3:00 p.m. She and U.S.S. STRINGHAM have just arrived from Boston and were the two most lately commissioned destroyers of the Navy. The DYER held her speed trials on June 30 (Fore River Shipbuilding Company), was accepted by the Navy and placed in commission at the Boston Navy Yard on July 2. Took on stores, ammunition, etc., left Boston July 7, arrived New York July 8, and sailed for active war service in Europe July 9. This is without doubt a Navy record. Captain Poteet is in command and the other officers are: Lieutenants Taylor, Slingluff and Paddock, and Ensigns McKaig and Sanford. At 5:00 p.m. we got under way and stood down New York Harbor, passing two of the five transports we are to escort, proceeded through Ambrose

Channel to the lightship, where we stood off and on at slow speed. At 8:00 p.m. the five transports, accompanied by the U.S.S. MACDONOUGH, passed out, and we proceeded to sea in the following order:

⛊ la France

⛊ Agamemnon   ⛊ Mt. Vernon   ⛊ America   ⛊ Orizaba

⛊ U.S.S. Dyer   ↓   ⛊ U.S.S. Macdonough

At dark we dropped back from the starboard bow to the starboard quarter of the AGAMEMNON. This is because on dark nights such as we are having now an escort ship is of no use and for the sake of safety takes the position where she can best maintain a sight contact with the convoy.

I am sleeping in Captain Poteet's stateroom and Captain McCauley, my Chief of Staff, has the spare officer's room forward. Poteet at sea sleeps in the chart room directly over the ward room and under the bridge. Sergeant Stratton, U.S.M.C., my orderly, is quartered with the Chief Petty Officers. He is already ill but will turn out to be a treasure, I think. He is a graduate of the University of Utah and afterwards, as a Rhodes scholar, of Oxford University. I am to leave him in France to join Smedley Butler's 13th Regiment. Everything went well on departure and the big camouflaged transports, most of which you know by other names, were crowded with men and were very weird as they showed up great black lightless masses during the night.

Today has been fairly smooth, absolutely so for a bigger ship than this. The U.S.S. MACDONOUGH left us this morning,

Wednesday, July 10, shortly after daylight to return to New York.

Thursday, July 11. I spoke too soon, it is pretty rough, even the troop ships roll and pitch. This little fellow is very lively though not as much so as the old destroyers would have been. Her motions are varied and thorough, but lack the snap of the whip quality of the older ones. One has to hang on all the time, never moving without taking hold with one hand before letting go with the other. Much of the crockery smashed; we cannot eat at the table even with racks, have to sit braced on the transom and hold the plate with one hand. Three officers ill, but so far I am all right—making a record!

Friday, July 12. A very different day—warm, bright, sunny and smooth, really smooth. Everybody happy again, also everything drying out. My companions are delightful. Eddie McCauley, Poteet and I are constantly together on the bridge or in the chart house and with the youngsters, Taylor, Slingluff and Paddock, and Ensigns McKaig and Sanford make a happy ward room. The two last are reserve Ensigns.

Saturday, July 13. A day full of excitement. At the faintest beginning of dawn I found myself instinctively out of my bunk and jumping for the ladder to the bridge. The alert whistle had blown and everybody was dashing to gun stations, etc. The lookout in the fore-top had reported a vessel ahead, quickly reporting another and another and another until we began to wonder if we had run into the whole German fleet. We had rung up full speed and were at the head of the convoy by this time. As we got closer and the light stronger the ships turned out to be twenty-eight merchantmen of the Hampton Roads convoy bound for England and headed across our bows on a slightly more northerly course. This was a slip-up on the part of the routing officers in New York and Washington. Two convoys are never supposed to cross courses near the same time. If the Norfolk convoy had been two miles further astern, or if we had been two miles ahead of our position, we would have run through them in the dark at eighteen knots and some bad smash-up would almost surely have followed. At 10:00 a.m. S.O.P., Captain on the MOUNT VERNON, signalled with his flicker that the transports were about to change course to the northeast, our base course for the last three days having been 90 degrees. In other words, after a short bend south of east after leaving New York we have been running due east between the 39th and 40th parallels of latitude and are now only 300 miles from Fayal and only a few miles north of it.

Upon receiving the signal we ran directly in front of the convoy and my flag was hoisted on the U.S.S. DYER at the maintop and we slowed down, passing between the MOUNT VERNON and AMERICA and waving "Good-bye" as we headed off south of east.

During the a.m. we held gun drill as usual and the precaution which Poteet had taken yesterday was probably responsible for several of the company being still alive. The two midship guns are mounted on a superstructure on each beam between the stacks. There was nothing in their mounts to prevent either gun from firing directly forward into the bridge, and Poteet had stops put in which prevented the guns from being trained closer than 5 degrees from the end of the bridge. During the gun trial a green youngster pulled the lanyard of the port gun when it was trained as far forward as it would go. McCauley and I happened to be standing in the port wing of the bridge, and when the blooming thing went off at the back of our heads and the four-inch shell went by only a few feet outboard, we thought the end had come. Captain Poteet seemed annoyed! This afternoon a periscope was reported by the lookout in the forward top. We headed for it at full speed about a mile away and fired three shots at it from the bow gun; then it turned out to be a floating keg with a little flag on it, probably thrown over by a passing vessel as a target to train the gun crews; otherwise it was a good experience for our crew. We are getting well on the voyage and I am learning much. Incidentally I am more than glad I came this way.

Sunday, July 14. All still well. A fine day, though a little more roll. I have read much, slept much and eaten much—very full of health. At lunch time more of the crockery disintegrated and we thought a torpedo had hit us when a big drawer full of knives, forks, spoons and dishes hopped out of the side-board and bounded across the ward room, narrowly missing all of us at the table. We are due to arrive at Fayal tomorrow. It is one of the westerly islands of the Azores and is the place where the Dabneys of Boston lived so long as Consul General, also the scene of the famous fight of the privateer "General Armstrong" in the War of 1812 against two British men-of-war. The harbor and town of Fayal is called Horta. We shall spend a few hours only, then proceed the 120 miles further to Ponta Delgada on the Island of San Miguel. This is our naval base and I shall hope to find Admiral Dunn there. By the way, do not read this part of the letter outside the family. Tell Anna and James and Elliott to look up these Azores places on the map.

Monday morning, July 15. Last night just after sundown one of our engines broke down and we made little progress for five hours. This morning we sighted Fayal rising out of the mists at 10:00 a.m. and ran down to within three miles of it; then our other engine heated up also, so here we lie, within ten miles of the harbor, motionless, but expect to make repairs and get in by 1:00 o'clock. You know this ship is just out of the builders' hands and has had no chance for a "shake-down" trial, in fact this run across is her "shake-down" and we must expect things like this to happen. I see no reason for staying more than a few hours here, so if our engines are repaired we will proceed on to Ponta Delgada this evening, arriving in the morning. The island of Fayal

379

looks lovely from here; lots of little pure white houses dotting the slopes and well cultivated small fields, and above towers the big old volcano 3500 feet high.

Monday evening, July 15. We have had a most interesting and delightful afternoon at Horta. Because of engine trouble we did not drop anchor until 1:00 o'clock. A tiny harbor behind a breakwater, and a most fascinating, colorful town along the beach, running up the steep hillsides. We were called on by the Port Authorities and the Admiral of the Portuguese warship. Then I went ashore with McCauley and Poteet and got a motor car through the Ex-Consular Agent of the United States, a Portuguese who spoke English. We called on the Governor and then went to the British Consul, who lives in "Fredonia," the old Dabney house, a splendid big old place overlooking the harbor. Then we motored up about 1500 feet where we had a wonderful view of the harbor and part of the interior valleys, a most picturesque spot. I wish we could have explored some more, but we had to get off again at five and are now at sea again, headed east for the Island of San Miguel.

Tuesday, July 16. Ponta Delgada is in sight and some of our ships are in the harbor. Both engines again heated up when we were six miles from the breakwater. We lay motionless for a half hour, keeping, of course, a careful lookout, but absolutely unable to move. When we got into the harbor we heard that at the particular moment we were lying to a submarine was seen following a Portuguese ship off the breakwater. Of course we would have been an easy mark, but if the submarine did see us she decided to avoid the destroyers, as all wise submarines now do. We shall be here twenty-four hours for oil and supplies. I will try and post this, though it will probably be a month or so before it reaches you.

U.S.S. DYER *at sea, July 18.* I have had a strenuous three days. We left Ponta Delgada at daybreak this morning and I sent you a line at midnight on the slim chance that a ship would stop in there on her return voyage.

Our few hours at Fayal on Monday were very delightful,—an out of the way little spot which lives very much on the memories of the Dabneys and the old American merchant marine, whaling ships, etc.

Tuesday we arrived at Ponta Delgada at 10:00. We were received by Admiral Dunn, and the Portuguese High Commissioner and his Admiral came in state and were revisited in state—a whole battalion of infantry at the palace, etc. The rest of the day was given up to inspection of our various naval activities and a nice quiet dinner with Dunn and his staff.

The Admiral has done excellent work here, but certain disturbing elements must be removed.

Yesterday we visited a wonderful private park belonging to a family named Canto—a collection of trees and plants from all over the world and especially curiously marked colored leaves. Almost anything will grow in the Azores for the temperature is about the same at all times and one sees bamboo next to English oak and even white pine.

Then at noon came a formal banquet at the palace of General Machallo, the High Commissioner. His wife spoke nothing but Portuguese but most of the others spoke French, so I managed to struggle through a ten-course dinner and many different kinds of cakes, sweetmeats, and relishes, and to make a speech toasting the Republic of Portugal.

After lunch we went on a very long motor trip, first across the Island to the northern side—a wonderful cultivation and all most picturesque,—very little change I imagine in the last 200 years. The peasants are respectful and evidently very keen about the American Naval Officers, many of the women wearing the long dark blue cloak and huge Poke bonnet still. We passed along the wonderful cliffs for miles and then mounted high up in the alpine scenery with outcroppings of rock, and dwelt in only by cows, goats and shepherds. Suddenly we came to the lip of what was once an enormous crater, three or four miles across and in the bottom a wonderful scene—several villages, valleys and parks, deep blue lakes and springs that threw out clouds of steam. It is called Furnes. We examined the springs and tasted the waters. The trip back was rainy and the Portuguese General, whose French was worse than mine, and I ran out of conversation, on the back seat, and so we slept peacefully. Then came the closing banquet at Admiral Dunn's. The Portuguese High Officials, the British Consul, the Naval Commander, our Consul and Dunn's staff. More speeches, of which I made two, and at midnight, last night, I returned to the DYER and wrote you a note.

Our engines are running again all right and we sailed at daylight this morning. Our destination is not what I expected on leaving owing to a telegram from Sims, and I expect to be in London on Sunday afternoon. Today is fine, though a little rough and I have done much sleeping to make up for the strenuous Azores days, but my sea-legs have been wonderful throughout—not sea sick once!

Friday, July 19, U.S.S. DYER. A gusty, squally day with occasional rain. Luckily the wind is behind us so the sea does not bother us much, though occasionally our bow is under the spray. Today we are off the Bay of Biscay, though far out from the Bay. A Norwegian tramp passed us and we looked him over pretty carefully before resuming our course. By tomorrow morning we shall be in the active submarine zone. Today we fired one of the guns and a depth charge for practice—all went well, though of course it takes much more than ten days to get a crew efficient. Poteet is an excellent commanding officer and an awfully nice friend.

Saturday, July 20. It has been rough and squally but sea still aft and no one has minded it. Very little motion for a destroyer. We were all got on deck at 4:00 a.m. by the alert signal and saw a passing convoy far off. This is the second time I have sprinted for the bridge in pajamas and bare feet. I realized my costume today and apologized to Poteet before descending but he said it made an excellent and distinctive uniform for a flag officer as long as the Secretary of the Navy does not try to change it to the old fashioned night-gown and carpet slippers. This evening we should sight land if all goes well, and will be in London tomorrow afternoon. I wish I could travel all the way in my destroyer costume,—my own invention,—khaki riding trousers, golf stockings, flannel shirt and leather coat. It does not soil or catch in things! Our delay at Ponta Delgada and change of plans as to destination will probably alter what I told you in regard to going to Queenstown first. I can tell you nothing further until I get to London. I do wish you would write me if you can think of any small thing Mama or the children would like me to get. I would ask you to do the same thing in regard to yourself but I fear you would suggest table-cloths or feather dusters. We must come over when the world is safe again but I will not ask you to try a destroyer, though I have loved every minute of it.

July 21, u.s.s. DYER. On deck at daylight, with the south coast of England in sight in the distance to port, running at 25 knots and zigzagging as this is a favorite place for submarines. By 7:00 we passed the cliffs of the Isle of Wight proper and in accordance with radio received last night we reached the given rendezvous off the southeast end of the Isle of Wight at sharp 8:00 a.m. We were picked up by one of the British P-Boats and followed her up the channel leading to Portsmouth. I got some good pictures of the harbor on the way in and one of the h.m.s. VICTORY, Nelson's Flagship, looking very much out of place among the destroyers, light cruisers, monitors, and P-Boats. We ran along the quay, where I saw a large group of officers awaiting us—they at once came on board—Vice Admiral Sims and his aide, Com-

mander Babcock; Rear-Admiral Everett, the Naval Secretary
to the First Lord of the Admiralty; Pay Inspector Victor S.
Jackson, USN, who is to be with us; Rear-Admiral Gay,
R.N., Commander of the Portsmouth Dock Yard; Commander Guy Gaunt, until very recently Naval Attaché at
Washington; etc., etc., etc. We sent our baggage to London
by train with Sergeant Stratton and then accompanied
Admiral Gay on an inspection of the dockyard, one of the
oldest and largest in England. Very little building was going
on but much repair work, including that of a torpedoed
merchantman. In one of the docks was a monitor, and we
obtained an excellent view of the queer-shaped blisters, a
successful British invention forming a projection along each
side of the ship, which has saved many ships from going to
the bottom. Also we saw in another dry dock one of the big
British submarines mounting a 15" gun. I do not think the
British have been impressed with the success of this type.
We went out to the VICTORY and went all over her. Her
general upkeep is far superior to what we have done in the
cases of the "Constitution" and "Constellation." A retired
Commander is responsible for her and a constant inspection
has prevented her from the periodic decay which has over-
taken our ships. They have a nucleus crew assigned to her
but this crew lives ashore, going out to her every morning.
On the way back, we stopped at the dock-yard museum. We
might easily have had equally interesting museums at
Brooklyn and Boston if the service itself had not allowed the
Navy Lyceum to go to pieces. We lunched with the Commandant ———— and we were joined by Vice Admiral ————,
the Commander-in-Chief of the Station. This Station ex-
tends a short distance eastward, where it joins the Dover
Station and quite far west, almost to the Plymouth Station.
At 3:00 p.m. we left for London by motor, I going ahead
with Admiral Everett in one of the Admiralty's Rolls-Royces.
I am told it is a very great honor to have had Everett sent

down to meet me. Personally, I think it is because they wanted to report as to whether I am house-broken or not. We went straight to the Ritz Hotel and have a magnificent suite as the guests of the British Admiralty.

Ritz Hotel, July 21. We arrived safely here at six and found Livingston Davis, Elliot Brown and Mr. Camalier, who had come over on the OLYMPIC—happy reunion, dinner and went to a big entertainment for all the American and Canadian Officers and men in uniform. House packed with khaki and a few of my Navy men.

July 22. This morning I called on Sir Eric Geddes, accompanied by Sims, McCauley, Jackson, Brown and Davis. Sims, McCauley and I were shown into the First Lord's room and after the formal introductions I held some formal conversation with Geddes, while Sims and McCauley sat opposite us. This type of interview is not calculated to get anybody anywhere, either officially, unofficially or personally. Memorandum for future occasions—either leave the Staff in the anteroom or sit it down in the corner and turn your back on it. Finally Geddes and I got started—he had awfully nice eyes and a smile, but is more like a successful American business man than any British Cabinet Officer one is accustomed to picture. He showed us a model of the new British project for the channel, even Sims knew nothing of this until today. Finally Geddes told me that he was leaving for Pembroke, in Wales, Queenstown, etc., tonight and asked me to accompany him. Of course I said I would, and will take only McCauley and Lieut-Commander Royes, our Assistant Naval Attaché here. I lunched with Mr. Balfour, Lord Milner, Secretary of State for War—Sir Ian Malcolm, whom we knew in Washington, also there. It was an awfully nice party and before I left I had a chance to tell Mr. Balfour of my worry about the Italian Naval situation and he is going to discuss it with Lloyd George and talk to me again about it before I leave for the Continent.

Lord Milner seemed interested in my opinion that the German offensive in March was more responsible than any one thing for thoroughly arousing the United States and that the whole tone of things in Washington had changed since then. After lunch I went to our Navy offices. Met all the officers, did some shopping and now in a few minutes leave on a few-days' trip with Sir Eric Geddes. Most interesting every minute, little time to sit down.

Friday, July 26. London, England. I am back again after a very successful trip of three days with Sir Eric Geddes. I think I wrote you on Monday that I lunched with Mr. Balfour, Lord Milner and Sir Ian Malcolm. That night I met the First Lord at Paddington. He took Admiral Everett and Commander Steele—I took Captain McCauley and Lieut-Commander Royes as aides. After a comfortable night on the train we arrived at Pembroke Dock-Yard in Wales, inspected it, and at 10:30 went on board the U.S.S. KIMBERLY, one of our new destroyers, commanded by Commander Johnson, whom you will remember on the CUNNINGHAM at Campobello in 1916,—4th of July. We ran at 25 knots the 125 miles to Queenstown. I asked Sir Eric if I might not have the honor of flying the Admiralty Flag on the KIMBERLY, but he told me something I did not know before,—that the Admiralty Flag may only be flown when two or more Commissioners of the Admiralty are present on board together. It was fairly choppy and the KIMBERLY took some water over the bow. Sir Eric did not feel like much lunch and both he and Admiral Everett remarked that our destroyers are more lively than British destroyers of equal tonnage. I hope to go on a British boat later and compare them. On arrival Admiral Bayly, R.N., Captain Pringle, Senior U. S. Officer, and others met us. We stopped at Admiralty House and had a nice dinner party of American and British Officers. Wednesday, Geddes and I inspected the dock-yard, American Flying Base, American Hospital Base and lunched on the U.S.S.

MELVILLE. Everything is running there in a most excellent way and the cooperation between the two forces is complete. At lunch time Geddes took me aside and asked me what I felt about the success or othewise of Admiral Sir Lewis Bayly. I told him frankly that our people from Sims down to the youngest destroyer officers felt that he was the ideal man to command this station. In the afternoon Geddes again took me aside and told me that he had decided to retain Bayly in command. This is a very unusual compliment as Bayly has already been here three years in command of the Irish Station and the usual tenure is two years. In fact, this action is so out of the ordinary that I think Geddes especially wanted my hearty approval in order to persuade the Sea Lords. That evening we went on board H.M.S. PATROL and woke up in the Bristol Channel off Newport in Wales, having been convoyed all night by the U.S.S. KIMBERLY. Geddes and I sent some radio messages, which you may have seen in our papers as I cabled them to Mr. Daniels in the interest of the entente cordiale. I hope he gave them to the press.

On Thursday morning we landed at Newport; motored to Chepstow and Beachleigh, and saw two of the National Shipyards they are building to turn out standard merchant ships. Then train to Port Bury, near Bristol, on the south side of the Bristol Channel, where we saw another shipyard and then train to London where we got back at 8:00 p.m. last night. Today I have worked at my office and the Admiralty. At the Admiralty I spent two hours with Admiral Hall, Chief Intelligence Officer. Their Intelligence Department is far more developed than ours and this is because it is a much more integral part of their Office of Operations. Of course, one of our troubles has been that our Intelligence is in a different building from operations. Much of this trouble will be eliminated when we get into the new building. I called on Mrs. Edwardes, who was quite overcome at seeing me. I am to tea with Gay on Tuesday. Tomorrow I go to Cliveden to the Waldorf Astors for Sunday. All my plans for next week are still uncertain,—it is either Scotland or France. I do so wish you could see all this in war time: in spite of all people say, one feels much closer to the actual fighting here. The counter attack in the Rheims salient has heartened everybody enormously, our men have undoubtedly done well. One of my Marine Regiments has lost 1200 and another 800 men.

Sunday, July 28, Cliveden. I wrote you on Friday of my Irish trip with Geddes. That afternoon I went to see Mrs. Reid at Red Cross Headquarters. That night Livy and I dined with Ned Bell at the St. James Club and had an old-fashioned talk. Yesterday morning I went down to Baring Brothers, saw two of the partners, went to the army and navy stores for silk pajamas at 61 shillings a pair!! Thence to my office at 30 Grosvenor Gardens where I am installed next to Sims. Livy and I lunched with Jean Reid, now Lady Ward. Mrs. Reid also there. Jean sends you much love. She looks just the same except that her hair is quite gray. At 4:30 Livy and I picked up Lord Eustace Percy in the Admiralty car, which has been placed at our disposal, to motor out here. We found the Brands, who have a cottage on the place, the Spender-Clays and Mr. Hutchens, the head of the Campbell-lairds, who are doing most of our destroyer repair work at Liverpool. Mrs. Astor is just the same, enthusiastic, amusing, and talkative soul as always, and I particularly like Waldorf Astor, who is doing wonderfully well and is now the Parliamentary Secretary of Ministry of Food. Both he and she have done splendid work all through the war and very unostentatiously. Of course this place is wonderful and I am so glad to see it. They live in the big house with only women servants—everything comfortable, food about like ours, only a scarcity of sugar and butter. Within a five-minute walk is the big hospital which they started in the tennis courts building but which the Government took over and enlarged to 1100 beds. It is not more than a quarter full just now but of course will be again when another batch comes over. I went all through it after attending the little hospital chapel this morning. The men get very good care and the walking cases have the run of the Cliveden gardens and grounds. Mrs. Astor is wonderful with them, I think, and they all adore her. Down on the bank overlooking the Thames, the Astors have turned an Italian Garden into a really perfect little cemetery for the overseas men who die in hospital. The hospital itself is run by a Canadian unit and most of the men are Canadians and Australians with only a few Americans so far. Tonight I shall motor back to London for dinner as I am to see the King at 10:30 tomorrow morning. I have two strenuous days ahead and then shall probably go through to Paris. Nothing has been decided about the Italian trip but I shall see Mr. Balfour about it tomorrow. I have had such nice letters from various people asking me to stay,—Mrs. Woolsey, Frances Archer-Shee, Mrs. Cochran, who was at Campobello, the Countess of Stratford, etc., but I cannot even get down to see Muriel this time but will stop there on the way back. It has rained much, in fact every day since my arrival until today. I will get off a line before crossing and also wire you on arrival in Paris.

July 30—London, England. A very interesting day yesterday, came in from Cliveden in the morning, dressed and went to Buckingham Palace at 10:30 and had forty minutes all alone with the King. We drove to the "new front" of Buckingham Palace, which has been pasted on since I was here in 1905. I say "pasted" on because from almost any angle you see the other sides of Buckingham Palace, and the new façade is obviously an unsuccessful attempt to hide the earlier style. I was accompanied by Admiral Everett and Captain McCauley and we passed through several corridors lined with paintings of naval actions that I would have given anything to stop and look at; thence up a half flight to a charming little room with some very good Chinese lacquer ornaments, etc. I hope they were presents from the Chinese Imperial Family, and not acquired as a result of the expedition of 1900. I am moved to make this remark by a story I have just heard about the wife of an American official in Peking. A year after the Boxer trouble she gave a formal dinner for one of the Imperial Princes and after dinner in the drawing room asked the Prince how the Chinese all seemed able to tell the difference between really good jade and the commoner varieties. The Prince said that to a Chinaman jade showed the same difference of quality as precious stones would to an American or European. The hostess insisted on pursuing the topic and finally said—"Now, Prince, I wish you would tell me whether that piece of jade on the mantel-piece is really good or not." The Prince's face did not change and though ten feet away from the mantel-piece he replied—"That is a truly excellent piece." The American woman said—"But how can you tell without examining it?", and he answered—"Because I gave it to my Aunt, the Empress, on her last birthday."

A gentleman in a frock coat soon conducted us up another half flight to the King's study. I was then introduced, shook hands and presented Captain McCauley, who also shook hands and then retired with the gentleman-in-waiting. The King has a nice smile and a very open, quick and cordial way of greeting one. He is not as short as I had expected, and I think his face is stronger than photographs make it appear. This is perhaps because his way of speaking is incisive, and later on when he got talking about German atrocities in Belgium his jaws almost snapped. We talked for a while about American war work in general and the Navy in particular. He seemed delighted that I had come over in a destroyer, and said his one regret was that it had been impossible for him to do active naval service during the war. Then the subject switched to the Germans and he told me a lot about the atrocities in Belgium and northern France—many examples which had been proved true but which were too horrible to be placed even in the French official report or the report of Lord Bryce. Our troops had just reoccupied Château-Thierry and had found examples of wanton destruction of property by the Germans before they left, such as the smashing of pictures, breaking of furniture, etc. The King said he hoped that this at least would persuade the American people that the stories of outrageous destruction were true, and I agreed with him that there had been a singular unwillingness in the United States to accept even the official reports of England and France.

I then remarked something about having been to school in Germany and having seen their preparation for the first stages of the war machine. The King said he went to school in Germany, too, for a year; then with a twinkle in his eye— "You know I have a number of relations in Germany, but I can tell you frankly that in all my life I have never seen a German gentleman."

The King said he had just had a nice letter from Uncle Ted, thanking him for one he had sent at the time of T.R.'s illness last spring. We had just received news of Quentin's probable death, and the King expressed much sympathy.

He was a delightfully easy person to talk to, and we got going so well that part of the time we were both talking at the same time. I understand that this type of interview is supposed to last only fifteen minutes, but it was nearly three-quarters of an hour before the King made a move. I said— "Good-bye"—and went back to the Chinese room, where I found McCauley and the gentleman-in-waiting looking at each other hopelessly.

Luncheon was given to Sir Eric Geddes and me by the Anglo-American Luncheon Club, a big affair at the Savoy and we both spoke. In my speech I took occasion to give the British Navy due credit for what they had done in transporting and escorting American troops to Europe in the greatly increased numbers of the past few months and I gave, for the first time, the official figures showing that during the month of June over 60% of our troops came over in British transports and under British escort. Slightly over 30% were in American transports and 5% in French and Italian. I much hope these figures will be telegraphed home, but I doubt it as the representatives of the Committee on Public Information over here have done nothing. In the afternoon I went down to the Liberty Hut, a Y.M.C.A. building for our troops and spoke to a great gathering of American soldiers, with a sprinkling of Canadians, Anzacs and our Blue-jackets. Last night one of the famous Gray Inn's dinners, a really historic occasion in honor of the War Ministers. Lord Curzon spoke most wonderfully for an hour. A defense of the War Cabinet, or rather a résumé of what England has done and is doing. Sir Robert Borden responded for Canada, General Smuts for South Africa and to my horror the Italian Ambassador and I were called on without warning at the close to speak for the Allies. Today a luncheon for me at the Embassy, Lloyd George, Mr. Balfour and various Navy people and Mrs. Page, the only woman. She sent her love to Mama. I had a very good time with Lloyd George. Lloyd George is just like his pictures; thick set; not very tall; rather a large head; and rather long hair; but what impressed me more than anything else was his tremendous vitality. There is no question that the great majority of Englishmen are standing solidly behind him on the sole issue of winning the war. The Conservatives who used to despise him as a demagogue; the Liberals who used to fear him as a radical; and most of the Labor people who now look on him as a reactionary, may hate him just as much as ever and be unwilling after the war to trust reconstruction to his hands, but they will stand by him just as long as his administration keeps the winning of the war as its only political aim. Strikes are threatened at the present time at a number of munition plants and shipyards. Mr. Lloyd George and I talked over the labor situation here and at home. He said of course the weakness of the British Government's position has all come from the failure to adopt conscription at the outbreak of the war and I suggested to him that in the same way we should have had vastly more trouble if we had not had the selective draft law as the final lever to insure continuation of work. I ventured to suggest that in my opinion the British Unions would obtain no sympathy from our Federation of Labor in any action involving a tie-up of war work and that on the contrary a firmer attitude on the part of the British Government would receive hearty applause from the United States. He seemed very greatly pleased and intimated that he had decided on a firmer stand in the future. Tea with Lady Edward; nice reminiscent time; and to end off, a dinner at the House of Commons by Sir Ian Malcolm, Mr. Balfour, Lord Robert Cecil, Dawson of the Times, Lord Londonderry, Sykes, M.P., who drew a picture for me on the dinner card, Sir Auckland Geddes, the First Lord's brother, and Minister of National Service, and two others. A long talk with Mr. Balfour afterwards while we walked up and down the terrace in the dark. What has pleased me more than anything else is the apparent determination of the British Cabinet to go through with the war to a definitely successful end. The past month has I think clearly marked the turning point of the war. June marked the high tide of the German advance, although the Channel Ports may still be considered in danger. The latest German offensive along the Marne and in the Château-Thierry salient has been not only broken up but during the past ten days has developed into what is apparently a definite retirement to the original lines. For the first time people realize that the American troops are to be the deciding factor. Mr.

Balfour said that everyone understands that it was the American Second Division with the Brigade of Marines which stopped the rush at Château-Thierry and which opened the definite counter-offensive at Soissons, which has pinched the salient into untenability. We also talked about the Italian Naval situation; he said that he had discussed with the Cabinet the advisability of my going to Italy in a further attempt to get some action and that they had heartily approved. I am to see Geddes in the morning to discuss the matter further. We are off in the morning, all of us, for France and should have a wonderfully interesting time. Calais and Dunkirk on the way, and motor all the way behind the lines. I will not add to this as it is late and I have not finished packing.

Saturday, August 3. Hotel Crillon, Paris. A line in haste to tell you that I am off in the morning to the front and the scene of the wonderful advance of the last few days. We crossed the channel on Wednesday in a British destroyer. We got to Dover at noon and were met by Admiral Sir Roger Keyes. My staff went to the hotel for lunch and McCauley accompanied me to the Admiral's house and the headquarters of the district, i.e., the channel station which runs almost to Portsmouth on the west and just short of the Thames on the east, including therefore the Folkstone and Dover crossings and the whole of the German-occupied Belgian coast. Admiral Keyes' operations room was of tremendous interest and this station is of course far and away the most active and interesting of all. Responsibility for the bulk of the troops crossing the channel and the supply transportation is on Keyes. This, of course, involves an enormous amount of patrolling, mine laying, escorting, etc., as well as offensive operations such as the expeditions against Zeebrugge, Ostend and the long range bombardment of the German land positions, by monitors, etc. We lunched with Lady Keyes and immediately afterwards went on board one of their latest destroyers, H.M.S. VELOX, Captain ———. As I came over the side my flag was broken out at the main, the first time this sort of thing has ever happened on a British ship. We passed out through the net gateway at the eastern entrance to the inner harbor and found the channel literally as smooth as a millpond. We were accompanied by four of the high speed P-boats which Admiral Keyes sent out to give me a demonstration of the artificial fog. We were doing 25 knots and the little boats ran well ahead of us at 35 knots, turned and ran back past us, laying a fog screen. It seemed to be wonderfully effective and Elliot Brown and I got some excellent photographs showing its development. It seems to be much more effective than the usual heavy oil smoke screen of destroyers. It can scarcely be detected when laid at horizontal range and in drifting it holds its consistency well and hugs the water. In other words it is almost an exact duplicate of the natural fog rolling in with the wind.

The run to Dunkirk took just two hours and we saw many of the lighters in which such a large proportion of the British Army supplies are towed over. Before the war no one supposed that lighters could stand the English Channel sea. They have not only done this, but their light draft makes them practically immune from torpedoing. The last ten miles before reaching Dunkirk was up a specially buoyed channel along the French Coast; this is because mine fields start at this point and run east. I was glad to see great numbers of French fishing boats—I am told that they practically wholly abandoned fishing in the Channel during the first two years of the war, but the improved patrol and the new mine field, with which I had something to do in the summer of 1917, has made it safe again. In fact Sir Roger Keyes told me that he did not think more than five submarines had passed through the channel since January 1. As we were running into the narrow mouth of Dunkirk Harbor, it became perfectly clear why our first Navy Aviation

Squadron has had such a bad time. There is not a whole house left in this place. It has been bombed more than any other two towns put together, in fact. It may be truthfully said it has been bombed every night that flying was possible for three years. It is not so much the buildings that have been completely demolished as the fact that every single house in the place has been damaged to some extent. For instance, I did not see one pane of glass in the town, and almost every house-front is pock-marked by fragments of shell, and a large percentage of the houses have been actually hit or damaged in part by explosion in an adjoining house.

We were met at the pier by Vice-Admiral Ronarch, the French Commandant of the District and the man who has won everlasting fame as the Naval Officer of the famous French Naval Brigade in the touch-and-go days of 1914, when the Boche almost broke through at the first battle of Ypres. I had unfortunately very little time to talk to him as I was hurried away by my old friend Captain Hutch I. Cone, who is in charge of our Naval Aviation. Admiral Ronarch welcomed me officially on behalf of the French Ministry of Marine and placed at my disposal two magnificent limousines, each with two Poilus on the front seat and rifles in a rack in front of them. Cone had two aviation cars for the rest of the party, and a baggage truck which I sent to Calais immediately with Sergeant Stratton to take our trunks and heavy pieces by rail to Paris, to await our arrival. Cone then started our inspection by taking us around the head of the harbor to our flying boat base. They have about a dozen planes and for many months have done excellent work under the greatest difficulties. This was by many weeks the first actual American flying base in Europe. Their task has been mainly that of patrol, and it is especially hard service as the hunting ground is within reach of the German fighting planes on the Belgian Coast, and of course a seaplane has absolutely no chance against a single- or double-seated land plane. We have been very lucky in not having had greater losses. The station itself has been frequently bombed, and I went down into one of the bomb-proofs in which the entire aviation force has had to descend, not occasionally but night after night, sometimes early in the evening, sometimes in the middle of the night and again not until nearly dawn. Here too we have been very lucky, for while bombs have fallen in front, behind and between the hangars, making holes in the canvas, planes and hulls themselves, they have not registered a single direct hit, and I think only one or two men have been wounded by fragments. I met all the officers and reviewed the men, and was sorry not to have had time enough to go out in one of the planes over the mine fields. On leaving we passed through most of the city; we saw much of the population of men, women and children, who are still here taking the nightly raids as we would take a thunder-storm, appreciating the danger perfectly but accepting a gambler's chance that the next bomb will hit their neighbor's house and not theirs. Considering the number of raids that have been made on Dunkirk and its harbor works, however, it is very extraordinary that more really effective damage has not been done. Very little harm has yet been done to the docks, railroads, and canal terminals, and I had no idea that the British were sending in so many supplies through this place. It must be remembered that while Dunkirk is in France, it is so close to the actual trench line that it has been shelled off and on by large calibre German Naval guns, i.e., not the type that shelled Paris, but the regulation naval fourteen or fifteen-inch. We passed eastward on the main Calais highway, and after a short run arrived at a flat field where the most easterly of our bombing squadrons is to be located. There in the midst of a vast, flat field, intersected with trench ditches, was a typical American construction camp and 150 youngsters who had joined the Navy to go to sea were engaged in putting tile pipe into drains and covering them over, cutting and harvesting wheat, putting down an artesian well, erecting a new mess hall, built solely out of packing cases, erecting two hangars, and building road. They got here just ten days ago, and if the farmer can be persuaded to remove the wheat from the two hundred acres or so, they have been told to have everything in readiness for flying within ten days from now. This field is called "Oie," and is for one of the day bombing squadrons. The other three fields, one for day bombers, and two for night bombers, are further west, in fact just beyond Calais.

We spent only half an hour at "Oie," but it gave us a good chance to see how an aviation field for service flying is started. At this particular place the hangars and also the wooden barracks and officers' quarters are absolutely in the open, in a stretch of country that has not got a tree for miles, and I suggested that it would probably be heavily day-bombed by the Boche. They told me, however, that the enemy does very little day bombing and they are sufficiently far behind the lines to avoid the occasional fast plane that comes over by daylight. Of course at night a field of this kind is practically safe as it is much more difficult to locate than a town like Dunkirk or Calais. The day bombing planes we shall use are to be D.H. 4's and the first are expected within about ten days.

We proceeded toward Calais, passing through the little town of Gravelines which had apparently been overlooked by the Boche bombers for only perhaps a third of the windows had been blown in. Belgian and British troops were billeted here, as I suppose they have been since the beginning of the war. We ran through the center of Calais—an obviously official party of four cars—so we were not even stopped by the sentries. Calais has been badly bombed. It is actually true that a large number of houses have been either really demolished or so badly wrecked that they must be wholly rebuilt, and yet they tell me that practically no military damage has been done. Calais and Boulogne have, of course, received not only the great majority of the troops sent from England to France but also the bulk of the supplies and munitions, and in spite of the bombing which has gone on almost every night, the work of transportation has proceeded without interruption. The harbor and quays have never been out of commission, and the canal and railway have been continuously used. Dunkirk had seemed like a town half deserted—little military activity and what there was they seemed to hide as much as possible. Calais on the other hand teems with movement—many troops, including replacements coming forward, leave men and wounded going back, and an enormous force working on transport; also great activity on the canal and the railroad. They tell me that it is only lately that serious attention has been paid to aeroplane bombs; in other words, up to very recently the bombs dropped have been very small, first 50 lb., then increasing gradually to 100, to 200 and even to 300 lb., but a bomb of that size does damage to little more than the object which it actually strikes and the radius of damage is only a few feet. Very recently, however, the Boche night bombers have dropped some huge bombs, variously estimated at from 800 to 1200 lbs. These have smashed things up over a large radius; for instance, I saw a spot where one had landed in the middle of a street—about six houses on each side of the street were completely wrecked by it and many people killed. The old type would probably have done little more than blow in the windows, with possibly no loss of life. The U. S. Navy happens to have an answer, however. Our new night bombers, which are being completed in Italy and will start to fly here over the Alps next week, will carry a bomb weighing 1750 lbs. In Belgium, of course, we shall try to avoid hitting any town. They are intended for the harbor works and batteries at Zeebrugge and Ostend—for ammunition dumps, airdromes and military objectives. One of our pilots dropped one on Middlekerke a few days ago from a British night bomber and the photographs show a big area demolished.

A few miles beyond Calais, on the road to Boulogne, we turned to the left and soon came to a charming little château surrounded by woods. This was the headquarters of one of our night bombing squadrons, and they have rented the château and about 200 acres that will make an excellent flying field after the wheat has been cut about two weeks hence. Here our party divided, McCauley, Jackson, Camalier, Cone and I remaining, and Davis, Brown and Royes going on eight miles west to another flying field, Saint Inglebert. Our run had been the first of many dusty ones, and I changed from my blue seagoing suit to khaki trousers, leather puttees and a gray coat. After a rather tough supper, due to the fact that they had only been here a few days and had not yet found a good cook among the enlisted men, we motored over to Saint Inglebert in the hope of seeing the night bombing squadron leave. Young Lovett, the son of Judge Lovett, is in command at Saint Inglebert and he seems like an awfully nice boy. At that place the officers have taken over a very charming old stone château, enclosed in a high wall and approached under a fine old archway. We will not have to establish a new field as we shall use the big British field adjoining, but we are putting up three big hangars at our end. I also saw Leverett Bradley, who is the Y.M.C.A. Secretary for our Naval Unit. I had no idea that he was in this work, but they say that he is doing very well. We walked down to the British Hangar and I learned much about this night bombing work from the British Commanding Officer. I also had a long talk with a Major who rode up on one of the finest thorough-breds I have ever seen and who is in charge of the big British re-mount station nearby. He told me some extraordinary figures to show the small percentage of loss among his horses, i.e., between the time the horses

leave the British base and the time he sends them forward
into active service. I think it was about 1/10th of one percent, and this includes a channel crossing and several weeks
at his camp. I have had little opportunity to note British
horse transport so far, but this Major says it is far and away
ahead of the French. We waited for nearly two hours in the
hope that the slight ground mist would decrease, but at
10:00 p.m. the Commanding Officer decided not to send out
the bombing squadron that night. Six of them were to have
started, one of them piloted by one of our Navy youngsters
and three of the others with American observers—in fact it
is this field that has been giving the finishing touches to the
pilots and observers who will handle our U.S. Navy night
bombing squadrons. I shall try to stop here on the way back.
The first of our Caproni's flew across the Alps from Turin to
Paris today. They will come along rapidly and our first
squadron will be operating from Saint Inglebert within
two weeks.

August 1.[1] We spent a comfortable night at the château
and had our first experience of night bombers—not very
exciting but proving at least that night bombing exists.
About 11:00 p.m. we heard a high-pitched note overhead
and shortly afterward could see shrapnel and anti-aircraft
guns at Calais bursting in tiny star points, and we could also
hear the sound of guns or explosions in the direction of
Boulogne. Evidently the Boche did not think the ground
mist too heavy.

This a.m. we left for Paris, going first to Saint Inglebert
to pick up the rest of the party. Cone and McCauley were
in one of the French Government cars with me, Camalier
in the other French limousine with the bags, all alone in the
roomy tonneau with suitcases, duffle-bags, etc., and two fero-

---

[1] The letter-diary was compiled chronologically according to F.D.R.'s activities and not according to the postmarks on the letters. Hence, one of the
two entries for August 3rd was placed ahead of the account for August 1st.

cious looking Poilus armed with rifles on the front seat. The understanding was that he was to follow us and join the other car at Saint Inglebert, but when we got there we looked around in vain, and after waiting ten minutes it became perfectly apparent that Camalier had been kidnapped by the Poilus. One of our own Frenchmen remarked that his companions of the other car undoubtedly knew that our ultimate destination was Paris. We had visions that having lost us these pirates would push through at top speed for the Hotel Crillon. Knowing what top speed to a Poilu means and the inability of Camalier to say even—"Go slow" —in French, we had visions of his pleasant day. More of this anon.

The rest of us ran south to Boulogne, passing around to the eastward of the old walled town; hence we did not see much of the bombed portion. Little attempt was made by the Germans to damage Boulogne until recently. Since the March drive they have visited it pretty regularly every night as part of the attempt to get the British out of the channel ports. I do not believe that much military damage has been done. Boulogne is used more for supplies and munitions, Calais being primarily for troops. From here we went almost due south over a wonderful road through Samur to Montreuil. I suppose there is no harm in saying now that Montreuil is the British General Headquarters,—in other words the permanent base of General Haig and his staff. We stopped to call on the American Liaison Officer, who to my delight turned out to be Major Robert Bacon. In the office I also found Gavin Hadden. We could stay only a few minutes, but I went over Major Bacon's map showing the latest moves along the British front. I imagine that things are in a very different condition from what they were even a month ago. The March, April and May German offensive shook the British Army to its roots. The whole theory of their General Staff up to March 21 had been not merely to discourage but

to prohibit any reference to or thought of a retrograde movement or the creation of defensive positions in the then
existing line. They felt that an army taught to think only of
going forward could never be forced back. The result was,
of course, that when the Germans on March 21 struck with
a great superiority of forces on a wide front and actually
broke through, as is now admitted, the British had no prepared plans for meeting the emergency. It was only magnificent fighting of the "back to the wall" kind that Haig called
for, and the inability of the Germans to push their advance
fast enough, that prevented the loss of the channel ports
and possibly a debacle of the British Army. But it left, after
the two main attacks, one on the Amiens salient and the
other between Lille and Ypres, a very badly jolted British
Army from the General Staff all the way down. Every plan
had to be re-cast, and more than that, their confidence was
badly shaken and they realized that the strip of land behind
them was altogether too narrow for comfort. I do not know
what the exact date was, but it probably coincides about with
the stopping of the German thrust down the Marne towards
Paris when our Marine Brigade acted the principal part of
"stopped." This was early in June and at the same time the
British stopped losing ground on their front and began to
take a little of it back. That time marks the "come back"
of the British Army. Perhaps today they are a better fighting
machine than if they had not had that reverse,—Major
Bacon, at least, is very well satisfied with the way things are
going here now. We pulled out along the same wonderful
road and made Abbeville just before noon. Of course the
surface of the road is not entirely smooth, in fact it is missing
in spots. This you realize when in perfect French you first
request your Poilu at the wheel to reduce his speed from 85
kilometers an hour to about 60 kilometers. He says "Oui
Monsieur" and does so for just three minutes before resuming 85 kilometers. You then direct him to reduce speed

in tones of command—the effect of this lasts about six minutes. We shed a silent tear for Camalier and wonder whether he or the suitcases are on top in the tonneau. Abbeville is the place practically on the coast which the German drive against Amiens would have reached, thereby cutting off the British from the French Army. Since Amiens has been under shell fire, the north and south rail communication has gone through Abbeville, and the Germans have, therefore, attacked it rather heavily. Everything in the vicinity of the railway station has been badly knocked about, and we saw the effects here of one of the few really big bombs, probably a thousand pounds, which the enemy have dropped. It fell in the middle of the street and the damage extended not only over a radius of about 200 feet but had really wrecked houses permanently. The fine old church did not seem to have received a direct hit, but the stained glass is at least half demolished and the statues and carvings of the façade have been badly chipped by fragments. We made inquiries here of the sentries as to whether they had seen anything of an innocent American being kidnapped by two Poilus. The sentries beamed their understanding and told us that the runaways had passed there about two hours before. We figure that this means an average speed of 120 miles an hour. When we reach Paris we shall inquire where the Protestant burying ground is. After filling up with "gas" we continued to Beauvais. The road on which we have been travelling since leaving Calais is one regularly used by staff cars and fast through motor traffic. It is, of course, well behind the lines and is comparatively little used for troops, supplies and ammunition. We have, of course, crossed a number of militray railways leading up to the front and we have also passed a good many divisions which are resting up or in reserve in these back areas. All towns and villages have troops billeted in them,—nearly all British down to Abbeville and from there on almost wholly French, though in two towns we saw

American troops, evidently only battalions. This is a "route militaire" so that there were sentries at each end of every village, but the character of the party was quite obvious and we were stopped only three or four times in entering the principal towns. They are much more strict, however, at this distance back from the front than they are at the front itself, it being assumed that any car which has succeeded in passing these rear guards has a right to be at the front. The French road sentries are noticeably more alert in saluting than the British or Americans.

We got into Beauvais at 1:30, just in time not to miss luncheon. As we pulled up to the hotel a white-faced figure came out to meet us, crying—"Thank God you are here." Our fears had been partly realized for though he was not quite dead and had not been carried through to Paris, Camalier had had an awful morning. His Frenchmen had run through not only at top speed but in what they admitted was record time. The prisoner in the rear had tried English, pure and cusswords,—and they had merely smiled encouragingly. He had hopped around that tonneau like a piece of popcorn and after waiting for us in Beauvais for 1½ hours, was almost ready to buy a ticket to New York. Luncheon, of course, was delicious—the first French meal always is. We saw many French and a few British Officers here, this town being the largest inhabited one near to this section of the front. The civil population has not yet been permitted to return to Amiens. Instead of taking the direct and rather rough road to Paris we proceeded through Clermont and Creil to Chantilly. This part of the road is really fairly close to the French front and we saw many new trench lines and wire entanglements. At Chantilly I insisted on driving through the château grounds, and apparently no damage has been done here by aircraft. From here it was a straight and uninteresting road into Paris, and we drew up at the Crillon at five o'clock. Captain R. H. Jackson, our Naval Attaché, and Lieutenant Maas met us. We have wonderful rooms on the troisième, southwest corner, as guests of the French Government. Within a few moments Commandant Pamard of the French Navy had called. He bore the greetings of the Minister of Marine and of Vice Admiral de Bon, Chief of the General Naval Staff, and asked me if I would mind postponing the official calls until tomorrow, owing to the lateness of the hour, and come this evening to dine informally with Admiral de Bon. Pamard is to be my aide while I am in France and he seems to be the kind to fit in excellently with my party.

I called Aunt Dora on the telephone and would have gone to see her if I had had more than a few minutes to unpack and dress for dinner. She insisted on coming to the Crillon and we had a nice chat. McCauley, Brown and Jackson accompanied me to the Ministry of Marine at 7:30. The building is next door to the Crillon, the building east of it on the Place de la Concorde, which is built as an exact duplicate. Admiral de Bon as Chief of Staff has quarters in this building in the Entre Sol. He had four officers of the General Staff to meet us so we made a delightful little dinner party of ten. To my delight and rather to my astonishment there were no toasts. I appreciated for the first time the value of French, and bad as it was, managed to keep a general conversation going during the whole meal. Admiral de Bon is one of the most delightful Frenchmen I have ever met. We are all singularly fortunate in having him at the head of the French Navy during this war. From everything I hear he is not only a good Chief of Staff for the French Navy but he is an excellent representative on the Inter-Allied Naval Council and gets on well with Admirals Wemyss and Sims. Incidentally he has a fine old face and a sense of humor. After dinner we stayed for an hour and I had a good chance to talk to some of the other French officers. All of these senior officers, French and British, seemed overcome at the thought that I came over in a destroyer. It is undoubtedly because their own destroyer days are several decades behind them.

Friday, August 2nd. Breakfasted with Aunt Dora and dashed back to the Crillon to put on the formal clothes for an official day. At 10:00 o'clock Admiral de Bon called on me officially and at 10:30 I went to the Ministry of Marine to call on M. Leygues, the Minister. He was very cordial and we chatted about ten minutes. Though these calls in full regalia and accompanied by staff are never very satisfactory, I expressed an interest in the splendid rooms and he showed me through the wonderful suite on the front of the Premier, —several wonderfully proportioned reception rooms including the council room where the Inter-Allied Council meets. Many of the decorations, some wonderful tapestries, vases and paintings have been removed for safe keeping since the long range shelling commenced. In London or Washington they would have left untouched the bare wall behind the tapestry, but here they have replaced it with damask. It is the same spirit which enabled the French during the "touch-and go" days of 1914, when the Government had gone to Bordeaux and the Germans were literally outside the gates, to keep on with the planting of the flower beds in the Tuileries and the repairing and cleaning of streets. They seem to lose their heads even less than the Anglo-Saxons,— very different from what we thought four years ago. It is this spirit that kept every village official in his own little village when the Germans over-ran northern France. Even though half or three-quarters of the population had fled southward, M. le maire and M. le curé were always at their posts.

Next we went to see M. Pichon, Minister for Foreign Affairs. I was told beforehand by a French official that this gentleman does not carry as much weight as his title would indicate. From there we went to the Embassy and I had a nice talk with Mr. Sharp. I had already spoken to Admiral de Bon and M. Leygues about my Italian visit. They had heartily approved. I discussed the question quite frankly with Mr. Sharp, and though he knew little about the subject personally, he read me a long letter from Thomas Nelson Page which confirmed me in my decision to go as soon as possible. I am frankly rather fearful that the British will want Sir Eric Geddes to go and have me accompany him. I am convinced that this would be just the wrong move, as the whole situation is at the present time deadlocked between the British and the Italians, and my business is to find a way out or a compromise. I cannot do this if the Italians think the British are bringing me along as "Exhibit 1" to prove that America takes wholly the British position. Therefore I shall leave for Rome next Wednesday night, immediately on our return from the front.

At 12:30 I went to the Elysée Palace and met the President and Mme. Poincaré. The entrance of the guests was even more informal than at the White House and I had to explain who I was to both M. and Mme. Poincaré. It was a big luncheon, about forty people, Mme. Poincaré the only lady. Most of the Cabinet were there—not Clemenceau—and it was really given in honor of Mr. Hoover, who arrived here several days ago. I sat between M. Leygues and a Senator, whose name I think was Du Puy. I thought the meal was rather sticky. After lunch I chatted with Mme. Poincaré and George Rublee, who had just come from London, had not expected this kind of a party and turned up in a yellow-brown tweed suit, the only man who was not at least in a cut-away coat. On the whole I thought the whole entertainment very much like similar ones at the White House except that here the wines were perfect of their kind and perfectly served.

Later I gathered up Captain McCauley at the hotel and we drove across the bridge again and called on M. Tardieu. I did not keep him long as he was in the middle of business hours, and I think from what I have seen in Washington and what I have heard here that he is the best executive administrator in the French Cabinet. Since returning from Washington he has succeeded in creating for himself a new position. He might now be called the Liaison Minister not only in Washington but in Paris, but the great feature is that he has obtained, in some way, the authority to carry the Liaison work into effect. The result is that if anything is needed by any branch of the American Army or Navy in France our officer in charge can go to Tardieu and get it done. This means in a sense that he has authority over the Ministers of the other departments. It is a beautiful and practical plan and it is showing results every day because every one knows what French Government "Red Tape" still is, and it is even more difficult for an American to untie. But it means also, I fear, that a good many other people in the Cabinet resent Tardieu's interference and are jealous of him. He expects to return to the United States about the time I do, and in the meantime I am to dine with him when I get back to Paris.

At 4:00 o'clock we went on to the office of the Premier, and McCauley, Pamard and I were shown into his room almost immediately. I knew at once that I was in the presence of the greatest civilian in France. He did not wait for me to advance to meet him at his desk, and there was no formality such as one generally meets. He almost ran forward to meet me and shook hands as if he meant it; grabbed me by the arm and walked me over to his desk and sat me down about two inches away. He is only 77 years old and people say he is getting younger every day. He started off with no polite remarks because they were unnecessary, asked me three or four definite questions about our naval production and what I thought of the effect of the submarine campaign on the troop transportation. He seemed delighted at the present rate of progress and I told him that I was over here solely to learn how to make everything move even faster. He jumped up, took me over to a big map with all the latest troop movements and showed me the latest report from General Degoute, covering progress north of Château-Thierry up to one hour before—a fine advance by the French and American troops north of Fère-en-Tardenois and to within a very short distance of the Vesle. Then he launched into a hair-raising description of the horrors left by the Boche in his retreat—civilian population carried off—smashing of furniture—slashing of paintings—burning of houses, and he said—"These things I have seen myself"—for the wonderful old man leaves his office almost every Saturday in a high-powered car, dashes to some part of the front, cheered by troops everywhere he passes, visits a Corps Commander, travels perhaps all night, goes up a good deal closer to the actual battle line than the officers like, keeps it up all day Sunday and motors back in time to be at his desk on Monday morning.

Then still standing he said—"Do not think that the Germans have stopped fighting or that they are not fighting well. We are driving them back and will keep them going back because we are fighting better and every Frenchman and every American is fighting better because he knows he is fighting for the Right and that it can prevail only by breaking the German Army by force of arms." He spoke of an episode he had seen while following just behind the advance— A Poilu and a Boche still standing partly buried in a shell hole, clinched in each other's arms, their rifles abandoned, and the Poilu and the Boche were in the act of trying to bite each other to death when a shell had killed both—and as he told me this he grabbed me by both shoulders and shook me with a grip of steel to illustrate his words, thrusting his teeth forward towards my neck.

We dined at the Crillon and several of the Paris staff joined me.

Saturday, August 3. I spent the morning working out the itinerary of our trip to the front during the next four days and sending telegrams about our visit to Rome, for which McCauley and I will leave on Wednesday night. Also Admiral de Bon came to the hotel and we had a long conference about the Italian Naval situation.

I went for Aunt Dora at noon and with her went out to Neuilly to see Cousin Hortense Howland, then back to pick up Cousin Charlie Forbes Gaston, Gabriel de Choiseul and Nina Barreau for luncheon in a neighboring restaurant.

At 3:00 I went with McCauley, Jackson and Pamard to call on Maréchal Joffre at the "École Militaire." He seemed very glad to see me and I came within an inch of getting my "accolade." I have escaped this charming little ceremony so far. The Maréchal looked to me older than when he was in the United States, and his face had a gray look. We had a delightful and intimate talk about the days in May 1917 when our decision to send a really great army to Europe hung in the balance. He was quite frank in telling me of his discouragement during his first visit to Washington, how it seemed impossible to get from the Secretary of War or the Army Staff any definite statement as to our plans, how they had generalized as to numbers of troops, time of departure, program for guns, deliveries of material, etc. etc., and he kept insisting that the friendly advice I had given him from the very first day when I met him with the MAYFLOWER at Hampton Roads had in the end enabled him to obtain the answers for which he had come to America. Of course we did not talk much about the military operations for the Maréchal is not very much a part of that just now, but I think he felt, and rightly so, that only a small part of the million and a quarter Americans now in France would be here had it not been for his mission at the outbreak of the war.

I went out at tea time to see Ted and Eleanor and found them in a nice little house just beyond the Arc de Triomphe.

Archie was there also, looking horribly badly. Everyone is trying to get him home but he refuses. I talked of the benefits of a sea voyage and a quicker recovery thereby. Ted still has one leg on the sofa, looks well and will be about again in a few weeks. Jeanetta Alexander Whitridge was also there. Ted and Archie were wonderfully interesting and they can't say enough for the American troops. They both have really splendid records.

On my return I found Fabry and Willie Eustis, the latter in fine form and doing really useful work in Paris. Colonel Fabry in civilian clothes looks much smaller and thinner than he did as a chasseur alpin in Washington. He still suffers a good deal with his leg, but has taken a position as military writer for the newspaper called "Oui." I am to dine with him on my return.

In the evening the staff and I dined early and went to the theatre, a "Revue." The most extraordinary audience I have ever seen—nine men out of ten in uniform; officers and enlisted men of all kinds, Army and Navy, French, British, South Africans, Anzacs, Canadians, Belgians, Serbs, Americans, Italians, etc., and between the acts everybody at the tables or the bar in the Foyer packed to suffocation. The average table contained one French girl and five foreigners, generally of different kinds—everybody extremely happy, no rowdiness, and wonderfully little intoxication. Nobody in uniform can be served with spirits, and French beer and wine are even weaker than in pre-war days.

We all piled into a taxi to go back to our hotel because we could not find the official car in the dark. The next day we found that our Poilus waited for us until 2:00 a.m.

Sunday, August 4. Our trip to the front started this a.m. from the Crillon at 8:00, Captain Jackson, Pamard and I in the first car, McCauley, Royes and Brown in the second, and Jackson, Davis and Lieutenant Watson of the Army in the third. We passed out of Paris toward Meaux on an excellent road, but found it more crowded with camions and divisions on the move than the Beauvais road. Our progress was, therefore, rather slow, but it was very interesting to watch the faces of the French troops, some of the divisions obviously coming out of the fighting and others going in. Also we passed a group of German prisoners, fresh from Château-Thierry, and still dirty and tired. They did not impress me as being physically unfit, but there is an awful contrast between the amount of intelligence in their faces compared with the French Poilus.

All this movement has to do with the offensive on the Château-Thierry front which began just thirteen days ago and which has been so far such a wonderful success. Meaux itself was congested with troops and hundreds of refugees who had fled down the Marne from Château-Thierry. Just beyond the city we turned to the right into a château park where Pershing has just begun the installation and organization of the staff of the First American Army. The Chief of Staff of the A. E. F. remains at Chaumont, and Pershing will be for a while at least not only Commander-in-Chief of the A. E. F. but Commanding General of the First American Army. Later on a second, third, etc., American Army will be formed. I met the Staff but spent only a few minutes as they have just begun to organize. From Meaux to Château-Thierry the road was increasingly congested, a good many refugees returning to their homes, in nearly all cases not knowing whether they would find a home left or not. They went with big carts drawn by a cow or an ox and a calf trotting behind, bedding, chickens, household goods and children, and some times a grandmother, piled on top, all of them taking it perfectly calmly, remembering always their good fortune in having got away before the arrival of the Boche, ready to start in again even from the ground up, but constantly impressing upon their children what the Boche has done to northern France in these four years.

Today or tomorrow, whichever way you count, begins the fifth year of the war for the people of France. The papers have mentioned it, but it has occasioned surprisingly little public comment. The Boche line is still further forward than ever except along the Marne, but if one can judge by the public press or by talking to the civil population or to these refugees, there is just as much quiet determination in France to see this thing through to victory or to go down fighting as there was in the beginning. And now since the American First and Second Divisions have helped to stop the drive and with other Americans at this moment are helping to conduct the most successful allied offensive of the whole war, these people show for the first time a complete confidence in the outcome.

A few miles before we reached Château-Thierry we passed through several villages rather badly wrecked by artillery fire—German artillery, but the Boche had never entered them. In one of them we were held up for an hour by an American artillery train, French guns, mostly 155's, but American-manned. One of the limbers had broken down, of course at a narrow turn, and all traffic was held up in both directions. I got out and walked to the scene and found two very junior youngsters making a bad mess of the tangle. Just then our Colonel appeared and in about ten quiet words had straightened things out and traffic proceeded. We came over a rise and there in the valley below us lay the bend of the Marne and Château-Thierry itself. On the ridge to the left lay a wrecked village, four times shelled—first by the advancing Boche; then by the retreating French; next by the advancing Americans of the Second Division, and finally by the retreating Boche. This was complete destruction, only detached walls remained—complete reconstruction will be necessary. We were now in a purely military area. No refugees have been allowed back as yet, and from now on no road sentries stopped our cars. We came into Château-

Thierry on the north bank of the Marne and spent half an hour searching for the French Army headquarters—one officer sent us across the river and another one back again, a somewhat difficult proceeding because all the bridges have been blown up and we had to cross by some precarious floating wooden affairs. One thing rather surprised me and that was that in the ten days that the French have been back in Château-Thierry no apparent attempt has been made to rebuild the bridges, either highway or railroad. Later in the day we found that the single track railway which runs north from this place into the Tardenois had not been touched by the engineers; in other words, although the troops have advanced twenty miles in these two weeks, the railway communication has not been advanced one mile. I could not help feeling that forethought in providing bridge steel would have made a better record. At last we found French headquarters just established an hour before in one of the few buildings in town with an almost complete roof. General Degoute, commanding the whole army in this sector, arrived a few minutes after we did. He is a splendid type of soldier, small, wiry and very cordial to us, insisting, although there were nine in our party, that we take luncheon with him. He apologized quite unnecessarily for the meal, for it was excellent although the cook, food and all, had barely arrived before we did. On my right sat M. Flamang, the very well-known painter who is on the staff. It was a most congenial luncheon and as soon as I found that the General was willing to talk I asked questions of every kind about the advance. He was especially nice about our Marines and told me that he had been the one who had issued the order changing the name of Bois de Belleau to Bois de la Brigade de Marine. (I have later learned that there was a mean piece of hokus pokus by some narrow-minded army officer in this connection. Degoute, as he told me with his own lips, announced the change in a general order to his entire army, in which among other things he gave especial praise to the Marine Brigade for their work in Belleau Wood. Somewhere down the line, whether it was in the Corps Headquarters or in the Division Headquarters, or perhaps even back at American General Headquarters, a public announcement was made that the French had changed the name of the wood to Bois des Americains. I put this on record because some other jealous individuals may seek further to prevent the Marine Brigade from getting this official recognition, but there is no question as to the action of General Degoute who was in command of the operations.)

While we were at luncheon Lieutenant de Tessan came in. We knew him when he came to Washington in 1917 with Maréchal Joffre. He gave me a copy of his book on that visit. After luncheon we went into the map room and I told Degoute frankly that the trip which Captain Jackson had laid out for the afternoon was wholly unsatisfactory to me. It was to include a visit to Bois de Belleau and thence to a dozen or so ruined villages all in the neighborhood of Château-Thierry, and where the fighting had ended days before. The General grasped the situation and detached de Tessan to take us up the line to as close to the actual fighting as seemed prudent, and he insisted that we return for dinner. I am sorry to say that this was the final straw on the back of the Naval Attaché. From now on for four days I ran the trip, especially as I had discovered that the plans called for late rising, easy trips and plenty of bombed houses thirty miles or so behind the front. We were to have slept in a comfortable hotel at Chalons, but I accepted the General's invitation to dine here at 9:00 p.m. and to sleep on the floor of some unoccupied house. We left immediately, passed out of Château-Thierry to the northwest over the ridge just in front of where the Marines first went into action when they checked the advance, and thence on a couple of miles to the eastern edge of Belleau Wood. We walked to the edge of the woods and looked east. No wonder this was the key to the salient. In front the ground, while rolling, was in general lower and more open, and even a civilian's eye could see that the few wooded higher points could be turned without offering half the defensive strength of the jungle we were about to enter. In the field in front of us frequent little crosses marked the men who had fallen in the open, nearly all Boche, and just beyond at the fork of the road a group of about two dozen American and Poilu crosses showed casualties in the taking of the farm buildings, whose much shattered walls had given the Boche machine gunners safety in spraying the whole edge of the wood itself in the neighborhood of where we stood. In order to enter the wood itself we had to thread our way past water-filled shell holes and thence up the steep slope over outcropping rocks, over-turned boulders, down trees, hastily improvised shelter pits, rusty bayonets, broken guns, emergency ration tins, hand grenades, discarded overcoats, rain-stained love letters, crawl-ing lines of ants and many little mounds, some wholly un-marked, some with a rifle stuck bayonet down in the earth, some with a helmet, and some, too, with a whittled cross with a tag of wood or wrapping paper hung over it and in a pencil scrawl an American name.

Over the top of this first rise [we walked] but a short dis-tance for the ground was so cut up with ridges, ravines, boulders, tree trunks and the remains of what had once been underbrush that it would have been a formidable task to work one's way through to the other side. It must be re-membered that the Marines had not only worked their way through the wood from one side to the other, a distance of more than a mile, but they also had worked their way length-wise in the wood, spreading out to cover a front three miles long, for when they went in they did not do so on the whole face of the wood. It was an operation a little like crossing a well-defended river. The point of entrance was like a bridgehead, small at first but widening out by continuous fighting, not only in front but to the right and left. This would have meant, of course, enfilading fires under the best of conditions, but where, as here, the ground was broken-up, tumbled, irregular ridges and gas-filled ravines, it meant offensive fighting of the most extraordinary merit. There is no use going into the details of those two weeks, of the days when food and ammunition could not be brought up, of the wounded who could not be brought out, of the detachments which could not maintain contact, and of the darkness and constant fighting without rest or sleep. It is enough to know that not one day passed without some advance, until an enemy defending force, first and last three times our number, had been wholly cleared from every foot of the Bois de la Brigade de Marine.

Entering the motors again we moved north and east through a number of villages nearly all of which had been heavily shelled and many of them showing the marks of machine gun and rifle fire on the walls. After crossing the railway which runs north from Château-Thierry we turned south and came to a little switch running a few hundred feet into a clump of woods. A hundred feet inside the trees was a small circular clearing and in the middle a great pit, ten or fifteen feet deep, containing the concrete foundations, the steel turntable and mechanism for a gun of very large calibre. No one knows definitely which size gun was mounted here or whether, indeed, the Germans had had time to place any gun in place. The work on the elaborate concrete and steel platform must have taken several weeks, and in view of the fact that no heavy piece was located here by the French observers, we can only suppose that this foundation was destined for another long-range gun to fire on Paris, but that the Franco-American advance made all this preparation useless. We moved on a few miles and suddenly found ourselves in the midst of many American troops. Up a delightful driveway, we came to a typical French château near Fresnes, now the headquarters of General Liggett. We waked the General from the first nap he had had for several days and he showed us the maps of his sector as Corps Commander of several American Divisions now in front of us. Again I had to insist that I did not want to see any more back areas as planned by Captain Jackson, and the General showed us how we could go into Fère-en-Tardenois, and thence, if the shelling is not too heavy, a few miles further to Mareuil. Just as we were leaving I saw to my delight Roland Redmond and Lydig Hoyt, both now on Liggett's staff. They looked very fit and have had a wonderful opportunity by being in this beginning of the general offensive.

From this point on, the road became more and more congested with motor trucks. At last we came to the first sign of actual operations, an observation balloon which the French had hauled down preparatory to moving it farther forward during the night. We passed through Cierges and Sergy, two villages which held up the advance for several days about one week ago. Both places show the effect of hard fighting. They were badly shelled and the walls were pock marked with bullets. The little church in Cierges remained just as the Boche had left it. It had evidently been used as a hospital, for litters of straw were still on the floor and various articles of Hun clothing. Every altar ornament and embroidery was gone and the houses themselves were cleaned out and more furniture broken than could possibly happen by shell fire. For instance, you could go into a small room, the walls and even the ceiling of which were completely intact, and in the corner you would find a wreck of three chairs, one leg of a table gone, and smashed china on the dresser. That kind of work was done deliberately and maliciously by the Huns. Turning west again, we drove into Fère-en-Tardenois and met here the artery of communications for this sector; camions, artillery and moving troops filled the road in both directions, but the stream never stopped. We turned sharply north just as a series of exploding shells followed by little white puffs indicated a Hun plane, probably doing photographic work. Our pace slowed up as the road was almost wholly filled with camions. Several large piles of shells on both sides of the road, ammunition dumps, proved how fast the Germans had had to get out at this point, abandoning most of their ammunition, and a huge circle of torn trees and turned-up ground indicated one of these ammunition dumps which had been exploded either by one of our shells or by the Boche themselves to prevent it from falling into our hands. We dropped down into a little valley, crossed a temporary bridge over the stream and came into the small straggling village of Mareuil. Just as we descended from the motors a loud explosion went off very close by. Some of the party jumped perceptibly, realizing that we were within easy range of the Hun artillery. It was, however, only one of our own 155's so cleverly camouflaged in a tree just off the road that we had not noticed its presence. Mareuil had been little damaged by shell fire, and we found General ———— established with the headquarters of the ———— Division in the empty inn—boards and boxes for tables and chairs, and none of the comforts of the Corps Headquarters in the château we had visited. This was about 5:00 p.m. and the Boche had actually been in the place last night. In the meantime we have hurried his retreat, and the fighting line is now about three or four miles farther north and we have actually, at one or two places, reached the Vesle River. It is indeed quite evident that we are on the battlefield. To our sensitive naval noses the smell of dead horses is not only evident but very horrid. These Army people do not seem to notice it at all. In the last kilometer or two we passed many carcasses, and the "cleaning-up outfit" had not yet got far enough forward to even sprinkle them with lime. This "cleaning-up" is, however, wonderfully organized, and the units have not been more than twenty-four hours behind the advance. There were a number of dead Boche in the fields and in one place a little pile of them awaiting burial. The casualties though were light on both sides at this point, as the enemy were pushing for the defensive line of the Vesle at top speed. That line will be a hard one to crack, and from what I can gather if the enemy attempt serious resistance there and do not continue the retreat as far as the Aisne, the French will try to turn them out by a flank attack from the neighborhood of Soissons. (Later it turned out that this eventually happened. We were held up on the Vesle for many weeks, and there was a good deal of shelling by both sides, Mareuil and the vicinity being constantly under fire.)

We visited the other guns of the battery of 155's, fired one of the guns, and then returned all the way to Château-Thierry over the dark road, a distance of about seventeen miles. The road was even more congested than in the afternoon and we passed an entire French Division which had been relieved and was going to the rear to recuperate. It was broken up [into] groups of every size and kind—platoons, companies, whole regiments, artillery, camions, then more infantry, ammunition wagons, and even a small body of cavalry. The men looked pretty thoroughly tired and were trudging along at the same rate as the slow moving transport animals but these Poilus after many days of constant fighting and shell fire still looked awake and intelligent, very different from the stolid, stupid look on the faces of the German prisoners, whom we also passed in small groups. We got back to General Degoute's headquarters just before 9:00 and after washing off layers of dust, joined him and his staff at an excellent dinner. The members of my staff have begun to realize what campaigning, or rather sight-seeing, with the Assistant Secretary means, and Captain Jackson is still visibly annoyed because I upset his comfortable plans for an inspection of regions fought over a month ago. However,

Brown and some of the others backed me up valiantly in my partially successful efforts to see the real thing. Before we left General Degoute, he gave me his own map used in the advance from Château-Thierry to the Vesle, with the sectors of each corps and division marked on it.

We motored through inky darkness and winding streets over the Marne bridge of boats to a suburb south of the town and came to two houses which were intact and were to be our quarters for the night. One electric torch served to light us up the rickety stairs and to the doors of our rooms. By using six matches I discovered a table, chair and a bed with a mattress and a *duvet* on it. I managed to get my boots and leggings off and fell in—1:00 a.m. and a thoroughly successful day.

Monday, August 5. Before 6 o'clock we were up; went across the street to a French hospital which had been established near a college building and begged some coffee and bread and butter, and the head doctor took me upstairs to see the damage done by Hun airplanes in the rear of the building. All the windows had been blown in and two of the sheds in the courtyard destroyed. A soldier was on the operating table when it happened and the window glass was showered all over him and the doctor, but neither was seriously injured. I was told that the enemy must have known that it was a hospital. It had been so used for many months, and the two big white crosses marked out on the ground must have been seen many times by Hun observation planes. The attack was made in daylight, the bomber circling above the hospital for fully ten minutes.

At seven we all started eastward along the south bank of the river toward Châlons-sur-Marne. A very short distance out of Château-Thierry we came to the lowest point on the river which the Germans actually crossed. From here on they held a long strip of the south bank. I have explained before how the advance down the north bank of the river from

Château-Thierry was started in the first days of June, with the assistance of the Marines. The enemy, on June 15, swung this attack a little further east, got across the river, and hoped from this new point of vantage to work down the south bank. The road we were passing over was just above the river bank and many shelter pits had been dug along it. Barbed wire, ammunition piles, and a good deal of debris were everywhere to be seen. The slope along the route, rising from the river, was pitted with shell holes, and the Boche must have had a very uncomfortable time hanging on by his eyelids to the comparatively narrow strip south of the river. All along this part there were more signs of artillery fire than in the Tardenois, where we were yesterday. Apparently the German command placed high hopes on this advance, for it threatened not only the road to Paris on the right, but on the left came very close to pinching off the narrow neck through which the French were hanging on to Rheims. Not only the villages but the fields and trees on both sides of the river gave evidence of great artillery concentration.

We passed through Mézy and Dormans, where we crossed the river to Verneuil, on the north bank, because the other road was congested with traffic. This is the official reason given for our crossing. The real reason was that my good friend Commandant Pamard got into a discussion with Captain Jackson as to how to read a road map, and I could not persuade anybody concerned to stop at the perfectly clear sign boards. I might state here that we started off from Château-Thierry this a.m. with the general object of finding the U.S. Marines at some point to the eastward. Each of the three members of the party had definite information, "high official authority" as to the Marines' location. These locations were, to be sure, all to the eastward of us, but each was many long miles from the other.

Near Châtillon-sur-Marne we passed the most easterly place, marked by much barbed wire, where the Germans had got across, and here too we recrossed the river to the south bank and proceeded east to Epernay, thence over a splendid highway to Chalons and on in a southeasterly direction, still following the Marne, to Vitry-le-Francois and St. Dizier. We lunched at ———— and made wonderful attempts to locate the Marines by long distance telephone. Some of our army friends had apparently never heard of them. Some thought they were still fighting at Château-Thierry, so we decided to continue to Toul and make further inquiries there.

From here we traveled at high speed over a magnificent "Route Nationale" through a beautiful part of France which I had never seen before, putting into Toul about 2:30. A good many American troops were in this neighborhood, for Toul and Nancy are the two big towns behind the sector of the front we are now holding, running along the southeast side of the St. Mihiel sector and past Pont à Mousson. Here we found definite information that the Marine Brigade is billeted just outside of Nancy and that General Lejeune, with Division Headquarters, is in Nancy itself. We continued our journey and finally pulled up before Headquarters at 4.

All of us had a delightful reunion, for we knew all of the Marine officers and some of the regulars. General Lejeune has just been given command of the whole Second Division, and Nevil has the Brigade of Marines. Dick Derby is also with the Division and a lot of other younger officers whom I knew. Orders have just been received sending part of the Second Division up to the trenches. I am a little surprised, and I think the Division was, too. They were due to go to the rear for a rest period after the Belleau Woods fighting, during which they had about 40 per cent. of casualties. Instead they were sent into the attack again at Soissons and lost over 20 per cent. more. At last they were taken out, only a week ago, and sent here to Nancy to rest and take in their replacements. Now part of their resting is to be done in the front line trenches near Pont à Mousson. I can say what none of them have even whispered to me, and that is that the high command has seen fit to give the Second Division more hard and continuous actual fighting than any other two American Divisions put together. Officers and men alike are nevertheless at heart very proud of this, and there is no complaint, except perhaps from tired bodies that crave even one consecutive week of let-up. There is no question that up to date the Second Division is "par excellence," the most tried and true unit of the A.E.F.

Accompanied by General Lejeune and Nevil we motored out to a little town and suburb of Nancy, and there I inspected one battalion of the 5th Regiment of Marines. They were drawn up the length of the narrow village street, and I passed down both lines. The men looked wonderfully well and their faces were not as drawn as I had expected to find them after these two months of constant operations. The majority were in the khaki of the army, their own olive drab having been worn out long ago. The replacement troops were easily recognizable by the olive drab. It gave one a pretty good idea of the heavy casualties which had taken place in the last fighting near Soissons.

We moved on one mile further and came to a sloping field, where the Machine Gun Battalion was drawn up. These men had very greatly distinguished themselves, contributing to the holding of every foot of the advance which we made. Continuing, we came to another village and I inspected the other Battalion, this one belonging to the 6th Regulars. The replacements seemed in about the same proportion as in the other two units. I noticed, however, that the men in the army khaki could scarcely be distinguished from the army troops. General Lejeune suggested that the Marine corps button could be worn on the collar points of their army shirts, but that he lacked the authority to allow this. I told him that I would assume responsibility and then and there issued an order that this device be worn in recognition of the splendid work of the Marine Brigade. I went back with General Lejeune to his quarters, where I was to spend the night, an attractive private house in a delightful garden. Here the General and his aide had been billeted at 1 Franc each per day. The French family had moved into the top story and during four years had been living thus, with different high commanding officers occupying the ground and second floors from time to time. The 1 Franc per day does not include food, and Lejeune's orderly cooks the General's breakfast in complete harmony with the family cook.

We cleaned up and went to a delightful restaurant in the famous Place Stanislas, where we found the rest of my party and half a dozen officers of the 2nd Brigade, including Brigadier-General Nevil and Brigadier-Generals ———— and ————, both of the army. There was no scarcity of the good things of life, and we sat at table talking war until one o'clock in the morning. It was a most interesting evening, and without question the Second Division has every right to think themselves, as they do—the best unit in the Army. That kind of feeling is all to the good when it is backed up by a real record and the desire to add to it.

Tuesday, August 6:—After a very early farewell to Lejeune (breakfast at 6:30 a.m.) we started on another breakneck motor spin, first retracing our steps through Toul and Void and Ligny-en-Barrois, where we turned to the right and ran into Bar-le-Duc. From here we ran north over the famous "Voie Sacrée" about 30 miles to Verdun. This is the famous road over which most of the troops and supplies were moved during the terrific fighting of 1916, for it must be remembered that the tip of the St. Mihiel Salient reaches to within nearly 15 miles of Bar-le-Duc on the east and the Argonne Forest comes down a similar distance from the northwest. The Voie Sacrée itself was made wide enough for two constant streams of traffic in both directions. Thousands of men were constantly engaged on its repair, and as we approached Verdun itself hundreds of shell holes on either side showed how these men had thwarted the attempts of the German artillery to cut the communications. All the villages along the road had been heavily bombed. As we approached the city itself from the south we could see only the citadel crowning the hill, for Verdun lies along the river on the northern slope. We went at once to the headquarters of Colonel de Hay, Commandant of the citadel now, as he has been, all through the siege. He took us at once into the tunnel which leads into the citadel, for the 4000 men forming the garrison live 60 feet under ground in vaulted galleries laid out like streets.

Before lunch Colonel de Hay took us to the top of the citadel and to the Cathedral and Bishop's Palace. Even up here there were many communication trenches. The Colonel told me that during many months so many shells were constantly falling that it was unsafe to cross from one side to the other, a matter of 200 yards, without using the trench, and that in fact many troops had been killed on top of the citadel and in its immediate vicinity. The Cathedral and Bishop's Palace have been badly damaged.

All this was nothing, however, to the sight that met our eyes when we looked down over the town. Great gaps showed where buildings had once stood. Detached and jagged walls were everywhere, and of the houses still standing not one roof remained intact. It was a scene of colossal destruction, but not the obliteration we were to see on the battlefield itself; but to me the great miracle was the bridges across the Meuse, for although not a house remains intact, not one of the six or eight bridges was hit by a single shell. Colonel de Hay said that this had been a saving chance for the supplying and reinforcing of the heroic men on the ridges across the river.

We returned to lunch in the tiny underground dining

room of the Commandant and his staff. The first thing that met our eyes on one of the walls was the memorable original signboard which was posted near the entrance to the citadel during the siege, and on which the thousands of troops going forward to hold the line read the words which, for the French people, will sum up for all time their great watchword of four years—"ils ne passeront pas." Here too were representations of what the advance of Verdun had meant. The Legion of Honor conferred on the city and the great "Book of Privileges," in which statesmen of all nations had written their appreciation.

After a very good meal Colonel de Hay showed us through the citadel. Frankly, I should hate to have to live in this spot. The troops sleep, eat and live in these low vaulted passageways in an atmosphere that is distinctly close and damp, and as for sanitary and toilet arrangements, they are practically non-existent. The men have a little chapel and two canteens, one for food, etc., the other for beer and wines, and a kind of recreation and writing room; but all of this is a part of the same system of tunnels, all the air they get being forced in by pumps.

On coming out we were given helmets and gas masks and proceeded in two automobiles across the Meuse to the famous battlefield. First we came to the splendid "Casernes" of the pre-war garrison, now mere shells of buildings. Near them was one of the battle cemeteries, thousands and thousands of graves tightly packed together, where the men had been laid under shell fire, and in fact only a few hundred yards short of the actual fighting line. These southern slopes of the ridge down to the Meuse itself were bare enough of trees and the ground terribly churned by shell fire, but as we reached the top of the ridge, just west of Fort Souville, the greater part of the battlefield came in view. For a few moments it didn't look like a battlefield, for there was little or nothing to see but a series of depressions and ridges, bare and brown and dead. Seen from even a short distance there were no gashes on these hills, no trenches, no tree trunks, no heaps of ruins—nothing but brown earth for miles upon miles. When you look at the ground immediately about you, you realize that this earth has been churned by shells, and churned again. You see no complete shell holes, for one runs into another, and trench systems and forts and roads have been swallowed up in a brown chaos. This ridge on which we paused for a moment or two marks the final and successful stand by the French. In front is the "Valley of Death," and beyond it, crowning the second ridge, Fort Douaumont. After the loss of the latter the French fell back into the valley and from then on, day after day, the Germans poured men down one side and the French the other, and it is probable that over a hundred thousand men were actually killed in this little stretch of valley. From the bottom the Crown Prince launched that last terrific attack which broke down at the very rim of Souville Fort itself and which marked the high tide of German arms.

As we started to descend we crossed the valley and came to the sharp turn known as "L'Angle de Mort," the spot so often described by American Ambulance drivers, who passed there so often by timing the intervals between the shells, and where many of them were hit in spite of all precautions. On the slope to the left Colonel de Hay pointed and said, "There is the village of Fleury." Not even a brick on the tumbled earth could verify his statement. We stopped to take a photograph, but the Colonel hurried us on as he spotted one or two Boche observation balloons off to the north and said that we undoubtedly had been seen and that they would begin shelling the road in a minute or two. We passed on to the south slopes of Fort Douaumont, a quarter of a mile beyond, and sure enough the long whining whistle of a shell was followed by the dull boom and puff of smoke of the explosion at the Dead Man's Corner we had just left. The

Colonel used this as the text of a wonderful description of German methods—their wonderfully planned and detailed operations where everything went by rule and clockwork. "For instance," said the Colonel, "that Boche battery has orders to fire at that angle in the road every six minutes for one hour in case traffic is reported as passing that point. As he spoke the second whistling shell came over and exploded at the angle, and was followed by another every six minutes as the Colonel had stated.

We sent the motors back a short distance to conceal themselves behind some dugouts and the party walked up the narrow hand railway to Fort Douaumont and entered the tunnel. I was so much interested in going through its narrow winding tunnels that the rest of the party failed to appreciate my enthusiasm and that of the French Commandant. He has 400 men living here underground, but while little remains of the exterior of the fort they have been busy repairing the interior damage and gettings things ready for a possible future attack. The loss of Douaumont by the French is not one of the heroic chapters of the siege. Through some mistake in orders it was held only by a Lieutenant and a handful of men who were overwhelmed almost without firing a shot by the rush of the Germans. The French artillery thereupon proceeded systematically to smash it to pieces so that when, months later, their counterattack came, its walls and "fosses" were leveled and the Germans were unable to use it as a point of support. They did use it, however, to good advantage during the fighting in the valley below and in the attack on Souville, for they were able to bring troops into it up the north slope and thence down through a very deep channel which they dug far underground and out into the valley in the south. This tunnel yielded hundreds of prisoners when the French swept them back later on. The armament of the fort, when we were there, consisted of only two big guns mounted in armored turrets and many machine guns protecting the north slope. Looking down on this north side we had a wonderful view of the present trench lines about a mile away and two-thirds of the way up the opposite ridge. The Boche trenches were about 40 yards from the French, but there was literally no sign of life in the two or three miles of front trench lines that we could see. We know only that they are manned at all times, though there has been little action in this sector of the front for months. Behind the German lines the same rolling country extended for miles, but every ridge was a forest. This was the way these ridges of the battlefield had been two years before. Now not even stumps are left.

After rejoining the motors we passed to the westward following the course of the battlefield and crossing the Meuse to Fort de Dacherauville. Here we had a splendid view of the angle of the Meuse and off to the left the high towers of Montfaucon. The Germans made several attempts to turn this left wing of the French position, and Colonel de Hay was personally in command at this point for several weeks.

On our return to the citadel we cleaned up as best we could and had a delightful dinner with the Colonel and several other French officers who had arrived on an inspection visit.

Wednesday, August 7th:—Personally, I should not care to be permanently stationed in the citadel. All of the air for the tunnels has to be forced in by pumps and last night I could not help the feeling that it is the same air being breathed over and over again. After a good breakfast with Colonel de Hay and his staff we said farewell and returned over the Voie Sacrée to Bar-le-Duc. At this point I missed my suitcase and was rather upset, as it contained some important papers. I did not dare return in person owing to the departure for Rome to-night, so Elliot Brown and Davis went back and finally located it at a "Post Militaire." It had been placed on the running board of the car and fallen off and been found by some honest poilu. Meanwhile the rest of us continued on to Paris, via Vitry-le-Francois and Cesson, getting back to the Crillon at 4, just in time to hear the last few shots from the long range gun. One of them exploded just north of the Louvre, and the report is that a number of people were killed in a restaurant. (Note:—These were the last shells fired into Paris. The Franco-American line was all along the Vesle and [a] further advance was beginning north of Soissons. The Germans evidently began to move out this gun or guns from the supposed location in the forest of St. Gobain.)

After an early dinner Captain McCauley and I, accompanied by Sergeant Stratton, left for Rome.

Thursday, August 8th:—When we woke up our train was passing Aix les Bains, and at 9 we arrived at Modane. We were met by a private car of the Italian Government and a very nice naval aide to look after me while I am in Italy,— Lieutenant Genori. We reached Turin at 6 and had two hours there. Were met by various officials, Italian Navy, American Army & Navy, American Consul, etc. Drove for an hour round the town; a heavenly day, with the surrounding mountains standing out clearly. They gave us a banquet in the station restaurant and we boarded our car again.

Friday, August 9th (Rome):—This morning we arrived at noon. Were met at the station by an enormous delegation, the Italian Minister of Marine—Admiral Del Bono and his staff; Peter A. Jay, Charges d'Affaires, and our embassy staff; Mr. Byrne and other Red Crossers; Colonel Buckley, our Military Attaché and his staff; Captain Hodges, our acting Naval Attaché; and about a dozen of our Naval officers. I was taken to the Royal waiting room and met everybody; then came to the Grand Hotel with the Minister of Marine.

We unpacked; had a quiet lunch in our salon; talked over the situation with a number of our people, and at 4 o'clock, in silk hats, etc., called on the Minister of Marine, then on

Signor Baron Sonino, the Foreign Minister, who did a very unusual thing in not only receiving me but in talking to me for half an hour. Jay said he had never known him to be so chatty and cordial, as he has rather the reputation of a bear.

Saturday, August 10th:—Last night Gussie Jay gave us a dinner; about 25 people, including the Minister of Marine and a number of Italian, American, British and French officers. I had some interesting talks, though here they are more anxious to know what we are doing and going to do than to speak of their own work. This whole Italian situation is difficult. I hope my visit will really help, and that this continued pressure and especially a fresh viewpoint from the United States will result in closer naval co-operation and more activity in the Mediterranean and Adriatic. This morning I gave a reception to the Italian press, a large gathering downstairs, refreshments for all. I was welcomed by the Minister of Public Information, Gallenga, and then spoke for three-quarters of an hour while he translated and the press asked questions. It was an unusual occurrence for Italy and they loved it apparently, and it did good. After it was over we spent two hours sightseeing, St. Peters, Sistine Chapel, etc. Lunched late and then a long conference with the Minister of Marine and the Chief of Staff, Admiral Thaon di Revel. We went over the whole naval situation and I insisted on keeping to the main point, the enormous superiority of the combined French, Italian, British, Japanese and American naval strength in these waters over Austria, and the lack of practically any offensive operations. Of course, this is due to the Italian policy of wishing to keep their capital ships intact to the end of the war. I think there is clearly divided opinion in the Italian Navy. Nearly all the younger officers want more action on the part of the regular navy ships, but Admiral Thaon di Revel is the absolute power behind Admiral Del Bono. The Minister is insistent on allowing no risks to be taken by the battleships. I remarked to them in our conference that the Italian Battleship Fleet had not gone outside of Taranto Harbor for over a year, that they had had no fleet drill and target practice. Thaon di Revel leaned forward and said, "Ah, but my dear Mr. Minister, you must not forget that the Austrian Fleet have not had any either." This is a naval classic which is hard to beat, but which perhaps should not be publicly repeated for a generation or two.

This evening an official dinner for me, Ministers of Marine and War and all the head allied naval officers, Jay the only civilian besides myself.

Sunday, August 11:—This morning had a most interesting long talk with Signor Orlando, Prime Minister. Things have worked out all right. I have proposed a plan for the creation of a General Naval Staff in Mediterranean, Adriatic and Aegean waters, to be composed of a Britisher, probably Jellicoe as senior member or chairman, and one member each from the French, Italian, American and Japanese Navies. This obviates the Italian and French objections to a British Commander-in-Chief, and while it does not give complete unity of command it would be a distinct step towards unity of action and a policy directed more along the lines of an offensive. I also told the Italians that if in any new operations against islands on the Dalmatian Coast, a land force of fifteen to twenty thousand men were needed, the American Navy could undoubtedly supply them before the close of the year. All of this will be taken up at the next Inter-allied Naval Council.

I have been much struck on this visit with the excellent work of the American Red Cross. They have been wonderfully effective in explaining the broad American point of view in the war and have reached almost every class in the community, and so have made up in part for the lack of actual American troops on the Italian front. We have only one regiment there and I think it of the greatest importance that we should send one or two others immediately. That one regiment was marched and counter-marched through various cities until it gave the impression of several divisions, but it is quite natural that the Italians who know should ask why we have been able to spare only three thousand men out of 1,250,000.

I lunched quietly with the American Naval Staff and am only sorry that I could not go down to Corfu, where Captain Nelson and the submarine chasers are based. Commander Train, our Naval Attaché, is in Malta with Admiral Strauss attending the Naval Conference on the mine barrage across the Adriatic. Train seems to have made an excellent impression in Italy. We left about two, in the same private car, accompanied by Lieut. Genori.

Monday, August 12: This a.m. we passed along the wonderful blue waters of the Gulf of Genoa. Lunched at Turin and reached Modena in the evening and said good-bye to Lieut. Genori. He has been a delightful companion and most helpful in all the arrangements. The private car takes us through to Paris.

Tuesday, August 13. The train was late and we did not reach Paris until noon. The staff was awaiting us and I packed and went around to see Admiral de Bon to tell him of my conference in Rome. In the evening the whole party left for Bordeaux, McCauley, Victor Jackson, Brown, Davis, Camalier, and Capt. Craven, second to Captain Cone in our Naval Aviation.

Wednesday, August 14: We arrived at Bordeaux early and started off on a long motor run to Moutchic and Pauillac. Moutchic is southwest of Bordeaux on a fine little lake not far from the ocean. This is where our naval aviators get their physical instruction in bomb dropping and machine gun practice. The camp has about 600 men and has been put up almost wholly by Bluejacket labor in a charming grove of pines beside the lake. They gave us an exhibition of bomb dropping on a fake submarine out in the lake and machine gun fire on a floating target. This visit was a sample of many which are to come. Only one hour could be spared as we had many more miles to cover, but I saw everything and through the staff was able to gather much information and the points of view of many officers.

We lost our way in the flat pine country and did not get to Pauillac until nearly lunch time. My old friend Taylor Evans met me with the entire personnel of nearly 5000 men turned out. This Pauillac camp is a wonderful location. It is on the south bank of the Gironde, not far from the mouth, and all it had to commend it was a long dock and rail communication. Every building, every hangar, and every workshop has been put up by us with American material. The new mess hall, where we lunched with 3000 enlisted men, is built almost entirely out of seaplane packing cases. I said a few words to the men and splendid entertainment was furnished by a jazz band, quartette and others. There is, of course, any amount of talent among the enlisted men, especially now,—actors, musicians, professional ball players, etc. etc. The first Navy paper to be published in Europe has been started under the name of the "Pauillac Pilot." The first number was published by mimeograph, but now it has become a dignified, illustrated, regularly printed newspaper. Captain Evans took me all over the camp and I spent a good deal of time with Lieut. Commander Briscoe going through the shops and checking up certain matters on which our Navy Dept. has fallen down rather badly. This base receives and assembles all airplanes and material from the U.S. Part of the material, such as the Liberty Motors, has arrived in bad condition, showing faulty inspection at home and necessitating much work here; for instance, one motor which was passed as ready to run was found to contain two pounds of sand in the cylinders. Then, also, many parts are lacking entirely; for instance, we have in France over a hundred seaplanes but only two self-starters. As a result of all this I sent a telegram to the Secretary of the Navy setting forth in detail the lack of certain parts and the lack of inspection. I made the telegram somewhat vigorous on purpose. It would make the office of aviation and the different Bureaus hopping mad, but they will be so mad that they will get busy and correct the trouble in future (all of which they have since done). I saw Ned Lane and he, like most of the others here, feels very much out of the fighting; but as I told the men at lunch it is just as important to do this work as it is to be on the actual firing line, and they must always realize that hundreds of thousands of other men in uniform at home would give anything in the world to change places with them. I went up for a "hop" in one of the seaplanes, flying up and down the Gironde, and getting an excellent idea of the geography in this region.

On our way back to Bordeaux we ran south about 15 miles to the wonderful new radio station which our Navy is putting up for the French Government at Croix d'Hins. Lieut. Commander Sweet, my old friend of the Pacific Coast trip, is in charge. None of the steel for the 8 great towers is up, but the material is rapidly arriving, and when completed this station will be exceeded only by the new radio station at Annapolis. We got back to Bordeaux at 7:30, very dusty and most of the party thoroughly exhausted. McCauley and I went to the house taken by Helen Astor, who is running the YMCA canteen and hut here. Ethel Harriman Russell is with her, and we found comfortable rooms and a real bath awaiting us. We dined there quietly.

Thursday, August 15: Met General Connor after breakfast and crossed the river to the docks, which have been taken over by the army. The length of the docks is being doubled and when the work is completed ten ships can unload at the same time. Temporary storehouses and additional trackage facilities have been put in along the docks, but it is not intended that any army supplies should remain here more than over night. After the enormous storage base, about 6 miles away, is completed and filled, and after railroad equipment becomes sufficient, it is the intention to move all the incoming cargoes direct on to the flat cars and thence by rail up to the supply bases back of the front. Thus the big supply base outside of Bordeaux will become a huge reserve to be used only in case of emergency, as, for instance, in case heavy German ships should get out of the North Sea and temporarily stop the flow across the trans-Atlantic lane. By shipping the cargoes in normal times direct from the ship to the front one process of handling will be avoided.

The bulk of the unloading is being handled by negro troops, and General Connor told me that he is now getting out an average of about 700 tons per ship per day. This is a splendid achievement, even when compared to the best commercial practice, but Connor is not satisfied and hopes eventually to get out over 800 tons per ship per day. It should be borne in mind that according to the plans Bordeaux and St. Nazaire are to handle the greater part of the army stores. Some will come in through smaller ports, and the principal troop debarkation port will continue to be Brest.

We commandeered a locomotive and flat car and moved out over a new line of track to the big storage base, 6 miles north. Its layout is excellent. All incoming freight comes in on the Bordeaux side, and the plant itself is divided into four main sections for different kinds of stores. The storehouses themselves are one story sheds, but of sufficiently durable character to last a great many years. The outgoing end at the farther side connects with the main line of railway to the north. German prisoners are at work on the grading and seem well taken care of.

After a hurried lunch at the hotel in Bordeaux we all left by motor, crossed the river and went down the right bank of the Gironde, arriving at Royon. Vincent Astor met us.

He is the Port Officer and has charge of the reporting of all vessels entering and leaving the Gironde. Captain McCulley, who is in charge of this district, seemed pleased with Vincent's work and especially with his success in laying a cable across from Royon to Pauillac. Royon is jammed with people, many of them those who have left Paris because of the "Bertha." We had a delicious swim, dined with Vincent, and went to an open air "Varieté."

Friday, August 16: Left Royon after an early breakfast, crossed the ——— River in a suspended car hung from a high bridge and arrived at Rochefort, Captain McCulley's headquarters. There is a French Navy Yard at this point, and I visited it with the French Admiral and my staff. It serves as a base for our converted yachts and other small craft operating in this district.

∾∾

At this point the diary-letter account of the trip ends, and the next letter is the last existing item of F.D.R.'s personal correspondence for 1918.

BREST, FRANCE
AUGUST 20, 1918
TUESDAY

Dearest E.

It has been a frightfully busy week—on the road each day from 6 a.m. to midnight—and we have done all manner of interesting things all the way from south of Bordeaux to here —all by auto—flying stations, ports, patrols, army stores, receptions, swims at French watering places, etc., etc.

Spent one night at Bordeaux with Helen Astor and Ethel Harriman.

There is so much to write of, but though I am behind on my diary it will all go in.

I have no news of Uncle Fred but hope to hear in Paris tomorrow. I shall be in France and Belgium one week more, and then a week in Scotland and England. So you may see me about Sept. 15, though the dates are of course very uncertain and I will telephone to H.P. on arrival.

Somehow I don't believe I shall be long in Washington. The more I think of it the more I feel that being only 36 my place is not at a Washington desk, even a Navy desk. I know you will understand.

I have seen Bob Huntington here, also Archie—they may give you news of me as they are both returning.

Kiss the chicks—I wish I could see them each day and tell them of the wonderful things our country is doing here.

A great deal of love from

Your devoted

F

The former Helen Dinsmore Huntington, Helen Astor was the first wife of Vincent Astor and the daughter of Robert P. Huntington, also mentioned in this letter. Ethel Harriman was the only daughter of Mrs. J. Borden Harriman, who served during the war as chairman of the Council of National Defense's Committee on Women in Industry, and later, in F.D.R.'s Administration, became Minister to Norway. Ethel Harriman was at this time married to Captain Henry P. Russell a prominent member of postwar Parisian society. Frederic A. Delano had resigned from the Federal Reserve Board to enter the Army in June, 1918; he was attached to General Atterbury's transportation staff at Tours, later promoted to colonel and appointed deputy director of transportation at Paris. "Archie" refers to Archibald Bulloch Roosevelt, T.R.'s third son by his second marriage, who was with the A.E.F. in France as a captain in the Twenty-Sixth Infantry Division.

F.D.R. was somewhat optimistic as to the date of his homecoming. After carrying out the itinerary enumerated in this letter, he boarded the U.S.S. *Leviathan* on September 8th, but the ship lacked coal and did not sail from Brest until the 12th. His return to New York on the 19th was not a festive one, for after several days at sea he was bedridden with double pneumonia and arrived home on a stretcher.

∽∽

It was not until the middle of October that F.D.R. was well enough to journey to Washington and turn in the official report of his trip, which he summarized with the remark that "we have very good reason to be proud of what the Navy has done." This accomplished, he went ahead with his plans to resign from the Department and join the Navy; but before he could do so the war in Europe came to a triumphant conclusion. During October, 1918, the Allied troops had completed the rout of the German forces that began with the offensives described by F.D.R. earlier in the summer. The American Meuse-Argonne campaign and the British and French push to the west had smashed the Hindenburg Line and driven the Germans practically out of France. On October 6, 1918, the German government sent a note to Wilson requesting him to aid in securing peace, stating that Germany was willing to accept the Fourteen Points and arrange for an armistice. Negotiations were carried on during the month that followed, and on the morning of November 11, 1918, the armistice was signed and the war officially ended.

A two-month armistice period elapsed between the cessation of hostilities and the opening of the Paris Peace Conference. During this time it was decided that F.D.R. should return to Europe early in 1919 to supervise the demobilization of naval personnel and equipment.

With the prospect of being present on the scene where the peace was to be arranged and a league of nations organized, 1918 closed joyously for F.D.R. and his family. The "war to end wars" had ended victoriously; the long years of bloodshed and sadness were past history; now the world could relax and look forward to the establishment of a real and permanent peace. Said A.E.R. in *This Is My Story,* "the feeling of relief and thankfulness" that marked the end of the year "was beyond description."

XI

"... They Are Beginning Again at the Beginning..."

ASSISTANT SECRETARY OF THE NAVY

1919-1920

THE TASK of reconstruction and reorganization which confronted the statesmen of the Allied countries at the end of the war was enormous. The problems of peace were at least equal to those of war. Approximately nine million soldiers had lost their lives in the conflict, nearly twenty-two million had been wounded in battle; and these figures did not include the huge total of civilian casualties resulting from the war, or the countless millions who suffered from the famine and pestilence accompanying the hostilities. Financially, the First World War was the costliest that had ever been fought. Direct expenditures by the principal belligerents had amounted to nearly two hundred billion dollars, a figure which did not take into account the economic loss from the interruption of trade and the destruction of property. These human and economic totals, almost incalculable figures, added up to a single, overwhelming truth for the peacemakers who convened in Paris: world war was a cataclysm which civilization could not afford to experience again.

Paris was chosen as the site for the conference in recognition of the heroic role played by France in the war. Early in 1919 the delegations of the various nations began to converge upon the French capital. In addition to the President of the United States, eleven prime ministers and twelve foreign ministers arrived on the scene. It was decided that those nations which had either declared war on Germany (Communist Russia excepted) or severed relations with the Central Powers should be represented at what was to be a dictated peace rather than a negotiated one.

In addition to their ranking plenipotentiaries, each country sent a delegation of experts of all kinds and an enormous clerical staff to assist in the formulation of peace terms; in some cases the delegations were made up of several hundred members. For the world Paris became the center of a united prayer for peace, while within the city itself the gathering of dignitaries produced a festival air; diplomatic protocol reached hitherto unknown heights, with official dinners and receptions rivaling private parties as the main evening activity. This was the Paris for which A.E.R. and F.D.R. sailed aboard the *George Washington* on January 2, 1919, a city caught between the tides of somber reality and unrestrained gaiety.

F.D.R.'s official orders for his second European trip granted him full authority to determine the status of all major contracts and financial obligations of the United States Navy, as well as the authority to approve and enact the settlement of any obligations and claims resulting from U.S. naval operations. He was granted this absolute authority because of the numerous complications involved in the settlement of the Navy's large European enterprise. The variety of the problems of demobilization precluded any overall decision; their solution was most feasible through a central authority. Fifty-four shore bases of varying kinds in the Azores and

European areas, twenty-five port offices, a railway battery of five fourteen-inch guns, several radio stations, and three hundred and fifty-nine vessels not participating in the transatlantic service—these were some of the overseas naval operations which F.D.R. had to dismantle; and there were also the seventy-five thousand enlisted men and five thousand officers to be gotten home. The task was further complicated by questions of property rights, governmental agreements, and the multitude of other factors arising from operations in foreign lands.

So that F.D.R. might cope with this huge task, Admiral Sims was directed to furnish him with all necessary facilities and personnel. In addition, F.D.R. took along Thomas J. Spellacy (at this time U.S. District Attorney and later mayor of Hartford, Conn.) as his legal adviser, Livingston Davis as his special assistant, and Commander John M. Hancock as his naval aide. Because of his recent recovery from pneumonia, A.E.R. was granted permission to accompany her husband on the trip, and as a result the correspondence of these weeks abroad is similar in nature to that written during their honeymoon. On this occasion, however, F.D.R. had little time to devote to letter-writing; five of the seven long letters to Sara Roosevelt were therefore written by A.E.R. These letters are here given in full.

U.S.S. "GEORGE WASHINGTON"

JANUARY 3, 1919

FRIDAY

Dearest Mama,

So far we've had a splendid crossing and this ship is very steady. There is nothing to make it different from other crossings except we are more comfortable, always have an orderly outside the door and everyone has to attend "abandon ship drill" daily with one's life preserver tied on!

I saw Roosevelt this a.m. and didn't recognize him till he

444

During the inspection tour of Europe in 1918—
F.D.R. and Admiral William S. Sims.

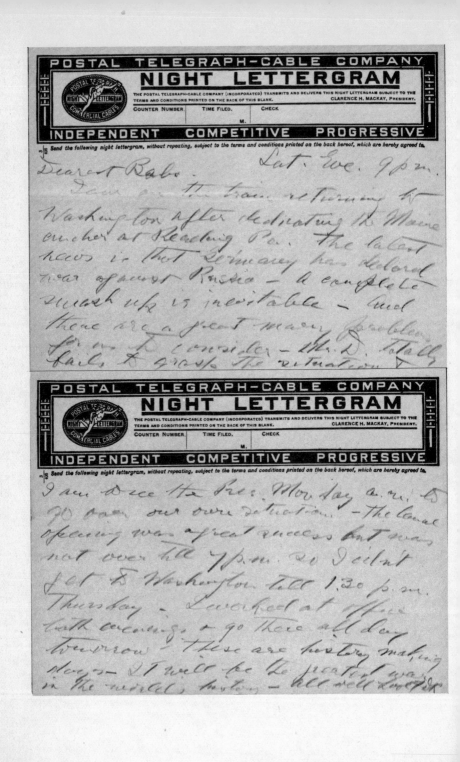

POSTAL TELEGRAPH-CABLE COMPANY

NIGHT LETTERGRAM

THE POSTAL TELEGRAPH-CABLE COMPANY (INCORPORATED) TRANSMITS AND DELIVERS THIS NIGHT LETTERGRAM SUBJECT TO THE TERMS AND CONDITIONS PRINTED ON THE BACK OF THIS BLANK.   CLARENCE H. MACKAY, President.

COUNTER NUMBER   TIME FILED   CHECK

M.

INDEPENDENT   COMPETITIVE   PROGRESSIVE

Send the following night lettergram, without repeating, subject to the terms and conditions printed on the back hereof, which are hereby agreed to.

Dearest Babs.   Sat. Eve. 9 p.m.

Dear on the train returning to
Washington after dedicating the Maine
anchor at Reading Pa. The latest
news is that Germany has declared
war against Russia — A complete
smash up is inevitable — And
there are a great many problems
for us to consider — Mr. D. totally
fails to grasp the situation &

POSTAL TELEGRAPH-CABLE COMPANY

NIGHT LETTERGRAM

THE POSTAL TELEGRAPH-CABLE COMPANY (INCORPORATED) TRANSMITS AND DELIVERS THIS NIGHT LETTERGRAM SUBJECT TO THE TERMS AND CONDITIONS PRINTED ON THE BACK OF THIS BLANK.   CLARENCE H. MACKAY, President.

COUNTER NUMBER   TIME FILED   CHECK

M.

INDEPENDENT   COMPETITIVE   PROGRESSIVE

Send the following night lettergram, without repeating, subject to the terms and conditions printed on the back hereof, which are hereby agreed to.

I am din the Pres. Monday a.m. to
go over our own situation — The Canal
opening was a great success but was
not over till 7 p.m. so I didn't
get to Washington till 1.30 p.m.
Thursday — I worked at office
both evenings & go there all day
tomorrow — these are history making
days — It will be the greatest war
in the world's history — All well Love Pops

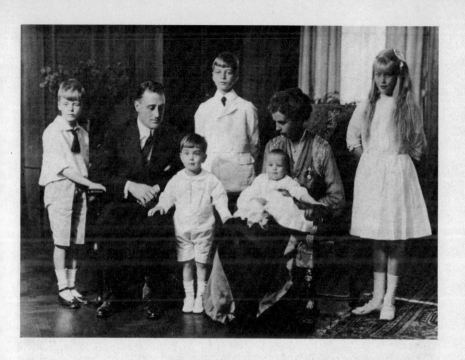

Franklin and Eleanor Roosevelt with their five
children; Elliott, Franklin, Jr., James, John, and
Anna.

A note written hastily by F.D.R. to his wife in
1914 at the outbreak of war in Europe—"A complete smash up is inevitable. . . ."

At his desk in Washington, the Assistant Secretary
of the Navy in 1919.

On the steps of the Capitol—William Jennings
Bryan, Josephus Daniels, Woodrow Wilson, and
F.D.R.

At Campobello during a wartime summer—Henry
Hooker, F. D. R., Sara Delano Roosevelt, and Aunt
Annie Delano Hitch.

The Walter Campers in 1917—"We exercised this A.M. at 7:30."

At an American base in France, F.D.R. inspects
Navy personnel during his tour of duty in 1918.

At the Navy Department in Washington, F.D.R.
with Admirals McKean and Sims.

Returning from Europe aboard the *George Washington* in 1919, F.D.R., Woodrow Wilson, and
Sheffield Cowles.

F.D.R., Josephus Daniels, and the Prince of Wales.

During the campaign of 1920—Presidential candidate James M. Cox and his running mate.

The Vice-Presidential candidate had a flashing
smile.

After a game of golf during the 1920 campaign, with his manager, Louis McHenry Howe, Democratic leader Thomas Lynch, and F.D.R.'s secretary, Marvin McIntyre.

On the stump campaigning for Cox. In the background at right stands Marvin McIntyre.

After his defeat and return to private life, F.D.R. and his children aboard the *Half Moon* at Campobello.

Warm Springs, Ga.
Saturday.

Dearest Mama —

We are here safely & I think Eleanor has written you this morning — I spent over an hour in the pool this a.m. & it is really wonderful & will I think do great good, though the Dr. says it takes three weeks to show the effects —

Everyone is most kind & this afternoon Mrs. Loyless has taken us for a motor trip through the surroundings,

A letter to his mother in the dark days—"I spent over an hour in the pool this a.m. . . . Everyone is most kind. . . ."

spoke to me and then we went and found F. but Roosevelt was just getting ready to go on deck for duty so we didn't have much talk.

F. does exercise with Mr. Camp daily and plays shuffle board and quoits and to-day they started to do a little work. Ad. Benson wired he wished to see F. at once so after two days in Brest we go to Paris which simplifies crossing the channel. I shall wire Aunt Dora when we land.

Thursday, Jan. 9th. We've had some rough weather but I've been a marvellously good sailor and attended every meal and all entertainments. We were shocked by the news of Uncle Ted's death and I think much of Aunt Edith for it will leave her very much alone. Another big figure gone from our nation and I fear the last years were for him full of disappointment. I have nearly finished "Henry Adams," very interesting but sad to have had so much and yet find it so little.

There is a good quintette in the orchestra which played for us one afternoon and we gave a tea for the Chinese delegation and Sunday night we all attended a concert in the crew's theatre and Franklin spoke well, followed by Mr. Schwab who seems to be a great favorite and certainly makes a good speech. I like him very much and had a little walk and talk with him to-day. To-night the crew gave a play with wonderful "ladies" and we all have had a wonderfully comfortable and entertaining trip. Franklin looks very well. Mrs. Spellacy has spent 3 days in bed with a bad eye and came out to-night for the play. I only hope she is not going to be laid up. Livy also has had a cold and is worried about himself. I will say he has a bad color and I wish he and Mrs. S. were safely at home.

We get in to-morrow a.m. The Chinese are being met by a Chinese delegation of 4 and have a special to Paris in the p.m., so all are to lunch on board with us and in the evening we are to have Ad. Wilson, the French admirals and their wives and we hope Gen. Smedley Butler to dine on board with us. We have wired asking if Sheffield and Josephus Daniels [Jr.] are still near to let them come to Brest to see us. We do not know yet where we go in Paris but hope to hear to-morrow. I fear there is difficulty about rooms or Ad. Benson would have sent a radio already, but then he is always rather slow so it may be just slowness.

Roosevelt came to tea with us on Monday and spent an hour in our cabin. He hopes to get out on completing this trip and spoke of wanting to go into railroading in Chile. I'm told there is quite an opening there so perhaps it will be just the thing for him, as he says he couldn't stand an office. He tells me Russell has left college and gone into some dye concern because he has a girl, did you know it? If not, don't repeat!

I think constantly of the chicks and wonder how Elliott gets on and how the babies are. I can hardly wait for news and I suppose our first letters will reach us in London as F. expects to reach Paris Sunday a.m. and spend 6 days. We are wiring Baring Bros. to-morrow to forward cables however, and I shall be glad to hear from you. I hope you have no anxieties while we are gone and I can't tell you what it means knowing you are there to see to everything. I forgot to tell you that Franklin keeps a balance of $376 in the house account but if this month's bills take more than F. gave you just draw on the balance!

Much love dearest,

Ever your devoted
ELEANOR

F.D.R.'s cousin, Roosevelt Clark, was a sailor on the *George Washington,* which was commanded by Captain Edward McCauley, F.D.R.'s aide on the inspection trip. "Russell" was Roosevelt Clark's younger brother.

Admiral Henry B. Wilson at this time had command of U.S. Naval Forces in France: in June, 1919, he was appointed Commander-in-Chief of the Atlantic Fleet and he later served for four years as Superintendent of the Naval Academy.

T.R.'s unexpected death occurred while he was asleep early in the morning of January 7, 1919. He had been ill during the autumn of 1918, but since his condition was never considered to be a serious one, his sudden passing stunned the country. Vice-President Marshall summarized the nation's views when he said that "death had to take him in his sleep, for if Roosevelt had been awake, there would have been a fight."

∽∽

U.S.S. "GEORGE WASHINGTON"
JANUARY 10, 1919
FRIDAY

Dearest Mama and Children,

We were up at daylight—just entering the port of Brest and now we are at anchor in this wonderful harbor outside the breakwater. My Marine Corps aide, Major Kilgore, has reported on board and is very nice. Soon Admiral Wilson will call on us, and a Chinese delegation to welcome the Chinese Mission on board. I shall have all the Chinamen and the Mexican Mission at a farewell luncheon and they will leave for Paris tonight. This evening we have a dinner on board for the French Admirals Moreau and Schwerer and their wives, also Admiral Wilson and General Smedley Butler.

We hope to see Sheffield Cowles and Josephus Daniels, Jr., both Lieutenants in the M.C.

The crossing has been a fortunate one—though the sea was heavy for two days it was from aft and this ship is the steadiest I have ever crossed on, even more so than the Leviathan.

There have been entertainments several times a day—a band, an orchestra, a violin quartet, several singers, moving pictures, and finally last night a musical play by the crew.

447

You would all have loved the sailors dressed up as chorus girls! This is what we call in the Navy a "Happy Ship" from Capt. McCauley down—and it makes a lot of difference to one's comfort and satisfaction.

I think we shall stay in Paris until the 17th or 18th and then go to London. This change in plan was due to a radio from Admiral Benson and it will be more satisfactory as we can stay in London until about Feb. 5 and then go back to France and sail from Brest about the 20th.

A great deal of love and many kisses to you all.

Your devoted
F.D.R.

∽

PARIS
JANUARY 11, 1919
SATURDAY

My dearest Mama,

We have had a busy time since I last wrote but everything is made so comfortable really that one can do a great deal. I think I closed my last letter on arriving in Brest Friday a.m. Jan. 10th. F. received visitors on board and we had Mexican and Chinese delegations lunch with us, then went ashore and he returned calls on French officials and then set to work with Capt. Craven on the aviation situation while Ad. Wilson took me on a lovely motor drive. He practically rules Brest and I am told has done much for the poor and is much beloved. We saw a good deal of coast which is beautiful, but savage and constant rain in winter without great cold keeps walls and fields green, though many are uncultivated, and all the peasants wear black and in town every other woman wears a crepe veil to her knees. That evening Josephus Daniels, Jr. and Gen. Butler, who is in charge under the Army of the evacuation camp near Brest, came to dine on board. Gen. B. is doing wonders under horrible conditions, the mud in camp is knee high, roads do not exist as the trucks have ruined them, the Army will send him 60,000 men when he has accommodations for 30,000, and there are not enough transports to take them home. The one cry on every side is "we want to go home" and they say only the troops actually in Germany are at all contented. In spite of everything Gen. B. has less than 1% of illness in camp but he says the Army colonels of every variety visit him daily and drive him nearly mad. He has had a "food Col., a drainage Col., a sanitation Col., a transportation Col. etc. and not one knows a d—— thing about looking after men!"

Sat. a.m. Jan. 11th F. and the men inspected this camp. Mrs. Spellacy and I took another drive with Ad. Wilson and at 12:30 Mr. and Mrs. Spellacy, Ad. Wilson, his aide, Com. Todd, Capt. Halligan, ourselves, Mme. Grin, Ad. Exelman, a French aide and his wife all lunched with Ad. and Mme. Moreau in the Préfécture Maritime, a lovely old house and garden and delightful hosts. They knew the Laboulaye's and told me of the death of poor little Monique from "flu" three days after landing here. I felt terribly and sent a note with flowers as soon as I got here, and then Capt. de Blanpre came to call and told me his wife had been ill ever since she landed with "flu" and all the Laboulaye's except M. de L., the 3 other children not so seriously, but Mme. de L. nearly died last Saturday, so yesterday I went to inquire and was told she was better. Hasn't it been dreadful for them? I didn't write Anna about Monique but you had better tell her.

To go back after our lunch, F. went to work and Ad. Wilson took Mrs. S. and myself to the naval hospital, an old monastery, gloomy but all painted white now in the interior and clean and the men looked well cared for and seemed cheerful, then to the Navy Y.M.C.A. which is, however, full of soldiers as there is no place provided for them in town. They have a Navy band and movies every p.m., a gym, a reading and writing room, and rooms for games and a restaurant which looked clean. Next the Navy store and the

Navy p.o. from which the mail is distributed direct to Navy camps and ships *without* delay. Mrs. S. sat in the car exhausted the last part of the time and we left her at the Admiral's apartment and he and I walked to a little shop he helped start to sell the work of war widows. It is patronized by the Fr. Ad's wives so I bought a 50 franc collar as F. thought I ought to, though I thought it expensive and not very pretty! We took our train for Paris at 5:30 and had a special car so we could take in Miss Delano of the Red Cross and Ad. Benson's son. There is quite insufficient transportation, so there was a riot at every station for people couldn't even get standing room, and at last a French officer broke one window of our car, climbed in, and tried each compartment and found all full! We got in about 8, an hour or more late, and found Ad. Long, Capt. Maas, and Commandant Pamard awaiting us. We have two cars and F. and I went off at once with Ad. Long and a Navy truck and orderly brought the trunks, Livy and the others followed in the other car. We have a sitting room, bed room and bath at the Ritz, looking out on the garden, great luxury! Livy has a room here and the others are at the Continental. We were made happy by your cable to Baring's and now I can hardly wait to get to London as I hope for letters there. I think we will sail for home about the 15th of Feb. as work is going fast, possibly with the President. In any case we'll cable when to stop writing. I miss you and the children dreadfully in spite of the fact that I am having a wonderful time.

I never saw anything like Paris. It is full beyond belief and one sees many celebrities and all one's friends! People wander the streets unable to find a bed and the prices are worse than New York for everything.

Sunday, Jan. 12th. After breakfast I bathed, unpacked and dressed and F. had a stream of visitors. We lunched with Aunt Dora and Uncle Fred was there so we had a nice talk. U. Fred looks grayer and older but well and I think A. Dora is well but Cousin Fay has been ill, De Coursy is nearly blind and that family are pretty wearing. Cousin Pauline comes in every time we go to A. Dora's but she isn't very sweet to A. Dora, who does everything for them. After lunch F. came back and worked and I walked in the Tuileries and over the Seine which is very high but going down fortunately. Paris is wonderful, though we never see the sun and Mrs. Benson says she is "much disappointed and wishes she could return to Washington!" All the Champs Elysées, Places, etc. are lined with German guns, captured *before* the armistice. At four I took the car, left some cards, and went to the Am. Church for service, as there was a sermon on Uncle Ted and then I went to tea with A. Doe where F. joined me and Gabriel and his wife came in. He has just been given the Legion of Honor. The staff, all except Mrs. Spellacy who had gone to bed, dined with us here. We saw Mr. Robert Bacon who asked us to stay at the front with him a night, Mr. Davidson, etc. and Munro Robinson who came up later to our rooms. His face looks stronger and coarser but since the armistice he's been very gay (not to be told). Now he's on the water wagon, and they say he's been wonderful for bravery, had 150 motors under him and did fine work and was cité, and all the officers have been off more or less since the armistice I'm sorry to say but conditions here are very hard for our men. Munro wants to go home and I hope he gets there soon. He told us very interesting things too long to write but with his own hands he put in his car in a village (out of which the Germans were driven and from which the civilians were evacuated on account of heavy shell fire) 8 little girls between the ages of 11 and 13 enceinte from the Germans. He said his men were crying and all would have murdered any German in sight.

Monday Jan. 13th. F. went to his office and A. Dora came for me about 11:30, we called for Mrs. S., went to St. Ives with your bags which will both be done over in velvet as that is the fashion for the price of about 70 francs cash, isn't it awful? Then we went to Worth and I ordered 2 dresses, paying far more than at home but wonderful materials and I only hope you'll like them and won't die at my extravagance, F. bore it like a lamb. Then back and F. and I had Mrs. Whitehouse, Livy, Munro, and Com. Sweet for lunch here. F. worked till he came home for tea at 5:30 and I paid more calls and then A. Dora, Mrs. Benson, Capt. Blanpre, Col. and Mme. Rémond, Ad. Bristol, 2 Captains and Roland came to tea. Tell Sara he looks well and we are dining with him to-night and going to the "Français." He hopes to go home with the President. We dined with A. Dora at 8 and brought U. Fred home after dinner.

Tuesday, Jan. 14th. F. again went to his office and I washed out some guimpes, gloves, etc., went for a fitting and to see Mrs. Spellacy who is having a bad time with her eye. F. and I lunched here with the Grews to meet the Lansings. Mrs. Harjes (pretty but ordinary in uniform and decorated), Mr. Berenson, a French Gen. and Fr. lady whose names I never got. Mrs. Jack Carter was near us so I spoke to her and she said she would tell her daughter to come to see me in London. The Grand Duke Alexander was near us also and his acquaintances curtsied to him, the Duchess of Rutland and Lady Diana Manners were pointed out. The curious thing is all the women in the Restaurant look to me exaggerated, some pretty, all chic but you wonder if any are ladies and the contrast with the black in the streets is striking. After lunch F. went to see M. Leygues (Minister of Marine) and I wrote James and sent the others p.c's and wrote some notes and at four left more cards, picked A. Dora up at 4:30 and went to see Mme. Howland. Very old but sweet and spoke affectionately of you, and Louis fat and unattractive was there. I left A. Dora at home and came back here and went up to see Mrs. Barclay Parsons. She has been here 2 yrs. and will take me Thursday to her hospital. F. saw Tardieu at 6 and his biggest deal is done, the Fr. gov. will take the big radio station and pay 22,000,000 frcs. This is a big success but don't mention it! We dined with Belle and Kermit, her sister and Ted there. B. and K. are a delight and I liked Ted. He went to the hospital after dinner to have his knee operated on this a.m. Just as we were leaving Major Robert Bacon, Gen. Frank McCoy and Col. Jimmie Logan appeared and we stayed on to talk, the last two could find no bed for the night so Belle arranged two and we took Maj. Bacon to someone else's apartment where he got in! They'd all been decorated yesterday with various degrees of the Legion of Honor and also awarded D.S.C.'s, at least the last 2 had both and Maj. Bacon one I think but all were very happy. Gen. McCoy is now to be Uncle Fred's chief and I know they will like each other.

Wed. Jan. 15th. Have written you a few p.c's and now must go to see how Mrs. S. is. Love to you dear from us both and kiss the chicks for us when you see them.

Your devoted,

ELEANOR

In so far as the settlement of naval property was concerned, A.E.R. was correct in considering the sale of the Lafayette Radio Station at Croix d'Hins, near Bordeaux, as F.D.R.'s "biggest deal." This high-powered station had been erected jointly by the American and French governments to assure communication between Washington and the U.S. Army and Navy units operating in France, since reliance on the cable system alone was too precarious in view of the submarine menace. However, the armistice was signed prior to the completion of the station, and, because its high power greatly exceeded the needs of the French, that government attempted to delay a settlement. In the hope of obtaining a swift decision, F.D.R. informed the French minister, André Tardieu, that all uninstalled equipment and material would be reshipped to the U.S. unless the French government agreed immediately to take the station over. Tardieu perforce replied that France definitely wanted the station finished, and would pay for it on the basis of cost to the U.S., which was tentatively estimated at the price noted by A.E.R. "Roosevelt knows how to handle the French," remarked a naval officer who had been unable to arrange a decision on the matter prior to F.D.R.'s arrival.

"Ted" refers to Theodore Roosevelt, Jr., at this time a lieutenant colonel in the A.E.F.'s First Division. During the early years of the Harding-Coolidge Administration he held the post of Assistant Secretary in the Navy Department, and later became a publisher, returning to active duty in World War II as a brigadier general with his old division. He died in France shortly after the Allied invasion in 1944.

∽∽

LONDON
JANUARY 20, 1919
MONDAY

Dearest Mama,

I got a letter off to Elliott on Friday and I meant to write you also but we had a very busy day and for some strange reason I thought I was coming down with "flu" but we reached London last night and now I must go back and tell you all we have done.

Wed. Jan. 15th. After writing you I paid Mrs. Spellacy a little visit and her eye was still very painful. Finally it was decided that she and her husband should stay in Paris until next Wednesday the 22d in the hope that she would be entirely well. Then I went and lunched at the Crillon with Mrs. Benson, the other guests being Mrs. House and Mrs. Lansing. We had a very nice time and much discussion about the President's not having yet been to the front which is worrying the French very much. They feel he should see the devastated regions before the conferences and of course our own boys are very anxious to have him see where they have fought and existed, for one couldn't call it living. Also he has been to no hospitals and Mrs. Wilson only to two so far which causes much comment. Col. House has been wretched and I think it is gall stones, but Mrs. House seemed to think he was better. When I got home I found a lot of roses from Mr. Baruch and hardly got them arranged before it was time to start in the car for Franklin. He had lunched with Mr. Swope, Livy and some other journalists there, and they are all furious because they get so little "news." I met Arthur Willert on the street however and he tells me the President has done very well in England and made a very good impression on their peace delegates. Everyone here thinks his coming over was vitally important and no foreigner can understand the row at home. I gave Mrs. Barclay Parsons a lift in the car and F. and I first left cards at the "Elysée" and then went to tea with Mrs. Wilson. The Palais Murat is lovely, with a glorious garden surrounded by the high wall and it seemed to me everyone had left Washington and congregated there! Among others were the Sam Howlands who promptly invited us to dine but we were unfortunately not able to accept. Then we went to Mme. de Blanpre's and had tea and her entire family was there, a really nice French family but I've decided there is very little real beauty in France! When we got home we had only a few minutes to dress but Lydig Hoyt came to see us. He looks well but like everybody else is dying to get home. When he left we hopped into our clothes, went to "Paillards" where Roland gave us a delicious dinner, and then to the Français where we saw "Amphytrion." A beautifully given play, wonderful clothes, wonderful scenery and very good lines.

Thursday Jan. 16th. Arthur Willert came to breakfast at 9:15 so as to talk to F. and we discovered that he had been knighted but he seems to intend to keep it very dark. Franklin went off a little before ten to a conference at the Crillon with Mr. Hoover and later I went with Major Kilgore to look over the big German tank in the Place de la Concorde, and then we walked up the Champs Elysées looking at the guns and how some had exploded and some had blown up until we turned off to go and see A. Dora but she was out. We walked back and I dressed and Franklin came for me and we lunched with Admiral and Mme. de Bon. One daughter and several naval officers and Ad. Long our Naval attaché there. It was a pleasant lunch, good food and good talk, much discussion about the attitude of the Germans in the Rhine provinces toward our troops. The Germans are being so nice to them. They are billeted in the best rooms which is a contrast to French barns and then the Germans are cleaner and bring them hot water, and the mayor had all the pre-war prices posted and they cannot be charged more. In France of course everything soars and then far more of our men speak German than French, so they find themselves pretty well off and it isn't a very safe situation, except as Kermit says they won't soon forget that the men were killing their mates and a few other things they've seen, though of course they will be friendly with the women and children. After lunch I drove F. and Ad. Long back to the office and went to Worth for a fitting and at four Mrs. Parsons took Mrs. Wilson, Miss Benham and me to Dr. Blake's hospital where she has been working. It was very interesting but a very sad sight. Some of those men have lain there with strange appliances on their legs and arms for 6 months. One poor man had both legs suspended in a kind of cradle, but no complaints only the one wish "we hope to get home soon." The hospital is being evacuated and will soon be closed but it is huge and Dr. Blake has done a remarkable work. Ted was there and his knee was doing well and I found David Gray there with a leg broken in 2 places.

He'd been there five weeks but he's nearly well. After Mrs. Wilson left I went back and sat with Ted and David till 6 and then went to see Mrs. Spellacy and then home to find that F. had been home early and gone up to A. Dora's hoping to find me there. He paid her a nice call and came home in time to dress and we dined with Gerry Chadwick. A very nice dinner, Mr. Schuyler Parsons, Chester Burden, and a lovely Miss Eleanor Colton whom we took home as taxis are hard to find in Paris.

Friday, Jan. 17th. Went up with F. to his office and saw A. Dora and asked her to lunch with me. Went home and Mme. de Blanpre came to see me and to my surprise Lord Reading. I protested that F. was not here but he insisted on coming up and I found he wanted to see our rooms as he thought of taking them! We had a nice chat and he soon left and Mme. de B. and I had a long talk and she left about 12:15 when I hurriedly wrote Elliott and went down to meet Aunt Dora, Ad. Long and Roland who were to lunch with me while F. and Livy lunched with Uncle Fred to meet all sorts of Colonels and Generals! He enjoyed his lunch very much and so did we. Aunt Dora is dear but she never asks people she meets to her house, it is always family. She came up to my room for a time and then I began to pack and at 3 I went out and paid all leftover calls, went into the hospital for a minute with a box of candy for David and stopped to ask for the Laboulaye's. She is out of danger and Paul has gone to his own grandmother and the babies are out again. Then I went for F. but he had to be left to see Mr. Hoover so I went to say goodbye to Mrs. Spellacy and then hurried home as Col. Murray was coming to see F. He came and Capt. Gherardi came and then F. came and later Capt. Evans' wife. We got out at 6 and paid a long call on the Jusserand's and then F. stopped to see Lord Reading but he was resting so he only had a chat with Sir Ian Malcolm and we got home just in time to dress and go and dine with

A. Dora (Gabrielle and Marie, Cousin Pauline, Cousin Charlie and Uncle Fred were the other guests). It was very nice but at 10 we had to leave to go home to pack. It has been a busy week but fun and the best is to come.

Saturday—Jan. 18. Dearest Mama and Children—We have had a very wonderful day and one which we shall never forget. At 7:15 this morning we started by motor from Paris. Eleanor and Livy and I and Major Manning of the Army in the first car; Com. Hancock, Major Kilgore and Capt. Cook in the second and the valises in the third car— (the Marine Corps orderly who rejoices in the name of "Nipper" is to take our trunks by rail and meet us in Boulogne). We proceeded due North from Paris, coming first to Senlis where the Boché committed such outrages in 1914, then began to see trench systems and wire entanglements and presently to Compiegne through part of its wonderful forest. Just beyond there was the point to which the Boche came in the great Spring drive of 1918—and from this point on all day we were in scenes which saw the heaviest kind of fighting up to such a very short time ago. First came Noyon, occupied by the Germans from September 1914, retaken by the French in 1917, lost again last spring and finally retaken while I was still here this summer. There is much destruction though nothing to what we saw later. The fine old Cathedral badly shelled and the stone figures around the arch of the doorway deliberately chiselled off. Hardly a house has escaped damage, and all the surrounding country is pockmarked with shell holes. Continuing North we came to Guiscarel and Ham, all damaged, but most of it here done in the organized retreat of the Boche in 1917 when they cut down the fruit trees and deliberately wrecked the countryside in the retreat to the Hindenburg line. Less was done the past Autumn in their forced retreat—they did not have time. At Ham the remains—a few stones—of the famous old Tower where Louis Napoleon was kept a prisoner prior to 1848. It served no possible military value but the Boche sought to destroy an historic monument. Turning Eastward we came in a few miles to the Hindenburg line itself. Tremendous trench systems in an open rolling country which is now bare and bleak and untilled. Trench after trench—wire after wire—serving well to hold up the British and French within sight of St. Quentin and very heavy losses occurred in these open stretches of country. St. Quentin itself is pitiful. Far more damage than Noyon and reminding me more of Verdun than anything else I had seen. We drove to the great skeleton of the splendid Cathedral. It is wrecked beyond repair I fear—roof blown in, towers partly down—all glass gone—main arches tottering. It had been spared almost wholly by French and British while they were advancing, but as soon as the Boche evacuated the town he turned around and poured shell after shell into it. We ate our lunch in the Cathedral "place"—on the base of a monument—the figure itself carried off to Hunland for metal and even the metal wreath around the inscription. Eleanor has a very achy side and shoulder but insists on doing everything, getting out of the car at all points of interest. We continued at one via Le Catelet to Cambrai—the road following almost the whole way the centre of the Hindenburg line. The same rolling open country—every village either wholly flat or a few standing walls only. The Huns thus had a command of an open shelterless country where they could see every movement for miles. The trench systems running north and south and with a depth of about two miles were most elaborate, and the nature of the soil, limestone, made concrete work and revetting unnecessary. A punctured tire gave us an opportunity to explore some of these systems with their many dugouts. We were following up the line of the main German defense and soon came to the St. Quentin Canal and the Bellecourt Tunnel where the canal runs underground for

3½ miles. Here is where the wonderful feat of the Americans and Australians and British took place last autumn—a break through the Hindenburg line in September which forced an almost immediate withdrawal for many miles and indentally the fall of Cambrai. The Canal runs in a cut south of the Tunnel and here the British attacked in a thick fog, went down into the prison—say 60 feet, swam or waded the Canal and went up the other side and held on—all in the face of concentrated machine guns—an almost incredible feat. Meanwhile just North, where the Canal goes into the hill the Americans (30th Div. and I think 80th) went forward 2500 yards through line after line of trenches and wire and were able to push South on the far side of the Canal to the support of those who had crossed the Canal itself. All the losses were heavy. Maj. Manning and Capt. Cook who were both in the fight say it was only possible because of the heavy fog, and that it was remarkable that any kind of contact was kept between the troops. We climbed down the cut and went into the mouth of the Tunnel. The Boche had blocked the end with concrete to hold the many canal boats in the Tunnel. In these and in chambers cut into the walls was room for many thousands of men and 3,000 were actually taken prisoner in the Tunnel.

A few miles further we came into Cambrai, one of the pivotal points of the German defense. The destruction was terrific—most of it caused by the Boche mines which they left behind them on evacuating and which continued to go off for days afterwards. For instance *every house* facing the large square was totally destroyed and the Hôtel de Ville badly burned out—the signs on it forbidding entrance because it is still mined. I wandered into a side street and met a French sergeant with the Croix de Guerre with Two Palms. He had with him his two little children who he had not seen since August 1914. They were caught in the Boche rush, carried off to Belgium, and now the family is reunited in the wreck of what is still their home—the roof gone but the lower story inhabitable and they are beginning again at the beginning. A few dozen families have moved back to Cambrai, and already a little school is running for the children.

From Cambrai we motored South, past the Hindenburg lines, the famous Bourlon Wood, through villages which were villages only because a sign on a pile of bricks said so, and then into Bapaume—the long sought and dearly bought objective of the Somme drive. Thence on in the twilight straight across the waste of the Somme Battlefield to Albert. This stretch was ghastly in its desertion—no longer pockmarked fields but the whole surface torn and dug and thrown apart. After Albert things became more and more normal and presently we came to the limit of the German 1918 advance 8 or 10 miles N.E. of Amiens. It was dark by now and suddenly we came on a sad but rather ludicrous accident. Two British officers in a Ford had collided with a big two-wheeled market cart, upsetting it and its load of 3 old ladies, one old man, many vegetables and several bottles. Everything spilled, horse ran away, nobody hurt, the Ford smashed too—and the officers, three old ladies and one old farmer having it out in the dark, in the middle of the road.

We arrived at Amiens at seven and had a most amusing mixup between the French and English authorities over our rooms. Also found the English (who control the St. Quentin-Cambrai area) had expected us in the morning and had orders forbidding any ladies to go up into the battle area. We meanwhile had gone into it by the back door via Noyon —no one had stopped us and it was a fait accompli. Eleanor's shoulder and side hurt her much and she had a good deal of fever but there is nothing to do here but push on to London.

Sunday Jan. 19.

We left Amiens at 8—Eleanor a little better. Visited the Amiens Cathedral. Not much damage done though more by

461

luck than Boche intent. Thence out North to Doullens (where the Boche first bombed the British hospital then came down low and used machine guns on the rescuers and patients in the open). Thence to Hesdin and a few miles beyond turned left to Château Brunhautpré leased by Lt. Col. Robert Bacon our liaison officer with Gen'l Haig—the latter's château being next door. Mr. Bacon met us and gave us an *excellent* lunch and we dashed off immediately after and caught the boat to Boulogne at 2:30 by the skin of our teeth—a very smooth crossing, and got to London at 7:30, met by Admiral Sims at the station and came here to the Ritz—comfortable rooms on the 6th floor—dinner upstairs and then bed.

Monday—London.

Muriel came this morning, sent a doctor to see Eleanor and he says she has a slight attack of pleurisy—must stay in bed a day or two. She is better though today and will have a very quiet time for this London visit. It is a comfort to have Muriel here. She and the chicks are very well and send you all much love.

I have found much work and will be very busy until we leave here Feb 1. Then I hope to go to Brussels and the Rhine—though I doubt if Eleanor is permitted to do more than Brussels—and would go to Paris where I would join her three days later. Ladies are not welcomed by the British or us in the occupied part of Germany.

Much love to you all—Your devoted

F.D.R.

Your letter and Anna and James made us happy and we also have your cable of the 19th so I know Elliott must be all right. Connachie is no good for picnics, well, we must remember and not try her again. I am so sorry for you however. Dearest love

E.R.

Beginning with the January 18th entry, this letter was written by F.D.R.

"The row at home" is a reference to the repudiation of Wilson in the Congressional elections of 1918. In spite of his campaign plea for the election of Democrats, the trend which had appeared unmistakably in 1916 resulted in a Republican majority in both houses of the Sixty-sixth Congress. Already hostile to Wilson's sponsorship of the League of Nations, Congressional leaders became further enraged when he failed to include them in the American delegation to Paris. The *New York Tribune* noted that "the President goes abroad a rebuked and discredited leader in his own nation." Nevertheless, Wilson's actions during the course of the peace conferences were based on the assumption that the American people had endorsed his program. It is an outstanding fact of modern history that this misinterpretation largely doomed the League of Nations at the time of its inception.

Miss Edith Benham, who later married James M. Helm, was Mrs. Woodrow Wilson's social secretary. In 1933 she returned to the White House to serve in the same capacity for A.E.R., and since 1945 has assisted Mrs. Harry S. Truman. Miss Elspeth Connachie was a Scotch governess A.E.R. employed at this time for the children.

LONDON
JANUARY 25, 1919
SATURDAY

Dearest Mama,

Our last letter left I think on Wednesday, but I really have rather little news as I've had to be pretty careful. I've run a little temperature, never much over 100 but it makes one feel tired and I think I've had a touch of "flu"! F. saw Mr. Walter Long (the new 1st Lord of Admiralty) on Wednesday and liked him very much. F. works morning and afternoon but gets home for lunch and tea about 5:30 and he's really not overworked.

Thursday a.m. I went to Liberty's and got what I hope will be a lovely blue velvet dress for Anna. It is rather the "Alice" shade but I hope will fit and be becoming. I also got Muriel's baby a little silk smock and the monkey loves clothes so much that she wished to put it on at once! She tries to rub and scratch a great deal but looks well and Nannie is wonderful with her. I think Muriel has a treasure in her. Muriel and the boys lunched with us and I've lost my heart to them, they are such ducks and so manly and devoted to her. We had a good many people for tea, among others Elfrida Orme-Clark and her husband. He looks about to die. In the evening we dined with Ad. Sims and saw a movie of the surrender of the German fleet which was good. At the end we were bidden to the green room to partake of sandwiches and champagne.

Friday Jan. 24. Capt. Pringle and Frances Archer-Shee came to lunch. She is entirely unchanged, same clothes, and same manner! She sent you so much love and longs to get home to her own family and friends and surroundings! Can't you hear her? Martin went to see F. at the office and we dine with them next Tuesday and to-morrow we go down for lunch at least F. does and I shall go if I can induce him to let me! I went out at 4 and paid some calls and had tea with Lady Grant. She and Muriel do not picture a very happy future for Sallie with her family-in-law and we all feel very sorry for the child. It appears that Mrs. Fellowes-Gordon thought the boy was marrying an heiress and is furious and looks on what they have as nothing. She won't come and meet them and Muriel has to take them into her wee house by moving out of her own bedroom if they stay in London. A sister who lives near by will come to meet them but can do *nothing* for them. It all sounds very *hard* Scotch and not very well bred though Muriel says they are nice people. Lady

Grant wants F. to write old Fellowes-Gordon and I hope he will. I fear we miss them all or we might have done something for her. Muriel does not look a day older and she is a wonder. I went in late to see her and found the Cochran's there and Edith looked much the same also. Mrs. Fort and a sister-in-law called Isabel were there also. We dined last night with Hancock and Kilgore and the Spellacy's joined us later at the play which was Elsie Janis in a light musical comedy. We all enjoyed it and walked home after it to see the crowds. We like Major Kilgore especially, he is so thoughtful and unselfish and a very gentle personality. His wife lives in New York and I've promised to try and see her on my way through.

Saturday Jan. 25th. Muriel and I went out to find some things for F. this a.m. but we had no success as there are no novelties and F. insists he wants something original! Admiral and Lady Browning, Capt. Tobey and Muriel lunched with us and it went very well I thought. They left about 3 and F. and I were to go and pay calls together at 4 on Lady Gertrude etc., but he insisted on taking my temperature and discovered it was over 100 and wouldn't let me go out. I was furious for I don't feel ill, it is just my old cough for the pleurisy is all gone and staying in does no good. However, here am I and he has gone to call and he dines tonight with Mrs. Copley Hewitt and he made me back out to my rage!

Your letters of the 4th and 6th came two days ago and I was so glad to hear of Elliott able to coast. I am glad Connachie recovered a little towards the end! I hate to think of you without Durrant but one cannot count on any of them and if you don't get along comfortably without a parlor maid do get one for it isn't worth making yourself uncomfortable. I am anxious to hear how you find my household but don't expect I shall get those letters till I'm back in Paris.

Much, much love dearest Mama, I hate being away from

you and the children and the next time we must all come together if we come!

Devotedly

ELEANOR

∽∾

The letters covering the interval between this and the next letter were not found among the family correspondence, and apparently were lost by Sara Roosevelt.

∽∾

PARIS
FEBRUARY 8, 1919
SATURDAY

Dearest Mama,

It was nice to get your cable and hear "all well" but I am afraid from your asking about me you must have been worried, and really there never was anything to bother about and I'm very well now, even my old friend cough is almost gone! Franklin cabled you to-day. I got here Wednesday night about 8 after a good trip but I was glad Commander Hancock was looking after me, for the red tape now is appalling and it is slow for I left Muriel at 8:30 a.m. It was rather a relief to be out of England before all the railroads struck! Livy arrived in the hotel with us, he went with F. as far as Brussels after all and then motored back through a most interesting and much fought-over part of Belgium and France. It took 2 days but he had some nice officer companions so it must have been a very satisfactory substitute for not going with Franklin. On arrival here he found that for 12 hrs. he must occupy a room without a bath and I thought the poor manager's head would be blown off! I have decided that trips of this kind either make very firm friendships or mar them. Hancock is not very attractive though he is very able but he wears well and you like him more and more. Kilgore is a dear, adaptable and thoughtful, unselfish and resourceful, the Spellacy's are nice but of such

466

a different kind that there is little common meeting ground for anything beyond acquaintanceship, but Livy is lazy, selfish and self-seeking to an extraordinary degree with the outward appearance of being quite different. Franklin is too loyal ever to change in his feelings but I am deciding more firmly every day that the estimate I've been making of him for over a year is not far from right.

Thursday morning I telephoned Aunt Dora and lunched with her and Uncle Fred was there and then I took her in the Navy car to the Val de Grace and went in with her. I don't see how she stands it and yet one must grow accustomed for she seemed to like hearing about all the horrible operations and I could hardly bear to look at the men with the horrible face wounds. The Spellacy's and I dined alone. Friday morning I took Mrs. Spellacy shopping and lunched alone with Aunt Dora and in the afternoon Aunt Dora came with me and did some odds and ends and I enjoyed being with her. I got 6 prs. of gris perle gloves and I have your bags but I am so afraid they won't be what you wanted. Mrs. Meyer and Julia Brambilla are here and they had asked me to tea so I went in at five and found Janet Auchincloss and we had a very nice time and Mrs. Meyer was sweet. I know she would like us to get her home on the George Washington but I haven't spoken to F. and I feel sure he will say it is impossible. From 6 p.m. on I began to hope for Franklin, and Commander Hancock came to dine at eight and still no sign, so we dined and at 9:30 Livy also came upstairs but at 10:30 he grew sleepy and went to bed. At 11:30 Hancock felt it wouldn't do for him to wait longer so he left and about 12:30 Franklin, Major Kilgore and Martin Archer-Shee walked in laden with all kinds of "loot" from battle-fields and Germany! Admiral Long met them in the hall and came too and I had a little cold supper waiting on the chance of their arrival as no food is served after 9:30. They had motored about 230 miles and were full of an interesting

and delightful trip which Franklin will write you about.
Much love always,

E. R.

∽

Dearest Mama,

Franklin says there is little use in writing as we will
probably arrive before the letter but I'll just send this off
on the chance!

Last Sunday I went to church with A. Dora, and Franklin
and I lunched with the La Grange's, the only other guests the
Lubersac's (she was Constance Livermore). In the afternoon
we both went to the memorial service for Uncle Ted and
then had tea with Aunt Dora, and Bishop Perry who had
preached a very good sermon came in to see Franklin. U.
Fred and Lawrence, Herbert Swope, Martin Archer-Shee,
and our party minus the Spellacy's dined here and after
dinner Martin went off to England, Livy to write letters and
all the rest came up to our sitting room to listen to Herbert
Swope talk! He told us some lovely tales of the President's
trip to England from the journalist point of view. Incidentally they were wonderfully looked after in England and
in consequence all returned pro-British and more critical
than ever of the French who do not understand the proper
treatment of the American newspaperman!

Monday morning Madame Lechartier and I went out and
I bought two pretty but very expensive lingerie blouses.
We lunched with Mme. de Blanpre, all French and very
nice except for two American officers. I saw Mme. de
Laboulaye in the afternoon for the first time and she still
looks very ill and very sad. I doubt if they come back to
America. I came back in time for tea and Mrs. Meyer, Julia,
Polly Hare and Janetta Whitridge and Alice Carter came in.

The latter looks young as ever and sent you much love. I think Janetta is nicer looking and much improved. We dined with A. Dora and all the Forbes family and she kindly asked Com. Hancock and Maj. Kilgore also and I think they liked seeing somebody's "home." Lady Hood asked us to dine to meet a lot of the English peace people but I felt as it was the only night we could go to Aunt Dora we ought not to disappoint her, so you see I did just what I always scold you for doing, which shows I'm really becoming a real Delano! Anna and James' letters of the 19th came and they sound very gay and happy. I am so glad and isn't it fine they've kept so well. I am sorry Anna got her cold again so soon; it must be the climate! I do hope Elliott is really well and doing well at school.

Sheffield turned up yesterday looking very well and is attached to F. till we leave, then he goes back to La Rochelle. I'm glad he's not here, it is no place for the boys, especially the younger ones, and the scandals going on would make many a woman at home unhappy.

I'm in this a.m. to write and sew and later Major Kilgore is coming to go for a little sightseeing with me before I call for F. and we go to lunch with Captain Edie. To-night we dine with U. Fred (and he is letting us bring Sheffield) at the Tour d'Argent and I've asked Mrs. Lansing, Mrs. House, Mrs. Benson, A. Doe, etc. to tea.

To-morrow afternoon I am going to one of the privately run French hospitals with a Comtesse de Rohau-Chabot whom I met at lunch. I think it is Duchesse de Rohau's hospital and she is going to show it to me which will be interesting after seeing one in England.

My love to the chicks and to you, dear, in which Franklin would join were he here.

Ever your devoted,

ELEANOR

∼∼

469

F.D.R. and A.E.R. sailed for home on February 15th aboard the *George Washington*. President and Mrs. Wilson were also on the ship, and the Roosevelts joined in the triumphal parade and reception accorded the President upon the arrival of the *George Washington* in Boston. Wilson was returning to sign bills passed by the 65th Congress in his absence, and he brought with him the first draft of the League of Nations.

Far more concerned about the punishment of Germany, most of the delegates to the Peace Conference were indifferent to the League, and Wilson had been forced to use his great prestige, as well as to make vital concessions, in order to secure consideration of the Covenant before any other business. Wilson's high hopes for the creation of a lasting peace were only shared by his contemporaries to the extent that the final terms had to be within the scope of their national aims. The overwhelming lesson provided by the war had not been learned by many of the peacemakers. Wilson soon came to be regarded as a visionary, while the other delegates freely admitted that sacrifices could not be made to their nationalism. On the grounds that a functioning League of Nations would eventually rectify injustices written into the peace, Wilson fought hard for the adoption of the Covenant as the first article of the treaty. Although his perseverance eventually triumphed, in so doing he made costly mistakes, the greatest of which was a failure to recognize the intrinsic isolationism of the American people.

At the time of his rousing welcome in Boston, Wilson was unaware of the precarious position he had assumed. It was not long after this reception, however, that the opposition to the League came directly into the open and vigorously expressed itself. Just before the expiration of Congress, thirty-seven Republican Senators signed a declaration that they would not ratify the peace treaty if it contained the Covenant of the League of Nations. On March 4th Wilson announced that if it was necessary to fight Congress by taking the issue directly to the people, he would do so as soon as he returned from Paris with the treaty prepared for ratification. The next day he sailed again on the *George Washington* for France.

Three months later, on the fifth anniversary of the assassination of Archduke Ferdinand, the Treaty of Versailles was signed. "Yielding to superior force, and without renouncing our view of the unheard-of justice of the peace conditions," the German envoys placed their signatures on the eighty-thousand-word document, thereby depriving Germany of her colonies, reducing her to military impotence, and requiring the payment of reparations totaling two hundred billion gold marks. Wilson admitted that he was not altogether satisfied with the treaty, but it contained the precious Covenant of the League, and he hopefully left for the United States on June 29th to present it to the Senate.

For two months during the summer of 1919 the treaty was under consideration by the Senate Committee on Foreign Relations, and in the meantime objections to the League spread throughout the nation at a rapid rate. Article X of the Covenant, which would have pledged the United States to send troops abroad to uphold the "territorial integrity" and "political independence" of any member nation, aroused the greatest opposition. The opponents of the treaty were unable to visualize submitting "domestic" problems to arbitration by "foreigners." Late in August, Wilson became convinced that Republican support in the Senate would not be forthcoming, and on September 3rd he started on a tour of the country in order to explain the Covenant to the people directly and force its passage through the pressure of public opinion.

〜〜

For A.E.R. and F.D.R., the spring and summer of 1919 was a period of readjustment. Washington was not the hectic place it had been during the war; quieter days necessitated an alteration of the daily routine. Frequently A.E.R. had to make trips to New York to settle her household problems, and these journeys account for the next few letters of this chapter.

471

Dearest Babs,

The house seems exceedingly empty and we all miss you and the babies so much. There is nothing to report except a contretempo between Conny and Elliott at bed time!

A., J. and I dined together and at 8:15 I went down to the meeting and had a dull evening.

Now I am off to bed at midnight having put out Chief and signed 400 commissions.

I do hope you had a good trip and I foresee a hectic day for you tomorrow.

Your devoted

F

"Conny" refers to the aforementioned Miss Connachie, while "Chief" was young Anna Roosevelt's police dog. J. D. was abroad at this time and thus F.D.R. had to sign the "400 commissions."

∞

Dearest Babs,

Your note is here on my return, so glad you are all safe in New York.

Mr. Homer and I brought Anna back to lunch at the house and soon A. & J. and I go down to dinner.

Sad news just came that the C-5 broke away from her moorings and is drifting away over the ocean, no one on board. This ends one of our hopes of crossing the Atlantic.

The chicks are well and send much love. All quiet at the office. I expect J.D. to land Saturday p.m. but not to come down here till Sunday.

I have finally bought my preliminary steel for the new ships, and today we had the last Council meeting under my auspices. Department will be *up to the minute* when the Sec'y gets back!

Your devoted

F

When the Navy dirigible C-5 departed for Newfoundland to attempt a transatlantic flight, hopes were high that a momentous advance in aviation development was about to be realized. The C-5 had passed tests considered equivalent to an Atlantic crossing, and it was anticipated that the airship would make the great flight without too much difficulty. Several hours after it arrived at Trepassy, N.F., however, a strong wind came up and threatened to break the dirigible from its moorings and carry it out to sea. When Lieutenant Little, the commanding officer, pulled the cord that would have deflated the gas bag, the men on the anchor ropes relaxed their hold; but the rip cord broke in Little's hands, and the dirigible broke from its moorings. Little jumped from a height of twenty feet and sprained an ankle, while the C-5 drifted out to sea in a northeasterly direction. Destroyers pursued the dirigible but could not keep pace with the forty-mile-an-hour wind, and the C-5 was subsequently given up as lost.

Since the building authorized by the Navy bill of 1916 would expire on July 1, 1919, and work on new ships had to be started before this date, a decision was reached at "the last Council meeting" presided over by F.D.R. to order 14,000 tons of steel for the construction of four battleships. Bids for this order had been previously rejected on the ground that they were too similar to have been arrived at competitively. In announcing the Department's change of policy, F.D.R. was quoted by the *New York Times* of May 15, 1919 to the effect that the contract was given to the Carnegie Steel Company because "that company was the only complete bidder on the entire schedule of requirements. By placing the order with one company the Navy felt assured of better service and a more convenient and economical inspection."

∽

Dearest Babs,

I wrote you yesterday morning to Hyde Park, tho' I doubt if you get it before you leave tomorrow morning—so I hope this will get you in N.Y.

Today we have had a peaceful and happy time. Connie took the chicks to Church while I disported myself at Chevy Chase, but I got back at 1:15 and we all four lunched with Mrs. Leavitt! Then a long motor drive including Chief—back at 5:30 and soon A., J., and I dine.

Last night I met the Sec'y and Mrs. D. at the station and came back and dined with the chicks and later went down and spent an hour at the Dept. getting news or rather trying to get it from the two missing planes.

Tomorrow we shall all be awaiting you and I will meet you at the train. I do hope you won't be exhausted.

Your devoted

F.

Mrs. James T. Leavitt was an old friend of A.E.R.'s father. "The two missing planes" refers to another transatlantic flight undertaken by three Navy seaplanes, the NC-1, the NC-3, and NC-4. As it included the Azores as a refueling point, this crossing was not intended to accomplish the feat of a non-stop trip from Newfoundland to Europe; nevertheless, the flight was followed with keen interest because it was considered a prelude to the latter. While the NC-4 arrived safely at Ponta Delgada in the Azores, the other two planes lost their bearings in a heavy fog and landed in the sea to await greater visibility. Before the fog lifted, however, the heavy sea so damaged the NC-1 that it had to be abandoned, and the NC-3 was forced to taxi two hundred miles in a gale to Ponta Delgada, arriving there badly damaged and unable to continue the trip to Lisbon. A month later, on June 15, 1919, the international efforts toward a non-stop transatlantic flight were finally realized when British Captain John Alcock and Lieutenant Arthur Whitten-Brown flew the 1900 miles between Newfoundland and Ireland in sixteen hours and twelve minutes, thereby opening a new era in the history of aviation.

∽∽

Dearest Mama,

Eleanor got back safely last night and the 3 children and I met her at the station. All are well. We had a nice lunch with Mrs. Leavitt on Sunday and afterwards I took A., J., E., and Chief for a long motor drive into the country.

J.D. is back and I will have less to do—tho' that is not an unmitigated blessing. I am enclosing cheque for $250— second installment on repairs to 49 E 65. Two more will come to you out of next year's rent. Mr. Lamont's secretary has wired him to ask if he wants the house next winter. I did not have the face to ask an increase after last year's raise.

Kiss the boys. This house seems very quiet without them. A great deal of love.

                    Your devoted

                              F.D.R.

As Sara Roosevelt never cashed it, the cheque for $250 is still to be found in the original envelope to this letter.

∽∽

Dearest Babs,

I am more dead than alive and at last will get to bed early and try to make up!

Yesterday I went on at noon to Atlantic City, got there at 6, dined, spoke, took a 10:30 trolley to Philadelphia, trans-

475

ferred from the ferry to West Philadelphia and stayed there in the station till 3 a.m. when the sleeper from New York came along and I got on and had four hours sleep! I did this in preference to going to a hotel and getting up at the crack of dawn as I *had* to be here for the Pessôa party to Mt. Vernon on the Mayflower. That started at 12:30 and now I am just back and going to dine alone and turn in.

Yesterday before telephoning you J.D. told me he is to be away Monday and the Naval Affairs Com. needs a lot of data which I must present. Also the news had just come about the sinking of the German ships and we didn't know what action might be necessary.

The four days in Cambridge were hectic, great fun and a grand success in every way.

I took very good care of myself in every way except sleep. Yesterday—no, Friday—I lunched with Mary Miller and she said she never saw me looking better. That afternoon on my way home during a rain squall a piece of tree hit me in the right eye. It was a little cut but is almost well.

I miss you a lot and hate not to get back but this arrangement is better as we can have four days and nothing ahead.

Your devoted

F

From the time of the talk with President Wilson aboard the *George Washington* during the return voyage from Europe, F.D.R. had become a staunch supporter of the League of Nations, and in the course of the spring and summer of 1919 he made numerous speeches urging its ratification by the Senate. His address in Atlantic City was not given sufficient coverage by the press to reveal his views, but on an earlier occasion his remarks were reported at some length:

. . . I have faith that the League of Nations will go through in the end with the support of the great majority of our nation to the unutterable delight of millions of downtrodden in Europe. I have faith that it will work out and that we and the other nations will use an unselfish effort to make it the best thing in the world, so that under it our relations with mankind will go from better to better.

I have read the draft of the League three times and always find something to object to in it, and that is the way with everybody. It is impossible to draw up such a League that would satisfy two people. But there is no doubt that, generally speaking, the people here, as in Europe, are in favor of some sort of agreement stronger than the Hague conventions—an agreement with teeth. And if we are willing for this we must be willing to give up something, even if it be a sovereign right of our nation. . . .

Personally I am willing to make a try on the present instrument. It does not fulfill something greater than what we would like to see done individually. Among all the peoples of the Allies, and I believe Germany, too, there is a demand that out of this war we shall get more than a mere treaty of peace—something nobler and higher. If this demand is not fulfilled many of those people will throw up their hands and say, "Well, if the forms of government existing today cannot give us the answer, some kind of an answer, why not try some other form?"

Chief of the Brazilian delegation to the peace conferences and a champion of amicable relations between the U.S.A. and his country, Dr. Epitacio Pessôa was at this time president-elect of Brazil. Returning from Paris to take up his new duties, he was given a warm reception in the United States, including the traditional wreath-laying ceremony at the tomb of George Washington mentioned by F.D.R. After his three-year term as the head of the Brazilian Republic, he served from 1924 to 1930 as a justice of the Permanent Court of International Justice located at The Hague.

The hoisting of a red flag at noon on June 21, 1919, was the signal for the crews of the German warships interned at Scapa Flow to scuttle the fleet. As all the explosives had been removed, this feat was accomplished by opening the sea cocks; and while the crews either swam or rowed to shore, the fleet sank slowly out of sight, to the consternation of the Allied personnel stationed at Scapa Flow to guard against violations of the armistice terms. All the battleships and battle cruisers except one were thus destroyed, together with numerous smaller vessels; eighteen destroyers were beached by tugboats. The British Navy later refloated nineteen of the ships, but the rest could not be salvaged and were subsequently dynamited. The responsible German commanders claimed that the scuttling of the fleet was in pursuance of orders given by the Kaiser early in the war that no German man-of-war was to be surrendered, but the Allies refused to accept this absurd contention and later exacted reparations for the loss.

F.D.R.'s luncheon date was with Adolph Miller's wife, the former Mary Sprague.

∽

NEW YORK
SUMMER, 1919

Dear old Lang—

Sure will I accept that bully responsibility in re L.P.M. Jr.! You and Mary are so good to want me, and the only thing that breaks my heart is that it is really impossible for me to get up to N.E. next Sunday. I would make a special trip were it not that I have been booked for a long time to make three speeches in Western N.Y. the end of this week, Sat. and Sunday and Monday. So I fear a proxy will have to respond and you can know that I am doing so in spirit at least at the same time.

When you all get back we will have a christening party.

Give Mary and him my love. So sorry to miss you—am off to the Rifle matches and back to Wash. this evening.

As ever
FDR

478

This letter is one of the few holograph items in Langdon P. Marvin's collection of his correspondence with F.D.R. It was written in July or August, 1919, in response to an invitation to act as godfather to Langdon P. Marvin, Jr., at the christening ceremony in Northeast Harbor, Maine.

∽

Dearest Babs,

It is surely a rainy time. It has poured ever since I got here, on the half and half system. Deluge one hour then sunlight one hour and the papers say continuation! I find a lot of work accumulated, last night I dined at the Club and tonight I dine at home. Lunched on desk both yesterday and today and have seen no one of interest.

J.D. leaves for the coast on August 1 and will be gone I think till September 15.

This a.m. I was awakened at 6 a.m. by a drip, drip, drip and found your bureau afloat, rushed upstairs and found the sun parlor a lake. Worked hard for an hour in my pyjamas with bath towels and tooth mugs and saved the house! Westcott will send a man.

It is fearfully muggy, not so hot but all the doors and windows won't move from the damp.

Do hope you had a fairly good trip though I fear you too were in the rain.

Kiss the chicks and I miss you so much. Wasn't it a nice 9 days at Hyde Park.

Your devoted

F

∽

Dearest Babs,

The riots seem to be about over today, only one man killed last night. Luckily the trouble hasn't spread to R Street and though I have troubled to keep out of harm's way I have heard occasional shots during the evening and night. It has been a nasty episode and I only wish *quicker* action had been taken to stop it.

I had a quiet dinner alone at home last night and did a lot of work. There is little news except that the rain has continued and I hope will let up for a game of golf which I go to in an hour. Probably I will stay out and dine at Chevy.

No letter from you at all. I do hope you got to Fairhaven safely last night and that it wasn't too wet or slippery on the road.

A letter from Mama this morning. It will amuse you as she says everything is going *very smoothly!*

Kiss the babies and Elliott and take care of yourself.

Your devoted   F

The race riots in Washington during July of 1919 were indeed a "nasty episode." On July 20th, aroused by stories of Negro attacks on white women, a band of several hundred servicemen, supported by an estimated crowd of a thousand civilians, retaliated by hauling innocent Negroes from streetcars and other vehicles, and attacking them on the streets. For several days the police force was unable to cope with the situation, and it was not until the Reserve was called out that order was restored to the capital, which the *Washington Herald* subsequently declared to be "the most lawless city in the Union."

∽

WASHINGTON
JULY 25, 1919
FRIDAY

Dearest Babs—

Your telegram came last night at ten—as I was in my pyjamas and couldn't get Western Union I did not answer it till this a.m. as soon as I got to the office.

Gee it was hot that night! I dined at home and took a cold bath at 9 and read till midnight—too hot to sleep.

I am wondering why letters are so slow from and to Fairhaven. Yours of Wed. a.m. only just came last evening. I wrote you Tues. and Wednesday and yesterday.

I don't know whether I shall be here Sunday or not. I have given up Norfolk—Sylph out of commission.

I *may* go to Harrisburg to make a speech Sat. night and come back here Sunday.

I long to have you back—very lonely, also hot again!

We dine Chevy Chase Monday Eve.

All well—I will meet you at train 8:30.

Your devoted

F

A.E.R. did not take the family to Campobello for the summer of 1919, but went instead to Fairhaven for a month, leaving the children there in the care of their nurses at the end of July and returning to the capital to spend the remainder of the summer with her husband. Hence F.D.R.'s correspondence was not resumed until late in October, when he went on a hunting trip to New Brunswick with Livingston Davis and Richard E. Byrd. F.D.R. and the famous explorer had become close friends early in the war when the latter was assigned to the *Dolphin,* and this intimate friendship continued in the years that followed, being highlighted in 1940 when F.D.R. decorated Admiral Byrd with the gold star in recognition of his services as commander of the U.S. Antarctic Expedition.

∽∽

During the interval between this letter and the next, Wilson's efforts to secure ratification of the Versailles Treaty collapsed with the failure of his own health. During the course of his speaking tour of the country, Wilson was stricken with paralysis. Although he recovered sufficiently to carry on important business from his bedside, the President was henceforth a very sick man and no longer able to deal directly with Senatorial opposition to the League of Nations.

For two months while he was convalescing, the Senate had debated the treaty, which had been finally reported out of committee with a number of amendments. These reservations included a clause whereby the U.S.A. would not be obliged to carry out the provisions of Article X without the authorization of Congress. Furthermore, according to these amendments sponsored by Senator Lodge, only Congress could determine whether or not the United States was to fulfill its obligations to the League. Wilson refused to accept any alterations of the treaty and instructed his supporters in the Senate to vote against the amended version. On November 19, 1919, the roll was called on the Lodge-sponsored treaty, which was then defeated by a decisive 55 to 39 vote, with forty-two Democrats abiding by Wilson's request and voting against the changes. A vote was then taken to ratify the treaty without alterations, and this in turn was defeated, by a 53 to 38 tally, with seven Democrats and forty-six Republicans voting in the negative. As the deadlock appeared insurmountable, Congress adjourned after six months in extra session.

On March 19, 1920, a third vote was taken on a new version of the treaty worked out in conference by both Democrats and Republicans. Although containing more mild amendments, the final draft lacked seven votes of the necessary two-thirds for ratification, with twenty-four Democrats adhering to Wilson's continued insistence that the Versailles Treaty be adopted without changes. Announcing that the Senate was unable to ratify it, Congress returned the treaty to Wilson and subsequently passed a resolution declaring the termination of the war with Germany. Calling it "an ineffaceable stain on the gallantry and honor of the United States," Wilson vetoed the Knox resolution, and as the House was unable to override the veto, the United States continued to be technically at war with the Central Powers. It was not until July, 1921, and the advent of a

Republican administration that peace resolutions officially ending the war were adopted.

Although ten months later F.D.R. became directly involved in the controversy over the League, at the time of his departure for New Brunswick these international problems were entirely forgotten in the excitement of spending a week "in the heart of the woods."

∽∽

FREDERICTON, NEW BRUNSWICK
[OCTOBER 20, 1919]
MONDAY

Dearest Babs—

Got here, Fredericton, in time for lunch, leave here tomorrow morning at 5 for Chatham, and go right in to the woods. Yesterday I had a nice day at Portland. Maude met me at the station with Mrs. Hopkins Smith in the latter's car and we went to the Smiths for lunch, I getting a bath first. Just Mr. and Mrs. S., Maude and I there, David not yet back from his horse competition. After lunch golf with Dr. George Derby, then tea at Maude's, several old ladies in, then dinner to which Mrs. Sills, wife of the President of Bowdoin College came. I left at 9:30 and found Liv and Dick Byrd on the train.

It is *very* cold but a wonderful day. We have had a walk— played a rubber of 3 handed bridge—and now are going to supper and to bed early.

All well so far, and I do hope you and the chicks will keep very well all the time I am gone.

Don't forget to write.

Your devoted

F

Like his father, Dr. Hasket Derby *(vide supra)*, George Derby became a prominent ophthalmologist, holding a professorship in the Harvard Medical School for a number of years and serving in the Army Medical Corps during the war as assistant consultant in ophthalmology to the A.E.F. Kenneth C. Sills was an assistant instructor in English at Harvard during F.D.R.'s first two years in college; after filling several academic positions at Bowdoin College, in May, 1918 he was appointed its president, a post he has since held for more than thirty years.

~~

Dearest Babs,

I am taking this opportunity of sending a line out of the woods by Livy, who leaves us this morning to go down 30 miles to the mouth of the Tabusintac to shoot duck and geese, and his automobile driver will mail it in Chatham tonight. We are literally in the heart of the woods and are getting very full of health. No moose or deer so far, though we have seen several and I had a shot at a moose through the underbrush and evidently did not touch him. It is "still hunting"—i.e., walking mile after mile through the woods as noiselessly as possible and hoping to come on game before they see or hear us.

We got to Chatham Tuesday at 10:30, drove 20 miles, lunched at Mr. Connell's son's house, drove on 8 miles more, then walked in 5 miles to the camp on a bluff beside the Tabusintac River. We have a comfortable cabin, two rooms and the living room, and the guides live in the cook house next door. The food is good and in addition to McDonald the cook, we have Mr. Connell and his son as guides. Wednesday morning Mr. Connell and I started at 7 and got back at 5, walking about 20 miles and very stiff walking at that. Thursday and Friday the same and yesterday I pulled off a record, not getting back till 7 p.m. and covering 29 or 30 miles! We are thoroughly tired by evening, but go to bed at 8:30 after a rubber of bridge, and get plenty of sleep. My feet are the only things that have gone back on me, but they are better.

484

I think it is doing me a world of good, and I wish you could be here with me, but you couldn't do the hunting. Byrd and I will stay on, unless we should get moose in which case we would join Livy. We all leave Chatham in any event on Saturday morning and I should get to Hyde Park Monday morning—and I am so looking forward to seeing you and the chicks again.

Your devoted
FDR

∽∽

F.D.R. returned to Washington from his hunting trip via Hyde Park. There he resumed his regular routine, now expanded to include the entertainment of numerous European dignitaries who were visiting the U.S.A. at this time. Since the Roosevelt family was together almost all the time during F.D.R.'s few remaining months in the Navy Department, only the two letters that follow appear in his personal correspondence for the first half of 1920.

METROPOLITAN CLUB
WASHINGTON
[1920]
WEDNESDAY

Dearest Babs,

Just a line to tell you that all is well and that I fear J. D. will go away Friday to Monday, so that means no Hyde Park for me till Tuesday!

He hasn't made up his mind but it is probable.

Yours of Monday was welcome this a.m.

Last night Livy and I and Jim Wadsworth dined with the Homers!!

Tonight we have a Class of 1904 Dinner here to celebrate Prohibition.

Devotedly
F

The exact date of this letter cannot be determined, but in view of the letterhead and the party "to celebrate prohibition" (which was declared in effect by the Secretary of State on January 16, 1920), it is placed at this point in the correspondence and was probably written between January and June, 1920.

James W. Wadsworth was at this time United States Senator from New York; he held the senatorial seat from 1915 to 1927, and four years later was elected by New York's Forty-first District to the House of Representatives, where he has since served eight terms. His wife, the former Alice Hay, was the president of the National Association Opposed to Woman Suffrage during the months when the Nineteenth Amendment to the Constitution was under consideration by Congress.

∽

WASHINGTON
FEBRUARY 11, [1920]
WEDNESDAY

Dearest Mama—

You are not only an angel which I always knew, but the kind which comes at the critical moment in life! For the question was not one of paying Dr. Mitchell for removing James' insides, the Dr. can wait, I know he is or must be rich, but of paying the gas man and the butcher lest the infants starve to death, and your cheque which is much too much of a Birthday present will do that. It is so dear of you.

We have had a quiet three days, though Eleanor has had to look after F. and John in Ada's absence. Tomorrow night I take Elliott and 5 small boys to a party at the Cathedral school. Anna is laid up with an upset tummy, not very serious I think. Otherwise things are quiet and will be for some time and even the office is less busy, the Sims episode being quiet for the moment and of less public interest as time goes on.

It has been warm these days and the streets are more pass-

able. I fear N.Y. must still be in bad shape. Give James a
kiss from us all, we miss him much.

Your devoted son

F.D.R.

Miss Ada Jarvis was an English nurse whom A.E.R. employed for the younger children at this time.

In *The Wilson Era,* Daniels explains that the "Sims episode" was part of a Republican plan to "smear" the Democratic Administration's conduct of the war as a prelude to
the national election of 1920. The "episode" began late in
1919 when Admiral Sims, who resented Daniels' earlier
refusal to approve all his recommendations of officers to
receive medals, himself refused the Distinguished Service
Medal and attacked the Navy Department's whole policy in
the matter. Daniels convened the Naval Board to reconsider the question; and when he published the Board's findings, which were that Sims's charges were ill-founded, the
latter was stimulated to make a sensational announcement.
He said that the "failure of the Navy Department to immediately send its full force of destroyers and anti-submarine
craft prolonged the war four months and occasioned the loss
to the Allies of 2,500,000 tons of shipping, 500,000 lives, and
$15,000,000,000." Such a charge by a high-ranking naval
officer could not go unheeded. In addition, it represented
an excellent opportunity for the Republicans to place the
Wilson Administration in a poor light, and consequently,
in March, 1920, the Senate Naval Affairs Committee began
hearings on the operation of the U.S. Navy during the war.
Three months later, after more than three thousand pages
of testimony, the hearings were concluded with the repudiation of Sims's charges, and the Navy's contribution to the
war effort was praised in glowing terms by both Republican
and Democratic leaders in Congress. According to Daniels,
no effort was made to court-martial Sims because such pro-
ceedings would have enabled him to pose as a martyr. When
approached on the matter, Wilson agreed with the decision

to forego punishment, remarking that "since Sims has ruined himself, why not let him stay in the hole he has dug for himself?"

≍

The months that followed this letter were a prelude to the national political conventions. Early in June the Republicans convened in Chicago, and on the tenth ballot nominated Senator Warren G. Harding of Ohio for President, with Governor Calvin Coolidge of Massachusetts as his running mate. The Democrats met in San Francisco later in the month, and did not agree so easily on candidates to succeed Wilson and Marshall. Even at the time of the convention the prospects of the Democratic Party in the coming election were not very bright. The two decisive defeats of Wilson's efforts to win approval for the League of Nations were a clear indication that the Republican trend of the past four years was not going to halt at the gates of the White House; and within the Democratic Party itself anti-Wilson sentiment had grown rapidly since the war. Furthermore, the convention was in a quandary because Wilson refused to express any preference as to his successor, merely advocating the nomination of a man who would support the League of Nations. F.D.R. journeyed across the country to attend the convention and do what he could to enlist support for a candidate who sympathized with Wilson's policies. In particular he favored Alfred E. Smith, who was then serving his first term as governor of New York; and he seconded Smith's nomination. However, the two most powerful aspirants for the nomination were Wilson's son-in-law, William G. McAdoo, and Attorney General A. Mitchell Palmer; and when a deadlock over these two candidates ensued, enough support was shifted to Governor James M. Cox of Ohio to bring about his nomination on the forty-fourth ballot. As Cox was not identified with the Wilson forces, the party leaders agreed almost unanimously that the Vice-Presidential nominee should be selected from the Wilson wing of the party. Hence, with Cox's approval, on July 6, 1920, the Democratic convention nominated F.D.R. by acclamation as its second standard-bearer.

F.D.R.'s nomination necessitated his resignation from the Navy Department, and it is appropriate to conclude this chapter with two letters which passed between Daniels and himself as their official association in the Wilson Administration ended. Although these letters are chronologically out of order, they pertain far more to the aspects of F.D.R.'s development and life portrayed by this and the preceding chapters, than to the Vice-Presidential campaign during which they were written. Both J.D. and F.D.R. painstakingly wrote each other in longhand, and these letters are the intimate expressions of a sincere and tested friendship—final evidence that the association between the two men had resulted in mutual admiration and affection.

THE ASSISTANT SECRETARY OF THE NAVY

WASHINGTON
AUGUST 6, 1920

My dear Chief:

This is not goodbye—that will always be impossible after these years of the closest association—and no words I write will make you know better than you know now how much our association has meant. All my life I shall look back,—not only on the *work* of the place—but mostly on the wonderful way in which you and I have gone through these nearly eight years *together*. You have taught me so wisely and kept my feet on the ground when I was about to sky-rocket—and in it all there has never been a real dispute or antagonism or distrust.

Hence, in part, at least, I will share in the reward for which you *will* get true credit in history. I am very proud—but more than that I am very *happy* to have been able to help.

We will I know keep up this association in the years to

come—and please let me keep on coming to you to get your fine inspiration of real idealism and right living and good Americanism.

So *au revoir* for a little while. You have always the

Affectionate regards of

Franklin D. Roosevelt

∽

THE SECRETARY OF THE NAVY

WASHINGTON

AUGUST 7, 1920

Dear Franklin:—

Your words of sincere friendship were very grateful to me and I am happy to know that the years of service have strengthened the friendship which began, I think, upon our first acquaintance. Love at first sight is rare with men, but sometimes I flatter myself in believing that I have some of woman's intuition, and on the day the President asked me to become Secretary of the Navy I told my wife I would recomment your appointment as Assistant Secretary if it was agreeable for you to be a co-worker in the Department. I was pleased to find that it was in line with your taste and congenial to your long interest in naval matters. And so, with mutual regard and mutual consecration, we have spent seven and a half years in the service of our country. We little thought then of the great responsibility we were assuming, but we were not of the type of men who run from work or seek to escape responsibility. I am happy that we were given the great job in the World War, and it will always be a matter of gratulation that the team work of naval direction resulted in such efficient contribution to victory.

I always counted on your zeal, your enthusiasm, your devoted patriotism and efficient and able service, and always found you equal to the big job in hand. My thought and feeling has been that of an older brother and your nomination to the great office of Vice President by our party pleased me very much, and I shall always rejoice in your successes and victories and be glad if in any way I can contribute to them. More intimately I shall share with you the happiness that [comes] to you in your beautiful home life and we will be brothers in all things that make for the good of our country.

My wife joins me in love to your wife and mother.

Faithfully your friend,

Josephus Daniels

∽

XII

"... Perhaps in This Life Things Have to be Evened Up in the End ..."

CAMPAIGN FOR VICE-PRESIDENT

July 1920-July 1921

ON JULY 21, 1920, the *Poughkeepsie Eagle,* a paper which had followed F.D.R.'s career with mixed feeling of Republican sponsorship and local pride, editorialized that F.D.R. "is a nice young man but that he cannot win in a year when parties and principles and not individuals are the important considerations. His nomination was a compliment; his defeat is a certainty." Although the next few letters reveal that F.D.R. was optimistic about the outcome of the election, there can be little doubt that he was aware of the situation which the *Eagle* shrewdly summarized. It did not matter whom the parties nominated in 1920. Personalities could not influence the clearcut line that divided the platforms of the two major parties; no one person would be able to persuade the electorate to alter its views of the actions and policies pursued by the Democratic Administration in the months that followed the war. The individual either believed that the sovereignty of the United States should be partially surrendered to the League of Nations, or he didn't. There was no middle road on this issue; and in 1920 the people of the United States overwhelmingly favored a continuation of American abstinence from the affairs of Europe.

In addition, the internal crises of the war had not yet subsided and "the return to normalcy" had not yet been achieved. Prices and rents were high in 1920, labor was unwilling to yield its high wages and business was anxious to restore its competitive system, coal was scarce, veterans were demanding a bonus for their war service, bootlegging emerged as a profitable and almost respectable enterprise, the I.W.W. was employing violence to radical ends, and, all in all, the domestic scene was one of insecurity and disorder. War had left a notable mark, and as far as the electorate was concerned, the incumbent administration was either at fault or it was not; again there was no middle road. Most Americans were convinced that the national situation was not a complicated end result of war, but proof of the Wilson Administration's failure.

Yet, as F.D.R. returned from San Francisco, with a stopover in Columbus, Ohio, to meet Governor Cox for the first time, political realities were temporarily forgotten in the excitement of the moment, as can be gathered from the next three letters to A.E.R.

WASHINGTON
[JULY 17, 1920]
SATURDAY

Dearest Babs,

All goes well, though of course very busily. On arrival yesterday I was met by Howe, McIntyre, Peoples, and lots of cameras and newspaper men, came home, bathed, breakfasted, again photographed and got to the Department at 10, to find things decorated with flags, flowers, Admirals, stenographers and the faithful Prior.

Lots of people of course all day, and the mail is appalling

—over 2,000 letters and telegrams and I am organizing a complete additional staff to handle it.

At four a reception for the officers and Department employees, all passing through my office, and at 4:30 the Navy Yard employees marched up outside and I went down, received a gavel made from the handrail of the "Mayflower," spoke to them, etc., etc. Then back to work till 7, then home, bathed and dined alone with Warren and Irene. Back at 9:30 and worked till midnight with Howe.

Today I went down at 9, and at 2 went to the station and met Governor Cox,—a huge cheering crowd, more enthusiastic than any Washington crowd I have ever seen, must have been 5,000 people there.

I drove up to 16th with him and the Ansberrys, got out and went back to the Department. At 4:30 I went out to the Ansberry's, came home to dress and have been dining there tonight. They live out in the park to the left of the Wardman Park Inn, only Victor Murdock, George White of Ohio in addition to the four of us.

Now I am really going to bed by 11.

Tomorrow we see the President at 10:30 and I shall work on mail till we take the train at 4:30. Nothing more definite about plans. I still hope to leave Saturday p.m. and be with you all Sunday evening. I can hardly wait. I miss you so so much. It is very strange not to have you with me in all these doings.

Kiss the chicks. It is almost a month since I saw them.

Your devoted
F

Marvin H. McIntyre was at this time a special assistant to the Secretary of the Navy responsible for the Navy's public relations, and was subsequently engaged by F.D.R. to take charge of the campaign train during the latter's several speaking tours of the country. He later became a

Washington representative of the newsreel companies, returning to F.D.R. in 1932 to become business manager of the Presidential campaign, and thereafter a notable member of the secretariat. Rear Admiral Christian J. Peoples was an assistant to the chief of the Bureau of Supplies and Accounts at the time of F.D.R.'s reception in Washington. He later became the Navy's Paymaster General, and for the first six years of F.D.R.'s Administration was director of the Procurement Division of the Treasury. A former Congressman from Ohio, Judge Timothy T. Ansberry placed F.D.R. in nomination at the San Francisco convention; while Victor Murdock, also an ex-Congressman, was at this time chairman of the Federal Trade Commission. Three days after F.D.R. wrote this letter, George White, another former Ohio Congressman, was selected as chairman of the Democratic National Committee, a post he held for two years; in 1931 he was elected governor of Ohio and served in this capacity until 1935.

∽

COLUMBUS, OHIO
[JULY 20, 1920]
TUESDAY

[Dearest Babs]

Sunday was a very wonderful experience. I don't quite like to write of the meeting with the President, so will wait till I can see you on Sunday. Yesterday was a busy day of conferences at the State Capitol here and now we are going to the meeting of the National Committee to get the plans of the campaign under way.

Mrs. Cox is so nice and the baby is sweet.

Reports are distinctly encouraging about the sentiment throughout the country.

I go back to Washington tonight getting there at 1 p.m. tomorrow.

Kiss the chicks. I long to be with you all.

Your devoted   F

495

A mild controversy exists among historians as to the nature of the interview between Cox, F.D.R., and Woodrow Wilson on July 18, 1920, the event which F.D.R. refers to as "a very wonderful experience." Many biographers claim that the meeting was arranged so that Cox might meet Wilson for the first time, and thereby show the electorate that the Democratic Party was politically united. It has also been said that until the time of the interview Cox had not decided whether he would make the League of Nations a key issue of his campaign, and that it was only his compassion for the President (whose illness and great suffering were clearly discernible) which made him announce his outright support of the League. But in his book, *Journey Through My Years*, Cox indicates that this interpretation of the event is entirely false; that "for eight years" prior to 1920 he had a "very close relationship officially and personally" with Wilson; and that, although not announced, the decision to make the League of Nations the major campaign issue had been reached long before the occasion of this conference at the White House. Cox substantiates this with a letter to himself from Claude G. Bowers, U.S. Ambassador to Chile, in which the latter recalls a discussion of the matter with F.D.R. while he was President. In this letter Bowers quotes F.D.R.'s recollections of the "wonderful experience" as follows:

. . . After the convention at San Francisco I stopped off for a conference with the Governor in Columbus to discuss the character of the campaign. The Governor advised that he was going to see President Wilson the next week.

I accompanied the Governor on the visit to Wilson. A large crowd greeted us at the station and we went directly to the White House. There we were asked to wait fifteen minutes, as they were taking the President to the portico facing the grounds. As we came in sight of the portico we saw the President in a wheel chair, his left shoulder covered with a shawl which concealed his left arm, which was paralyzed, and the Governor said to me, "He is a very sick man."

The Governor went up to the President and warmly greeted him. Wilson looked up and in a very low, weak voice said, "Thank you for coming. I am very glad you came." His utter weakness was startling and I noticed tears in the eyes of Cox. A little later Cox said, "Mr. President, we are going to be a million per cent with you, and your Administration, and that means the League of Nations." The President looked up again, and again in a voice scarcely audible, he said, "I am very grateful," and then repeated, "I am very grateful."

As we passed out we came then to the Executive offices and in this very room, Cox sat down at this table . . . and asked Tumulty for paper and a pencil, and there he wrote the statement that committed us to making the League the paramount issue of the campaign. It was one of the most impressive scenes I have ever witnessed. . . .

This last remark is similar to the statement F.D.R. made to the press after the interview: "I wish every American could have been a silent witness to the meeting between these two great men. Their splendid accord and their high purpose are an inspiration." On July 21, 1920, the *Poughkeepsie Eagle* commented that these were "strange words from this hitherto upstanding and independent Democrat . . . just another surrender to the arch-politicians and a clambering aboard the party's rickety old wagon." However, as can be seen from F.D.R.'s letter to A.E.R. and his talk with Bowers, as well as from his vigorous campaign for the League, his feelings about the interview with Wilson were not politically motivated; he had been genuinely moved.

∽

WASHINGTON
[JULY 21, 1920]
WEDNESDAY

Dearest Babs,

Back again in Washington. A terrific day yesterday which threatened all sorts of trouble over the selection of a National

Chairman. I poured oil on the troubled waters and the selection of George White is an excellent one. He is a *splendid* man and you will like him.

I have just bathed and shaved and am off to the office to try to catch up a little further on those 2500 or more letters and telegrams.

I will drop you a line tomorrow though I doubt if it reaches you before I do.

You, I and Anna go to Dayton for the notification of Gov. Cox on August 7. Our own at H. P. is Monday the 9th. All my love.

F.

The "trouble over the selection of a National Chairman" was occasioned by the withdrawal of the incumbent, Homer S. Cummings (later F.D.R.'s Attorney General), as a candidate for reelection, and by personal friction among the national committeemen over the choice of his successor. It was considered advisable that the new chairman be a native of Ohio, as both Presidential candidates were leading figures in the Buckeye State, where the campaign was figured to be hotly contested; but when the most likely person for the job, Edmond H. Moore, who had managed Cox's pre-convention campaign, refused to accept the position, "all sorts of trouble" developed. Cox preferred Cordell Hull, at this time a Congressman from Tennessee and an active participant in Cox's campaign, but Moore objected to Hull because of a misunderstanding at the convention. After seven hours of deliberation George White was finally chosen. As the latter was not on the National Committee— which, according to the rules, could only be headed by one of its members—his elevation to the chairmanship was preceded by Moore's resignation as the Ohio committeeman and the election of White to replace him. In 1921 White was succeeded by Hull, who then held the post for three years.

Several days after writing this letter F.D.R. journeyed to Campobello to enjoy a brief rest with his family. Thence he went to Washington to close his affairs, and on August 6, 1920, he officially concluded his duties as Assistant Secretary of the Navy. After attending the notification ceremonies of Governor Cox in Dayton, F.D.R. returned to Hyde Park for his own notification on August 9th. The *Poughkeepsie Enterprise* described the joyous event with superlatives:

Hyde Park was dressed within an inch of its life for the debut in the great affairs of the nation and was bubbling over with eagerness to make the day a smashing success. Business was suspended and partisanship forgotten. Republicans and Democrats joined hands in recognition of the honor that has come to one of their neighbors and their friend. All those who attended carried away impressions too poignant to ever pass away with the beat of the drums and the melody of patriotic airs.

The party's campaign got into full steam ahead and the celebration in full swing. Hyde Park had the greatest day in its history all between sunrise and sunset.

The acceptance speech came at the end of a long program in which high-pitched enthusiasm ruled the day. The delegates were conveyed by every form of vehicle from limousines to ox-carts, taxicabs, omnibuses and "shank horses" to see the candidate and pay their respects in tumultuous political emotionalism.

About one o'clock the surging throngs began to tramp on one another's toes and the Democratic nominee had to abandon the hope of shaking hands with the eager crowd. He stood and smilingly waved acknowledgments to the cheering delegates as they crowded around him.

The huge crowd gave Mr. Roosevelt at various intervals during the afternoon a crescendo of cheers and indulged repeatedly in loud bursts of applause. . . .

F.D.R.'s speech of acceptance, which he delivered from the front porch of the Roosevelt home, was in fact a sum-mary of all the issues he later enlarged upon in the campaign. In order to portray the nature of that campaign, and further to cast light upon F.D.R.'s subsequent development as politician and statesman, this address is given in full at this point in the correspondence.

Mr. Cummings and Ladies and Gentlemen of the Committee:

I accept the nomination for the office of Vice-President with humbleness and with a deep wish to give to our beloved country the best that is in me. No one could receive a higher privilege or opportunity than to be thus associated with men and ideals which I am confident will soon receive the support of the majority of our citizens.

In fact, I could not conscientiously accept it if I had not come to know by the closest intimacy that he who is our selection for the Presidency, and who is my chief and yours, is a man possessed of ideals which are also mine. He will give to America that kind of leadership which will make us respect him and bring further greatness to our land. In James M. Cox I recognize one who can lead this nation forward in an unhalting march of progress.

Two great problems will confront the next administration; our relations with the world and the pressing need of organized progress at home. The latter includes a systematized and intensified development of our resources and a progressive betterment of our citizenship. These matters will require the guiding hand of a President who can see his country above his party, and who, having a clear vision of things as they are, has also the independence, courage and skill to guide us along the road to things as they should be without swerving one footstep at the dictation of narrow partisans who whisper "party" or of selfish interests that murmur "profits."

In our world problems, we must either shut our eyes, sell our newly built merchant marine to more far-seeing foreign powers, crush utterly by embargo and harassing legislation our foreign trade, close our ports, build an impregnable wall of costly armaments and live, as the Orient used to live, a hermit nation, dreaming of the past: or, we must open our eyes and see that modern civilization has become so complex and the lives of civilized men so interwoven with the lives of other men in other countries as to make it impossible to be in this world and not of it. We must see that it is impossible to avoid except by monastic seclusion those honorable and intimate foreign relations which the fearful-hearted shudderingly miscall by that Devil's catch-word "international complications."

As for our home problem, we have been awakened by this war into a startled realization of the archaic shortcomings of our governmental machinery and of the need for the kind of reorganization which only a clear-thinking business man, experienced in the technicalities of governmental procedure, can carry out. Such a man we have. One who has so successfully reformed the business management of his own great State is obviously capable of doing greater things. This is not a time to experiment with men who believe that their party can do no wrong and that what is good for the selfish interests of a political party is of necessity good for the nation as well. I as a citizen believe that this year we should choose as President a proved executive. We need to do things; not to talk about them.

Much has been said of late about good Americanism. It is right that it should have been said, and it is right that every chance should be seized to repeat the basic truths underlying our prosperity and our national existence itself. But it would be an unusual and much to be wished for thing if in the coming presentation of the issues a new note of fairness and generosity could be struck. Littleness, meanness, falsehood, extreme partisanship—these are not in accord with the American spirit. I like to think that in this respect also we are moving forward.

Let us be definite. We have passed through a great war, an armed conflict which called forth every effort on the part of the whole population. The war was won by Republicans as well as by Democrats. Men of all parties served in our armed forces. Men and women of all parties served the government at home. They strived honestly as Americans, not as mere partisans. Republicans and Democrats alike worked in administrative positions, raised Liberty loans, administered food control, toiled in munition plants, built ships. The war was brought to a successful conclusion by a glorious common effort—one which in the years to come will be a national pride. I feel very certain that our children will come to regard our participation as memorable for the broad honor and honesty which marked it, for the absence of unfortunate scandal, and for the splendid unity of action which extended to every position of the nation. It would, therefore, not only serve little purpose, but would conform ill to our high standards if any person should in the heat of political rivalry seek to manufacture political advantage out of a nationally conducted struggle. We have seen things on too large a scale to listen in this day to trifles, or to believe in the adequacy of trifling men.

It is that same vision of the bigger outlook of national and individual life which will, I am sure, lead us to demand that the men who represent us in the affairs of our government shall be more than politicians or the errand boys of politicians—that they shall subordinate always the individual ambition and the party advantage to the national good. In the long run the true statesman and the honestly forward-looking party will prevail.

Even as the Nation entered the war for an ideal, so it has emerged from the war with the determination that the ideal shall not die. It is idle to pretend that the war declaration of April 6th, 1917, was a mere act of self-defense, or that the object of our participation was solely to defeat the military power of the Central Nations of Europe. We knew then as a Nation, even as we know today, that success on land and sea could be but half a victory. The other half is not won yet. To the cry of the French at Verdun: "They shall not pass"; the cheer of our men in the Argonne: "We shall go through"—we must add this: "It shall not occur again." This is the positive declaration of our own wills:

that the world shall be saved from a repetition of this crime.

To this end the Democratic party offers a treaty of peace, which, to make it a real treaty for a real peace *must* include a League of Nations; because this peace treaty, if our best and bravest are not to have died in vain, must be no thinly disguised armistice devised by cynical statesmen to mask their preparations for a renewal of greed-inspired conquests later on. "Peace" must mean peace that will last. A practical, workable, permanent, enforcible kind of a peace that will hold as tightly as the business contracts of the individual. We must indeed be, above all things, businesslike and practical in this peace treaty-making business of ours. The League of Nations is a practical solution of a practical situation. It is no more perfect than our original Constitution, which has been amended 18 times and will soon, we hope, be amended the 19th, was perfect. It is not anti-national, it is anti-war. No super-nation, binding us to the decisions of its tribunals, is suggested, but the method and machinery by which the opinion of civilization may become effective against those who seek war is at last within the reach of humanity. Through it we may with nearly every other duly constituted government in the whole world throw our moral force and our potential power into the scale of peace. That such an object should be contrary to American policy is unthinkable; but if there be any citizen who has honest fears that it may be perverted from its plain intent so as to conflict with our established form of government, it will be simple to declare to him and to the other nations that the Constitution of the United States is in every way supreme. There must be no equivocation, no vagueness, no double dealing with the people on this issue. The League will not die. An idea does not die which meets the call of the hearts of our mothers.

So, too, with peace. War may be "declared"; peace cannot. It must be established by mutual consent, by a meeting of the minds of the parties in interest. From the practical point of view alone a peace by resolution of Congress is unworkable. From the point of view of the millions of splendid Americans who served in that whirlwind of war, and of those other millions at home who saw, in our part of the conflict, the splendid hope of days of peace for future generations, a peace by resolution of Congress is an insult and a denial of our national purpose.

Today we are offered a seat at the table of the family of nations to the end that smaller peoples may be truly safe to work out their own destiny, to the end that the sword shall not follow on the heels of the merchant, to the end that the burden of increasing armies and navies shall be lifted from the shoulders of a world already staggering under the weight of taxation. We shall take that place. I say so because I have faith—faith that this nation has no selfish destiny, faith that our people are looking into the years beyond for better things, and that they are not afraid to do their part.

The fundamental outlook on the associations between this Republic and the other Nations can never be very different in character from the principles which one applies to our own purely internal affairs. A man who opposes concrete reforms and improvements in international relations is of necessity a reactionary, or at least, a conservative in viewing his home problems.

We can well rejoice in our great land, in our great citizenship brought hither out of many kindreds and tongues, but to fulfill our true destiny we must be glad also for the opportunity for greater service. So much calls to us for action, and the need is so pressing that the slacker of peace is a greater menace than the slacker of war. Progress will come not through the talkers, but through the doers.

It is for this reason that I am especially happy in the pledges given in the platform of the Democratic party. That document is definite. It is a solemn pledge that, given the authority, our party will accomplish clear aims.

Among the most pressing of these national needs I place the bettering of our citizenship, the extension of teaching to over 5,000,000 of our population above the age of ten who are illiterate, the strengthening of our immigration laws to exclude the physically and morally unfit, the improvement of working conditions especially in the congested centers, the extension of communications to make rural life more attractive, the further protection of child life and of women in industry. All of these demand action. If we raise the standard of education, of physical fitness, of moral sense, the generations to come will have no difficulty in coping with the problems of material economics.

So also with regard to the further development of our natural resources we offer a constructive and definite objective. We begin to appreciate that as a nation we have been wasteful of our opportunities. We need not merely thrift by saving, but thrift by the proper use of what we have at hand. Our efforts in the past have been scattered. It is now time to undertake a well considered, co-ordinated plan of development, so that each year will see progress along definite lines. The days of "pork-barrel" legislation are over. Every dollar of our expenditures for port facilities, for inland waterways, for food control, for the reclamation of swamp and arid lands, for highways, for public buildings, shall be expended only by trained men in accordance with a continuing plan.

The golden rule of the true public servant is to give to his work the same or even higher interest and efficiency than he would give to his private affairs. There is no reason why the effectiveness of the National Government should not at least approximate that of well-conducted private business. Today this is not the case. I may be pardoned if I draw on my experience of over seven years in an administrative position to state unequivocally that the government machinery requires reorganization. The system, especially since the war, has become antiquated. No budget system, much as we need that, will correct the faults.

First of all, the methods of the legislative branch of the National Government, especially in the upper House, require drastic changes. It is safe to say that the procedure of the Congress has progressed less with the times than in any other business body in the country. Yet it is upon the Congress that every executive department must wait. Appeals to the House and Senate in the last session fell on apparently deaf ears.

In the administrative branch also great changes must take place. The functions of the departments should be redistributed along common-sense lines and methods provided to standardize and prevent duplication of effort. Further, it is high time that Government employment be placed upon a proper level. Under the safeguard of civil service the salaries must approximate those paid in private employ. Today we are faced with the fact that the majority of the most efficient Government employes leave the service when they are becoming most valuable. The less useful remain. Many millions of dollars could be saved to the taxpayers by reclassification of the service, by the payment of adequate compensation and by the rigid elimination of those who fail to measure up to a high standard. All of this also has been called to the attention of the present Congress without result, and Congress only can authorize the remedy.

It is a particular pleasure to know that if we are sustained by the people in the election, the country will have as its chief executive a man who has already amply established his reputation as a successful administrator by the reorganization of the business methods of a great State. He is an engineer-statesman. The task before the National Government can also be assisted by a sympathetic co-operation between the executive and the legislative branches, and in this work partisanship must not enter.

In the consideration of the needs of the country and the conduct of its affairs I like to dwell particularly on that part of Lincoln's immortal phrase which speaks of "Government for the People." Service on the part of men and women in the Government is not enough; it must be unselfish service, it must be service with sufficient breadth of view to include the needs and conditions of every kind of citizen, of every section of the land. Such a body of workers would make impossible a return to the conditions of twenty years ago when men in the halls of the Congress and in the executive branches almost openly represented special interests or considered the obtaining of appropriations for their own localities as of more weight than the welfare of the United States as a whole. Such a spirit of unselfishness would prevent also the formation of cliques or oligarchies in the Senate for the retarding of public business.

Some people have been saying of late: "We are tired of progress, we want to go back to where we were before; to go about our own business; to restore 'normal' conditions." They are wrong. This is not the wish of America. We can never go back. The "good old days" are gone past forever; we have no regrets. For our eyes are trained ahead—forward to better new days. In this faith I am strengthened by the firm belief that the women of this nation, now about to receive the National franchise, will throw their weight into the scale of progress and will be unbound by partisan prejudices and a too-narrow outlook on national problems. We cannot anchor our ship of state in this world tempest, nor can we return to the placid harbor of long years ago. We must go forward or flounder.

America's opportunity is at hand. We can lead the world by a great example, we can prove this nation a living, growing thing, with policies that are adequate to new conditions. In a thousand ways this is our hour of test. The Democratic program offers a larger life for our country, a richer destiny for our people. It is a plan of hope. In this, chiefly let it be our aim to build up, not to tear down. Our opposition is to the things which once existed, in order that they may never return. We oppose money in politics, we oppose the private control of national finances, we oppose the treatment of human beings as commodities, we oppose the saloon-bossed city, we oppose starvation wages, we oppose rule by groups or cliques. In the same way we oppose a mere period of coma in our national life.

A greater America is our objective. Definite and continuing study shall be made of our industrial, fiscal, and social problems. Definite and continuing action shall result

507

therefrom, and neither the study nor the action shall be left to emotional caprice or the opportunism of any groups of men. We need a co-operation of the ablest and the wisest heads in the land, irrespective of their politics. So we shall grow—sanely, humanly, honorably, happily—conscious at the end that we handed on to those that follow us the knowledge that we have not allowed to grow dim the light of the American spirit brought hither three hundred years ago by the Pilgrim Fathers.

The coming years are laden with significance, and much will depend on the immediate decision of America. This is the time when men and women must determine for themselves wherein our future lies. I look to that future for progress: in the establishment of good will and mutual help among nations, in the ending of wars and the miseries that wars bring, in the extension of honorable commerce, in the international settlement which will make it unnecessary to send again two millions of our men across the sea. I look to our future for progress; in better citizenship, in less waste, in fairer remuneration for our labor, in more efficient governing, in higher standards of living.

To this future I dedicate myself, willing whatever may be the choice of the people to continue to help as best I am able. It is the faith which is in me that makes me very certain that America will choose the path of progress and set aside the doctrines of despair, the whispering of cowardice, the narrow road to yesterday. May the Guiding Spirit of our land keep our feet on the broad road that leads to a better tomorrow and give to us strength to carry on.

Two days later F.D.R. departed on his first speaking trip through the West. The year 1920 was the first election year in which women could vote and it was the last national campaign conducted without the use of the radio; therefore, following the precedents he had set while campaigning for the State Senate, F.D.R. twice toured the country in a whirlwind manner. His complete campaign itinerary called for nearly one thousand speeches, a figure not including the countless impromptu addresses he made in the course of the three-month ordeal. His railroad car, the *Westboro,* was attached to regular trains according to a careful plan; at the time, his campaign was considered the most extensive ever conducted by a candidate for national office.

As there was scarcely enough time to prepare his speeches in advance of the schedule for their delivery, much less write letters to his family, and as A.E.R. joined him on the second tour of the country, only one item written during the campaign was found among F.D.R.'s personal correspondence. This was the following letter, written to A.E.R. at Campobello during the first week of the trip.

ST. PAUL, MINNESOTA

AUGUST 15, 1920

SUNDAY

Dearest Babs,

A line before I dash back to the car to resume our journey. I have had a delightful family day with the Ames'. I got in this a.m. and went up there and sat around all morning, also doing some preparation on new speeches.

We had a large family lunch of 19! Lesley and his wife, Margaret, several other Ames cousins and old Mrs. Ames, C.W.A.'s mother, the most cheerful and wide awake old lady of 80 I have ever met.

This p.m. I played golf "sub-rosa" with Lesley and Linda and a family supper followed.

This is the *last* day of rest till September. I have had a wonderful experience so far but it *is* tiring. The Chicago meeting on Wednesday was a wonder. Thursday in Wisconsin *very* strenuous. Friday only 2 speeches, one in Minneapolis and one here, but both in big auditoriums. Yesterday 5 speeches in four towns of South Dakota and a motor trip of 80 miles. There is no wire from you and I fear you did not get mine. All my love. I do hope all goes well. Keep some kind of diary *please* or I know I will miss some of the things that happen!

Your devoted

F

The Ames family were distant relatives of the Roosevelts from Boston. Charles Wilberforce Ames assisted his father in editing the *Christian Register,* and in 1881 moved permanently to St. Paul to become a publisher in his own right. His wife, the former Mary Lesley, was the assistant librarian of the American Philosophical Society for five years, and in 1907 became president of the St. Paul School of Fine Arts.

F.D.R. concluded his campaign with a speech in New York's Madison Square Garden on October 30th, then retired to Hyde Park to await the outcome of the election. On November 2nd the returns came in. Joseph P. Tumulty, Wilson's private secretary, described the result as "not a landslide" but "an earthquake." Harding defeated Cox by seven million votes. In the House of Representatives the Republicans acquired the greatest majority ever achieved by a single party, electing 309 members as against 132 Democrats; in the Senate the Republican margin was 59 to 37. The nation's "return to normalcy" commenced in grand style as President Wilson observed: "We had a chance to gain the leadership of the world. We have lost it, and soon we shall be witnessing the tragedy of it all."

F.D.R., it will be seen, accepted defeat philosophically as a good experience. On January 1, 1921, he returned to active work in the law firm of Emmet, Marvin & Roosevelt, and at the same time became a vice-president of the Fidelity and Deposit Company of Maryland, in charge of its New York office. Before resuming the life of a private citizen in New York for the first time in ten years, he went on a short hunting trip in the marshes of Louisiana with his brother-in-law. This brief effort to recuperate from

the strenuous campaign was the occasion for the next two
letters to his wife.

Dearest Babs,

A rainy day all day, so good for travelling, except that I
couldn't see the splendid hills between Bristol and here. I
have been writing and paying cheques all day, this is the 25th
letter!

I hope Hall will get on at 11 p.m. If he doesn't we are
to meet at the Grunewald in New Orleans.

Yesterday was very busy—many conferences in New York
and Washington, and I really think that Woodbury person
is either crooked or pin-headed! I got my shells and think
my outfit is all right, though possibly thin! Hall told me we
would live in bathing suits and I see the thermometer was
50° in New Orleans this a.m.!

Keep Huckins' letter for the address, I have answered it.

This cheque is only for the last account. I still owe you
either $1104 or $1404, I know not which, by the time I get
back enough money will have accumulated to let me pay
you!

I so wish you could be with me on this trip—it sounds not
the least bit like roughing it, and we could have such fun
together. When I join Clove Valley you *must* shoot too, even
if you missed the birds occasionally!

I am writing James. I think *frequent* reminders will be
in line with the "follow up system."

Kiss the chicks and love to Mama and oceans for yourself.

Your devoted

F.

"That Woodbury person" is probably a reference to
Gordon Woodbury, one-time proprietor and editor of the

Manchester (N.H.) *Union,* and F.D.R.'s successor in the
Navy Department for the seven remaining months of the
Wilson Administration. The autumn of 1920 was James
Roosevelt's first semester at Groton, and the "follow up
system" refers to the common parental method of frequently reminding children that continued residence in a
boarding school requires much study and hard work.

∽∽

HOTEL GRUNEWALD, NEW ORLEANS
NOVEMBER 28, 1920
SUNDAY

Dearest Babs,

We got into Birmingham an hour late last night and I
did not find Hall for the very good reason that he had gone
to bed on the local sleeper. This a.m. at 8:30 he came into
my car and we breakfasted together and got into New
Orleans half an hour late at 11:30, came here and were met
by Mr. M. L. Alexander, the Louisiana Conservation Commissioner. We cleaned up and went to his house to lunch,
a nice unassuming family party, two daughters, two brothers-
in-law, two swains of the girls who came in later and a nice
capable Mrs. Alexander. I talked over the phone with John
Parker in the Governor's House at Baton Rouge. He has to
go North to the Conference of Governors so I shall miss him,
but he promised to let us know the next time he comes to
New York. After lunch we took a long motor drive through
the city. Tonight we go out at 11:30 and get to Lake Charles
at 7 a.m., thence as far as we can make out go by motor to
Lake Arthur where we get on the houseboat. This looks like
no shooting tomorrow, but Alexander says there are millions
of birds, especially plentiful this year.

My address will be c/o W. B. Conover, Lake Charles, La.
unless you hear to the contrary by wire.

Your telegram is most welcome tonight and I feel like

a pig in leaving you all alone at Hyde Park this way! I do so
wish you were with me.

Hall seems very fit and sends much love.

My present plan is to get back to New Orleans 8 a.m. the
8th, leave at 8:30, get to Dayton the 9th about 3 p.m., and
leave that night getting to Washington on Friday morning
the 10th.

This all depends on very close connections and one slip
will throw me back a whole 24 hours.

A great deal of love and kisses.

Your devoted

F

John M. Parker served as governor of Louisiana from
1920 to 1924; he was nominated as T.R.'s running mate by
the Progressive Party convention of 1916, but the deterioration of the party following T.R.'s withdrawal prevented
Parker from achieving the status of either victor or van-
quished in the election.

∽∾

After the hunting trip F.D.R. went to Hyde Park to
enjoy the Christmas vacation with his family, and to close
out the business left over from the campaign. In so doing he
wrote the following letter to Stephen T. Early, who had
obtained a leave of absence from the Associated Press to
serve as his advance publicity representative during the
campaign. Mr. Early explains that he and F.D.R. "did most
of our exchanging orally. And, if there are any 'personal'
letters in my files somewhere, memory does not tell me what
or where they are. I am rather certain I do not have many
anywhere. However, there is one 4-page longhand letter I
have treasured through many years. To me it explains the
reasons F.D.R. had in mind when, as President-elect, he
called me back to service—after the 1920 hitch. It certainly
explains why I responded and stayed 12 years plus in that
service when I agreed in '33 for a two year enlistment."
Thus, as it is distinctly personal correspondence, and as it

clearly reveals F.D.R.'s reaction to his crushing defeat in the election, this letter is included here.

HYDE PARK
DECEMBER 21, 1920
TUESDAY

Dear Steve,

It is awfully nice to hear of your new work. One of us at least has landed in the Senate Chamber, though I think your job will be more interesting than the one I was after. At any rate it is fine to know that the A.P. has you to cover the story of that Den of Thieves. I often thought how lucky you were in campaign to avoid all, or at least most of my perorations. Perhaps in this life things have to be evened up in the end, at least you will have nice "chatty" times with V. P. Coolidge.

By the way, I have meant to send you the enclosed for a month or so. It is the balance due you from the Nat. Committee on your travel account. I have settled up all my accounts with them. Incidentally they are not as hopelessly bankrupt as I thought they would be.

We move to N.Y.—47 East 65 Street on January 3, and will be there from Monday to Friday every week—so if you come up at any time we really count on your letting us know, or if you can get off for a Sunday come up here and spend it with us—very quiet but plenty to eat and wash it down.

We particularly want to arrange a reunion of the party in New York. I told Louis H. to get everyone to choose the same date for an evening in the "big city." Also I want to have a talk with you about the situation in general. You were so perfectly fine in the way you helped in the campaign, and I value your judgment so much that I look to you for many things in the days to come. Thank the Lord we are both comparatively youthful!

Eleanor joins me in warmest regards.

Always sincerely
FRANKLIN D. ROOSEVELT

514

The contemplated "reunion of the party" eventually became an annual dinner given by F.D.R. for those who had formed his staff during the Vice-Presidential campaign. The "Cuff-Links Club," so named because after the election F.D.R. gave the members gold cuff-links with their initials engraved on one link and his own on the other, included Messrs. Howe, Camalier, McIntyre, and Early, all previously mentioned; and also James Sullivan, a general secretary; Tom Lynch, an old friend from Poughkeepsie, who was the disbursement officer on the *Westboro;* and Stanley Prenosil, the only newspaperman continuously assigned to the Vice-Presidential train.

In view of the circumstances under which it was written, this letter is perhaps the most striking example in F.D.R.'s correspondence of one of the most significant features of his personality: his optimism. "Thank the Lord we are both comparatively youthful," he writes almost immediately after an overwhelming political defeat, and this feeling pervades his letters, especially those written during the years of recovery from infantile paralysis. Even where his basically optimistic outlook is not specifically revealed, it is none the less glaringly present in the total absence of pessimism.

∾

F.D.R. easily made the adjustment to private business and life in New York, and in *This Is My Story* A.E.R. recalls that during the first six months of his return to an active practice "my husband was working hard." This brief period is not covered by his personal letters, as the family was together in New York from Mondays to Thursdays and in Hyde Park over the weekends. It was not until A.E.R. took the children to Campobello in July of 1921 that F.D.R. resumed his correspondence. Continued efforts on the part of several Senators to smear the Navy Department's record during the war prevented F.D.R. from spending the entire summer with his family; as he had to be present at committee hearings until late in July, he did not get to Campobello until the first week of August.

In this particular "smear" F.D.R. and Josephus Daniels

515

were denounced for methods used by the Navy Department in investigating wartime scandals among enlisted men at the Newport Training Station. Crowded living conditions at the Rhode Island base had led to the development of immoral practices which the majority report of the Senate investigating committee called "a scandal of an unprintable nature." When Daniels first heard of the conditions at Newport early in the war, he sent F.D.R. to verify the reports, and upon F.D.R.'s confirmation an investigating commission composed of naval personnel was established to obtain the evidence necessary for appropriate action. Unbeknownst to J.D. and F.D.R., the investigating commission at first employed immoral practices to secure the evidence, and although these tactics were stopped as soon as they came to the attention of J.D. and F.D.R., the ranking officials in the Navy Department were charged with sanctioning this method of investigation. In violation of a promise to F.D.R. that he would have a hearing on the matter before the majority report was filed and published, Senators Ball and Keyes submitted their opinion on July 5, 1921. F.D.R. rushed to Washington to uphold the Navy Department's action; then, upon his return to New York, wrote the next letter to A.E.R.

NEW YORK
[JULY 21, 1921]
THURSDAY

Dearest Babs,

I left Washington in awful heat yesterday p.m., got a good night at 47, and today is much cooler.

It was a joy to find your dear letters here this morning, and tomorrow one should come telling of the Bibescos' visit. I wish Elizabeth had fallen off the Vireo instead of Mlle. I think she would float quite high out of water!

As all good things go by three, tell Mlle. to postpone her next bath till she can fall off the rocks on our next cliff walk. I am sorry to have missed the boys on the yacht. It turns out they were in the Fly Club.

It would be too long a story to go into all the Washington details. Of course as I expected I found all the cards stacked, only even worse than I thought. At 10 a.m. Monday I asked to be heard, and told them of their former promise to do so. They (the majority) told me they had thought it unnecessary as I had testified before the Dunn Board. I told them I had not seen the 9 volumes of Dunn Board testimony and their own 30 witnesses' testimony. They then offered to let me see it (15 volumes, 6,000 pages) and make a statement at 8 p.m. At 4 p.m. the newspaper boys told me the majority report was in the hands of all the papers for release the next p.m. and that Senator Ball had declined to hold it back or amend it in any way.

As this was before I had even been heard it proved the futility of trying to get any fair treatment. I worked very hard up to 8 p.m., then went before them with a statement covering every mis-statement in their report and another statement of objections on the ground that they had twice used bad faith—also a request for various "findings" all borne out by uncontradicted testimony.

Steve Early was a great help and the papers (on the whole) have mentioned my complete denials fairly well. The "Times" account was by far the most unfair in its whole makeup.

I have done the only other thing possible—demanded an *open* hearing before the whole Naval Affairs Committee (which I don't believe will be paid any attention to) and this week-end I shall prepare and file with the whole Committee a complete statement in answer to every paragraph of the Majority Report.

Senator King was all right—worked hard, though too late and I have no fault to find with his report. As it came out the next day it of course did not get the same publicity.

I have talked to a good many people today and lots of them want to rush into print. But in view of the fact that no papers have taken it up it may seem best to drop the whole thing as far as letters to the papers are concerned and seek only for the present at least to file the complete brief and facts with the full Senate Committee, and watch what if anything they will do.

Lots of mail and work on both my desks so I shall be very busy. I will go up to Hyde Park on Saturday at one and stay till early Monday morning.

Tomorrow Hamilton comes over from Balto. and we dine together.

Tonight Harriet gives me supper at home.

Tell Louis I expect those boats to be all rigged and ready when I get up there and I am very greatly put out not to be there now.

Kiss all the chicks and many many for you.

Your devoted

F.

By the way, look at the bricks in the sitting room fire place. I fear some have fallen out, though they were supposedly new. Are the extinguishers all refilled? Is the swimming pool operation started?

FDR

The "Bibescos" were acquaintances from Washington's diplomatic circle. Prince Antoine Bibesco had served for sixteen years as a member of the Rumanian Legation in London before being appointed Rumanian Minister to the United States in 1921. His wife, the former Elizabeth Asquith, was a daughter of Herbert Henry Asquith, whose premiership during the tumultuous years between 1908 and 1916 was later said to have "left an ineffaceable mark on English history." In order that his children could learn to sail, F.D.R. had purchased a small sailboat, the *Vireo,* after turning the *Half Moon* over to the government. A.E.R.'s letter to F.D.R. of July 18, 1921, describes Mademoiselle's experience on the *Vireo* as follows: "Mlle. fell in again this a.m. while cleaning the 'Vireo' and I've just had to give her a little of your gin in hot lemonade as she has never warmed up since."

F.D.R.'s "statement covering every mis-statement" contained in the majority report of the Senate Naval Affairs Subcommittee explains further the complications of the Newport case; it was issued on July 18, 1921, as follows:

The Senate Naval Affairs Sub-committee, two Republicans, Senators Ball of Delaware and Keyes of New Hampshire, and one Democrat, Senator King of Utah, was appointed in January, 1920. On February 12, 1920, Captain Leigh, Admiral Niblack and I went before them to give a preliminary outline of what the Navy Department knew of this Newport investigation. No details were gone into, and Senator Ball, the Chairman, stated that after they had received other testimony we would be given an opportunity at a later date to come before the subcommittee and present the department's case.

Senator Ball, three months later, in May, 1920, confirmed to me that after the Dunn Board had reported we would be given an opportunity to be heard. The Dunn Board report was acted on March 4, 1921. I never received any word from the subcommittee. Only last Thursday I received a telegram from an outside source that Senators Ball and Keyes had on July 5, filed their majority report with the full Committee on Naval Affairs.

This was, of course, a clear breach of faith. This is, however, only the first instance.

I telegraphed at once, demanding a hearing, and Senator Ball wired me they would hear me Monday in the morning, but the hearing was postponed to the evening. As soon as I arrived I was informed by Senator King, the minority member, that he had an understanding with Senator Ball that the report would be withheld from publication until Friday. Senator Ball also said to me that the subcommittee could still withdraw or amend the report.

Yesterday afternoon I was informed that, in spite of these

assurances, and before I have been heard, the report was to be published without change today, Tuesday afternoon. There is, therefore, no possible use in giving my testimony, but I shall do so just the same. This is the second case of a deliberately broken word. All this shows a premeditated and unfair purpose of seeking what they mistakenly believe to be a partisan political advantage.

None of this worries me, nor does the report itself worry me personally. As an American, one deplores bad faith and a conscious perversion of facts on the part of any Senator. As an American, irrespective of party, one hates to see the United States Navy, an organization of the nation, not of party, used as the vehicle for cheap ward politics. It rather amuses me to know that these Republican Senators consider me worthwhile attacking so maliciously and savagely. Perhaps they may later on learn what a boomerang is.

As to the majority report of Senators Ball and Keyes, little need be said. I have today for the first time been given an opportunity to see the whole evidence—fifteen books of nearly 6,000 pages of testimony and exhibits.

In a nutshell, the clear facts known to the subcommittee and shown by the evidence are these: Early in 1919 thousands of Navy men were still at the Newport Training Station. The conditions in the vicinity in regard to illicit liquor and drug selling and immorality were exceedingly bad. The local navy commandant and the officers in command of the training station tried to investigate and stop these conditions by using local officers and enlisted men to catch the criminals. The Department of Justice was asked by me to take a hand, but it failed utterly to stop the trouble. Then as a last resort, and on the recommendation of the commandant of the training station, the Chief of the Bureau of Navigation, the Morale Officer and the Judge Advocate General, I approved the formation of an investigating squad under a naval reserve doctor and a chief petty officer. These men were recommended to me by all concerned and by the Red Cross officer at Newport, sent to me by Governor Beeckman of Rhode Island.

Emphasis was placed by the Newport officers on the need for secrecy in order to prevent blocking the work in Newport, and for this reason the squad was placed for purely technical purposes relating to disbursements, travel, etc., first under Naval Intelligence and later under my office. Their work, however, was at no time supervised by me personally, as it related solely to personnel questions under the charge of the Bureau of Navigation and the Judge Advocate General.

No one other than partisan politicians could ever, in their wildest dreams, assume or charge that the squad was under the "direct supervision" of the Acting Secretary of the Navy.

It is curiously enough a fact that a Secretary or an Assistant Secretary has plenty to do in the general management of a navy of hundreds of ships and hundreds of thousands of men without attempting to manage the details of an investigation of one small place by a dozen or so navy men. It is doubly true when it is considered that in the Spring and Summer of 1919 the heads of the navy were trying to bring the army back from France and, at the same time, to demobilize the navy itself from 500,000 men to peace-time strength.

In September, 1919, I, as Acting Secretary, and Captain Leigh, as Acting Chief of the Bureau of Navigation, were, for the first time, informed by two friends of a local Newport minister, who had been tried in a local court and acquitted, that some of the members of the investigating squad had used highly improper and revolting methods in getting evidence. Immediate orders went out from me and Captain Leigh that day to stop it. There is no charge that any wrong-doing occurred after that. That is all there is to the Senators' unwarranted deductions.

Their insinuations that I must have known, that I supervised the operations, that I was morally responsible, that I committed all sorts of high crimes and misdemeanors, are nowhere supported by the evidence directly or indirectly. The Senators cannot cite the evidence in their support.

Throughout their report I accuse them of deliberate falsification of evidence, of perversion of facts, of misstatements of the record, and of a deliberate attempt to deceive.

This business of using the navy as a football of politics is going to stop. People everywhere are tired of partisan discussion of dead history. If these Senators want to go on with the question of how effective our navy was in the war, then take it out of the Senate, out of partisanship, and put the facts up to any good, average jury of twelve men in any court in the land. I am quite willing to abide by the result. I only ask fair play.

The facts in complete answer to the subcommittee's majority report will be immediately filed by me with the Senate Committee on Naval Affairs.

After F.D.R. filed "the complete answer" with the Senate Committee interest in the Newport case diminished, and the charges against him were subsequently dropped.

∽∽

Ten days after writing this letter F.D.R. departed for Campobello in the company of Van Lear Black, at this time publisher of the *Baltimore Sun* and the leading figure in the Fidelity and Deposit Company of Maryland. The trip was made aboard the latter's yacht, the *Sabalo*. Several days later F.D.R. arrived at Campobello to enjoy a prolonged visit with all his family except his mother, who was spending the summer in Europe. The leading event of this vacation constitutes the correspondence of the next chapter.

XIII

"Dearest Mama—Franklin Has Been Quite Ill..."

Summer of 1921

ON WEDNESDAY afternoon, August 10, 1921, F.D.R. took his
family out on the *Vireo*. During the course of the sail a forest
fire was sighted, and F.D.R. brought the boat into shore to
fight it. Several hours later, after stamping out the fire and
going for a swim on the other side of the island, the family
returned home. F.D.R. sat around in his bathing suit looking
over his mail, but within a short time he felt chilled and
retired to his bed to avoid catching a cold. However, the
chill turned out to be more complicated than a cold, and he
was bedridden for many months, the first ten days of which
were described by A.E.R. in the following letters to F.D.R.'s
half-brother.

CAMPOBELLO
AUGUST 14, 1921
SUNDAY

Dear Rosy,

We have had a very anxious few days as on Wed. evening
Franklin was taken ill. It seemed a chill but Thursday he

had so much pain in his back and legs that I sent for the doctor, by Friday evening he lost the ability to walk or move his legs but though they felt numb he can still feel in them. Yesterday a.m. Dr. Bennett and I decided we wanted the best opinion we could get quickly so Louis Howe (who, thank heavens, is here, for he has been the greatest help) went with Dr. Bennett to Lubec and they canvassed the nearby resorts and decided that the best available diagnostician was the famous old Dr. W. W. Keen of Philadelphia and he agreed to motor up and spend the night. He arrived about 7:30 and made a most careful, thorough examination and the same this morning and he thinks a clot of blood from a sudden congestion has settled in the lower spinal cord temporarily removing the power to move though not to feel. I have wired to New York for a masseuse as he said that was vital and the nursing I could do, and in the meantime Louis and I are rubbing him as well as we can. The doctor feels sure he will get well but it may take some months. I have only told Franklin he said he could surely go down the 15th of Sept. He did say to leave then but not before on account of heat and to go to New York but it may have to be done on a wheel chair. The doctor thinks absorption has already begun as he can move his toes on one foot a little more which is very encouraging. He has told the Dr. here just what medicines to give and what treatment to follow and we should know in the next ten days or two weeks how things are going.

Do you think you can meet Mama when she lands? She has asked us to cable just before she sails and I have decided to say nothing. No letter can reach her now and it would simply mean worry all the way home and she will have enough once here but at least then she can do things. I will write her a letter to quarantine saying he is ill but leave explaining to you or if you can't meet her to Uncle Fred or whoever does meet her. I hope you will think I am doing right and have done all I could. Of course write me if you think of anything else. I do not want particulars to get in the papers so I am writing the family that he is ill from the effects of a chill and I hope will soon be better, but I shall write Uncle Fred what I have told you and Langdon Marvin as F cannot be at the office to relieve him.

Affly always,
ELEANOR

My love to Betty.

∽∽

Dear Rosy,

Franklin asked me to send you the enclosed and ask you on your return from Herkimer to attend to it.

Yesterday and to-day his temperature has been normal and I think he's getting back his grip and a better mental attitude though he has of course times of great discouragement. We thought yesterday he moved his toes on one foot a little better which is encouraging. Dr. Keen wrote me a long letter saying that the longer he reflected the more he inclined to discard the clot and think the inflammation had caused a lesion in the spinal cord which might be a longer business than his first estimate. He also sent his bill for $600! I dread the time when I have to tell Franklin and it wrings my heart for it is all so much worse to a man than to a woman but the 3 doctors agree he will be eventually *well* if nothing unfavorable happens in the next ten days or so and at present all signs are favorable, so we should be very thankful.

Much love,
ELEANOR

Love to Betty and Helen. Mama arrives Aug. 31st she writes.

∽∽

Dear Rosy,

Many thanks for your telegram and both letters. Uncle Fred is meeting Mama on the 31st and Aunt Kassie seems to be going down to see her also. I will get Uncle Fred to make reservations for her on the 1st as she could not leave the day she landed and there is no hurry for no change can occur here. The doctors agree that there is no doubt but that F. is suffering from the after effects of a congestion of the lower part of the spinal cord which was of unusually short duration so far as the acute symptoms. (His temp. has been a little subnormal the past few days but is up to 98 to-day.) It is too early yet to say positively if all this came from his chill and exposure which brought to a focus an irritation that had existed some time, or from an attack of Infantile Paralysis. The symptoms so far would be much the same. On Uncle Fred's urgent advice, which I feel I must follow on Mama's account, I have asked Dr. Keen to try to get Dr. Lovett here for a consultation to determine if it is I.P. or not. Dr. Keen thinks *not* but the treatment at this stage differs in one particular and no matter what it costs I feel and I am sure Mama would feel we must leave no stone unturned to accomplish the best results.

Franklin cannot be moved before Sept. 15th and then by boat to N.Y. to avoid jar and he must stay in N.Y. first, because it is only there that he can have all the after treatments necessary and second, if, as he hopes, he can carry on his various business activities it can only be done there.

I will wire you after consultation which I hope will be Thursday. Love to Betty and Helen and to you. Franklin was much cheered by your letters.

Devotedly

E. R.

Dearest Mama,

Franklin has been quite ill and so can't go down to meet you on Tuesday to his great regret, but Uncle Fred and Aunt Kassie both write they will be there so it will not be a lonely home coming. We are all so happy to have you home again dear, you don't know what it means to feel you near again.

The children are all very well and I wish you could have seen John's face shine when he heard us say you would be home soon.

Aunt Jennie is here with Ellen and we are having such lovely weather, the island is really at its loveliest.

Franklin sends all his love and we are both so sorry he cannot meet you.

Ever devotedly
ELEANOR

Dr. Robert W. Lovett, a well-known Boston specialist in poliomyelitis, arrived at Campobello on August 25th, and at the consultation mentioned in A.E.R.'s last letter to James Roosevelt Roosevelt disagreed with Dr. Keen's analysis and made a definite diagnosis of infantile paralysis. As noted by A.E.R., this decision necessitated an alteration of the treatments, which were prescribed by Dr. Lovett in a letter written to Dr. E. H. Bennett on September 2, 1921, as follows:

. . . Drugs I believe are of little or no value, and not worth giving if they impair appetite. Bromide for sleeplessness may be useful. Massage will prolong hyperaesthesia and tenderness, and the high sensitiveness should be watched from this point of view. There is nothing that can be added to the treatment, and this is one of the hardest things to make the family understand. The use of hot baths

527

should I think now be considered again, as it is really helpful and will encourage the patient, as he can do so much more under water with his legs. There is likely to be mental depression and sometimes irritability in adults, as you heard me say to Mrs. R. I should have the patient sit up in a chair as soon as it can be done without discomfort. . . .

As Frederic Delano arranged for a private railroad car which could be switched in Boston so as to make the trip to New York without changing, F.D.R.'s departure from Campobello on September 13th was not made by boat as originally planned by A.E.R. Louis Howe, always on the alert for any possible injuries to F.D.R.'s political career, engineered the transfer from Campobello to the train at Eastport in such a way that the people gathered at the dock did not get a glimpse of F.D.R. until he was comfortably settled on the train. The ruse was accomplished by misinforming the reporters and the crowd of wellwishers as to the time and place of arrival of F.D.R.'s launch from Campobello. In addition to preventing F.D.R. from exposure to public view while prostrated on a stretcher, Howe delayed releasing the story of F.D.R.'s "paralysis" as long as possible so that when the story was finally given nationwide coverage, it also included the notation that "the patient is improving."

Upon his arrival in New York, F.D.R. was taken in an ambulance to the Presbyterian Hospital and put in the care of Dr. George Draper, whom F.D.R. had known at Harvard and who was an associate of Dr. Lovett. While in the hospital F.D.R. occupied his time dictating answers to the many notes of sympathy he received from all over the country. Although not personal letters in the strict sense, three of these notes, with carbon copies of F.D.R.'s replies, are included here to help indicate his outlook during this trying and depressing period of his life.

Mr. F. D. Roosevelt.

Fellow Sufferer,

Through the enclosed clipping, I have just learned the pretty and truthful name of that from which I have suffered for eleven years, compelled to walk with a cane, though a young girl, only 87½ years old. Except for that, though so young, I should clip around like a young girl, as are others of my age.

Hoping your trouble will not stay as long as mine has,

Yours very respectfully

ELIZABETH CARLETON

∽∾

NEW YORK
SEPTEMBER 23, 1921
FRIDAY

My dear Miss Carleton:

I appreciated your little note very much and enjoyed reading the poetry.

If I could feel assured that time could treat me so lightly as to leave me at eighty-seven and a half years with all my vigor, powers and only a cane required, I would consider that my future was very bright indeed. There are not many people who can equal that record, even though they have been fortunate enough not to have been fellow-sufferers, with you and me, of infantile paralysis.

Very sincerely yours,

FRANKLIN D. ROOSEVELT

Miss Elizabeth Carleton
3200 Stevens Ave.
Minneapolis, Minn.

∽∾

529

Hon. Franklin D. Roosevelt
Presbyterian Hospital
New York City.

Dear Mr. Roosevelt:

This is just a line to assure you how glad all your old friends were to get reports that you are coming along all right.

I am only one of that very great number, but I wished you to know how anxiously I have followed reports and to recall and hope to repeat the old days when Delano, McAdoo, Davis and you formed my "Flying Squadron" and we "double-quicked" in Potomac Park!

Yours very sincerely,

WALTER CAMP

Pray remember me to Mrs. Roosevelt.

∽

NEW YORK
SEPTEMBER 28, 1921
WEDNESDAY

Dear Mr. Camp:

Thank you for your nice little note.

There were days in the old "Flying Squadron" when I felt that "double-quicking" around Potomac Park came very near [the] classification of hard work, but I can assure you that if I could get up this afternoon and join with Messrs. McAdoo, Davis and Delano in a sprint for the record, I would consider it the greatest joy in the world.

However, the doctors are most encouraging and I have been given every reason to expect that my somewhat rebellious legs will permit me to join in another course of training sometime in the future.

Very sincerely yours,

FRANKLIN D. ROOSEVELT

Walter Camp, Esq.
New Haven, Conn.

∽

AMERICAN NATIONAL ASSOCIATION OF SUPERVISORS

Washington Branch
United States Naval Gun Factory

WASHINGTON

SEPTEMBER 26, 1921

The Hon. Franklin D. Roosevelt
General Presbyterian Hospital
New York, N. Y.

Dear Mr. Roosevelt:—

It is with the deepest regret that the members of the supervisory force of the Washington Navy Yard learn of your severe illness. They, therefore, desire to express through me, the hope that you will have a speedy and permanent recovery.

Very sincerely

R. M. CARNAHAN

Secretary.

∾

NEW YORK

OCTOBER 3, 1921

MONDAY

Dear Mr. Carnahan:

Will you please express to the members of the supervisory force of the Washington Navy Yard my thanks for their interest and thoughtfulness in sending me their good wishes. It is most pleasant to feel that they still think of me kindly and that the very pleasant relations I had with them as Assistant Secretary of the Navy have not been forgotten.

You will be glad to know that the doctors consider me a prize patient and are much gratified at my progress toward recovery.

Very sincerely yours,

[FRANKLIN D. ROOSEVELT]

Mr. R. M. Carnahan
2407 Irving St., N.E.,
Washington, D. C.

∾

These letters are an indication of the attitude F.D.R. gradually evolved toward his illness. He was thirty-nine years old when stricken with polio, approaching the peak of maturity and on the verge of great success. He had always been a very active person; that he was fond of the outdoor life and thrilled at the use of his body, is witnessed by the letters written during hunting trips. His intrinsic optimism, his stability, his independent nature, his good humor—all these characteristics were intricately connected with his good health. The loss of the use of his legs was thus not only an unexpected setback, but one which required great courage if the consequences were to be confined to merely physical disability. Dr. Lovett had written "there is likely to be mental depression."

The obstacles to complete mental adjustment that confront an adult more-or-less permanently crippled are innumerable; to the surmounting of these F.D.R. devoted the next six or seven years of his life. Dr. Draper had announced that "he will not be crippled," that "no one need have any fear of permanent injury from this attack"; and F.D.R. determined to realize this prediction. His "somewhat rebellious legs" became a challenge not dissimilar to organizing the Navy's resources for war or to campaigning throughout Dutchess County in a bright-red Maxwell. He did the prescribed exercises regularly and diligently, learned to walk on crutches, and, all in all, would not admit that he was anything but a perfectly normal, able-bodied person.

However, the barriers to a swift mental recovery were not all within himself. Sara Roosevelt, who had always had fears concerning his health, insisted that he retire to Hyde Park and become a country gentleman. The rest of his family, as well as the attending doctors, objected to this, and it soon became evident that F.D.R. too rebelled at the idea of retirement. Hence, in the autumn of 1922, F.D.R. actively resumed his business affairs and began making daily trips to his insurance office. On January 1, 1925, he formed a partnership with Basil O'Connor and established offices in the Equitable Building. He retained the chairmanship of the Boy Scouts of Greater New York, and became very active in the raising of funds for the expansion of that organization. Also included among his various activities was the national directorship of the fund to secure ten million dollars for the completion of the Cathedral of St. John the Divine. In this way did F.D.R. return to active life in New York during the 'twenties.

In Warm Springs, Georgia, he was even more energetic. There he set about establishing a permanent institution for those suffering from infantile paralysis. The organization of the Georgia Warm Springs Foundation was a personal matter, directly pertaining to his own efforts to regain the use of his legs; and his interest therein largely dominates the remaining letters of this volume.

In the meantime, in order to revive her husband's interest in politics, A.E.R. entered political work and became an active member of the Democratic Party. Louis Howe, too, devoted himself entirely to the reconstruction of F.D.R.'s career, refusing the offer of a position with a lucrative salary and taking up residence in the Roosevelt household.

Thus the background of F.D.R.'s endeavors to recover his health and become accustomed to a new kind of life. Chapter Fourteen contains personal correspondence written during this six-year interval. Politically it was an interlude. Personally, it was the most overwhelming period of his life.

XIV

"... The Walking Progresses Slowly but Definitely ..."

YEARS OF CONVALESCENCE

1923-1928

F.D.R.'s PERSONAL CORRESPONDENCE during the six years that
he was out of public service is varied and somewhat sparse.
In the effort to regain his health F.D.R. went on fishing trips
off the coast of Florida, on rest cures to Warm Springs, and
on summer vacations to 'Marion, Massachusetts, where he
also received special treatments. These months spent away
from New York account for the majority of the letters of this
chapter, and for their variety. Inasmuch as the correspondence for this period pertains mainly to F.D.R.'s endeavors
to recover the use of his legs, it has all been grouped together; and since the general nature of his business and law
work in New York during the time has already been mentioned, the intervals between letters are not described in
detail.

Two factors explain the relative scarcity of letters for these
crucial years: first, the family was united a great deal of the
time; and second, neither A.E.R. nor the children saved the

letters F.D.R. wrote to them during the 'twenties. It is only the fact that F.D.R. occasionally dictated letters to his children (with carbon copies retained in his own files) that any early letters he wrote as a father are still in existence. There are no personal letters at all for 1922, as it was not until late in this year that F.D.R. was able to leave his 65th Street home and be separated from his family. Hence the first item of correspondence following the infantile paralysis attack was written on a fishing trip off Florida in 1923.

∽∾

"WEONA II"
MARCH 5, 1923
MONDAY

Dearest Mama,

I have written Eleanor quite fully and I know she will read it to you. It has been a wonderful week and we are on our way back to Long Key. The West Coast country is wholly wild and tropical. I have been in swimming four times and it goes better and better. I'm sure this warmth and exercise is doing lots of good. The remains of the flu are all gone and I am sunburned and in fine shape. Cass and Ruth and Henry and Frances have been dear and look after me all the time. They are great fun to have on board in this somewhat negligée existence. All wander round in pyjamas, nighties and bathing suits!

Later—March 6th. Just got in to Long Key and I have your two dear letters. So glad to know all is well and that the chimney fire was not more serious. I suppose you have to pay a fine for having a fire which calls out the engines! I hope it didn't get everything dirty in the house.

We have had fine luck fishing, though nothing very large except a 42 pound Jewfish which Cass landed after 25 minutes' hard work.

We shall stay near here fishing today and tomorrow and the Ledyards leave the p.m. of the 8. Lucy and Johnny

Lawrence get here the next morning and we go south to Knights' Key for 3 days and get back here the 12 to let the deRhams take the train.

Lots of love and I hope you'll get this safely before you sail. Give Rosy and Betty much love. I know you'll love it in Bermuda.

Your devoted son,

FDR

The *Weona II* was a houseboat F.D.R. rented for his fishing cruise off Florida waters. As A.E.R. had to be in New York a great deal of the time and could only go South with F.D.R. for a few weeks during each winter, the family encouraged his friends to take turns visiting with him so that he would not have to be alone on the boat. The friends mentioned on this occasion were the families of Lewis Cass Ledyard, Jr., Henry de Rham *(vide supra)*, and John S. Lawrence. The first-mentioned, several years ahead of F.D.R. at Harvard, was a member of his first law firm; while John Lawrence was in the class of 1901 at Harvard and later became a prominent Boston merchant.

On February 26, 1923, the *Poughkeepsie Enterprise* reported that for a short time the "chimney fire" at 47 East 65th Street "created some excitement in the neighborhood": "The family was at dinner when it was discovered that smoke was spreading throughout the house. An alarm was turned in and on the arrival of the firemen it was found that the soot in one of the chimneys had ignited. The blaze was extinguished quickly without damage to the house."

∾

F.D.R. returned to his work in New York in the spring of 1923; the summer was spent mostly in Hyde Park, and the following autumn he was back in New York. The next winter F.D.R. again went South for health reasons, only this time he was part-owner of his own houseboat. After the pleasant experience of the first fishing cruise he and John Lawrence decided to purchase a houseboat which they could use whenever it was desired. The new vessel was christened the *Larooco* (being a merger of the first two letters of "Lawrence," the first three of "Roosevelt," and the abbreviation of the word "company"). A log was kept of the three winters spent aboard the *Larooco*, and as it is largely a personal document, the entries made by F.D.R. are included in his personal correspondence at the appropriate chronological points. In addition to the written entries, which were made with pen and ink and are mainly in the third person, the log consists of pictures, poems, and other incidental material acquired on the three trips. With the object in mind of revealing F.D.R.'s outlook during these early years of recovery from infantile paralysis, entries known to have been made by him have been excerpted from the photostatic copy of the logbook at the Franklin D. Roosevelt Library, and are included here without abridgment.

In addition to the crew, F.D.R.'s companions on "Cruise No. 1" were his private secretary, Miss Marguerite Le Hand, Livingston Davis, and Maunsell Schieffelin Crosby. The former, who is referred to in the log as "M.A.L." and who was generally known to the family as "Missy," worked in F.D.R.'s Vice-Presidential headquarters and came to Hyde Park for a few weeks after the election to clear up the correspondence. A temporary job became a permanent one, and Miss Le Hand not only was F.D.R.'s private secretary for the remaining years of her life, but became a close friend of the family. Maunsell S. Crosby was a neighbor of F.D.R. from Rhinebeck, a prominent amateur ornithologist who went on numerous collecting expeditions for the American Museum of Natural History. Crosby was a member of the class of 1908 at Harvard.

∽∾

Saturday, February 2, 1924.

At Jacksonville, Florida. F.D.R. went on board and put Larooco in commission. Sailing-master Robert S. Morris and Mrs. Morris spent the day getting provisions, and the trunks etc. were duly unpacked, fishing gear stowed and Library of the World's Worst Literature placed on shelves.

Sunday, February 3, 1924.

Gave all hands opportunity to go to Church. No takers. Hence left dock at 11:30 a.m. proceeding down St. John's River, about 18 miles, thence South into Canal. Very narrow channel and little water. Most of the way a straight cut through young pine lands. Moored to old piling at 5:30 p.m., 2 or 3 miles short of the Toll Chain. Pondered deeply over interior decorations (of boat—not self)—green or light blue —or both?

Monday, February 4, 1924.

Started at 9:30, coming out soon into a marshy river— strong head wind. Anchored at St. Augustine at 2:30 p.m. A hard rain in the late afternoon produced some new leaks in the cabin and in my (port) stateroom. Got some delicious oysters and whitefish.

Tuesday, February 5, 1924.

Shopping by Dora etc. in the afternoon. The Captain found a 23 foot sea-skiff (dory-type) 7 ft. beam, 2 cycle Bridgeport engine. Tried her out in St. Augustine bay for an hour, then bought her from Mr. George Washington Corbett for $375.00. At six Maunsell Crosby came on board, just in from N.Y. Yesterday when approaching the town we saw the flags at half mast—President Wilson died Sunday morning. Our own ensign will remain at half mast for 30 days.

Wednesday, February 6, 1924.

Got under way at St. Augustine at 9:30 passing South through drawbridge, thence up river into some very narrow places. At noon, just after passing Matanzas Inlet the steering cable slipped and we blew sideways and gracefully on to a sand bar. Tide going out. Larooco soon high and dry and at an angle. M.S.C., M.A.L. and F.D.R. went fishing in the inlet. Caught one sea trout. M.S.C. identified 33 different species of birds, including a very large flock of black skimmers. Also a flock of Greater Snow Goose. All hands played solitaire. M.A.L. ate too much. At 9 p.m. the incoming tide lifted Larooco clear, and Capt. Morris in the darkness and without a searchlight got her into the mouth of the Canal where we tied up for the night. Fine piece of piloting.

Thursday, February 7, 1924.

Under way at 9:30. Ran five miles and were stopped by a ship in the Canal. Freight boat aground. Seven other boats, including 2 other houseboats and Larooco soon lined up. The N.W. wind had driven the water out. Dredge working towards the shoal place. Will reach there in two months at present rate of progress. M.A.L. and F.D.R. in launch fishing in p.m. No luck. M.S.C. and Geo. Dyer the engineer hunting towards the beach. Additional birds identified. Painted 3/4 of a chair—booful blue.

Friday, February 8, 1924.

Wind still N.W. See no chance of release today. All these days have been brilliant sunshine but chilly air and really cold at night. At 10 M.S.C. and Capt. Morris went South about 10 miles to the toll bridge and store and came back (from "Ocean City") with a live turkey, a big fish (bought) and other grub. The houseboat "Priscilla" astern of us, a Mr. and Mrs. DeVorse of Detroit and children almost starving. They also shopped and all is well. The "Lounger III" belonging to some Uppercu persons tried to be smart and rude by pushing by us. Stuck in sand. Bent propeller. Just deserts etc.

Saturday, February 9, 1924.

Very cold night. Waited for the N.E. wind to blow some more water into the ridiculous Canal. At 4 p.m. the freight boat got through, then the Lounger, then "Larooco" and the 2nd boat back of us stuck. We were lucky to get ahead, but in a few minutes the port shaft hit a rock and bent. Tied up at the toll bridge 5 miles South.

Sunday, February 10, 1924.

A little warmer. Passed into the Halifax River, reached Ormonde Bridge at noon—draw out of order! M.S.C. and M.A.L. to see the famous beach. Through the draw at last at 4:30. Anchored off Daytona at dark. M.S.C. ashore for telegrams and brought back sad news of death of M.A.L.'s father. Arranged for train berth etc.

Monday, February 11, 1924.

Our party broken up by M.A.L.'s departure for Boston at 7 a.m. Hauled out Larooco at Mathews Ship Yard. Removed shaft, had it straightened, put back—afloat again at 4:30. Proceeded through bridges to S. of Daytona—anchored for night. Clutch of port engine on the blink. One thing after another.

Tuesday, February 12, 1924.

An uneventful day—engines have apparently recovered from what sounded like pneumonia. We left Daytona at 9, and kept on South till we stuck in the mud just before reaching the "Haul-Over." Anchored for the night. Much playing of solitaire and Parcheesi.

Wednesday, February 13, 1924.

Off at 8:30. Stopped at the Haul-Over for a chicken and some very superior eggs. Came into the broad expanse of Indian River and kept on till 5:30 p. m., a fine day's run of 48 nautical miles. Engines working OK.

Thursday, February 14, 1924.

Yesterday Maunsell took a bath. Reason clothed in mystery. Now it develops that today is his Birthday. Having no other gifts I took a bath also, in his honor. It is a heavenly warm day, shirtsleeve weather for the first time. We painted two dining room chairs blue and liked it and will do the others. Proceeded ever Southward. Anchored off Fort Pierce at 6 p.m. and had cake and some flowers for the Birthday dinner. This Indian River is a wonderful body of water, stretching N. and S. for miles, and separated by a narrow stretch of beach from the ocean. It is however very shallow almost everywhere.

Friday, February 15, 1924.

M.S.C. and Mrs. Morris went shopping at Ft. Pierce and we took on more gasoline. Left at ten and it is a wonderful hot day—we are getting to the nearest point to the Gulf Stream. At 3, while passing through Peck Lake we ran aground and stuck aft. Engines would not move her. Channel 50 feet wide. We got our hawser to a mangrove tree and by the united efforts of the engines and Mac in the motor boat and the Capt. and Maunsell and Roan on the windlass she came off in an hour. Passed through the lovely winding Lower Jupiter Narrows into Hobe Sound where we anchored for the night off the Olympia Beach Club.

Saturday, February 16, 1924.

Left Olympia of the Very Mortals at 9:30, and took our time, going aground two or three times, finally reaching Palm Beach at 4. M.S.C. ashore for mail and papers. Spent several hours trying to find out why the world continues to move on in our absence.

Sunday, February 17, 1924.

In the morning M.S.C. and I went ashore and motored all over Palm Beach for an hour; not having been here since 1904 I found the growth of mushroom millionaires' houses luxuriant. The women we saw went well with the place—

and we desired to meet them no more than we wished to remain in the harbor even an hour more than necessary. Up anchor at 1 and with starboard engine running well and port engine coughing spasmodically we got down to the South end of Lake Worth and anchored for the night.

Monday, February 18, 1924.

During the night we dragged and all hands were called to get her under way and back into the channel. Started through Canal at 9. Very bad as there are many boulders along it and in it. Port engine very sick—too sick to be moved most of the time, so we had Mac ahead towing us in the launch. Tied up in Canal just above Hillsboro Inlet.

Tuesday, February 19, 1924.

Maunsell to date has seen 98 different varieties of birds. He had a walk ashore last evening and added 8 species. We ran aground six times today—very bad water—at one place, just below New River Inlet, the yacht Capts. accuse the local Fort Lauderdale people with dumping rocks into the channel to make repairs necessary and bring trade! Painted chairs most of the p.m. We had to wait just below the inlet for 3 hours till the tide rose.

Wednesday, February 20, 1924.

Started at 7. All went well till we got to Dumbfoundling Lake—well named. Ran aground at S. end trying to let another yacht by. Port engine in comatose condition again. Just as we got to N. end of Biscayne Bay we blew into the bushes—broke two windows—a barge came along and towed us four miles, part way down the Bay. Anchored. M.S.C. went on to Miami for food and telegrams. They had just left when we had an hour of bad rain squalls. At 4 started up again. Ran through the bridges successfully, both engines working, went up the Miami River and moored to dock on right bank just short of the first bridge. Miami or Bust. Bust lost. So endeth a three [weeks'] voyage.

Thursday, February 21, 1924.

Miami. M.S.C. shopped, opened bank account for me etc. in the morning. Engine doctor began diagnosis. In p.m. with M.S.C. motored to Miami Beach, called on the James M. Cox's who were out, went to Cocoanut Grove, called on Wm. J. Bryan, who came out to the car and we had a nice talk.

Friday, February 22, 1924.

Miami. Engine doctor still at work. His patient may respond to heroic treatment. M.S.C., Mac, Roan and I left at 10:30 in the launch, ran down to Bear Cut, trolled for an hour or so, got one small mackerel, went ashore at the point on South side where we spent three delightful days last year, had lunch, and Maunsell and I took off all raiment and swam and lay on the sand for two hours. Got back to Larooco at 5.

∽∽

MIAMI, FLORIDA
FEBRUARY 22, 1924
FRIDAY

Dearest Mama,

At last we are in Miami after many adventures with sand banks, etc. There is a good deal to be done to the boat so we shall stay here till Monday. For the past week the weather has been really heavenly and Maunsell and I have sat around in our bathing suits, though it has been too cold to swim in the inside waters. From now on however the waters of the Gulf Stream are close at hand. Today Maunsell and I took the motor boat to an inlet, fished, got out on the sandy beach, picnicked and swam and lay in the sun for hours. I know it is doing the legs good, and though I have worn the braces hardly at all, I get lots of exercise crawling around, and I know the muscles are better than ever before. Maunsell has been a delightful companion and we have any number of tastes in common from birds and forestry to collecting stamps! For the happy thought of asking him you are responsible!

February 28th. I did not post this in Miami. We got away a day late because of a violent storm and we had a fairly difficult trip down here to Angelfish Creek as it was still blowing and the Larooco is impossible to steer in a wind as she is so shallow and high and has not enough power.

We have fished and caught nothing, though Roan who stayed on board caught a dozen delicious Perch and Grunts with a handline over the stern!

I am apparently still perfectly uncertain about people coming down, no chance of deRhams, and Lang and Mary are still vague. I shall go back to Miami on March 2, and if the Marvins are not coming will try to get the Cox's to go down the Keys with me until Johnny and the girls come March 23rd.

I have loved your letters. You must have had a lovely visit at Algonac. But you say nothing of the knee and it worries me not to know that it is really better. I am very glad that you are going on for James' confirmation on March 9th. He and Elliott have both had hard times this term. I wrote Eleanor that if Elliott's cold is not wholly gone, he had best come down here for his *whole* vacation.

I am in *fine* health and spend my time painting chairs, making boats and writing a history of the United States!

A great deal of love and give my love too to the Aunts and to Uncle Fred when you see them.

Your affectionate son

FDR

Will you send this to the Poughkeepsie Savings Bank for Anna's account?

The "Cox's" were James M. Cox and his wife. John S. Lawrence's "girls" were named Eloise and Isabel; his wife, the former Emma Atherton, was a leading figure in Boston and North Shore society, as well as a distinguished horse-woman and a contributor to *The Atlantic Monthly*.

∽∽

The rough draft of F.D.R.'s "history of the United States" was recently found along with his aforementioned script on John Paul Jones. Penned on yellow 8½″ x 14″ lined paper, the fourteen-page document contains innumerable ink blots and arrows where F.D.R. corrected words and sentences and then linked them with each other. Like his John Paul Jones effort, F.D.R. did not complete this history of the United States; he barely entered upon an analysis of the conditions which led to the discovery of America. The first page of the draft has been lost, but the remainder of the text is printed herewith in the corrected form that F.D.R. intended, except that incomplete sentences where he planned further revisions have not been altered.

The manuscript is both interesting of itself, and appropriate to a collection of letters whose main purpose is to trace the growth of personality. It is the only material evidence of a frequently expressed contention, that F.D.R. spent the years of convalescence mainly engaged in philosophical speculation, which in due course gave birth to the doctrines that he sponsored as governor of New York and President of the United States. This claim is perhaps over-balanced. He did do more philosophic thinking than in previous years, but it was certainly not his primary pursuit. The "History" further reveals the extent and nature of F.D.R.'s academic investigations during this period. It indicates that he was not only a firm advocate of the cause and effect theory of history, but also that he was particularly concerned about the relation of the various classes of society to each other.

. . . for lack of general record. It is therefore more correct to say that the Columbus discovery was the first which became a part of the world's knowledge.

Many other factors contribute to the thought that the period itself was the discoverer of America, and Columbus the agent of his time. Medieval history, the "feudal age" was coming to a close; modern history—the revival of learning—was arriving. To understand the next century of further discoveries it is needful to examine the background.

Europe in the year 1000 was highly primitive. Peoples were not far past the tribal state. Horrible barbarities were still the rule. Learning was looked down on by the war lords, unknown to the populace, indulged in only by a minority of the priesthood. From this chaos came the feudal system, a beginning of the modern permanent organization of society. With it arose a defining of land ownership, a clear division of humanity into classes, a lessening of barbarous and inhuman practices, an institution of a code of conduct, and a distinct surge of religious faith.

This last found voice in the epoch of the Crusades. It is little realized that the spiritual enthusiasm which launched seven major expeditions and a dozen minor efforts against the Mohammedan from 1096 to 1270 accomplished in the end more for civilization and democracy than any previous event. Knighthood and overlordship took on responsibilities to others. Feudal barons were taught to look beyond their own castle domains, and to work with other individuals to a common end. With travel came the desire for the products of other lands and organized trade commenced by land and sea throughout Europe. From this quickening of intercourse and growth of travel came however the most important result, for the Crusades required money, and equipment, and the interchange of goods and supplies. It was natural that at once the growth of villages into towns and cities became marked. Merchants became a class, skilled artisans developed the dignity of trades, money lenders who financed the needs of the feudal lords grew into bankers. Thus a middle class grew up, different from the serfs upon the land, different from the fighting men-at-arms, and with their acquisition of money and property came the demand for certain rights of government. By the end of the fourteenth century the burghers of the cities of Europe were to be reckoned with as a factor in wealth, in learning and even in battle.

One other element had entered into the political life of the times. The great Ecclesiastics wielded powers more secular than priestly. Bishops made and unmade kings, led armies, owned vast tracts of land and exercised wholly feudal relations to their countless tenants. The Church became a political factor.

Down at the bottom of the heap of humanity, but comprising by far the greater part of the whole, lay the serfs—slaves to their barons or bishops—servants to their burghers. Actually there was far less freedom as we know it for the great mass of the European population than their ancestors had enjoyed under the tribal conditions which prevailed in the days of Roman supremacy. In all Europe, even in England, the land was wholly owned by the greater and the lesser nobles and the dignitaries of the Church. A mere handful of humanity, certainly less than one in a hundred, owned and controlled the very lives and fortunes of the other ninety-nine.

All through the eleventh, twelfth, thirteenth and fourteenth centuries Europe was an armed camp. When the overlords were not making a mad dash for the Holy Land they were waging hot war against their neighbors. Ruling houses rose and fell. Kingdoms and duchies were created and fell apart. Brothers fought brothers, sons overthrew their fathers, rival Popes excommunicated one another, whole fair provinces were bartered away, and to us moderns these years seem a mad kaleidoscopic scramble for power and plunder. The rule was that the man went under who did not attack and crush his neighbor first.

Yet through these centuries up to the year 1400 certain events of truly great significance to the future of civilization took place. Commerce produced better roads on land and better ships at sea. The Crusades gave some knowledge of the East and an interest in geography. Independent communities in which at least some fair share of the inhabitants had a voice in the government came with the growth of towns. In England the bill of rights called Magna Charta was granted. The beginnings of the Swiss Confederacy were formed, and it is safe to say that by the early part of the 15th Century a larger number of people than ever before were talking of what we would call the rudiments of science and art and letters and government. At best this number was but a handful, yet it gave promise of the great strides to come.

In 1450 came the discovery of printing; in 1453 occurred the fall of Constantinople resulting in the search for a new way to the East, and a dispersal of the Eastern scholars through Europe carrying with them the classics, and a new enthusiasm for the sciences. Beginning in 1461 Louis XI of France put down the power of the great feudal lords and established his absolute monarchy. In all countries a growing protest over the abuses of the churchly power; in Spain the conquest of Granada and in Portugal the important discoveries of the Madeira, Cape Verde and Azore Islands, and the West Coast of Africa under the patronage of Henry the Navigator. Universities had increased in number and patronage.

In short, by the year 1492 the imagination of thousands in Europe was on fire. Not the populace by any means, but at least more than a handful of people were thinking in larger terms than ever before. Scholars were interchanging theories and facts by means of printed books, and these very books were being read by mere laymen. So too the commercial needs of times demanded new worlds to conquer. The short route to the East was shut off by the Turk, yet the story of what Marco Polo had found in the Far East was still remembered. New profits were dreamed of by the merchants, new adventures by the knights and sailors, new kingdoms by the rulers and princes.

This was the atmosphere in which Columbus grew to manhood, and that is why it has been said that America was discovered by the era. It is perhaps not stretching the point to assert that definite knowledge of America to the European world was bound to come at the end of the 15th Century.

EXPLORATION

For nearly a century and a quarter colonization of America held back. The time was not yet ripe. By colonization we mean an emigration from the older world by men and women and children who, leaving their homes, intend to establish new homes and with their descendants live and die in the new land. Thousands of Europeans came to the New World from 1492 to 1607, but they came for exploration, for conquest, for gold, for fur, for fish—all, except a handful, intending to return richer in pocket or in knowledge or in power to their Old World homes.

We are often inclined to think that aside from the Spaniards in Panama and Peru and Mexico only a very few explorers visited the other parts of North and South America. We have read for instance of the voyages of the Cabots, of Vespucius, of Balboa, of Cortez and Pizarro, of Jacques Cartier, of deSoto and Ponce de Leon, of Coronado and Frobisher, Landonnière and Grenville. Our school histories tell of these and a dozen more, and historical research has revealed the names of several score others who led expeditions to the new land. Are we then to assume that in all that century a few hundred ships only crossed the Atlantic to North

America? Such is the impression given, yet it is wholly false. What a ridiculous assumption to teach that Henry Hudson in 1609 was the first to enter the river that bears his name; or that Chesapeake Bay was first seen by the Virginia colonists in 1607; or that the Pilgrims were the first to see Cape Cod in 1620.

First of all Spain obtained the honor of capitalizing the discoveries. During the whole of the 16th Century, indeed, no other nation seriously undertook to develop the new world. English mariners grew rich indeed in the occupation of robbing the Spanish galleons, but these galleons were heavy laden with treasure because of the enterprise and imagination of the subjects of His Most Catholic Majesty. The conquest of Mexico, and of Peru, the founding of great cities in Central and South America, the building of cathedrals, the establishment of universities, the whole creation of a new civilization in the Spanish parts of America—all had been undertaken, had reached their zenith and had commenced to decline before ever Jamestown or Plymouth were conceived. It was a false glory, that of Spain. For mostly men came, leaving behind them their mothers and sisters and wives. So it was that a hybrid race grew up, part cavalier, part Indian, later on in part negro. All was staked on the great adventure. Glorious riches to be gained for little labor, all in a land whose fabled wealth was magnified a thousand times beyond reality. Nothing in the method of these Spanish cavaliers made for a sound and permanent colonization. Their whole object from King to soldier was exploitation— to get as much out of it in as short a time as possible.

Everything from Mexico and Florida southward to Magellan's Straits, was under the influence of the Spanish and the Portuguese, and their ships in vast numbers plied the waters on both the Atlantic and Pacific coasts. It would be unwarranted to assume that their mariners, well versed by now in the arts of navigation, were never visitors to the more northern coasts of what are today the United States and Canada. When we consider that the records of only a very small percentage of the Spanish voyages to the southward have survived to this day, it is not to be wondered at that we know practically nothing of their navigators who saw and visited the shores of the Carolinas, the Virginias and New England.

From the other approach came many vessels also. As early as 1504 French fishermen were on the Grand Banks, and soon hundreds of vessels from France and Northern Europe were drying their nets on Newfoundland and Nova Scotia. Surely some of them, seeking new grounds, became familiar with our whole Atlantic coast line. Other shipmasters seeking furs or the ever hoped for Northwest Passage to the Indies skirted our shores.

Thus it was that before even the English colonies were settled scores, probably hundreds of vessels, had visited the region. It is easy to understand why we have such scanty records of these voyages: Everything militated against their recording. First of all there was the need of secrecy. To publish the news of a new harbor, or of a place to fish, or of a friendly tribe of Indians ready to sell furs meant competition the following year; furthermore it might mean armed attack by other nations. If some French fishermen established a base in some safe harbor from which to conduct their operations, a printed recital of their doings might bring down on them English or Spanish marauders. So it was that there came to be a premium on secrecy, much to the loss of history.

The other cause of the paucity of records is the lack of learning of the time. Shipmasters could navigate by rule of thumb but it did not follow that they could read or write or draw maps, and it was an exceptional case when any record of a voyage was set down on paper at all. Books, even a hundred years after Gutenberg, were an event; publication only of facts of apparent grave importance to the world was undertaken. Newspapers were non-existent; their predecessor handbills were read and used to light the fire. The only wonder is that we have any surviving records of the voyages of those early days. All we can surely say is that thousands saw and knew our shores, but none remained.

Near the bottom of the fourteenth page of the original draft, F.D.R.'s "history of the United States" terminates. The log of the *Larooco* is now resumed.

∽∽

Saturday, February 23, 1924.
Port engine still being worked over. M.A.L. arrived at 1. Much hard work making the boat spick and span. Grand tea party in p.m. Gov and Mrs. Cox, Tim Ansberry, Ed. N. Hurley, Col. and Mrs. Van Tassel. They stayed till after seven. M.A.L. poured tea, and M.S.C. mixed "Larooco drinks."

Sunday, February 24, 1924.
We all, including Capt and Mrs. Morris, went down to Bear Cut in the morning in the launch. Fished in rain, landed at Beach on South side, had lunch and then a grand swimming party followed by sun bath. Home at 5, a final parcheesi match and M.S.C. left for home at 10 p.m. He saw 99 different bird species on the trip. We shall miss him much.

Monday, February 25, 1924.
M.A.L. and Mrs. Morris ashore shopping. In the p.m. a drive to Miami Beach to call on J. C. Penney etc.

Tuesday, February 26, 1924.
Tied up at dock all day because of engine repairs—too much wind to go down Biscayne Bay anyway.

Wednesday, February 27, 1924.
Left Miami at 10 and went down the Bay and anchored inside Pumpkin Key, close to the mouth of Angelfish Creek.

M.A.L. experienced the first pangs of Mal de Mer as it blew hard on the way down from the West and gave us a good roll. In late p.m. tied up inside Creek.

Thursday, February 28, 1924.

Went in launch with Mac and M.A.L. to get mail etc. at Key Largo. On way down were greatly delayed by trolling and failing to find N. entrance to Jewfish Creek. Finally started on return trip at 6:30 p.m. It was dark by the time we got out of Jewfish Creek. Steered by the stars for the South entrance of Steamboat Creek—missed it—passing it at least three times within 100 feet in the dark. Gave it up at 9 p.m. Tried to find the channels W. of the Island, found one line of stakes—lost the next—aground badly three or four times, got through at last—made Pumpkin Key by great luck and ran into Angelfish Creek without even seeing the marker which we must have passed within 50 feet. Back on board at 11:30 p.m.!

Friday, February 29, 1924.

Recuperating at Angelfish after yesterday's adventures. Caught a few small fish.

Saturday, March 1, 1924.

Went back to Key Largo in the launch, taking lunch with us this time, caught no fish, but found a lot of mail. Got back in time for one of Mrs. Morris's delightful suppers.

Sunday, March 2, 1924.

A lovely warm lazy day. Fished for angelfish, grunts, etc. and got enough for a meal.

Monday, March 3, 1924.

Left Angelfish Creek after breakfast and ran through to Miami in 5½ hours. Tied up again in the River and took on supplies and did shopping.

Tuesday, March 4, 1924.

At Miami. Got the sad news that John Lawrence—½ owner of and partner in this ancient craft cannot come down to join us as he has to go abroad. A few hours later however a wire came from L. Davis saying he is coming soon. Sent many telegrams and letters and telephoned several people in Miami.

Wednesday, March 5, 1924.

A wire from E.R. says Anna probably cannot come but that Elliott will. Just after lunch Miss Eleanor Hennessy, an old friend of M.A.L.'s arrived from Palm Beach for a week on board. At 4:30 we had another tea party on deck, Mr. and Mrs. William H. Kelly of Syracuse—the Democratic leader,—and Mr. J. C. Penney, the chain store man who has a large farm near Hopewell Junction, Dutchess Co. Much discussion of cows, politics and boy-scouts.

Thursday, March 6, 1924.

Left Miami early and ran down the bay to Barnes Sound, anchoring about half way between Steamboat and Jewfish Creeks. Caught a nice mess of crawfish in the evening. I forgot to mention that Geo. Dyer left us in Miami to go home to Rhode Island. He was not really happy on board and was also I think not well. I do not know that he was inefficient with his engines but he certainly did not keep them clean. Mac (Myles McNichols) has taken over George's work and has from his own account had a good deal of engine experience.

Friday, March 7, 1924.

Moved into Jewfish Creek. Rain, high wind, and engine trouble. E.H., M.A.L. and F.D.R. fished in the Creek and caught various mangrove snappers, grunts etc. Roan is however the enthusiastic champion with the small fish.

Saturday, March 8, 1924.

Left Jewfish Creek about 11, lunched on deck enroute, and got down to the mouth of Tavernier Creek about 4. The Captain went ashore, got mail and some provisions.

Sunday, March 9, 1924.

As a blow threatened we moved Larooco into Tavernier Creek. E.H., M.A.L. and F.D.R. went through the Creek to the Ocean and landed at the Alburys' little dock at Tavernier. Almost all inhabitants of the settlement are Alburys —those not so named are at least close relatives. We swam in the p.m.

Monday, March 10, 1924.

It blew too hard to go fishing on the reef, so we fished in the creek and went swimming again at the delightful beach on the Bay side of the settlement.

Tuesday, March 11, 1924.

All hands went reef fishing in Mr. M. R. Albury's launch. It was pretty rough and we only got two Cero Mackerel and two Barracuda.

Wednesday, March 12, 1924.

Miss Hennessy left us at noon—very sad not to be able to wait to meet the attractions of Davis who comes next Sunday.

Thursday, March 13, 1924.

Blowing hard all day. Stayed in Creek.

Friday, March 14, 1924.

Ditto. This year has been considered a very poor one as to weather down here—a lot of wind, large temperature changes etc.

Saturday, March 15, 1924.

A grand fishing party in the Albury launch to the reef. We got nearly 20 Barracuda, Cero Mackerel and Spanish Mackerel. Mrs. Morris caught several and the water was smooth. A grand day.

Sunday, March 16, 1924.

Livingston Davis arrived at 1 p.m. weighted down with sundry wet and dry goods,—he looks like a sick child and is recuperating from shingles, boils, bunions and cold in the head. A blowy day and we stayed in Tavernier Creek, L.D. unpacking fishing gear and I making boats.

Monday, March 17, 1924.

Water too cold to swim and wind too high to go to reef. L.D. went to the R.R. bridge to fish and came back minus trousers—to the disgust of the two ladies. Earlier he had exercised on the top deck a la nature. Why do people who *must* take off their clothes go anywhere where the other sex is present? Capt. Morris remarked that some men get shot for less.

Tuesday, March 18, 1924.

To the reef with L.D. in M. L. Albury's launch. At Pickles reef we found a lee from the swell and got all the fishing we wanted. Caught in all—35 fish—L.D. 17 and F.D.R. 18—mostly Cero Mackerel and Barracuda—but including 2 Yellow Jacks and several Spanish Mackerel. A shark took a mackerel I was bringing in and I played him for several minutes before he went off with my fish, spoon, and wire inside of him. Our day's catch ran well over 250 pounds of fish.

Wednesday, March 19, 1924.

L.D. went off to the stream alone with Albury, gone all day. It was very hot and the mosquitos began, so at noon we moved Larooco out of the Creek. M.A.L. and F.D.R. went swimming.

Thursday, March 20, 1924.

After lunch fished with Albury for small grunts and sailor's-choice off Tavernier Key on the Ocean side. On our

556

return we picked up Mrs. Albury and Marjorie, aged 4, to show them the Larooco. When we got to her a heavy storm was rapidly approaching from the West. We tried to get up anchor to enter the Creek but in backing the rowboat was swamped, all her insides were scattered broadcast over the face of the waters—Albury picked most of them up. Then his painter got foul of our port propeller. Hell to pay. Davis got the awning off but had to disrobe to do it as it was raining. We got out the other anchor and tied everything down and trusted to Heaven that she wouldn't blow ashore. Mrs. Albury and the little girl stayed on board and they all slept on the cot and big mattress in the living room.

Friday, March 21, 1924.

Mac ashore in the launch to get the mail etc. He was held up by the tide at the RR bridge. It blew a gale all day. He showed up at 6:30 p.m., stopped his engine too soon, couldn't start it, drifted off into the darkness and Capt. Morris rowed downwind and found him aground. They got back safely. All this day we have feared she would drift or the anchor chain go, but she has come through it all right and the wind is dying down this evening.

Saturday, March 22, 1924.

Wind much moderated. Engines both working. Off early.

∽∽

No entries for March 23rd to April 4th appear in the *Larooco* log.

∽∽

Saturday, April 5, 1924.

L. Davis waved from the train departing for Key West at 8:30 a.m. He was seen by Mrs. Morris who shook a towel at him in reply. We had a quiet morning and after lunch M.A.L., Mrs. Morris and I went round to the Ocean side of

Long Key and had a fine "bathe" in shallow water—sharks playing outshore from us—At 5 Mr. Schutt Jr., the manager of the Fishing Camp, and Mr. Bow, the Division engineer of the Florida East Coast Ry., came on board and we had a pleasant hour. In the evening word came from Mr. M. R. Albury that he or his brother would come down in their launch from Tavernier tomorrow.

Sunday, April 6, 1924.

A quiet morning answering lots of mail and exercising with canes and crutches. In the p.m. M.A.L. and I went up and down the Trestle for 2 hours in the launch with Capt. Morris and had a very exciting time. At the start I hooked a tarpon on a spoon on my light rod and reel with no brakes on it. He jumped twice at the start, took out two hundred feet of line, burned a bad blister on my thumb but was still on. I got him in a little, he jumped again, ran out again and I stopped him by letting the handle of the little reel bump past my palm. He was on for 8 minutes and then the hook pulled out! He looked like a fish of about 30 pounds.

That was only the start. In a few minutes I landed a fine Kingfish, about 12 pounds, then M.A.L. got a grouper, next a very big 7 lb. snapper—then we ended up with two jacks, another big grouper, another snapper and two Spanish Mackerel.

At 8 p.m., after dark, the Albury launch turned up, in a fairly rough sea, with M. R. Albury's brother. Capt. Morris was wondering why he did not come aboard more quickly, "heard a squawk," asked what that was and Albury answered, "I've got my wife and baby"! So here is the whole family— wife 17 years old and baby 16 months. They are about to go to bed in the guest stateroom.

Monday, April 7, 1924.

It blew hard all morning. M.A.L. went ashore to pay the bill at the Fishing Camp. At 2:30 we got under way as the wind seemed decreasing and with starboard engine running fitfully and the Albury launch lashed to port side and the little motor pushing astern we ambled along about 17 miles to near McGinty Key and anchored for the night. Mrs. Albury Jr. and Baby left at Long Key and took train!

Tuesday, April 8, 1924.

A heavenly day. Under way at 8, and anchored off Tavernier—landside at 10—We had a grand swim while the Capt. and young Albury went ashore. Mr. M. Albury, the storekeeper, came over to the beach and we had a long talk about the possibility of his starting a gas, water and yacht supply base at Tavernier. At 1:30 M. R. Albury came on board with his wife and Marjorie, 4 years old, grand chance to go free to Miami! They were given the guest stateroom! We started and kept on going without a hitch, through Jewfish drawbridge and anchored for the night in Barnes Sound.

Wednesday, April 9, 1924.

At 7:30 M.A.L. and Mrs. Morris went to Key Largo to see if any telegrams were there and to tip the telegraph man, Mr. Barcus, who has been very kind. We got under way at 10 and had a splendid run with the wind aft. Starboard engine running well and the Albury launch pushing on the port side. Just before we got to the channel two miles S. of Miami the launch engine went wrong and we anchored for the night.

Thursday, April 10, 1924.

Started on the last leg of the cruise. Just after we rounded the point to go into the Miami River the steering cable broke but we had enough headway to get to the Royal Palm dock. The good old craft is thus safely moored after many adventures. The engines have of course given all sorts of trouble, in fact they have been the source of every untoward happening but we knew when she started from N.Y. that the engines were old and would give trouble, and only people with bad indigestion, chronic grouch or bad nerves worried when things went a little less smoothly than if we had the engines running right.

Friday, April 11, 1924.

Seeing people about laying up Larooco and putting new engines in her. Also started packing, and putting away linen, china, etc. In the p.m. went in the launch to Bear's Cut and had a fine swim.

Saturday, April 12, 1924.

To Bear's Cut again in the launch for a swim. Busy packing and getting ready to go out of commission.

Sunday, April 13, 1924.

Capt and Mrs. Morris, M.A.L. and I went to Bear's Cut for a picnic lunch and final swim. At sundown Larooco went out of commission and at 10:30 p.m. ½ owner F.D.R. left for N.Y. Larooco goes to yard tomorrow and will be cared for during summer by Atlantic Boat Works. So ends Cruise No. 1.

~~~

Soon after F.D.R. returned from Florida, on May 1, 1924, he assumed the management of Governor Alfred E. Smith's pre-convention campaign for the Democratic Presidential nomination. Smith's record during his second term as governor of New York had greatly increased his stature, and when the Ku Klux Klan announced its support of the other leading contender, William Gibbs McAdoo, his candidacy became a formidable movement. As his strength continued to grow throughout the Northern states, Smith and his associates decided to conduct an active pre-convention campaign; but it was not so easy to find a director for the organized movement. Charles F. Murphy had died several months before and the heir to his position had not yet appeared; the New York delegation was therefore without any close connections in national politics. The choice of F.D.R. as chairman of the campaign committee was a natural one: he and his wife had both announced their support of Smith's candidacy early in February; he had a name which added national prestige to the movement and provided the necessary contacts outside of the state; and his endorsement meant greater recognition by all the Wilson Democrats. Some of Smith's advisers furthermore believed that F.D.R.'s crippled state would not enable him to be an active director of the campaign, and that their will could therefore be freely exercised.

F.D.R. was not disinclined to become more active in politics. He had kept in touch with political developments during his convalescence, and his desire to participate directly in political events had revived. He felt that the management of a campaign was not of such long duration as to counteract his efforts to regain his health, and he thus accepted the position, taking full and vigorous charge of the campaign.

Late in May, after having searched futilely for a prominent and capable speaker to place his name in nomination, Smith finally asked F.D.R. to make the address. It was not the usual procedure to choose one's campaign manager to give the nominating speech, but Smith could visualize no alternative and F.D.R. again accepted his offer. The Democratic convention met in New York's Madison Square Garden late in June, 1924; on the twenty-sixth F.D.R. was brought to the rostrum in a wheel chair, used crutches to advance to the speaker's desk, and then delivered one of his most famous speeches:

. . . He has a power to strike at error and wrongdoing that makes his adversaries quail before him. He has a personality that carries to every hearer not only the sincerity but the righteousness of what he says. He is the "Happy Warrior" of the political battlefield. . . .

The campaign chairmanship and address at Madison
Square Garden was F.D.R.'s only major, public political
effort between 1921 and 1928, and it was everywhere received with great enthusiasm. Only July 1st, the day after
the balloting began, "Looker On" remarked in the *Herald
Tribune:*

. . . While the results of the futile ballots were droned
from the platform in the Garden yesterday, there sat in
the exact center of the great hall the one man whose name
would stampede the convention were he put in nomination.
He is the only man to whom the contending factions could
turn and at the same time save their faces and keep square
with the folks at home. And that man does not want the
nomination and actually would be alarmed if he knew what
people were saying about him in the delegations and
in the lower labyrinths of the building. . . . From the time
Roosevelt made his speech in nomination of Smith, which
was the one great speech of the convention, he has been
easily the foremost figure on floor or platform. That is not
because of his name. There are many Roosevelts. It is because, without the slightest intention or desire to do anything of the sort, he has done for himself what he could not
do for his candidate.

Believing Roosevelt to be out of reach, the delegates cast
a lingering look at him over their shoulders and renewed
the search for somebody who could be nominated. . . .
But always back to Roosevelt their gaze would go, and
more than once it was found expedient to hush a little delegation which was talking about sending up his name, lest
unforeseen results might happen. . . .

Six days later the *Evening World* also commented on
F.D.R.'s activities at the convention:

. . . No matter whether Governor Smith wins or loses,
Franklin D. Roosevelt stands out as the real hero of the
Democratic Convention of 1924.

Adversity has lifted him above the bickering, the religious bigotry, conflicting personal ambitions and petty sectional prejudices. It has made him the one leader commanding the respect and admiration of delegations from all sections of the land. . . . Roosevelt might be a pathetic, tragic figure but for the fine courage that flashes in his smile. It holds observers enchained. . . .

F.D.R.'s work for Smith proved to be in vain. After the deadlock between Smith and McAdoo had continued past a hundred ballots, the convention wearied and finally agreed upon a compromise candidate, John W. Davis of West Virginia, a conservative and able lawyer who had been Ambassador to England during the last years of the Wilson Administration. In order to appease the more radical elements of the party, Governor Charles W. Bryan of Nebraska, brother of "W.J.B.," was nominated for Vice-President.

In the meantime, the Republicans had met in Cleveland, where on the first ballot they overwhelmingly named Calvin Coolidge and General Charles G. Dawes as their standard bearers. The former had convinced the electorate that he had not been aware of the oil scandals of the Harding Administration until after they were brought into the open; this fact assured the President's nomination by his party. In the course of the campaign the Democrats accused Coolidge of indirectly participating in the Harding scandals, but the accusations were proven to be ill-founded. The real opposition to continued Republican rule came from another source. Claiming that Coolidge "had literally turned his back on the farmer," Senator Robert M. La Follette organized an Independent-Progressive party composed mainly of insurgent Republicans dissatisfied with the conservatism of the Harding-Coolidge Administration. With the endorsement of the Farmer-Labor Party, the Socialist Party, the executive council of the American Federation of Labor, and the railroad brotherhoods, the third party nominated La Follette for President and

Senator Burton K. Wheeler of Montana as his running mate at Cleveland on July 4th.

As Smith had served the customary two terms, later in July F.D.R. was offered the Democratic nomination for governor of New York, but he quickly turned it down with the announcement that he would not seek public office until he no longer needed crutches. There being no other suitable candidates, the precedent was broken and Smith accepted his third nomination for the post.

~~~

F.D.R.'s refusal to participate further in politics was based on a sincere desire to return to the political arena only when equipped for all eventualities. Furthermore, George Foster Peabody, a New York banker and philanthropist, had recently told F.D.R. of a young man afflicted with infantile paralysis who had learned to walk with canes by spending several summers swimming in a pool at an old resort in Warm Springs, Georgia. Peabody had recently bought an interest in Warm Springs's Meriwether Inn, a dilapidated, rundown hotel; and through the lessee-manager of the Inn, Thomas Loyless, Peabody had heard the account of Louis Joseph's improvement. F.D.R., impatient to find a swifter cure for his legs, was impressed by the story. Hence, early in October, 1924, he went with A.E.R. to Warm Springs to spend three weeks investigating the seemingly impossible recovery of Joseph, and it was on this eventful occasion that he resumed his family correspondence.

WARM SPRINGS
[OCTOBER, 1924]
SATURDAY

Dearest Mama,

We are here safely and I think Eleanor has written you this morning. I spent over an hour in the pool this a.m. and it is really wonderful and will I think do great good, though the Dr. says it takes three weeks to show the effects.

Everyone is most kind and this afternoon Mr. Loyless has taken us for a motor trip through the surrounding country—many peach orchards but also a good deal of neglect and poverty.

The cottage is delightful and very comfortable and with Roy and Mary the cook bequeathed to us by the Hart's who own the cottage we shall be most comfortable. The Loyless family are next door.

It is too bad that Eleanor has to leave so soon, but she and I both feel it is important for her not to be away the end of the campaign as long as I have to be myself.

I will write you again soon and in the meantime you can be sure that I am really taking all the precautions of a cure and getting every minute's worth out of it.

A great deal of love and kiss the chicks.

Your devoted son
FDR

The "Dr." refers to James Johnson of nearby Manchester, who later became the consulting physician to the Georgia Warm Springs Foundation. He knew very little about polio at this time, but from the case of Louis Joseph was able to advise that "it takes three weeks to show the effects." Thomas Loyless had formerly been the editor of the *Atlanta Constitution,* but had been forced to relinquish his position with the rise of the Ku Klux Klan after the war. William Hart was a regular resident of Warm Springs, while the two other persons mentioned were F.D.R.'s servants for these first few weeks.

∽∽

WARM SPRINGS
[OCTOBER, 1924]
SUNDAY

Dearest E,

It is just a week since you left, but the time has passed almost without our realizing it, as the life is just the same day after day and there is no variety to give landmarks. The mornings are as you know wholly taken up with the pool and four of the afternoons we have sat out on the lawn or as Roy calls it the "yard," and I have worked at stamps or cheques or accounts or have played rummy with Missy. The other three afternoons we have gone motoring with Mr. and Mrs. Loyless and have seen the country pretty thoroughly. I like him ever so much and she is nice but not broad in her interests, but she chatters away to Missy on the back seat and I hear an occasional yes or no from Missy to prove she is not sleeping.

The legs are really improving a great deal. The walking and general exercising in the water is fine and I have worked out some special exercises also. This is really a discovery of a place and there is no doubt that I've got to do it some more.

Various people came over Sunday. The Harts to stay with the Hudsons a block away, and today the pool was very gay, at least twenty people.

Thank Louis for the papers and tell him I hear nothing of interest.

I have a hunch that Davis' strength is really improving, but I still think the election will go into the house. Anyway, I am philosophic enough to think that even if Coolidge is elected we shall be so darned sick of conservatism of the old money-controlled crowd in four years that we [will] get a real progressive landslide in 1928.

Much love, take care of yourself.

Your devoted

FDR

F.D.R.'s belief that "the election will go into the House" prevailed in the ranks of both major parties. It was based on the argument that La Follette and his third party would carry enough of the Western states to prevent a majority in the Electoral College, therefore throwing the election into the House of Representatives. On election day, however, Coolidge swept the nation, gaining a popular plurality of seven million votes and an electoral majority of 382 to 136 for Davis. Although La Follette received four and a half million votes, a half-million more than T.R. was accorded in 1912, he was able to carry only his own state of Wisconsin and its 13 electoral votes. In Congress the Republicans won a majority of fifteen in the Senate and sixty in the House; their victory was so overwhelming that the insurgent third party was stripped of its power. Yet F.D.R.'s prediction of "a real progressive landslide in 1928" was not altogether ill-founded, for the mid-term elections of 1926 witnessed a public reaction to the "conservatism of the old money-controlled crowd" to such an extent that the Republican majority was wiped out in the Senate, and reduced to thirty-six in the House.

∽

WARM SPRINGS
[AUTUMN, 1924]
SUNDAY

Dearest Mama:

It is most exciting to hear that you have actually rented the house from November 15th and I hope they are nice people and that you got at least $10,000. When I get back I will clean out all my stuff from the closet in your house, so you can let the tenants have that and lock up only your own closet under the stairs. Also the actual getting of the stateroom on the Italian line makes the trip seem very close. When I get back I hope to come up to Hyde Park practically every Sunday till you go and to take a whole week at Christmas.

I enclose three cheques for Anna's account in the Savings Bank and also cheque for $210.30 for the wood account which I entirely forgot to give you.

The heavenly weather here continues, we have not had a single rainy day since coming, and I spend my full two hours at the pool every morning. Every other afternoon I have been driving with the Loyless's and have got to know both the surrounding country and most of the neighbors. On Wednesday the people of Warm Springs are giving me a supper and reception in the Town Hall and on Friday evening, our last day, I am to go to Manchester, 5 miles an hour for another supper and speech. I think every organization and town in Georgia has asked me to some kind of a party, and Missy spends most of her time keeping up a huge and constant local correspondence.

When I get back I am going to have a long talk with Mr. George Foster Peabody who is really the controlling interest in the property. I feel that a great "cure" for infantile paralysis and kindred diseases could well be established here.

Roy is faithful and seems to like it. He is chauffeur as well as butler and valet. Mary the cook is typical southerner but her cooking is good and all she needs is supervision!

Much love. I will be back in New York on Monday morning and hope to get up to Hyde Park on Wednesday evening.

Your devoted son

FDR

As can be gathered from these last three letters, F.D.R. was immediately enthusiastic about the possibilities of Warm Springs as a cure both for himself and for other paralytics. During his first brief visit to the Meriwether pool he had made greater progress with his legs than in all the three preceding years. As a result of his visit he felt life in his toes for the first time since August, 1921; this improvement alone was enough to make him become a frequent visitor to Warm Springs. And a kindred feeling for all who suffered as he did sponsored his idea of making Warm Springs into a center for the treatment of infantile paralysis victims.

F.D.R. did not know at the time the medical reasons for the improvement he experienced through swimming in this pool fed by natural warm springs, but he did know that it was a great help to paralyzed muscles. The remedial effects of the pool at Warm Springs derive from the temperature and enervating quality of the water. Prior to F.D.R.'s first visit to Georgia, Dr. Lovett had found that greater success in treating infantile paralysis could be achieved with swimming and exercises in warm water. Water relieves the limbs of the weight of gravity, thereby allowing weak and unused muscles to respond more easily and to be exercised for greater lengths of time without strain. Dr. Lovett preferred warm water because the patient could exercise longer without being chilled. The peculiar quality of the water at Warm Springs, which enables a patient to remain in it for one or two hours without being fatigued, was thus of great value in the treatment of infantile paralysis. Geologists have since explained this natural phenomenon by the fact that the rain which falls on Pine Mountain, several miles away, runs down 3800 feet to a vast pocket of rock, is then warmed by the inner earth, and returned to the surface at a temperature of 88°F. and at a rate of 800 gallons per minute. Engineers estimate that twenty tons of coal a day would be required to equal this gift of nature.

F.D.R. returned to New York early in November of 1924 convinced more than ever before that the recovery of his leg power was soon to be realized. His increased optimism is even evident in the somewhat routine letter to his uncle which is the next item of his correspondence.

NEW YORK
JANUARY 15, 1925.
THURSDAY

Dear Uncle Fred:

I am glad to know by Monday's bulletin that Aunt Tillie's fever is running a moderate course. It is too bad that she is so uncomfortable, but having had typhoid twice I can realize that this is a necessary accompaniment of the trouble. Also, it is undoubtedly better that she have a normal case of real typhoid rather than the paratyphoid which never reaches a definite turning point and is marked by a series of small flare ups.

Give her my love and tell her that the chief comfort of typhoid is that after getting over the attack itself one's general health is always vastly better.

Affectionately yours,

[F.D.R.]

Frederic A. Delano, Esq.,
Washington, D. C.

This letter is taken from a carbon copy. "Monday's bulletin" was a note about his wife's health which Frederic A. Delano had mimeographed and sent to all the members of his family.

∽∽

Two weeks after writing this letter F.D.R. departed for Florida and "Cruise Number Two" aboard the *Larooco*. Miss Le Hand and Maunsell Crosby again joined him on the second voyage, and he also took along his chauffeur, Montfort Snyder (who later went with him to the White House in the same capacity). In addition, he entertained numerous guests for brief visits, among them the de Rham family, Henry Morgenthau, Jr., F.D.R.'s neighbor and old friend from Dutchess County, Thomas Lynch, his early political adviser, and his son James. Before making the first entry in the log, F.D.R. explained the location and condition of the *Larooco* during the interval between cruises with a few introductory remarks.

1925
Larooco
Cruise Number Two
Foreword

During the past summer and autumn Larooco was laid up at Atlantic Boat Yard, Miami, and was re-engined with

2 Regal Motors. Also the steering wheel was shifted from fore cabin to top deck, and new electric light motor was installed.

The new work seems to be right, but the Yard took very bad care of the boat. Chairs and various small articles were stolen. New canvas was laid over whole of top deck. Capt. and Mrs. Morris went on board to live the end of November and helped get things in shape for going into commission.

Wednesday, February 4, 1925.

F.D.R. arrived Miami—train just 24 hours late, due to floods in Georgia and the vagaries of the Florida East Coast R.R. Went straight on board and Larooco went into commission. Rest of day spent in unpacking and shopping by Mrs. Morris and M.A.L.

Thursday, February 5, 1925.

More shopping, replacing stolen furniture (at expense of yard) and laying in supplies. In the afternoon the Executive Council of the Am. Fed. of Labor with wives etc., thirty in all, came on board and I had interesting talk with William Green, the President, and other leaders.

Friday, February 6, 1925.

More shopping etc. Bought a new rowboat to replace the one stolen.

Saturday, February 7, 1925.

After filling up with water and gas, got under way at 12:30 and proceeded down Biscayne Bay. Engines working finely. Ran into Angelfish Creek and tied up to bushes at 5:15 p.m. LeRoy Jones caught the first fish, a mangrove snapper, and enough others were caught by him and Monty Snyder to give us a meal tomorrow.

Sunday, February 8, 1925.

A quiet day in Angelfish Creek. After lunch M.A.L. and I out in launch and caught 2 big Angelfish, 3 snappers, 2 Grunts and a large Turbot.

Monday, February 9, 1925.

Left Angelfish Creek at 9:30 and had a quick run through Jewfish Creek etc., getting to Tavernier at 1:15 p.m. F.D.R. steered most of the way. Had a good swim in the afternoon and sent ashore for mail to the Albury's. The Aquarium on top deck—two wooden tubs—did not work—the fish were dead in the morning. Probably too many of them in it.

Tuesday, February 10, 1925.

Sent off a lot of mail, and had a swim in the morning. At 12:30 took launch through Creek to the Albury's at Tavernier on the Ocean side. Saw most of the tribe. Made arrangements for them to take the black kitten, the daughter of "Tweetie," last year's houseboat guest. Too rough for outside fishing so we came back. M.A.L. caught 3 jacks and a big snapper just outside the Railroad culvert.

Wednesday, February 11, 1925.

A violent thunderstorm and very heavy rain at 5 a.m. Too cold to swim today. At 1 went through Creek and out to Couch Reef with young Lou, an Albury nephew. Got some fine Barracuda fishing, over a dozen and all large size. F.D.R. landed a 35 pounder with 12 thread line and a light rod and reel without any brake on it. On way back a heavy squall with rain broke on us, we transferred to our launch at the Albury dock and came through the Creek, darkness and rain notwithstanding. Found Larooco near W. mouth of Creek, pounding heavily. Came along side, M.A.L. climbed on board safely, F.D.R. fell on floor of pounding launch and tore knee ligaments. Had to be passed in through galley window. Heavy wind and rain all night, but anchors held.

Thursday, February 12, 1925.

F.D.R.'s leg possibly broken so got under way at 10 and ran till dark getting within 2 hours of Miami.

Friday, February 13, 1925.

Reached Miami 11 a.m. M.A.L. ashore for Doctor, who came on board and diagnosed only torn and pulled ligaments and strapped leg up. Tried in vain to locate Maunsell Crosby but he had evidently left for Tavernier to find us.

Saturday, February 14, 1925.

At 1 a.m. a shout from Royal Palm Dock announced arrival of Maunsell Crosby, who had gone to Tavernier, found our message, and come back. Slept late. In p.m. had visits from Mort Newhall and Col. Van Tassel and M. Helm, the two latter in real estate business here.

Sunday, February 15, 1925.

A quiet day. Got off mail. Doctor Turner came and reported F.D.R.'s knee mending slowly. F.D.R. still in bed.

Monday, February 16, 1925.

Under way at 10:30, and made a fine run getting to Tarpan Basin at 5:30 p.m. Capt. Charles Watkins joined before leaving and will pilot us—act as fish guide below Long Key. After dark they got us a fine mess of Crawfish and a Grouper for chowder. The Parcheesi Contest got actively under way.

Tuesday, February 17, 1925.

Left Tarpan Basin at 9 and reached Tavernier at 11. M.S.C. and the Capt. went ashore and got mail and some eggs and 2 live chickens. Under way again. F.D.R. got stiff brace on leg and was carried on deck. Arrived Long Key at 4, got more mail and telegram from Tom Lynch saying he arrives tomorrow.

Wednesday, February 18, 1925.

Went to Long Key dock for gas—which we found was 34¢ though only 26¢ in Maine. Ran down to anchorage inside of

573

Channel Key as it looks like a Norther. Went back in launch for T.L. but he will not come till tomorrow.

Thursday, February 19, 1925.

Tom Lynch arrived safely on board about 9:30 a.m. looking pale (see below). Got under way and ran down to Knights Key, anchoring N. of track inside Hog Key. After lunch M.S.C. and T.L. went fishing and brought back a large mess of fish—2 jacks, 1 grouper—2 porgies and over 20 grunts.

Friday, February 20, 1925.

At anchor Hog Key. M.A.L. and T.L. went fishing—1 jack —and T.L. looks less pale. An enormous mess of crawfish in eve.

Saturday, February 21, 1925.

Back to Long Key after lunch. Got mail and ran down to Channel Key. T.L. no longer pale, is in fact putting anything on face which his friends suggest.

Sunday, February 22, 1925. Birthington's Washday.

F.D. de Rham arrived 3 hours late, but was met by the gents in launch. She caught her lunch on way back. She also looks pale. T.L. today is at opposite extreme and somewhat sensitive about it. After lunch all off to Duck Key and swam in shallow water among the sponges. Business of washing each other's backs with sea soap. After grog Missy and Frances rowed over to "Whileaway" and nearly got more grog, only they didn't know it was Mort Newhall shaking it at them. Service on deck in eve, conducted by Capt. Charlie.

Monday, February 23, 1925.

Another washday. All much disturbed in night by M.S.C. who dreamed he was a pink Bazoo. Ran up to Long Key and took on water and gas, before which F. and M.S.C. and T.L. thoroughly explored Channel Key which we have determined to own. They planted three cocoanuts near landing, and brought back corcooloulus minor and other flora. Parcheesi tournament is progressing in favor of M.A.L. T.L. has kindly consented the use of his face in place of the port running light. It will save oil. In p.m. took launch around to E. of Long Key and all swam. T.L. caught 1 jack and 1 grouper on return trip, and F.D.R. nearly got one about 6 inches long. Grog in midst of glorious sunset which was almost as poetic in coloring as F. and M's nighties. Colors remained hoisted. Much complaint. Answer "We're loadin' ice." Roy rescued our nautical reputation.

∿∿

The entries in the log for the month between the 24th of February and March were made by other members of the *Larooco* party.

∿∿

Tuesday, March 24, 1925.

Left Channel Key at noon, soon after arrival of James, who came through from Groton. After lunch fished the trestle and H.M. Jr. got a 12 pound Jack and J.R. a Mackerel. In the p.m. the clouds came up and fearing a Norther we ran up to Jewfish Key anchorage. The H. Morgenthau Jr.'s left at 7 p.m. in the dory and got soaked on their way to Long Key in the dory to take the train. Heavy rain but not much wind.

Wednesday, March 25, 1925.

At Jewfish Key, N. of Long Key. James and I fished the trestle in the morning, went outside and got a mess of bottom fish including a Turbot. Heavy rain in p.m. At 6, Fortuna with R. Talbot, Judge Corrigan, Judge Fred Kernochan, Dr. Rushmore, Willy Post, and Gallatin Pell came to anchor near us. A fine poker party in the evening.

Thursday, March 26, 1925.

Ran back before lunch to Long Key to get last mail and telegrams, and then headed North on the homeward journey, getting into Tavernier Creek at four and tying up to the bushes in the basin right by the Railroad culvert.

Friday, March 27, 1925.

Jimmy and I left at 9:30 with Rodney Albury in latter's launch, ran to Couch Reef and started fishing. Sea too much for JR's breakfast. Got a mackerel and a number of big Barracuda, Monty Snyder one of 22 lbs. and I one of 25 lbs. Mine measured 3 ft. 4 inches, not as big as the Feb. one. Anchored half way to Pickles Reef—still fished and I hooked on to a Monster of the Deep and stayed on just an hour and a half. He hardly moved, would take out 10 feet of line and then I would get it back again. What he was no one will ever know! Got back to Larooco at 6:30 thoroughly exhausted.

Saturday, March 28, 1925.

A bad blow and rain in the night. Under way at 1 o'clock and ran well against strong head wind, reaching Jewfish Creek Drawbridge at 4:20 and anchored just beyond it. After supper J.R. and I rowed around near and through the bridge and got a big Mangrove Snapper, a big Jack and five Lady-fish, the latter great fun as they jump many times, and one nearly came into the boat. While we were gone Monty hooked a 7½ foot shovel-nose shark from the deck and he and LeRoy had a hard time before they got it in close and shot it with my revolver.

Sunday, March 29, 1925.

J. R. and Monty fished after breakfast and we got under way at 11:30 and ran straight through to Bear's Cut just below Miami. It has turned much colder.

Monday, March 30, 1925.

Left Bear's Cut at 10:30 after J.R. had had a cold swim. Docked opposite the Royal Palm and J.R. went ashore for mail etc.—shopping etc. in p.m. by James and Mrs. Morris and I packed up with LeRoy.

Tuesday, March 31, 1925.

Miami. Packing and having hair cut in morning. At 1 James and I, in Scott Watkin's (Capt. Charlie's son) car went to Fort Lauderdale and made arrangement at Pilkington's Yacht Basin to take care of Larooco during the summer. After our return we went down to Cocoanut Grove and spent 1½ hours with Mr. and Mrs. William Jennings Bryan.

Wednesday, April 1, 1925.

Placed "Larooco" out of commission at 6 p.m. and took train for Warm Springs, Georgia.

> *Here ends a very delightful*
> *2nd Cruise*
> *of the Good Ship "Larooco."*

∽∽

F.D.R.'s second trip to Warm Springs was somewhat different from his first visit. This time he was concerned not only about his own health, but also about other paralytics who had found their way to Warm Springs. During his October sojourn he had had an interview on the Presidential campaign with two reporters from Atlanta; and as he was in the pool when the reporters arrived, one of them later wrote an article about his efforts to regain his health which was syndicated in newspapers throughout the country. Although F.D.R. was annoyed by the publicity of his "Swimming Back to Health," the consequence of the article was the arrival at Warm Springs of no less than ten infantile paralysis victims during his April visit; by the end of 1925 a total of seventeen patients, all uninvited and uncared for, had come to the Meriwether Inn, which was thrown into a turmoil because the regular resort guests objected to the use of the pool by polio victims for fear of "catching" the disease. Protests were next raised against the eating facilities, and Tom Loyless had to provide a special dining room for the paralytics. F.D.R. partially solved these difficulties by building a small treatment pool thirty yards from the public one for the use of his "gang," and he also fixed up cottages for the crippled strangers to occupy.

Thus F.D.R. came to be known during these early years at Warm Springs as "Dr. Roosevelt," for it was he who advised the first patients how to exercise in the water. There were no polio specialists at Warm Springs at this time, and F.D.R. undertook the task of teaching what he had learned from Dr. Lovett. He prepared crude muscle charts, and on the basis of these and consultations with Dr. Johnson he devised new methods of exercise which seemed appropriate to this natural warm-water pool. This new activity at Warm Springs, which was just beginning when F.D.R. wrote the next two letters, was the prelude to an era of development culminating in the establishment of the National Foundation for Infantile Paralysis, with its more than 2700 local chapters all over the country.

WARM SPRINGS
APRIL 28, 1925
TUESDAY

Dear Rosy:

Canon Jones wrote me that you came back with a bad knee and I hope it is not bothering you. My own knees are really gaining a lot of strength,—this exercising in warm water seems to be far and away the best thing, and I think you will be delighted with the progress I have made. It is so good that, as you know, I have decided to stay down until the 15th.

A telegram from the Bishop last night said that $10,000,-000 is assured. I take it that that does not include the balance (about $1,500,000) which Haley Fiske's division says they can raise in addition to their present million. I think we all have cause to be happy. Even if the total net cash from this campaign does not exceed $10,000,000 it will take so long to spend it that we shall not offend the public or the rich donors by staging a final appeal 8 or 10 years from now. In the meantime a lot of quiet work can be done to get people to add bequests to their wills.

It is lovely down here—about a month ahead of Hyde Park so I will get a double spring. I hope to come up the first Sunday I get home.

Affectionately yours,

Much love to Betty.

[F.D.R.]

This letter to James Roosevelt Roosevelt concerns a campaign to raise ten million dollars for the Cathedral of St. John the Divine. F.D.R. was chairman of the campaign and on the board of trustees of the cathedral; his half-brother was the oldest trustee, the only one who had been present at the laying of the cornerstone in 1892. The eastern end of the great church, as well as its auxiliary buildings, had been constructed by 1916, but, with the exception of the baptistry, nothing had been done for the next ten years; the ten-million-dollar fund was to complete the work. Robert Ellis Jones was canon of the cathedral from 1905 until his death in 1929. "The Bishop" refers to William T. Manning, who was bishop of New York from 1921 until he resigned in 1946; he was honorary chairman of the fund-raising committee. Haley Fiske, another trustee of the cathedral, was president of the Metropolitan Life Insurance Company.

∽∾

WARM SPRINGS
APRIL 30, 1925
THURSDAY

Dear Jimmy:

I am awfully glad to get your letter and it is too bad that the debate did not end in a victory. That word "has" was certainly a difficult thing to get around. As you undoubtedly pointed out, the only actual proof that aircraft has come into its own is the fact that the more advanced naval and military men believe it will be perhaps of primary importance in the next war, and are therefore at the present moment preparing along these lines.

The baseball scores look as if we have a chance at least of beating St. Marks. I am glad we won the Middlesex game.

My application for the 2 boat race tickets has gone in to Cambridge, but I do not suppose that I shall get them much before the first of June, and will then forward them to you. You owe me nothing for them; they are on me!

I am glad that Elliott got through his exams, and I do hope he is working for a better standing in the June exams— he would be so much happier if he could have a free summer without having to worry about work.

Mother, Anna and Mr. Howe get here tonight. Of course the old car had to break down this morning. Mother will get 4 days of rest I hope, though it is awfully cold here today and yesterday and the swimming is unpleasant except when one is under the water. Anna I think is bringing Chief who will probably get full of "jiggers" and ticks when he goes into the woods. These friendly parasites will then communicate themselves to all of us, but I hope the family will be disinfected by the time you and Elliott return.

I am staying on until May 14th. The legs have really improved a lot. There is no question that this place does more good than all the rest of the exercising etc. put together.

Affectionately
[Father]

This dictated letter to his eldest son was an answer to James Roosevelt's letter of April 27, 1925, from Groton. F.D.R.'s remark about the use of aircraft in war came in reply to the following paragraph:

. . . The Middlesex debate was held last Thursday. We lost, although it was very close. The subject was, "Resolved: that Aircraft has supplanted Naval Armament as a means of first line defense in Modern Warfare." We had the pro, and used these arguments: airplanes, which carry poisonous gas as well as high explosive bombs, are able to resist attacks by air, land, and sea, whereas dreadnoughts, while vastly more expensive to build and keep up, are capable of protecting the mother country only by sea, thus making Aircraft the logical first line of defense; airplanes are much cheaper, and when an airplane is fighting a battleship two men are fighting two thousand; Japan, France, and Germany are all building them by the hundred, etc. Middlesex, while admitting that someday the given situation might come about, put all their emphasis on the 'has'. As there had not been a war since 1918, we could not give any actual proof in rebuttal to the contrary, and the judges decided that on this more-or-less of a quibble, the evening should be given to the con. . . .

∽∽

Around the middle of May, F.D.R. left Warm Springs and returned to New York, from where he dictated the next letter to his son Elliott.

NEW YORK
MAY 21, 1925
Dear Bunny: THURSDAY

I wish I could get up to school this spring but I will have to put it off until the autumn. Granny and Anna will be up there next week and go down to the game. I do hope we will win this year.

Your report has come and the Rector says at the bottom ———. I do hope you will make a grand extra special effort the balance of the term and it would be fine if you could get through *all* your exams. You would have a wonderful feeling of freedom for the summer.

Jimmy says you are in the squad of which he is Corporal. Don't try to beat him up while you are a mere private in the ranks—you might get court-martialed and shot!

Do please drop your old Daddy a line to tell him something

about your activities. How is the baseball coming? Are you going in for any running in the spring meet, etc. etc. Also, don't forget to step on the gas for those exams! Start now!

Affectionately,

[Father]

The Rector's remarks were not included in the carbon copy of this letter. Evidently F.D.R. wrote them personally in the original so as to emphasize further his advice.

∽

[NEW YORK]
JULY 20, 1925
MONDAY

Dearest Sister:

It was good to hear your voice yesterday and to know that all goes well with you, and I wish I could get out to Geneva to play around with you for a few days. By Golly, if I have to call you up next Saturday for failure to hear a line I will jolly well reverse the charges!

I forgot to give you the inclosed to sign before you left. Will you fill out the necessary places and return it to me as I have a letter waiting to go with it to Mr. Sibley, the Secretary of the College of Agriculture.

I have been awfully busy with Mr. Clinton getting prices on lumber, stone work, plumbing, etc. and yesterday telegraphed a bid to Mother and Nan and Marion on behalf of Clinton & Roosevelt, which, if they take, will save them over $4,000! Your Pa is some little contractor! The pool is practically finished.

Monty got back last night with the car from Campo. I dined at the Morgenthau's last night. I am busy as a one-armed paper hanger with the itch!

Your affectionate father,

[FDR]

P.S. Will you please sign the inclosed on page 2 and page 3 and get it sworn to before a Notary Public in Geneva, re-

582

turning it to me. The Notary will charge you 25¢ which I will reimburse you when next we become acquainted with each other.

[FDR]

This letter to Anna Roosevelt, then studying agriculture at the experimental station in Geneva, N.Y., is also taken from a carbon copy of the original.

Nancy Cook and Marion Dickerman became close friends of A.E.R. several years before when she first entered active political work in the women's division of the Democratic State Committee. Their friendship, further strengthened when Miss Dickerman bought the Todhunter School in 1927 and made A.E.R. her associate principal, led F.D.R. to give all three some land east of the family home in Hyde Park. The property was called Val-Kill. F.D.R. built a swimming pool on it so that he could carry out his exercises when he was in Hyde Park, and Misses Cook and Dickerman planned to make it their permanent residence. F.D.R. and Henry Clinton, a local Poughkeepsie contractor, undertook to build their cottage, as proudly mentioned in this letter. Later the Val-Kill Furniture Factory, put into operation under the direction of the three women, was located there. The building, remodeled into a home in 1936, has been A.E.R.'s residence since her husband's death.

〰〰

[NEW YORK]
JULY 22, 1925
WEDNESDAY

Dear Rosy:

I inclose the sheet of the minutes of the meeting of June 23rd which relate to the report of the Fabric Committee. Is the report at the bottom correct? I *thought* the report of the Committee on Fabrics was *approved*. If so, the minutes must be changed at the September meeting. I send you this lest I forget it and be unable to attend the September meeting myself.

All goes well. Eleanor and the rest of the caravan reached Campobello in safety, the only accidents being first, Franklin cutting his foot with the ax, instead of the tree; 2nd, sliding off the road into the ditch and having to be pulled out; and 3d, upsetting a dray just as they approached Lubec and dumping the load of lumber and the small boy who was driving it—total cost of damages, $10!

Clinton and I have taken the contract for the cottage and the estimate is $4,000 under that of the Poughkeepsie contractors. The swimming pool is just about finished and I hope to swim in it next Saturday.

I spent Monday trying to prevent the road cutting into Mr. Fred Newbold's garden, by pushing it over into the hospital ground instead; also, I still think I may be able to get the engineers to run it east of Aunt Ellen's 2 cottages and bring the new road out into the old one north of the priests' gate.

Mama's shingles are, I think, practically well, and Mrs. Low is staying with her and will continue there for a month or more, going with her about August 15th to Beverly, Portland and Bar Harbor.

James and Elliott are tremendously enthusiastic about the West, and want to prolong their stay.

I do hope you will really get a lot of benefit from the cure. I wish you would really consider coming to Warm Springs, Georgia next spring when you get back from Bermuda. The reports from there show that all the patients—rheumatism, infantile etc. have been tremendously improved.

Much love to you both. Let me know if there is anything I can do for you here. I shall be at the office and at Hyde Park right along until September 23rd except for a little over 2 weeks in August at Mr. Howe's beach.

Affectionately yours,

[F.D.R.]

Frederick Newbold was a brother of Thomas Newbold *(vide supra)*; Mrs. Augustus Low, who is referred to in later letters as "Cousin Mamie," came from Brooklyn and was a close friend of Sara Roosevelt.

∽∽

[NEW YORK]
JULY 29, 1925
WEDNESDAY

Dear Jimmy and Elliott:

As I have no idea what day or hour you get to Chicago, I have not done anything about your accommodations. I am inclosing, however, the information in regard to trains and the amount I figured it would cost you to get home. If I do not hear from you I will send a check to the home ranch about August 10th, and leave it to you to get your accommodations in Chicago and Montreal. I do not believe there will be much difficulty about this at this time of year.

If you want, however, I will try to reserve the pullman accommodations for you if you will tell me the train and day.

I go to the Beach with Louis Howe next Tuesday—address me there care Louis McH. Howe, Westport Point, Mass. I will be there until August 25th, returning that day to New York. Mother joins me at the beach August 6th for a few days, then goes to pick up Anna, and stops again at the beach on their way to Campobello.

It is perfectly grand that you are getting so much out of the trip. I have an awful feeling that neither of you took trout rods and that you are needing them in the Yellowstone country.

I am having a very busy summer,—lots of work at both offices and I hope some of it will be profitable. The swimming pool is done and the foundation for the cottage is poured.

[Your affectionate Father]
[F.D.R.]

585

This letter is taken from a carbon copy of the original, thus the abrupt ending, to which F.D.R. probably added a few words in his own hand.

∽

Dearest Mama,

It is good to get your letter tonight and you can think of me as leaving tomorrow morning at 7:30 for Westport Point. The car will as usual be crowded, Louis and I on the back seat with various packages tucked around and under us, one colored treasure on a little seat, the other in front with Snyder and several score suitcases, braces, crutches, canes, sandwiches thrown in for good measure. However, it saves $11 for each person to travel thus to the Beach!

I have had a frightfully busy day. Got my work all cleaned up and Missy has left for her vacation in northern New York.

I will try to go to see McDonald Thursday or Friday, depending on the tide, as I have to go from cottage to road after half ebb tide and get back before half flood.

A letter from Eleanor says she has a note from Anna saying she is feeling perfectly well. Love to Cousin Mamie. I am *so* glad she is with you and I do hope she really will make you headquarters till December.

Much love.

FDR

Dr. William McDonald was a well-known neurologist who had developed on his own a special treatment for infantile paralysis. Originally from Albany, McDonald later practiced in Boston and Providence, and while treating a friend's child for polio, he evolved a treatment which differed somewhat from the prevailing one. His first case proved to be so successful that he became more and more a specialist in the field. He bought a house in Marion adjacent to the quiet water of the upper harbor, where he accepted four cases at a time for treatment. At first he had no assistants, and did all the exercises with each patient, as well as supervising their swimming from a nearby stone pier. When F.D.R. heard of McDonald's work, it was not difficult to persuade him to undergo the treatment for a month. F.D.R. never tired of exploring new possibilities for recovery; just as he had investigated the almost absurd stories about Warm Springs, he followed up the reports on McDonald. First, however, he spent several weeks vacationing with the Howes at Westport Point.

∽∽

HORSENECK BEACH
WESTPORT POINT, MASS.
AUGUST 18, 1925
TUESDAY

Dearest Mama—

Eleanor has doubtless read you my telegram and letter so I will not repeat about the grand plan of going to Dr. McDonald next Monday for a month. He is very encouraging and will take me in hand at once, tho' he had made up his mind to take no more cases this year. His work is evidently very strenuous for the patient, so I shall devote myself to it wholly.

I hope to get a wee cottage two doors from him and to move in with Ray and Ricketts.

Why don't you sometime while I am at Marion drive over in the car to Fairhaven and stay a few days and come over and see me? I will let you know all about my hours.

Mr. Howe and I are motoring over to Marion this p.m. as the tide serves and we will find out all about the cottage.

A great deal of love

F.D.R.

Sara Roosevelt was also quite excited about the "grand plan" to take treatments from Dr. McDonald, and she wrote on August 23, 1925: "I was very glad to get your letter of Tuesday the 18th, and all my thoughts are in Marion, and tomorrow I can think of you there and beginning the treatment. I feel so hopeful and confident! Once able to move about with crutches and without braces, strength will come and now for the first time in more than a year I feel that *work* is to be done for *you,* my dearest. . . ."

~~

MARION, MASS.
AUGUST 26, 1925
WEDNESDAY

Dearest Mama—

I am safely installed and the work is underway. Got here with Louis on Monday at 2. Dr. McDonald came at four and gave me the complete muscle tests. Yesterday I swam for 1½ hours in the morning, had the exercises with the Dr. at 4 and then tried the walking board for ½ hour. He seems pleased with the general line-up and I feel with him that things have now got to the point with the muscles in general where there is something to work on and I can go right after it. Braces are of course laid aside, he is hot against them, and confirms what I have told you for two years and you would not believe.

The swimming work is just what I did at Warm Springs, only the water being much colder I cannot stay so long.

After lunch yesterday, I drove over and saw Catherine and Xander and Laura.

When you get to Fairhaven, I think I can come over to lunch on Sunday and stay all afternoon and perhaps for dinner too, as Sunday is apparently an off day.

Why don't you come back with me and spend Sunday night? I am on a diet also and hope to get off 10 lbs.

Eleanor and the boys according to latest plans get here

the 9th, she going on that night by boat with the two little boys and James and Elliott spending 2 nights with me.

It is warmer today but the paper says colder tonight.

Three other cases here—one little Edward Parish—all showing remarkable improvement.

Mr. Edward Hamlin (who has given me this perfectly sweet little cottage) is three doors away. Miss Harriet Hamlin next door and the Doc. three doors at end of street.

Louis is in N. Y. meeting his family. Missy has just arrived and will be here off and on. Louis comes back tomorrow to report on the host of things he had to do for me in N. Y. as of course this change of plans made all sorts of complications with my work and various activities.

Love to Cousin Mamie and tell her I loved her letter.

Devotedly

F.D.R.

Mrs. Charles (Bertie) S. Hamlin (*vide supra*), who was then living in nearby Mattapoisett and who had taken an interest in Dr. McDonald's work, later wrote an article telling the story of F.D.R.'s recuperative months at Marion. On July 25, 1948, the *Boston Globe* summarized Mrs. Hamlin's account and explained F.D.R.'s activities on the "walking board" as follows: "For two or three hours a day he went round-and-round an oblong of wood with a railing around it. He leaned on the railing, and hand-over-hand he talked, laughed, and dragged his legs after him." Mrs. Hamlin also enlarged upon F.D.R.'s inference that McDonald believed in recovery through independence of mechanical devices such as braces:

. . . One night Franklin and Eleanor came to visit with me in Mattapoisett. Two men carried him in to a seat at the dining-room table. He told the men not to return until 9:30.

When dinner was over, Franklin pushed back his chair and said, "See me get into the next room." He got down on the floor and went in on his hands and knees and got up into another chair himself.

It seems that Dr. McDonald taught his patients this way of helping themselves so they would have a feeling of freedom to move if necessary. . . .

"Catherine" refers to F.D.R.'s cousin, Catherine L. Delano, who married Alexander Grant (known by the family as "Xander"). Edward and Harriet Hamlin were Charles S. Hamlin's brother and sister, permanent residents of Marion.

∽

MARION, MASS.
NOVEMBER 1, [1925]
SUNDAY

Dearest Mama—

Ever so many thanks for sending the blanket and also the Zwiebach and the book! There is little of news here—Aunt Kassie and K. & S. and G. & C. come to Fairhaven tomorrow, and will all come to tea with me Tuesday afternoon and I go over to dine with them that night. Poor Dr. McD. has been laid up all week, and I have had no treatments; he strained his heart carrying Janet Wright into the Stadium at the Brown-Yale game a week ago. It is only a temporary thing and he is nearly all well again. Meanwhile I have been doing my walking regularly and the muscles continue to improve.

Saturday I motored all the way to Groton, 102 miles, and saw the boys, also Warren Robbins. James played a good game, but has a bad tendon, which however will be in good shape for the St. Marks game on the 11th. We won 20—7 from Huntington School.

I have seen Bertie Hamlin several times and she goes to Washington in a few days.

I find each day very fully occupied and everything is going well. A great deal of love.

Devotedly
F.D.R.

Ever since childhood zwieback had been a favorite biscuit of F.D.R. The initialed arrivals were Aunt Kassie's daughters, Katherine and Sara, and their husbands, George B. St. George and Charles Fellowes-Gordon. Janet Wright made a complete recovery from infantile paralysis and married John Crawford Byers, a member of the class of 1923 at Williams College. There is a discrepancy between F.D.R.'s account of the Groton-Huntington game and the report of the *New York Times*, which lists Groton as the winner by a score of 20 to 0. Groton also won the St. Mark's game the following week by a 13 to 6 count.

∾

MARION, MASS.
NOVEMBER 17, 1925
TUESDAY

Dearest Mama,

Eleanor's nice visit is over. We all went to see old houses on Cape Cod on Friday p.m. and at Plymouth on Saturday p.m. and the weather was actually warm, but now it has turned cold again. The walking progresses slowly but definitely and I have walked a block with crutches and only the left leg brace. The Dr. is all right again.

You must have had a nice visit from Una and Charley and Cousin Anna Swift. Eleanor writes that the boys seem all right again and that Mammie has left for a couple of weeks rest cure.

So glad James's knee is no worse and I only feared some nerve injury. It was certainly hard luck but it was some comfort to him to have the team win.

Last night the McD's came in for bridge and this p.m. I have been to Fuller's antique shop in New Bedford to look over a lot of old books. Tomorrow night the two little infantile paralysis girls dine here.

When you go to Poughkeepsie will you get this picture at Raymond's and pay the bill. I will repay you!

Love to Rosy and Betty. I hate to miss them before they

591

sail, but it will certainly be better for him to get to a warmer clime.

A great deal of love.

Devotedly

FDR

Glad Anna seemed well. She seems to be really interested in the life and the work and it will do her loads of good in a thousand ways in her after life.

> Charles M. Connfelt and his wife, the former Una F. Soley, as well as Anna Swift, were distant cousins of F.D.R. His connection with the Connfelts was more than family, as Mrs. Connfelt's father, James Russell Soley, was a Harvard graduate (class of 1870), a lawyer, a naval historian, and had been Assistant Secretary of the Navy during the Harrison Administration. "Mammie" refers to Mlle. Seline Thiel, a Swiss governess A.E.R. employed for her younger children. The "work" of F.D.R.'s daughter was a continuation of her aforementioned interest in farming; she was at this time taking an agricultural course at Cornell. The following spring she married Curtis B. Dall.

∽∽

> After having been so impressed by his continued improvement while at Marion that he changed his original plan of staying only a month and remained until December, F.D.R. returned to New York and Hyde Park for the Christmas holidays; thence, on the first of February, he and A.E.R. departed for Florida and a third cruise aboard the *Larooco,* where he resumed the log of the "Good Ship."

Foreword

After Larooco went out of commission last April 1 Capt. and Mrs. Morris took up to Fort Lauderdale to Capt. Pilkington's Yacht Basin about four miles up the River. Capt. and Mrs. Morris continued to live on board during the summer and autumn. Twice boats near her in the yard caught fire but she came through safely. A new engine was put in the dory but little else was done except the usual painting and overhauling before commissioning. The bowsprit, broken off last year, was left off entirely, thereby greatly improving her looks. John Entwistle, my chauffeur, arrived Saturday Jan. 30 and Capt. Charlie on Feb. 1.

Tuesday, February 2, 1926.

Eleanor and I arrived at Fort Lauderdale at noon, only three hours late instead of over a day late as last year. Roy with us. Drove out to Pilkington Yacht Basin where we found Mrs. Morris and Capt. Charlie waiting us. Larooco went into commission and we had lunch. In p.m. E and I drove into town and did a lot of laying in of supplies.

Wednesday, February 3, 1926.

Intended to start early, but a very heavy rain blocked plans and later the tide ran ebb too strong to make the try to go down River. Wrote and sent off mail and telegrams.

Thursday, February 4, 1926.

Started—false alarm. Got down the River a mile and both engines went on the blink. Tried to get Roy Haines the engine doctor from Miami and failed. Got local man who apparently in the late p.m. did the necessary.

Friday, February 5, 1926.

Under way at 9, but current too strong so sent down for 2 tugs who finally came and at 1 we were towed down to mouth of River—one tug ahead and other steering astern. A very congested, tortuous River and will be even more difficult to navigate when new bridges are finished. Headed for Miami but sundry engine troubles halted us from time to time and we made slow progress, tying up finally at the

S. end of the well named Snake Creek just before reaching Biscayne Bay.

Saturday, February 6, 1926.

Our unlucky spot—vide log of 1924. Got under way at 9 and promptly ran on a lump in the usual narrow place. Stuck fast. At 10 A.E.R. took dory with Capt. Charlie to try to reach Miami before bank closed, meet Maunsell Crosby and Ethel Douglas Merritt. While the dory was away I got Larooco off by warping to shore, but then both engines balked. At 4, after a narrow escape from being raked by a tug and 3 loaded lumber barges, we started and with one engine and the dory towing ahead got down to 1 mile above Miami upper bridge and anchored. Eleanor came out in the Col. Thompson launch with M.S.C. and E.D.M. Henry Breckinridge paid us a short call.

Sunday, February 7, 1926.

At anchor above Miami all day. Nothing of note. On lookout for possible arrival of Lady Cynthia Mosley and Oswald Mosley. First swimming party by M.S.C. and E.D.M. Pâté de foie gras No. 1 for supper (with accompaniment).

Monday, February 8, 1926.

Roy Hayes, Engine Doctor, came on board early and pronounced port shaft bent. After lunch took Larooco in tow of dory, and with starboard engine running, successfully passed through bridges and up to Vogal's Yard where we were hauled out. The ladies and Maunsell do much shopping.

Tuesday, February 9, 1926.

On the ways at Vogal's Yard all day. New port shaft put in and bottom painted. More shopping, and M.S.C. motored E.D.M. out to Coral Gables and other swindles.

Wednesday, February 10, 1926.

Came off ways at Miami at 11 a.m. and got under way at once, taking Roy Hayes along to watch engines. Proceeded from Biscayne Bay and tied up in Jewfish Creek at 5 p.m. Sent Hayes back to Miami by 10:20 train.

Thursday, February 11, 1926.

Fished in vain during morning. Met M.A.L. at Key Largo at 2—only 7 hours late. Fished again in vain in p.m.

Friday, February 12, 1926.

In Jewfish Creek. Water very murky still—no fish. In p.m. went through drawbridge and anchored off new dredged channel to Key Largo. The Mosleys wire they cannot get off till Monday from Palm Beach. At 10 p.m. E.R. goes to train bound home. Fine mess of crawfish.

Saturday, February 13, 1926.

Left Key Largo at 11 and ran down to Tavernier, anchoring off the "Bath Tub" at the Hull's house. In p.m. all go in for bath in Bath Tub. Much appreciated. Crawfish for lunch.

Sunday, February 14, 1926.

At anchor off Tavernier. M.S.C.'s birthday. Cake with candles. Also Valentines for all hands. Swim off boat. In p.m. ran into Tavernier Creek and tied up near R.R. bridge. Caught a few very small Sailor's-Choice and trolled in vain.

Monday, February 15, 1926.

Another wonderful day. Went in to Tavernier at 2 and met the Mosleys who brought us the first fishing luck, several small jacks, a grouper and enough small fish for supper. At 9:30 Ethel Merritt left us to rejoin her family at Fort Myer.

Tuesday, February 16, 1926.

Grand trip to the Reef in Leonard Low's new fishboat. Not very rough but too very for M.A.L. At Pickle Reef

Crosby brought in an 18 lb. barracuda. We then ran north to Molasses Reef and got two smaller barracuda, then back to Pickle where the fun began. All hands caught fish—including an 18 lb. jack, the biggest I have ever landed and a nice "grumper," which were duly photographed by Lady Cynthia. In the evening the men caught a 79 lb. hammerhead shark, hooked through the side and duly shot by Mosley. During the day Roy got a mess of grunts, so that with the crawfish caught last night and the arrival of an order of groceries we shall not starve for a week.

Wednesday, February 17, 1926.

Cloudy and showers in morning. Capt. Morris ashore to get oranges and grapefruit from the Hull grove by kindness of Bobby Burns.

〜〜

The February 17th entry was completed by Sir Oswald E. Mosley, at this time a prominent Member of Parliament, later the leader of the British Union of Fascists. His wife, the former Cynthia Curzon, daughter of the ex-Viceroy of India, made the February 18th entry in the log.

〜〜

Friday, February 19, 1926.

Left trestle 2 anchorage early and ran to Long Key. Took on water, gasoline, mail and telegrams. At 2 it looked like a Norther, so we ran up to Jewfish Bush. Norther in full force with heavy rain and wind at 3:30. The Mosleys simply had to make evening train, so we gave them tea, wrapped them up in slickers and sent them in to Long Key in the dory at 5. When last seen most of Florida Bay was dashing over the good old dory. The Mosleys are a most delightful couple and we shall miss them much. Dory got back safely with mail. A bad blowy night.

596

When F.D.R. presented his sons Franklin, Jr.,
and John with certificates as charter members of
the Woodrow Wilson Foundation, he sat for this
portrait, said to be the first made after his long
illness.

"Dr. Roosevelt" and fellow victims of poliomyelitis were able to do their exercises all the year around in the pool at Warm Springs, Georgia, when a roof was erected with funds donated by Henry Ford.

An enthusiastic horseman from early childhood, Franklin Roosevelt continued in spite of his handicap to ride at Warm Springs during the years of his convalescence.

In the Presidential campaign of 1924, F.D.R. came
back once again to politics to appear with the
candidate, John W. Davis.

At the 1924 convention at Saratoga, New York—
John W. Davis and F.D.R. with Alfred E. Smith
in the background.

In the town of Marion on the South Shore of Massachusetts, F. D. R. sought the help of Dr. William McDonald at whose home he spent two summers taking exercises and working on the walking board.

Assisted by Dr. McDonald and a servant, F. D. R. posed for this first picture showing him back on his feet during the transition between crutches and canes.

Aboard the *Larooco* where he convalesced in Florida, F. D. R. took this photograph of the ship's mascot.

The houseboat *Larooco* in Biscayne Bay . . .

. . . and ashore inland above Fort Lauderdale, where she was driven in the hurricane of 1926.

This Log
is
Dedicated to

St.
Ananias

St.
Sapphira

THE PATRON SAINTS
OF ALL
TRUE FISHERFOLK

The dedication page of the *Larooco* log in which
the protection of St. Ananias and St. Sapphira,
patron saints of liars, was sought by the ship's
artist, Louis McHenry Howe.

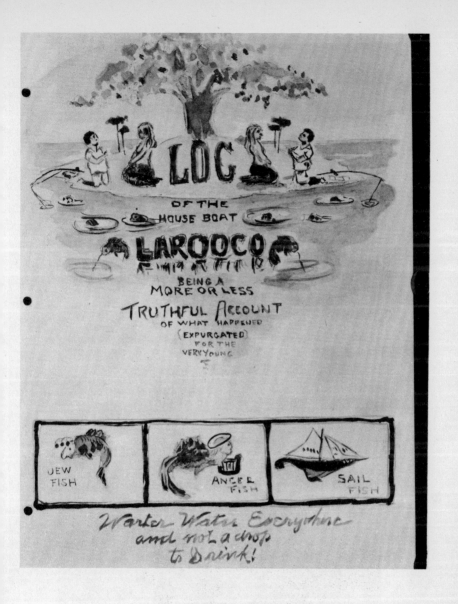

The entries in the log were made alternately by F. D. R. and the many friends who were his guests on the *Larooco* cruises, but this colorful pen-and-wash title page, like all the other illustrations, were Louis Howe's handiwork.

Everyone on board took turns posing with the large jewfish Elliott caught when he spent his winter vacation in 1926 with his father.

F.D.R. on the beach near Miami with several of his *Larooco* house-guests—Mrs. Henry de Rham, Maunsell Crosby, and Lady Cynthia Mosley.

Gradual recovery brought back the possibility of
F.D.R.'s enjoying once again the fishing and
camping trips which had been so much a part of
his life.

Presidential candidate Alfred E. Smith at a rally
in Brooklyn during the 1928 campaign shares a
joke with gubernatorial candidate Franklin D.
Roosevelt.

Four generations of the Roosevelts of Hyde Park
. . . the Governor-elect, his new granddaughter,
his mother, and his daughter Anna.

Saturday, February 20, 1926.

Sent in to Long Key for Tom Lynch—ice and food. T.M.L. arrived looking sunburned and reports Rip Saw all connected. After lunch we ran down to Stirrup Key, fine little harbor.

Sunday, February 21, 1926.

Rip Saw working most of night. T.M.L. sawed a lot of wood, M.S.C. accompanying him on his saxophone with a hole in it. M.A.L. appreciates wood and jazz, but has enough for the Winter. Made a fine run past Pigeon Key where a large yacht is hard and fast aground, through drawbridge and to anchor in New Found Harbor, next to Peliwar Key.

Monday, February 22, 1926.

In morning to Boca Chica where the new bridge cuts off— an old anchorage [two words illegible] Island. Tried for Tarpon in evening but did not raise anything. A nice swim at the point.

Tuesday, February 23, 1926.

A heavy blow looked imminent so we ran round to Key West at noon and went to the gasoline dock for supplies and sundry repairs. All went for a drive in the p.m. and went out the new road 15 miles over Boca Chica Key. The land F.D.R. nearly bought at $450 an acre is now selling at over $2,000.

Wednesday, February 24, 1926.

A quiet day—Charles S. Peabody and William Hart (the latter of Columbus, Ga.) arrived and we began talking over the possible purchase of Georgia Warm Springs from Geo. Foster Peabody and his nephew. Various repairs to engines, etc. In p.m. went out in launch and caught some small bottom fish.

Thursday, February 25, 1926.

Went around to Navy Yard and were greeted by Capt. and Mrs. Stearns—Maunsell Crosby left us, much to our regret. Went motoring in p.m. and received callers in p.m., including Col. Robt. M. Thompson and Ad. Brownson who are moored alongside in the "Everglades."

Friday, February 26, 1926.

At Navy Yard Key West. Tom Lynch left us by evening train and M.A.L., Hart, Peabody and I dined with the Stearns.

Saturday, February 27, 1926.

At Navy Yard. Peabody and Hart left by the evening train. Went for another drive in the p.m.

Sunday, February 28, 1926.

At Navy Yard. Grand motor boat and swimming race all afternoon which we saw from deck of Larooco. Calls from Mr. and Mrs. Meacham, the Porters, etc.

Monday, March 1, 1926.

John S. Lawrence, joint owner of this good craft arrives on board and the Eastern Y.C. burgee replaces the N.Y.Y.C., and the J.S.L. red private signal the blue of F.D.R. His first visit in the 3 years we have owned her. J.S.L. accompanied by Edwin Farnham (Far-from) Greene of the Pacific Mills. We leave Navy Yard at 1, steering wheel knuckle breaks as we leave, tie up to destroyer, replace and at 4 run out of yard and anchor under Mangrove Key at N. of harbor.

Tuesday, March 2, 1926.

Ran from Mangrove Key to inside Taylor Key, about 20 miles. Starts to blow. Try fishing but get only a few small bottom fish.

Wednesday, March 3, 1926.

At anchor inside Taylor Key. Blowing too hard outside to move. In p.m. took launch 6 miles South to Cudjoe Key, fishing on way and getting a jack and a grouper.

Thursday, March 4, 1926.

Off at 9 and tried to go East outside but were driven back by heavy seas. In p.m. went in to Cudjoe Key Station and sent and received telegrams.

Friday, March 5, 1926.

Started early and got safely round to Big Spanish Key Channel and anchored behind No Name Key and we went in to the "Shark Factory" where we got the mended steering knuckle at Big Pine Key Station. Then back on board—out to Bahia Honda. The port exhaust manifold cracked and we anchored. During night began bumping bottom and had to move to deeper water.

Saturday, March 6, 1926.

Mended manifold temporarily and ran to Hog Key, close to Marathon. Got groceries and mail. In p.m. went through to Marathon Harbor, caught grouper and jack.

∽

"LAROOCO," NEAR LONG KEY
MARCH 7, 1926
SUNDAY

Dearest Mama—

It was of course a very great shock to get your telegram when we got into Long Key in the motorboat last night. With it came your letter of a week ago, telling of the family dinner before Uncle Fred sailed, and I am so glad you could

599

all have been together then, and it will be a great blow to Uncle Fred on the ocean. Your telegram though from Newburgh says "Doctor present" so I have fears that neither you nor Aunt Doe were there, and that the attack must have been very sudden.

Still I know it is as dear Aunt Annie would have wished it, active up to the last. You know what a shock it is to me for in so many ways Aunt Annie and I were sympathetic, and her passing [is] as I would have mine be. She was so keen about everything and with it had such a twinkle in her eye that it is no wonder people in every walk of life in Newburgh loved her. I shall always be glad that she and Aunt Doe spent the last Christmas with us at H.P.

I shall think of you this week all going to Fairhaven. I wish I might be with you all. Somehow down here I feel just as far away as if it were Europe, for six days we have been out of touch with H.P. and telegrams and letters stuck on the West Side between here and Key West because of heavy gales.

John Lawrence and Edwin F. Greene are on board and stay till the 14th. Missy goes on Tuesday the 9th. Elliott gets here the 16th and possibly Lewis B. Brown (Lathrop's cousin) and probably Livy on the 15th.

I had a nice visit from Chas. Peabody and it looks as if I had bought Warm Springs. If so I want you to take a great interest in it, for I feel you can help me with many suggestions and the place properly run will not only do a great deal of good but will prove financially successful.

I go there from Miami March 27th and hope to find it warm enough to use the outdoor pool.

It has been very windy down here and the fishing poor in consequence.

Devotedly your son,

F.D.R.

A great deal of love to all the family.

The death of Annie Delano Hitch on March 6, 1926, not only caused great sorrow in the Delano and Roosevelt families, but also was deeply felt by the town of Newburgh, where her charitable endeavors left a permanent mark on the life of the community. She was the first woman to be elected an honorary member of a men's service club, having been made a member of the Newburgh Chapter of the Lions International. That the latter organization was proud of her membership is witnessed by their eulogy carried in the *Newburgh Daily News* a year later, on April 12, 1927:

. . . Her influence as a gentlewoman made an indelible imprint here never to be obliterated while Lions live and cherish her memory as a rich legacy. She was a lover of children, a friend of the unfortunate. She was not a charitable spendthrift, but a practical philanthropist with a highly cultivated mind. Her disposition was radiant, and while she might command the loftiest social altitude in America, she was not bothered by cheap personal ambition. She was too big to bend below the standards of a queen. . . .

In her own unique way Sara Roosevelt expressed similar sentiments in a letter to F.D.R. of March 15, 1926: "It seems very strange here without darling Annie, and we miss her terribly but I do feel thankful that she left quickly and without pain. She would have been unhappy to have lived on and to give up all her active interests. She was so wonderful in every detail, following people to the door with flowers and gifts, and yet doing big things so well. The feeling in Newburgh is deep and widespread, flags at half-mast and shops closed (for an hour) the day of the funeral."

Appointed by President Wilson to the First Industrial Commission in 1919, Edwin Farnham Greene was at this time president of the Lockwood Greene Company and chief executive of the Pacific Mills. Charles Peabody was a brother of George Foster Peabody, from whom F.D.R. purchased the property at Warm Springs after his arrival there late in March. The modification concerning the financial possibilities of Warm Springs was added by F.D.R. to

his main purpose of doing "a great deal of good" primarily
because Sara Roosevelt was worried lest her son "bankrupt"
himself.

∽

Dearest Mama—

I am thinking of you on another sad visit to Fairhaven
and I wish so that I could be with you all. I know Lyman
will have made all the arrangements well. It must have been a
terrible shock to you on reaching Algonac, but I am thankful
Aunt Doe and Miss Dreier were there. Poor Aunt Doe will
indeed feel in a way as if she had lost her home, for I suppose
Uncle Fred will really move to Algonac next summer or
autumn, and Aunt Tillie will give a very different atmosphere.

Eleanor wired me about Dr. Newton. I feared he would
not long survive the stroke as he was never really strong. It
is going to make a vast difference at Hyde Park, but I hope
we will get a young man and that there won't be any effort
to call the Rev. Montgomery!

I enclose several business things:

1. A cheque for $33.33, your share from Papa's estate of
$100 which I collected from Stratton for a quit-claim deed
for one of the old lots. You can treat is as a present and *not*
report it as income!

2. You told me you would give me the new fishing reel—
the bill for it is $71.00!

3. There is a grand mix-up over the Terrace Garage Bill.
Dec. 31 Bill. My car did not get to N.Y. till Dec. 15 and was
at H.P. Dec. 23–27 and again Dec. 30–31, so it was only
stored 10 days or 1/3 of $50 = $17.00. The shutter was not
mine that I know of, nor the tube repair, nor that vast

amount of gas and oil! I figure about 20 gals. of gas and 3
qts. oil were mine or about $6.50.

Total Dec.   23.50

January—both cars in town
½ bill is mine
none of the Feb. Bill is mine 83.30
I therefore owe you on these 3 bills   106.80 .
But I paid in Dec. a Terrace Garage bill
of $214.19 of which I figure your share
was $147.08 as per enclosed slip.
Therefore to sum up

You owe me—July—Oct.	147.08
" " " Fishing reel	71.00
	$218.08
I owe you Jan/Feb.	106.80
Balance due me	$111.28

Will you pay the bills or send me cheque whenever you
want?

Missy left yesterday and I am practically cleaned up but
from now will have to work 2 or 3 hours every day, long
hand. Nothing definite from the Peabodys but I think they
will accept my terms.

Johnny Lawrence leaves on Monday and Elliott arrives
Tuesday and will be alone with me as Livy wires from
Nassau he cannot come.

Address up to Mar. 23rd Miami Grocery Co. I go to Warm
Springs the 27th.

Devotedly
F.D.R.

F.D.R.'s remarks about his Aunt Doe (Mrs. Paul R.
Forbes), who had lived with her sister Annie in Newburgh
since the death of her husband in 1921, was a reply to a
comment in his mother's letter of March 6, 1926: "Aunt
Doe is lovely and brave but in one way it is worse for her

than for anyone, as she has no children and this is home, the only one she knows."

After fifteen years as pastor of St. James's Church, the Reverend Edward Piersons Newton died of a heart attack on March 8, 1926, and F.D.R.'s remark about "a vast difference at Hyde Park" echoed the sentiments of the entire community. His successor was Alban Richey, Jr., who was under thirty at the time, thereby fulfilling F.D.R.'s preference for a "young man" instead of the Reverend Hardman P. Montgomery of nearby Millbrook, who was born in 1873. In her letter of March 15, 1926, Sara Roosevelt concurred with her son's preference: "I am glad you told me you want a young rector. I will try to 'work it.' "

These are the only two existing family letters F.D.R. wrote during his third cruise on the *Larooco*, the log of which is resumed with the March 7th entry.

∽∾

Sunday, March 7, 1926.
Ran up to Channel Key and in p.m. J.S.L. and Greene went in to Long Key for mail, etc. It has been blowing steadily for five days. Fine bath in shallows.

Monday, March 8, 1926.
All out to reef in launch. On way back after catching only 1 grouper it came on to blow hard from N. Made Long Key, got mail and back to ship at 7 p.m.

Tuesday, March 9, 1926.
J.S.L. and Greene left to go to Cuba. Capt. Charlie Watkins to go to Miami to pay his income tax. Blowing hard—the weather—not Capt. C.

Wednesday, March 10, 1926.
M.A.L. and I cleared up a lot of files and correspondence. In p.m. went in from Channel Key to Long Key and on way back M.A.L. got a 12 lb. Jack. Still blowing.

Thursday, March 11, 1926.

Wind shifted from E. to S.W. Looked stormy. After lunch started and ran past Long Key to Jewfish Bush. Heavy rain. At 8:30 M.A.L. left to take train home.

Friday, March 12, 1926.

Still blowing—anchored all day at Jewfish Bush. J.S.L. wires he will not arrive till tomorrow. Capt. Charlie came back from Miami. F.D.R. improved his solitary confinement by much exercising on deck, doing accounts, playing solitaire, reading Oppenheim, and eating less heavily.

Saturday, March 13, 1926.

Stayed at Jewfish Bush till the p.m. when I moved Larooco up to Long Key. Had a visit from Mr. Schutt. ½ Owner Lawrence turned up in evening from Havana, rather sleepy but had a very good time!

Sunday, March 14, 1926.

J.S.L. and I trolled all afternoon, out to reef beyond trestle 2 etc. Got a couple of jacks and a grouper. Back to Long Key. Much discussion of the cotton industry, New England conference, etc.

Monday, March 15, 1926.

William Hart comes from Columbus, Ga. and J.S.L. left for the North at 11 a.m. Hart and I discussed plans for Warm Springs all day and evening. The Fortuna arrived and we had a call from Dick Talbot, Cassy de Rham and Dr. Rushmore. Bill Post too ill to come. At Long Key all day.

Tuesday, March 16, 1926.

Elliott arrived early, looking rather pale. W. Hart left at 11 and we got under way and ran up before lunch to 2 miles N.W. of Bow Leg Key. Elliott and I and the two Capts. and

Roy took the row boat and launch through a cut, then in a
N. direction about 3 miles past 3 Keys on the right. Got into
rowboat and pushed her over mud to a wonderful deep pool
between 3rd and 4th Keys. Pool full of fish of all kinds and
apparently never visited. Got a dozen or more very large red
snappers, some up to 5 lbs. and also a very large gag—about
10 lbs. This pool is a real discovery.

Wednesday, March 17, 1926.

Blowing hard in a.m. so we went back 2 miles through
main cut and anchored in behind Bow Leg Key. In p.m.
Elliott and I went back to our pool, but spent our time trying
to harpoon whip-rays. Struck one but harpoon pulled out
after a few minutes. Got another big grouper on the way
back, so we look forward to more chowder.

Thursday, March 18, 1926.

Sent dory in to Long Key for mail and after lunch we ran
up to Tavernier and anchored off the Hull Cottage. Elliott
and I went in for a swim in the Bath Tub and his "tan"
came off under the application of soap!

Friday, March 19, 1926.

Tavernier. Off early for a day on the reef in Mr. Leonard
Low's excellent launch. An onshore breeze made it a bit
choppy and Elliott was about to succumb when a 12 lb.
grouper struck his hook. For a minute it was a grave question
as to whether grouper would come in or breakfast go out.
Grouper came in, and Elliott beat Jimmy's record by retain-
ing his insides. We made a record catch of groupers, 15 in all
and 1 barracuda. Total weight well up to 150 lbs. as I got one
of 21 lbs. and Capt. Charlie one of 20 lbs. This was the best
day's grouper fishing I have had.

Saturday, March 20, 1926.

Tavernier. An expedition to Hammonds Point netted us
many dozen delicious grapefruit from the Hull grove. They

are not picked and "Bobby Burns" told us help ourselves. After lunch we ran up to Key Largo, and anchored off the new canal to the station.

Sunday, March 21, 1926.

Another grand day—Elliott and the Capt. ashore to see the two excursion trains bearing 2,000 people from Miami to view the "great" Key Largo development. Free ride, free lunch, free motor trip, free lecture, free chance, to agree to buy a lot for $2,000, worth $20! In p.m. Elliott and I fished to the westward and got 3 ladyfish. A norther looked imminent and we moved Larooco through drawbridge into Jewfish Creek.

Monday, March 22, 1926.

Last night we caught the record fish of all time! Elliott had put out a shark hook baited with half a ladyfish and about 8 o'clock we noticed the line was out in the middle of the Creek. It seemed caught on a rock and we got the rowboat and cleared it. It ran then under Larooco and with E. and Roy and John and the Capt. pulling on it we finally brought a perfectly enormous Jewfish along side. We could just get his mouth out of water and put in 2 other hooks and a gaff. Then Roy shot him about 8 times through the head with my revolver. As he seemed to be fairly dead we hoisted him on the davit which threatened to snap off at any moment. He was over seven feet long, over 5 feet around and his jaw opened 18 inches. We put him on the hand scale this morning, which registers up to 400 lbs. He weighed more than this, as he was only 2/3 out of water, so we figure his weight at between 450 and 500 lbs. We borrowed a Kodak and films at Key Largo, and took many photos of him.

After lunch E. and I trolled and he caught 3 good-sized red groupers south of Jewfish Creek using a bait troll.

Tuesday, March 23, 1926.

Awakened at midnight by a man from Chicago yacht "Adventurer" lying near us, asking for a Doctor. They had gone shark fishing in their launch which caught fire and two of the men were quite badly burned. We gave them some olive oil unguentine.

At 10 a.m. left Jewfish Creek and ran up to Angelfish Creek. Elliott and I and the two Captains caught a large mess of grunts, porgies, pork-fish etc.

Wednesday, March 24, 1926.

Angelfish Creek. Elliott went sponging with the two Captains and they came back with a dozen or more nice sheep wools. After lunch we went fishing again, our last day, and caught over 30—large grunts, yellow grunts, porgies, runners, pork-fish, parrot fish, black angelfish and yellow angelfish! A fine final day. "Adventurer" came in and anchored close to us and the men with burns are much better.

Thursday, March 25, 1926.

Another glorious day. Left good old Angelfish Creek after breakfast and ran up to Bear Cut near Miami and after lunch Elliott ran in to the City with Capt. Bob while F.D.R. and Roy spent the afternoon packing things up. There are 18 or 20 large vessels anchored off shore, waiting to get in to Miami. We wonder if the channel is again blocked.

Friday, March 26, 1926.

Spent the day peacefully near the "ole swimming hole" on the South side of Bear Cut. Completed packing up various things to be sent to Warm Springs, as Johnny Lawrence and I have decided to offer good old Larooco for sale, and we have a superfluous quantity of china, linen, etc. In the afternoon we ran into the Miami River and got things ready to leave.

Saturday, March 27, 1926.

At Miami. Completed all final arrangements and said farewell to the good old boat. Elliott and I left on the evening train for Warm Springs.

End of 1926 Cruise

∞

Postscript

In September 1926 a violent hurricane swept the East Coast of Florida. The Houseboat Larooco was laid up at the Pilkington Yacht Basin, about 2 miles up the Fort Lauderdale River. This was near the center of the hurricane area. Most of the yachts were in the big shed, and were destroyed when the river rose and the shed collapsed. "Larooco" was moored outside, along the bank and made fast to two palm trees. As the river rose far above its banks, the two trees were pulled up by the roots, and Larooco started inland on her last voyage. Driven by the hurricane and disregarding river course or channel she finally brought up in a pine forest four miles inland and as the waters receded she settled down comfortably on the pine needles, at least a mile from the nearest water.

As the old strains to the hull were made worse, salvage was impracticable, and she was offered for sale as a hunting lodge—and finally sold for junk in 1927.

So ended a good old craft with a personality. On the whole it was an end to be preferred to that of gasoline barge or lumber lighter.

∞

F.D.R. arrived in Warm Springs at the end of March, and on April 29, 1926, he acquired the property, which consisted of the springs, the hotel, and the cottages, as well as some twelve hundred acres of land. He then began to experiment on a much larger scale with the curative possibilities of Warm Springs. The noticeable improvement of every paralytic who had spent time in the pool during the previous year convinced F.D.R. that it was time for medical experts to investigate the cure. As the American Orthopedic Association was then holding its national convention in nearby Atlanta, F.D.R. suggested that it undertake experimentation at Warm Springs. After much difficulty, because of his layman status, he succeeded in winning unofficial approval by the Association, which agreed to an experimental period and to an investigating committee of three of its members, all eminent specialists. The committee was to receive reports from a physician in charge of the experiment, and for this job F.D.R. obtained the services of Dr. LeRoy W. Hubbard, the orthopedic surgeon of the New York State Department of Health, who had had nine years' experience in the after-care of poliomyelitis. Dr. Hubbard brought with him an assistant, Miss Helena T. Mahoney, a graduate nurse and a trained physiotherapist. Together with a swimming instructor they carried out the first medical experiment at Warm Springs. Twenty-three patients, all in the after-care stage, were observed for periods of from five to seventeen weeks, covering the months of June to December. The findings, which indicated improvement in every case, were then sent to the three orthopedic surgeons of the A.O.A. Individually and together their verdict was one of approval of the work accomplished by Hubbard, and they further recommended the establishment of a permanent hydrotherapeutic center at Warm Springs.

While leaving the strictly medical aspects of his new enterprise to Dr. Hubbard and Miss Mahoney, F.D.R. engaged wholeheartedly and energetically in the development of Warm Springs. At first A.E.R., who had been forced to shoulder greater independence as a result of her husband's illness and who consequently was at this time just learning that no job was too big to overcome, was somewhat skeptical of F.D.R.'s new enterprise in Georgia. On May 4, 1926, she wrote:

. . . I know you love creative work, my only feeling is that Georgia is somewhat distant for you to keep in touch with what is really a big undertaking. One cannot, it seems to me, have *vital* interests in widely divided places, but that may be because I'm old and rather overwhelmed by what there is to do in one place and it wearies me to think of even undertaking to make new ties. Don't be discouraged by me; I have great confidence in your extraordinary interest and enthusiasm. It is just that I couldn't do it, but then I couldn't contemplate doing what Nan is proposing at Hyde Park! . . .

∽∽

Although not "discouraged" by his wife, F.D.R. did not remain with his "big undertaking" during the summer, but left the experiment with Dr. Hubbard and returned to New York several days after receiving this letter. He spent the summer of 1926 at Marion, where he rented a house for his family so that they could also enjoy a vacation away from New York. Dr. McDonald's treatments had been so helpful the previous summer that F.D.R. decided to continue his exercises; it is at this point that his correspondence is briefly resumed.

MARION, MASS.
[AUGUST 10, 1926]
TUESDAY

Dearest Mama,

Eleanor left Sunday night for N.Y. from Weekapaug whither we had motored that morning to lunch with the Morgenthau's. I got back here at 8:30 and gave Elliott his Latin. Yesterday I lunched with Bertie Hamlin, saw Catherine, the children afterwards. Today F. & J. motor to Providence, where E. meets them and they go to Weekapaug and motor back here Friday. On Sunday we have 24 to lunch —the Grants, Martineau's, Aunt Kassie, etc. F. Jr.'s Birthday party. I do so wish you could be with us.

Elliott takes the Monday a.m. boat and you will see him Tuesday early. James wires he leaves Thursday, so I take it he will get to St. Andrews Saturday morning.

A great deal of love, also to Cousin Mamie and the Adams and Archer-Shee's. Your letter makes me very homesick for Campo!

Devotedly

F.D.R.

F.D.R. did not gratify his "homesickness" for Campobello until the summer of 1933, after he had completed his first famous hundred days as President of the United States. On this occasion he expressed to the welcoming crowd his happiness at finally returning to the island:

I think I can address you as my old friends of Campobello —old and new. I was figuring this morning on the passage of time and I remembered that I was brought here because I was teething forty-nine years ago. I have been coming for many months almost every year until twelve years ago, when there was a gap.

It seems to me that memory is a very wonderful thing, because this morning, when we were beginning to come out of the fog off Quoddy Head, the boys from the lookout in the bow called out "Land ahead." Nevertheless, memory kept me going full speed because I knew the place was the Lubec Narrows. . . .

The day after writing this letter F.D.R. received a printed form from the Dean of Harvard College, C. N. Greenough, stating that his eldest son had been admitted and requesting information on James' "special characteristics." The Dean explained that "Harvard College is so large that its teachers and administrative officers have great difficulty in knowing their students as individuals," and that to overcome this problem the parents were being asked to supply the data "which we can acquire only very gradually but which you already have as no one else has it in the case of your own son." F.D.R. was also informed that his reply would be "regarded as absolutely confidential and that the more frankly you write to us, the more we can help your son." Several days later F.D.R. answered this form. His reply, which is distinctly a personal letter although he was only casually acquainted with the addressee, is extraordinary, far more revealing of father than of son.

MARION, MASS.
AUGUST 15, 1926
SUNDAY

My dear Dean Greenough:

This is a more or less personal note in reply to yours of August 11th regarding my oldest boy James who is about to enter the Freshman Class.

He goes to Harvard with the usual advantages and handicaps of having spent six years at Groton. He did very well there in athletics and leadership, rather poorly in studies— lower half of the form—but passed all his College Board Examinations, two with honors.

He is clean, truthful, considerate of others, and has distinct ambition to make good. He has at the same time, I think, too much of a love of "social good times" (like the rest of his crowd), and for that reason, although a former Overseer, etc., I hesitated for some time before letting him go to Cambridge at all. In other words, I know enough of the club and Boston life of the average private school freshman to fear the lack of individuality and the narrowness which comes to so many of them.

One of the principal troubles with most of these private school undergraduates of yours is, I am convinced after a good deal of investigation, that their parents give them a great deal too much money to go through college on. To this is added in most cases, automobiles, and all sorts of expensive toys in the holidays.

You people in authority have done and are doing a great work in aiming at greater simplicity of college life, and incidentally your fine efforts for higher scholarship, i.e., more work, is bearing good fruit.

I, as one graduate among many, want to cooperate with you in this. During this past summer my boy has worked as a laborer in a Canadian pulp and paper mill. Most of the Groton boys will have college allowances well over $2,000 a year. James and his room mate Harrison Parker, Jr. will have only $1500 or $1600.

I should like them in addition to find some sort of employment while at college so that they could earn part of their education, even if it covered only the $300 tuition. In my own days such a thing was rare and difficult. Waiting on table at Memorial was about the only method, and the college office made very little effort to encourage boys to find jobs. I hope this phase is better handled now.

Concretely in regard to my boy I feel that the following should be the objectives:
1. Better scholarship than passing marks. 2. Athletics to be a secondary not a primary objective. 3. Activity in student activities such as debating, Crimson, etc. to be encouraged. 4. Acquaintance with the average of the class, not just the Mt. Auburn Street crowd to be emphasized. 5. Opportunity to earn part of his education.

I hope to get up to Cambridge this autumn and to have a chance to see you. Very sincerely yours,
                                    Franklin D. Roosevelt

F.D.R. never mailed this letter, which is still enclosed in its original envelope with an uncanceled stamp. Instead he first sent it to his son at Campobello for approval, and as James protested to part of the contents, he rewrote it in a less provocative vein. However, this does not mean that he did not believe what he had written, but rather that he respected his son's sincerity and realized that James was aware of the purpose of a college education. This letter indicates the part of his heritage which F.D.R. rejected; it contains the same principle which caused discord between himself and his mother. By its very nature, by the establishment of "social good times" as an end in itself, F.D.R. visualized his heritage as fostering a "lack of individuality"; it was a source of "narrowness," a characteristic which, as his personal correspondence clearly reveals, was diametrically opposed to his personality.

∽∾

That F.D.R. and A.E.R. sought to impress these values upon their children is disclosed by James' protest against the letter to Dean Greenough.

CAMPOBELLO
AUGUST 17, 1926
TUESDAY

Dear Father,

Elliott has just given me your letter to Dean Greenough. I'm sorry I couldn't have talked with you before you wrote, especially on two points: (1) the working the way through, and two, "the social good times." I know how you and Mother feel on the subject and to a certain extent I agree with you, but on one point in your letter I not only disagree but object very strongly. When you say "He has at the same time, I think, too much of a love of 'social good times' (like the rest of his crowd)." Now it seems to me that to say that strongly implies that "my crowd" is a wild, pleasure-loving crowd, which is not so at all. Of course every boy and girl likes to have a good time, it is only normal to do so but boys from Groton, St. Marks, etc., do not do so any more than any others, as you imply. We are not all necessarily [name deleted] or [name deleted] you know and I think it distinctly unfair to tell Dean Greenough that we are a pleasure loving crowd. High school boys and all boys enjoy dances and "social good times" but I *know* and believe that you will come to see that a large majority of us know when to stop and to behave as gentlemen in the true sense of the word. Therefore I think it hardly fair to give the Dean the false impression that I and others from Groton are over-social. We know and I will prove that work is foremost and that we really intend to get something out of college.

The second point about working one's way through seems to me to come down to this: if one intends to study, play games and participate too in hard extra curriculum activities, such as the Crimson, there is really no time left to do the other. If on the other hand you feel that you can only afford to give me so much I will without hesitation give up debating, etc., and earn my board. It can be done but I feel that I can get more out of college by taking part in outside activities, but I know also that with the work (scholastic) it will be necessary for me to do, I cannot combine and do everything thoroughly. If you feel that by giving me $1800 I will be free to spend socially I will gladly give you an itemized account of every penny I spend and turn the surplus back to you at the end of the year.

I hope you will realize that I have written this because I really feel it and not because I am obstinate and trying to justify myself. It is frank and I hope you will understand what I mean, because I do want you to understand, and it is the only way isn't it to understand each other.

Affectionately,

James

~~

At the end of the summer F.D.R. returned briefly to New York; then, late in September, he and his mother journeyed to Warm Springs, where Dr. Hubbard was just finishing up the experimental period of observation. Two weeks afterward Sara Roosevelt departed for Hyde Park, whereupon F.D.R. wrote the following letter.

WARM SPRINGS
OCTOBER 13, [1926]
Dearest Mama,   WEDNESDAY

Your cheque book can't be found, nor Missy's book, but your work bag has gone to you.

I miss you a lot and I don't have to tell you how I loved to have you here, and I know you were really interested in seeing what I think is a very practical good to which this place can be put and you needn't worry about my losing a fortune in it, for every step is being planned either to pay for itself or to make a profit on.

Missy and Barbara Muller are very unobtrusive house guests and we play bridge every evening which makes it impossible for me to hear the story of "Hilda's" life repeated!

The weather continues heavenly. I'm so glad you had those nice two days with Uncle Fred—it would be grand if he would come here in the Spring. The rug comes tomorrow!
                                                  Devotedly
                                                  FDR

Barbara Muller was a friend of Miss Le Hand; the following year she married the business manager of the hydro-therapeutic center at Warm Springs, Egbert T. Curtis. Miss Hilda Emmott had made F.D.R.'s acquaintance through a mutual friend, and came to him seeking legal advice on a matter which required the enumeration of "the story of her life." After the service was rendered, she persisted with the acquaintance and with her story.

∾

WARM SPRINGS
OCTOBER 29, 1926
Dearest Mama,   FRIDAY

I am sending you by Parcel Post a somewhat belated Birthday present with my love and the hope that you will love it as much as I do. It came via a Scotch sailor who is beating his way from New Orleans to Baltimore and it was probably stolen or undoubtedly was smuggled in. Both Miss Emmott and I think it a really fine speciman, and it is of the rather rare variety which has different shades as you view it from different sides! It came over in the ship with the sailor who swears he got it in the Mediterranean, would not be more definite! Now aren't you intrigued!

I'm busy every second. Miss Emmott fell down a week ago and sprained both ankles. She leaves on Thursday next.

My house is started and they have dug the cellar and are beginning the foundations.

Expect to leave here the 8th. A great deal of love.

Devotedly
FDR

A.E.R. cannot recall the nature of F.D.R.'s birthday present to his mother, although the story of its acquisition was compounded to tease his mother. The cottage F.D.R. was building at this time was not the "Little White House" in which he died. This latter building was constructed in 1932, and after his death was turned over to the State of Georgia in accordance with F.D.R.'s will. His first cottage, which is mentioned in this letter and which was the beginning of the "cottage colony" that came into being within the next two years, was sold after F.D.R. moved into the Little White House.

∽∽

F.D.R. again returned to New York for the winter holidays, and while there, in January 1927, he formed the Georgia Warm Springs Foundation. This step was taken on the basis of Dr. Hubbard's report and the subsequent recommendation of the investigating committee. In addition to F.D.R., the incorporators of the non-stock, non-profit institution were George Foster Peabody, Basil O'Connor, Herbert N. Straus, and Louis McH. Howe. Dr. Hubbard accepted the position of chief physiotherapist and director of nurses. We "will see our dream carried out," F.D.R. wired Thomas Loyless on January 18th; with keen anticipation he departed for Georgia the following month. Shortly before leaving he dictated the next two letters to his brother-in-law and uncle.

NEW YORK
FEBRUARY 3, 1927
THURSDAY

Dear Hall:

I haven't answered your letter of January 10th before this because Barron Collier has been down in Florida and now I am going away next week. However, I am asking Louis to see Collier as soon as the latter gets back.

As you probably know, Eleanor had her tonsils out last Friday and is now back home, the trained nurse still there, but everything is going finely and Eleanor will probably go up to Hyde Park tomorrow if the weather holds good. She goes down to Warm Springs with me on February 12th.

John broke his arm last Friday, but is getting along all right and is back at school. James has been home with the flu, but is now back in Cambridge and all seems to be going well.

My, but those ducks were good and I cannot tell you how much they were appreciated by everybody.

Affectionately yours,

[F.D.R.]

G. Hall Roosevelt had written F.D.R. about a method of exploiting the earth's oil resources in which he had become interested: ". . . in general, the operation is to locate a dome by placing a number of seismograph instruments at known distances from charges of dynamite and secure curves which can be interpreted to give reliable indications of the substrata." In need of land on which to carry out the "operation," A.E.R.'s brother asked F.D.R.

to sound out Barron Collier, a prominent New York capitalist and the largest landowner in Florida, on the possibilities of leasing his land. F.D.R. and Collier had become acquainted mainly through their mutual interest in the Boy Scout Foundation of Greater New York, for which F.D.R. had directed the raising of funds and of which Collier was acting president.

∾

NEW YORK
FEBRUARY 4, 1927
FRIDAY

Dear Uncle Fred:

I wish much that I could stay with you. However, I have to give the annual dinner to the 1920 newspaper boys and also have to see crowds of senators and congressmen, and it is really much easier for all concerned for me to go to the same hotel that I spent the night at last year—I think it is the Continental—near the station.

I get down there Friday afternoon, the 11th, and will be there all day Saturday and count on seeing you. Can't you come in some time Saturday afternoon? Eleanor will not be in Washington, but I join her on the train for Warm Springs Saturday evening. She has had her tonsils out, as you probably know, and her throat is still pretty sore and we are keeping her as quiet as possible before the trip. The same day as the tonsil operation, Johnny fell down and broke his arm and James was home from Cambridge in bed with quite a bad attack of the flu, so we have had a hospital in the house.

Affectionately yours,

[F.D.R.]

∾

WARM SPRINGS
[FEBRUARY 1927]
WEDNESDAY

Dearest Mama—

It is good to get your letter and we shall think of you taking the boys to Hyde Park next Sunday. We are safely installed in the *old* cottage, not unpacked as we hope to move into the new cottage by early next week. The new cottage is *too* sweet, really very good in every way, the woodwork covering all walls and ceilings a great success, and the new furniture fits perfectly and is just the right color. Of course I am taking a good deal of stuff out of the hotel but there is much to buy and today Eleanor and Missy have gone to Atlanta to buy a stove and a refrigerator and a lot of small things, and they get back about six.

This morning I have driven with Mr. Curtis and Miss Mahoney over the "Pine Mountain Scenic Highway"—five miles long, out to the Knob, marvellous views all the way and cost me only $1050! I've been in the pool each day and done all the exercises and stretching and am feeling finely. The weather is warm and bright, the peach blossoms coming out, everything is nearly a month early and the local people say we shall have a cold, rainy March to make up for it. I am going ahead with the big work of preparing for 50 patients and hope Major Proctor will soon raise some money—the golf course comes along well and is going to be very good.

Love to you all and I hope you have a lovely Sunday at H.P.

Devotedly

F.D.R.

The exact date of this letter cannot be determined, but it appears to have been written during the first February after the Georgia Warm Springs Foundation had been incorporated. The high cost of F.D.R.'s drive "out to the Knob" probably refers to the fact that he purchased some land to add to the farm he had bought the previous year. The farm, comprising 1750 acres, was located three miles south of Warm Springs on the summit of Pine Mountain, and F.D.R. operated it mainly to raise cattle for market; he purposely refused to allow his foreman to grow cotton in order to show that it was not a necessary crop in the South for a profitable farm operation. Redfield Proctor, an officer in the engineer corps and governor of Vermont from 1923 to 1925, was a member of the Harvard Infantile Paralysis Commission.

During the interval between this letter and the next F.D.R. remained in Warm Springs busily organizing the work of the Foundation.

~~

Dearest Mama,

DeGroff arrived safely Thursday evening and is comfortably installed in the cottage colony, and goes in for his first swim today. I have not seen him yet as I haven't been out of the house since we moved into the old cottage on Tuesday. Missy stood the move very well, and heart action was greatly improved, but since Wednesday p.m. she has had a *serious* attack of dysentery, or colitis and is rather low and very miserable. Another nurse comes from Atlanta today and I am wiring for either her brother Dan or his wife.

I have had of course no opportunity to do anything else and therefore cannot set a definite date for return till we know more.

Please be sure to get that diagnosis from Hibbs and also please a history of his case from his Poughkeepsie Dr. It is absolutely necessary for Dr. Hubbard to have these.

After a week or two will give DeGroff charge of the lawns and grounds with 2 negroes under him.

Much love.

Devotedly

FDR

John DeGroff had been a coachman at the Hyde Park home for nearly ten years, and when he was stricken with chronic arthritis, F.D.R. arranged for him to work at Warm

Springs and at the same time to undergo the cure. Sara Roosevelt answered her son's request for a history of DeGroff's illness in her usual precise manner: ". . . As to DeGroff, all I can tell you is that Dr. Hibbs told me that 'it is arthritis of the spine, and nothing will cure him; he will be off and on *very* suffering as long as he lives.' The attacks of pain began years ago, before he came to me and the last three illnesses have come only a few months apart. I cannot see that his month in the Orthopedic Hospital did any good except that he rested, and had x-rays, massage, etc., and his teeth were examined and cleaned! Dr. Cronk says the trouble is *sciatica*, and has often treated him; also he has been helped once by Dr. Cook the osteopath. Lately he tried a chiropractor, who did *no* good. . . ."

∽∽

A week after writing this letter F.D.R. left Warm Springs to spend the summer at Hyde Park, with occasional trips to his New York office.

NEW YORK
JUNE 29, 1927
WEDNESDAY

Dearest Auntie Bye:

I have been very remiss in answering your note, but I know what the taking of Rosy has meant to you as well as to me. It is very hard to realize when I am at Hyde Park that he is no longer there and in so many more ways than I had realized, I depended on his companionship and on his judgment.

I am sending you some of our folders about Warm Springs. The work of starting a combined resort and therapeutic center has been most fascinating for it is something which, so far as I know, has never been done in this country before.

We have already 30 patients there this summer and our total capacity for this coming year will be only 50, a figure I think we shall reach in a few weeks.

623

Most of the patients are suffering from infantile paralysis though we have two arthritis cases at the present time and expect several others, and also hope to have a good many people come there next winter for a few weeks of after-cure succeeding operations or serious illness. It ought to be a success as the doctors are most enthusiastic and, at the same time, the climate is a delightful one all the year round. The elevation of 1000 feet makes it cool enough even in summer and it is far enough south to make it dry and bracing, and yet warm enough during the winter.

Aside from the therapeutic value, we have so many natural resources for the families or patients that the swimming, golf, riding and quail shooting ought to appeal to those in perfect health. The whole property I have put under the Georgia Warm Springs Foundation and am now busily engaged in trying to raise two or three hundred thousand dollars to carry out the improvements and pay the mortgage on the property.

Oh, I do wish that you could be wafted down there and placed gently in a chair and slid gracefully down a ramp into the water. You would love the informality and truly languid southern atmosphere of the place! My one fear is that this gentle charm will appeal to some of our rich friends who are suffering from nervous prosperity and that they will come down there and ruin our atmosphere. Cousin Susy Parish talks of a visit there, but I am not certain that she could endure our southern cooking.

Do send me some nice souls this coming winter, but not the kind who would insist on full dress for dinner every evening.

Always affectionately yours,

[F.D.R.]

As can be seen from this carbon copy of a letter to Mrs. W. Sheffield Cowles, the Georgia Warm Springs Foundation began auspiciously. By the end of 1927 seventy-one patients had been treated and the staff had increased to one hundred and ten. The letter bespeaks F.D.R.'s enthusiasm about the work. After returning from Bermuda late in April, James Roosevelt Roosevelt was bedridden with bronchitis; on May 7, 1927, at the age of seventy-three, he died in his Hyde Park home.

∽∽

[HYDE PARK]
[SUMMER, 1927]

Dear Bunny:

Sorry not to see you before you go. Do please wire us when you get safely to Maine and also when to expect you back.

Do you realize that your license is only good for driving on my business and that no police officer would construe this trip as such!

Be *very* careful—if you smashed up I could not collect any insurance aside from any question of injury to you!

Affectionately

Pa

The date of this holograph letter from F.D.R. to his son Elliott cannot be definitely ascertained, but it was written sometime early in the summer of 1927, on the occasion of the latter's departure for Campobello by auto.

∽∽

HYDE PARK
AUGUST 29, 1927
MONDAY

Dearest Mama—

The coal has come and I enclose receipted bill for $89.76.

It's a crime about DeGroff's attitude—he needs a talking to.

The small boys took the ponies up yesterday at 7 p.m. and went up today at 10 to stay alone at the Fair till p.m.

Eleanor has gone to N. Y. for a few hours and gets back this evening.

We had a busy week end. The Teads' left Sunday p.m., Lady Willert last night and Sir Arthur this a.m. with Eleanor.

I have never seen so much rain, it fell steadily from Friday p.m. to this morning and now we are in the midst of a thunderstorm.

I wish much I could get on for Livy's wedding in Bar Harbor, but I am to lunch with them in N. Y. on Friday.

Much, much love from us all.

Devotedly,

F.D.R.

Dr. Hubbard had advised Sara Roosevelt that John DeGroff's arthritic condition was such that he should not work in the stable upon his return from Warm Springs. DeGroff resented this medical opinion, and his "attitude" caused F.D.R. and his mother some concern. The "Teads" refers to the family of Ordway Tead, the prominent editor and educator who later became chairman of the Board of Higher Education of New York City. Livingston Davis' second marriage was to Georgia Appleton of New York.

Late in September F.D.R. again journeyed to Warm Springs to pursue his own cure, and to be on hand for the continued and rapid development of the Foundation.

WARM SPRINGS
[SEPTEMBER 30, 1927]
FRIDAY

Dearest Mama,

I loved your description of the christening! Some party! Garden fountain, vested choir, jewels, light blue maids, negus, perfume and lip stick! It's wicked to laugh, but *entre nous* it's a joy!

I'm so glad you're going to Groton. F.D.R. Jr. seems to be

doing well and enjoying it all, and he will love to have you come.

It seems to me that $500 is too much for that other horse. I told that Archer man not over $300 and Narissa thrown in. I'd insist on it if I were you. The grey is enough as an expensive horse and at this time of year I'm sure we can get a good one for $300 and Narissa.

The weather continues warm and heavenly and I'm busy every minute but am doing my exercises morning and afternoon with regularity and Miss M. says I am doing finely.

Much love to you and Johnny. The house must seem very empty.

Devotedly

FDR

Thanks for the Courier.

Sara Roosevelt's "description of the christening" was contained in her letter of September 27, 1927:

. . . [she] dressed the baby and hung pearls around her neck, and during the ceremony at the fountain in the garden, hung a pink pearl on a fine chain around her neck (baby behaved perfectly). There was the Rhinebeck choir, three hymns, and *such* vestments, and all the neighbors were there. We drank *not* candle, but a punch with a decided *stick* in it. I found one glass quite enough, but some took two or three! Delicious caviar sandwiches and others— two maids, dressed in very bright blue, handed each person a programme, giving the hymns. One hymn being "Holy, Holy, Holy"—is it appropriate for a baptism? The scene was lovely and the day warm and perfect. I *wish* you had been there! . . .

The same letter also explains Sara Roosevelt's complicated efforts to purchase a new horse and sell the old one, Narissa:

. . . The bay horse came yesterday on trial. Johnnie went up in the truck. I have him on trial for a week. Dr. Roy says he is sound and twelve years old, but he ought to be good for ten years yet, so I think the *age* is not so bad. Price $500 and *no* exchange, so I am going to see what to do with Narissa—as I can't have so many. Johnnie rides all, but *much* prefers Natoma, as she is *narrow* backed. He says *"I can't* exercise them all," and I want him to *drive* the bay and "Silver" when he wants to. . . .

∽

WARM SPRINGS
[AUTUMN, 1927]
WEDNESDAY

Dearest Mama,

It is fine to have your nice long letter of Sunday, and I'm glad that Uncle Fred thinks Aunt Tillie is really better and that you had such a nice visit from him. I do wish he could come down here to see Warm Springs. Of course I can't be responsible for *all* the silly and untrue stories which gossip spreads. *No* circular about Warm Springs, no statement or authorized account has spoken of Warm Springs as being the only place which has helped one. You have I think a copy of the medical pamphlet, if not I enclose another. If Dr. McDonald is hurt I am sorry, but he has no cause to be. I am not giving to the public any history of my own case— if I did I should include Dr. Lovett, Mrs. Lake, etc. etc. Why Dr. McDonald's name should appear in literature about Warm Springs I really can't see—the literature is not about me. Furthermore Dr. M. has been constantly begged by me to come down here and look things over. Finally, as Dr. M. is not an orthopedist none of the orthopedists who are in touch with the work here would care to have him associated.

By the way I wrote Dr. M. several times last Spring, and I had several nice letters from him. In May I wrote him most carefully that we would not come to Marion for the summer as we planned to stay at Hyde Park. I told him I hoped to go to Fairhaven for a week in July and another in September and to take treatments then. You know why these little visits did not materialize.

628

As to the Library—Uncle Fred's plan is of course *fine* for a much larger place than Hyde Park and a much richer one, but I cannot see how it could possibly work out successfully. I have several times explained the question involved in *maintaining* the Library. Under Uncle Fred's plan it becomes necessary in addition to the income of $500 a year from your endowment to raise about $1500 by subscription or memberships. You know as well as I do that this is wholly impossible in Hyde Park. If the Rogers, Newbolds, Betty and Mr. Vanderbilt and Eleanor and I each gave $100, how much more could you raise in the village. Possibly $200 by a food sale or dances! The money *won't* be *given*. The only practical way is to have it taken from either the town taxes or the School District taxes. After all it is not *felt* that way and yet every taxpayer contributes a small share where they will not make it a gift. Also while there is no difficulty about the maintenance of the Library during your or my life time, there is no reason why School District trustees cannot run it after you and I are both gone as well as the trustees suggested by Uncle Fred.

I have read Jefferson's Bible many times. He had a very versatile mind! And incidentally while a gentleman he had a better insight into the Republican form of government than did G. Washington or A. Hamilton. A century and a quarter have proved this!

I'm spending two days in the house as I've had a sore throat for 10 days or rather a raw palate, nothing serious. I feel finely.

Everything goes very well. We have 34 patients and need some new cottages and are working hard on our campaign. The weather has been like September and we shall soon pay for it with cold and rain I fear.

Ever so much love. I must get this off to the mail.

Devotedly

FDR

As it is a reply to an undated letter from Sara Roosevelt, the exact date of this letter cannot be fixed, but it is definitely estimated to have been written in the autumn of 1927. F.D.R.'s remarks about Dr. McDonald, to whom F.D.R. was always grateful for his treatments and who in later years sometimes came to the White House to adjust his braces, was occasioned by the last three paragraphs of his mother's letter:

. . . Uncle Fred heard from Bertie Hamlin, and also, in a round about way, from the young lady you got to go from New Bedford, that Dr. McDonald was much hurt that all accounts and circulars speak of Warm Springs as being the only place that had helped you. Also he feels badly that as he expected you at Marion, you not only did not go there, but you did not write him.

Uncle Fred defended you, but it occurred to him that in any subsequent circulars you could give credit to Dr. Lovett and Dr. McDonald if you think they helped you. For instance in lauding the Springs you might say what great work such men as Dr. Lovett and Dr. McDonald could have accomplished in such a place.

I asked Uncle Fred to allow me to write you this, as you *ought* to know, and I consider that the first *real* improvement you made was with Dr. McDonald. Have you read "Thomas Jefferson's Bible"? If *not* Uncle Fred will send you a copy. . . . Please *mark, read* and *ponder*. . . . Your loving, Mummy.

The controversial pamphlet, which Sara Roosevelt preserved along with F.D.R.'s letter, gives a detailed history and description of the hydrotherapeutic center at Warm Springs. It is quite lengthy, and only devotes a few words to F.D.R.:

. . . In the summer of 1924, Mr. Franklin D. Roosevelt, who had an attack of poliomyelitis (infantile paralysis) in 1921, learned through Mr. George Foster Peabody, then owner of the property, of a young man who had also suffered from the same disease, which rendered him practically helpless. . . . In the fall of 1924 and the spring of 1925, Mr. Roosevelt went to Warm Springs and spent several weeks there, exercising and swimming in the pool and he also had an opportunity to observe several other patients with poliomyelitis who came there in 1925 as a result of newspaper publicity, and spent most of the summer taking exercises with practically no medical supervision.

He was so impressed with their improvement, as well as his own, that he decided in the spring of 1926 to purchase the property and conduct some experimental work during the summer under supervision. Dr. LeRoy W. Hubbard . . . was chosen to direct the work. . . .

For his mother's edification F.D.R. underlined in ink the words "He was so impressed with their improvement, as well as his own."

The question of maintaining the library which F.D.R.'s mother had opened earlier in the year in memory of her husband was complicated by the fact that she did not want to incorporate it. In March of 1926 she had purchased a lot on the main street of Hyde Park, and, sixteen months later, the James Roosevelt Memorial Library, a small two-story building, was opened for use by the residents and school children of the district. As F.D.R.'s plan for maintaining the library could not be worked out to the satisfaction of either his mother or the community, Sara Roosevelt during her lifetime paid all expenses in excess of the $3500 collected in membership dues. After her death in 1941 it was maintained by F.D.R., and in 1947 the town of Hyde Park purchased it from his estate for $4500. The library has since been operated by subscriptions as a community enterprise. Although its name was changed to the Hyde Park Free Library, the name of F.D.R.'s father is still to be seen in stone over the doorway.

Dearest Mama,

Ever so many thanks for the check for 1/3 of the horse. I enclose a money order from Trecartin which I have endorsed to you. You can cash it I think at the Hyde Park postoffice.

I'm distressed to hear about Douglas and am writing Helen. I do hope he won't be left with much paralysis. Thank the Lord I haven't seen him for months, otherwise some people would always feel I gave it to him.

Has Baumgarten started to put in the book cases in the schoolroom? If not will you phone him to hurry up?

Much love.

Devotedly

FDR

F.D.R. had paid the bill for the aforementioned horse called "Silver," and the opening sentence of this letter refers to the receipt of a $159 check from his mother as her share of the horse. A slight lameness in one leg was the eventual result of Theodore Douglas Robinson, Jr.'s mild attack of infantile paralysis. The "schoolroom," which F.D.R. made into an office for himself at the time that he had the bookcases installed by Baumgarten, the local carpenter, is downstairs in the north wing of the Hyde Park home.

∽

Dearest Mama—

I'm so sorry about Douglas. Eleanor writes it is a mild case, but apparently both arms and one leg are hit. I shall offer no advice of course, but only wrote Helen that rest and avoidance of muscle stretching and contractions are all important for at least 3 months. We have so many cases here that come to us from the so-called leading doctors where the treatment has been *criminal* and left permanently bad results that could with knowledge have been avoided. We don't of course take any cases till all soreness is gone, but we know from the history of dozens of cases what awful mistakes are made. I'm so glad the Tuxedo meeting was such a success. Forbes is a wonder. I'm writing to Kassie, etc. etc. etc.

Mr. Pope has been here for two days. Charles Peabody came today. Mrs. Caldwell comes Tuesday. Very cold these past few days but we only missed one day in the pool this past week.

I get to H. P. probably at 6:30 a.m. on Monday, December 5th from St. Louis.

Much love   Devotedly   F.D.R.

Is this yours? It says "Lincoln" on it so suppose it is.

The "Tuxedo meeting" was called by F.D.R.'s mother and her friends to consider the possibilities of raising money for the Georgia Warm Springs Foundation. Forbes Amory, a distant relative of the Roosevelts from Boston whose family later built a cottage at Warm Springs, was a strong and persuasive advocate of the need for helping the Foundation. Henry Pope of Chicago, whose daughter had had polio, became one of the first trustees, and later gave the Foundation some twenty thousand dollars for further experimental work. As mentioned in this letter, F.D.R. went to Hyde Park during the first week in December, but his visit was only a brief one and a month or so later he returned to Warm Springs.

∽

HOTEL WINECOFF
ATLANTA, GEORGIA
[MARCH 17, 1928]
SATURDAY

Dearest Mama,

I came up here last night with a party to buy furniture! Your cottage, Missy's cottage, **Mrs. Pattison's** and **Mrs.**

Curtis'! They are all in process of erection, and when you get here in April you will see yours up, though probably not finished till about the first of May.

Kitty Gandy has come and swears at the weather and everything else, but her language is worse than she is! She looks forward much to your coming, and by that time I hope the rain will really be over. They have had a lot of it all over the South, even Florida, for this past month.

I do hope you are really getting rid of that horrid tonsilitis germ. It has certainly stayed on a long time, but when you come in April it will go quickly and finally in the sunshine. I'm *so* looking forward to having you and crazy to have you see all we've done,—53 patients with us now, and accommodations for 12 more will be ready in April. We have a "waiting list" now, and we are coming out a little better than even on operating expenses.

The Edsel Fords were with the Piersons for a week and I liked them both very much. He gave me a *fine* cheque for the Foundation yesterday.

All well. Much much love and do be sure to take care of yourself.

Devotedly

FDR

A victim of infantile paralysis, Mrs. Lee Marion Pattison, wife of the well-known concert pianist, had been one of the first patients at the Foundation. Like the others mentioned, she erected a cottage on the property in order to be able to consider Warm Springs a home.

Mr. and Mrs. Lynn Pierson of Detroit had taken over the Hart cottage at Warm Springs in which F.D.R. lived during his first visit in 1924. Edsel Ford's gift to the Foundation was accompanied by the following note:

March 15, 1928

Dear Mr. Roosevelt:

Mrs. Ford and I are deeply impressed with the wonderful work which is being carried out here at Warm Springs and we would like to do something towards the development. I am sending herewith a check for twenty-five thousand dollars which I hope you will accept for the Foundation with our best wishes for its complete success.

Sincerely,
Edsel Ford

∽

The automobile manufacturer's subscription, which was used to build a glass-enclosed patients' pool, marked the beginning of a new era of growth for the Foundation; it makes an appropriate conclusion to this chapter. F.D.R.'s efforts to recover the use of his legs did not, of course, end at this time, but in the months following March of 1928 he became more and more active in politics. He was entering the next phase of his life. The Foundation had passed from the fledgling to the expansion stage of its development, and, now that its success was assured, F.D.R. could forget any reluctance he may have had about returning to the political world.

The correspondence in this chapter clearly demonstrates that the loss of the free use of his legs at the age of thirty-nine did not effect any substantial change either in F.D.R.'s personality or his outlook. Instead—and this can perhaps best be seen in the log of the *Larooco*—life as a cripple intensified all the characteristics shown in his letters prior to 1922. His stability became more stable, his optimism more optimistic, and, notwithstanding his inability to walk, even his independent nature was intensified. Hence the argument which attributes to the polio attack, as well as to the several "contemplative" years that followed, the evolution of F.D.R.'s Presidential qualities is easily refuted. He became more steady as a result of his illness, but he did not basically change; thus whatever development he experienced during these six years, and later applied while in the White House, was partly the same growth that would have taken place had he been able to walk as any other healthy person.

∽

XV

"... I Have Had a Difficult Time Turning Down the Governorship ..."

ACTIVE RETURN TO POLITICS

April - November, 1928

During the two years prior to 1928 F.D.R. openly and actively worked to secure Alfred E. Smith's nomination for President at the forthcoming convention. Smith's continued progressive record in New York not only substantiated what F.D.R. had said in his address at Madison Square Garden in 1924, but made him more determined than ever to put Smith across. His efforts in the latter's behalf were mainly carried out in the South during the many weeks he spent in Warm Springs. As early as May of 1927 he had announced that the South would support Smith, who "of all the Democratic candidates, would have the smallest number of electoral votes to make up to obtain the two hundred and sixty-six required for election." At the time that F.D.R. wrote the next letter, the usual emotions with characterize a national election year were beginning to appear, and political matters enter into F.D.R.'s correspondence along with concern and elation over the improved condition of his legs.

Dearest Mama—

Yours of Friday came this morning and though I always hate to have you on one side of the ocean and me on the other, yet in one way it would be a good time for you to go over this summer, and of course I should be much happier to have you go over with Sallie and Charley, and the date is excellent, for I have to leave for Houston just 4 days after June 16th.

Also, if Smith is nominated, as he probably will be, I shall have to do a lot of organizing work in July and the first part of August, with little time at Hyde Park. And I plan *not* to do any work to amount to anything after Sept. 1st and you will be back by then. So the plans "of you and me" would work in well together!

Those talked-of plans for the following summer are merely theoretical! I *doubt* very much (entre nous) if I go over, for I cannot see the object of sitting around hotels in Europe while the others "sight see" and I can get more good out of Warm Springs than any place like Nauheim. You will see a big gain when you come next week I think!

Do let me know what you decide about motoring down, what day you arrive. It is glorious here, all the trees and blossoms coming out, and I'm *so* glad you're coming soon.

Devotedly

F.D.R.

P.S. Brother is really better. I keep him in the sun all day long and I am feeding him up. He will leave Saturday and get to N.Y. Sunday and go to Groton Monday.

"Brother" was a family nickname for Franklin D. Roosevelt, Jr.

F.D.R.'s prediction about the outcome of the Houston convention proved to be correct. With the discrediting of the Ku Klux Klan the main opposition to Smith had been removed and his candidacy could no longer be denied. He was nominated on the first ballot with 849½ of the 1100 votes. Senator Joseph T. Robinson of Arkansas was chosen as his running mate. In the meantime the Republicans, although faced with an "I do not choose to run" statement from President Coolidge and a similar announcement by the next most influential man in the party, Charles Evans Hughes, found little difficulty agreeing upon a candidate at their convention in Kansas City on June 12th: Herbert Hoover, who for the past seven years had efficiently served as Secretary of Commerce.

Although Smith's "kitchen cabinet" handled his 1928 pre-convention campaign, F.D.R. was the logical choice to place his name before the convention. Hence, while his mother departed for Europe in the company of his son James, F.D.R. went to Houston and for the third time addressed a Democratic national convention on Smith's behalf. Except that the location was different and that this time he had replaced his crutches with a cane, history was repeating itself when F.D.R. stepped forward on the platform in Sam Houston Hall: his speech was not only similar in nature to his "Happy Warrior" speech in 1924, but it too was everywhere received with the same great enthusiasm. On June 28, 1928, under the title of a "A High-Bred Speech," the *New York Times* editorialized its approval in no uncertain terms:

Mr. Franklin D. Roosevelt, in his speech last night nominating Governor Smith, proceeded like a gentleman speaking to gentlemen. There was nothing strained or fantastic or extravagant in what he said. It was the address of a fair-minded and cultivated man, avoiding the usual perils of national convention oratory, and discussing in an intelligent way the qualifications which should be sought for in the President of the United States and the ability of Alfred Smith to meet every fair test of capacity. Mr. Roosevelt went further than that. He declared that many men could be found with sufficient mental and moral equipment to be a reasonably satisfactory President. But if the country wishes to have a great President it must inquire for something more. That one thing additional which is needed, Mr. Roosevelt singled out in a passage of great simplicity and yet of moving appeal:

"It is that quality of soul which makes a man loved by little children, by dumb animals; that quality of soul which makes him a strong help to all those in sorrow or in trouble; that quality which makes him not merely admired but loved by all the people—the quality of sympathetic understanding of the human heart, of real interest in one's fellowmen. Instinctively he senses the popular need because he himself has lived through the hardship, the labor and the sacrifice which must be endured by every man of heroic mold who struggles up to eminence from obscurity and low estate. Between him and the people is that subtle bond which makes him their champion and makes them enthusiastically trust him with their loyalty and their love."

It is seldom that a political speech attains this kind of eloquence. Indeed, the entire address of Mr. Franklin Roosevelt is a model of its kind—limpid and unaffected in style and without a single trace of fustian. It was not fitted to provoke frenzied applause, but could not be heard or read without prompting to serious thought and sincere emotion. . . .

∽

After the convention F.D.R. went briefly to Warm Springs and thence back to Hyde Park, from where he wrote the next letter to his mother.

HYDE PARK
JULY 14, 1928
SATURDAY

Dearest Mama,

I have been a disgrace about writing and I honestly don't know where this past month has gone, but as you know

I have been "on the jump" and at last am back at Hyde Park. It was good to get your cable letter yesterday and to know that all goes well. I haven't had a chance yet to talk to Plog but everything seems all right and the household is going on well. During my absence first F. Jr. and then John have been really miserable. John is out today for the first time.

The Convention went smoothly as per schedule in every way, but as I was floor manager for Gov. Smith's nomination I had to be on the job all the time. The nominating speech went much better than I had anticipated and seems to have been approved by both Democratic and Republican papers, and there have been a lot of really nice editorials, and flocks of letters and telegrams. I haven't half caught up answering them yet as I could do little work at Warm Springs and this week in New York have been again occupied with the National Committee meeting.

It was very hot in Houston, also at Warm Springs, and this week in New York was even hotter!

We had a tragedy at Warm Springs just before I left. That dear little Pattison girl, "Tishy" the younger, died very suddenly after being ill for only a few hours, acute acidosis, and we were all much upset. The new winter pool is started and everything else is going well, with every bed taken.

There has been much rain everywhere, and the streams are full. The big field south of Avenue is out and the grass lying soaking on the ground. The Women's City and County Club is here this p.m. for a lecture by Mrs. Brown on "Historic New York." Caroline O'Day is here for Sunday, also Mrs. Ross, lately Governor of Wyoming, very nice and she is to have charge of the Women's Division in the campaign. I declined the National Chairmanship, and will decline the nomination for Governor.

James wrote you seemed much more rested and I do hope you will keep it up and I know the regime of the "cure" will do good. Give lots of love to Aunt Doe when you see her. I am glad James' trip seems to be successful. Elliott got out to the Ranch from Houston, partly by airplane from Phoenix, Arizona to Salt Lake City over the Grand Canyon. Much much love—we miss you much. I go to New York Monday and return Friday, and have the State Council of Parks meet here next Saturday, about 25 for a stand-up lunch.

Ever your devoted

FDR

Patricia ("Tishy") Lee Pattison was the daughter of the aforementioned Lee Marion Pattison. Mrs. Caroline Love Goodwin O'Day, eminent New York social worker and widow of David T. O'Day, a Standard Oil heir, was at this time associate chairman of the New York Democratic State Committee and the outstanding Democratic woman leader of the state. She and A.E.R. had become intimate friends when A.E.R. first entered into political work. In 1935 she was elected to Congress as representative at large from New York, and during her four terms in office supported F.D.R.'s Administration in all major issues except the 1939 repeal of the arms embargo and the 1940 Selective Service Bill. On January 4, 1943, one day after the expiration of her fourth term, Mrs. O'Day died in her home at the age of sixty-seven. At this time a vice-chairman of the Democratic National Convention, Mrs. Nellie Tayloe Ross was the first woman to serve as governor of any state. She was elected to that office in Wyoming on January 5, 1925, to complete the unexpired term of her husband, William Bradford Ross, who had died the previous October. She held the post for two years. In April, 1933, she was appointed Director of the Mint, the first woman to hold this position.

The *Poughkeepsie Eagle* of July 16, 1928, reported that two hundred persons attended the lecture by Mrs. Henry Collins Brown of New York "for the benefit of the budget of the Women's City and County Club." The event was held at Val-Kill and the newspaper noted that while A.E.R. presided over the meeting, F.D.R. did not attend the lecture. At this time F.D.R. held the chairmanship of the Taconic State Park Commission, and thus the State Council of Parks held its meeting at his Hyde Park home.

~~

The same reasons which led F.D.R. in the previous letter to write "I plan not to do any work to amount to anything after Sept. 1st" also lay behind the remark here that "I declined the National Chairmanship, and will decline the nomination for Governor." The rate of recovery had quickened considerably in the past year, and he was determined not to let anything interfere with the final stages. His doctors had even expressed the belief that he would be able to discard his cane if he continued the cure through the next winter. He could do this now, thanks to the enclosed pool which Edsel Ford had provided and which was certain to be completed by October. Hence there was every reason for F.D.R. to decline a major political job, and during the summer it appeared that no eventuality could make him change his mind.

Although he turned down the national chairmanship, F.D.R. questioned the selection of John J. Raskob for the post. As chairman of the Finance Committee of General Motors, Raskob was chosen by Smith on the ground that the Democratic Party could not gain victory in the election without the support of "big business," a faction of which Raskob was an outstanding member. F.D.R. objected to this reasoning on the theory that as a very prominent Catholic and an ardent wet Raskob would further increase the prejudice in the South and West against Smith, an increase which would not be compensated by his influence in the East. F.D.R. had witnessed the prejudice at first hand, and was fully aware of its potency. The reduction of the power of the Ku Klux Klan did not mean that the average Southern Democrat was going to change his views about the advisability of a Catholic Presidential nominee; on the contrary, the campaign was marked by the dissemination of "vile propaganda" throughout the Southern states. However, the "kitchen cabinet" did not think it mattered that both Smith and Raskob were wets and Catholics. They believed that the key issue of the campaign was "prosperity," and in this sense Raskob had every qualification for the job.

Smith and his associates were also certain that victory could only be achieved if the Democrats carried New York State. It was therefore deemed vital that Smith's successor as Democratic gubernatorial nominee be chosen from among the leading figures of the party, be someone whom New Yorkers knew and respected. There was only one logical person for the post: F.D.R. No other person commanded the respect and had the contacts that F.D.R. did in 1928, and it was a hard blow to Smith and the national committee when he declined the nomination and announced his intention to spend the winter in Warm Springs. In spite of pressure from all sides, F.D.R. could not be deterred from his decision to realize the ultimate goal of his seven-year struggle. So, after doing what he could for the campaign during the summer, he left New York in the third week of September for Warm Springs and several weeks' rest before making his last few speeches on Smith's behalf.

∽

WARM SPRINGS
SEPTEMBER 21, [1928]
FRIDAY

Dearest Mama,

I wish much that you were here today for your Birthday or that I were at Hyde Park. I wired you last night in the hope that you will get it before you depart for points unknown in New England. This I am sending to Campo. I am anxious to hear all about your trip and how you find the boys and how things are on the Island.

I got here safely Wednesday evening and the weather is heavenly. The pool is lovely and I'm getting a real rest.

Kitty Gandy is here, also Mary Amory and Kitty. The new winter pool comes along well and will be ready in a month.

I am borrowing the money for the Foundation to put in new water supply. It simply has to be done.

Ever so much love.

Your devoted

FDR

Mary and Kitty Amory, distant cousins of F.D.R., were Forbes Amory's mother and sister.

During the interval between this letter and the next, New York Democrats began to convene in Rochester to choose a gubernatorial successor to Smith. Everywhere there was a clamor to draft F.D.R. In the course of the nine weeks which had elapsed since his refusal to run, it became more and more evident that his candidacy was essential to Smith's election. The national vote was expected to be so close that New York's 45 electoral votes would be the difference between victory and defeat. Within the state itself the race was considered an even closer contest, perhaps a matter of a few thousand votes only. F.D.R. had come to be regarded as the key figure of the whole campaign. If he ran, he would carry New York for Smith; if he didn't run, the Democratic State Convention had grave doubts as to Smith's election. Consequently, the clamor in Rochester soon developed into a general feeling of desperation, which by phone and wire extended to F.D.R. at Warm Springs. While on the way to Rochester after his campaign through the West, Smith called F.D.R. from Milwaukee on September 29th, and asked him to reconsider his earlier refusal. But, as noted in the next letter, F.D.R. could not be dissuaded from adhering to the advice of his doctors, who were, as he wired Smith, "very definite in stating that the continued improvement in my condition is dependent on my avoidance of cold climate and on taking exercises here at Warm Springs during the cold winter months."

Dearest Mama,

I think of you as being at school today and getting back to Hyde Park tomorrow. It must have been lovely at Campo and I loved your letters.

I have to stay here to make a speech to a big meeting in Columbus on Thursday, then go on Friday straight to Cleveland, speak there Saturday night and get either to Hyde Park or New York Sunday afternoon, I don't know which yet.

I spoke in Atlanta twice last Wednesday and there is an appalling amount of vile propaganda in circulation all through the South. Still I think Smith will carry these states.

I have had a difficult time turning down the Governorship, letters and telegrams by the dozen begging me to save the situation by running, but I have been perfectly firm. I only hope they don't try to stampede the Convention tomorrow and nominate me and then adjourn!

Ever so much love.

Your devoted

F

F.D.R. did not have to fear that the state convention would nominate him and then adjourn; instead, the nomination was postponed in order to allow for new persuasive efforts to make him change his mind. Telephone calls were renewed; Smith again, and Thomas Lynch, and Herbert H. Lehman, who was subsequently nominated for the lieutenant governorship; letters and telegrams continued to be sent "by the dozen." "Go ahead and take it," his daughter wired. F.D.R.'s reply was equally crisp: "You ought to be spanked." A.E.R. went to the convention and finally was persuaded to get F.D.R. on the ticket. As the Todhunter School opened on October 2nd, A.E.R. could only spend a few hours in Rochester, and in her letter to

F.D.R. of September 30, 1928, she expressed her views on this abbreviated trip shortly before undertaking it:

I have to go to Rochester but I wish I didn't have to, for everyone makes me so uncomfortable. They feel so strongly about your running and even good explanations can be made to sound foolish. The Governor called me yesterday and I told him to call you. . . .

Early in the morning of October 1st, Smith and F.D.R. again conferred by phone and F.D.R. again refused to yield to the pressure. Smith conceded the futility of drafting F.D.R. and sent word to the nominating committee that another candidate would have to be selected. The committee answered that there was no alternative: F.D.R. had to be the nominee. Thus, for the third time within forty-eight hours, the efforts to secure his consent were resumed. Suspecting that the pressure had not ended, F.D.R. went on a picnic during the afternoon, and was not located until the evening while he was making a speech in support of Smith at the hall in nearby Manchester. F.D.R. was finally reached on his return to Warm Springs. The persuasion continued with Smith and Raskob taking over once his wife reached him. Lehman came on with a further reason for acceptance: as lieutenant governor, he would willingly handle the heavy work whenever F.D.R. wanted to be in Warm Springs. Finally Smith returned to the phone and put the matter to F.D.R. on a personal basis, almost as a favor. When F.D.R., having found it increasingly difficult to remain "perfectly firm," hesitated over the question of whether or not he would accept if nominated the next day, Smith hung up the phone. On October 2nd F.D.R. was nominated by acclamation and he did not decline the honor.

New York's Republican papers made much capital of this dramatic episode. The *Herald Tribune* editorialized that "the nomination is unfair to Mr. Roosevelt. It is equally unfair to the people of the State, who, under other conditions, would welcome Mr. Roosevelt's candidacy for any office." The *Evening Post* attacked Smith for making "this most loyal of friends agree to serve his ambitions at a price that is beyond all reason," and called the drafting a "pathetic and pitiless" act.

At a press conference the following day Smith responded to these argument with a simple and reasonable answer: "A Governor does not have to be an acrobat. We do not elect him for his ability to do a double back-flip or a handspring. The work of the Governorship is brainwork. Ninety-nine percent of it is accomplished at a desk."

Sara Roosevelt, too, had a few illuminating comments to make in her letter of October 2nd:

Eleanor telephoned me before I got my papers that you have to "run" for the Governorship. Well, I am sorry if you do not feel that you can do it without too much *self* sacrifice, and yet if you run I do not want you to be defeated! I feel just as Rosy did. However, all will be well whatever happens. . . .

Although perhaps momentarily regretting the event, F.D.R.'s first reaction was similar to his mother's: since he had been nominated, the election should be won. Accordingly, on October 5th he issued a statement to the press shortly before leaving for Cleveland:

I am amazed to hear that efforts are being made to make it appear that I have been "sacrificed" by Governor Smith to further his own election and that my friends should vote against me to prevent such "sacrifice." Let me set this matter straight at once. I was not dragooned into running by the Governor. On the contrary, he fully appreciated the reasons for my reluctance and was willing to give up such advantage as he felt my candidacy might bring him in deference to my wishes. I was drafted because all of the party leaders, when they assembled, insisted that my often expressed belief in the policies of Governor Smith made my nomination the best assurance to the voters that these policies would be continued.

It was because they felt, and I feel, that the whole splendid structure of State Government built up by Governor Smith and all the high ideals of service to the people which he had established were in peril that caused me to accept the nomination. New York must not lose its proud position as the State which leads in efficiency and democracy. That is something too important to let any personal consideration weigh in the slightest. I am in this fight not to win personal honor, but for the carrying forward of the policies of Governor Smith.

I do not believe that appeals to personal friendship should form any part of a plea to the electorate. But if I did, my own appeal would be: "Not only do I want my friends to vote for me, but if they are my real friends I ask them to get as many other people to vote for me as possible."

I trust this statement will eliminate this particular bit of nonsense from the campaign from the beginning.

F.D.R. spoke in Cleveland on October 6th; another speech in Boston concluded his out-of-the-state speaking commitments for Smith, and on the 16th the formal acceptance ceremonies were held. The next day F.D.R. began his campaign. In contradiction to the belief which prevailed even within his own party that his health would prevent a whirlwind tour of the state, he campaigned with the same vigor and enthusiasm that marked his four previous candidacies. Speaking from the back of an automobile, he again visited as many of the small hamlets of upstate New York as could be fitted into a crowded schedule. It was not long before people forgot that F.D.R. was an invalid; indeed, he was convinced himself that his personal struggle had ended in victory, that he was physically capable of returning to active public service. In one way the realization of this triumph meant more to him than the election itself.

But 1928 was the height of the era of prosperity, of the golden 'twenties, and the American people generally credited the Republican Administration with the flow of goods and dollars. Smith's personal charm could not deter the Hoover landslide, while his religion inevitably gave it further impetus. On November 6, 1928, the Democrats suffered their most disastrous defeat since the Civil War. Hoover received 444 electoral votes to Smith's 87. Four Southern states, Virginia, North Carolina, Florida, and Texas, voted Republican for the first time in their history. Hoover carried forty states and gained a popular majority of nearly seven million. In Congress, too, the Republicans won an overwhelming victory.

In addition to six states of the "solid South," only Massachusetts and Rhode Island were carried by Smith. While the defeat was everywhere complete for the popular New York governor, most humiliating was his failure to carry his own state. In the end it did not matter that F.D.R. had been on the Democratic ticket, not to Smith at any rate. Perhaps Hoover's margin of 103,481 votes would have been larger had F.D.R. not been the Democratic candidate, but, in any case, it was certain that the phone calls to Warm Springs early in October were in vain, based on unreal estimates.

At the time when Smith conceded the election to Hoover, late in the evening of the 6th, it was generally thought that F.D.R. would also be defeated by his Republican opponent, Albert Ottinger. When the news reached F.D.R.'s headquarters that Smith had lost New York, F.D.R. went home convinced that he was not to be the Happy Warrior's successor. This was near midnight, with Ottinger sufficiently in the lead for the morning papers to go to press with the news of his election. But Sara Roosevelt would not leave until the decision was final, and several hours later the tide began to turn. At four o'clock in the morning she heard the tally men announce that her son had been elected by 25,564 votes.

Where they would not vote for him for President, the people of New York supported Smith by voting for his gubernatorial successor, whose vigorous campaign, straightforward manner, and past record had appealed to them. F.D.R. defied the Republican sweep of the country, and his victory, narrow as was the margin, was a great compliment, like a promise of future advancement.

After the election F.D.R. went to Warm Springs until the middle of December, and then returned to Hyde Park to spend the Christmas holidays with his family. It was a joyous few weeks. He was back in public service, his legs were no longer a liability, his family was united, and there was everything to look forward to in the days ahead.

The inaugural ceremonies were held in Albany on January 1, 1929. At this point F.D.R.'s personal correspondence will be resumed, in a third and final volume covering the period from 1929 until his death in 1945—the period of American history which is best characterized by the initials F.D.R.

INDEX

INDEX

* Mentioned in Index to "F. D. R. His Personal Letters. Early Years."

Pussie. Hunt. *See* Morgan, Mrs. W. Forbes

rabbit, death of, 231-32
race riots, Washington, 478-79
race track gambling bill, 164, 165
Radio station, French, sale of, 453
Rainsford, Laurence and Kerr, 33, 34
*Rainsford, Rev. William S., 33, 34
Ranelagh, 12, 13
Raskob, John J., 643
Reading, Pa., dedication of *Maine* anchor, 233-35, 240
Redfield, William C., 245, 246
*Redmond, Mr. and Mrs. Roland L., 242
*Reid, Jean. *See* Ward, the Honorable John Hubert
*Reid, Mr. and Mrs. Whitlaw, 10
renomination for the state senate, 193-98
Reserve, naval. *See* Naval Reserve
resignation as assistant secretary of the navy; exchange of letters with Daniels, 489-91
return to politics, 635-50
Richards, Eliza. *See* Jusserand, Ambassador and Mme. Jean Jules
Richardson, Margaret. *See* Roosevelt, Mr. and Mrs. G. Hall
Richelieu, Duc and Duchesse de, 307, 308
riches, opinion on; differences with mother, 274-75
Richey, Rev. Alban, Jr., 602
Rigby, Rev. Hazen, 95, 97
Rigby, Helena, 95, 97
Riley, Elizabeth R. *See* Roosevelt, Mr. and Mrs. James Roosevelt Roosevelt
riots, race, in Washington, 478-79
Roach, J. & Co., 212-13
Robb, Mrs. Thayer, 11

*Robbins, Muriel Delano. *See* Martineau, Mrs. Cyril
*Robbins, Mr. and Mrs. Warren Delano (Irene de Bruyn), 63, 65, 77, 78, 206-08, 332, 333
*Robinson, Mr. and Mrs. Douglas (Corinne Roosevelt), 5, 6
Robinson, Helen Roosevelt, 93
Robinson, Joseph T., 638
Robinson, Kenneth, 43, 45
Robinson, Munro, 451
*Robinson, Mr. and Mrs. Theodore Douglas (Helen Rebecca Roosevelt), 12, 14, 94
Robinson, Theodore Douglas, Jr., 14, 632
Rodgers, Admiral Thomas S., 206
Rogers, Rae, 49, 51
Rogers, Locke & Milburn, 256
Rojas, Ezequiel, 221, 222
Rome in wartime, 432-35
*Roosevelt, Alice. *See* Longworth, Mr. and Mrs. Nicholas
*Roosevelt, Anna. *See* Cowles, Captain and Mrs. William Sheffield
Roosevelt, Anna (daughter of F. D. R.). *See* Dall, Mr. and Mrs. Curtis B.
Roosevelt, Archibald Bulloch, 412, 440
*Roosevelt, Corinne. *See* Robinson, Mrs. Douglas
*Roosevelt, Elliott (father of A. E. R.), 150
Roosevelt, Elliott (son of F. D. R.), at Groton, 581-82
birth of, 150
spanking, 286
*Roosevelt, Ethel. *See* Derby, Dr. and Mrs. Richard
Roosevelt, Franklin D., Jr. (first), birth and death, 150
*Roosevelt, Franklin D., Jr. (second), 637
birth, 250

3 Commando Brigade